THE
FAIR RIVER VALLEY

◆

Strabane through the Ages

THE
FAIR RIVER VALLEY

◆

Strabane through the Ages

JIM BRADLEY *et al*

EDITED BY
JOHN DOOHER
MICHAEL KENNEDY

THE
ULSTER HISTORICAL
FOUNDATION

IN ASSOCIATION WITH
THE STRABANE HISTORY SOCIETY

THE STRABANE HISTORY SOCIETY
AND THE ULSTER HISTORICAL FOUNDATION

gratefully acknowledge the financial support
provided by the following towards this publication

Strabane District Council
Strabane Lifford Development Commission –
ARTS Programme 2000/2001
Ulster Local History Trust
Community Relations Council

Published 2000
by the Ulster Historical Foundation
12 College Square East, Belfast, BT1 6DD
in association with the Strabane History Society

All rights reserved. No part of this publication may be reproduced,
stored in a retrieval system or transmitted in any form or by any means,
mechanical or otherwise without permission of the publisher.

© Ulster Historical Foundation, 2000

Printed by Betaprint, Dublin
Design and production, Dunbar Design

ISBN 0-901905-96-8

This book has received support from the Cultural Diversity Programme
of the Community Relations Council, which aims to encourage acceptance
and understanding of cultural diversity. The views expressed do not necessarily
reflect those of the NI Community Relations Council.

Contents

Preface		VII
Dedication		IX
Notes on Contributors		XI

1	Out of the Shadows – Early Settlers in Strabane The Golden Years – The Christian Settlement Strabane in the Middle Ages – Invasions and Tribal Conflicts JIM BRADLEY	1
2	The Foundation of Strabane JIM BRADLEY	17
3	The Nine Years War in the North-west WILLIAM ROULSTON	39
4	The Plantation and Seventeenth-century Developments MICHAEL COX	57
5	The Development of Strabane in the Eighteenth Century, 1700–1770 JOHN DOOHER	81
6	The Emergence of a New Leadership – Strabane *c.*1770–1800 JOHN DOOHER	97
7	The Abercorn Family and Political Control in Strabane, 1690–1800 ANTHONY MALCOMSON	130
8	The Growth and Development of Strabane, 1800–1850 JOHN DOOHER	151
9	Economic Development in Strabane, 1800–1900 MICHAEL HARRON	179
10	Mills and the Rural Economy WILLIAM ROULSTON	196
11	The Convent of Mercy and the Industrial School MICHAEL HARRON	207
12	Parliamentary Elections in North Tyrone, 1885–1921 WILLIAM ROULSTON	218

13	Local Government in Strabane, 1800–1925 JOHN DOOHER	232
14	A Literary History of Strabane JACK GAMBLE	250
15	Strabane in the Wider World – Famous People from the Area JIM BRADLEY	267
16	A History of the Church of Ireland and Methodism in Strabane CANON FREDERICK FAWCETT	286
17	Strabane Presbyterianism WILLIAM ROULSTON	298
18	The Catholic Church in Strabane since *c.*1600 JOHN DOOHER	314
19	River, Road and Rail MICHAEL KENNEDY	333
20	Education in Strabane MICHAEL KENNEDY	352
21	The Arts in Strabane MICHAEL KENNEDY	368
22	Strabane in the Twentieth Century, 1900–1950 BRIAN CARLIN	388
23	Corridors of Memories – Personal Recollections JIM BRADLEY	396
	Acknowledgements, Notes and Sources	405
	Strabane History Publications – A Select Bibliography	414
	Index	417

Preface

The publication of A.A. Campbell's *Literary History of Strabane* in 1902 was a landmark synthesis of the historical and literary work of the area and a demonstration of its rich and varied heritage. In the following decades, however, there was little building on the foundations laid by Campbell, and Strabane's history was kept alive mainly by oral dissemination, with a small number of scholarly figures being looked to as the repositories of knowledge about the past. It was in such a scenario that Jim Bradley was initiated into the local history field, and he quickly built up an encyclopaedic knowledge about not only Strabane and its immediate environs but also about the surrounding counties and even further afield. Yet Jim was not content simply to disseminate information; he constantly sought to supplement his own knowledge base and to encourage others to challenge and research further into the history of the town. Under his tutelage and guidance a more comprehensive account of the past was being assembled and there was little doubt that Jim Bradley should be the person to collate the varied strands of historical information in a publication that would be accessible to all and yet incorporate the highest standards of scholarship. Unfortunately, he did not live to see the completion of his project and it has been left to others to attempt to bring together a history that would do justice to his vision and provide a detailed examination of the history of Strabane and its neighbourhood. Jim Bradley was a great believer in inclusiveness and it is hoped that this history will go some way towards meeting the needs of a wide section of the population and allow local history to be seen both as a reconciler and as a celebration of diversity. Some gaps in research and information clearly remain, and this publication will have served a very useful purpose if it can stimulate others to address the shortcomings and further the process of historical investigation.

A large number of people have contributed to making this work possible and tribute is paid to all who submitted articles and other material. Not all contributions have been included but thanks are due to everyone who wrote articles and a special thanks is extended to those who re-edited and refined their work in order to suit the editorial criteria. A number of people helped by making photographs and other illustrations available, and their assistance is much appreciated. John Mills assisted with the proof reading of the manuscript and a special word of thanks is due to Jack Gamble who provided a great deal of help and support, especially in locating and providing illustrations and in helping with the bibliographies while William Roulston was always ready to assist in preparing the completed work. It took a considerable length of time to bring this book to publication and in this context sincere thanks must be paid to Shane McAteer and the Ulster Historical Foundation for all their help in the editing processes and in smoothing the path to eventual completion. The design team were prepared to work long hours to ensure that the production timetable was met and we are deeply indebted to them. Tribute is paid elsewhere to those bodies who helped finance the project and it is our earnest hope that the active encouragement and positive contributions from such a wide range of people will be repaid at least in part by this Strabane history publication. It has been a humbling but pleasant task to bring the vision of *The Fair River Valley* to this stage of completion in tribute to the memory of its inspirer and initiator, Jim Bradley.

JOHNNY DOOHER
& MICHAEL KENNEDY, EDITORS
DECEMBER 2000

Jim Bradley and 'The Fair River Valley'

A Personal Introduction

FR. OLIVER CRILLY

Jim Bradley was a significant and influential figure in Strabane for many years. He played a central role in local administration and in the cultural life of the town and the area. His love for Strabane expressed itself in his abiding interest in local history, which for him was not only place-lore but also people-lore.

The landscape of Strabane is full of memories of Jim. He was rooted in the landscape himself, and he helped to shape the landscape of Strabane over the years. Jim was involved, for instance, in the naming of most of the housing developments of the last few decades. Jim could identify the rich associations in the landscape and raise them up so that we might see them and be inspired by them, whether it be a modern reference like Delaney Crescent, celebrating an Irishman's victory in the Olympic Games, or older and deeper associations, like Lisnafin – *Lios na Finne* – from the river Finn, or Belldoo – *Beal Dubh* – the dark opening, literally the dark mouth, of the stream or drainage channel which came out into the river Mourne below the golf course.

There is one name in particular which I think has a special relevance, and says something about Jim's vision for our community. The other names I mentioned come from the Irish tradition. Carlton Drive was named for a man whose associations are from the British tradition. Guy *Carleton* was born in Strabane, and he became Governor of British North America – what we would call Canada. He fought the Americans to retain Quebec as part of Canada, but then he fought the British Government so that the people of

Quebec – Frenchspeaking and Catholic – could have cultural and religious freedom. In proposing the name of Carlton Drive, Jim was making an important statement about cultural and religious diversity in our community here in Northern Ireland.

When we walk into Jim Bradley's landscape, we walk into a place of roots and resonances. Jim's special gift was like the gift of the water diviner: he had the skill and sensitivity to identify the underground streams and deposits, and to locate the position from which their riches might be tapped and brought to the surface. It reminds me of a visit I made to Jacob's Well in Nablus, in the Holy Land. The guide dropped a pebble into the well, which was narrow and very deep. After a long silence, we could hear the pebble striking the water, and the echoing resonance of the sound in the well, and we could see the water far below, like a wee eye winking in the darkness.

It is this sense of resonance which makes me think also of Jim's association with drama. He was one of the founders of the Lifford Players, and was deeply involved in drama and Pantomime over the years. When Jim was producing Pantomime, he showed the same reverence to the youngest child taking part as he showed to the leading man or leading lady. Drama for Jim wasn't just make-believe. The actor taking part in the drama was offering a living body and a living voice to amplify and transmit resonances of the mind and of the spirit.

Jim was a personal friend and adviser to an extraordinary number of people. He gave of himself both in the formal context of school boards of governors and community projects, but also in the one to one informal personal response of a good neighbour who was available without question when he was needed. Like his beloved landscape – the fair river valley – Jim never imposed himself in a heavy-handed way, but he will be remembered as a man of stature, a generous and gentle presence, a leader, not by coercion, but by inspiration.

Notes on Contributors

BRADLEY, JIM – For many years the acknowledged historian of Strabane, he had contributed to local publications and lectured to a wide variety of groups on the heritage and history of the area. In the late 1980s he was commissioned by Strabane District Council to write a history of the area but died before he could complete the project. He had worked for a number of years as clerk of Strabane Urban Council until its amalgamation with the rural council in 1973, when he became development officer for local government in the north-west area.

CARLIN, BRIAN – Currently chairman of the Strabane History Society, he has been active in the committee since the re-formation of the society in 1988 and has helped collate material for the society publications. He is a teacher in St Mary's Primary School and has contributed to the society's lecture programme on a number of occasions.

COX, MICHAEL – Lives in Lothian in Scotland and is deeply involved in the Scottish local history scene, being on the executive committee of the Scottish Local History Forum and a frequent contributor to their local history magazine. He has strong local connections and was an active participant in local studies in Strabane and Ulster in the 1970s, helping in the publication of a booklet, *The Plantation of Ulster in the Strabane Barony*. He has also contributed in recent years to *Concordia* and is keenly interested in researching family history.

DOOHER, JOHN – Actively involved in the local history scene in Strabane and also in Ulster, being chairman of the Federation for Ulster Local Studies in the years 1996 –8. He has contributed to *Ulster Local Studies* and was editor of the journal for a number of years. He produced the booklet on the *Hiring Fairs in Strabane* and wrote a number of articles for *Concordia*, the magazine of Strabane History Society. He has taught History in St Colman's High School for over thirty years.

FAWCETT, REV. CANON FREDERICK – Until recently the Church of Ireland rector in Camus-Juxta-Mourne parish and an active participant in the workings of Strabane History Society. He has written and lectured on Columba and was the joint editor of the recently updated and revised edition of Canon Leslie's compilation, *Clergy of Derry and Raphoe*. He has since retired but retains a strong affinity with the local history scene in Strabane and elsewhere.

GAMBLE, JOHN A. – A native of Strabane and now an antiquarian bookseller in Belfast. He has retained a strong interest in local history and has given talks to numerous societies, including Strabane, on various aspects of local studies. He has contributed in various ways to community relations and sponsored *A Poem for Peace* competition run by the Strabane Teachers Centre in the late 1980s.

HARRON, MICHAEL – A retired teacher who has become very involved in researching various aspects of local history and searching for hitherto unfamiliar local sources. He has contributed to local publications and is currently involved in compiling databases for local research purposes.

KENNEDY, MICHAEL – One of the founding members of the re-launched Strabane History Society in the late 1980s, he has helped steer the society since then and has been a regular contributor to the lecture programme as well as helping to edit *Concordia*. He has himself published a very successful and acclaimed history of Strabane, *By the Banks of the Mourne*, and is currently principal of St Colman's High School, having previously worked as education officer with the Western Education and Library Board.

MALCOMSON, DR ANTHONY – The former director of the Public Record Office of Northern Ireland, Dr Malcomson has long been regarded as the expert on the Abercorn Papers. His most important publication, *John Foster: the politics of the Anglo-Irish ascendancy* (1978) is regarded in both Irish and British historical circles as a classic. Under his guidance PRONI became a major research source for local historians and his encouragement has done much to stimulate investigation and publications

ROULSTON, WILLIAM – Currently doing research work for a PhD in Archaeology, William has been very active for a number of years in the field of local studies, contributing to *Ulster Local Studies* and to *Concordia*. He had written a chapter on Tyrone politics in the county history series and has been active in researching family history while working with the Ulster Historical Foundation. His recent publication, *The Parishes of Leckpatrick and Dunnalong*, has been widely acclaimed in local history circles and has proved highly successful.

1 Out of the Shadows
Early Settlers in Strabane

JIM BRADLEY

Beltany stone circle

It may seem presumptuous for a local historical outline to commence with an excursion into the obscure ages of prehistory, about which the most eminent scholars will always have differing theories. However, encouraged by the words of the illustrious Newman, 'that to do some substantial good is a compensation for much incidental imperfection', the writer hopes that this opening chapter will throw some light on the original settlers in the general Strabane area and on the antiquities of structure and place name that have survived at least three millennia. Who were these people and what is the derivation of the names they gave so many years ago to the familiar features of our local landscape, both natural and man-made?

The First Settlements

The first indication of the existence of man in Ireland can be traced back to the beginning of the mesolithic period or Middle Stone Age, i.e. around 6000 BC. Many remains of structures, flint implements and food debris from this period have been excavated at Mount Sandel, Coleraine, and it has been established that in the north-west of our island these early settlers lived by hunting, fishing, and collecting shellfish, nuts, berries, leaves and roots.

During this period, development locally, as elsewhere in the island, was a slow and laborious process. The early settlers were few in numbers and limited in technology. Climatic conditions, which in earlier centuries had stimulated dense forest growth, gradually changed, and it was only in the 2,000 years preceding the birth of Christ that man was able to make inroads into the forested lowlands.

Early local settlements were generally restricted to island sites (crannogs), sandy soils, river banks and higher ground where the forest growth was less dense. The principal obstacle to development was the absence of any form of technology other than stone tools, which were of limited use; and, because of the complete absence of tin in this area, stone implements remained in constant use throughout the Bronze Age period.

Across the Foyle in the townland of Argry, Ballindrait, many Stone Age axes and flint knives were found in the days of the horse-drawn plough, and especially on the farm of the late Andrew Lowry, a noted Donegal antiquarian. Many of these finds can be seen in the Co. Donegal Historical Society Museum in the Franciscan Friary in Rossnowlagh.

Closer to home, namely between Rossgeir and the Foyle, Strabane man Mickey Doherty, a keen pearl fisherman and in his youth a national sprint champion, discovered in the bed of the Deele (a Foyle tributary) a Stone Age axe and polished flint knife. Similar finds made on the west side of the Foyle indicate that a substantial settlement existed in the Lifford area as early as 4000–3000 BC. There is a close similarity between the local finds and those from the Mount Sandel excavations.

Although lacking in technology, our ancient locals succeeded, to a greater degree than elsewhere in Europe, in constructing everlasting monuments in stone as tombs for their dead, or for the purposes of religious or social assemblies.

Monuments in Stone

The most striking local monument of the period is the imposing stone circle, some eight miles from Strabane, at Beltany, Raphoe, probably the principal druidic place of worship in the area around Strabane.

> Here, 67 gigantic standing stones, each 6 to 10 feet high above ground and weighing from 3 to 10 tons each, have been formed into a perfect circle 50 yards in diameter, the largest of its kind in Ireland.

The name Beltany derives from Baal Tinne, the god of fire, and it is suggested that the druids lit a fire on a particular day in each year in honour of one or other of their gods, possibly the sun. In a recent book, *Walking Along the Border*, Colm Tóibín, who visited the site with the present writer, concluded his observations on the Beltany stone circle in words that surely speak for themselves:

> We walked down the hill, leaving the stones to their magic, away from the reminder that there once was a time in this place when there were no Catholics or Protestants; the dim past standing there on the crown of the hill, for once a history that could do us no harm, could not teach us, inspire us, remind us, beckon us, embitter us: history locked up in stone.

Throughout the district, and particularly in the parish of Ardstraw, a number of these ancient monuments still exist – a portal tomb near Baronscourt, a cist burial site in Glenock and one in nearby Crosh, a court tomb at Clady Halliday, a pillar stone at Killen, and the same at Ardstraw and Shannony East, immediately adjoining the district of Gallen (the name Gallen means a pillar stone).

There is also a cist burial site in Evish, traditionally referred to by the people of the area as 'Dermott and Gráinne's Bed'. Toland, in his critical history of the druids (*A Critical History of the Celtic Religion and Learning, Containing an Account of the Druids*), says that altars of stone chests were always given this name by the 'vulgar Irish', and there are numerous examples of these cist tombs throughout the north-west. Dr Madden, in his *Shrines and Sepulchures of the Old and New World* says that 'all these rude, gigantic, uninscribed monuments which bear no marks of the chisel or hammer are not only sepulchral monuments but very early ones'.

Right in the very heart of Strabane town in the old graveyard at Patrick Street, unrecognised and unrecorded, is a standing stone of the same period, circa 2500 BC, a reminder in stone that over 4,000 years ago people lived here around a site that was later to be the location of a Christian foundation and the nucleus of the early settlement that was to become the town of the 'Fair River Valley'.

The above monuments can all be placed in the period 4000–2500 BC, though there is a great deal of debate as to their precise origins and chronology. A number of other stone monuments have also been placed in this period. There are numerous examples of stone circles in the Sperrins, particularly in the area around Plumbridge. One of the largest and most impressive stone circles in Ireland is at Beltany, near Raphoe, which may have originally consisted of around 80 stones. The simplest of all megalithic monuments is the standing stone, the precise purpose of which is something of a mystery. An interesting example may be found in the boundary fence between the townlands of Lisdivin and Sandville, where two upright stones stand side by side. The tradition regarding these stones is that they

There are four principal types of megalithic tombs:

A court tomb consists of a gallery divided into a number of burial chambers with a forecourt at the entrance to the gallery. The stones forming the forecourt normally stand upright. The area behind the court is enclosed in an earthen mound or stone cairn, usually trapezoidal in shape. There are considerable variations in the form of these tombs, but one of the most typical in Ireland today is to be found at Clady Halliday, near Ardstraw.

Portal tombs or dolmens are very simple in construction, consisting of a single chamber roofed by a sometimes enormous capstone. The capstone is supported by a number of upright stones, the two largest of which stand on either side of the entrance. At Killynaught, just north of Artigarvan, is a megalith known as the 'Rocking Stone'. It is actually a collapsed portal tomb, the

The 'Rocking Stone', a megalithic monument near Artigarvan, evidence of settlement in the district in the later Stone Age period.

upright stones having given way under the weight of the capstone.

Passage tombs consist of a normally circular earthen mound with a passage leading from the outside of the monument to a central burial chamber. Often there are several smaller burial chambers off a central area. The best known passage tomb in Ireland is at Newgrange, Co. Meath. At Kilmonaster, near Lifford, there is a large 'cemetery' of passage tombs, most of which have been destroyed.

Wedge tombs are the most numerous type of megalithic monument in Ireland. They take their name from their wedge shape and typically contain a central burial gallery roofed with stone slabs. There is usually a second wall of stones around this gallery holding the cairn in place. An excavation of the wedge tomb at Loughash revealed a bronze blade and an axe mould.

W .R.

formed part of a fertility rite whereby livestock were driven between them in order to ensure healthy offspring the following year.

The First Arrivals

Mythology suggests that many groups or races were to people this area throughout its history. The ancient Irish manuscript popularly known as the *Book of Invasions* (*Lebor Gabála Éireann: The Book of the Taking of Ireland*), tells of successive expeditions: the Nemedians, the Formorians, the Firbolgs and (immediately preceding the Milesians) the Tuatha De Danann (Peoples of the Goddess Dana), the least reviled of these prehistoric colonisers.

The most ancient of our local place names are attributed to the De Danann, the diminutive and artful, yet peaceful, people overcome by the Milesians, who distorted their memory over the centuries into the fairies and leprechauns of Celtic folklore.

John O'Donovan, the renowned topographer and translator of the *Annals of the Four Masters*, tells us that Knockavoe, the hill that guards our town, is referred to in the Annals as 'Knock a Bove Dearg' (Hill of Bo Dearg), being so named in memory of a prominent De Danann chieftain who at one time reigned in the north-west of Ireland.

Our own River Mourne (originally Morne) is reputedly named after a De Danann prince and Foyle is said to be a corruption of 'Feabhail' (son of Lodran), who was drowned in the waters that were ever afterwards to commemorate his name. It is fascinating to realise that these local names, which roll off our tongues daily, were in use many years before the coming of Christ.

In Ptolemy's map of Ireland in the second century AD, the upper Foyle is shown as Argita – the ancient name of the River Finn. According to Joyce (*The Origins and History of Irish Names of Places*), a sister of Fergorman (one of the Fianna heroes) named Finn (Fionn: 'fair' or 'lovely') was drowned in the lake now known as Lough Finn, trying to reach her dying brother. The lake was thereafter called Loch Finne, and the river issuing from it was known as Finn from the first years of the third century.

One of our oldest local ballads is presently enjoying a well-deserved revival in popularity. For many years 'The Flower of Sweet Strabane' was high on the limited repertoire of the street singers who entertained the fair day crowds of our youth. A line in the original ballad, recently updated, ran as follows: 'She was one of the fairest creatures of the whole Milesian clan.' The old ballad writer had a keener sense of history than the modern arrangers who usually omit the word 'Milesian'. The ancient annals preface the account of the Milesian invasion of Ireland with a long narration on the origin of that colony in eastern Europe and its wanderings by land and sea to and from Spain until its eventual arrival in Ireland in the eighth century BC.

The Arrival of the Clans

The Milesians derived their name from their leader, Miledh or Milesius ('leader of 1,000 troops') and they were the principal, if not the earliest, Celtic invaders of Ireland. The initial expedition, which was led by Ith, the uncle of Milesius, is reputed to have landed at Inis Saimar, a small island in the Erne estuary at Ballyshannon.

Two of the sons of Milesius were Heber and Ir, from which derive the early Latin names of the island, 'Hibernia' and 'Irlanda'. All the old Irish families claim descent from the Milesians or early Celts, and, accordingly, the local ballad writer of the last century was honouring his Celtic ancestry when he used the word 'Milesian' in the song which has long been the unofficial anthem of the Strabane district.

The most distinguished of the Milesian clan was Niall of the Nine Hostages, High King of Ireland, who reigned at Tara at the end of the fourth century. Two of his twelve sons, Eoghan (Owen) and Connail, journeyed north and appropriated territories later to be known as Tyrone ('land of Owen') and Tyrconnell ('land of Connail').

At the same time, a third son named Enna claimed that fertile part of east Donegal on the west banks of the Finn and Foyle. This statelet, known as Tír Enna, corresponded to the territory known earlier as Magh Ith and later as the Laggan of Donegal. The rulers of Tír Enna were unable to maintain sovereignty, and the area was eventually annexed by the descendants of Owen and Connail, whose territories lay on its northern and western borders.

The respective dynasties and descendants of these two brothers were to be known as the Cinel Owen ('Clan Owen') and Cinel Connail ('Clan Connail'), and although the present territorial boundaries of Tyrone and Donegal differ from the original minor kingdoms established by the brothers, their respective clans still predominate in the original homelands under such names as O'Donnell, Boyle, Sweeney, Gallagher, McGlinchey, McMenamin, Ward, McGinley and Bonner in Donegal, and O'Neill, McLaughlin, Doherty, McShane, Devine, Quinn, McHugh and McNamee in Tyrone.

The original dividing line between the old historic territories of Tir Owen and Tir Connail was the passageway then and still called Barnesmore ('Great Gap'), the scenic landmark on the road from Ballybofey to Donegal town. The twin peaks guarding the gap each have place names dating back to the fifth century. The peak on the left-hand side going towards Donegal is Cruach Eoghanagh (Hill of Owen), and its twin on the western side is Cruach Connallach (Hill of Connail). The lands from Barnesmore west to the Atlantic Ocean were part of the ancient territory of Tir Connail, while the former Tir Owen included the present Co. Tyrone, the peninsula of

Church, it was abandoned in favour of a church erected by the earl of Abercorn in Strabane (which will be referred to later). The graveyard at Camus is still occasionally used for burials of Protestants and Catholics, and similar facilities were available in all the old graveyards attached to the various monastic and church sites in the district.

For many generations the people in the neighbourhood of Camus handed on a tradition that a large stone discernible in the River Mourne was the font of the old monastery. In 1950 voluntary workers under the supervision of the late John O'Kane Sr, building the Lourdes Grotto in Strabane on the site of the former Church of St John at Townsend Street, retrieved the 1-ton block from the river bed and placed it in the grounds of the grotto.

Other local religious foundations in the Strabane area were at Urney, Donagheady, Artigarvan and Ballycolman. The foundation at Urney ('Place of Prayer', 'Oratory') was a Brigidine nunnery and was in existence by AD 738 when it was under the direction of Samthainn of Cluan Bronaigh (Longford), who died the following year and whose feast-day is 19 December. A little-known cleric named Girvan or Garvan founded a church at the site ever afterwards known as Artigarvan ('Height of Garvan's House'), so called because only the ridge of the house or church was visible from the surrounding countryside.

The parish of Donagheady ('Donnaigh Caoide': the Church of Caoide) takes its name from St Caidinus or Caoide who founded a monastery close to the present village of Dunamanagh ('Fort of the Monks'). He was described as an abbot, and it was recorded that his bell and staff were at one

Camus, known as the 'bend in the river' is still preserved in an ivy-covered site, close to the river Mourne at Bearney

time preserved in the original abbey there. He was associated with St Columbanus of Bangor, and his feast-day was observed on 25 October.

There are significant remains of a Franciscan abbey founded *c*.1465 in Corickmore townland on a site overlooking the confluence of the Owenkillew and Glenelly rivers. In 1837 Lewis described the ruins as 'highly picturesque' in his *Topographical Dictionary of Ireland*. The remains of another Franciscan foundation can be seen at Scarvagherin near Spamount, while Pubble graveyard near Newtownstewart marks the site of a further monastery belonging to this religious order. At Camus, just a couple of miles south of Strabane, are the remains of the pre-Reformation parish church, featuring part of the frame of a small Romanesque window.

The parish churches of Badoney and Leckpatrick both claim to have associations with St Patrick. High up in the Glenelly valley, the present Badoney Church of Ireland stands on the site of the pre-Reformation building. Nothing remains of the medieval parish church of Leckpatrick, which may have been located within the confines of the old graveyard just north of Ballymagorry. Another early religious site in this area was at Grange, near Bready, the site now marked by the old graveyard. Nothing now remains of the monastic buildings, but Lewis described them as 'extensive' in 1837.

An early religious foundation within the present town of Strabane was at Ballycolman, reputedly founded by St Colman (AD 555–611), abbot of Fahan, a nephew of St Colmcille and at a later stage a member of the Iona Columban community. No sign of this foundation remains in what is now the most populous part of the town, but the older generation will remember the Ivy Pillar, an ivy-covered round stone pillar of considerable girth, which was traditionally associated with the old abbey and demolished a quarter of a century ago to make way for a private housing development opposite the Ballycolman Industrial Estate.

Early Church Leaders

St Eugene, patron saint of the diocese of Derry, was born in Leinster, but his mother was a native of Mugdornia (Mourne river valley). He and a fellow student, Tighernach, were taken to Alba (Scotland) as captives by marauding pirates, but through the influence of Ninian, the abbot of Rosnat (White Thorn), the ruler of the area was induced to liberate both youths, who then continued their studies at White Thorn.

On returning to England, Eugene was again made captive by slave-traders and taken to Gaul, and on his subsequent release returned to Scotland once more to pursue his studies. After their ordination, Eugene and Tighernach established several monasteries. Eugene's first foundation was at Kilnamanagh in Wicklow; he presided over this establishment as abbot for fifteen years until, in obedience to his superiors, he came north with

Tighernach to establish further foundations.

His companion selected Clones as a site for his new monastery, while Eugene journeyed on to his mother's country. On the banks of the Derg, on the site that is now Ardstraw, he founded the monastery that was to become an episcopal see and where he was to remain until his death on 23 August 618. (According to Brian Bonner in his recent scholarly work, *An Outline History of the Diocese of Derry*, the church at Ardstraw was originally built by MacEirc, a youthful disciple and student of Patrick, and his foundation was enlarged into a famous and outstanding monastery by Eugene over 100 years after its establishment.)

Although Eugene is the patron saint of the diocese of Derry, he was never bishop of Derry but was bishop of Ardstraw. The original see of Ardstraw, which comprised the greater part of Co. Derry, all of Inishowen, part of Donegal and a great part of Tyrone (including all the Strabane district), was transferred to Maghera in 1150. In 1158 the episcopal see of Derry was founded, and this new see was formally amalgamated with Ardstraw in 1285. The new see was now co-extensive with the ancient territory of the Cinel Owen, while the see of Raphoe covered exclusively the Cinel Connail territory in part of Co. Donegal only.

Although the monastery of Ardstraw maintained its pre-eminence as a religious house for many centuries, it had a troubled history. It was burnt on four occasions – 1069, 1099, 1101 and 1109 – by the native Irish (on one occasion, in 1101, by Muireartach O'Brien, High King of Ireland, on his way to destroy the palace of Aileach then occupied by the MacLochlainns), and by the Normans under John De Courcy in 1198.

The abbot of Ardstraw had the privilege of presiding over the obsequies of the dead lords of the Uí Fiachrach, and subsequently over those of the local O'Neill chieftains. (In *The Root and Branch of the Irish Nation*, it is recorded that, even as late as the eighteenth century, the remains of descendants of the branch of the O'Neills known as the Clann Arte were brought to Ardstraw for burial from various parts of Ireland and even from the Continent.)

Because of its ecclesiastical importance, the termon or church land of the monastery at Ardstraw was very extensive, being four times greater than that of the average church holding. On the occasion of Primate Colton's visitation in 1397, the entertainment given to his immense retinue was reputed to be outstanding, a sure indication of the substantial resources of Ardstraw and its pre-eminence in the Irish Church.

The monastery finally suffered the fate of other religious houses during the dissolution of the monasteries by Henry VIII, and the only remains extant today is the graveyard, which was rudely bisected in the last century for the purpose of constructing the present county road.

Such then is the chronicle of the religious foundations established locally

The Ruins of Scarvaherin, 1999
The photograph shows the old wall, graveyard and tomb stones of the historical site at Scarvaherin, near Crew Bridge, between Castlederg and Ardstraw.

in the years following the coming of Patrick. The place names of the settlements in themselves are historic cameos – it is doubly important that they should always be jealously preserved.

Any notes referring to the coming of Christianity to this district must include some reference to Adamnáin (otherwise Eunan), direct descendant of Niall of the Nine Hostages and patron of the diocese of Raphoe. Eunan, who was born in AD 624 at Ballindrait (Lifford), otherwise Droichead Adamnáin (the Bridge of Eunan), was elected ninth abbot of Iona in 678. At the synod of Tara in 697, which was attended by the Ard Rí, forty-seven tribal leaders from all over Ireland, the abbot of Armagh, and thirty-nine other principal ecclesiastics, the influence of Eunan was responsible for the adoption by the assembly of a collection of laws called in his honour Cáin Adamnáin.

One of these laws exempted women from the burden of attending hostings and expeditions or otherwise engaging in war, as had been customary in pagan times. At a time when the status of women in Ireland seemed to be low (they are rarely mentioned in the various annals as significant persons in their own right), Eunan can rightly be regarded as their champion. The venerable Bede says of him that he was a good and wise man well versed in the Scriptures.

In his lifetime Eunan, a noted scholar in Hebrew, Latin and Greek, wrote a most authoritative life of St Colmcille, 'in Latin of the most remarkable purity'. This manuscript is said to be the most valuable specimen of the literature of the period. He died on 23 September 704, and his name is today honoured in the Catholic cathedral of Letterkenny and the Church of Ireland cathedral in Raphoe.

The period from the sixth century to the ninth century was the brightest era in the history of the land and of our own valleys, when the most significant entries in the Annals were those recording the succession of kings and chieftains and particularly the milestones in the spread of Christianity. Unfortunately, this idyllic state of affairs was not to last.

Strabane in the Middle Ages – Invasions and Tribal Conflicts

In the eighth and ninth centuries, the coast of Scandinavia was peopled by a savage race under the various names of Norsemen, Danes and Vikings, for long the scourge of western Europe. By 806 they had reached as far as Iona, which they laid waste, following which they turned their attention to the settlements around the coast of Ireland, then enjoying relative peace and stability. The monasteries were the first objects of attack. Here were deposited the most valuable articles in the land – gold and silver chalices, and precious manuscripts prized mainly by the invaders for the gold and jewel-encrusted cases in which they were enclosed.

By 832 these fierce invaders had made their first inroads into Lough Foyle, marking their arrival by destroying the monastery of Rath Lurac in Maghera. In the next few years they were making regular forays up the River Foyle, creating settlements on its banks, notably at Dunnalong (Fort of the Ships) and finally at Port na Trí-Namhad (Port of the Three Enemies – the old name for Lifford).

The frequency of the Danish invasions was such that they gave to Tir Connail a new name that survives today – Donegal ('Dún na nGall': Fort of the Stranger). Although the Danes never established a permanent power base in the Strabane/Lifford area, they destroyed or pillaged all the religious houses in the district.

Long before the power of the Danes in the rest of Ireland was broken in the Battle of Clontarf in 1014, they were vanquished on the banks of the Foyle by Aedh Finnliath, successor in 863 to Malachy, High King of Ireland. This celebrated and formidable warrior had his residence at Aileach, overlooking the Foyle and the Swilly, but it was on the Foyle, as far inland as Lifford, that he prosecuted with vigour one of the most savage of many wars between the Gael and the Gall. The final victory of the Gaels in the Strabane and Lifford district in 864 is recorded thus:

> After Aedh, King of Ireland, had learned that this gathering of strangers was on the borders of his country he was not negligent in attending to them, for he marched towards them with all his forces and a battle was fought fiercely and spiritedly on both sides between them. This victory was gained over the foreigners and a slaughter was made of them. Their heads were collected to one place in the presence of the King and twelve score

heads were reckoned before him which was the number slain by him in that battle, besides the numbers of them who were wounded and carried off by him in the agonies of death and who died of their wounds some time afterwards.

Following the victory of the forces of Aedh Finnliath, the Danish incursions into the Foyle valley ended. Some of those who had recently settled there withdrew to their homeland, while those who remained were assimilated, frequently through marriage, into the native community, and their descendants can be recognised today under such names as McCusker (son of Oscar) or Sigerson (Sigurd's son).

The end of the Danish wars did not necessarily mean better days for the local monasteries. The turbulent and lawless times which followed were not favourable to the systematic observance of religion. The ravages of the Danes had struck the first blow at such schools of learning as Clonleigh and Ardstraw, and paved the way for regular violations of the monasteries from time to time by native clans professing Christianity.

The reasons were twofold – the decline of ecclesiastical government and discipline during the Danish wars, and the greed of the native chiefs, for whom the restored monasteries, with their modest treasures and livestock, were soft targets. Thus the round towers built by many of the monasteries in these years were intended as a defence against native as well as foreign attacks. By the tenth and eleventh centuries, the power struggles between the native clans in this region were in full swing. The MacLochlainns (McLaughlins), O'Neills, O'Donnells and O'Dohertys were the principal protagonists in the inter-tribal strife that was to be the most outstanding feature of life in the Foyle and Finn valleys for the next 500 years.

In the eleventh century the great druidic foundation of Grianán, for many years the court of the chieftain of Aileach, a territory embracing Inishowen and west Ulster, was the residence of Donnail MacLochlainn of the Cinel Owen, High King of Ireland and head of the MacLochlainn clan, then the principal ruling family in the north-west. In 1101 this royal palace was destroyed by the O'Briens of Thomond and never rebuilt.

Although Aileach was destroyed, the kings of the Cinel Owen retained the name of Aileach in their title, but in the reign of Donnail MacLochlainn, the last resident king of Aileach, the seat of power was transferred to Inchany (Inish Enaigh) in the parish of Urney, three miles from Strabane and less than a mile from the ancient abbey of Urney. No trace now remains of the last residence of the MacLochlainns, but oral tradition associates it with Urney Fort, a grassy plateau at Inchany.

In 1120 Donnail MacLochlainn, wearied by years of battle and strife, left Urney and retired to the monastery of Doire Colmcille to spend the remainder of his days in prayer and contemplation. His death in 1121 is recorded in the *Annals* in the following words:

> Domhnaill Son of Ardghar, King of Ireland, the most distinguished of the
> Irish for personal form, family sense, prowess, prosperity and happiness,
> died at Derry Colmcille after having been twenty-seven years in sovereign-
> ty over Ireland, and eleven years in the kingdom of Aileach in the seventy-
> third year of his age.

Further Tribal Conflicts

After MacLochlainn's death, quarrels arose between his followers and the
O'Neills for the supreme position in Tyrone, until finally in 1243 the
O'Neills, with the assistance of the O'Donnells, defeated the
MacLochlainns, and Brian O'Neill became 'The O'Neill'. It was at this
point that the ceremonial crowning of the kings of Aileach moved from An
Grianán to Tullahogue near Cookstown and the principal seat of their power
was established at Dungannon, with sub-branches at such places as
Newtownstewart and Omagh.

The unfortunate non-combatants, religious and lay, had little peace in
these barbaric years of civil strife, but worse was yet to come. The Norman
conquest of Ireland, which had begun as a gradual process in the east and
south, reached this area before the end of the twelfth century under Sir John
de Burgh, the Red Earl. The new invaders destroyed the monastery at
Ardstraw in 1198 and followed this with the destruction of Clonleigh,
Donaghmore and Urney.

In addition to the usual inter-tribal wars, the ordinary people now had to
contend with the new threat from the well-equipped Norman soldiery. All
of these warring factions fought for their own personal gain, oblivious of the
suffering caused to the ordinary people, particularly the weak and unpro-
tected. The annals for the period record the battles and praise the victorious
native chiefs, but remain silent on the anguish of the mothers, the sick and
the old.

The alliance of the O'Neills and the O'Donnells, which vanquished the
MacLochlainns in 1243, was short-lived. In 1275 the O'Neills invaded
Tyrconnell and destroyed Nagthan O'Donnell's castle on the Finn
(Castlefin). In the same year the O'Donnells under Dónal Óg O'Donnell
defeated the O'Neills in the parish of Ardstraw. The *Annals of the Four
Masters* states that on that occasion the O'Neills lost 'men, horses, arms and
armour'. Six years later the O'Neills defeated the O'Donnells in a further
major battle in which Dónal Óg O'Donnell was slain.

These wars, not for the last time, weakened the capacity of both the
O'Neills and the O'Donnells to resist the common enemy, and in 1286 the
Norman forces of De Burgh invaded and conquered both Tyrone and
Tyrconnell 'in which they did not leave a cloth upon an altar nor a mass

book in the churches of Cinel Connell'. The eventual decline, as a result of internal dissension, of Norman power in the north-west of Ireland led to renewed and increased strife between the Irish chiefs, particularly the old enemies O'Neills and O'Donnells, and the principal cockpit was the site of what would later become known as Strabane.

In 1380, 1395, 1398 and 1400, the local wars were resumed. This was a period which modern writers agree was 'the darkest of the Middle Ages'. It had seen the coming and going of the Danes and the Normans and much evidence of the cruelties of which they were guilty, but the severest wounds inflicted on Irish society were self-inflicted – truly the enemy within!

Castles and fortified buildings

One of the most remarkable Gaelic fortifications in Ireland stands on a low hill just outside Newtownstewart. Built in the latter part of the fourteenth century, this castle, known as Harry Avery's after the O'Neill chieftain believed to have been responsible for its construction, has as its most distinctive feature a double-towered building, with the entrance between the towers. This 'gatehouse' has parallels with gatehouses of English castles of the same period and shows a borrowing of ideas by Gaelic chieftains from the English.

The remains of another Gaelic castle stand on a small island in Lough Catherine in the grounds of Baronscourt. Island MacHugh castle was probably built in the later fifteenth century and consists of a small stone keep about 20 feet high, attached to which is a small bailey. The site has a very long history dating back to the neolithic period (*c.* 4000–2000 BC), when it began as a crannog or artificially constructed lake dwelling which was later extended in the Iron Age (*c.* 500 BC – AD 400). Other castles and tower houses were built in this area in the sixteenth century, but nothing now remains of the fortifications at Dunnalong, Newtownstewart, Strabane and elsewhere.

2 The Foundation of Strabane

JIM BRADLEY

The Franciscan Community

The Submission of Turlough O'Neill to Sir Henry Sidney after the death of Shane O'Neill in 1567 as illustrated in John Derrick's The Image of Ireland.

In 1231 the Franciscan order of Friars Minor arrived in Ireland for the first time and over the next century founded many religious houses. By 1326 a group of friars is said to have established a religious foundation on a green plateau overlooking the Mourne and close to the riparian battlegrounds of the Finn and the Foyle. The site is now the old graveyard at Patrick Street, and, not for the first time in Ireland, the church buildings were erected beside the standing stone previously mentioned – the triumph of Christianity over paganism!

This foundation, which was to last for almost two hundred years, is not listed by Franciscan historians, whose records tell us of a Franciscan house in Strabane town in the unlikely years of 1681 and 1682, long after the Strabane community had merged with a community of Third Order regulars at Scarvagherin, Castlederg.

Various terms have been used to designate Franciscan foundations such as the one in Strabane, e.g. abbey, convent, friary, or monastery. Abbey and monastery are misleading terms. 'Monastery' implies a community of monks, but there is a clear distinction between monks and friars – Franciscans were not monks. 'Convent' would be a correct canonical term for a Franciscan house, but in its present-day usage the term relates solely to a community of nuns. 'Friary' is the best name, and this appellation was used in the English language as far back as 1538 to designate a house of Franciscan friars.

The ordinary day-to-day existence of the local friars would have consisted of the usual round of masses, offices, other spiritual exercises and manual work. Some were engaged in preaching, some in studies, and some in work around the house and garden, turf-cutting in the local bogs, as well as timber-felling and fishing in the prolific Mourne and Foyle. The friars were the sole educators of the people of the district as they tried with some limited success to introduce Christian ideals into the tribal struggles and warring campaigns of the time.

The Life of the People

The friary, and the cluster of cabins on its south-eastern side inhabited by families seeking protection and instruction, formed the nucleus of the pre-plantation settlement that became known as 'An Srath Bán', meaning 'the fair holm' or 'fair river valley' – though some authorities hold that the name Strabane means 'white strand', deriving from the whitish gravel deposits in the river as it passes through the town. It seems likely that the original settlement was largely confined to the area that, centuries later, became known as Bowling Green and Barrack Street.

For over half a century after its foundation, the Gaelic-speaking settlement was reasonably free from trouble, although there was no significant development in the area. The cabins would have been small timber constructions roofed with peat or thatched with rushes. The local peasantry knew little of building, and the few houses that were made of stone were of dry masonry, as the use of mortar was unknown. The cabins were round in form and consisted of only one apartment with no chimney, smoke from the centrally located fireplace issuing through a hole in the roof.

There was little husbandry, no roads or bridges, and the whole district was heavily wooded – a contemporary chronicler claimed that there was a continuous forest from the Foyle to Lough Derg. There were occasional clearings for the growing of corn, barley and flax, and a limited range of vegetables, principally beans and peas. Grazing was carried on under the system known as creaghting, involving the movement of cattle between summer and winter pastures, all unfenced.

The spectre of hunger or want was never far removed from the lives of many who could, by the standards of the time, be regarded as living above the poverty line. The diet of the ordinary people in those years, long before the introduction of the potato, generally consisted of coarse oaten bread, salted meat, and milk, butter and buttermilk when available. Their chief drink was ale brewed from barley.

In those years the usual dress of the Ulster peasant consisted of a smock or shirt made of linen and of an overall mantle of wool with an edge of shaggy material. This latter was described in the state papers as 'a garment by day and a house by night – it makes the wearer by continuous use of it more apt, and more able, to lie out in the bogs and the woods. They plough, they ditch, they thresh with their mantles on.' Some of the men wore skin-tight trews and calfskin sandals or shoes, but many of the poorer classes wore neither trews nor shoes and so went barefooted and barelegged.

The Quarrels of the Clans – Strabane in Turmoil

In 1380 the period of relative calm in the district was broken when the O'Neills and the O'Donnells resumed hostilities in a major battle during which an English expeditionary force under Viceroy Edmund Mortimer took the opportunity to raid and destroy much property, ecclesiastical and lay, including the castle of Newton O'Donnell at Castlefin.

During the next century there was intermittent warfare between the related clans of O'Neill and O'Donnell, so it was logical that early in the sixteenth century Neil Connolly O'Neill, a leading member of the Clann Art or Slua Art branch of the O'Neills, then living in the castle at Ballynua (Newtownstewart), should build a castle or large fortified house in Strabane on the banks of the Mourne close to the site of the present Health Centre in Meetinghouse Street. This was to be the bridgehead for future attacks on the O'Donnells, whose traditional assembly point in neighbouring Tyrconnell was at Drumleen, a hill adjacent to Rossgeir, reasonably secure from surprise cross-river attacks.

In June 1522 a major confrontation, remembered in the folklore as the 'Battle of Knockavoe', took place between the traditional enemies. This surpassed in ferocity the countless wars and glorified faction fights previously waged across the Finn and the Foyle.

Prior to the combat, the O'Neills under Conn Bacach (Con the Lame) made their preparations with great secrecy and care, and succeeded in enlisting the support of the Connacht clans of McWilliams, O'Connor, O'Kennedy, O'Carroll, Burke, McDermott and O'Brien, as well as the Ulster clans of McGuinness, McMahon and O'Reilly, and a contingent of English mercenaries from Leinster who were willing to 'help the son of the

Earl's daughter', for Conn was the grandson of the earl of Kildare. Conn intended this particular battle to be the final showdown between his clan and the O'Donnells, whose prospect of victory seemed very slim.

Battle at Knockavoe

Manus O'Donnell, son of the chieftain of Tyrconnell, in no way daunted, summoned the help of the minor Donegal clans of O'Boyle, MacSweeney and O'Gallagher, and the combined O'Donnell forces, having marched from Donegal town through Barnesmore Gap, pitched their camp at Drumleen, where they were joined by a contingent of the finest of the O'Doherty warriors from Inishowen. At the same time the main O'Neill forces were encamped at Knockavoe, overlooking the river valley, awaiting the arrival of some of their allies from Connacht and Leinster.

In the early hours of 15 June 1522, the O'Donnells made a surprise two-pronged attack across the Foyle on the O'Neill camp, with complete success. Following a savage encounter, which lasted throughout the long summer day and ranged from the Greenbraes of the Foyle to Lough Moneen (the old name for Murlog), the outcome, according to the annals, was that 'the O'Neills were defeated with the loss of nine hundred men and many of their best leaders and great quantities of armour, provisions and strong liquors were seized by the victors'.

Many of those who perished in the battle were buried with Christian rites in mass graves on the hillside (now Church Street) below the friary. In the early years of the twentieth century, long-buried remains were unearthed during pipe laying operations in the Church Street/Patrick Street area. The latest of those morbid finds was as recent as 1960 during rebuilding operations on the facade of Melly's public house (known until recently as Kelly's Bar and now Farrell's). It should be noted, however, that the main source for the details of the battle is the *Annals of the Four Masters*, which may not be impartial, given the compilers' association with the O'Donnells.

In 1523 the O'Donnells again invaded Tyrone and burned the available buildings, including the friary at Strabane. The annals record that on this occasion the O'Donnells 'left nothing worth notice in it without burning'. It was at this time that the Strabane friars left the settlement to merge with the Scarvagherin community. This settlement was confiscated by the Crown in 1609 and its lands were granted to Robert Leicester.

In 1524 and 1525 there was continuous internecine strife between the local clans, and in consequence Manus O'Donnell, now the O'Donnell chieftain, commenced, in 1526, the erection of a castle in Lifford (immediately downstream on the Foyle from Lifford courthouse). O'Donnell hoped that the erection of the Lifford fortification would bring 'peace in his time'. For a period his optimism was fulfilled, and for the next thirty years there was relative calm in the Strabane/Lifford area.

In the year 1532 Manus, now resident in his new castle in Lifford, embarked on a project completely different from his previous warlike activities – a compilation of all existing documents and poems in Latin and Old Irish relating to the life and times of Colmcille. The preface to this monumental work translates in the following words:

> Be it known to the readers of this Life that it was Manus son of Hugh, son of Hugh Roe, Son of Niall Garve, son of Tirlough of the Wise O'Donnell, who ordered the part of this Life which was in Latin to be put into Gaelic and who ordered that what was in difficult Gaelic should be modified so that it might be clear and comprehensive to everyone; and who gathered and put together the parts of it that were scattered throughout the old books of Erin; and who dictated out of his own mouth with great labour and a great expenditure of time in studying how he should arrange all its parts in their proper places as they are left here in writing by us; and in love and friendship for his illustrious saint, relative and patron to whom he was devoutly attached. It was in the Castle of Port-na-Tri-Namhad that this Life was indited when were fulfilled 12 years and 20 and 500 and 1000 of the age of the Lord [Note: Port-na-Tri-Namhad, 'Port of the Three Enemies', was the old name for Lifford.]

This *Life*, written in a large vellum folder, is preserved in the Bodleian Library at Oxford and was only made available in a published translation in 1918. It has been republished again recently.

On 12 June 1541, a parliament was held in Dublin at which the novel sight was witnessed of Irish chiefs sitting for the first time with English lords. An Act was passed conferring on Henry VIII the title 'King of Ireland' instead of 'Lord of Ireland', by which title he and his predecessors had been known. Although O'Neill and O'Donnell kept aloof from this parliament they both made their submission to the Crown in 1542. O'Neill renounced the Irish title of 'The O'Neill' and was created earl of Tyrone. O'Donnell was granted the title of earl of Tyrconnell, but this honour was not formally conferred until the accession of Rory O'Donnell in 1603.

In 1555 Calvagh O'Donnell, the ambitious eldest son of Manus O'Donnell, aided by Scottish mercenaries, seized the reins of power from his father, whom he made prisoner in Lifford until his death at the age of 71 years, which is recorded in the annals in the following words:

> 1563 O'Donnell, Manus son of Aodh Dubh son of Aodh Rua son of Niall Garbh son of Turlough of the Wise Lord of Tyrconnell, Inishowen, Fermanagh and North Connacht. He was fierce towards his enemies, friendly and bountiful to the learned and the poor, to ollamhs and literati, to religious and clergy. A skilled and learned man. Died February 9 in his

Shane O'Neill

One of the best-known, if not best-loved, names in Irish history is that of Sean an Dionmuis (Shane the Proud), son of Con Bacach O'Neill. His name has been vilified by English historians, and it is difficult to excuse him even in an age when violence and wrongdoing were commonplace. He was, on the other hand, reputed to be chivalrous and generous, and was generally accepted as an outstanding Irish military strategist of the sixteenth century. His life and times, including his attendances upon Queen Elizabeth, are so well documented that it is unnecessary to dwell upon them in these pages except in so far as they form part of the history of this area.

On the death of his father, Con Bacach, in 1558, Shane assumed the O'Neill chieftaincy, and in accordance with a unique and barbarous custom of 'first hosting', whereby a newly elected chief was expected to raid the territory of an enemy, he decided to take advantage of the dissension in the O'Donnell camp following the usurpation of the leadership by Calvagh.

For this purpose in the summer he mustered an expeditionary force of sixty gallowglasses (Scottish mercenaries) and sixty Irish fighting men at Carricklee, between the rivers Finn and Mourne, where he was joined by Hugh O'Donnell, the second son of Manus, who disapproved of the overthrow of his father by Calvagh. In this emergency Calvagh actually consulted his imprisoned father, who, despite the treatment he had received from his son, was mindful of the old enmity between himself and the O'Neills, and proposed the strategy to use in the forthcoming encounter – briefly, to avoid a pitched battle and to rely on the merit of a surprise attack.

O'Neill's men entered Tyrconnell unimpeded and encamped at Balleighan near Newtowncunningham, and, following a plan similar to that adopted by Manus thirty-five years earlier in the Battle of Knockavoe, the O'Donnells struck without warning before dawn on 1 May 1558 and proceeded 'to slaughter the men of Tyrone without resistance' (*Annals of the Four Masters*). Shane was one of the few survivors, and he escaped 'by swimming across three rivers' on his way to the Sperrins and thence to Dungannon. This was the second of the great battles of the sixteenth century fought along the banks of the Finn and the Foyle, but it was not to be the last.

In 1561 Shane returned in a surprise raid on Tyrconnell, and at the Franciscan friary of Killydonnell near Letterkenny, he captured Calvagh O'Donnell and his wife, who later became Shane's very willing mistress. After being held captive in fetters for almost two years, Calvagh was ransomed (by the surrender of territory) and he resumed leadership of those of his clan who remained loyal to him. It was while he was leading his followers at Derry on 26 October 1566 that he fell dead from his horse from natural and unexplained causes 'in the heyday of his health and vigour' (O'Sullivan Beare – *Historiae Catholicae Iberniae Compendium*).

At this time the Irish explained the sudden death of Calvagh as a divine punishment for the desecration of the church of Doire Colmcille by the English who had been garrisoned there by Calvagh to prevent Derry from falling into the hands of Shane O'Neill.

On the death of Calvagh, his brother, Hugh Dubh, succeeded to the O'Donnell chieftaincy and immediately became a bitter enemy of Shane, although he had been on his side in the battle between Calvagh and Shane at Carricklee in 1558. The new O'Donnell, encouraged by the English government and promised a measure of support, launched attacks into Shane's territory, which of course included Strabane and its hinterland, and this action so exasperated Shane that he mobilised a substantial force and invaded Tyrconnell, crossing the Swilly at Farsetmore.

Well prepared for the expected attack, the forces of O'Donnell were once more successful in routing the O'Neills. The annals record that about 1,000 of the O'Neill forces were slain in battle or drowned in the Swilly in this encounter, which took place on 8 May 1567, and Shane only managed to escape with his life by swimming over the swollen Swilly. He believed that he could retrieve the situation by an alliance with the McDonnells of the Glens, previously his bitter enemies.

He fled to Antrim with his mistress, the widow of Calvagh, and a small following to seek the assistance of the McDonnells encamped at Cushendun. In the course of a drunken feast on the night of 2 July 1567, Shane and his followers were slain by their hosts, possibly in an attempt to curry favour with the government, and in this manner the way was clear for the entry onto the scene of the most renowned of the Strabane O'Neills – Turlough Luineach, son of Niall Connolly O'Neill, chieftain and builder of Strabane castle.

The Rise and Fall of Turlough Luineach O'Neill

Because Turlough was the most important figure ever in the history of the Strabane area, this chapter must dwell at some length on his life and times, despite the fact that he was reported to have been as bloody-minded as any of his kinsmen. Recent research, however, tends to suggest that Turlough Luineach was far from the buffoon and drunkard often portrayed in contemporary English sources, and the fact that he was able to keep the government at bay for the next thirteen years is testimony to his adroitness and political skills.

Turlough, later to become Sir Turlough, was at this time the territorial leader of the Clann Art branch of the O'Neills, whose traditional castles were at Newtownstewart and Strabane. He had earlier been renowned as one of Shane's most vigorous lieutenants in his wars against the English and the O'Donnells, until, as a result of a quarrel over the succession, the alliance was broken and he became Shane's rival. He was named Luineach because of his having been fostered by the O'Luineach sept in the Munterloney district of the Sperrins, and as he was the most powerful member of the O'Neill clan following the death of Shane, he was elected out of four contenders to succeed him, despite the fact that Shane had left two sons.

According to the Irish chroniclers, Turlough was an easy-going man of amiable disposition – the English referred to him as 'facile and brittle and without ambition', and the Dean of Armagh, Terence Donnelly, wrote that the new O'Neill was a 'savage but timorous man'. Whatever he was, he was certainly not timorous in the cowardly sense. He had fought fiercely in the past and would do so in the future, and he could scarcely be regarded as unambitious, having, five years prior to being crowned 'The O'Neill' at Tullaghogue, arranged the murder of the youthful Brian O'Neill who would have been a possible contender for the chieftainship.

Turlough's first hosting in the year following his accession was a complete disaster. He sent a raiding party under the leadership of Shane's grandson, Con Boy McHenry, into Monaghan to convince the ruling McMahons there that a recent renunciation of his overlordship of their territory in favour of the Queen had been merely a polite formality. The raiding party was badly defeated – its teenage leader was killed, as were 300 of Turlough's men.

For the next year Turlough occupied himself in the building of a 'fine castle' on the old Danish settlement of Dunnalong on the Foyle and was reasonably peaceful, apart from a successful raid on Newry in August 1569 in which his men carried off 3,000 cattle belonging to Sir Nicholas Bagenal, in retaliation for an insulting reference by Bagenal to the sister of Turlough's deceased wife.

A Scottish Alliance

It was about this time that Turlough, then a widower, was sending regular proposals of marriage to Lady Agnes McDonnell, daughter of the earl of Argylle, which partly explained his anxiety for a new castle. His wooing of the noble Scots lady may also have prompted his short-lived rebellion in 1569, when he demanded all the rights enjoyed by his ancestors, protested against the attempted plantation of Clandeboy and displacement of the Scots residing there, and warned against any harm being done to Sorley Boy MacDonnell of Antrim.

Turlough's marriage soon afterwards to Lady Agnes on Rathlin Island was negotiated by his principal bard, Ferdoragh MacNamee, who was described in the state papers as 'the richest Rhymer in Ireland'. The MacNamees, whose traditional homeland was Cúirt an Bhaird ('Home/Court of the Poet', now the Baronscourt desmesne), were the hereditary poets to the O'Neills. Their most illustrious kinsman, Gilbride MacNamee, had in 1260 composed a poem in which he made the gruesome boast that the O'Neills had a chess board formed of the bones of their one-time foes, the Leinstermen. A translation from the Irish reads:

> Chess of the shinbones of Leinstermen
> In our workshop was constructed
> Smooth chessmen were on the tables of our ancestors
> Of the bare bones of the Leinstermen

Many historians assert that Lady Agnes brought with her to Strabane as her dowry 1,000 Scots mercenaries. This was a frightening innovation for the English government, and we know from later state papers that the English government tried to force Turlough to reduce his Scottish mercenaries to no more than 300 men. Whatever number of Scots were in Turlough's employ, it was more than he could afford, but it made him the chief power in Ulster.

Turlough spent a fortnight on Rathlin to celebrate his wedding and the consequent link forged between the O'Neills and the McDonnells. The relationship between these powerful clans was further cemented by the marriage at the same time of Turlough's eldest son Henry (killed in battle in 1578) to Lady Agnes's third daughter by her previous marriage (the other two daughters of Lady Agnes, Catherine and the redoubtable Iníon Dubh, having respectively married Shane O'Neill and Hugh O'Donnell).

These marriages between members of the ruling clans were seldom love matches, and in Turlough's case they increased his political power, which was further enhanced by the subsequent marriage of one of his daughters to Con MacCalvagh, a strong contender against Hugh O'Donnell for the leadership of the O'Donnells, earlier held by his father Calvagh and grandfather Manus.

In 1569 the recently appointed Lord Deputy Sydney landed at Carrickfergus and received there the formal submission of Turlough. On several occasions following his break with Shane, Turlough, presumably in anticipation of future events, had proclaimed himself The O'Neill – which action in itself was considered by the Crown as an act of treason – and he had repeated this 'offence' at his coronation, hence the necessity for his submission. Despite this formal renunciation by Turlough of his rebellious ways, the lord deputy was aware that in the early days of his chieftainship Turlough had evinced an unmistakable anxiety to put an end to English interference in the affairs of his clan.

The care with which he was watched, and the aversion with which he was regarded by the English, was remarkable. Deputy Fitzwilliam, in his letters to the State Offices in England, often referred to Turlough's 'pride', his 'treachery', his 'insincerity', his 'friendship for the Scottish McDonnells in Antrim', his 'assumption' of the proscribed title of 'The O'Neill' and his 'continued employment of Scottish mercenaries' who, at that time, were too numerous and troublesome in Ulster for the peace of the Crown.

In 1569 Lord Deputy Sydney reported to his imperial masters that Turlough had 'with him in Strabane one thousand Scots and is working in the old manner of his lewd predecessors and has an understanding with all the rebels in the kingdom'. Accordingly, as a necessary precaution, the English government decided to groom the young Hugh O'Neill, second son of the deceased Matthew, the illegitimate half-brother of Shane, as a possible rival for the O'Neill chieftaincy. This was part of the divide and conquer policy that the English used so often and so effectively in their dealings with the Irish clans. Turlough's comment on this devious policy was that 'the English were rearing a whelp which would bite their hands' – a prophetic comment that would be remembered when Hugh would achieve fame (or notoriety) as the great earl of Tyrone.

Turlough and the English Administration

When Turlough was elected leader, the clan expected him to act and think as an Irish chieftain, and for a time he proved a thorn in the side of the English desire to control Ulster. The annals mention that there were many poems addressed to him inciting him to shake off English rule and become monarch of Ireland like his ancestors. However, it seems that Turlough, advancing in years, had little stomach for taking on the English and was being influenced by his new wife Lady Agnes in the ways of peace and obedience to the Queen. In recognition of her role as 'wise counsellor' (quoting the words of Lord Deputy Sydney), Lady Agnes was presented with one of Queen Elizabeth's magnificent velvet dresses, which, however, was so damaged in places by the queen's untidy fashion of eating that it had to be provided with a new lap before presentation (Gerrard to Walsingham).

It was at this time, on being presented with gowns and robes by the lord deputy for his occasional visits to the Irish parliament in Dublin, that Turlough was reputed as saying he did not much 'fancy these weades'. He asked the lord deputy to allow one of the latter's chaplains to go with him through the streets of Dublin clad in 'trousse' (trousers) as worn by the Irish, saying 'The boyes will then laugh as much at him as now they do at me.'

By 1574 Turlough's most trusted captain in the field of battle was his favourite son-in-law, Con McCalvagh, nephew and rival of Hugh Dubh, the reigning O'Donnell chieftain. Con was then in possession of his grandfather's castle at Lifford, the ancient castle of Nagthan O'Donnell at Castlefin, and all the lands in the Finn Valley. When Essex was carrying out his illadvised expedition in the north-west, he attempted unsuccessfully to enlist the aid of Con McCalvagh in a foray against Turlough, but Con refused to join, out of loyalty to his father-in-law. As a result he was arrested on the orders of Essex and sent to Dublin Castle, to the great joy of his uncle Hugh, who promptly seized possession of Con's strongholds in Lifford and Castlefin. On his subsequent escape from Dublin Castle, Con, now homeless and without followers, was given a home in Strabane at Castletown (West), and for the next few years he became the recognised commander of Turlough's field forces.

In the great rebellion of the earl of Desmond in 1579, Turlough sought by bribery to induce the neighbouring Hugh O'Donnell to join with him in support of Desmond, his kinsman, which O'Donnell refused to do. In December of the same year the Lord Chief Justice of Ireland wrote to the Council in England that 'Desmond had daily messages' with Turlough and that the latter was procuring Scottish mercenaries to go to Munster to support Desmond against the Crown. The *Book of Howth* at that time described Turlough 'as not to be trusted for he had killed his brother and in his drunkenness had slain three of the best gallowglasses he had, causing all his gallowglasses to refuse to continue in his service as a result of which he was unable to make all the wars he would'.

Although there was no love lost between Turlough and Hugh O'Neill, there was a temporary peace in 1579 when Hugh divorced his wife Joan (née O'Donnell) and went through a form of marriage with a daughter of Turlough by an earlier marriage. On the same occasion Turlough nominated Hugh as his tánaiste or successor. These arrangements increased the enmity between the O'Neills and the O'Donnells, for Joan was a daughter of Manus O'Donnell and a sister of the O'Donnell chieftain.

Lord Ernest Hamilton in his flawed work, *Elizabethan Ulster*, writes that on the occasion of Turlough's journey to the Blackwater Fort for the 'marriage' of his daughter to Hugh O'Neill, he was still recovering from a severe stomach injury caused some little time before by a leaden ball 'from a caliver' which his jester Donnolly had accidentally let off during a drunken carouse in Turlough's castle in Strabane. Being too weak to ride, Turlough was carried forty miles in a litter to the Dungannon meeting place. Hamilton goes on to say that on the journey Turlough wore the high steeple-crowned taffeta hat given to him as a wedding present from his father-in-law, the earl of Argylle. The state papers, referring to the shooting incident three months after it happened, inform us that 'Turlough is not yet whole of his hurt'.

In the year 1581 Turlough entrusted the command of his available forces to Con McCalvagh for a foray into Hugh O'Donnell's territory at Kiltole near Raphoe, in which it was recorded that 600 of the O'Donnells were killed. After the battle, peace negotiations were carried on across the Foyle by the wives of Turlough and Hugh O'Donnell, i.e. Lady Agnes living in

Dunnalong and her daughter, the renowned Iníon Dubh, living in Mongelvin Castle on the opposite side of the Foyle. (The ruins of this old castle, which was the birthplace of Iníon Dubh's son, Red Hugh O'Donnell, can be seen along the disused railway line between Porthall and St Johnstone.) The outcome of the peace negotiations was that the castles of Lifford and Castlefin were restored to Con McCalvagh, the rival branch of the O'Donnells, while their chieftain Hugh was to hold the castles at Donegal Town and Mongevlin. On the death of Con McCalvagh in March 1583, Hugh O'Donnell retook possession of the Lifford castle.

If we are to fully accept the writings of Lord Ernest Hamilton, the year 1583 must have been an eventful one for Turlough. This author quotes from a letter written from Privy Councillor Fenton to Walsingham, dated 19 June 1583, that at that time Turlough's military ardour 'had abated' and that he had left active operations in the field of battle to others while he devoted himself exclusively to the wine flagon. Hamilton goes on to say that so deep were Turlough's 'potations' that a short time previously he was actually reported dead and 'laid out with honours in his castle of Strabane', and that the inevitable sycophant galloped over to Dungannon and imparted the glad tidings to Baron Hugh O'Neill, who immediately betook himself to the crowning stone at Tullahogue and there went through the ceremony of investiture. According to Hamilton, 'Turlough was not dead but only very drunk, and after lying in a deathlike trance for twenty-four hours he astonished the assembled mourners by getting up and walking unsteadily away.'

The Burning of Strabane

If the above narrative is untrue, and it certainly stretches credibility, there is no doubt that 1583 was a disastrous year for Turlough. Apart from the death of his son-in-law, Con McCalvagh O'Donnell, the person Turlough loved more than any other, we find it reported in the annals for the same year:

> The town of O'Neill namely Srath Bán was burned by O'Donnell (Hugh the son of Manus) and great injuries were done to O'Neill beside the plundering of the town for it was on this occasion that O'Coinne (Quinn) the son of McHugh and many others beside them were slain by O'Donnell.

That encounter took place in September 1583, following an earlier and unsuccessful attack on the O'Donnell camp at Drumleen.

Early in 1584, the lord deputy, Sir John Perrott, marked out seven counties in Ulster, including Tyrone, for which sheriffs, commissioners of the peace and coroners were appointed, and in the following year he summoned a parliament, which met in Dublin on 26 and 28 April and which was memorable for the great number of Irish lords and heads of septs who attended. The official attendance roll was headed by the name of Turlough O'Neill, followed by Hugh, Baron of Dungannon, who was formally created earl in this parliament. The principal business of the assembly was to attain for treason the earl of Desmond and 140 of his followers – seven years earlier Turlough was inducing others to join in Desmond's rebellion and now he was sitting in judgment on those he had secretly supported! A prime example of the poacher turned gamekeeper!

A further enactment of the same parliament was the appointment of Turlough, Baron Hugh and Marshall Bagenal as a triumvirate to be responsible for the government of the northern province. This arrangement was short-lived. Turlough, disregarding his new-found responsibilities, tacitly approved of intermittent raids into Hugh's territory by the embittered sons of the dead Shane, who were at that time living in the Strabane district in a small castle long since demolished but remembered in the present-day name of Castletown East. Hugh O'Neill quickly retaliated by burning Dunnalong Castle at a time when Turlough was temporarily living in Lifford in a house of Hugh Gallagher, a minor Donegal chieftain – his Strabane castle was still in ruins following its destruction by Hugh O'Donnell in 1583.

Despite the outward show of recognition by the government of Turlough's importance, his position was being steadily eroded, a process which was accelerated when, in 1587, the Crown compelled him to lease to Hugh for seven years the greater part of the territory of Tyrone, i.e. everything lying to the south-east of the mountain of Mullaghcarn in the Sperrins to the Blackwater. Turlough's control was confined to the north-western part of the principality of Tyrone, corresponding largely to the present Strabane District Council area.

Turlough Loses Power

This arrangement considerably advanced Hugh in power and esteem, while Turlough, still the titular head of the clan, was steadily losing power, privileges and income. It was the privately expressed hope of the English that within the seven years of the lease Turlough would be dead of old age or through his continual use of alcohol, and that the English-reared and English-educated Hugh would then succeed to the overlordship of the whole county of Tyrone defined by Perrott.

From this time on, relations between the two O'Neills deteriorated rapidly and over the next three years there were intermittent bloody skirmishes between their respective adherents at various places, including Mountjoy near Omagh and at historic Ardstraw. Finally, at the close of April 1588, Hugh, earl of Tyrone, led an army against Turlough and encamped at Carricklee as his half-uncle Shane had done in 1557.

Despite their earlier estrangement as a result of the treatment meted to his sister Joan by Hugh O'Neill, Hugh O'Donnell joined forces with the earl while the family of Calvagh O'Donnell supported Turlough, who was also aided by English auxiliaries from Connacht under a Captain Moyston and by the followers of Turlough's friend, Hugh Gallagher. Despite the fact that the combined forces of the earl of Tyrone, amounting to 1000 men, outnumbered the 400-strong force led by Moyston and the elderly Turlough, the encounter which took place along the banks of the Finn on the first day of May 1588 ended in the withdrawal in disarray of the earl's followers.

By 1591 a virtual state of war existed between the joint rulers of Tyrone. The following letter from Deputy Fitzwilliam to Burghley in 1591 gives some idea as to the state of affairs in the county at that time:

> I, and this Council being now but six in number, must be, the last of this month (God pleased) at Dundalk for the ending of a great controversy between the earl and Sir Tyrlagh O'Neale, by reason of a fray fallen between them in which the dutiful old knight Sir Tyrlagh was shot through the shoulder with a bullet and stricken with a horseman's staff in the small of his back, two grievous wounds but (God, I thank) well recovered. I sent him a surgeon with a great deal of stuff for his dressing.

Writing less than a month afterwards to Sir George Carew, the Deputy mentions the 'affaire' in the following words:

> In the quarrel between the Earl of Tyrone and Sir Tyrlagh O'Neale it was complained that the Earl was altogether in fault but on examination (having them both here and at the Newry) it fell out that Sir Tyrlagh was therein fair to blame. I and the Council have so ended those causes as they are both returned home with good contentment and have given both their consents to have Tirone reduced to shire ground and to accept a Sheriff [*Calendar of Carew MSS*, 3rd series, pp. 55, 57]

By the end of 1591 Turlough had rebuilt the castle at Strabane, in ruins since its destruction by Hugh O'Donnell in 1583. By this time, however, his main body of Scottish mercenaries had deserted him and he had only the support of a small group of English soldiery under the command of a Captain Humphrey Willis. On his return to the Strabane castle, Turlough handed over to Niall, the son of Con McCalvagh, the new stone house of Hugh Gallagher in Lifford which he had occupied since the O'Donnells burned his Strabane castle.

Turlough the Middleman

On 3 May 1593 Hugh O'Donnell, then living in Donegal town, abdicated the chieftaincy of Tyrconnell in favour of his son, the illustrious Red Hugh, who, following his inauguration and in accordance with the ancient custom, resolved to make his 'first hosting' without delay. Not surprisingly, he embarked on an excursion into the Strabane district, which he laid waste, and then forced Turlough O'Neill and Captain Willis and their English soldiers to flee for asylum to the castle of Rory O'Cahan (O'Kane) in Dungiven. Because the fugitives found refuge under the roof of a chieftain friendly to the O'Donnells (and one who had been Red Hugh's foster-father), the O'Donnells agreed to a request by O'Cahan not to molest Turlough and his adherents on condition, amongst others, that Turlough would dismiss his English guard forever.

Due to his delay in doing so, Red Hugh again entered Strabane and attacked the rebuilt castle. This incident is described in the following words in a history of the O'Donnells, written in Irish in 1603 by Micheál O'Cleirigh:

> When he (Red Hugh) came to his castle at Donegal he remained there and his physicians were brought to examine his feet (he had suffered the loss of his two great toes through frostbite in his acclaimed escape from Dublin Castle). The illness remained with him for the space of two months and he allowed the troops to rest for that time. It seemed to him long that O'Neill (Turlough) and his English followers should not have been attacked during that time. He assembled his troops after two months preparation and they went off through Bearnas Mor, across the Finn, across the Mourne to Strabane to the place where the English and O'Neill were, to see if he could do them harm. Since the English did not leave the strong part of the castle to attack them, as they were anxious they should do, what they did was to kindle and light up fires and conflagrations in the four quarters of the town and they did not go away until they had burned and plundered all the houses close to the walls outside and until they drove off immediately many of a large number of horses which they met wandering about confused by the thick cloud of smoke which came a long distance from the town. It was on the 18 July 1592 this took place. As the English did not come meanwhile to guard or protect the town from them they left it after wasting it in this way and returning to their homes without opposition.

Under the combined military pressure of the O'Donnells, of the Crown's growing anxiety for the promotion of Hugh O'Neill, who was rising steadily in the esteem of his clan, and finally of his own weight of years, Turlough was, in May 1593, forced to resign the headship of the O'Neills after a much-troubled reign lasting over a quarter of a century. Thus Hugh, the earl of Tyrone, became the sole leader of the O'Neills and the seat of power, such as it was, moved away from Strabane for ever.

If we are to believe the writings of such historians as Lord Ernest Hamilton or the contemporary accounts of English observors, Turlough was by now a slave to drink and in poor circumstances. The rent agreed to be paid by Hugh O'Neill under the seven-year lease was three years in arrears and could not be enforced. (In a letter written by Fitzwilliam to Burghley, it was stated 'that the old O'Neale is quite past government being overcome by the drink which he is daily in'.)

To add to Turlough's problems, his two sons, Art (now living in the Dunnalong castle) and Cormac, had fallen out with him and had joined forces with his long-standing rival, the earl of Tyrone. In addition, his wife, Lady Agnes, was detained in Scotland as the virtual prisoner of her brother Angus.

In the rebellion which began in 1594 and was to be named the Nine Years War, Turlough, though old and broken, offered the Crown the use of his castle in Strabane and also offered to take to the field and reduce all Ulster to obedience if the Queen would make him certain concessions and allowances in the way of troops. His offer was not taken seriously and by the end of March 1595 he was writing to the lord deputy for assistance as his followers had all deserted him and he was at variance with his son Sir Art, who at that time was conspiring to have Turlough's castle in Strabane possessed by the earl of Tyrone.

In response to his request, a long-time friend, Captain Merriman, and 100 men were sent round by sea from Dublin to the Foyle in HM *Popinjay*, with instructions to bring Turlough to Dublin to spend his remaining days in peace and comfort, as he was past making the overland journey. Turlough was not destined to make the voyage, for in September 1595 he died in his castle at Strabane and was buried in Ardstraw in the burial grounds of his ancestors.

Although Turlough died loyal to the Crown, little respected by his clan and estranged from his sons, the *Annals of the Four Masters*, always prepared to see the good in everyone, chronicles his death in the following words:

> He had bestowed most wealth and riches upon the learned, the Ollamhs and all who sought gifts of any of the Lords of Ireland in his time for he had often issued a proclamation throughout Ireland to all those who sought gifts inviting them to come to him on the festivals of the Nativity of Our Lord and when they came not one of them departed dissatisfied or without being supplied. He was a Lord who had many soldiers in his service for pay and wages, a Lord prosperous in peace and powerful in war until age and infirmity came upon him...

So passed from our local scene one of its most colourful characters – an opportunist who changed his religion and his allegiances repeatedly without a scruple; a chieftain renowned for his generosity to his friends and cruelty to his enemies, brave and foolhardy in war, yet cunning enough to escape the fate of so many of his short-lived kinsmen.

The O'Neills Lose Out at Strabane

On the death of Turlough, his eldest son, Sir Art, then living in Dunnalong Castle, was successful in getting the Crown's agreement to his entering into possession of his father's lands and castles in north and mid Tyrone. However, in his father's declining years, Art had formed an alliance with Hugh O'Neill, the old man's long standing-rival, so it was not surprising that he would join forces with Hugh, commencing in June 1598.

As part of the military strategy involved in the rebellion, Art was actually responsible for the partial demolition of the castle in Strabane – erected by his grandfather, destroyed by the O'Donnells and lately restored by his father. This action was taken to prevent the castle falling into the hands of those branches of the O'Neill and O'Donnell clans at that time supporting the Government.

The tortuous relationship which had always existed between these two clans was much complicated in the second half of the sixteenth century by the fact that within each clan there were serious internal divisions. On the O'Neill side, there had been the long-standing rivalry between Turlough and Hugh; while in the O'Donnell camp, the descendants of Calvagh, namely Con McCalvagh and his son Nial Garbh, were in active opposition to Hugh O'Donnell and his son, the renowned Red Hugh, whose interests were being energetically and ruthlessly advanced by his mother, the forceful Iníon Dubh.

Viceroy Fitzwilliam, commenting on the friction in the O'Donnell camp, remarked that 'it was good to let them cut their own throats without which the kingdom will never be quiet'.

These words could have been applied with equal force to the O'Neills. For many years the local O'Neills (Clann Art) were in alliance with the branch of the O'Donnells descended from Calvagh, while the main line of the O'Donnells under Hugh and his son, Red Hugh, was usually in alliance with Hugh O'Neill. Consequently, in many of the battles in which these clans were involved, the opposing sides included members of both tribes.

The English forces in the area at this period were not a dominant factor and usually relied on the support of the shifting loyalties of the Irish. Future events would shortly alter for ever the whole balance of military power in the north-west of Ireland.

On 16 May 1600, a fleet arrived in Lough Foyle from England, having touched at Carrickfergus to take on board some troops that had marched there from Dublin. The fleet finally conveyed to the Foyle a total of 4000 foot soldiers and 200 horses under the command of Sir Henry Docwra, together with large supplies of military stores, building materials and other accessories for the construction of forts at Culmore, Derry and Lifford.

On 1 June 1600, Sir Art O'Neill, whose allegiances were as fickle as those of his father, made his formal submission to the Queen's representative and joined forces with Docwra. Sir Art came over to the English in the hope that the Crown would assist him in attaining the headship of the O'Neills from Hugh, who was now very much out of royal favour. By this time the English were beginning to appreciate the truth in Turlough's words many years earlier that, in favouring Hugh, 'They were rearing a whelp that would bite their hands.'

In the summer of 1600, Red Hugh, after successful forays against Docwra's forces, went on one of his too-frequent warring expeditions as far south as Co. Clare. In his absence the command of his forces at home was entrusted to Neal Garbh, his cousin and brother-in-law, and that worthy promptly joined forces with Dowcra and surrendered Lifford castle to him. Docwra now had the support of both Neal Garbh and Sir Art O'Neill and their followers. However, the last named was not destined to be of much assistance for long – following his submission, Art had been established by the Crown with a small force of English soldiers in the Dunnalong Castle erected by his father, where he died allegedly of alcoholic poisoning on 13 October 1600. In recording his death, the Annals briefly mention that he 'died with the English'.

Neal Garbh O'Donnell, whose name, rightly or wrongly, was reviled by many Irish historians, was poorly rewarded for his perceived betrayal of the native interest. Following the defeat of the Irish forces at the Battle of Kinsale in 1601, Red Hugh, the reigning chieftain, made his way to the Continent to seek Spanish help in a fresh rebellion. He died the following year in Spain in mysterious circumstances – some historians claim that he was poisoned by a spy acting in English interests, the foremost of which would have been to ensure that any proposed rebellion was nipped in the bud.

In 1603 the newly crowned James I received the submission of Rory O'Donnell (Red Hugh's brother), the new chieftain, and conferred on him the title of earl of Tyrconnell, held in suspense since 1543. On hearing of Red Hugh's death, Neal Garbh had hastily proclaimed himself 'The O'Donnell', a procedure and a name that were anathema to the Crown and that eventually prompted his removal to the Tower of London (for alleged conspiracy in Cahir O'Doherty's revolt), where he was confined until his death in 1626.

By 1603 Lifford was a strong English garrison town, while Strabane, which had sustained so much damage all through the troubled sixteenth century, had been finally reduced to ruins on 27 May 1601 by Donal O'Cahan and was to remain so until the commencement of the Ulster plantation a decade later.

On the death of Sir Art, the headship of the Clann Art branch of the O'Neills had passed to his half brother, Cormac McArt who, with most of his followers, had remained faithful to Hugh O'Neill and were in revolt since 1598. On 1 April 1601 Cormac was pardoned by the Queen but as a result of a subsequent disagreement with Docwra he went into rebellion for the second time in August. By 1604 Cormac was still in revolt but by then he and his diminishing band of followers had been virtually isolated in the Sperrins, in an area roughly corresponding to the present parish of Badoney.

In the absence of Cormac the final devolution of the headship of the Clann Art was to Turlough McArt, the eldest of the four surviving sons of Sir Art. The young Turlough and his brothers, then living in their castles at Dunnalong and Newtowne, had given their services regularly to the Crown and were at war with Hugh O'Neill. They expected, and were led by the Crown to expect, that despite the impending plantation, they would be allowed to remain on the lands and residences at Strabane, Newtowne and Dunnalong enjoyed by their ancestors.

The O'Neills Moved Out

Following the close of the wars against the northern earls and their subsequent escape to the Continent, the government felt that it was no longer dependent on the support of any of the native septs and that the urgency of the proposed plantation of Ulster would not permit the claims of the O'Neill brothers to be recognised. Some years before the plantation, Lord Deputy Chichester had taken it upon himself to grant a custodiam to Turlough McArt of the two castles at Newtowne and Strabane with the desmesnes belonging thereto. In his 'Notes of remembrance', the Deputy made the following entry:

> I have delivered the possession of the Newtowne with some three ballybetaghs of land about 3000 acres to Turlough and Neal McArt, the children of Sir Art O'Neill, in respect of the good service they did against the traitor O'Doherty and the relief they gave to the Liffer [Lifford] upon the burning of Derry. I think this sufficient for them but they do not. If the King will be pleased to reserve the town of Strabane which stands upon the lands now assigned to them and give them a greater scope on the other side I think it would be best for his service for divers Scottishmen will plant there and make it a pretty town albeit it was all burned to the ground by O'Doherty which was the cause they the young O'Neills were permitted to take it at this time.

The brothers made as good a fight as they could do for better terms, and Turlough, the eldest of the four, undertook the risk and expense of a trip to London that he might personally lay their case before the Council. He brought back a letter from the Council in the following words:

> We recommend the bearer Tyrloghe O'Neale eldest son of Sir Arthur

O'Neale Knight for two middle proportions (3000 acres) in the precinct of Dungannon in Tyrone. He sought from us all the land in Ulster called Slewsheese (about 1100 acres) which formerly belonged to Neal Conelagh O'Neale his great grandfather. Of these lands he only had a custody grant from you of the castles of Strabane and Newtowne with some ballybetaghs of land belonging to them. He now prays that he may have in addition to the proportions we have recommended for him the castles of Benburb and Knockincligh in the Barony of Dungannon but this we leave altogether to your judgement as to you is left the placing of the natives. Considering his acceptable services and his willingness to be transplanted we hope he may be extraordinarily respected in the greatness of his proportion and in the choice of a good seat for his greater comfort. One other middle proportion should be divided among the three other sons of Sir Arthur O'Neill, namely Neal, Con and Bryan. [Note: Slewsheese, or the 'Mountain Going North', was then the local name at Strabane of the great range now known as the Sperrins.]

Despite his earlier sentiments and the recommendations contained in the letter from the Council, Chichester forced the brothers to transfer by 1609 to the Barony of Dungannon without allotting to them the old castles there which they were anxious to secure. The removal of the brothers to the Dungannon area virtually ended the long association of the Clan Art with the Strabane district – the Crown now had free access to the whole Barony of Strabane, containing some 240,000 acres.

Two years earlier, on 14 September 1607, the earls of Tyrone and Tyrconnell with their followers had met at Ballindrait on the first stage of their journey to Rathmullan and permanent exile on the Continent – the leaders of the great families that for generations had fought savagely across the Finn and the Foyle were ironically united in the inglorious venture that has been romanticised in history as 'The Flight of the Earls'. With the departure of the earls and the removal of the local O'Neills, the Strabane and Lifford area was ripe for plantation.

Postscript

Most of the principal families in the Strabane area at the end of the sixteenth century were followers of Cormac O'Neill and were pardoned with him in 1601. They included McCannys (48 pardoned), McGushanans (27 pardoned), McEnallys (15 pardoned) and McNamees (8 pardoned).

It is not certain how many of those pardoned rejoined Cormac in his renewed revolt against the Crown and his final rearguard action in the Sperrins. A government list prepared at the time of Cormac's submission records that Cormac, his nephew Turlough McArt, and his cousin Neal were each the possessors of 2000 cattle and that four minor chiefs, O'Quinn,

McHugh, McBrien and McQuiry (McGurk), had each between 500 and 1000 head.

Addendum

The following is the substance of an agreement entered into for the division of Tyrone between the earl of Tyrone, Hugh O'Neill, and Turlough Luineach:

Article of Agreement made at Dondalke (Dundalk) on 28 June 1593:

1 First the Earl of Tyrone had the command of 50 horse equivalent to a sum of 6361 9s 4d yearly and Sir Tyrlough to have this command transferred to him during his life according to the Queen's injunction he finding the said horsemen to serve her majesty at the Earl's expense.

2 Sir Tyrlough to receive the yearly rents and duties payable by Maguire the Lord of Fermanagh according to the Queen's grant, the Earl being bound to compel Maguire to pay the same to Turlough should they at any time refuse to do so.

3 The Earl to pay Sir Turlough so many cows yearly as shall after the rate of 20s ster. the cow, make up together with the said command and Maguire's rent the sum of £2000 stg. provided always that if the said command do in the life of the said Sir Turlough surcease by the death of the Earl or otherwise then the Earl or his heirs or assigns shall pay to Sir Turlough the said sum of £2000 or in default of money a choice cow for every 20s sterling; such cows as shall be delivered at May yearly to be in calf and the cows to be delivered at Hallowmas (November) yearly to be sufficient beefs, 5s extra to be paid for every cow not delivered at the said feasts. The said money or cows to be paid at Strabane or Benburb.

4 Sir Turlough to have for life the town and lands of Strabane and Largie Uirnevie (Urney) and also the lands adjoining Strabane between the Finn and the Derg free from all duties and other charges.

5 Sir Turlough shall quietly and without any molestation from the Earl receive three score cows yearly from O'Doherty and also one half from the duties due from Lough Foyle and the Bann; the other half to be received by the Earl.

6 Sir Turlough demanded of the Earl some increase of pension over and above the £2000 to which the Earl was unwilling to yield but the arrangement of this point was left to the Earl's brother Cormac O'Neill and to his sons in law, Donal O'Kane and Henry Og O'Neill, Sir Turlough to name an arbitrator also. [A dispute existed between Sir Turlough and his son Arthur regarding certain lands then in the

possession of the latter, and the Earl attempted to enforce the decree of the arbitrators for the settlement of this controversy.]

7   Sir Turlough to receive such rents and duties out of the lands of Slewsheese owned by his father Neal Connolly O'Neill as were due to him by such as dwell in Tyrone and to cause Maguire and O'Cahan to pay Sir Turlough the arrears due upon them.

8   The Earl and his heirs to hold the territory of Tyrone against Sir Turlough and his heirs discharged of all such title and demand as Sir Turlough claimed to have in and to the same.

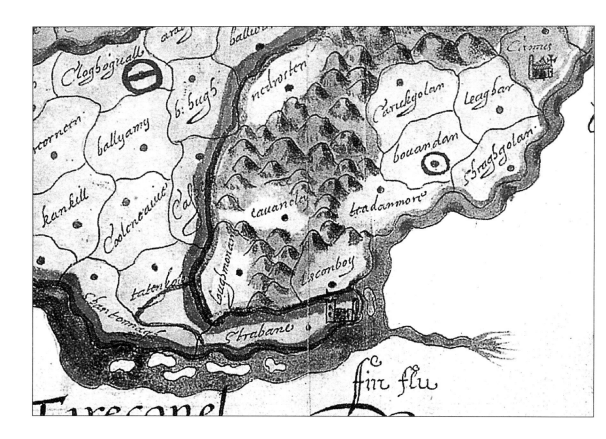

Part of the Bodley Map of Strabane in 1609, just before the Plantation

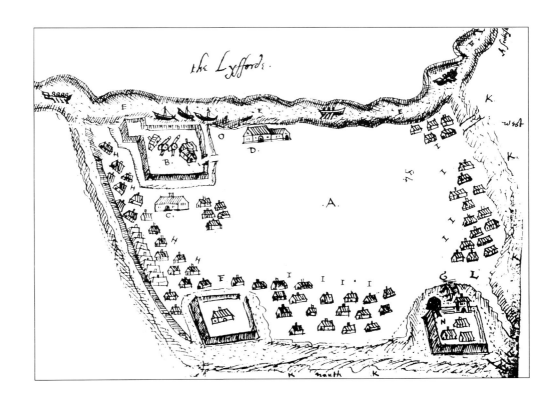

3 The Nine Years War in the North-West

Dunnalong, Lifford and the Conquest of North-west Ulster 1600–1603

WILLIAM ROULSTON

Lifford Fort in 1600

At the beginning of the seventeenth century, Ireland was caught up in a bloody and savage war between the Gaelic chieftains on the one side and the forces of the English Crown on the other. It is not necessary here to discuss the complex origins of this conflict, known to history as the Nine Years War (1594–1603). Suffice to say that in 1595 Hugh O'Neill, the earl of Tyrone, was declared a traitor and from that time on was in open rebellion against the government. He gathered around him a confederation of Gaelic lords headed by Hugh Roe O'Donnell, chieftain of the O'Donnell clan. To begin with, the war was a disaster for the English, culminating in their defeat at the Battle of Yellow Ford in 1598, when an entire army was wiped out. For a time it seemed that Dublin itself was under threat of attack.

It was clearly recognised that the confederates' strength lay in their stronghold of west Ulster, an area almost unknown to the English and separated from Dublin by a long and precarious march. The Dublin administration had also come to the realisation that the confederates in Ulster could not be defeated by a single invasion force. As early as 1596 the Council of War had drawn up plans for sending an expeditionary force to Lough Foyle. However, it was not until the appointment of Lord Mountjoy as lord deputy of Ireland that it was decided once and for all to send an English army by sea to north-west Ulster. The man appointed to lead this force was Sir Henry Docwra, a Yorkshireman who had gained considerable experience fighting the Spanish in the Low Countries.

Docwra was not just expected to tackle the forces of the confederacy in their own backyard. He was also instructed to find out which of the Gaelic chieftains were dissatisfied with the leadership of Tyrone and O'Donnell and could be induced to side with the English. Those chieftains who were believed to be wavering in their support for the confederacy included Sir Art O'Neill, Niall Garbh O'Donnell and Sir John O'Doherty. Sir Art was the son of Turlough Luineach O'Neill and a rival to the earl of Tyrone for the headship of the O'Neills. In a similar vein, Niall Garbh was a rival to Hugh Roe O'Donnell (Red Hugh), his kinsman, for the leadership of the O'Donnell clan. Both were hoping to use English intervention in northwest Ulster to further their own ends. The aim of this chapter is to provide a general overview of the English conquest of north-west Ulster, focusing on the war in west Tyrone, and in particular examining the role of the fort at Dunnalong in the period 1600–03.

The Establishment of an English Garrison at Lough Foyle

Departing from Carrickfergus on 12 May 1600, the English fleet entered Lough Foyle two days later, but because of poor piloting the ships became grounded several times and it was not until the 16 May that Culmore was reached. Here Docwra decided to build a fort capable of holding 200 soldiers. While this fort was being built troops, were sent on reconnaissance to find out more about the surrounding countryside. One company came upon Elagh, the chief castle of Sir John O'Doherty, which the Irish had abandoned and had attempted to pull down. Captain Floyd and his company of 150 men were stationed here by Docwra. A few days later unsuccessful negotiations took place between the English commander and O'Doherty, though Docwra held out hope that the Irish chieftain would eventually come over to his side.

Shortly after the English arrived in Lough Foyle, Sir Art O'Neill invited Docwra to come and visit him at his residence at Dunnalong. However,

Docwra, reluctant to venture far from his base at Culmore, and having been informed that Dunnalong was 'moist and unwholesome' to build upon, instead invited Sir Art to visit him at Derry. It was at Derry that Docwra was to establish his headquarters and to it he marched with the main part of his force on 22 May, leaving Captain Alford and 600 men at Culmore. On 1 June, Sir Art O'Neill and a company of foot-soldiers and horsemen entered Derry, only just escaping a force of confederate soldiers who were hard on their heels. Docwra and Sir Art immediately began their negotiations and, on the advice of the Irishman, Docwra sent Sir John Chamberlain, one of the senior English officers, into O'Cahan's country (now Co. Londonderry) with 700 men. The aim of this expedition, to capture a large herd of cattle, was successfully completed. Through this Sir Art won Docwra's trust, and the commander resolved to plant a garrison at Dunnalong as soon as the weather permitted.

The Construction of a Fort at Dunnalong

On the first day of July, Docwra, having decided that the time was right to establish a fort at Dunnalong, sent 800 men upriver in boats to the site of one of Turlough Luineach O'Neill's former castles. Docwra himself accompanied this force. Landing the next morning the soldiers immediately began building a fortification. On the following day some soldiers foraging for wood were attacked by troops in the service of the earl of Tyrone who had moved 1,200 of his men at Strabane closer to Dunnalong when the English had landed. Minor battles were fought all that day with the English driving back the earl's forces and reputedly killing between 100 and 120 of his men. Tyrone responded by dividing his force in two and placing 600 of his men in camp between Dunnalong and Derry. However, apart from this he basically left the fort to its own devices. Satisfied that the fort was secure, Docwra left six companies of foot at Dunnalong under the command of Sir John Bolles and later sent 50 horsemen there.

The fort at Dunnalong, like the forts at Culmore and Derry, was constructed with a strong earthen rampart surrounded by a ditch. The *Annals of the Four Masters* explains that this type of fortification was stronger than forts of stone or of lime and stone, and constructed more quickly. Docwra himself gave a good explanation of the purpose of these forts when he wrote, 'one of the chiefest uses we intended these garrisons for was to make sudden inroads upon their country to spoil and prey them of their cattle', upon which the Irish economy depended. In its immediate context the garrison at Dunnalong was expected to make incursions upon both O'Cahan's country and north Tyrone. However, it was also true that satisfying the personal whim of Sir Art O'Neill was also a major factor in the establishment of an English garrison here.

Later in the summer Docwra wrote to his superiors that Dunnalong was only really taken to satisfy Sir Art who wanted it to be a focal point to which his followers could be drawn. However, much to Docwra's dismay, many of the Irish came and went as they pleased, their submissions, it would appear, only lasting as long as it suited them. Sir Art, who lived with the English garrison at Dunnalong, was becoming increasingly troublesome to Docwra and continually pestered him for more money. Docwra responded angrily, telling the discontented Irishman to earn this by doing something useful. At the same time Docwra realised that, despite his failings, it was better to keep Sir Art on his side and give in to his demands.

A short time after this, a rather unfortunate incident occurred in the fort at Dunnalong. For some time relations between the English soldiers under Bolles and the Irish followers of Sir Art had been deteriorating, though this is hardly surprising given the differences between the two groups, particularly with regard to language. Crisis point was reached when a major brawl broke out between the two factions, and in the ensuing fight an Irish soldier was killed. Sir Art was furious and demanded immediate justice; when this was not forthcoming he became even angrier. Docwra, concerned that in his rage Sir Art would take the life of an innocent man, withdrew the Irish chieftain to Derry with the intention of sending him to Dublin where, after meeting with Mountjoy, his grievances would be redressed.

In other ways things were not going particularly well for the garrison at Dunnalong. Contrary to what might have been expected, the biggest threat to the English presence in Lough Foyle was not the armies of Tyrone or O'Donnell, but rather disease, which swept through the garrisons with devastating effect. At the end of August Docwra wrote to Cecil, Queen Elizabeth's chief government minister, that he could only muster 300 fit men in Derry and a further 400 at Dunnalong, and that out of a force of 4,000. Precisely what this sickness was is not known, but it was probably due to a lack of hygiene among the soldiers, possibly brought about by drinking water they themselves had contaminated. However, as Cyril Falls has pointed out, this level of sickness was not uncommon among soldiers at this time, and troops stationed in camps were more likely to succumb to disease than those housed in towns. It was also recorded that a number of English soldiers were deserting Dunnalong and going over to the enemy.

The Submission of Niall Garbh O'Donnell

Throughout this time there had been no contact between Niall Garbh O'Donnell and the English. When Hugh Roe O'Donnell went into Thomond in early August, he left Niall Garbh in charge of Tyrconnell. During this time Docwra and Niall Garbh negotiated secretly. On 3 October, Niall Garbh came over to the English side, though this happened sooner than had been intended due to the discovery by Hugh Roe of the impending desertion of his kinsman. This, together with a good recovery rate among the English soldiers, put Docwra and his forces in a much stronger position by autumn 1600.

Niall Garbh immediately made himself useful to the Crown by encouraging Docwra to take Lifford, for he had heard that Hugh Roe was returning to Donegal from Connacht. Therefore, on 8 October 1600 Sir John Bolles and a force of 500 foot-soldiers and 300 horsemen were sent with Niall Garbh to capture the O'Donnell fort at Lifford. The venture was successful, with the defenders being put to the sword. The English soldiers then raised large mounds of earth and stone to shelter themselves, the Irish defences being rather insubstantial. Hugh Roe O'Donnell was both surprised and furious that his cousin should desert to the English and on 11 October arrived at Lifford. However, despite some skirmishing, O'Donnell did not make a serious attempt to storm the fort and soon afterwards returned to the main part of his forces.

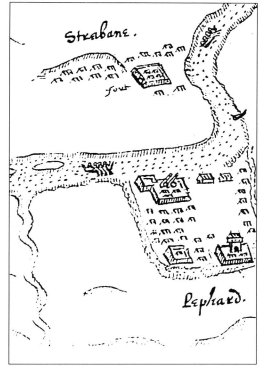

Strabane and Lifford, 1601

The strategic value of Lifford had been recognised for some time by the English. One of the officers on the expedition, Captain Willis, had suggested in a letter despatched from Derry, presumably just prior to the capture of Lifford, that this fort would be a good place to take. Furthermore, he recommended that soldiers be taken from Dunnalong to garrison Lifford, with Dunnalong being left in the hands of one company as well as some merchants and others who would live there. The mention of merchants at Dunnalong is a further indication of its commercial importance, something that would have been encouraged further by the large numbers of English soldiers stationed there. However, the proposal that the garrison at Dunnalong be reduced to one company would imply that there were those within the Lough Foyle force who did not regard Dunnalong as being of prime importance in the reduction of north-west Ulster to Crown control. At the same time, Willis did recognise that Bolles and his men would be reluctant to leave Dunnalong because of all the building work they had carried out there.

The building work to which Willis referred included the construction of a brewery at Dunnalong in October 1600. Docwra ordered the erection of this brewery in order to supply cheap beer to the garrisons in Lough Foyle, something that was a major concern in the ranks. Certainly the Irish made their own beer, which they sold to the English soldiers, but at exorbitant prices. The beer produced at Dunnalong was transported down river to Derry by means of a specially adapted horseboat. In the spring of 1601 a somewhat amusing incident took place involving the transportation of beer to Derry. The horseboat, laden with beer, was making one of its regular trips to Derry when a sudden squall arose. The boat was badly buffeted on the water and eventually overturned, with the consequent loss of its cargo, and was driven a mile below Derry.

In an effort to retrieve the boat Docwra sent some of his men to where it was grounded. The soldiers managed to secure the boat to the shore using a cable, but because of the intensity of the storm they decided to wait until it had abated before attempting to pull the boat ashore. However, watching what was happening from the opposite side of the river were some of O'Cahan's men. One of them, braving the storm, set off in a small boat to where the horseboat lay. Managing to cut the cable, he drew it over to the eastern side of the river, where he and his associates smashed it to pieces and then set it on fire, much to the chagrin of the English.

On 28 October, Sir Art O'Neill died at Dunnalong after three days illness brought on by what Captain Willis described as 'immoderate drinking'. A realistic assessment of Sir Art would show that he had been of only limited value to Docwra and at times was rather troublesome. Nevertheless, the governor trusted his Irish ally and called him a 'faithful and honest man'. Shortly after the death of his brother, Cormac O'Neill approached Docwra claiming to be Sir Art's lawful successor and hoping for 'good entertainments from the Queen'. However, soon after this Sir Art's son Turlough approached Docwra, and it was he, rather than his uncle, who was accepted by the Crown as the rightful heir. Because of his youth, Turlough was not of great use to Docwra, though the latter had high hopes for him.

The Layout of the Fort at Dunnalong

Around the middle of December 1600, Captain Humphrey Covert, controller-general of muster and surveyor-general of victuals in Lough Foyle, was despatched to London by Docwra. Contained among the various notices which he carried with him were four maps including an overall map of Lough Foyle and three individual drawings of the forts at Derry, Dunnalong and Lifford. These maps were not signed, so the identity of the artist remains a mystery, though it was possibly Docwra himself. Covert arrived with the maps in London on December 27 after a very quick journey. From these drawings it is possible to derive a reasonably good idea of what the forts on the Foyle actually looked like.

The map of Dunnalong, entitled 'Dounalong' and with its compass directions wrong (north should be where east is), has a number of explanatory

Dunnalong Fort, 1600

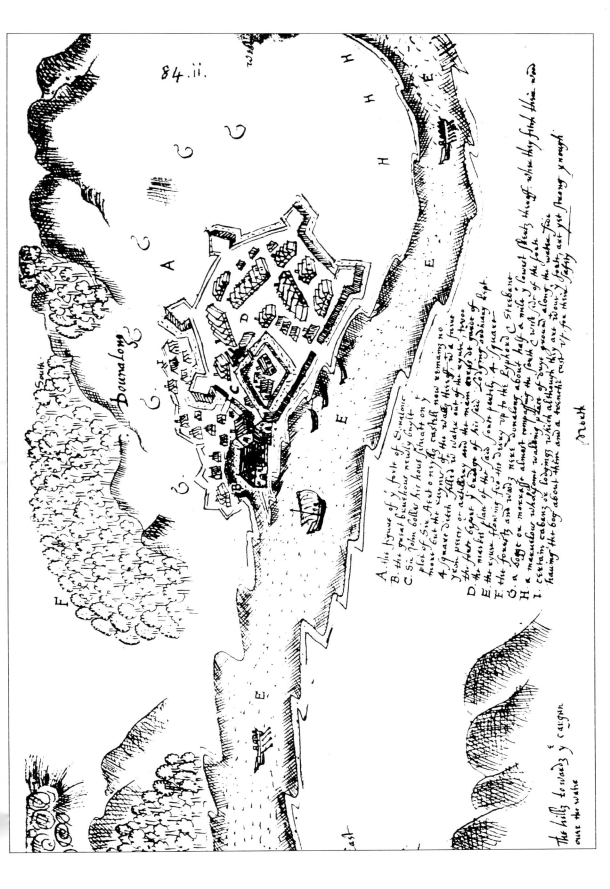

notes attached to it. The first is simply a description of what the map shows – 'the figure of [the] forte of Donalong'. The second note refers to the recently built brewery. The map shows the 'great bruehous' to be a fairly large building, set on the edge of the river at the north end of the fort. Note C refers to Sir John Bolles' house which he had built on the site of the original castle of which only the ruined walls remained. Surrounding it was a 'faire 4 square ditch filled [with] water out of the ryver', though whether this was a new construction or simply part of the original defences of Turlough Luineach's castle is not clear. Beside the bridge leading to this artificial island, Bolles placed two pieces of artillery as well as the main 'corps de garde' of the fort. It would appear that Bolles intended his house to be the citadel for the garrison supposing a successful attack was launched on the fort and its ramparts breached.

The fourth explanatory note refers to the marketplace located inside the fort, where the merchants traded with the soldiers and possibly also with the local inhabitants who had submitted to Bolles. The marketplace would appear to have been an integral part of the fort, both because of its positioning and its extent. Note E refers to the River Foyle, while note F refers to the woods located about half a mile from Dunnalong which provided the garrison with its timber needs. The next note mentions the bog which almost surrounded the fort on its east and south sides and which provided it with a reasonable degree of protection. Note H describes the land running upstream from the fort as a 'marvelous wholesome walking place of drye ground'.

The final explanatory note refers to 'certain cabans or lodgings' which were located to the immediate north and east of the fort and which, although located outside the ramparts, were fairly secure, having the bog about them and also a 'trench cast up for their safety'. The inhabitants of this 'village' may have been the local Irish and its origins may have dated to the time of Turlough Luineach's castle. Alternatively, it may have sprung up in response to the revival of Dunnalong's importance, following the establishment of a large English garrison there in July 1600. It may even have been where the merchants and their followers lived. At the same time the houses are shown as having chimneys, which at that time was a distinctly English feature. Apart from possibly Bolles' house, the buildings inside the fort would not have been of permanent construction. For example, the brewery was built using 2,000 deal boards sent specifically for that purpose by a Mr Newcome[n]. This goes a long way towards explaining the virtual absence of any traces of the fort today.

At about this time a muster at Dunnalong recorded the fort's strength as being 1,050 foot soldiers, which is a good indication of just how large this garrison was. Also, in December 1600 a spy was captured by soldiers from Dunnalong. When interrogated by Bolles, the man at first claimed to be a servant to one of the soldiers of the garrison and then said he was one of O'Doherty's men. Bolles, being unsure what to do, sent the man to Derry where he continued to tell tales, before Docwra had him executed as a spy.

The Submission of Cahir O'Doherty of Inishowen

The fortunes of the Lough Foyle force took a new turn around Christmas 1600 when Sir John O'Doherty died. A succession dispute broke out between O'Donnell's candidate, Phelim Oge, brother of Sir John, and Cahir, son of Sir John and foster-child of Hugh Boy MacDavitt. Shortly before this Hugh Boy MacDavitt had been the main instigator of a failed plot to capture Culmore fort. However, he now came to Docwra on behalf of Cahir. Docwra, still suspicious of Hugh Boy, made friendly overtures to Phelim Oge, though without reply. He therefore decided to recognise Cahir as the rightful heir. However, no sooner had he done this than messengers arrived offering the submission of Phelim Oge. Docwra also received word that O'Donnell was coming up to Lifford with a large force. In a bit of a quandary, Docwra gave a temporary truce to both Phelim Oge and Cahir. However, O Donnell soon returned to Connacht and the troops he left behind were attacked and defeated by Niall Garbh and the garrison at Lifford.

Fresh supplies having arrived and the truces with the O'Dohertys having expired, Docwra blocked the routes into Inishowen and marched into the peninsula with a force of 300 men, Hugh Boy acting as their guide. However, Phelim Oge, his son and several of his men fled, leaving Inishowen in the hands of Cahir O'Doherty with Hugh Boy as his guardian. Both now formally submitted to Docwra, who reinforced his hold on that country by erecting forts at Carrigans and Colmackatreyne (near Newtowncunningham) and a number of other places. Hugh Boy now became a valued ally of Docwra and immediately proved his worth to the governor by informing him - correctly as it turned out - that a Spanish army of 6,000 men would land that year (1601) in Munster.

The Killing of Bishop Redmond O'Gallagher

At about this time an incident occurred which must have given the Dunnalong garrison a degree of notoriety. Being the last region in Ireland to be reduced to Crown control, the north-west was also the last part of Ireland in which the Roman Catholic church survived with at least some kind of organisational structure. The Catholic bishop of Derry, Redmond O'Gallagher, who was about eighty years of age at this time, was a major fig-ure in the confederacy and had made a number of foreign trips to solicit help for Tyrone and O'Donnell from Spain and the papacy. This made him a prime target for the Lough Foyle garrison under Docwra, whose arrival must have hindered his activities. For around ten months he managed to evade capture. However, on 7 March 1601, Sir John Bolles was able to write to Cecil that O'Gallagher, 'the first and general contriver . . . with the Spaniards', had been captured and put to death by soldiers from the garrison at Dunnalong. This force must have been acting on information received from an informer and Bolles, almost apologetically, explained to Cecil that the soldiers, in their exuberance at finding O'Gallagher, killed the aged prelate before he (Bolles) had caught up with them.

There has been considerable debate as to the precise location where this incident occurred. In *Derriana*, Bishop O'Doherty pointed to a manuscript, the original of which is in the Bodleian Library, written about 1670 by a Dr John Lynch which describes how Docwra and his troops 'seized him [O'Gallagher] in Cumalia, an out-of-the-way hamlet about a mile from Derry, on the way which leads to Strabane, where there was a parochial church'. In his analysis of the above document, Bishop O'Doherty pointed out that in the early seventeenth century the only road between Derry and Strabane passed through the villages of St Johnston and Carrigans. Consequently, O'Doherty fixed the site of the incident in Co. Donegal and furthermore argued that the parochial church referred to in Lynch's document was at Killea where the ruins of a church had existed until a few years before his time of writing (1902).

However, the accuracy of both Lynch's manuscript and O'Doherty's interpretation of it are highly questionable, since most of the surviving evidence would seem to suggest that the bishop's death took place on the eastern side of the river. Firstly, the fact that Bolles and soldiers from Dunnalong were involved would make it highly probable that the incident took place on their side of the river. If the event had taken place in Donegal as O'Doherty believed, then surely troops from Lifford or Derry would have been involved. Lynch, in fact, got the date wrong, for he stated it to have taken place in 1602 when in reality it took place on Ash Wednesday 1601. The content of the rest of Bolles' letter to Cecil would also point to the killing having taken place on the eastern side of the Foyle. The account of O'Gallagher's death in the *Annals of the Four Masters* also supports this theory for it stated that he was killed by the English in '*Oireacht Ui Chathain*' (O'Cahan's country).

More evidence to support this theory can be found in a description of his diocese by the Protestant bishop of Derry, George Montgomery, written about 1607. Referring to the parish of Cumber, Montgomery wrote, '*Reimundus ultimus Episcopus Hibernicus inibi occisus per Anglos.*' Translated this means, 'Redmond, the last Irish bishop, was killed in that place by the English.' While the treatment meted out to the elderly bishop was rather extreme, the Dunnalong garrison would undoubtedly have been extremely proud of the fact that it was they who had eliminated this 'troublesome' individual. In fact Bolles went so far as to write that it was God who had given Bishop O'Gallagher into their hands.

The expedition from Dunnalong that Ash Wednesday achieved a great deal more than the capture and execution of Redmond O'Gallagher. Bolles and his soldiers successfully engaged in fighting with some of O'Cahan's men, with whom they fought for five miles, killing between 80 and 100 and also capturing 80 cows. In this encounter the English suffered six casualties, only one of which was a fatality. They also captured an individual whom Bolles described as a 'scholar', perhaps a bardic poet or a Brehon lawyer. The man was apparently of no use as a soldier, and so Bolles decided to ransom him for corn and horses, of which there was the greater need. This action would appear to have been rather unprecendented, for Bolles actually apologised to Cecil if he happened to be wrong in doing this.

The commander of the garrison at Dunnalong, Sir John Bolles, was a particularly interesting figure, and an insight into his character and the state of the war in Lough Foyle can be gleaned from the frequent letters he wrote to Cecil. Quite often he painted a rather bleak picture of the situation and at times seemed to have little confidence in his commanding officer, Sir Henry Docwra. For example, he was highly critical of the trust Docwra placed in Hugh Boy MacDavitt. On another occasion he felt the need to defend himself on a charge of negligence, though for precisely what is not known. In March 1601, Bolles complained to Cecil that there were not enough men on the eastern side of the Foyle, perhaps implying that he believed that too much attention was being focused on Donegal at the expense of the Dunnalong hinterland. Certainly the garrison at Dunnalong was steadily being reduced in size in order that men could be spared to fight elsewhere. The muster of April 1601 revealed that there were only 557 men at Dunnalong compared with over 1,000 the previous December.

At the beginning of March 1601, for example, Bolles, as ordered by Docwra, sent Captain Ralph Bingley with his company to capture the abbey at Rathmullan in MacSweeny Fanad's country, which they successfully completed. It is highly probable that many of the troops sent on expeditions into north Tyrone were also from Dunnalong. Bolles also made frequent requests to Cecil that he might be relieved of his command so that he could return to England. He claimed that the steward of his estate had died and consequently he needed to go home and investigate its finances. However, although occasionally a fairly poor picture may be drawn of Bolles, he was a competent soldier, and he also seems to have possessed a rare insight into the situation in Ireland.

In one of his letters to Cecil, he commented on the numbers of Irish, including priests, who were coming over to the English side. He pointed out that many of the priests earnestly desired peace so long as they were not persecuted on account of their religion and were permitted to have their own churches. Furthermore, he suggested that these priests could be very useful in encouraging the bulk of the people to submit to the Crown, since no-one dared to disobey them. However, Bolles also offered a more extreme scheme to reduce the country to Crown control whereby only those fighting men who could prove their trustworthiness would be allowed into the garrisons while the rest of the Irish would be kept outside to starve.

In the spring of 1601 Docwra began measures designed to ensure MacSweeny Fanad's submission and so invaded his territory in north Donegal, capturing 1,000 cows in the process. The Gaelic chieftain then submitted to Docwra, though a short time later, and without any compulsion, he went back to O'Donnell. It was not until December of that year that MacSweeny genuinely surrendered to the Crown, and that was only after Docwra had devastated his lands, causing great hardship to its inhabitants. In April 1601 Docwra invaded an area in west Tyrone inhabited by a clan known as the Sleught (Slua) Art, and captured Castlederg, where Captain Dutton was left with 100 men.

Seeking revenge on Cahir O'Doherty and Hugh Boy for deserting him, O'Donnell drew up his forces to Donegal in preparation for an attack on Inishowen. On 7 May, O'Donnell's army crossed the bog at the base of Inishowen, using man-made bridges. Docwra, aware of what was happening, had already ordered the cattle to be driven to the other end of the peninsula, where they were guarded by Hugh Boy, his brother, and 200 English soldiers under Captain Willis. Marching further into Inishowen the following day, O'Donnell's troops encountered the English defences, which they attacked only to be repulsed with the loss of 40 men. O'Donnell then called off his attack on Inishowen.

The 'Battle of Dunnalong'

Throughout the spring of 1601 minor raids had been carried out on the fort at Dunnalong, mainly attempts to steal some of the horses or cows grazing around it. Following the destruction of the horseboat, some of O'Cahan's men, in high spirits, appeared outside the fort. Giving a 'bravado', they attempted to steal some of the horses belonging to the garrison and would have succeeded in doing this but for the swift action of Bolles and his men. These 'subtle and desperate ambuscadoes' by O Cahan's men upon the garrison at Dunnalong continued for several weeks, though without any serious consequence. However, in May 1601 an incident occurred which can perhaps be called the 'Battle of Dunnalong', even if it was only on the small scale.

It would appear that in conjunction with O'Donnell's attempted invasion, Tyrone had brought a large part of his forces to the Strabane area to cause as many distractions for the English as possible. Naturally his attention turned to the garrison at Dunnalong. On the day before the 'battle', Tyrone and his men had made a minor raid on the fort, managing to capture some grazing cows, which were being tended by a priest of Sir John Bolles. Buoyed by his success, Tyrone returned the next day expecting to find more easy pickings. However, what he and his soldiers encountered this time was much more serious.

While O'Donnell was invading Inishowen, Docwra realised that a large part of Donegal was left virtually unguarded and, in an attempt to capitalise on this, instructed Niall Garbh to go on a wasting expedition as far as, if possible, Donegal town itself. Niall Garbh immediately set out to do this, but at that moment he received word from one of his spies about Tyrone's intentions concerning Dunnalong. On hearing this, Niall Garbh adjusted his plans and made a detour to the fort at Dunnalong, taking with him Captain Windsor and 100 English soldiers. Arriving at Dunnalong, this force gave out a great roar and launched a ferocious attack on Tyrone and his men, who had been lying in wait a little way beyond the fort. The confederates were so taken by surprise that they were thrown into total confusion and immediately took to flight, leaving all their equipment behind, including a large number of Spanish pikes. The forces of Niall Garbh and Captain Windsor were joined by soldiers from the Dunnalong garrison and together they chased the confederate soldiers for six miles, killing many of them and nearly killing the earl of Tyrone himself, who was often 'within a stave's throw' of death.

Tradition has it that the earl's chief pursuer was none other than Niall Garbh, who reputedly called after Tyrone to turn and fight if he were a gentleman. However, Tyrone, believing discretion to be the better part of valour, declined the challenge and, probably because he was better mounted than Niall Garbh, managed to escape from the fearsome young warrior. At the same time this must have been the closest that Tyrone came to death during the Nine Years War, and it would have been ironic had it occurred while attempting to steal some cows from Dunnalong, the old castle of his former rival, Turlough Luineach. In all, 300 of Tyrone's men were killed in the encounter. One hundred of these were killed when the initial attack was launched, with eventually 200 more by the time the pursuit was called off.

As well as killing large numbers of Tyrone's men in the fighting around Dunnalong, most of the confederates' weapons were captured and also thirteen of their best horses. Only one English officer and four English soldiers were killed. Sir Art's son Turlough, fighting for the English, was shot in the thigh, but recovered. From this time on neither Tyrone nor O'Donnell made another attempt to interfere with the English in their strongholds along the Foyle. With Spanish aid expected at any time, it would appear that the confederate leaders had decided against attempting to drive the English out of

Lough Foyle before the arrival of this help.

The War in West Tyrone

Still not ready to establish a garrison at Ballyshannon, Docwra turned his attention to the lordship of Tyrone. On 24 May 1601, he drew two pieces of artillery to the castle at Newtownstewart and bombarded it until it surrendered the next day. It was a strong fortress with an iron gate and high walls, and here Docwra left Captain Atkinson with 100 men. To assist Atkinson, Docwra left Turlough Magnylson, who had come in with Sir Art O'Neill and had performed many good services for the Crown. However, Docwra warned Atkinson to be wary of the Irish and not to allow any of them inside the castle.

About this time a general muster of the army in Ireland was carried out. At Dunnalong it was recorded that there were 650 men, with 400 of these ready for the field. These men were divided up as follows: 150 under Sir John Bolles; 150 under Captain Floyd; 150 under Captain Badby; 100 under Captain Sidley; and 100 under Captain Bassett. These figures show that Dunnalong continued to be important in terms of garrison size, even if it was now used as a stopping-off point for soldiers being sent into north Tyrone and the western part of what is now Co. Londonderry. By the summer of 1601 the fort was no longer a frontier outpost on the eastern side of the River Foyle from which the garrison was frightened to venture too far.

On 20 June 1601, Docwra took the cannon to Enagh, a castle belonging to O'Cahan standing in a lough near Derry. This castle was bombarded and it was discovered the next day that the warders had fled during the night. This was a blow to O'Cahan's pride because he had considered the castle impregnable. On 19 July Docwra received a letter from Mountjoy instructing him to come to the Blackwater for a meeting. But having prepared his troops for the journey, Docwra discovered that he had insufficient match for firing the gunpowder and so had to abandon his plans. Docwra wrote to his lord deputy apologising for this but received a rebuking letter in reply. However, Docwra turned this setback to his own advantage, for he learned that O'Donnell had drawn the greater part of his forces to the Blackwater to confront Mountjoy, thereby leaving his own part of Donegal unguarded.

Docwra, therefore, sent Niall Garbh with Captain Willis and 500 men to take Donegal town as a first step towards capturing Ballyshannon. He also instructed Cormac, Sir Art's brother, to drive cattle on the expedition. Yet willing as Cormac was, his men simply refused to obey him and so Docwra travelled to Strabane, where he hanged two of them with the result that the rest then yielded, although a few later deserted. The troops arrived in Donegal town on 2 August and established themselves in the old Franciscan friary. Shortly afterwards O'Donnell returned and laid siege for several months, during which time the defenders experienced incredible hardships in one of the most exciting episodes of the entire campaign.

At this time Docwra experienced two setbacks. Firstly, Turlough Magnylson betrayed the Newtownstewart garrison, which was put to the sword. Secondly, on the same day Art Mergoh and Hugh Mussey betrayed Captain Dutton at Castlederg: this time, however, the garrison was spared. Although Docwra was surprised at the actions of these supposedly trustworthy Irishmen, unknown to him a large Spanish force had already landed at Kinsale and so these men may have been trying to win favour with Tyrone through their actions. The arrival of the Spanish was to the relief of the garrison at Donegal friary because the siege was lifted as O'Donnell drew his forces south. With O'Cahan's troops also having journeyed to Munster, Docwra invaded his unguarded country, inflicting a great deal of devastation on it.

On 24 December 1601 the Battle of Kinsale was fought, the result of which was the decisive defeat of the forces of Tyrone and O'Donnell by Mountjoy. The Spanish troops surrendered and were allowed to return to Spain, while O'Donnell also went there to press for further help. As Docwra himself put it, following Kinsale, 'the axe was nowe at the roote of the tree, and I may well say, the Necke of the Rebellion as good as utterlie broken'. However, it was a further fifteen months before Tyrone submitted, mainly because Elizabeth insisted that he surrender unconditionally rather than give way on his own terms.

Docwra now resolved once and for all to capture Ballyshannon and therefore sent four companies of foot soldiers and 50 horsemen to Asheroe as a prelude to taking the castle. The cannon was also sent by sea and once it arrived the garrison at Ballyshannon did not hold out for long, surrendering on 25 March 1602. This success was followed up by the capture and execution of Turlough Magnylson and the recovery of Newtownstewart by Turlough, Sir Art's son. The betrayers of Castlederg were also captured, and on 20 April Cane Ballogh MacRickard, a chieftain in O'Cahan's country, delivered into English hands his castle at Dungiven on condition that it be returned to him after the war.

The Final Stages of the War

In June 1602, Docwra made the journey he should have made a year earlier when he travelled to the Blackwater to meet Mountjoy, leaving a garrison at Omagh on the way. Docwra arrived at the Blackwater on 26 June and, with Mountjoy, spent the next ten days despoiling the surrounding countryside before withdrawing to get more supplies. On his return to Derry, Docwra received word from O'Cahan that he was prepared to submit to the Crown. Believing O'Cahan to be genuine, Docwra immediately negotiated an agreement with him which granted the Irishman his whole country except his castle at Enagh and a triangle of land between the rivers Foyle, Faughan and Burngibbagh. O'Cahan also surrendered a piece of land on the River Bann on which a fort, designed to prevent Tyrone from escaping by sea, could be built.

The loss of O'Cahan was a serious blow to Tyrone, as he had been one of his most important supporters. With the armies of Docwra, Mountjoy and now Sir Arthur Chichester, from his base at Carrickfergus, converging on Tyrone, the stranglehold on him tightened, and the earl and his remaining soldiers were confined to the rugged fastness of Glenconkeyne (an area in what is now southeast Co. Londonderry). On 10 August, as ordered by Mountjoy, Docwra journeyed to Omagh, with Hugh Boy following on the next day. However, before reaching Omagh, Hugh Boy was set upon by a gang of 'loose fellows' and killed. Although many distrusted him and did not lament his death, Docwra grieved sincerely at his loss. While waiting for Mountjoy, Docwra became involved in a fierce skirmish with some soldiers of the confederacy, and in the encounter the young Cahir O'Doherty distinguished himself by his bravery. Because of this he was knighted by Mountjoy on 30 August.

For the next week the two commanders carried out various activities before Docwra was sent back to Derry with orders to bring the cannon to Omagh, where he was to remain until the harvest was in. Although unable to bring the cannon at this time, Docwra met with Mountjoy and Chichester and together they captured the castle at Augher. On his return to Derry, Docwra destroyed an old castle that belonged to Henry Hovenden, one of Tyrone's foster-brothers: the castle stood in a lough near Newtownstewart and had been taken over by some followers of Tyrone. This must have been the castle on Island MacHugh of which traces still remain. Eventually, with the situation becoming hopeless, Rory O'Donnell promised his submission to Mountjoy; his brother Hugh Roe had already died in Spain.

On 18 November 1602, Docwra received word from Chichester that Tyrone and his remaining forces were once again in Glenconkeyne. However, it was a further month before Docwra could assemble a sufficient force to travel to those parts. Even then, when he realised how difficult it would be to capture Tyrone in the dense woodland, he decided to abandon the expedition, leaving behind 100 loyal Irish soldiers to guard the routes in and out of the area. Eventually, it was the shortage of food that forced Tyrone to surrender. Mountjoy, who had previously been ordered not to accept Tyrone's submission until his forces had been totally annihilated, was finally given permission by a dying queen to accept Tyrone's surrender. Tyrone therefore submitted to Mountjoy, with the agreement being formalised in the Treaty of Mellifont on 30 March 1603. However, unknown to Tyrone, Elizabeth had been dead for nearly a week.

Aftermath

In a war which had thrown up a number of disasters for the English, the Lough Foyle expedition had been a creditable success. In the words of G.A. Hayes McCoy, the military historian, Docwra's campaign in north-west Ulster 'fatally weakened the Ulster confederacy and . . . following the defeat at Kinsale, ensured its downfall'. Docwra himself must take a great deal of the credit for the expedition's success. Perhaps the best tribute paid to him can be found in the *Annals of the Four Masters*, where he is described as 'an illustrious knight of wisdom and prudence, a pillar of battle and conflict'. As a reward for his services, on 8 February 1604 the government made him governor of Derry for life. However, he quickly became disillusioned with life in Derry, and in July 1606 was permitted to surrender his title to Sir George Paulett. Thus Docwra ended his association with an area whose recent history he had so helped to shape.

The Gaelic chieftains also found it difficult to adjust to the new situation. Those who had assisted the English during the war were generally disappointed with the reward for their services. When Turlough O'Neill asked for the castle at Newtown which had been promised to him, he was told that it was being given to the earl of Tyrone instead. Niall Garbh O'Donnell was extremely angry at being overlooked for the title of earl of Tyrconnell, which was given to his kinsman and rival, Rory. The earl of Tyrone and the newly created earl of Tyrconnell continued to be objects of suspicion and had many enemies in the Dublin administration. Eventually, Tyrone and Rory O'Donnell decided to leave Ireland and sail to Spain. On his way to meet O'Donnell at Ballindrait on his final journey through Ulster, Tyrone passed through the Strabane district, pausing briefly to rest by the banks of the River Dennett. From Ballindrait they travelled on to Rathmullan from where they set sail with nearly 100 of their followers. They never did reach Spain, and Tyrone died in Rome in 1616. Following the 'Flight of the Earls' the government declared their lands forfeited and began to make plans for their disposal.

One more episode further cleared the way for plantation. In April 1608, Sir Cahir O'Doherty attacked and burned Derry. The fort at Lifford under the command of Sir Richard Hansard became the focal point for resistance to this rising. To it the small garrison at Dunnalong fled for safety, as did a colony of Scots at Strabane. These Scots had presumably settled here in the aftermath of the Nine Years War and were probably closely connected to the pre-plantation colony at Derry which, though mainly English, included a small Scottish element. O'Doherty was killed soon afterwards and his rebellion petered out. Niall Garbh O'Donnell was accused of being the main instigator of the rising and was sent to the Tower of London, where he died in 1625.

Although the lands around Strabane were originally intended for Turlough O'Neill, to whom the castle at Newtown was finally given as a reward for his loyalty during O'Doherty's rising, in September 1608 it was recommended that these lands should be reserved to the Crown as part of their intended plantation scheme. Turlough was instead allocated lands in the Barony of Dungannon. The fort at Dunnalong was abandoned after O'Doherty's rising and virtually no trace of it remains today. Dunnalong continued to be important to the people of the area as a ferry crossing and also for its renowned horse fairs. However, even these are now no more than a distant memory.

Plantation castle remains at Mountcastle, near Donemana

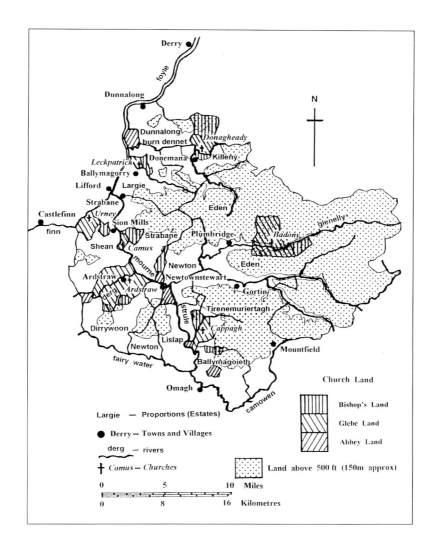

4 The Plantation and Seventeenth-Century Developments

MICHAEL COX

The plantation estates in the Strabane Barony; note also the church lands reserved for the Church of Ireland.

From 1603, when James VI of Scotland became also James I of England, Ireland, Scotland and England became known as the 'Three Kingdoms'. Each had its own government comprising the king, Privy Council and ministers. The parliaments met only occasionally to make laws and raise money through taxes. Ireland had to follow the directives of the English government. The principal landowners' place in society and the extent of their landholdings depended on their 'services and loyalty to the crown'. The majority of people lived in the countryside, leading a somewhat precarious life. During the seventeenth century, the three kingdoms witnessed major periods of civil and religious strife, which impinged on life in and around Strabane. In turn, this strife affected the somewhat basic administrative, legal, and educational systems. A move towards a market economy developed as the century progressed.

End of an Era

The beginning of the seventeenth century saw an end to local conflicts between Gaelic leaders both within Ireland and within Scotland. In Ulster, these had often been fought using Scottish mercenaries. Although there had been disputes between Turlough Luineach O'Neill of Strabane (c. 1531–95) and Hugh O'Neill of Dungannon, second earl of Tyrone, (c. 1550–1616), both men and other Ulster leaders objected to the extension of Dublin rule after the formation of counties in Ulster. This led to the Nine Years War (April 1593 – March 1603).

In 1605, James I rewarded a cleric, George Montgomery, one of his Scottish supporters in England, by appointing him Bishop of Derry, Raphoe and Clogher. At that time religion in all countries of western Europe was controlled by governments. As England had an Episcopalian Protestant church, Ireland had to follow suit. The Bishop took control of all the church land in the parishes of Donagheady, Leckpatrick, Camus-Juxta-Mourne (Strabane) and Ardstraw. In 1607 James I summoned the two earls, Tyrone and Tyrconnell, to London. Hugh O'Neill set off on his journey. However, intelligence reached him that he and Tyrconnell were likely to be detained upon reaching London. Having learnt that a French ship was on its way to Lough Swilly, the two earls decided that they would go to Spain to seek support for the Gaelic cause there. O'Neill returned to Dungannon, collected his family, hurried through the Sperrins to Dunnalong and on to Rathmullen. On 4 September 1607, the two earls set sail with about 100 people, eventually reaching northern France, and not Spain as intended. This pleased Spain, as it had made peace with England in 1604. Thus ended Gaelic lordly power in Ulster.

Filling the Vacuum

In April 1608, Sir Cahir O'Doherty of Inishowen, who had become a supporter of Docwra, fell out with his successor, Sir George Paulett. He attacked Derry with about 100 men and was joined by the O'Cahans and O'Hanlons. Rebellion threatened. The English government asked the Scottish government to send a force to help subdue the rebels. Captains

William Stewart and Patrick Crawford, with 200 men, reached Carrickfergus in June, moving across to Strabane. Meanwhile, O'Doherty's force had gone south, and Strabane was burned as it had been ten years earlier. Between 60 and 80 Scots living there took refuge in the fort of Lifford. Who were these Scots? Could they have been mercenaries who had not returned to Scotland and had married local women? In July, O'Doherty's men were attacked and defeated near Kilmacrenan, seven miles north of Letterkenny, Co. Donegal, and by August all the pockets of resistance had been dealt with. Some of the O'Neills had supported the English forces during this rebellion: Turlough O'Neill, the grandson of Turlough Luineach, survived, whilst Sir Henry Oge O'Neill (nephew of Hugh O'Neill) and his son Turlough Oge, were both killed.

It was then proposed and agreed by James I that six of the nine counties of Ulster should be colonised. He had earlier tried a form of colonisation, then called 'plantation', within Scotland, using lowlanders to curb some of the unruly highlanders, with mixed results. The form the plantation was to take was planned, and surveys of the land to be allocated to the 'planters' (colonisers) took place in 1608 and 1609. For the second survey in 1609, all the Co. Tyrone jurors met the surveyors in August for a ten-day meeting at their tented encampment near Dungannon. The resultant maps of the Bodley survey were no better than sketches. A fundamental error was that all the 'balliboes' (later townlands) were considered to be the same size–60 Irish acres of profitable land. In reality, they varied in size, reflecting the quality of the land. Almost 200 out of the 289 balliboes featured on the two maps covering the Strabane barony have names corresponding to modern townlands.

It was decided that there should be three categories of grantees: English and lowland Scottish 'undertakers' (men who 'undertook' to fulfil the conditions of their grants, including the requirement that the settlers be Protestant); 'servitors' (government officials and military officers who had been employed in Ireland); and native Irish. There were to be three sizes of 'proportions' (estates): 2,000, 1,500 and 1,000 Irish acres (great, middle and small proportions), plus adjoining bog and wood for which no rent would be charged.

The beginning of the seventeenth century saw a period of economic stability in lowland Scotland. This had led to overpopulation, with Scots leaving their country in large numbers. Landlords, royal servants and officials in Scotland were the principal beneficiaries of this prosperity. It was from this group that the Scottish lowlander undertakers were drawn. In the Strabane area, grants of land were awarded to members of one of the leading Scottish families, the Hamiltons of Paisley: James Hamilton, first earl of Abercorn, his brothers, Sir Claud and Sir George Hamilton, and their brother-in-law, Sir Thomas Boyd. These four men were granted 8,000 plantation acres. In reality their estates covered 66,850 statute acres (27,000 ha), which excluded the higher hills and the Sperrin Mountains. At that time only the low-lying land near to, or alongside, the rivers and main streams, had been farmed.

Turlough O'Neill, grandson of Turlough Luineach, went to London early in 1610 to make representations to James that his family be granted the ancestral lands around Strabane. Turlough, having helped repel O'Doherty at Lifford, had expected that this service to the crown would be recognised. The king's council decided, however, that Irish landowners in Tyrone would be given land around Dungannon and in Armagh. Turlough O'Neill and his three brothers were granted 5,200 plantation acres, whilst Turlough Oge O'Neill's widow was granted almost 2,000 plantation acres, which passed to her son Sir Phelim O'Neill. Thus the two leading O'Neill families obtained around 7,500 plantation acres, almost as many as the Hamilton family with 8,000 plantation acres.

The Undertakers in the Strabane District

The conditions which the undertakers had to fulfil were quite onerous. They had to bring over to their estates twenty-four men, or ten families, to develop farms on each 1,000 plantation acre estate, for which they would pay a government tax (rent) annually of £5 6s 8d (£5.33). The undertakers had to give leases in accordance with English tenures, adopt English farming methods and build a castle surrounded by a 'bawn' or defensive wall. The type of castle envisaged was similar to a Scottish five-storey tower house. The Stewart castle in Newtownstewart (now undergoing restoration) is a typical example. Deadlines for the arrival of undertakers, for colonisation, and for payments of rent, as well as conditions for the building of towns, including churches and schools, were all laid down by the English government, which subsequently commissioned surveys on the progress being made, in 1611, 1613, 1618–19 and 1622.

The principal undertaker, James Hamilton, born 1575, was the eldest son of Lord Claud Hamilton of Paisley, near Glasgow. James Hamilton was appointed a privy councillor in 1598, and in 1603 was created first earl of Abercorn. Abercorn had not been one of the early applicants for land in Ulster, but was 'induced' by the king to become an undertaker 'for a countenance and strength to the rest'. In November 1611 he came over to Strabane with his wife and family. He had married Marion Boyd before 1603, and they had nine children.

Sir Claud Hamilton was born in 1577. He, like so many younger sons of Scottish landowners, married an heiress, Janet Hamilton, c.1603. Her father's estate provided him with an income. In Scotland, unlike England, estates could be passed to daughters if there were no sons to inherit. They also had nine children. He received favours from the king, becoming a privy councillor in Edinburgh in 1595 and in Dublin in 1613. However, he died in the following year, aged thirty-seven. The third brother, Sir George Hamilton, born c.1580, had come over from Scotland soon after he received his 'doquet' (warrant) for land in August 1610. These two brothers were practising Catholics, unlike their eldest brother Abercorn, who was a Scottish Protestant. At that time the Church of Scotland was basically Episcopalian but with leanings towards Calvinism. In 1618, following Abercorn's death, aged forty-three, his eldest son, James (fifteen), and William Hamilton (fourteen), eldest son of Sir Claud Hamilton, were placed under the guardianship of their uncle, Sir George Hamilton of the Largie and Dirrywoon estates. They were brought up as Catholics in Scotland. Thus one of the fundamental requirements of the plantation that undertakers should be Protestant was not fulfilled in the Strabane district.

Captain William Stewart, who had stayed on after the O'Doherty rebellion, was, as a servitor, granted the small estate of Kilmacrenan, Co. Donegal. His active development of this estate led James I to arrange for him to take over the middle proportion of Tirenemuriertagh, immediately to the east of Newtownstewart, in 1613. By 1630 he owned an estate in the Clogher area, as well as the proportions of Newton and Lislap, in the Strabane barony. This gave him control of all the land around Newtownstewart. (For more information on the development of Newtownstewart and the parish of Ardstraw, see J.H. Gebbie, *Ardstraw (Newtownstewart) – Historical Survey of a Parish, 1600–1900*, Omagh [1968].)

Development of two of the Plantation Estates

Abercorn's estate of Dunnalong, with its substantial fort and quays on the Foyle, had been an important O'Neill settlement in the late sixteenth century. The 1618–19 survey shows that there were six freeholders with 440 plantation acres and fourteen 14-year leaseholders with 540 plantation acres, but no castle, as the earl was living in Strabane. This low-lying land, halfway between Strabane and Derry, had attracted some minor members of the Hamilton network, John Hamilton and two Hugh Hamiltons. One of the latter was a freeholder and merchant. He built a stone house at Lisdivin. In 1615 he had the choice of paying his rent in cash or kind: either £6, or else wine, sugar, pepper and marmalade. By the time of his death in 1637, he owned houses in Strabane and had played a part in the development of the town. In the 1654 Civil Survey, his son, Hugh, claimed the estates of Lisdivin (72 acres) and neighbouring Loughneas (80 acres). Abercorn's agent, William Lynne, also lived on this estate. He undertook a survey of the district for the government in 1622. William Lynne's nephew, also William, had inherited and claimed the freehold of Cloghogle (72 acres) in 1654. (For more information on the Dunnalong estate during this period, see William Roulston, 'A brief survey of the manor of Dunnalong, 1610–41', in *Concordia*, iv [1997].)

Sir Claud Hamilton's estate of Killeny and Eden was in a less favourable area, lying mostly to the north-east and east of Strabane, including the Donemana and Plumbridge areas. By 1622, a four-storey castle without doors and windows and with a nearly complete bawn, plus six small houses, had been built at Donemana, with other houses built elsewhere on the estate. (It is unlikely that the castle was finished, as Sir George Hamilton of Largie, who then administered this estate (see below), was intending to live at the almost completed Dirrywoon castle.) There were six freeholders and fourteen lessees, but their holdings were half the size of those on the Dunnalong estate. Scottish settlers lived on the lower land downstream from Donemana. Upstream, and around Plumbridge, and further afield in the Gortin, Newtownstewart and Ardstraw areas, virtually all the tenants were Irish. In the period 1613–15 a local man of substance, Brian Groome O'Duffeme (Devine), rented at least eight modern townlands east of Donemana. He paid a rent of £32, plus 42 days service, 14 barrels of beer, 14 sheep, 12 pigs, 60 hens, two 4-year-old cows and calves, and a barrel of butter. Providing services to the landlord could on occasion mean joining the landlord's 'army' during a dispute, as happened after 1640. Money rents exclusively came mostly after 1650. Brian Groome O'Duffeme acted as an agent for Sir Claud Hamilton in 1613. He 'took £23.10.0. (£23.50) to Sir Claud in Scotland'. This would have been the surplus cash after expenses had been met, and more than covered the rent of £10 13s 4d (£10.67) which was due to the Crown. Following Sir Claud's death in 1614, Brian Groome in 1615 collected the rents of the estate, which was then administered by Sir George Hamilton of the Largie and Dirrywoon estates, since Sir Claud's heir, William, was a minor. With the death of Abercorn in 1618, Sir George then administered all the Hamilton estates. In 1640, the O'Duffeme family held a mortgage on four townlands to the north of Donemana, leased to Sir George Hamilton of Dunnalong by John Bramhall, bishop of Derry, thus holding on to what they had earlier controlled. (An O'Devine Catholic Church connection appears c. 1680, when James O'Devine is recorded as the parish priest of Donagheady.) Unfortunately, no other records have survived to provide similar information on life in the countryside elsewhere in the Strabane area.

For the settlers, it was important that they could cope with any attacks on their property or family, by man or beast – wolves were still found in the nearby forests. Periodic 'musters' of men and a listing of their arms took place. The 1630 muster roll shows that Sir William Hamilton, the late Sir Claud's eldest son, had only 43 men on his Killeny and Eden estate – 21 had a sword and pike, 18 had a sword and snaphance (flintlock gun), suggesting a population of around 120 settlers. Ten years earlier there had been about half that number. Whilst this estate had seen an increase in the settler population during the 1620s, the Dunnalong settler population had apparently fallen. There were 106 men with arms in 1619, but only 44 in 1630. Perhaps some of the Dunnalong settlers had returned to Scotland or moved to either Strabane or Derry as had happened elsewhere in north-west Ulster. (For a complete list of the men mustered on the Hamilton and Stewart estates, see Gebbie, *Ardstraw (Newtownstewart)*, pp. 21–30.)

Building a New Town

By 1618, Strabane had become the second largest of the plantation towns – only Derry was larger. Abercorn had built his new settlement away from the ruins of the earlier O'Neill castle (possibly near the old graveyard in Patrick Street). There was a 'strong and fair castle (tower house) but no bawn' (off Castle Street). Eighty houses had been built, many of stone and lime, the rest of timber. The nearby woodland, shown on a 1600 map, could have been a source of timber. On the Strabane estate there were 65 settler families, with 53 in the town. This suggests that Irish families might have been living in some of the houses; others may have restored the houses burned in 1608. Some Irish families in and around Strabane, retainers of Turlough O'Neill's family, may have moved with him to his new estate in south Tyrone. In 1620 the population of the town was probably about 250. A school had been built. The building of a church had commenced, as there had not been one in Strabane before. Its construction stopped when Abercorn died – its walls were then 5 feet (1.5 m) high. By 1622, there was a sessions house, a market cross of stone and lime with a platform on top and a strong room under it, in which to keep prisoners before they were sent to the gaol at Dungannon. There was a mill, probably located on the Cavanalee river beside the present grammar school. Thirty of the town's inhabitants were freeholders, each having a house, garden and small plot of land on which they could graze a cow. At the end of the first ten years of the plantation, we find that, unlike Derry, Strabane had neither walls nor a garrison. It had no land from which to draw an income and no 'free school'. The Tyrone 'free school' was at Dungannon.

The undertakers imported animals and goods required for building. Trade with Scotland flourished. Although a port was built at Derry, small ships made their way to Dunnalong and Strabane. The only port records to have survived cover the period 1612–15. A ship, the *Gift of God* of Strabane, master Robert Lindsiee, was used by Abercorn for both imports and exports to and from Renfrew, not far from his family's home at Paisley. Sir George Hamilton and other local merchants, such as John and William Hamilton and John Birsbean, also used this ship. One export consignment by the latter included, 5 cwt. (250 kg) cheese, valued at £1 13s 4d (£1.67) and three barrels, 3 cwt. (150 kg) butter, valued at £2. On one occasion imports included 1 ton of salt valued at 16s 0d (80p) and 12 tons of coal valued at £3. Only landlords and merchants could afford to buy coal. Goods were sent free of tariff during the early years of the plantation.

The Corporation of Strabane

Strabane received its charter in 1613, whereby it had a provost (mayor) to be elected annually, and twelve burgesses who could elect two members to parliament on the rare occasion when a parliament was summoned. The constitution was such that the membership of the corporation was a small self-electing group drawn from the merchants and leading freeholders living in or near Strabane. They were to hold a weekly court every Monday to hear civil actions not exceeding 5 marks (£3.33) and might pass bye-laws from time to time. The corporation could appoint municipal officers. The provost was empowered to be the clerk of the weekly Tuesday market and the two fairs on 1 November and 1 May. The corporation's limited income came from fees obtained from the markets, fairs and courts.

The first provost was Patrick Crawford. He was first in Strabane in 1608, when, with William Stewart and 200 men, he had helped to quell the O'Doherty rising. He then resided in Lifford. In 1610, as one of the servitor planters, he was granted the 1,000 plantation acre estate of Letterkenny. Abercorn, who would have selected the first burgesses, would have seen him as a man of substance who knew the area well. In 1614 he was asked to subdue a rising on the Isle of Islay and was killed in the fighting. Another burgess who had been living in Strabane before the plantation was John Browne. In 1607 he had received a patent to establish a ferry between Strabane and Lifford. He was the provost in 1628 and 1634.

A more eminent burgess was William Hamilton, a grandson of a bishop of St Andrews in Scotland. He lived initially on the Strabane estate, a freeholder of four townlands. He moved to the less well-developed barony of Omagh. He remained a burgess of Strabane, and was the provost and a justice of the peace (JP) in 1622. Quarter sessions were held before him in 1630, when he was again the Provost. He was a JP in 1632–5 and high sheriff of Tyrone in 1625 and 1638. In 1616 William Hamilton received a 'fee farm grant' (leasehold in perpetuity) of a 'messuage [dwelling] or tenement [site] and garden plot 64 feet [19.5 m] wide and 150 feet [45.5 m] long, and two acres [0.8 ha] in the holme [flat land by the river] of Strabane'. He could 'dig turf [peat] for his own use in any of the earl's mosses [peat bogs]'. He had to pay a rent of £1 sterling a year, plus six hens and two capons, and undertake two days work with a man and horse. The Civil Survey indicated that in Strabane in 1640, the 'land is lett in tenements and acres to the inhabitants of the Corporation, to most in fee farm'. James Hamilton, first earl of Abercorn, had set the pace for the building of the town. This work was continued by his brother, Sir George Hamilton, assisted by very able agents and tradesmen from Scotland.

The first earl of Abercorn increased his landholding in 1615, when he bought the Shean estate from his brother-in-law, Sir Thomas Boyd. In 1616 Abercorn's eldest son, James, aged twelve, was created baron of (Lord) Strabane by James I. This was given as a token of thanks to Abercorn for the progress he had made with the 'plantation' in the Strabane area. After Abercorn's death in 1618, young James Hamilton held the titles of second earl of Abercorn and first Lord Strabane. In 1620, when her husband's will was validated, the countess of Abercorn was given the income of one third of the estate during her lifetime. Her sons, James, George and Claud, were to share £2,555 11s 1d (£2,555.56) levied out of the rents. The first earl's widow stayed on in Strabane, occasionally visiting Scotland. She was a Catholic and, when in Scotland in 1628, was denounced as a 'papist' by the Presbytery of Paisley. In 1621, James, second earl of Abercorn, inherited his grandfather's extensive Scottish estates and continued to live in Scotland, becoming a member of the Scottish parliament. In 1633, a year after the death of his mother, he passed on his title of Lord Strabane to his brother Claud, who moved between Strabane and Scotland. In 1632 Claud married a member of Scotland's leading Catholic family, Jean Gordon, a daughter of the marquis of Huntly, Aberdeenshire. They had four children before he died in 1638, aged thirty-four, being buried at Leckpatrick. His eldest son James, aged five, became the third Lord Strabane, living with his mother in Strabane.

The town continued to grow during the 1620s. The 1630 muster roll for Strabane lists 208 settler men, both Protestant and Scottish Catholics. With the addition of women and children, there could have been a settler population of about 500, and a little higher if the Irish inhabitants were to be included. Strabane now ranked third amongst the plantation towns; only Derry and Coleraine were larger. A wide spectrum of Scottish names appears on the muster roll. Those occurring five or more times were Cunningham, Hamilton, Paterson, Robertson, Wallace and Home–the latter being a common Scottish Borders' surname, whilst Smith suggests an English origin. There were 22 who had 'Mac' names. These men would have been of Scottish Highland origin, some possibly even living in the district before the plantation. They mustered 140 swords, 53 snaphances, 45 pikes, 10 callivers (a firearm about 3.5 feet (105 cm) long), 4 muskets (handgun with a barrel 4.5 feet (125 cm) long), 2 halberts (large axe with a long shaft), with one man the 'bearer of colours'.

The estate-owning members of the Hamilton family continued to be

Royalists, and with three exceptions, Catholics, throughout the century. Some of the leading settlers were also known to be practising Catholics–James Crawford, the countess's agent, and Robert Algeo, Sir George Hamilton's agent. James Farrell, a merchant, was 'the chief harbourer of priests and Jesuits, in whose house the masses are most usually said'. These worshippers included forty Scottish Catholics. In 1628 there had been a 'great meeting of priests' in the town. In view of this, it is not surprising to find that both the bishop of Derry and the archbishop of Glasgow deplored the number of Scottish Catholics who had settled in the Strabane area during the 1620s. The former had complained that the civil authorities 'were wanting in the prosecution of catholic clergy in his diocese'.

The succeeding Hamiltons made no attempt to complete the building of the episcopal church in Strabane, whereas the building of St Columb's Cathedral in Derry had progressed to completion by 1633. In 1634 the bishop of Derry, John Bramhall, received a request from John Browne, the provost, that the building of the church in the town be completed and the parishes of Camus-Juxta-Mourne and Leckpatrick be joined because the two churches were some way from the town. The church at Camus was 4 miles (6.5 km) south and the one at Leckpatrick was 3 miles (5 km) north of Strabane. Nothing came of this request. Henry Noble was the Church of Ireland rector for Leckpatrick from 1622 to 1625, being succeeded by Alexander Spicer to 1636. Noble was also the rector at Camus from 1622 to 1636, when he was dismissed by Bramhall for 'professed popery'. This suggests that even the Protestant settlers attending his services were coming under his Catholic influence, there being no overt signs of Presbyterianism in the district. Indeed at that time, Presbyterianism, albeit within the episcopal church structure, was mainly to be found in the east of Ulster. (For a more comprehensive history of the plantation in the Strabane barony, see R.J. Hunter (ed.), *The Strabane Barony During the Ulster Plantation, 1607-1641*, Derry [1982].)

The Crises of the 1640s

For much of the seventeenth century there were wars between, and civil wars within, west European countries. Most of these were due to the spread of different Protestant churches, with conflicts between them and the Catholic Church. In 1632 Thomas Wentworth was appointed lord deputy by Charles I, and his despotic rule antagonised both the Catholic Church and the few Presbyterian congregations. Wentworth, created earl of Strafford in 1640, had increasingly upset the English Puritan parliament. He was recalled, impeached by parliament, and beheaded.

By 1640, after some poor harvests with rents unpaid, many Irish landlords in Ulster found themselves in debt. Sir Phelim O'Neill of Charlemont was one of these. Some had had to sell their land. Many of them, harassed by Wentworth's government, still resented having been moved from their ancestral heartlands thirty years earlier. With the death of Wentworth and the impending outbreak of the English civil war (1642–6 and 1648–9), Irish leaders saw the opportunity to redress their grievances. In Ulster, the Irish Rising or Rebellion, depending on one's loyalties, broke out on the night of 23 October 1641, with Sir Phelim one of the leaders.

Sir Phelim had said that Scots should not be attacked, but, following rumours and propaganda, there were local outbreaks of violence, with the paying off of old scores. Some settlers were killed. Those who fled to the woods most likely died of exposure or starvation. Some made their way to the comparative safety of Newtownstewart or Derry. Others returned to Scotland. In Strabane Andrew Hamilton died during that winter. He was listed as having 'no arms' in the 1630 muster roll. His widow Marion fled to Scotland and got 'relief' from the Presbytery of Edinburgh at the end of March 1642. The former rector of Donagheady, Rev. Edward Stanhope, died of a fever in 1642. The number of such occurrences is not known, but, twenty-five years later, the hearth tax lists show a significant reduction and change in settler family names throughout the Strabane area. In November 1641, Sir William Stewart of Newtownstewart and his younger brother, Sir Robert Stewart of Ramelton, received a request from Charles I, then in Edinburgh, that each of them should raise regiments of 1,000 foot and troops of horse to defend the Protestant settlers. Military supplies were sent to them from Scotland. The combined military groups became known as the Laggan Force, the Laggan being that part of east Donegal between Raphoe and Ramelton. One of their first engagements was likely to have been an attack on some of Sir Phelim O'Neill's men active in the Strabane area.

In the seventeenth century, with poor roads more like today's unmade forest tracks, military campaigns often came to a halt during wintertime. In the spring of 1642 O'Neill formed an army from amongst his supporters in Tyrone and Derry. In the third week of April, with 4,000 men and 6 troops of horse, he proceeded to Strabane and occupied it. He left a contingent, under Captain Murragh O'Divin(e), to hold the castle with Lady Strabane and her family under house arrest. O'Neill then proceeded along the River Finn to engage the Laggan Force, which had just returned from forays in south Donegal. It is not clear where the encounter took place, but O'Neill's men were forced to retreat. O'Neill left some men with O'Devin(e) in the castle and then returned to Charlemont, taking Lady Strabane and her family with him.

Three days later the Laggan Force crossed from Lifford, attacking the Strabane castle. O'Neill's force within was 'put to the sword', many making their escape by 'their fleetness of foot'. Murragh O'Divin(e) was captured and confined in the gaol at Derry. Friar O'Mellan, who recorded many of these events, commented, 'had the defenders barred the gates they would have been in no danger as they had plenty of military supplies and food'. Unfortunately for them, they did not know that the Laggan Force, by that time, had almost exhausted the supplies sent to them the previous year. Both sides then had to purchase their military supplies from merchants, one of whom was James Maxwell of Strabane. A new garrison was established at Strabane, led by Captain Wisher and commanded by Sir William Hamilton, most probably the son of Sir Claud Hamilton. He would have been a cousin of Lady Strabane's late husband, a Royalist who had become a Protestant before 1640.

Meanwhile, Sir Phelim had asked Lady Strabane to marry him. His wife had died the previous October. She refused his offer, as she had vowed on the death of her husband in 1638 not to remarry for at least five years. O'Neill then arranged for a Franciscan friar, Patrick O'Hammill, to escort the countess to the home of her brother-in-law, Sir George Hamilton of Dunnalong, then living in Munster. In 1629 he had married Mary Butler, a sister of the first duke of Ormond, who was lord lieutenant of Ireland in 1644-50 and 1662-9. Hamilton had received a dowry of £1,800 in February 1630 and the lease of the manor of Roscrea, Co. Tipperary. He, with his family, followed the future Charles II into exile. Three of their nine children will feature later.

By mid May 1642, General Monro and his army, which had earlier come from Scotland, returned to Carrickfergus from a campaign in south-east Ulster. Sir Phelim then decided to go north with the intention of capturing Derry. He had as allies Alasdair and Ranald MacColla from the Glens of Antrim. After reaching Strabane, O'Neill's men were attacked by the Laggan Force. They retired and regrouped, crossing to Donegal in early June. O'Neill's army engaged the Laggan Force on 16 June at Glenmacquin, near Raphoe. Again the Stewart brothers' military experience won the day, with possibly 500 men killed. With their military supplies now exhausted, the Laggan Force was unable to follow O'Neill's beaten army, which then returned to Charlemont. In July 1642, Owen Roe O'Neill, a cousin of Sir Phelim, returned from Spain, landing at Doe Castle on the north coast of Co. Donegal. On 13 August, after passing through the devastated country-side of Donegal and Tyrone, he reached Charlemont, taking over as commander of Sir Phelim's army. Sir Phelim then became involved with the Catholic Confederacy at Kilkenny, the Irish 'government in waiting'. Shortly afterwards Sir Phelim married again, but the marriage was of short duration. He then conducted a courtship of Lady Strabane 'through letters' and eventually married her in 1649. They had a son, Gordon (see below).

In 1643 the Presbyterian Church of Scotland launched its Solemn League and Covenant, which attempted to have the church accepted by the Scottish parliament. Presbyterian ministers came over to Ulster to tell the Scottish settlers about this great event and to seek their support. Some of these visiting ministers reached Raphoe towards the end of April 1644. They addressed members of the Laggan Force in the absence of Sir Robert Stewart who, however, did not support the 'Covenanters'. The ministers then went to Enniskillen, escorted by the Laggan Force, and did not visit Strabane.

Political and military confusion ensued in the three kingdoms for the rest of the decade. With the famine and destruction in 1642–3, everyone would have found it hard to survive. At the end of decade there was a change of sides, with Sir Phelim O'Neill supporting the Royalists, and the Laggan Force the emergent Puritan Republicans. There was again some military activity in east Donegal and Derry, with Strabane briefly held by a republican contingent moving south from Derry.

The Commonwealth of the 1650s

On 30 January 1649, Charles I was beheaded at the instigation of the Puritan parliament. England became a republic with Oliver Cromwell as head of state and called Protector from 1653. Cromwell arrived in Dublin on 15 August 1649 with an army of 10,000 men. The story of the mayhem, death and destruction he caused from Drogheda southwards to Wexford has been extensively recorded. He sent Col. Venables to extend his control over Ulster. By that time, Sir George Hamilton of Dunnalong had gone to France to support the future Charles II. In July 1650, Lady Strabane's eldest son, James Hamilton, third Lord Strabane, then just seventeen, joined the regiment of his stepfather, Sir Phelim O'Neill.

In August 1650 Charlemont was captured. Sir Phelim O'Neill and his men then hid out in woods. James Hamilton surrendered a week later to Sir William Coote, the army commander at Derry. However, he was able to rejoin his stepfather, Sir Phelim, in December. Legend suggests that they passed some of the time in hiding in the Dirrywoon (Baronscourt) area. In February 1653 Sir Phelim was eventually captured at Roughan Lough, near Coalisland. Sir Phelim O'Neill's trial took place in March, and, although many of the Irish leaders were spared in the trials that had taken place, he was found guilty and beheaded. The war was virtually over. The Commonwealth army continued to seek out royalist supporters. In 1655, James Hamilton, third Lord Strabane, then twenty-two, was finally tracked down to a kinsman's house, that of William Hamilton at Ballyfatton. He was flushed out, ran down to the Mourne and drowned. James's brother, George Hamilton, two years younger than his brother, succeeded as fourth Lord Strabane.

With all the turmoil of the 1640s, local as well as national administration had collapsed. In 1654 the Commonwealth government planned a confiscation of the rebels' land. A survey of the whole country was initiated to determine who the landowners were in 1640. The Civil Survey describes the boundaries of each parish, the proprietors of the 'balliboes' (townlands), their size (still in plantation acres), with a breakdown of the type of land to be found plus the value of each townland in 1640. Of the Hamiltons, only Sir William Hamilton, son of Sir Claud Hamilton, was noted as being a Scottish Protestant. The other three Hamiltons, James, third Lord Strabane, a minor, Sir George Hamilton of Dunnalong, and James, his eldest son, also a minor, to whom he had transferred his Largie and Dirrywoon (Baronscourt) estates, were all noted as 'Scottish Papists'. An Inquisition (inquiry) held at Strabane on 9 August 1658 confirmed that from 21 December 1657 the estates of Strabane and Shean, owned by James Hamilton, third Lord Strabane, had been taken over by the 'Commonwealth of England'. Edward Roberts, one of the Irish auditors-general in Dublin, then administered them. At the same time George, fourth Lord Strabane, was told to 'remove to Munster' and it was he who regained possession of the estate under the restored monarchy of Charles II. He, like his forebears, married an heiress with an estate, probably near Dublin.

Very few freeholders were named in the survey, which would suggest that many within this category had left the area during the 1640s. In the Dunnalong estate those named claiming ownership of a townland with a direct family connection to the original owners are William Lynn(e), Hugh Hamilton, John Hamilton and John Goodlet. In the Killeny and Eden estate, there were Hugh and Daniel McKee and John Leslie. Nearer Strabane, two Scottish Catholics claimed ownership of townlands: David Magee of Hollyhill (see below) and Robert Algeo (junior) of Tullyard and Conkill. The latter was a son of Robert Algeo of Woodend, who had been the agent for Sir George Hamilton at the beginning of the plantation. Robert Algeo (junior) was still living at Woodend in 1666. The Hamiltons of Ballyfatton are noted, with William Hamilton also claiming a mortgage on four townlands in the parish of Ardstraw. In the same parish, the son of one of the original burgesses of Strabane, William Birsbean, claimed ownership of the two Clady townlands. (William Hamilton of Ballyfatton was the elder brother of Hugh Hamilton of Lisdivin. Some of William's large family feature later. The descendants of this Hamilton family continued to live at Ballyfatton until the 1990s.)

After 1653 one group in Ulster did benefit from the Commonwealth—the growing Presbyterian Church. Following the visitation of Scottish ministers in the 1640s, a few distinct Presbyterian congregations were formed in the Laggan area, the first being that of Taughboyne in 1646. This development did not cross the Foyle/Mourne for almost a decade. William Moorcroft became the minister at Ardstraw (Newtownstewart) in 1654. A year later he was offering a Presbyterian form of worship. The Commonwealth provided stipends (salaries) to non-conformists. In Moorcroft's case, this amounted to

£100 per year. Other Commonwealth ministers included James Wallace, Urney (1654), John Adamson, Leckpatrick (1655), and Robert Browne, Strabane (1656–9). The first acknowledged Presbyterian minister in Strabane was William Keyes, who had come to Strabane from Cheshire in 1659. His income from the Protectorate was £140.

During this period many Catholic priests were exiled, with the 1650s becoming known as the age of the 'mass rocks'. In Strabane the saying of masses in the homes of prominent people would have continued, but people in rural areas would have attended services at remote spots such as the 'priest's bush' in Cavanalee or the mass rock in Hollyhill. The Catholic Church in Ireland experienced changes during the seventeenth century, with clashes between adherents of the Gaelic Church and the new reformed Tridentine Church. The Catholic diocese of Derry, in common with most other dioceses in Ulster, lacked any kind of effective administration during the whole of the century, with many clerics noted for drunkenness and having common-law wives. One of the worst offenders in the latter category was Terence O'Kelly, the vicar-general of the Derry diocese from 1629, who had lived in safety in the district, protected by the Hamiltons. In 1670 O'Kelly had his jurisdiction suspended by Archbishop Oliver Plunkett for 'thirty years of concubinage and simony' (buying or selling ecclesiastical privileges). Plunkett was later beheaded in London (1681), having been accused of being involved with the 'Popish Plot' by clerics he had antagonised.

The Restoration Period

In 1658 Oliver Cromwell died and was succeeded by his son, Richard, as Protector. He resigned in 1659. Following negotiations to restore the monarchy, Charles II returned to London on 29 May 1660. Although tolerant in religious matters, he attempted without success to alleviate the lot of Catholics who had suffered under the Commonwealth. The Church of Ireland, restored also, attempted to regain its position in the 1660s. In 1661 George Wilde, bishop of Derry, undertook a survey of the parishes in his diocese, which extended from Derry to Omagh and included Clonleigh (Lifford). Robert Wilson, Strabane, and John Adamson, Leckpatrick, are listed, albeit as Scottish Presbyterians. Wilson, ordained in 1655, had come to Strabane in 1660. The bishop deposed him, together with the other ministers living nearby. They were not harassed by the bishop of Derry, unlike four ministers in east Donegal, who endured house arrest for three years in Lifford in the 1660s at the behest of Bishop Leslie of Raphoe.

Although a school had been built in Strabane by 1618, no information regarding its size or subjects taught is known. The first mention of a schoolmaster was in the 1650s. He was a Mr Paton whom the 'townspeople turned out because of his incapability'. Later, in 1686, the parish schoolmaster was

Daniel Magee. Bishops were responsible for appointing the Church of Ireland parish schoolmasters from 1665. The nobility and gentry individually employed teachers for their own children.

In 1667, Robert Mossom, the bishop of Derry, noted that many churches were still ruinous since the war. At the end of April 1668, the bishop started on a two-month-long series of visits to all the churches in his diocese. He spent the morning of 4 June at Strabane, before going over to Lifford to stay for two nights with the warden (mayor), Major Richard Perkins, who had married Cecilia Hamilton, the sister of George Hamilton, fourth Lord Strabane. At each church, he attempted to put in train a church rebuilding programme.

Robert Wilson continued as the Presbyterian minister in Strabane until 1689. His congregation was only able to give him a stipend of £17 in 1674. John Hamilton, the Presbyterian minister of Donagheady, was asked to preach in Strabane and 'to deal smartly with the people in this matter'. It is not known if his stipend was increased as a result of this visit. It would seem that John Adamson was more Episcopalian than Presbyterian, as he was not replaced at Leckpatrick until 1665. Rev. John Sinclair succeeded him as Church of Ireland rector. He was also the rector of Camus (Strabane). Sinclair was a member of a landowning family in Caithness, north-east Scotland. After his death in 1702, his second wife erected a memorial tablet to his memory, extolling his 'humanity and hospitality to all (and his) enthusiasm for suppressing dissenters', both Catholics and Presbyterians. We do not know how he went about this! The memorial can be seen today in the Church of Ireland church at Leckpatrick.

Leading Citizens in and around Strabane in the 1660s

Only a few Church of Ireland and governmental records have survived to provide information about Strabane for the latter part of the century. Sir George Hamilton of Dunnalong had his Irish estates restored to him by act of parliament, after his return to Ireland at the Restoration. His nephew George Hamilton, fourth Lord Strabane, had also been successful in having the Strabane estates restored to him. On his death in 1668 aged thirty-four, his eldest son Claud, aged nine, succeeded as fifth Lord Strabane. Claud was active later in the affairs of the town and was high sheriff of Tyrone in 1683.

A census was carried out in Ireland in 1659, but the Tyrone report has not survived. However the 1666 hearth tax returns provide valuable information about the town at that time. There were 79 householders with one or more hearths on which a tax was levied. Dwellings without chimneys were not recorded, which makes it impossible to assess the total population. It was probably still a little lower than the pre-1641 total. There were 2 houses with three hearths, 18 with two hearths and 59 with one hearth. A comparison of the surnames of 1666 with those on the 1630 muster roll shows 151 different settler surnames in 1630, whereas in 1666 there were only 66. Of the latter, only 36 were the same as in 1630, suggesting that 115 settler families had 'disappeared' from the town during the previous 36 years, reflecting the effects of the intervening warfare. It is possible that some men feature in both lists. The 'new names' would confirm that George Hamilton, fourth Lord Strabane, was achieving some success in the 'replanting the town' with new settlers coming over to Ulster in the 1660s. In 1666 we find a few English surnames but only one 'Mac' name: Where had the 'highlanders' gone, or had they dropped the 'Mac' part of their surname? Were they still living in the town among the poorer people living in the 'cabins', basic dwellings without hearths?

Two families stand out. First the Moderwells, Andrew and Robert on the 1630 muster roll, and John Moderall, who lived in one of the two 'three-hearth' houses in 1666. Was this a restored manor or agent's house, with Moderall the agent for the Strabane estate? He was one of the two commissioners for Poll Money Ordinance in 1660. The other was Patrick Hamilton, a member of the Hamilton of Ballyfatton family, who was a merchant, firstly in Dublin and then in Strabane, becoming the provost in 1669. His sister Katherine had married John Moderall. These two men also feature in the subsidy rolls for Strabane in 1667–8. Moderall must have been highly regarded in Tyrone, as he was the high sheriff in 1678/9. The hearth tax lists also included John Hamell, who lived in a two-hearth house. He was the town clerk. His widow, Christian, went to Scotland after the Siege of Derry. In Edinburgh she asked the Scottish Privy Council for 'a pass to go to London' with one of her sons.

On 15 September 1664, Patrick Hamilton had obtained the lease of a house and garden from George Hamilton, fourth Lord Strabane. Four of the named lessees of adjoining plots appear in the 1666 hearth tax lists. These were Alan Cuthbert (a tanner living in a two-hearth house), John Hamilton, William Ewarts and Andrew Beard. The last named had taken over a plot from a carpenter, John Holmes, whose widow appears in the hearth tax list. Another family, the Delaps, featured in both the 1630 and 1666 lists. Their descendant, John Dunlap, achieved fame in America at the end of the eighteenth century. Also in 1666, Col. James Hamilton, the eldest son of Sir George Hamilton of Dunnalong, was an MP for Strabane. In 1661 this James Hamilton had expressed a wish to marry a Protestant heiress, Elizabeth Colepepper. His mother, an ardent Catholic, was against the match. Hamilton asked his uncle, the duke of Ormond, a Protestant himself, to intercede on his behalf.

In 1664 the bishop of Derry had asked the archbishop of Armagh to consider the amalgamation of the two parishes of Camus-Juxta-Mourne (Strabane) and Leckpatrick and to have only one church. This did

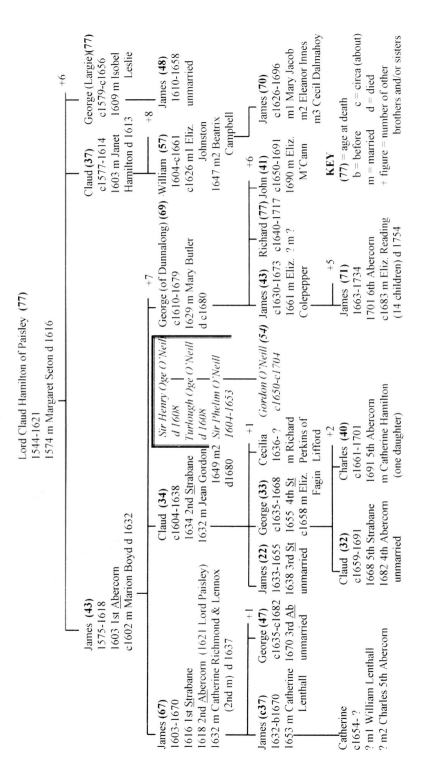

not materialise, as Rev. John Sinclair was appointed rector of Leckpatrick in 1665 and Strabane in 1668. Although Sinclair lived at Hollyhill from the 1680s, it is not known where he lived before then. In the 1654 Civil Survey, David Magee, a Scottish papist, claimed the tenancy of Hollyhill. In 1680 Elizabeth Hamilton, the widow of Col. James Hamilton, who had died during a naval engagement against the Dutch in 1673, granted the townlands of Hollyhill and Kenaghan to George Magee, the son of David Magee. For a period of eighteen months, from November 1681, the two townlands were leased to Gordon O'Neill of Crowe (Crewe) in the parish of Ardstraw. This is the first indication that Gordon O'Neill, the son of Sir Phelim O'Neill, had a link with the Strabane area after the death of his impoverished mother, probably a year earlier. In July 1683 George Magee sold the two townlands to John Sinclair. In 1686 Ezekiel Hopkins, bishop of Derry, visited his parishes to meet the key church people. At Leckpatrick the parish clerk was George Blewart and in Strabane, John Fergyshill. For both parishes the schoolmaster was Daniel Magee.

The Williamite Revolution

The events of the latter part of the seventeenth century culminated in one of the last European religious wars. Charles II had been engaged in wars against the Dutch in 1665–7 and 1672–4. When he died in 1685, his brother, James II, a devoted Catholic, succeeded him. In Ireland, Richard Talbot (1630–1691), earl (later duke) of Tyrconnell, set in motion the move towards giving Catholics public office and the creation of a Catholic army. In England, in 1688, James's attempts to re-establish the Catholic Church led to the Dutch William of Orange being invited to become the king of England–the 'Glorious Revolution'. James fled to France after William reached England in November. Many of his leading Irish supporters joined him there. They included Col. Gordon O'Neill, Claud, fifth Lord Strabane and fourth earl of Abercorn (following the death of his uncle George in 1682), and his uncle, Anthony Hamilton. These families were now ardent Jacobites. They, with the exception of Anthony Hamilton, returned to Ireland with James, who reached Kinsale on 12 March 1689.

A Catholic administration was initiated and a parliament summoned, being in session from 7 May to 20 July 1689. The two Strabane members of the 'Patriot Parliament', Christopher Nugent and Daniel O'Donnelly, were residents of Dublin, but the Co. Tyrone MP was Col. Gordon O'Neill. This parliament instigated an 'Act of Attainder', resulting in the confiscation of land owned by known supporters of William of Orange. Included in a list for the Strabane area was the small Hamilton of Ballyfatton estate. The grandson of the original William Hamilton, also William, did not lodge a claim with the Commissioners of Estates for its return until 1701. Earlier, in August 1688, the Corporation of Strabane was reconstructed, with the majority of the burgesses, if not all, being Catholics. The sovereign (mayor) was John O'Neill (Shane Mac Con Bacagh O'Neill). Of the twenty-one burgesses, fifteen were Irish, including Col. Gordon O'Neill and four other O'Neills. The remainder included Claud Hamilton (fourth Earl of Abercorn), the others bearing surnames which first appeared on the 1630 muster roll: Adams, Browne, Gamble, Cunningham and Hamilton. It is doubtful if this corporation played any significant role in the life of Strabane. With Ireland being run by a Catholic government, with a new Catholic army, the Protestant community became alarmed, afraid that there might be a repeat of the 1641 Rising, an event which still lingered in folk memory of so many of the descendants of the original 'planters'. On 9 December, when the earl of Antrim went to reinforce the garrison at Derry with men from the Catholic army, he had the gates of the walled city closed against him. Thus began the 'Siege of Derry'.

In mid March 1689 the Rev. George Walker, of the parish of Donaghmore, near Dungannon, who had raised five regiments of soldiers, set off for Derry. When he got to Strabane he was told to return to Rash, near Omagh and await further instructions. At the end of March he was told to proceed to St Johnstown. He crossed the Finn by the bridge at Clady, which was subsequently destroyed. In mid April, word reached Derry that King James and his army were coming north. They passed through Newtownstewart on the morning of 16 April and went on to cross the Finn at Clady. Walker, joined by Col. Crofton and his men, engaged James's army at Lifford. The next day, Walker retreated to Derry, whilst Crofton held James's army back a little longer until he ran out of ammunition. He also returned to Derry. Later that day James and his army reached St Johnston, with James staying at nearby Mongevlin Castle. By this time around 30,000 Protestants from north-west Ulster had fled to Derry and taken refuge within its walls. These included Strabane's Church of Ireland rector, Rev. John Sinclair, and the Presbyterian minister, Robert Wilson, and their families. During the confrontation, General Richard Hamilton, another son of Sir George Hamilton of Dunnalong, and commander of James's army, allowed upwards of 10,000 of the refugees to leave Derry, to make their way home or to safety in Scotland.

In view of the stalemate, after fruitless negotiations by the fourth earl of Abercorn with the leaders of the Protestant defenders within the walls of Derry, James decided to return to Dublin. He started his journey on 20 April 1689, staying that night at Cavanacor House, a couple of miles (4 km) north-west of Lifford. Small military contingents were based at Lifford, Strabane, and nearby villages. The church at Strabane became a hospital. The army was poorly equipped. After some skirmishes the Jacobite Royalist army decided to await the surrender of the city when their food ran out.

With Abercorn and his uncle, General Richard Hamilton, were the latter's brother, John, and Col. Gordon O'Neill. On the opposite side was another Hamilton. He was James Hamilton, the nephew of Richard and John Hamilton, and son of their eldest brother, Col. James Hamilton. This James Hamilton, sixth earl of Abercorn from 1701, brought up as a member of the Church of Ireland, had been a privy councillor for James II, but at the 'Glorious Revolution' in 1688, decided to support William of Orange. He brought arms by sea for the defence of Derry.

The siege of Derry continued until 30 July 1689, when relief came with the arrival of ships up Lough Foyle. King James's army on both sides of the Foyle beat a hasty retreat southwards, 'robbing and burning all before them'. Those on the east bank of the Foyle paused at Strabane but, learning that their army at Enniskillen had been defeated, they prepared to continue their retreat southwards. Before moving off, this part of James's army destroyed four of their large guns, burying some and throwing the others and twelve cartloads of arms into the river. They spent the night of 2 August at Newtownstewart, and it, like Strabane, was torched before they continued their retreat. The war continued for another year, ending with the signing of the Treaty of Limerick in October 1691. The Abercorn family suffered many casualties: John Hamilton was wounded and captured at the Battle of Aughrim, dying in captivity in Dublin; Richard Hamilton was captured at the Battle of the Boyne and committed to the Tower of London. He was exchanged for Lord Mountjoy and died in France in 1717. The fourth earl of Abercorn died on the way to France after the Battle of the Boyne, and Col. Gordon O'Neill returned to the continent and died there shortly after 1700. Although Rev. John Sinclair survived the siege, some of his ten children died. Only three of his children survived him when he died in 1702, aged fifty-nine. The Presbyterian minister, Robert Wilson, also died during the siege.

Rebuilding Strabane

No records have been found to provide information on the rebuilding of Strabane in the 1690s. A 1692 report on the state of the Derry diocese reveals that the church at Leckpatrick had been burned during the warfare. The church at Strabane had been severely damaged and was being rebuilt by the parishioners. The first Presbyterian ordination in Strabane was that of Rev. William Holmes on 21 December 1691. Two years later saw the completion of the building of the first Presbyterian meeting-house, which was in what is now Orchard Street. For most of the century, little information regarding the celebration of masses by Catholics or the names of priests in the Strabane district has come to light. From the 1630s services would have continued to be held in the homes of leading Catholics or at 'mass rocks' in rural areas. From 1691, with the new Anglican-led administration, a period of harassment returned, reaching a peak in the next century. Presbyterians and Catholics were both affected. In 1696 five priests held in prison at Strabane asked the Church of Ireland bishop of Derry, William King, to release them, as they had not been charged with anything. One of these was Fr Teig O'Luinsechan of Leckpatrick.

In 1691 the Strabane estates of the fourth earl of Abercorn were 'attaindered' (forfeited because of treason) by the now Williamite Crown. But in May 1692, Charles, fifth earl of Abercorn, obtained a reversal of the attainder, on which there was a mortgage of £3,000. He was able to pay this off in September 1694. New immigrants were coming to Ulster, many from Scotland. It is evident that there was again a thriving merchant community in the town which included Patrick Hamilton, John Gamble, James Hamilton (master of the ship Beattie of Glasgow) and John Love. In 1693 the latter went to Glasgow with his brother-in-law, Alex Herkes, a Derry merchant, to arrange an apprenticeship for his nephew, Thomas Herkes, with a surgeon, John Boyd.

The Countryside – Living and Dying

Most people lived in the countryside and the economy of the district depended on there being a surplus of agricultural products. One of the requirements for the 'undertakers' had been the adoption of English farming methods. The first earl of Abercorn and his brothers brought over lowland Scots. Their farming methods were akin to those in Ulster, with climate and soils being similar. The Celtic system of agriculture largely prevailed. 'Infields', cultivated areas close by clusters of farm houses (clachans), were usually divided into a number of plots not adjacent to each other ('rundale' in Ireland, 'rigs' in Scotland). The 'outfield', larger areas of poorer or hilly land, was used for grazing. In the Strabane area, in townlands near or alongside rivers and streams, a little over half the land was considered 'profitable', comprising arable and pasture land. By 1640 the parish of Urney was the best-developed district, with 85% 'profitable' land. Crops grown were oats, barley and, increasingly, flax; these, together with cows, sheep, pigs and poultry, provided farmers with most of their food and clothing requirements, plus the rent. Peat and timber were usually nearby. Years with poor harvests would have meant starvation for many country people, especially labourers.

Many families in the countryside had lived there for generations, the O'Duffemes (Devines) in the Donemana district for example. A fragmentary poll tax return of 1660 shows that over half the population in the parish of Donagheady was still of Irish origin, with twice as many servants and labourers as farmers. This is confirmed, in part, in the 1666 hearth tax lists, which show that all the farmers with hearths, in eight out of seventeen townlands, were Irish. Close to Strabane, in Cavanalee townland, four of the six hearth taxpayers were Irish and in the neighbouring Edymore townland, two out of six. Eighteenth-century Abercorn estate records show that descendants of two of the settler farmers in Edymore, Rabb and Finlay, who would have broken in steep hillside land, were still living there over 100 years later.

In the early part of the century, one way to make money was to sell timber from the extensive woods found in the district. The landlords rigidly controlled this activity, seeing timber as one of the disposable natural resources of their estates. Scotland was the main market for timber. By the middle of the century the woods were 'all wasted'. Surpluses from flax spinning and linen weaving also provided welcome cash. In 1700 there was active support for this, with the staging of an exhibition in the Strabane Town Hall to promote good spinning techniques. More lucrative for those living beside or near the Foyle/Mourne river system was salmon fishing. Salmon was exported widely, especially in the last quarter of the century. As indicated earlier, it is known that there had been direct trade from the Foyle to and from Scotland from the latter part of the sixteenth century and during the early days of the plantation. Unfortunately, no information on this trade to and from Strabane and Dunnalong after 1615 has survived. The use of the Foyle for freight transportation continued right up to and beyond the establishment of the Strabane Canal at the end of the eighteenth century.

The speed of travel was extremely slow. People had to walk or ride on horseback along roads similar to unmade forest tracks of today. From 1615 these had to be maintained on a parish basis. There were no bridges across the Foyle and Mourne, but bridges were built over smaller rivers. In 1633 five parishes were fined £40 for not contributing to the building of a bridge over the Douglas Burn on the 'king's highway' from Strabane to Newtownstewart. With difficult 'roads' to the south, most travellers going from Omagh to Derry would have crossed the Finn at Clady and travelled through east Donegal. Those wishing to cross the Foyle would have used the Strabane-Lifford, Dunnalong-Mongevlin or the Waterside-Derry ferries. The ferries were flat-bottomed boats called 'cots'. In the upper reaches of the Foyle and along the Mourne, people and animals would wade across the river when water levels were low, sometimes with disastrous consequences. As the century progressed, farmers would have increasingly used wheeled carts. Away from the 'roads' the use of 'slide cars' (carts without wheels) was more usual. These, as well as horses or donkeys with pannier baskets, were used when bringing home 'turf' (peat) from the landlord's 'mosses' (peat bogs).

In seventeenth-century Ulster people were often affected by ill-health, with diseases such as dysentery and consumption being quite common. Outbreaks of typhoid, hepatitis, smallpox and typhus were frequent, especially in the 1640s. Harvest failures in the 1630s, 1642, 1650, 1664 and 1674 led to famine and starvation conditions, with many people dying as a result. No information on any such outbreaks in the Strabane area has been found.

It is no wonder that life expectancy was lower for everyone in the seventeenth century. Of the seventeen principal landowning Hamiltons encountered during the century, only six lived more than fifty years. Marriages with large families were common and some have been noted. Many women died in childbirth. With high mortality and disease rates, many children did not reach adulthood. Men and women often remarried after their spouses had died because of the need to have a family to provide for them in old age. To have a tolerable life, people needed to experience good health and seasons, augmented by faith and good luck!

End Note

It has been possible to provide only glimpses of people and events in and around Strabane from 1622, as few governmental, church and private records have survived. The town of Strabane, a small village in today's terms, uniquely, yet sadly, was destroyed on four occasions in a period of 100 years. Only details of the second rebuilding, in the early plantation period, are known. These show a significant growth in the size of the town.

The many Irish families who did not go with the O'Neills to south Tyrone in 1610, and the incoming Scottish undertakers, the Hamiltons, together with some of their kinsmen, ensured a substantial Catholic population in the Strabane area: the Hamiltons gave a degree of protection to Catholic worshippers for many years during the century. The active development of the two small Protestant churches did not gain momentum until the latter part of the century. After 1691 both Catholics and Presbyterians were harassed, but that story continues into the next century.

Strabane greatly benefited from its geographical location. With poor roads to the south, few travellers other than armies came from that direction. The Sperrins were a barrier to travel to the east of Ulster. Strabane is located at the head of the tidal waters of the Foyle, with the small vessels of the period able to reach Dunnalong, and even Strabane itself. Trade with Scotland flourished, developed by an active Scottish merchant community living in the town. Both farmers and townsfolk benefited. The town grew, but had to cope with rebuilding and regeneration after periods of strife and disruption in the middle and latter parts of the century. Without doubt, during the seventeenth century, for everyone living in and around Strabane, life was 'rough and tough'. In the next century Strabane grew and prospered.

5 The Development of Strabane in the Eighteenth Century 1700–1770

JOHN DOOHER

Strabane area in the late seventeenth century from Petty's *Hibernia Delineato*, 1685

The Williamite Wars had ended a period of major unrest in Ireland, and Strabane had borne a share of the dislocation and suffering that enveloped the country. Defeats at the Boyne and Limerick had effectively ended native and Catholic hopes of a revival in their fortunes, and the future lay with the Protestants and the descendants of the plantation settlers. Little mercy was to be shown to the defeated and the subsequent penal laws represented both the desire for revenge and the determination to marginalise and control the defeated and dispossessed. The new order required a new leadership and a more exclusive approach to the political management of the country.

Information on Strabane in the early years of the eighteenth century is limited and it would appear to have been a period of regrouping after the dislocations of the previous decades. The Abercorn family had been caught up in the civil conflict of the Williamite wars and their hold over the Strabane area had suffered as a result. The main beneficiaries of the period of confusion were the merchants and freeholders of Strabane, and it seems that they were able to extend their own power at the expense of the Hamiltons. It appears also that the estate management was somewhat confused in the period, with little coherent agent control and planning. Leases may have been granted on what were later to appear as too favourable terms and from the 1740s the earl and his representatives were determined to recover lost ground and re-establish traditional landlord power. The Strabane Corporation and the tenants on the various Abercorn estates were to feel the impact of these attempts at re-establishing the lost power and authority. (This topic is treated in some detail in the chapter by Dr Malcomson.)

The Eighteenth-century Landscape

What were Strabane and district like in the early decades of the eighteenth century? Contemporary accounts stress a country suffering from an absence of population and an abundance of poverty over large areas. Chief Baron Willes described Tyrone as 'a dreary empty country, its boggy mountains dangerous to sportsmen, its stocks of food so low that a traveller would leap at a crust of stale bread and a mutton chop', while Bishop Nicholson, on his way to his diocese of Derry in 1718, wrote of the sorry slaves who lived in reeking sod hovels and subsisted on a 'rig' or two of potatoes. In 1721 he wrote of a sight of poverty that he witnessed from his own home. One of his coach horses had been killed in an accident and, before arrangements could be made for its removal, the animal had been cut up and carried off by the starving population of the district. Of course, these were outsider views but there can be little doubt that much of the population lived in constant dread of famine and its accompanying ailments.

Famines and Shortages

Reports suggest that Ireland suffered shortages in the summer of 1726, resulting from a poor harvest in the previous autumn, while a serious famine developed in the years 1728–9. It is difficult to know for certain whether such shortages impacted heavily on Strabane, but it seems likely that poor harvests would be countrywide in their effect and that there would have been considerable suffering locally. Further shortages in the 1730s culminated in a major famine in the years 1740–41 with an impact considered even more severe than that of the 'Great Hunger' of the 1840s. The disaster period began with a major storm and a long period of severe frost in the early weeks of 1740, with shipping unable to move in many places and potatoes destroyed in their storage pits and in the ground. A very dry and cold spring prevented growth and ensured that the crop for 1740 would be far below the usual levels. The combination of serious food shortage and the unusually cold weather led to a disease epidemic in the spring and early summer of 1741, with the result that the episode was designated *Bliain an Air*, the year of slaughter. Animals as well as humans suffered severely in the period, and the early months of that year saw the death and slaughter of many cattle through lack of fodder and inadequate care. It appears, however, that Ulster did not suffer quite so severely and one reason was the availability of imports, paid for by the export of linen products. An account from Strabane, published in a Dublin journal in August 1741, suggested a plentiful harvest and an area that had suffered little:

> The earth is loaded; potatoes never so many nor ever so good . . . I do assure you of peace and plenty at home, I mean the North of Ireland, where we are more industrious than any of the other provinces . . . [See David Dickson, *Arctic Ireland: The Extraordinary Story of the Great Frost and Forgotten Famine of 1740–41*, Belfast (1997)]

The smugness and sense of superiority of the writer may have coloured his description somewhat, but other evidence suggests that the North suffered considerably less than some other regions. Omagh, however, was apparently not so lucky and the dry summer of 1741 led to a town fire that is reputed to have destroyed much of the town, with only the public buildings left standing (Dickson, *Arctic Ireland*).

Strabane was shortly afterwards to suffer from a partial famine and the Abercorn correspondence of the years 1744–5 details the impact on prices and food supplies of a major local shortage, caused by poor weather in the harvest period of 1744 and the consequent upsurge in the price of oatmeal. By March 1745 Abercorn's agent was reporting on the starving cattle and desperate people; while a month later the poor people were said to be fighting for the meat of dead cattle, with many dying of starvation. Imported food supplies, paid for by the landlord and other people with money, ensured that widespread deaths were prevented over much of the area and a reasonably abundant harvest in the autumn of 1745 brought an end to the immediate famine. But the episode demonstrated that food supplies for many were at the mercy of the weather and that famine was never far distant for a large section of the poorer population. The simultaneous harvest failure and linen depression ensured that there was no back-up in a period of shortage, unlike the earlier 1740–41 episode, when proceeds from linen could offset local crop failures. (This topic is dealt with in greater detail in John Dooher, 'A Strabane famine in the 1740s', in *Concordia*, iv [1997].) It will be seen later that shortages were endemic in the eighteenth century and that landlords and their agents had to take them into consideration in assessing unwillingness or inability to pay rent when it fell due.

The Linen Industry and Economic Growth

Linen was clearly highlighted as one of the factors that made Ulster less prone to serious shortages than other parts of Ireland, and it is clear that Strabane was indebted to the spread of the industry in the district. The origins of the linen trade are shrouded in some dispute but it appears that the influx of Scottish settlers was an important factor in the early growth of the industry, especially in its commercial aspects. In the early eighteenth century, when transport and communications were slow and underdeveloped, linen was an easily transportable commodity and for many people the only source of ready money. References were made in the 1740s to the importance of linen in relieving many poorer people in Strabane from the worst effects of the famines that were ravaging the districts, and the correspondence to Abercorn from his agents in the mid eighteenth century frequently mentions linen and the flax mills. In the 1740s, when the earl was attempting to increase the income from his estates, the rents from linen mills and bleach greens were an important consideration. Markets and fairs were important trading opportunities and there was considerable dispute in the mid century over the markets at Magheracrigan, in the Derrywoon part of the Abercorn estates. Tenants were allegedly trying to prevent the growth of the market because they saw it as leading to an increase in their rents, and they claimed the right to have some recompense, including a share of the tolls. The market was itself situated near glebe land (not under landlord control) and, according to John Colhoun, this prevented proper regulation of the activities at the fair:

> The markets at Magheracrigan are surely improving but what discourages it at present is yarn buyers who wait perhaps a quarter of a mile from the market and stops yarn there by buying it; I could prevent this on all sides but where the glebe land comes so near us, there is the loss and I know not if I can discourage such practice there or how.

Both landlord and tenant were clearly suffering from the loss of tolls while the merchants/forestallers were reaping the advantages.

More tangible support for the growing linen industry is provided by the decision of the Strabane Corporation in 1750 to build a market house and brown linen hall. John Colhoun, Abercorn's agent in Strabane, informed him in October of the decision of the corporation and the likelihood of application being made for financial support, with the claim that the profits on the linen hall were to be used to provide premiums to encourage the further growth of the market. In February of the following year the provost of Strabane, William Hamilton, sought Abercorn's approval and active participation in the project and clearly with some degree of success. Nathaniel Nisbitt, the Abercorn agent based in Lifford, wrote in April 1751 of the response of the town:

> The people of Strabane were in great joy, on hearing that your lordship was so good as to subscribe to the market house and most of the better sort of people expressed themselves to me that nothing could be more agreeable to them, that the concernment your lordship took in its being erected in proper form, and the care your lordship took in the correcting of some errors in the plan laid before your lordship.

It appeared from a thank-you letter that Abercorn subscribed the sum of 40 guineas while Lady Abercorn provided a further 20 guineas to a building estimated to cost about £650, and with a Mr Price the builder. The decision to proceed with the building at that stage was both a reflection of the current strong state of the linen trade and a belief in its importance for the future. A strong and thriving linen market would greatly strengthen the local economy and ensure that the corporation had the funds to further develop the town and its markets.

The Corporation in Strabane

The issue of markets and the collection of tolls was a matter of some dispute between Abercorn and the corporation in mid century, and the correspondence from the agents suggests that it was for many years an irritating battle for the earl. It was tied in to the whole issue of political control and the claims of the Abercorns to the right of nomination of Strabane's two members of parliament. (This topic is explored in detail in Dr Malcomson's chapter.) Suffice to say that the earl believed that previous agents and disinterested earls had allowed the Hamilton family's rights to be eroded, and he was determined to win back the lost position. In 1747 he raised the issue of ownership of the Bowling Green, claimed by a political opponent, McCausland, and sought legal advice on his claims. In the following year it was suggested that the corporation claimed the area as a gift from the earl's grandfather. In late 1746 dispute had arisen over a house belonging to Hugh Browne beside the old market house. Abercorn's agent had persuaded Browne to pay rent to the Earl, and, when the corporation attempted to remove the building as a means of enlarging the market house, they were stopped by Nisbitt, who argued that the corporation had rights only over the area of the market house. It was clear that other parcels of ground were involved in the dispute and Nisbitt had no doubt that the corporation meant to lay claim to much more:

> They have got a new recorder in town, as they call him, who if he continues his schemes will be a very troublesome person; he is, I am told, putting the corporation on claiming a little piece of ground lying between Strabane and Lifford called the wheat fall; they say it was formerly the right of the corporation, and given by some of your lordship's family, but they don't pretend to have a deed; they also say that their charter gives them several waste lotts of ground whereon there are houses now built.

The corporation attempted to proceed with their demolition work at the market house but were warned off by Nisbitt who went on to detail to Abercorn some of the other claims of the corporation, including the right to arrest people over the bridge in the parish of Urney and the rejection of the right of the earl's seneschal to hold manor courts within the limits of the corporation. The agent was at a loss on what to do and concluded that 'they appear to me my lord as if they were bit by a mad dog'. Clearly this threat of legal action was enough to stay the corporation, and by December 1747 Hugh Browne was still in possession of his property and the extension of the market house had been shelved. It appears that enough members of the corporation refused to contribute towards the cost of legal action to test the claims of Abercorn, and a further letter in August 1748 reported that Browne had got approval from the Court of Chancery for repossession of the land at the market house that had been the original cause of the dispute. In February of that year Nisbitt had warned Abercorn that his claims did not appear to be totally secure:

> I have, my lord, from time to time taken all the care I could to find if any of your lordship's property was concealed or overlooked about Strabane and as far as I can judge your lordship has an acknowledgement out of every thing except the Bowling Green, the little house at the end of the market house, bridge tenement, and a bit of ground on the meeting house brae, in the possession of one Samuel Carson who lives in America.

Abercorn's position seemed, however, to have been strengthened somewhat in May when a number of shopkeepers, those nearest the market house, paid their rents to the earl, thus effectively accepting him as the owner of the land and property.

Conflict continued into the following decade, despite the apparent goodwill gesture by Abercorn in assisting the building of the new market house. In 1752 the corporation took their claim to the highest level and petitioned parliament for a reaffirmation of their rights to hold weekly markets in accordance with the original charter and with the unchallenged extension of the market since then. The issue seems to have concerned the tolls due on the Saturday markets and the conflicting claims of Abercorn and the corporation, and it would appear that the decision was in favour of the corporation in this particular case. Further claims arose in 1755 over the rights of the corporation-appointed town sergeant to control the shopkeepers and a mearing dispute between the corporation and land in the adjoining parish of Leckpatrick was raised in agent's correspondence with the earl. Much of the surviving information is from the Abercorn archives, but it seems likely that the growing prosperity of Strabane merchants and their efforts to expand their own power was at the bottom of the conflict with the earl in this period. The right of the town to develop in accordance with the wishes of the leading citizens rather than being restrained by the requirements of the rural hinterland and the patriarchal authority of the Abercorns, who had for long done little to help the struggling townspeople, was the major challenge to be resolved.

Estate Management

It was not only in the town of Strabane that Abercorn was attempting to extend his authority and control, and the letters of the agents in the 1740s and 1750s detail the areas of estate management that the earl was concerned with. It appeared that previous agents had been more than willing to give tenants favourable terms and it is likely that this would have happened in the immediate aftermath of major war and dislocation, when any tenant was preferable to none. By the 1730s, however, the sustained period of stability and the growth of the domestic linen industry suggested that the income from the estates should be more in line with the Abercorn expectations and requirements. A clear definition of farms and rental terms was considered essential, and from the mid 1730s the Abercorn estates were to be divided into individual holdings rather than the joint tenures that had prevailed in many areas prior to this. William Starrat, a well-respected and informed engineer/mapper, was employed to delimit individual farms and set manageable boundaries for them and the 'Starrat Marches' are still referred to up to the present time. In 1737 Starrat corresponded with Abercorn about draining and ditching that he was doing in the Townparks area of Strabane and some of the early Starrat farm maps still survive. (One example is the estate map of the Sinclair lands in Hollyhill and Keenaghan and this map is in the possession of Hamilton Thompson.) Correspondence from the Abercorn agents in the 1740s detail how they faced problems in getting tenants to accept new divisions and John McClintock advised the earl in 1744 to allow a continuation of the Rundale until the following year when access problems could be clearly resolved.

Correspondence from Nathaniel Nisbitt to Abercorn in the 1748–9 period highlight some of the problems faced by tenants and landlord in the period. Abercorn had himself remarked that he felt that many of the tenants were deliberately allowing their farms to run down as the lease drew to a close in order to get better terms and a smaller renewal figure, and Nisbitt agreed that this was certainly the case. He went on to argue, however, that leases for twenty-one years were not attractive and that tenants would be more motivated by the three lives lease, being prepared to pay higher fines or renewal payments for the longer term. Other landlords were offering the longer terms and Abercorn's agents were finding it difficult to move tenants to new leases except on the better terms. This would suggest a growing confidence among the tenantry and a willingness to hold out for improved conditions, even against the inclinations of the earl.

Exploiting Natural Resources

Land leases were only one aspect of estate management and the letters of the agents confirm that fishing rights, river transport and control of mills and waterways were all part of the landlord's rentals. In 1746 the agent reassured Abercorn that there was nothing wrong with letting the Edymore mountain for rough grazing despite the fact that this might reduce the acreage of turf land available; the people of Strabane, it was suggested, got too much turf free from Abercorn and could afford to pay for their supplies. Frequently the rentals for fishing in the Foyle were the subject of correspondence and in October 1748 Colhoun informed Abercorn of the need for new arrangements for the Strabane and Greenbrae fishing, both of which were out of lease and with prospects of improved rentals. This necessitated agreement with the Creighton estate on the Lifford side of the river and was not easy to dispose of quickly. The various woods were also considered part of the estate's wealth and the unauthorised cutting of timber considered a serious crime. Thus Colhoun could justify the appointment of a wood keeper for Cloughcor following the cutting of several sapling oak from there, while at a later stage an investigation was ordered into the appearance of fresh oak at one of the markets. Even bog oak or fir had to be accounted for, and tenants had to seek permission to use it for house building. Thus in 1748 one John McClintock sought permission to raise two tons of bog fir in Strabane bog for the purpose of rebuilding his house while John Sinclair, agent for the Donelong (Dunnalong) manor in the later 1750s, sought Abercorn's approval for searching for bog timber in the Moorlough area in order to build a store.

Likewise, ferries across the Foyle were liable to rent and McClintock in October 1744 bemoaned the fact that he was in difficulties getting new tenants at the existing rental and feared having to offer them for less. One of the problems for ferries, however, was access and rights of way, with tenants jealous of their rights and unwilling to allow passage except at a cost. In June 1745 Colhoun reported to Abercorn about Thomas Wensley from Donagheady landing boats at Ballydonaghey and transporting his goods from there through Frederick Poak's land without his approval. The matter was referred to the arbitration of Colhoun and Mc Clintock, but with Abercorn accepting that there was no right of passage through Ballydonaghey. In a period when roads were only starting to develop, short river crossings and indeed transport by water would have seemed very attractive, and it must have been the poor prospects at the end of 1744 that caused the difficulties in finding tenants for the ferries. Certainly the river Foyle seemed to thrive as a communication artery and reports in 1750–51 gave estimates of the volume of traffic that it carried. Nisbitt had been instructed to record the numbers, and his report in September 1751 suggested that 'there come up Lifford River from May 1750 to May 1751 about 200 boats'. It is clear that he was estimating trading boats in this calculation and thus pointing to the importance of river transport in the period; presumably the level of transport down river was similar to that coming from Derry. Roads were only being developed and were as yet unsuitable and slow for much of the transport that was needed.

Duty Work

The provision of roads and bridges was something that concerned the tenants of the Abercorn estates and there was increasing opposition manifested to the labour dues that were supposed to be part of the tenants' obligations. Main roads were the responsibility of the grand jury and a county cess was levied to pay for this. The collection and enforcement of labour dues, however, was often a matter for the local landlord and his agents and the Abercorn correspondence bears testimony to the problems that this could engender. In the 1740s William Edie appears to have been Abercorn's work manager at Baronscourt, and in June 1744 he reported on the progress of road building: '[T]he new road from Newtown towards Strabane is more than half finished; I intend to be as early as the season will permit at them and hopes to have some assistance from your lordship this summer in order to get the constables to do their duty.' This was a reference to the parish constables elected by the vestry and responsible for the collection of the various dues imposed on the tenantry. It was often difficult, however, to get the work done and Colhoun reported to Abercorn in August 1750 about the fines imposed on those who had not done their share of work on the roads. Work was progressing on the road from Newtownstewart to Omagh but little had been done on the Strabane to Ardstraw road – being a relatively minor road, this was the responsibility of the parish vestries rather than the county grand jury. Nisbitt, in the spring of the following year, suggested that the system of allowing tenants to pay a monetary sum (a fine) rather than work the stipulated number of days was not succeeding, since people were slow to pay and labourers sought high wages. A further report in September of 1751 suggested that little progress had been made on the Strabane to Ardstraw road despite the demands of the people of Sian (Sion) for a greater urgency and stiffer work allocation if necessary: '[T]hey began at the Strabane end of the road and made about a quarter mile of good road towards Bellicolman but I think the road too narrow all through the lands of Bellicolman and Ballifatton.' William Edie had little doubt that part of the problem lay with the overseer and compared his successful management of the Baronscourt district with the less developed roads in Urney parish; he sought Abercorn's approval and support in having himself appointed agent for the Strabane manor in the place of the recently deceased McClintock and placed in charge of the roads and the cess collection at the next vestry meeting. He did not get the position but his contribution demonstrated the difficulties that agents could encounter in the management of the estates, especially over road making and maintenance. What appeared a desirable road to the landlord or his agent might not appear so needy to tenants who felt they could better use their time or energy on their own farms.

Utilising the Bogs

In the same period, the use of the bogs became a matter of major interest to Abercorn and it is clear that he felt they were not realising their full potential. In 1755 Nisbitt was instructed to regulate Woodend turf bog, and by 1757 the estate surveyor was required to divide up the turf bog at Donelong 'in small lots for setting'. Nisbitt reported on his visit to Donelong in company with the agent for that estate, John Sinclair, and the surveyor, Michael Priestly:

> I took Mr Sinclair with me, to show him the new boat and to make him as sensible as I could of your lordship's meaning in the cutting of the wood and turf bog along the shore, for the future, and that there was to be no turf sold by any persons but those who would take lotts of bog by acre from your lordship.

The Strabane bog was organised the following year and it was clear that Abercorn was determined to have as full a value as possible from the natural resources on the estate. As early as 1753 Nisbitt had complained of the abuse of the bogs by cottiers; many of these would have been weavers and needed the turf for the drying of the linen. But cottiers were not normally direct tenants on the estate and would not have been subject to the same degree of control. Nisbitt had argued that they made no improvements and were simply wasteful of the bogs and resources of the estate. The division of the bogs into defined lots and the renting of these out at a rent was a new departure and a serious undermining of the ill-defined rights that many had previously accepted as the norm.

Fears of Jacobitism in 1745

Thus by the middle of the eighteenth century Abercorn was well on the way to establishing firm control over his estates and the people who lived there. Close attention was paid to all areas of estate management and opportunities taken for increasing the potential from the various manors. Despite periodic shortages there was some improvement in overall prosperity and much of the uncertainty of the early part of the century had gone. The land settlement was apparently there to stay, though the fear of a Catholic rebellion remained, and this is evident in the scare occasioned by the Jacobite rebellion in Scotland in 1745 and the repercussions in Ireland and in Strabane. In late 1744 Nisbitt had reported to Abercorn about the collapse of confidence in the markets on the rumours of invasion but it was not until the autumn of 1745 that the real panic set in with the landing of the Pretender in Scotland. John McClintock reported on the difficulties he was encountering in setting houses and believed that the low price for linen was directly related to the news of the Jacobite successes. He claimed that the country was greatly alarmed and such views were echoed by Nisbitt when reporting on the impact of the early victory of the Jacobites over General Cope: '[C]redit among the dealing people was never so low, and I am informed from Dublin there never was so great a run on the banks . . . there is scarce a person will buy a piece of cloth and yarn is very low.' The decision to mobilise the militia was seen as a confidence-boosting measure but had little immediate impact on trade. The agents were instructed to list the firearms available in each manor and the consequent reports were far from satisfactory. Donelong (Dunnalong) had 48 'in order' but 41 in 'bad order' and similar figures came from the other areas. Nisbitt was pessimistic about the state of Strabane's defences and Lifford seemed even worse:

> I have looked at what fire arms there are in your lordship's estate of Strabane, the town excepted; I find to the amount of 46 firelocks, and 2 cases of pistols, mostly in very bad order. This country is but in a very indifferent state of defence at present . . . There are present 750 firelocks and as many bayonets with equal quantity of ammunition in the barrack of this town (Lifford) for the militia of Donegal; but the arms are all in bad order and seem to be much neglected . . . I set a Protestant guard on them.

By November Colhoun was reporting that 'we are now more alarmed than ever about the rebellion in Scotland and in fear of some disturbances here; our trade is quite gone', while the following month Mc Clintock reported on the increasing fears of 'a visit from those rebels that are plundering our neighbouring kingdom, or some foreign invasion, either of which must be of terrible consequence to this country as there is no standing army in the North'.

At the local level the mobilisation of the militia and the appearance of regular troops were important reassurances to a fearful population who clearly believed that a Jacobite victory could mean their own ruin. One of the Strabane MPs, William Hamilton of Dunamanagh, called a public meeting to declare loyalty to the existing constitution and to mobilise popular support for any necessary defensive action and it was reportedly well attended:

> The Scotch rebellion has raised a spirit of great zeal and loyalty among Protestants of all ranks and denominations. There was a gathering of the Protestants of neighbouring parishes to this town on Wednesday last by order of Mr Hamilton, one of the Deputy governors of this county, when there was a very numerous appearance of Protestants who all showed the greatest zeal and loyalty for his Majesty and the present government. [John Mc Clintock to Abercorn, 16 October 1745]

There is no evidence of local repercussions against the Catholic population at the time but no doubt they would have been looked at with suspicion and made liable to the full rigours of the penal laws. The period of uncertainty continued until the halting of the Jacobites at Derby and their retreat from England in the early part of 1746, though even then there were still fears of reverses, and as late as March 1746 Mc Clintock reported on a further setback to a revival of the linen trade with the continued mobilisation of the Jacobites in the Highlands; the fears only abated with the duke of Cumberland's victory over the Jacobites at Culloden in April of that year.

The Penal Laws at Local Level

The penal laws were certainly enforced in the Strabane area in the early eighteenth century and the Abercorn correspondence provides some glimpses of the disabilities that Catholics, and to a lesser extent Presbyterians, had to endure. In May 1748 John Colhoun reported to Abercorn that the Baronscourt gardener, Broomfield, had been married in a Catholic ceremony by a 'popish priest'. The agent added that he had often warned the gardener 'of his drinking with bad company and from circumstances of this sort I doubt his conduct or neglect rather'. Abercorn instructed the agent to persuade Broomfield 'to get married again regularly' (i.e. in a Church of Ireland ceremony) and to mend his ways. At the same time Colhoun was instructed to inform Broomfield that he was not to bring his wife into the estate household, though he was to allow him to unofficially set up house for the wife nearby. This doubtless proved very difficult and by 1750 Broomfield had been dismissed from the Abercorn employment. No doubt the alleged reason was his failure to manage the business of the estate gardens efficiently, but the episode illustrates the difficulties that Catholics could experience in their everyday life. Abercorn would have counted himself a liberal in his outlook and favoured a relaxation of the penal laws in the 1770s, but his refusal to allow a Catholic in his household at the end of the 1740s demonstrates a level of unacknowledged and probably unconscious discrimination in the mid eighteenth century.

Another and more defined area of discrimination was over leases and there are frequent mentions of the restrictions on Catholics having leases on the same terms as Protestants. In 1762 John Hamilton reported on his new leases for Ballymagorry and added that 'there are two or three papists who could not have leases for lives but were desirous to have leases for 21 years'. Abercorn sanctioned this arrangement and in 1769 accepted that the proposed new houses at Irish Street, Strabane, would not be open to all: '[A]s the leases are to be for three lives, they can not, I am afraid, be let to papists.' This obviously placed Catholics at a disadvantage in offering for houses or land and was part of the legal framework designed to maintain a degree of control over this section of the population. One of the more remarkable aspects of the Abercorn correspondence is the relative absence of references to Catholics and indeed Presbyterians in the decades before the 1770s and it almost seems that they didn't exist; certainly they kept their heads down and got on with the problems of living in a restrictive environment.

The Tithe Question

One area where conflict did arise regularly was over tithes, an annual tax collected for the upkeep of the Church of Ireland and its clergy. In the early part of the century tithes would appear to have been collected 'in kind' – that is, one tenth of the crop – and this frequently gave rise to agitation and dispute. In the late 1730s two tenants from Cullion in the Dunnalong manor, James and Robert Dunn, wrote to Abercorn about the rector of Donagheady and his forcible seizure of the tithe on their crop. Other parishes had similar problems, and in 1744 Nisbitt reported to Abercorn that a number of tenants from the Ardstraw parish were to be brought before the Bishop's Court for judgment against them. A little over a year later the problem had moved to Strabane, with Nisbitt reporting that the church vestry had decided to levy and collect from the whole parish the salary for the parish clerk, a new departure that Nisbitt condemned and instructed tenants not to tolerate. Abercorn was clearly worried about the tithe issue, and his agents reported in late 1750 about the standard payments that were required in addition to the tenth proportion of the crops. From this it can be seen that there were payments required for possession of cows, sheep and horses, and dues to be paid on christenings, marriages and burials. In addition, payments were levied on gardens and on turf stacks, and every family was required to make an Easter offering. It was calculated that such payments amounted to one fifth of the landlord's rents, 'a very high tax on the country' in the view of Abercorn's agent, Nisbitt. The fact that parish vestries could and did impose additional taxes for salaries and other items of parish administration was a source of much discontent and frequently reported on in the correspondence from the local agents. It is clear that Abercorn had considerable sympathy with the grievances of many of his tenants and in correspondence with a Dr Hudson of Trinity College, Dublin, owners of part of the Ardstraw Glebe lands, he left no doubt about his attitude on the question:

> When first I went into Ireland I found numbers of my father's tenants labouring under the most grievous oppression in their tithes and this founded on cruel maxims said to be established by law, though most notoriously contrary to it. All the assistance I could give was very unequal to their distress, but the clamour raised against my endeavours convinced me they were not quite ineffectual.

That many of his tenants were Presbyterians or Catholics would have exacerbated the level of discontent in parts of the Abercorn estates and posed difficulties for the agents in management. From the letters it is clear that they had been instructed to help tenants defend cases against new impositions and to bring some influence to bear on the rectors and their collectors.

Problems of Tithe Collection

Ownership of an estate frequently allowed the landlord considerable influence in the appointment of rectors and Abercorn had the right of appointment to Donagheady in Tyrone and Taughboyne in Donegal where he owned a further estate. These positions were frequently allocated to relations or to other family friends and the death of Dr Hamilton in Donagheady in 1753 allowed the opportunity for a new appointment. The agent reported that much of the corn tithe due remained unharvested in mid October (about 550 acres?) and it was necessary for the church authorities to arrange for the collection of this tithe. Andrew Wood, the old rector's tithe manager, was requested to collect the outstanding tithes and these would have been paid to the estate of the late rector. These tithe agents were generally very unpopular and the correspondence from Abercorn's agents would suggest that they had little sympathy with the problems of the poorer people. The farming out of tithes to agents was frequently seen by the estate managers as inappropriate and insensitive but no doubt beneficial to the rector, who was relieved of the fluctuations that might result from poor harvests and bad seasons. Thus in 1758 Rev. Bracegirdle, appointed rector of Donagheady in 1753 on Abercorn's nomination, reported to his patron on the tithes problem, aggravated by the poor crops and linen depression of the time, and sought approval for the farming out of these in the years ahead:

> If my income were fixed and I knew what I had to depend on, I should be much better satisfied with my situation than I have yet been, or have had reason to be; but processes, decrees, citations, etc, etc, are horrid things, which I had never seen, or scarce heard of in England.

Abercorn was rather unfortunate in his clerical nominations in this period since Rev. Bracegirdle found Donagheady rather uncongenial and settled in Strabane rather than remain in his parish, while Abercorn's appointee in Taughboyne, Rev. Frederick Hamilton, was very much an absentee and could not be prevailed on to reside in his parish. Such absentees had little contact with their parishioners or their problems and saw tithes as a necessary part of their income. The death of Bracegirdle in 1768 was apparently mourned by few in his parish but posed problems for his family, and a son petitioned the earl for help in collecting the arrears of over £2,000 due to the late rector. His successor, Rev. James Hamilton, lost little time in appointing a tithe manager and arranging for the finances of his new living, staying in the meantime at Strabane:

> I continue Mr Burgoyne as my curate but go to Donaghkiddy every Sunday and am pretty often there on week days to set tithes and grow acquainted with the people; several of them are troublesome and force me to draw; a few of your lordship's tenants are among these but with Carey's help, who is my manager, I hope to deal with them all, but I must proceed at law with some of them, which is very disagreeable to me..

It is clear that the main concern at this stage was with the arrears owed to Bracegirdle's estate but Abercorn's agent was not entirely in sympathy with the whole tithe issue. John Sinclair, in reporting on the activities of Mr Carey, estate seneschal, felt that excessive use was being made of the legal processes and that insufficient attention was being paid to the inability of some of the tenants to pay in a period of depression and poor farm returns. Such actions could create a wider unrest in the whole neighbourhood and increase the difficulties of the agent in maintaining control and collecting rent.

Despite having no control over the other livings within his estates, Abercorn had to be attentive to problems raised in those areas by church matters and tithes was a major issue in widespread unrest in 1763 when a province-wide protest movement posed a serious threat to the established authorities. Until 1750 tithes appear to have been levied mainly on corn crops but there were disputes in the following years over attempts by tithe agents to include potato and flax crops for tithe purposes. This would suggest that these were only then becoming recognised as mainstream crops and helps to show the developing nature of farming in the period. This was to pose problems in the following decades when more land was brought under cultivation, especially in the more mountainous parts, leading to a demand from the rectors and parish authorities for an extension of the tithe payments. The issue emerged in both Camus and Donaheady parishes in the early 1770s with James Hamilton reporting in August 1772 on the attempts by the parish vestries to equalise the burden of payments, with strong opposition from the newly developed parts:

> The lower part of the parish of Donaghkiddy has for many years paid two thirds of the taxes, and they and those of the upper parts have always had distinct applotters; it is believed that now that the upper part is cultivated, it is perhaps equal to the lower part; at a vestry lately held, a number from each of those parts of the parish were chosen and appointed to make a valuation, so as to adjust the taxes, but those of the upper part refused to join, nor would they suffer the others to go on their lands but made prisoners of them on the high road when they found they were going out for that purpose.

The same problem had arisen over the Strabane parish when the town objected to paying two thirds of the dues and attempted to change the arrangements at the vestry. The problem was more difficult in this latter case since the rural parts of the parish refused to accept the authority of the corporation-controlled town vestry. Hamilton believed that the issue needed to be settled by the courts with some claiming that the vestry did not have the power to change the mode of taxing, only the amount. By this stage Abercorn was in control of the corporation and would have been under some pressure to give assistance to the inhabitants of the town who felt that they were owed something by the earl. In 1753 Abercorn had received a petition from the provost and the burgesses, supported by the minister and church wardens, seeking help in the restoration of the parish church, which was said to be 'in ruinous condition' and too small to accommodate the large number of conformists who were annually increasing. Those signing the petition included Sir William Hamilton (one of the corporation's MPs), William Auchinleck, William Colhoun, Robert Barcley, William Hamilton (Rev.), Robert Horne and William Orr, the two latter being designated church wardens. It is likely that some donation was made, but there was little sympathy between the corporation and the earl at that stage and any co-operation would have been grudging.

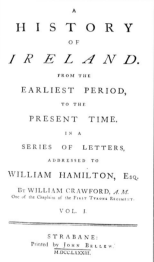

Title page from William Crawford's *History of Ireland*, published in Strabane in 1783.

6 The Emergence of a New Leadership
Strabane *c.* 1770–1800

JOHN DOOHER

The Growing Market Town

Following the re-establishment of Abercorn control in Strabane, much discussion took place on the need for repairs to the Town Hall or Market House, with Hamilton accepting in June 1765 that 'it is in a very ruinous state and will take the saving of many years'. Later that year estimates were prepared for repairs, and Hamilton suggested that the original scheme of the Town Hall/Market House as a money-making venture should be resurrected, with provision for a large number of linen buyers on the premises. Such work would have to be longer term and by June of the following year only sufficient repairs were made to prevent rain getting through the roof. Further improvements were made in the following years and by December 1769 the newly elected provost, James Stevenson, sought Abercorn's support in developing the market facilities of the corporation and erecting additional trader space. It was felt that the market house area was overcrowded and

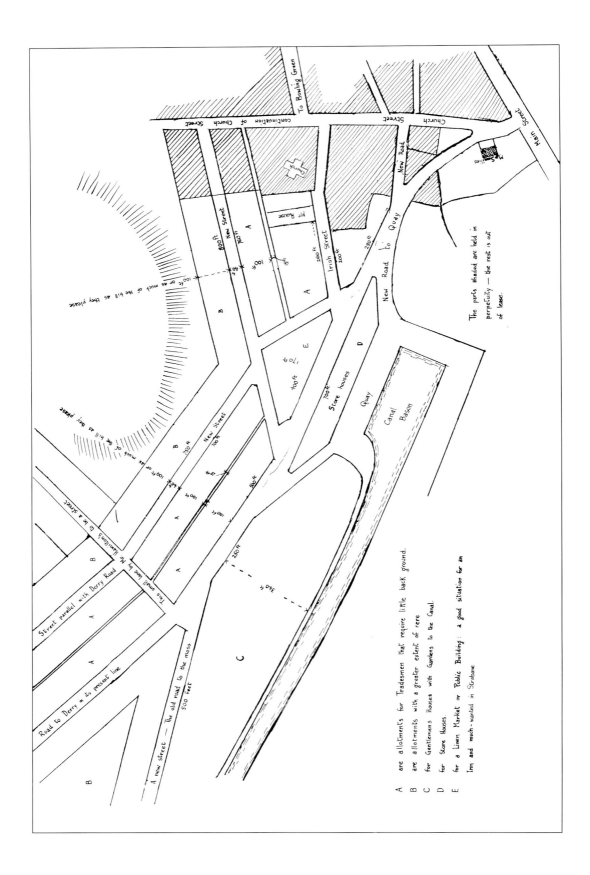

made less attractive by the various meat markets and butcher stalls and that it would greatly help if these could be relocated, possibly to the Bowling Green, which was described as 'now only a receptacle for dung hills'. The provost also remarked that he had got thirty-six lamps for lighting the town and suggested that the corporation had become much more financially viable. There were clearly reservations about using the Bowling Green as a shambles and meat market, especially with the further suggestion that a cattle market might easily be located there as well, and the agent's letters point to other possible locations for the market. In the event little was changed, and the next project was to develop the existing facilities at the market house. Yet it is clear that the corporation under Abercorn's control and financial support was prepared to look at the opportunities for the development of the town as a market centre. A document survives for Lifford in this period which demonstrates the range of activities an active corporation might become involved in to develop the markets and improve the administration of the town (Records of the Common Council of Lifford, 31 October 1765). The Common Council, composed of the freemen of the town, issued a series of regulations designed to improve cleanliness and encourage honest working. Anyone allowing pigs to wander in the streets was liable to a fine, and anyone found encouraging gambling was to be charged a fine of 10 shillings. Likewise anyone encouraging drinking or other forms of disorderly behaviour on the Sabbath was liable to punishment, while those who cleaned corn on the streets or public roads were to be fined. Other regulations banned the payment of more than 5s 5d to the boatmen, and labourers were forbidden to demand more than 9d per day in wages. Fines were to be imposed on those who sold by unjust weights, and it was stipulated that meal and potatoes could not be exposed for sale at more than the price prevailing at the Strabane market on the preceding market day. Such regulations necessitated the appointment of enforcement officers, but the series of fines levied would ensure the payment of their wages. The attempts to control prices and wages could only work in normal seasons and were probably envisaged as little more than guidelines since enforcement would have been difficult and highly unpopular. The corporations of Strabane and Lifford would have seen such regulations as helping to clean the town and encourage a spirit of thrift and enterprise.

Housing Developments

There was some expansion of the town in Strabane in the period after 1750 and plans were drawn for the allocation of new plots and the building of further housing. In 1757 Michael Priestley was instructed to draw plans for housing allotments adjoining a projected canal through the bog into the town. The maps were sent to Abercorn for his approval and he seemed

Plan for the development of the town in 1799

prepared to accept the proposals, informing Nisbitt that the scheme appeared viable. It was proposed to extend Irish Street, and Priestley had suggested that there was considerable interest in renting the plots, especially those near the projected canal. A further proposal envisaged extending the houses further out from the town and Abercorn was attracted by the project 'of streets leading towards Ballymagorry':

> In order to make a beginning I send you a scheme of ten lots that I propose to set, from the lane next the bleach yard, running towards Strabane . . . The chief conditions I will insist upon are that only one dwelling house shall be built upon each lot, that the houses and all their offices be slated, and that the houses be not less than twelve feet high in the side walls next the street.

He was concerned that the new developments would not be the typical Irish cabins that were to be found on the outskirts of most towns; hence the stipulations on size and material. Abercorn believed that he had a duty to ensure that travellers and visitors would not be put off by evidence of dirt and poverty on their approach to the town and instructed his agent, John Hamilton, to ensure that tenants obeyed the instructions in their leases:

> I desire that you will make the bailiff from time to time go through the Irish Street and from thence to Woodend and Ballymagorry, with directions that all those people must keep their doors clean, and put no dung hills or turf stacks before their houses, nor dress any flax, or do anything that is a nuisance on the road.

It is unclear whether the development took place as envisaged, though later plans would suggest that little came of the Priestley scheme, and in 1765 John Hamilton was yet again discussing plans for houses or tenements 'beyond Strabane church', with Abercorn stipulating that he would not like to see 'a set of new cabins there'. A few years later the agent was discussing the building of houses along Irish Street, and Abercorn again insisted that they should not be cabins and that they should be set on three life leases, thus precluding Catholics from renting them. Of course it was all very well to draw maps and suggest houses, but these had to be built by the tenants and the relatively short leases would not have been much of an incentive. The building of the Newtown and Irish Street areas made good sense for a landlord trying to augment his income, but the area did not necessarily prove as attractive to the middle class developers, and it seems likely that the area continued to favour the cabin-type poorer house rather than the more substantial buildings desired by the earl.

Crises in the Linen Industry

Yet that there were plans at all reinforces the impression that this was a period of growth and expansion for Strabane, much of the expansion being due to a thriving linen trade based around the weekly market for brown linen. One problem was that linen was subject to regular fluctuations and scares, and both workers and merchants frequently suffered as a result. The Irish parliament had recognised the value of expanding the industry by establishing a Linen Board in 1711 to provide encouragement and growth. This was especially so in years of agricultural failures and work shortages, when spinning wheels and looms would be provided at reduced cost to different parts of the country. In 1747 Abercorn had arranged for the distribution of 'fifty wheels and ten reels' on his estate and in 1753 had again sought support from the Linen Board to help with the food scarcity and high prices:

> Your lordship has got many blessings in Strabane for the wheels and indeed this season is much harder on the little people who live in towns than those that live in the country; provisions of all sorts being higher than ever I knew them this time of year. [Nisbitt to Abercorn, May 1753]

This was a particularly bad year for linen and reports at the end of the year mentioned the poor returns and the failures of many of the linen merchants. In 1757–8 the market had again collapsed with the local markets paying poor returns for both cloth and yarn and creating a near famine situation in many households. Recovery in 1758 was relatively short-lived, and by 1762 the industry was in another depression, which had a serious impact locally. The corporation had attempted to encourage the industry by building a market house and linen hall but were unable to prevent the fluctuations in the markets.

In 1765 the leading merchants in Strabane petitioned Abercorn to assist the recovery of a depressed trade and help the recovery of the town, thus reinforcing the agreement whereby he took control of the corporation and promised to help the development of the town:

> We therefore most humbly beseech your lordship to take us into favourable consideration and to lend your hand to trade, now tottering in our streets, by which it will revive, we shall flourish and your lordship will rejoice to see it.

Once again, however, the recovery was short-lived and the early 1770s witnessed a further depression in both agriculture and linen. The Linen Board was again asked to provide assistance and local relief measures were introduced. William Brownlow, an active supporter of the linen industry in Lurgan, wrote to Abercorn detailing the depth of the depression and adding that 'I am obliged to advance every penny I can spare at great risk to prevent as much as in my power the weavers in my district from being quite idle'. Abercorn's help at Strabane was much less costly than Brownlow's but he was expected to lend assistance in periods of crisis and seek to lessen the impact of poverty and suffering and assist in the recovery. Certainly by 1775 the recovery appears to have been well under way since in that year the corporation decided to expand the linen market from the narrow confines that it had previously occupied. A resolution of the corporation enacted 'that all brown linen cloth that shall hereafter be brought to the said market for sale shall be exposed for sale in that part of the front street of Strabane aforesaid beginning at the houses now inhabited by James Fleming and Robert Killen in each side of the street and downwards to the corner of the lane leading to the Castle'. Such expansion could only mean renewed confidence and a growing market that promised well for the progress of the town.

Poverty and Relief

The frequent depressions and near-famines were serious interruptions to the overall growth and Strabane suffered considerably during the latter part of the century just as it had suffered in the mid 1740s. The change from poverty to plenty and back again could happen suddenly, and by April 1752 John Colhoun wrote to Abercorn about the recent transformation: '[T]his country is greatly improved since your lordship left it, but I really believe the lower orders will lose their senses; many who lately were half starving appear now like gentlemen and cannot be spoke to; servants are hard to be got and day labourers must have double wages.' By the following spring, however, things had changed for the worse, though wages were still high, and Nisbitt believed that the urban workers were the main sufferers due to the very high food prices, 'higher than ever I knew them at this time of year'. A collapse in the linen markets later in the year was to prove very difficult for many of the poorer classes, and the frequency of the fluctuations made saving an impossibility. By late 1756 the threat of shortages pushed food prices upwards and the agents showed concern at the difficulties in collecting rents from a tenantry who were uncertain about the future and unwilling to sell farm produce too soon in case of even higher prices. In the early months of 1757 Abercorn was asked for assistance by Rev. Pellissier at Newtownstewart and by Archdeacon Hamilton, recently appointed to Taughboyne near Raphoe: the latter mentioned the severe winter and the great scarcity of food as the main causes of the deep poverty that he witnessed in his visit to the north. Again rents were a major problem and Abercorn's financial agent in Dublin, Henry Hatch, claimed that 'the reason this half year's rent was so long overdue proceeds from many of the poorest tenants who were not able to pay as eatables have been so very dear'. The plentiful harvest and the return to capacity of the linen trade soon removed the immediate problems, but the landlords often found that years of plenty were no better for them than years of shortages, since agricultural prices fell in the good years and posed difficulties for tenants depending on the sale of their produce. Thus in November 1759 John Hamilton reported on the problems in finding labourers because provisions were so cheap; lower living costs removed the necessity of working long hours for little return and a buoyant linen trade provided alternative sources of income.

There were further serious shortages in 1761–3, leading in the latter year to a protest movement among tenants against rents and the various taxes and tithes due to the established church. The next major famine, however, did not come until the early 1770s and a number of poor harvests and a near collapse in the linen industry caused severe dislocation. A poor harvest in 1769 led to serious shortages by the following spring, with Hamilton reporting on the lack of cattle fodder and the very high price of meal and food. By May it was reported that prices were as high as they had been in the famine year of 1742, and Hamilton won the support of Abercorn in importing meal for sale at below market prices. The agent's letters add that a collection had been organised in Strabane 'for the relief of the poor housekeepers of it' and that relief measures had to be continued until the end of July, when potatoes became available locally. Sales of imported meal continued through to September 1770 and James Hamilton acknowledged that they had all underestimated the extent of the shortages:

> We thought there was meal sufficient in the country but had it not been for the meal that came to Derry, we must have famished. I know farmers that pay upwards of 30s rent now buying meal.

Early hopes of a plentiful harvest were soon dashed, however, and by the end of the year prospects were most unpromising. Yet there was not the same panic in the following spring and early summer as in the previous year and it must be assumed that a portion of the crop had been saved before the onset of the severe weather that was widely reported. Reports in December 1771 suggested a bumper harvest with provisions cheap and every prospect of a return to prosperity for Strabane and its hinterland.

The Crisis Years 1772–3

Yet the following years were to see starvation and death sweeping over the district and a serious loss of confidence by many in their future means of livelihood. In July 1772 Hamilton reported to Abercorn of the unusually large number of beggars roaming the district in search of food and large numbers were reported going from neighbouring estates as emigrants to America. There was a clampdown on illicit distilling in an attempt to conserve barley supplies but Hamilton was apprehensive in his report to

Abercorn in October of the same year:

> The great backwardness of the tenants gives me very great uneasiness; the badness of our harvests these three years past, that occasioned the extravagant price of provisions, the sickness that has raged so long and the low prices of yarn and linen . . . have much distressed this country but our plentiful harvest this year which in general was got home safe will I hope lead the people not to go so much for subsistence.

The continued bleakness of the outlook posed problems for the agent in his distribution of relief. He suggested that many who would apply for grain at a reduced price and expect to be given one of the spinning wheels which were being distributed were not necessarily the most deserving and that more careful checking of relief claimants might be necessary. He had reported the existence of a violent fever in the Strabane neighbourhood and claimed that it had caused many deaths. Lifford Dispensary hospital was full and few districts had managed to avoid the illness. The corporation were moved to action and in March of 1773 they petitioned Abercorn to help relieve the long drawn out depression by seeking parliamentary support for the opening of a canal. Intensified emigration in the spring of that year demonstrated that people were greatly unnerved and despondent about the future while a report from Hamilton in May suggested that the fever was still as virulent as ever. All this led to very heavy arrears and possibly threatened the tenure of the agent. Yet the evidence of widespread poverty and death is compelling and Ireland as a whole suffered grievously in these years. Strabane, with its efficient estate management and with a landlord who was prepared to finance assistance, possibly suffered comparatively less than other areas but nonetheless the town and district was clearly worried at the protracted nature of the shortages and sought remedies for the future. The problem was that the causes of the famines had little to do with local factors and thus local solutions would make limited impact.

Helping the Poor

The relief of poverty and suffering was something that had become a matter of serious concern as the century progressed and there were frequent calls for some action to ensure that the desperate were given assistance. Begging was a way of life for a minority of the population, especially in the summer months when food prices were often highest. In periods of acute distress support was provided, as has been seen, by the distribution of cheaper meal and the postponement of rents. Yet there were the semi-permanent starving poor and how to provide for them was a matter of concern. Illnesses and recurring fevers were as serious as famines and the fear always was that diseases could be too easily spread by these travelling beggars. In the 1760s provision was made by the Irish parliament for the establishment of county hospitals or infirmaries to deal with the diseased and the members of the Tyrone grand jury decided to set up their county hospital and seek support from the landed gentry and other wealthy people. There was initially some dispute over its location, with Lord Northland favouring Dungannon as the base, but the majority held out for Omagh, and by July 1767 the decision had been made to rent a building and set up the hospital. Abercorn donated when requested but also stipulated that his agent, James Hamilton, be appointed as one of the visiting committee to oversee the administration of the project. Hamilton himself believed that the hospital project should be developed even further and his views illustrate the extent of the poverty issue in eighteenth-century Ireland:

> My lord I humbly submit whither this now intended good might not be made still more useful if this House might not also be made in some degree a workhouse, and that strolling beggars, some of whom are apparently miserable, might be sent there, if real objects, there to be taken care of, and as far as they were able, made to contribute to their support and as these houses are to be in every county, I do apprehend it would put an effectual stop to vagrants and add but few to the number of each house.

The early plan to establish the Donegal hospital at Letterkenny found little favour with Abercorn and he refused to contribute to it, requesting information instead on the Londonderry hospital since it would be accessible to a number of his tenants. When this plan was reversed in the early 1770s and the Donegal infirmary established in Lifford, Abercorn was happy enough to subscribe, believing that it would be beneficial to his Tyrone as well as his Donegal estate. The hospitals had proved their value in the fever epidemic of 1772–3 but Abercorn's generosity was not bottomless. His agent was requested to halve his subscription to the Tyrone hospital in order to finance his donation to the Lifford infirmary.

Floods and Flooding

Crisis years were often the results of poor harvests and exceptionally wet weather and the reports from the agents highlight many of the resultant problems. Rents were difficult to collect and threats of eviction achieved little. The years 1770–73 proved exceptionally severe weather-wise, with the agent reporting in May 1770 the long severe winter and the lateness of the crops. At the end of the year there were again severe storms and the harvest was only partially saved, leading to shortages in the following spring and summer. Reports claimed that many houses had been damaged, even Baronscourt suffering, while the end of 1771 saw even worse storms, beginning at the harvest time and continuing through until December, when Hamilton reported on great damage caused to the roads and especially to

Lifford Bridge. This had been an important source of trade and communication for Strabane and its building in 1755 had promised a new era of progress and prosperity. By early 1772 there was a feeling that the bridge and the linking road to Strabane were impossible to keep in repair, with it being reported that two of the three bridge arches had been swept away and the road impassable; the result was that many traders unloaded further down river at Dysert and brought their goods by road through the bog. This had not proved very satisfactory and the road problems at this time gave an added impulse to a revival of the canal project. Some money was forthcoming from the grand jury for road repairs but if the same road needed repairs regularly it was going to be difficult to get county sanction for such recurrent expenditure. It is clear, however, that the period of the early 1770s saw exceptionally severe weather that had major repercussions on the economy and living standards.

River Transport

Road travel was slow and expensive even in normal times, and it was estimated by John Colhoun in 1746 that the cost of bringing one hundredweight of goods from Dublin to Strabane cost 6 shillings in winter and 5 shillings in summer. The project of a canal was increasingly canvassed from the mid century onwards, with the example of other canal construction providing the stimulus. A memorial was sent to Abercorn in 1753 from the leading inhabitants in the town of Strabane seeking the construction of 'a canal from that part of Loughfoyle known as Blackfence to the said town by which boats, lighters and other vessels of burden might trade and import and export goods, wares . . . from the said town'. In 1757 Priestley had been engaged to plan houses fronting the projected canal and in the following year work was undertaken in fashioning a small canal through Strabane Bog and with access to the river Foyle. This canal seems to have been for both drainage purposes and for limited transport and appears to have been totally financed by Abercorn. Clearly it did not solve the transport problem and by 1768 Strabane corporation petitioned the earl for help in overcoming newly emerging threats to Strabane's trading position. They expressed concern at the plans of Mr Creighton of Lifford to build a pier there but were more concerned at the efforts of Bishop Hervey of Derry to raise the capital necessary to build a bridge across the Foyle. This was felt to threaten Strabane's position as a trading centre, with the likelihood that shipping would load and unload at Derry rather than risk the often shallow waters of the river towards Strabane. This did not suit the Strabane petitioners and they had no doubt that the Foyle could be made navigable as far as their town: '[W]e are capable of being made a port for reception of trading vessels, if not obstructed by the intended bridge . . . and by the monopoly of the city of Londonderry.'

Abercorn at first toyed with the concept of extending navigation through the Mourne to other parts of mid Ulster but John Hamilton advised against any such scheme, claiming that Strabane's interests would best be served by 'a canal made from Desert through the bog to Strabane . . . this will be the most effectual way to make this place flourish'. Lord Erne had ambitions to develop Lifford through improved navigation of the Foyle and it was claimed that certain interests wanted navigation extended to Castlefin but either option might take away from Strabane. The difficulty was in financing such a project, and Abercorn sought the help of William Brownlow of Lurgan in building support in the Irish parliament for the scheme.

The depression of 1773 led to the corporation renewing their call for assistance in the canal project and a further memorial was sent to Abercorn, seeking his active intervention as a means of rejuvenating the local economy. Hamilton in a covering letter highlighted the problems that traders encountered in their current navigation of the river, being often forced to transport goods by land from the shallows at Greenlaw. In addition, other vessels were often delayed by the tides and it was claimed that a merchant informed Hamilton that one of his boats with wine and other liquor had taken twenty days coming from Derry. An additional complication was that Lifford was presently the main port for the boats coming up river and the dues benefited them and raised the price of goods for Strabane. A Mr Ducart was at that period involved in the Newry canal and it was felt that his expertise would prove invaluable in the further development of the Strabane project. But things moved slowly and it was not until nearly twenty years later that the canal project was implemented. An improvement in roads and road transport in the interim had helped reduce the sense of urgency of the early 1770s and was eventually to prove the undoing of the canal.

Law and Order Enforcement

The letters of the agents only rarely examine the fears and problems faced by the ordinary people but life was often uncertain and protest action never far away. The system of law and order depended greatly on local enforcement, and each manor had its seneschal who acted as magistrate at the monthly courts. In the 1760s there were demands that the existing seneschal, Tristram Cary, be dismissed and a more active magistrate appointed; it was alleged by John Hamilton that his living outside the estates meant that he was not readily available and that a more committed seneschal was required. In January 1766 Hamilton proposed McKernan for the position and suggested that courts should be held monthly in each of the Abercorn manors and that it would prove very advantageous: '[T]he seneschal living in this town will be of great use to the different manors, as they have frequent business to it.' Cary was very quickly removed but sought to justify his alleged inaction and requested that he be given time to collect money owing to him on the various manors. He claimed that he had always sought arbitration and 'ever discouraged vexatious suits and where a dispute was started recommended a reference which generally agreed the parties'. The manors had their monthly fairs and these could often pose problems for law and order that the seneschal and his court might have to deal with or else have them passed on to the magistrates and the county court. Such a case would have been the incident at Dunamanagh fair in January 1743, when it was claimed that at a horse race near there 'a man was killed with a stroke of a stone on the spot and another is likely to die; tis said it was a designed quarrel'. These gatherings were likely to see quarrels carried over from previous meetings or fairs and in many such cases the local magistrate had to be summoned to ensure that peace was maintained. In the case of the McNaughten trial in December 1761, the justices came to Strabane for a special court and had Mc Naughten executed within three weeks of his murder of Miss Knox. Lifford gaol had to be used to hold McNaughten since the Strabane prison was not considered either secure enough or clean enough for such a prisoner.

Popular Protest Movements – 1760s and 1770s

Widespread unrest was generally avoided on the Abercorn estates and the 1745 menace had passed off quietly. The economic depression of the early 1760s caused much more serious opposition to the status quo and a peasant society, the Oakboys, emerged in Ulster demanding a reduction in tithes and a limit on other local taxation. Information is scanty but it appears that the movement spread to the Abercorn estates and threatened the wealthier sections of society. The main strength of the movement was in mid and west Ulster and members of the grand jury in Armagh and Tyrone were under pressure from the Oakboys to reject any demands for further road taxes. By July 1763 it was claimed that Derry was a city of refuge for rectors and tithe farmers, and the troops were called out to deal with this menace to property rights. There was a pitched battle near Newtownstewart between a large body of the Oakboys and three companies of regular troops, and the defeat of the rebels signalled the end of the movement. Abercorn, writing in late July 1763 to John Sinclair, his agent for the Donelong(Dunnalong) manor, welcomed 'the present appearance of the dispersion of the rioters in your neighbourhood' and instructed both James and John Hamilton to keep him informed about the trials of the captured Oakboys from his estates. It appears from the correspondence that none of the property owners lost from the outbreak but Abercorn was quick to point out that matters could have been serious: '[I]n how much worse a situation we should have been than our neighbours, with such an arrears in the hands of the Oakboys, if the confusion they occasioned had borne any proportion to their madness.' The tithe issue had frequently threatened to cause serious unrest and when taken in conjunction with the serious trade recession and food shortages of these years in the early 1760s it is probably rather surprising that the outbreak of unrest did not prove more serious and threatening. No doubt the lack of organisation and the absence of a supply of weapons made any serious upset to the status quo very difficult. Yet Hamilton expressed disquiet at the withdrawal of troops in March 1764 and felt that 'it could be wished we were not left quite destitute of men'. He sent to Abercorn a confiscated ballad, of the type commonly recited and sold at local fairs, suggesting that a future rising would occur and cautioned against any premature acceptance of normality.

Troublemakers?

In the next major depression in the early 1770s the Steelboys became the active peasant organisation but its main area of operation was in the east of the province and Hamilton was able to assure Abercorn that the Strabane area remained quiescent. Hamilton showed some sympathy for the causes of the Steelboy protest and agreed that it might have been provoked by injudicious treatment, but the movement did cause some anxiety and a number of soldiers were sent from Omagh to Strabane in case of trouble. And Hamilton's letters do suggest that there were some signs of unrest, despite his claim that the area was immune: '[T]hese disturbances are remote from us and I am persuaded there would not have happened any disturbances here if those deluded people kept from us.' It is clear from his other correspondence at the time that James Hamilton believed that the Presbyterians were the cause of the unrest and in sympathy with the Steelboys:

> Besides I must own that in general I think them a plodding discontented people, valuing themselves much on their consequence (which is no doubt greatly increased by the octennial bill) and striving by every means to be uppermost.

The emergence of a strong Presbyterian merchant class in Strabane was worrying to Hamilton and no doubt to other members of the establishment but for the moment they were no real threat and the few troops were withdrawn after a number of months of inactivity. The emergence of the Volunteer movement in 1779 and the later support for the United Irishmen in the Strabane neighbourhood suggests perhaps that Hamilton was right to be wary and somewhat fearful but by then circumstances had changed and the emergence of the Catholic question was to prove a weakening factor in any protest movement.

The Franchise at Local Level

In the eighteenth century the tenant-farmers were expected to accept the rules laid down for them and agitation was looked on suspiciously. At election times those few tenants who had the vote were expected to vote as directed by the landlord or his agent and this was made clear in the 1768 general election for Tyrone. One of the candidates was Claud Hamilton, brother of the agent James Hamilton, and distant cousin of Abercorn. But his contesting the election posed a serious dilemma for James who was also at the time an agent for part of the Blessington estate. The problem was that Blessington had thrown his support against Claud Hamilton and James could not be seen to encourage the tenants to vote against the wishes of their landlord. His neutrality did not endear him to his master, however, and the agency was removed from James Hamilton following the election. It appears that in Donegal large numbers of tenants ignored the wishes of the agents and voted for the popular candidate and James Hamilton was highly critical of their actions. Any signs of independence were to be deplored and not only over elections. In 1759, during a crisis in the Seven Years War, Ireland was faced with the prospect of invasion and an attempt was made to recruit a militia for the defence of the country. The agents on the various manors were instructed to encourage recruitment but the response was very disappointing. Nisbitt reported that the comparative prosperity was a major disincentive: '[P]eople are so full of bread at present that they care neither to work nor be under any command of any kind.' James Hamilton reported that he had called on the tenants of Derrywoon to serve their king and country but found the response very negative, with the weavers in particular much against their sons joining up. A similar situation existed in Newtownstewart, where not one recruit had joined up on market day, but Hamilton suggested that had they been allowed to recruit Catholics the response would have been much more favourable. What was most annoying, however, was the refusal of the lower classes to accept the exhortations and instructions of their masters and their inclination to make decisions for themselves.

The Lure of Emigration

Emigration was both a symptom of unrest and a release mechanism to remove such unrest and the economic depressions certainly encouraged a movement away from the estates. It appears that there was substantial emigration from the Strabane estates in the early decades of the century though there is an absence of verifiable evidence. One documented case is where a Presbyterian minister led a substantial portion of his congregation to the New World in protest against the restrictions of the penal laws, while a returned Presbyterian minister applied to Abercorn for a living as a Church of Ireland clergyman; this minister had apparently found life in the colonies less appealing than anticipated and was attempting to return to a position offering some security. But the main period of movement from the Strabane region appears to date from the 1770s, and the major trade and agricultural depressions of the early years of the decade were very influential in initiating the outflow. In 1770 and 1771, and before the worst excesses of the depression were apparent, Abercorn had attempted to recruit workers locally for employment in mines that he had purchased in Scotland. There was a reluctance to publicise the wages on offer and that may have been the reason why there were so few volunteers. Abercorn sought reasons why a supposedly starving labour force would not welcome this opportunity and James Hamilton attempted to provide some answers:

> I think it very strange that many were not desirous of going, especially as bread has been so scarce, but the few that spoke to me objected to the working underground, which they thought dangerous, and some asked me how much they would make a day; I could only say that I was persuaded that they could make more there than here.

Previous shortages had confirmed, however, that one year's hardships were not seriously considered but when this continued for two or more years then people could get seriously worried about the future. Such seemed to be the situation from 1772 and 1773 when the combination of linen collapse and agricultural dislocation threatened the ability of many to provide for their families in such an unnatural order.

The Disadvantages of Emigration

In March 1772 Hamilton confirmed to Abercorn that emigration was rapidly increasing but that as yet the earl's estates were not under threat since tenants knew that they would be hard pressed to find so benevolent a landlord. In July of that same year it was suggested that the levels of emigration were unprecedented and it was hinted that the Abercorn estates were losing some tenants, though fewer comparatively than other local properties. That year too had seen the launch of the *Londonderry Journal*, with Andrew Gamble the paper's Strabane agent, and its pages carried frequent advertisements about emigrant ship sailings and reports of previous crossings. In early 1773 the paper carried an advertisement about passage to Baltimore and the opportunities for tradesmen in that region, with an agent and contact point at Knox's Inn, Strabane. By that stage James Hamilton could no longer ignore the extent of emigration, reporting in March that 'I never knew so many preparing to go to America', but suggesting that many were from the Church lands of Ardstraw and these were gaining the passage money through the sale of their leases. Clearly the situation was becoming worrying and the *Londonderry Journal* must have been caught in something of a dilemma at the period. Its pages encouraged emigration through the advertisements from ship masters and emigration agents, but at the same time the editor found himself compelled to issue a word of warning about the financial drain and potential political impact. It was estimated that over 60 ships had taken emigrants from Ulster ports in the previous two years, with more than 20,000 of a population outflow:

> Their removal is sensibly felt in this country. This prevalent humour of industrious Protestants withdrawing from this once flourishing part of the kingdom seems to be increasing, and it is thought the number will be considerably larger this year than ever. The North of Ireland has been occasionally used to emigration, for which the American settlements have been much beholden. But till now it was chiefly the very meanest of the people that went off, mostly in the station of indented servants and such as had become obnoxious to their mother country . . . It is computed that the North of Ireland has in the last five or six years been drained of one fourth of its trading cash and the like proportion of its manufacturing people.

The fact that many of those leaving would have been the most provident of the tenants and the least likely to accumulate rent arrears made their going a serious threat to the prosperity of the landlord. Yet what could be done about it? Massive intervention to turn around an ailing economy was unthinkable and it was left to natural economic forces to bring about the recovery that would put a stop to the heavy emigration. The renewed confidence in the linen industry that occurred later that year and the harvesting of near bumper crops were crucial in ending the immediate crisis but emigration had become too deeply rooted to be eradicated and it was to remain a recurring theme in Strabane's and Ulster's history for the next century.

The Volunteers and 'Revolution' 1778–85

The emergence of the Volunteer movement in 1778 in response to the American War of Independence and the possibility of a French invasion of Ireland evoked tremendous enthusiasm in the country but was not always so welcome to those in authority, especially when these same Volunteers began to demonstrate some of the democratic tendencies of the American Revolution. The Volunteer movement began in Ulster and quickly spread through the country, but it appeared rather tardy in reaching Strabane, and the evidence suggests that it spread from Derry and Raphoe and then on to Strabane. Economic factors were likely to be of some significance in the origins and spread of the Volunteers, and a poor harvest in 1777 caused major shortages and scarcity by the summer of 1778. This food shortage aggravated an already worsening economic situation brought about by the embargo on trade with the American colonies; in 1776 James Hamilton was reporting on the difficulties being experienced in procuring flax seed, essential for the prosperity of the linen industry. By the early summer of 1778 Abercorn had been prevailed on to offer relief to his tenantry, and, according to Hamilton, the failures in trade, the lack of money and the shortages of food were creating major distress; it was calculated by July that in Donelong (Dunnalong) manor there were 140 families needing free meal, while Cloghogal had 79 families on relief and Newtownstewart had well over 100 seeking assistance. Such widespread distress could provoke serious unrest if it were not adequately controlled and the development of a Volunteer force needed to be carefully managed. Thus James Hamilton was cautious and, while reporting in July 1778 about the establishment of three companies in Derry, sought Abercorn's approval before giving the spreading movement any encouragement in the Strabane region. He was also emphatic that the time would be most inopportune for insisting on the payment of rents, claiming that tenants would be forced to sell their yarn and linen at a very low rate and thereby reducing their chances of being able to recover quickly from the current depression.

At the same time Hamilton provided some insights into how those in authority saw the blossoming Volunteer movement, reporting that a number of the leading citizens of Strabane had sought his support in establishing a local Volunteer corps, suggesting that it was necessary for internal security and preventing serious disorder in the country. Hamilton and Abercorn would be helpful in seeking government assistance in procuring weapons but equally important was the sense of determination evident in the approach. The local leadership had already fixed on their uniforms and Hamilton confessed that he would find it very difficult to dissuade them from their plans. He feared that 'it may cause idleness, nor do I wish to see a country in arms', but more worrying was the suggestion that the Volunteer leadership had no wish to take commissions from government, fearing that they might be sent to other parts of the country. This independence of thought and suspicion of government was something that was potentially threatening but Hamilton's dilemma was plain: '[T]hose people will no doubt go on learning their exercises and will probably get their clothing.' Was it wise to resist what appeared to be an irresistible movement at that stage?

A year later Hamilton had still not reconciled himself to the Volunteers and in early September 1779 again reported on the spread of the movement in his Strabane area. It was suggested that every parish had a company and the government's decision to provide them with arms was seen as a major boost. Hamilton took some credit for the fact that the Strabane company was one of the smallest, suggesting that he had refused to encourage it, but was also forced to report that a second company – larger than the original – was to be formed and that the local dissenting minister was a leading light in this recruitment. This was the Presbyterian minister, Rev. William Crawford, and other evidence suggests that he was indeed a firm supporter of the Volunteer movement. A sermon that he gave to the Strabane Volunteers, the Strabane Rangers and Urney Foresters, on Sunday 19 March 1780, titled *The Nature and Happy Effects of Civil Liberty Considered*, was later published and was mentioned in A.A. Campbell's *Literary History of Strabane* (1902). The title suggests that the Rev. Crawford saw the Volunteer movement as more than a local defence force, and he was to play an active part in the growing politicisation of the organisation in the following years, attending as a Tyrone delegate at the famous Dungannon Convention of 1782, when the Volunteers put forward their demands in unequivocal terms for legislative independence, leading to the famous Grattan's Parliament, and supporting the measures already passed in favour of greater emancipation for Catholics. Campbell's book also mentions another published lecture by Crawford to the Volunteer Company of Strabane Rangers on Sunday 12 September 1779, just days after Hamilton's letter to Abercorn. This lecture was titled *The Connection Between Courage and Moral Virtues*. A further published sermon by Rev. Andrew Alexander to the Urney and Strabane Volunteers the following month had an even more explicit title: *The Advantages of a General Knowledge of Arms*. Reform and greater freedom for dissenters and others excluded from the political process in the era of Church of Ireland supremacy were important to the Strabane Volunteer leaders and people like James Hamilton were seen as obstacles to that greater independence. Hamilton had reported in the letter of September 1789 that Crawford, along with another dissenting minister from the parish of Urney, probably the Rev. Alexander, had petitioned the government about weapons, and this was seen as both a rejection of the former leadership exercised through Abercorn's agent and clear evidence of a more radical and potentially revolutionary outlook by the numerically important Presbyterian community.

The Volunteers and Free Trade 1779

Abercorn was kept fully informed by a number of correspondents about happenings in Ireland and the 1779 Volunteer agitation for free trade was not seen as threatening to the long-term relationship between Britain and Ireland. In fact it was seen by many as a useful release valve in a period of economic depression and Abercorn seems to have believed that it would fizzle out. Writing to Hamilton in early November 1779, just when the Volunteer demand for the removal of British trade restrictions was reaching its peak, he commented on the poor prospects for the barley harvest in

Ireland and suggested that the patriots would greatly help this country if the nobility and gentry would drink their own beer rather than import expensive French claret. He went on to claim that he himself had earlier tried to encourage local industry but with little success:

> The first time I was at Strabane, I made up a suit of clothes of the cloth of the neighbourhood; it was dressed at a tuck mill, that was then I think at Sian. But nobody at Strabane followed my example. So I may reckon myself the oldest patriot, though I was then a very young one, and the last time I was in Ireland I certainly drank no liquor but Irish.

The success of the Volunteer campaign in the following month, when the British government pledged to remove the trade restrictions, suggested that the movement might easily be left without a cause. Such certainly was the hope of Abercorn and numbers like him, for example James Hamilton at Strabane, and the early parts of the following year seemed to convey that promise.

In the same letter in which Abercorn had given his views on the free trade protest movement, he also instructed Hamilton to send him on the weekly Strabane newspaper, and it seems that it had recently made its appearance. A.A. Campbell in his *Literary History of Strabane* claims that the *Strabane Journal* made its first appearance in 1771, with John Alexander as editor and printer, and that it gave extensive coverage to the Volunteer movement in the later 1770s and early 1780s. This would provide Abercorn with another view of the strength and hold of the protest movement in his area and allow him to counsel Hamilton in a more practical approach to an organisation over which the gentry were in danger of losing control. In a letter in early December the agent had been very alarmist in his assessment of the local corps and concluded that 'the volunteers are certainly driving at something more than defending us from invaders. I am sure that a free trade would not content the first stirrers up of it. When I was first forced in among them I feared their purposes, and accepted hoping that I might perhaps be some means of preventing their going very improper lengths.' His report dealt with the desire of the eleven companies in the Strabane barony to form themselves into a battalion and select a commander. He had been overruled in his opposition to such a move and was further perturbed on the day prior to the meeting to find that his nominee for the post, young Mr Hamilton, was not acceptable to his own Strabane company: '[I] was astonished to find a person dissenting from it; as civilly as they could they gave their reasons against it.' Hamilton was later informed that the two Strabane companies had approved a resolution that they would not serve under anyone who lived in England, referring no doubt to the same young Mr. Hamilton who had gained the support of a majority of the companies at the meeting. It seems that this same meeting of the Strabane companies had suggested James Hamilton himself as commander rather than the absentee and he sought

Abercorn's advice on what he should do in the circumstances. Would an open quarrel with the local Volunteers do anything to reduce their power or limit their movement? Clearly Hamilton did not think that defiance would achieve the best results for himself or the other worried local gentry and he ended his letter by seeking advice from Abercorn on this delicate matter.

The decision of the British parliament to remove the restrictions on Irish trade in December 1779 had the effect of defusing the immediate crisis and the role of the local corps of the Volunteers seemed to have moderated in the early part of the new year with Hamilton reporting in January 1780 that 'the people of this town seem better pleased than they were', while by May he was able to write positively about volunteering, accepting that while he still feared the time wasting and the expense yet he had to conclude that 'quarrels and riots are much suppressed by the Volunteers'. He went on to add that the reason may have been that the Volunteers had previously been the most likely originators of quarrels at the fairs and that their new discipline prevented them engaging in such activities. At the same time he was able to hope that the movement would fade away and cease putting pressure on the parliamentary representatives. In late May of that year he again expressed his unease and confirmed that the Volunteer movement was by then much more organised and critical of government policy. It was claimed that the original defensive motivation of the movement was rarely mentioned in public statements, and the reform of the laws and the need for more open government were increasingly being declared as the major objectives. Equally worrying from Hamilton's viewpoint was the general approval in the press for the Volunteer movement and the expressions of hostility directed towards those who opposed them: 'the newspapers every day more and more inflammatory and even threatening those who do not take active parts'. It appears that he was forced into remaining quiescent during this critical period and there is an absence of comment on the Volunteer movement in the following two years. It had moved outside his control and Abercorn, writing to one of his contemporaries, may have unwittingly recognised the strength of the increasingly radical organisation and its insatiability: '[I]t is becoming doubtful to me, whether the possession of free trade will have much other effect than that of irrefragably convincing the people that one of the great roots of their evils lies in their own domestic misgovernment and mismanagement.'

Few of the more committed Volunteer leaders could have better expressed the motivation of the movement and the need for clear action to establish a more responsive and democratically aware system of government. The Strabane leadership were thus in the vanguard of the movement for change and it seems clear that the Presbyterians, both lay and clerical, were prime movers in the Volunteer organisation at local level.

There was a Volunteer review at Strabane on 1 July 1780 and Hamilton was worried about the threatening tone of some of the speeches, where it was suggested that those not in active support of the movement were obstacles. Hamilton was careful not to display outward hostility to the Volunteers and it seems clear that Abercorn and many other landlords followed a similar policy. In some parts the landowners were the leading light in the organisation and Lord Charlemont of Armagh became the leader of the whole movement. Yet the Strabane Volunteers were clearly too populist for the local Ascendancy and the non-involvement of Hamilton and others of his ilk meant that a more democratic structure emerged. Rev. Crawford became an influential local figure and attended the famous Dungannon Volunteer Convention of February 1782 . He was appointed to a provincial Volunteer committee to co-ordinate action for the settlement of the Volunteer demands and it is clear that he was a highly regarded figure throughout Ulster and not just in Strabane.

The Volunteer Decline

The very success of the Volunteers, however, led to their rapid decline after the government granted the demand for legislative independence that was expected to lead to a government more responsive to the needs of the country. It was clear in a very short time that many of the more propertied members of the Volunteers were only too glad to curtail the activities of the organisation at this stage and wished that it would quietly fade into the background. The more radical elements wished to see it continue as a pressure movement for further reform but there were reservations about undermining the authority of the newly independent legislature. The result was that the pressure for further change became identified as dangerous tampering with the constitution and there were strong condemnations from influential figures. In Strabane the local leadership remained active and contributed to a further meeting at Dungannon in late 1783. Parliament's rejection of the reform petition in early December posed a serious challenge to the Volunteer movement. What was it going to do now? Abercorn was kept informed of political developments in Ireland by Lord Harberton, a kinsman and Kildare-based landlord, and there was a degree of rejoicing at the summary rejection by the Irish parliament of the Volunteer reform petition. The question of full Catholic Emancipation had been raised by some of the more radical reformers and this had alarmed a considerable number of former supporters. It seemed preferable to keep the unreformed system than endanger the whole political and social structure by the admission of the Catholics.

There were minor repercussions in Strabane, with a petition to Abercorn in late December 1783 from a section of people in the town who had considerable economic power but no opportunity for involvement in the running of the town. These would have been the people who supported the

Volunteer movement and its demand for reform but the fact that they were reduced to petitioning Abercorn suggests a recognition of the limitations of their power. James Hamilton was also called upon but managed to avoid meeting the delegation sent to see him and the fact that the reformists were now seeking to reduce the power of the local corporation and its appointed burgesses meant that the radical grouping was becoming increasingly isolated from mainstream political life. Hamilton was critical of the public statements of local Volunteer commander, Colonel Charleton, the nephew, it was stated, of Mr Maxwell, one of the town's burgesses, and his close association with the increasingly intemperate views of Bishop Hervey, earl of Bristol and bishop of Derry, was equally condemned.

Yet the Volunteer organisation did not simply disappear but remained as a semi-political movement meeting annually in parades and celebratory dinners. One such meeting was reported from Strabane on 23 July 1785 in the *Strabane Journal* when the earl of Charlemont reviewed the local Volunteers under the command of Lieutenant Colonel Charleton. A number of resolutions were passed at the meeting, with James Orr recorded as secretary of the Volunteer officers at the review. It is clear, however, that the Volunteers were no longer seen as a threat to the establishment since the town's provost, Nathaniel Edie, an appointee of Abercorn, welcomed Charlemont to Strabane and provided him with accommodation for the night. The continued leadership of someone like Charlemont was an additional guarantee that the movement would not become too democratic and property-threatening. At the same time a substantial number of ambitious young men had become politicised and they did not simply disappear into obscurity thereafter. Recent research has demonstrated a significant degree of continuity between the membership of the Volunteer movement and the later United Irishmen organisation and Strabane was no exception. Unrest with the status quo was to re-emerge within a short period and the new movement was to be seen as even more worrying for the people in control.

Poverty and Hardships in the 1780s

Economic factors were always liable to influence unrest and the early 1780s witnessed another period of poverty and instability. One symptom of hardship was rent arrears, and Hamilton was forced to provide Abercorn with an account of unpaid rents at the beginning of 1780. This showed a total of £2,441 outstanding from 1777 and no doubt a greater sum for the two following years. By April of 1781 Abercorn expressed grave concern that there had been only a decrease of £18 in the total arrears bill since the previous year, especially since prices had been high and thus beneficial to the farmers, and he instructed Hamilton to get tough on defaulters. There was no noticeable improvement by the end of the year and a number of ejectments were made in the following months. In September 1783 Hamilton was again threatening firm action when the harvesting was completed but the difficulty was that too many were in arrears to allow for wholesale dismissals. The power of the landlord was always curtailed somewhat by the potential demand for land and a further period of hardship in 1790–91 demonstrated the limits of Hamilton's threats. A poor summer in 1790 had led to rent arrears, but when a number of tenants were evicted in the early part of 1791 it was found impossible to get anyone to take over the farms. This was no doubt due to a combination of poor farming prospects and a determination by tenants to make a stand against evictions as a result of poor harvests. An early form of Ulster Custom and tenant solidarity in the face of unwarranted evictions was clearly in operation in the Strabane area in the latter part of the eighteenth century.

There was little doubt either that there was severe dislocation and the years 1782–3 saw Abercorn forced to intervene again to prevent serious poverty. A big flood in September 1781 had caused much damage to roads and bridges and had destroyed part of the crop of that year but it was in the early months of 1783 that serious shortages became apparent. One bad harvest was generally manageable but not two and the price of food had clearly rocketed by the late spring of 1783. By May Hamilton informed Abercorn that there were over one thousand cottiers and 160 widows and herds suffering serious hardship, claiming that 'I never knew more distress'. Abercorn instructed him to provide relief in money so as to preclude those not in urgent need and also to press on with work schemes that had been planned. Hamilton informed him in June that his work programme fed 'hundreds every day' and also reported on the efforts made in Strabane town to provide help. It was claimed that there were '40 badged beggars and perhaps twice as many beg through the town without badges'. This badging must have been a decision of the corporation or parish in order to identify poor people genuinely belonging to the town and thus deny relief to travelling or outside beggars. The towns became a favoured relief centre in periods of distress and the people of Strabane were then paying out about £15 weekly in support of the poor. Beggars from other estates could soon exhaust the sums collected locally for poor relief and it was expected that help would have to continue right up to August when the new harvests would become available.

There was thus a clear distinction between town and country in eighteenth-century Strabane, with Abercorn having a sense of responsibility for the welfare of the people on his estates but expecting the townspeople to provide support in times of hardship for those most in need. Weekly collections were raised to pay for such assistance and thus the desire was always strong to prevent waste in supporting outside beggars. The bountiful harvest of 1783 and 1784 ended the immediate problem of relief, but it was clear that action needed to be taken in the long run, and in 1786 a permanent poor fund was established in Strabane to provide help during the frequent temporary fluctuations. Abercorn was called on to help, and in 1789 there was a memorial of thanks to him from the corporation and leading citizens for his donation to the Poor Fund. Clearly starvation was never very far away from a section of the population in both urban and rural areas. In July of 1791 it was again reported that times were very hard on some of the poorer country people, though there did not appear to be the same need for active relief measures at that stage. Things were to worsen again by the end of the century with the onset of yet another famine.

The Evils of Poteen

In 1783 there had been some hesitation in accepting the severity of the situation and Abercorn was initially rather dismissive of the cries of poverty, claiming that it was the fault of the Irish poor in preferring to use their grain to make drink rather than for food. There was a big push on at this stage by government to cut down on illegal distilling and it was reported in January 1782 that there was no officially sanctioned distilling in Strabane. In February of 1783 additional troops were sent to the area to help in the suppression of illicit poteen making, and Abercorn was fully supportive of the new clampdown when writing in May. There was always the potential for conflict and reference was made in June to the 'unhappy fray' when there must have been some resistance to still seizures by the troops. Hamilton clearly adopted the Abercorn line and believed that 'it would be a pity not to entirely put an end to it, and if the breweries could be established soon, it would be a great help to it; the people would soon be brought to like it and in time give up whiskey'. In later correspondence with Abercorn he reported on the bonuses paid to the gaugers and those who helped them when stills were seized but lamented the fact that the stills could be too easily replaced and the poteen making started up again.

In late 1784 Hamilton provided a strongly worded condemnation of the whole ethos of poteen making and believed that 'the manners of the people would soon be changed' if only it could be destroyed. It would be much better if people could be persuaded to drink beer and he reported a conversation with a Mr Kerr from beyond Ballymagorry; this man had taken a licence to brew and sell ale and believed that people could be weaned from drinking spirits if an alternative was available. Hamilton was enthusiastic about the potential benefits:

> We should have but few quarrels, and though a person exceeded in that liquor (ale) he would be able to mind his work the next day which few can do who debauch in whiskey. The little whiskey houses that are all over the country ruin the people; they are full every market day, as they return home, and it is in them that quarrels are chiefly.

It was clear, however, that the attempts to suppress distilling in 1783–4 met with only partial success and it was again in the news in 1791 when the *Londonderry Journal* reported on the drink menace in the north west. Derry had no licensed distillers yet whiskey was plentiful and while Strabane had three licensed manufacturers it was reported that there was large scale unlicensed distilling to cater for the 231 publicans in the Strabane district. The making of poteen had become too much of an industry in some parts for it to be ended by limited and temporary sanctions and its manufacture survived in a number of rural areas in the Strabane district until comparatively recently. Clearly alcohol usage was considerable in the late eighteenth century and the figure of 231 publicans is startling. It is little wonder that people like Abercorn and Hamilton saw it as a major social evil and supported harsh measures to eradicate it.

Emigration 1780–1800

The other main consequence of uncertainty and poor harvests was emigration and this was highlighted in the years 1783–4 and in the early 1790s. In June 1783 Hamilton had expressed concern about numbers leaving the district and taking with them linen for sale in America. Clearly there was a downturn in the price of linen locally and some of the more enterprising of the weavers decided that the potential market in America would help offset the costs of emigration. Abercorn expressed scepticism about the potential market in the New World but did not yet see the emigration as worrying for the area. He was ready even to encourage it and in December of that year instructed Hamilton to provide some additional money to one former tenant who was departing for America. The worsening of the shortages in the following year, however, greatly increased the outward flow of people and Hamilton began expressing concern at the high level of population movement in the late spring of 1784.

The earlier emigrants were not seen as damaging to the estate and Hamilton claimed that despite the high numbers leaving from the emigrant ports in Ulster – there were an estimated 15,000 intending emigrants that spring – the Abercorn estates were not seriously affected, except for some young men. He also remarked that Catholics were now emigrating in much greater numbers than formerly and in the following month of June he again reported with confidence that while 'a great number of young men are going to America, I hear of but few families from this neighbourhood'. In August the extent of migration was clearly becoming worrying, and while Hamilton was still claiming that of the many who had gone off most were of the poorer sort and with few landholders among them, yet it might be necessary for parliament to intervene by insisting that intending emigrants give two months notice 'so that they might not steal away and defraud their creditors'. Such comments suggest that the economic standing of many of those leaving was not so lowly as Hamilton had earlier suggested and that people of some credit and possibly property were departing from the district. Certainly the idea of imposing restrictions was being actively considered by government at the time and one of Strabane's most famous emigrants, John Dunlap, made mention of the possible restrictions on the freedom to move from Ireland in a letter to his brother-in-law, Robert Rutherford, in May of the following year. He believed, however, that legislation would have little impact since only those outside its scope should contemplate emigration: '[P]eople with a family advanced in life find great difficulties in emigration but the young men of Ireland who wish to be free and happy should leave it and come here as quick as possible.'

In the following decades emigration continued, and with periodic upsurges such as in 1791 when Hamilton reported that 'the emigrations to America are double this season . . . and a good many entire families have left this neighbourhood', with no sign of abatement in the following weeks of May and June. Clearly these exceptional bouts of emigration were tied in to the prevailing economic circumstances on the estates and especially to the short term fluctuations in the linen industry. Regulations were imposed in 1793 against unrestricted emigration, with moves to prevent the movement of skilled men like weavers and mechanics (tradesmen) but a Hamilton report by 1795 suggested that the legislation was having only limited effect:

> The embargo upon mechanicks to America has tended rather to encourage and increase their emigration; many smuggle in women's cloaths. Upon the whole it is computed that more will go this season than for the last two. They are warmly encouraged by their friends and desire to bring out their property in cash, brown unbleached linen or livestock, by which they mean boys and girls of a certain age who cheerfully bind themselves by indentures for three, four or five years to men of good character who will pay their passage out, feed and cloath them for the time of their servitude.

The letter clearly shows the attractiveness of emigration and also its availability on terms that could be afforded by even the poorer sections of the population. What had especially worried government at this time was the outbreak of the war with revolutionary France and the need to use Ireland both for recruiting purposes and for the supply of food and munitions to the army fighting abroad. High emigration threatened both aims, but the poverty in Ireland was a major incentive to disregard government regulations. Thus in 1797 it was reported from Strabane that 'the emigration to America from the port of Derry has been this season very considerable, and chiefly of the younger parts of large families', while in 1807 it was claimed that 'there has been monstrous emigration this season to America'. It was in this latter year that James Wilson, grandfather of the future US president, Woodrow

Wilson, left Strabane as a young man of twenty years of age to seek his fortune in the New World.

Linen Fluctuations 1780–1800

The fluctuations in the levels of emigration can be related to the prosperity or otherwise of the local linen industry and the extracts from Hamilton's letters suggest that many of those who left were weavers or otherwise connected to the domestic based linen industry that seemed particularly subject to frequent fluctuations. The evidence from the estate correspondence suggests that 1783 was a year of uncertainty in the linen trade, with a number of emigrants taking brown linen with them to America. Abercorn had not held out any great hopes of the success of such a venture and he made further comments on the industry in the month of July when claiming that 'the linen manufacture can never flourish as it ought to do, till it can be carried on advantageously with what you call bought flax. Growing flax is no part of the business of a linen manufacturer any more than keeping sheep is the business of a woollen manufacture.' Such a major transformation of how the industry was organised was as yet far distant and Abercorn's comments should be seen as musings that had little practical reality in the circumstances of the late eighteenth century. He was in full support in October 1784 of the proposals to transform Scian (Sion) wheat mill into a bleaching mill, and Hamilton was enthusiastic about the gains from having three such centres in the Strabane area, claiming that 'we have not bleach greens sufficient to bleach the cloth bought in this neighbourhood; many are forced to send to greens upwards of 20, some 30 miles from this'.

The renewed high emigration of the 1790s was a reflection of further depression or slackness in the industry and posed problems for estate management, when rent payments often depended partly on cash earned from weaving. The area certainly owed much to a domestic linen industry if we take the evidence of the growth of the Strabane linen market as a guide. The corporation had petitioned Abercorn for an extension to the market in the 1770s and the selection of mill owner and linen bleacher, Nathaniel Edie, as burgess in 1784 and as provost in 1785 and 1786 demonstrated the importance attached to the linen trade. Figures are available for the volume sold in Strabane market in the latter part of the eighteenth and the early years of the nineteenth century, and they show clearly that the weekly market contributed substantially to the town's trade. The following table is from Dr W.H. Crawford's *Domestic Industry in Ireland*, Dublin (1972) and shows annual sales in comparison with other markets in Tyrone:

	1783	1803	1816	1820
Aughnacloy	26,000	41,000	—	4,618
Cookstown	6,240	26,000	67,600	43,509
Dungannon	78,000	182,000	208,000	81,295
Fintona		12,000	41,600	33,670
Newtownstewart	31,200	52,000	20,800	32,379
Omagh	—	—	47,840	51,520
Stewartstown	41,600	52,000	32,760	26,831
Strabane	36,400	78,000	123,760	77,502
Strabane % of county sales	15.75	17.37	22.12	21.32

Tyrone linen markets 1783–1820

Thus Strabane emerged clearly as the second largest linen market town in the county in the period under review and had an increasing share in the years of growth up to 1816. Clearly, Omagh had replaced Newtownstewart as a linen market centre in the second decade of the nineteenth century and may have impacted somewhat on Strabane in that period. But there was a general downwards movement in the domestic industry then and Strabane's decline was mirrored in the other traditional linen markets.

The Corporation and the Growth of Strabane 1780–1800

Much of the economic growth was a reflection of the support given by the corporation and their recognition that the whole town would benefit greatly from increased trade. Abercorn and Hamilton were careful in their appointments of the burgesses and tried to ensure that commercial interests would be well represented in the membership of the corporation. Yet nothing was left to chance and appointees left in little doubt that they owed their position to Abercorn. In 1783 it was decided to bring Nathaniel Edie into the corporation and the new burgess was profuse in his thanks and good wishes: '[T]hat your lordship may long live to be the patron of the industrious poor, to feed the hungry and clothe the naked, is mine as well as the wish of all those who sincerely desire the happiness of this country.' His elevation to the position of provost two years later was a demonstration of his attachment to the wishes of his benefactor but he could not be prevailed on to continue in the position for a third term. Hamilton reported in August 1786 of his conversation with Edie in which it had been claimed that it was both 'expensive and tiresome holding court every Monday and Tuesday, complaints about cloth and yarn, bad money and light gold'. For a man of business, and one actively involved in the development of his undertakings, such a voluntary commitment would have been excessive and unrewarding.

The prosperity of the growing town and the support provided by the opening of the canal in 1796 clearly signified prosperity, with the hope of more to come and the elections for the corporation showed no surprises. In the end James Hamilton had to undertake the position of provost, a position he maintained for much of the final decade of the century and into the early years of the new one. By that stage he had moved aside from active management of the estate, with his son, James Jr, taking over the running of Abercorn's affairs. The report on the election for the corporation for 1795, the year prior to the canal opening, showed the dominance of the Hamilton family as nominees of Abercorn. The full corporation was: James Hamilton (Sr), Rev. A.T. Hamilton (rector of Donagheady and son of James Hamilton), James Hamilton (Jr), Sir John Hamilton, MP, Mr T. Pemberton, Mr Edie, Mr Barclay, Dr Fenton, Mr Knox, Hon. H. Pomeroy, Rev. Mr Edwards, Mr McCausland, and Mr C. Crawford (in place of Mr Burgoyne). Most owed their position to Abercorn even if he did manage to allow the impression of a degree of independence.

The success of the canal and the stimulus given to the linen trade by the French wars was reflected in the development of the town's prosperity, with Hamilton reporting in April 1799 of 'the surprising increase in wealth and prosperity in the last two years'. He went on to describe how 'people of substance in trade' were flocking to Strabane to settle there and insisted that there would be strong competition for houses if Abercorn would build some in the New Town area adjacent to Irish Street and near the canal basin. He went on to add that 'the country is in a most flourishing state, the price of cloth and yarn most enormous'. This may have been part of a scheme to persuade Abercorn to proceed with further development and he employed an architect, Mr Woodgate, to draw up plans for undeveloped lands to the north of the town. Little came of this initiative, however, and Hamilton claimed in correspondence with Abercorn in 1802 that Woodgate had set too high a price on the building lots near the canal basin. The high prices on demand had deterred potential buyers who, it was claimed, had fitted up stores in parts of the town further away from the canal basin but at a lower rent. In 1805 Hamilton was still advertising for potential developers in the New Street area and claimed to have discovered a degree of interest. Clearly, the initial plan for Abercorn to build housing for rent had not been accepted and the attractiveness of easy access to the canal had proved less appealing than envisaged.

Much of Strabane's progress in the late eighteenth century has to be attributed to the work of the Hamilton agents and their keeping Abercorn fully informed about developments and opportunities in the area. James Sr had built up the estates and then helped to bring the corporation along with his and the earl's plans for the future, becoming provost during the critical years of the 1790s. Other members of the family benefited from the success of James, and in 1781 his son Andrew became rector in Donagheady when the parish became vacant. This was in the gift of Abercorn and the incumbent had traditionally been a relative of the family. James Hamilton saw the opportunity and his son Andrew, who had previously talked vaguely about a career in the law, applied to Abercorn for the vacant living, despite the fact that he had no training then in the church. Abercorn acquiesced with some misgivings and the Rev. Andrew became part of the Ascendancy grouping in the area, being also elected to the corporation of Strabane as a sound supporter of the earl, lately created marquis. The succession of James Jr to the management of the estate helped consolidate the family interest, and in 1804, when the rector of Strabane died, another brother, Stewart, was appointed to the vacancy through an agreement between the bishop of Derry and Abercorn. In this case there had been prior inclination towards life as a churchman, since Stewart had acted as curate in Donagheady for a number of years previously.

The United Irishmen and 1798 in North Tyrone

It was only right that the leaders in Strabane should praise themselves by the turn of the century since the whole area had come relatively unscathed through the tempestuous period of the 1790s and the deep unrest connected with the United Irishmen movement. But there were many times during the decade when things had not looked so bright and it had seemed for a period that the whole of the north-west would be engulfed in revolutionary activities. The economic depression in the early years of the 1790s had encouraged wider unrest, and assizes reports in 1792 suggested that all the jails were full from the increase in lawbreaking. Hamilton had reported in March 1793 of the dangerous leniency of the judge at the Tyrone spring assizes and this was to be a recurrent theme throughout the decade, whereby troublemakers were allegedly being set free by the courts at the expense of law and order locally. It was in this early part of 1793 that the United Irishmen movement began to spread throughout the Strabane and east Donegal areas, and reports to Abercorn were increasingly alarming about the revolutionary potential in the district. Strabane town, however, appeared settled, with the local militia demonstrating unflinching loyalty and obedience to their officers.

The reports from 1795 onwards became much more alarming, and Hamilton reported to Abercorn on the growing prevalence of sectarian conflict between Defenders and Hedge Masons in the Strabane neighbourhood. Late in the following year, the decision to establish a yeomanry force to deal with local unrest was a matter of concern for James Hamilton, increasing his fear that the arming of this largely Protestant force would exacerbate the sectarian divisions that he wished to avoid. It appears that Rev. Fowler, rector of Urney and Rev. Graham, rector in Strabane, were greatly perturbed at the worsening situation in Strabane and district and had written to government in November 1796 about the inactivity of the local magistrates, especially the provost, James Hamilton, in view of the alleged 150 men in the town of Strabane that had taken the oath of the United Irishmen. The provost had called a public meeting but this had concluded that the reports of United activity were greatly exaggerated and unnecessarily alarmist and contented itself with a declaration of attachment to the constitution. In the spring of the following year, however, Hamilton became much more alarmist in his assessment of the revolutionary potential and claimed that collecting rents had become much more dangerous and difficult. In April he was convinced that 'the spirit of discontent has become too general and however strong the measures now taken by the government may crush them for the present, if a favourable opportunity should present itself they will reunite'.

Military reports for February and March 1797 showed a high level of United activity, with a meeting of the Ulster directory of the United Irishmen taking place in Newtownstewart despite the attempts of the military to surprise the leadership, and other meetings taking place in Dunamanagh and St Johnstown. It was claimed that a Strabane schoolmaster, George Hamilton, had been forced to provide information on the activities of the local revolutionaries, and it was reported that troops had been fired at near Douglas Bridge when they attempted to intercept a group of rebels. The spring assizes in March had again been a major disappointment to the establishment leaders, with allegations of unnecessary acquittals and celebratory bonfires on the surrounding hillsides. One minor consolation remarked on by Hamilton was the emergence of Orangeism; this, he believed, would counteract the United men and prove a barrier against revolutionary change. The Orangemen had issued a challenge to the United Irishmen for the forthcoming Derg Bridge fair and though nothing happened there, it meant that the United men no longer had unchallenged opportunity for growth. It is clear that fairs were seen as major opportunities for official information gathering in this period, and both Hamilton and the military representatives remarked on the unprecedented level of sobriety displayed by the peasantry at these gatherings, a sure sign, they believed, of revolutionary intent.

The military embarked on arms searches in the summer of 1797 and parts of Donagheady parish were placed under martial law, with a number of people arrested and others persuaded to take the oath of allegiance. This, however, did little to lessen the fears of the Ascendancy leadership, and Hamilton rather acidly remarked on the more relaxed attitude to perjury, even among Catholics, who were, in his opinion, 'tenfold more loyal subjects than either Methodists or Presbyterians'. He saw the latter, and especially their ministers, as particularly to blame for the unrest and claimed that 'if every Presbyterian minister had been put out several years ago on board a tender to be scuttled when a dozen leagues at sea . . . we would now have a loyal

No Strabane Uprising 1798?

In the Rising period of May/June 1798, the Strabane area remained relatively quiet and the short-lived panic created by the uprisings in Antrim and Down soon subsided. There were large numbers of troops billeted in the district and it has been claimed that the failure of the United Irishmen leadership to provide guidance was the crucial factor in ensuring that the north-west remained peaceful. Hamilton reported a degree of panic at one stage, with an alleged army of 1,000 being seen one evening at Meenashesk mountain, and the danger of a Catholic uprising being widely discussed. The government offensive in the immediate aftermath of the failures in Antrim and Down led to the surrender of many weapons in Tyrone and Donegal and declarations of loyalty by some who might have feared implication. The leadership of the Catholic church in the north-west had come out strongly against rebellion, and local parish priests, Fr McHugh of Urney and Fr McBride of Newtownstewart, had forwarded declarations of loyalty from large numbers of their parishioners. Not everything went the way of the authorities, however, and Hamilton reported, rather unsympathetically, in August 1798 of the malicious burning of Rev. Fowler's parsonage at Urney: '[V]ery few people pity him; he has an overgrown fortune and he never took pains to be popular either among his parishioners or neighbours.' But the main danger to be faced in the latter part of the year was not the revenge of the erstwhile revolutionaries; rather it was the actions of the ultra-loyalists and their revenge against alleged republicans and United Irishmen.

It was reported that over 1,500 troops in Strabane and 600 more in Lifford were required to keep down unrest from the 'lower orders', and it was claimed that Catholics stayed awake on Christmas night, 1798, fearing a massacre by Orangemen. This was a reversal of the rumour on the eve of St Patrick's day earlier in the year, when Protestants had apparently feared a re-enactment of the Catholic attacks associated with the 1641 rebellion. In April of 1799 Hamilton expressed strong hostility to the continued lawlessness and had no doubt of the cause:

> This part of the North is in quite a ferment by the excesses committed by Orangemen, or people under that description, who had been obliged to fly the country for being most desperate United Irishmen. The Papists are almost driven to a state of desperation; some who had been cruelly treated I gave a warrant to and in the search after the Orange party a pike on a pole and several concealed arms were found.

No doubt a number of former radicals had decided to safeguard their future by joining the winning side, and sectarian divisions had been deliberately exploited by a section of the upper classes in the previous years. It was going to prove difficult to now tell those people previously encouraged and supported in anti-Catholic activity that they must desist and treat everyone as fully deserving of consideration and respect. The position of the troops was a case in point. They were needed to maintain order but in April of 1799 the magistrates of Strabane district petitioned the government on behalf of the inhabitants to withdraw the troops since their billeting was a serious burden on the local population.

The other major issue at the end of the eighteenth century was the question of the Union and Abercorn was very much in favour, with the consequent pressure on James Hamilton to gather local support. He reported success in July 1799 in gaining the 'signatures of almost all the respectable and wealthy merchants of Strabane and neighbourhood to your Lordship's resolutions relative to the Union', but was forced to confess by October that 'the bulk of the people in Strabane and around are unfriendly to union'. In the end public opinion made little difference and both of Strabane's MPs voted in support of the proposal to abolish the Irish parliament. The compensation of £15,000 for the loss of parliamentary representation for the borough of Strabane went to Abercorn, and the removal of the corporation's right of selection of parliamentary representatives lessened its role and importance still further. Power was very clearly with the Abercorn family and their local representative, and the refusal of government to take seriously the wishes of former provost Nathaniel Edie to be knighted in return for supporting the Union, clearly demonstrated the impotence of local political leaders. Rewards were only to be given to those who mattered. The century thus drew to a close with the future prosperity of the area still tied closely to the wealth and vitality of the Abercorn interest and little achieved in the struggle to establish local control or accountability. How lasting would be Hamilton's view that 'the country is in a most flourishing state'?

7 The Abercorn Family and Political Control in Strabane 1690–1800

ANTHONY MALCOMSON

Plantation Strabane was very much a personal achievement of the Abercorn family. It had not been part of the original plan of plantation of 1609 that the town should be incorporated as a parliamentary borough, and the government's decision to do this was probably taken in the light of the zeal and activity which the first earl of Abercorn had already displayed in planting his estate (totalling roughly a third of the surrounding barony). In December 1610, as a result of the lack of progress made with the towns which did form part of the original plantation scheme, the government decided not to entrust their future development to the projected corporations but to the neighbouring undertakers or servitors instead, and to grant to these latter the lands with which the corporations were to have been endowed.

Since Strabane had not formed part of the original scheme, the land on which it stood had already been granted to the earl of Abercorn, as the

Strabane Corporation Crest, dating from the Royal grant of corporation status in 1612 during the early plantation period.

neighbouring undertaker. But the change of policy meant that this situation was not remedied when the town received its charter of incorporation on 18 March 1613. Despite a petition in 1622 during a government survey of the plantation settlement no action was taken and the corporation continued to have no means of support independent of the Abercorns.

The corporation's financial dependence on the Abercorn family might be expected to have had the corollary of political dependence. This however was not strictly the case. Up to the Revolution, the earls of Abercorn may have exercised effective political control over the borough; but the likelihood is that their control was badly shaken by the Williamite war, when the fourth earl of Abercorn fought and died for King James and, as a consequence, the political and territorial survival of the family hung for a time in the balance.

The MPs returned for Strabane in 1692 may or may not have been nominees of his brother and successor, the fifth earl; one of them, Sir Matthew Bridges, is described as 'of the city of Dublin', and seems to have been a carpet-bagger who could have been anybody's nominee; the other, Capt. Oliver McCausland, was a local man who was to represent Strabane until his death in 1723, and by 1713 was definitely the nominee of the corporation and returned by them against the wishes of the Abercorns. This may have been the position in 1692; alternatively McCausland may originally have been the Abercorns' choice, but gradually have made himself independent of their control.

McCausland and his colleague in the 1695 parliament, Audley Mervyn, were Whig or 'country party' men, as was the fifth earl's kinsman and heir, James Hamilton, and presumably the fifth earl himself; so the Abercorns may still have controlled the return for both seats in 1695. The same was true in 1703, by which time James Hamilton had succeeded as sixth earl: McCausland and his new colleague, James Topham, were Whigs, like Abercorn, and Topham at any rate must have been Abercorn's nominee, as in the next parliament, that of 1713, he was returned for the other Abercorn borough, St Johnstown, Co. Donegal.

At this point, events in Strabane become obscured by the political and personal eccentricity of the sixth earl. In the period 1707–9, he moved over into the Tory camp, leaving McCausland and the Strabane corporation behind him, but for the time being accompanied by Topham. In 1711 and 1713, however, Topham as well as McCausland was classified as a Whig, while Abercorn remained a prominent, though highly individualistic, Tory.

In the latter year, Topham had transferred to St Johnstown, but McCausland's next colleague in Strabane, the Hon. Gustavus Hamilton, was also a Whig. A government-compiled (and therefore Tory) list of various constituencies in advance of the 1713 general election predicted that the members for Strabane would be McCausland 'and whoever he brings in'; but another government list of about the same date described Strabane as 'Lord

Abercorn's borough', so the government may simply have been unclear about what was going on. The information they derived from Abercorn himself at this time probably did not make for clarity: he affected to disapprove in principle of party being carried into constituency politics, declared his support for two Whig candidates in the Co. Donegal election, and expressed strong disapproval of the electioneering activities of the Tory bishop of Raphoe.

Significantly, the second Whig elected for Strabane, Gustavus Hamilton, was Abercorn's kinsman and the brother of one of the Whig candidates he supported in Donegal. Hamilton may have been McCausland's nominee, but he is more likely to have been a compromise candidate set up by Abercorn, who deemed it prudent to back someone who was at least personally acceptable to him, rather than risk backing someone who was not politically acceptable as well. The same motive may have induced him to return the Whig Topham for St Johnstown.

From 1714 onwards, reconstruction of events in Strabane ceases to be a matter of guesswork. In that year, the documentation from the Abercorn papers begins, although it takes the form of a designedly opaque letter which Abercorn wrote to the burgesses of Strabane in March, at a time when Queen Anne's failing health had given rise to a good deal of canvassing for the general election which would have to take place if she died. In the letter Abercorn promised that he would thereafter ask them to return only one nominee of his for Strabane, assured them that his nominee would be a fit representative and one who would attend to their interests, and guaranteed that he would leave the other seat to be disposed of as they thought proper; all he asked was that they should not elect as their representative someone in opposition to him in Co. Tyrone politics. He went on:

> I think it cannot but be obvious to all considering gentlemen that no person can be hearty for your interest who can be prevailed upon to act in contradiction to mine, I being of the same principles and having the same notions as to politics with yourselves . . . No inhabitant of, or friend to, Strabane will . . . [? suffer the] rendering that corporation so insignificant as not to be represented at all – which in effect would be the case if your two representatives voted different ways. And it would be odd if the gentleman I recommend should, as I daresay he will, vote according to your sense, and the other altogether of your own pitching upon should as far as in him lies obstruct what you desire should take place.

Privately, he explained to his friend, Edward Southwell, secretary to the lord lieutenant in the former Tory administration:

> I have reason to hope from the answer I received from the above letter that I shall be able to be better than my word, by getting the town of Strabane

> to return two good members; whereas I only ventured to promise an
> amendment as to one, mistrusting whether I should be able to prevail upon
> them to leave out Capt. McCausland, who lives among them.

If the letter to the corporation was intended to be meaningless, it fulfilled
the intention admirably. Had Abercorn and the corporation really been of
the same political principles, two Whigs would not currently be sitting for
Strabane; and though the letter could be interpreted as an offer to nominate
a Whig provided they nominated a Whig who was not opposed to Abercorn
in Tyrone politics (which McCausland presumably was), the explanation to
Southwell makes it clear that Abercorn hoped by nominating a Tory, to
induce them to nominate a second Tory instead of McCausland. When the
general election took place in the following year, Abercorn was in fact no
better than his word, as McCausland was re-elected. But he at least had the
satisfaction of replacing Gustavus Hamilton with a rabid Tory, the Hon.
Richard Stewart, a younger brother of his (Whig) neighbour at
Newtownstewart, Lord Mountjoy. This in itself was a considerable achievement, as the 1715 general election was characterised by a massacre of Tory
candidates and by the temporary overthrow of the influence of several Tory
borough-patrons.

Not only did Abercorn's influence survive: between 1715 and the mid
1730s he enjoyed the lion's share of the representation of Strabane. This was
because of the extraordinary construction which he managed to put on the
partnership arrangement made with the corporation in 1714. Normally,
when such arrangements existed, the terms were that at any given moment
each party should have one representative in parliament (such, for example,
were the terms under which the Creighton and Montgomery families agreed
to share the parliamentary representation of the next door borough of
Lifford, Co. Donegal, in 1727).

However, Abercorn's interpretation was that the corporation and he
should fill alternate vacancies, regardless of whose representative it was who
had created the vacancy. Thus, at a by-election in 1723 caused by
McCausland's death, Abercorn successfully claimed to fill the seat with a
nominee of his own, his relation Henry Colley of Castle Carbury, Co.
Kildare; in 1725, when Colley in turn died, the corporation nominated John
McCausland, probably Capt. Oliver's son, to succeed him; at the general
election of 1727 the representation was again shared between the Abercorn
and McCausland families.

The Crisis Period for the Abercorns

In 1732 the crisis in the political affairs of Strabane came, with the death of
John McCausland. At this time there seem to have been roughly four groups

in the corporation: the supporters of the Abercorn family, the supporters of the McCausland family, the supporters of one Hugh Edwards of Castle Gore, Co. Tyrone, and a kind of flying squadron headed by a local man called George McGhee. The composition and allegiance of these groups varied according to the viewpoint of the Abercorn family's conflicting sources of information – for example, McGhee was represented to them (whether rightly or wrongly it is impossible to determine) as their worst enemy in the corporation, although he represented himself as their best friend. For their part, the Abercorns did themselves no good by being absent from Strabane throughout the crisis, and by counteracting and contradicting each other in their tactics.

The sixth earl was now a very old man, and seems for some time past to have left the management of his political concerns in Strabane to his son and heir, Lord Paisley, with whom he was on poor terms. Both were so far united as to set up Paisley's eldest son, the Hon. James Hamilton, as their candidate in place of McCausland; but where Paisley took the offensive by disenfranchising McGhee as a burgess (a step of doubtful wisdom and still more doubtful legality), in order to gain a majority in the corporation, Abercorn went on the defensive by appealing, in still more suppliant tones than in 1714, to the agreement of that year. He also offered to support Edwards as candidate for a probable vacancy for Co. Tyrone, in return for Edwards's support in Strabane for the candidature of Abercorn's grandson: an offer which was particularly embarrassing to Paisley, who had already promised whatever influence he had, independent of his father, to Edwards's opponent in the county election.

In these circumstances, Paisley decided not to run the risk of setting up his son. Instead he turned, as a compromise, to a remote kinsman of the Abercorns, William Hamilton of Dunamanagh, Co. Tyrone, who was acceptable to certain burgesses opposed to the Abercorns, and who yet undertook to support the family's interest in the borough. William Hamilton was accordingly elected in the autumn and early winter of 1733, both as a burgess in place of the disenfranchised McGhee and as MP for Strabane in place of McCausland.

The election of William Hamilton was a serious mistake, for he soon afterwards made common cause, not only with Edwards, but with the Abercorn family's more serious and implacable enemies, the McCauslands. The result was that the Abercorns found their political influence in the borough eclipsed, except in the limited sense that the member of their family elected in 1727, the Hon. Charles Hamilton, continued to hold the seat until the general election of 1761. Whether their discomfiture was simply the result of miscalculation and of the difficulty, especially for people at a distance, of unravelling 'the many secret cabals of the burgesses of Strabane', or whether it was in some degree the result of deliberate misrepresentation, is a moot point.

Years later there occurs in the Abercorn papers a reference to the treachery of the family's agents at this time, who are charged with 'misleading the people and considering their own private interest more than that of their master and generous benefactor'. The charge probably relates to one Robert Patterson, who was either an under-agent of the sixth earl or else an agent employed separately by Lord Paisley. Patterson was the instigator of the proceedings against McGhee, a measure which Paisley entered into with some hesitation; and although the decision to elect William Hamilton was Paisley's, not Patterson's, and indeed was taken in opposition to Patterson's opinion, it seems that McGhee may have been a truer friend to the Abercorn family than Patterson, and may have given the sounder advice.

For example, as early as September 1732 – prior to McGhee's disenfranchisement and a year prior to Hamilton's election – McGhee had written to Paisley warning him that if Hamilton were admitted to the corporation he would join forces with the McCauslands and break the control of the Abercorns. The warning was not heeded, and what McGhee foretold came to pass. Whether this means that Patterson was guilty of actual treachery, or whether he simply misjudged the extremely complicated situation in Strabane, is anybody's guess ; either way, the result was the same from the point of view of the Abercorn family, who in any case had only themselves to blame for relying on second-hand information and failing to come to Strabane to make their own appraisal of what was going on there.

The political situation in Strabane was complex by the standards of any corporation borough; but in no borough was the influence of a patron likely to subsist for long if it was as seriously neglected as was the Abercorn influence in Strabane.

The Abercorns Attempt to Recover Control

The sixth earl of Abercorn died shortly after these events, in 1734, and Lord Paisley succeeded him as seventh earl. He did not enjoy his inheritance for long, and up to the time of his death in 1744 nothing seems to have been done by the Abercorn family to recover the ground lost in 1733. It was not until his son, the same Hon. James Hamilton whose candidature had been given up in that year, succeeded as eighth earl that a determined effort was made to do so.

On the face of it, the eighth earl's prospects of success were good. His supplanters in the corporation, Oliver McCausland (probably Capt. Oliver McCausland's grandson) and William Hamilton of Dunamanagh, MP for Strabane since 1733, were by then on bad terms with each other. A written agreement seems to have existed defining their respective interests in Strabane, but the cause of contention between them appears to have been that McCausland enjoyed the lion's share. Both men, as well as being at loggerheads with each other, were at loggerheads with some of their fellow burgesses; so much so that three vacancies in the corporation remained unfilled for several years prior to 1755 because of the impossibility of agreement being reached over the men to fill them. Moreover, both McCausland and Hamilton were in such pressing financial difficulties that by 1755 part of their estates were under sequestration for debt.

Nevertheless, the eighth earl of Abercorn proceeded cautiously. Initially, his counter-attack took the form of tentative probings. He seems to have made more frequent visits to Strabane than his predecessors: visits which, according to his agent, Nathaniel Nisbitt, effected a 'breach . . . in the corporation'. He made overtures to Lord Tyrone, whose agent, Mark McCausland, was a burgess of Strabane and a relative of Oliver McCausland, but without success; Lord Tyrone declined to interfere. He also took soundings from three or four burgesses thought to be venal or on particularly bad terms with McCausland or Hamilton.

In April 1750, for example, an under-agent reported to him that one burgess, John Davis, 'is more inclined to serve your lordship than anyone living, and desires I intimate this. We had no nearer discourse about it, but I believe she [Mrs Davis] was fishing to understand if anything would be offered. Midsummer is near, and your lordship knows best what to do.' He also took soundings from Hamilton himself, to see whether Hamilton could be detached from McCausland. Finally, he instructed Nathaniel Nisbitt to make a declaration of his intentions towards the borough should he recover control of it: 'If anyone speaks of my views upon the town, you may say I have no desire to have two of my family chosen for it, nor even one that would not attend in parliament, but that I stand up for the freedom of the town against all persons, and particularly against Mr McCausland, who has endeavoured to take it away.'

This was in 1751, but unfortunately it had no better effect than the tactful letter written by Abercorn's grandfather, the sixth earl, in 1714. Nor is this surprising. The attendance record of the member of the family currently sitting for Strabane, the Hon. Charles Hamilton, Abercorn's uncle, did not lend credibility to Abercorn's declaration; elected in 1727, Hamilton had not yet set foot in parliament and still had not done so when that parliament was dissolved thirty-four years later, in 1760. Unlike Abercorn's other uncle in the house, the Hon. George Hamilton, MP for St Johnstown, Charles Hamilton did not even attend in the 1753–4 session, to cast his vote on the unpopular Castle side in the celebrated money bill dispute. Both McCausland and Hamilton of Dunamanagh espoused the popular side in that dispute, and both were no doubt prominent at the 'great patriot meeting' held in Strabane in May 1755 which Nathaniel Nisbitt loftily dismissed as 'a drinking match'.

The dispute had a twofold effect on the struggle for control of Strabane:

it brought McCausland and Hamilton closer together, and it cast the Abercorn family in an unpopular role and so made it harder for Abercorn to win any of the burgesses over to his side. In the autumn of 1755, the three long-standing vacancies in the corporation were filled up; which meant, presumably, that McCausland and Hamilton had reached at least temporary agreement by then. It also meant that the first, and cautious, phase of Abercorn's counter-attack had proved a failure. After 1755, the second phase, which consisted of stronger measures, came into operation.

Abercorn Fights the Corporation

In that year he began litigation in the Court of King's Bench to prove that various acts of the corporation, particularly the disenfranchisement of McGhee in 1733 – in spite of the fact that this had been the Abercorn family's own doing – were illegal and invalidated all subsequent acts of, and elections to, the corporation. In this he was greatly hampered by the refusal of the provost and town clerk to allow his lawyers to examine the corporation books. (Indeed, the fact that the corporation books prior to 1755 do not survive raises the suspicion that his antagonists wilfully destroyed them.) Some limited information from the books was smuggled to him by a clerk in the provost's office, and his Dublin lawyer was hopeful that the town clerk 'is not so very virtuous as not to be prevailed upon by money'.

But the town clerk must have been virtuous, as no further information was forthcoming. Nor could Abercorn hope to obtain a court order for access to the books unless he was successful in the first stage of litigation in the King's Bench. He was confident of success; so confident that he exerted all his influence to procure for himself an advantage during the second stage. This second stage would take the form of a hearing before a special jury of Co. Tyrone, and it was vital both to Abercorn and his opponents that the sheriff of Co. Tyrone for the coming year should be their man, as the sheriff would have the picking, or rather packing, of the jury.

In the autumn of 1756 Abercorn busied himself lobbying the lords justices (who governed the country during the prolonged absences of the lord lieutenant), but without success; his opponents' man was appointed sheriff. In any case, this reverse did not matter, as he shortly afterwards suffered a more severe, and unexpected, reverse in the first stage of the litigation. The judges of the King's Bench decided that the transactions he complained of had taken place too long ago to be enquired into now, and also rejected the subsidiary points of law he adduced. In February 1757 his Dublin lawyer ruefully reported:

> I did believe . . . that the length of time was of no weight with them, but in giving their judgment that objection had the greatest, I might rather say the only, weight; for that an enquiry into this matter, after an acquiescence

of near twenty-four years, might disturb the elections of many subsequent
burgesses and be a precedent for embarrassing or overturning many other
corporations in this kingdom. And though the disenfranchisement of
McGhee might, if recently complained of, be very proper to enquire into,
yet it was not proper at this distance of time.

Thus ended the second phase of Abercorn's counterattack, and once again
he had been worsted.

The Abercorn Recovery

The third phase, which lasted from 1757 to 1764, also took the form of litigation, but litigation of a different nature. Abercorn now concentrated on
the present rather than the past misdeeds of the corporation: their claims to
tolls and to exercise jurisdiction in the adjoining parish of Urney and manor
of Cloughogle. Here he was on firmer legal ground; for the corporation,
having no land for its support, and its two leading members being financially embarrassed, had tried to raise revenue by extending its jurisdiction
unwarrantably. The financial embarrassment of the McCauslands and
Hamiltons had the other important effect of leaving them very ill-equipped
to bear the cost of such litigation; and in this, rather than in the legal rights
and wrongs of the matter, the strength of Abercorn's position lay.

Oliver McCausland himself had died in 1756, and the struggle was now
being carried on by his son, John, who received a financial fillip of £1,650
by selling one seat for Strabane to Robert Lowry of Millberry, Co. Tyrone,
at the 1761 general election. Hamilton of Dunamanagh, on the other hand,
continued to fill the other seat in person, and so got no money for the sale
of it. In 1763 he too died and was succeeded by his son, John, who succeeded him as MP for Strabane. Before long John Hamilton and
McCausland, like their fathers before them, were on bad terms. By February
1764 the financial effects of Abercorn's litigation had begun to make themselves felt, and Hamilton in particular was complaining bitterly about being
called upon for a half-share of the expense while McCausland continued to
enjoy more than a half-share of the patronage of the borough. In these circumstances, the provost for the year, one Barclay, who claimed to be a well-
wisher to them both, advised them that their best course would be to come
to terms with Abercorn.

Abercorn, for his part, was in no hurry to come to terms. 'I am ready', he
wrote to his agent, James Hamilton, 'to give him [McCausland] my friendship as sincerely as he can ask it and to pity the inconveniences his family
have brought upon him by their endeavours to oppress mine. But I really do
not dare to give what I think a great deal for what it may be at least doubtful whether I get or not at last, and [for what] may engage me in new
contests in exchange for the old ones . . ..' The 'great deal' which

McCausland had asked for his interest in the corporation was apparently £2,000 in cash, subsequently reduced to £1,000, plus an indemnity against the costs of all the suits still outstanding, plus a guarantee that he would have the disposal of the next seat in parliament which fell vacant.

In the end Abercorn acceded to these terms, except that he insisted that the £1,000 in cash should be a loan and not an outright payment. In this he showed both magnanimity and common sense. His agent, James Hamilton, had already forewarned him that Robert Lowry, the man to whom McCausland had sold the seat for Strabane in 1761, was dangerously ill, and that if McCausland was able to raise more money by a second sale of the seat he might be able to hold out against Abercorn for some time to come. This warning proved to be accurate; Lowry died just after the bargain between McCausland and Abercorn had been concluded, and McCausland made £2,000 by selling the seat to George Montgomery of Ballyconnell, Co. Cavan.

Hamilton of Dunamanagh was in a weaker bargaining position than McCausland, but Abercorn gave him handsome terms all the same. He agreed to lend Hamilton £500 to stave off his most pressing creditors, indemnified him against the costs of the outstanding suits and declared that it was his intention that Hamilton should always fill a seat for Strabane, provided, presumably, that Hamilton considered himself as Abercorn's nominee and conducted himself in parliament as Abercorn wished. He also continued both McCausland and Hamilton as burgesses of Strabane, and even, to the astonishment of McCausland and the consternation of the agent, James Hamilton, had McCausland elected provost for 1765.

Throughout the three phases of his counter-attack, Abercorn had shown that he wanted merely to be restored to what he considered to be his own and not to revenge himself on his dispossessors. In this he displayed a restraint remarkable among borough patrons in an age when boroughs were regarded as a species of private property and opposition to the patron as an invasion of property rights. So far was Abercorn from allowing righteous indignation to sway his conduct that he was content to wait twenty years before accomplishing his end, and in his choice of means showed caution, flexibility and moderation. To some extent all this can be attributed to his lack of interest in matters political: for example, after 1768, when his repossession of the borough was complete and both its members were nominees of his own, he does not seem to have exercised tight control over their parliamentary conduct. And in 1789, when his very politically-minded nephew succeeded to the Abercorn title and estates, he was dismayed by the rundown state of the family's voting strength in counties Tyrone and Donegal.

However, when every allowance has been made for Abercorn's indifference to political concerns, the fact remains that sound sense lay at the bottom of his tactics towards Strabane borough in the period 1744–64. He recognised that it would not be in his interests to drive either McCausland or Hamilton to desperation; in that event they would either sink their differences and present a united front against him, or else seek to sell their interest in the corporation to someone who might have the financial means they lacked to parry his counter-attack.

Electoral Harmony 1764 –76

Abercorn, moreover, was concerned to heal, or at least not to exacerbate, the divisions among the townspeople of Strabane which the events of the period 1744–64 inevitably had created. In this he was not disappointed. In October 1764 James Hamilton was able to reassure him that 'this revolution has given the people of this place universal pleasure'; and about the same time the people of Strabane testified to their pleasure by themselves writing

> . . . with hearts overflowing with joy, to return your lordship our hearty and unfeigned thanks for taking us into your favour and protection. Your noble ancestors set up, supported and established ours without a rival in trade, and they gave birth and maturity to the linen manufacture, our staple commodity, now falling into a languishing state, and 'tis not to be doubted but that your lordship would have continued the like favours to us had we been truly represented to you. We beg leave to assure your lordship from the most profound sincerity of heart that we always did, do and ever will truly and sincerely love, esteem and regard your lordship, your noble family and interest. We therefore most humbly beseech your lordship to take us into favourable consideration and to lend your hand to trade, now tottering in our streets, by which it will revive, we shall flourish, and your lordship will rejoice to see it.

Such sentiments, though hardly laudable, are understandable; they are indeed a commonplace of the unreformed electoral system. The townspeople of Strabane, apart from the few who featured among the thirteen burgesses, were excluded from the political life of the borough; and, since it was their lot to be dictated to politically by someone, their primary concern was that he should be a powerful individual who could promote their economic well-being to the best effect. On these criteria, there was great advantage from their point of view in being dictated to by Abercorn rather than by McCausland and Hamilton of Dunamanagh.

After the settlement of 1764 there was no further serious challenge to Abercorn's control of Strabane. The next general election took place in 1768 and passed off uneventfully. One local man, William Maxwell, who had been brought into the corporation by Abercorn in 1764, blotted his copybook by getting up a petition from the inhabitants to Abercorn asking him to return Maxwell for the borough. However, James Hamilton was able to warn Abercorn that the petition was not a spontaneous expression of the inhabitants' feelings, and Maxwell's designs were frustrated.

A minor difficulty also arose over George Montgomery of Ballyconnell, the man to whom McCausland had sold the seat for £2,000 in 1765. Montgomery felt, not surprisingly, that he had made a bad bargain of it, and expressed the hope that Abercorn would return him at a reduced price, or preferably, for nothing. Hard though his case was, it was certainly not Abercorn's responsibility, and Montgomery got nowhere with his request. Abercorn had in any case other plans for the representation of Strabane at the general election of 1768. One seat had of course to go to John Hamilton of Dunamanagh, in accordance with the agreement of 1764. The other Abercorn intended for his cousin, William Brownlow of Lurgan, should Brownlow fail to be re-elected for Co. Armagh.

Brownlow was a man of high reputation and great popularity in the north of Ireland and would have reflected credit on any constituency for which he sat. However, he was successful in his election for Co. Armagh and did not need the Strabane seat as a long-stop. In the end, Abercorn used it to bring in Claudius Hamilton of Beltrim, Co. Tyrone, a kinsman and the brother-in-law of James Hamilton. Claudius Hamilton had been beaten in a bitter and expensive contest for Co. Tyrone, and although Abercorn had not encouraged him in this contest, he readily returned him for Strabane by way of consolation prize.

The general election of 1776 was even less eventful. John Hamilton, who continued to represent the borough until 1797, was again returned, along with Henry Pomeroy of Newberry, Co. Kildare, whose mother was a grand-daughter of the sixth earl of Abercorn. In 1776, as in 1768, there seems to have been slight discontent among some of the burgesses. James Hamilton reported that two or three of them had thoughts of petitioning Abercorn to continue Claudius Hamilton, whom he had decided to drop, as their MP, but nothing came of this. Abercorn himself notified to Pomeroy's father his intention of returning Pomeroy in terms which sounded strangely diffident: 'I have expressed to my friends at Strabane my wishes in favour of your eldest son, and I believe he will meet with no difficulty in being chosen there this term.' But this was probably only the common form of borough patronage, and indeed the letter may have been intended for display to the burgesses of Strabane.

Abercorn and the Volunteer Movement 1779–83

At the general election of 1783, when Pomeroy and Hamilton were re-elected, Abercorn again spoke of Pomeroy's return in terms which suggested that he did not regard it as a foregone conclusion. This time he may have had good reason for his diffidence. The general election of 1783 took place against a background of Volunteer propaganda and activity which, although on the wane, temporarily toppled patron control in boroughs like Dundalk, Co. Louth, and Lisburn, Co. Antrim, where there were fairly large though normally acquiescent electorates; and Abercorn may have been concerned about the possible effects of this propaganda and activity on the thirteen-strong electorate of Strabane.

Certainly, he had all along treated the Volunteer movement with studied respect. In its early days he had been alive, like most landowners, to the usefulness of the Volunteers in their role of a local peace-keeping force; but even after the movement had become overtly political, he continued to keep on good terms with it. When a Barony of Strabane battalion was formed in December 1779, and his nephew and heir rejected as its colonel in preference to an outsider from the other end of Co. Tyrone, James Stewart of Killymoon, Abercorn did not register a protest, and even subscribed – though unpunctually – to the expenses of raising the battalion. In all this he was probably not without political motivation.

At this time there was discontent among a section of the Strabane townspeople that they were excluded from a say in matters of local 'regulation or taxation' and in the election of minor borough officials – discontent which shortly after the 1783 general election, in December of that year, found expression in a petition to Abercorn. The objects of the townspeople seem genuinely to have been as limited as they stated. But James Hamilton was worried that this might be an attempt to 'creep farther into the corporation, in order if they could to overturn it, which is the spirit of the people at present throughout the kingdom'; and his fears were borne out in March 1784, when one Richard Charleton, lieutenant-colonel of the Strabane battalion of the Volunteers, convened 'a meeting of the town to think of a proper address to parliament to open the corporation'. Nothing, however, seems to have come of all this.

By the early winter of 1784 the discontent among the townspeople appears to have subsided, helped on its way by minor concessions on Abercorn's part in matters of 'taxation or regulation'. Probably there had never been any serious danger of the thirteen burgesses of Strabane succumbing to Volunteer pressures at the time of the general election of 1783. But since they were virtually all of them townspeople of Strabane, Abercorn, with that mixture of consideration and shrewdness which was characteristic of him, had no doubt been anxious to behave towards the local Volunteers and towards the borough in a way which did not expose his burgesses to local resentment. By 1787 any worries which he may have had on the score of the Volunteers were over; for in that year Richard Charleton was lamenting that 'the Volunteer spirit' in the Strabane area had 'so fallen off . . . as to make it almost impossible to assemble the battalion so as to appear with either credit to themselves or the original institution'.

Strabane MPs in the Irish Parliament 1764–83

The political line pursued by the members for Strabane in the three parliaments during which the eighth earl of Abercorn controlled the return is not always easy to trace. Abercorn himself, as has been seen, was not politically minded. He was an instinctive conservative, uneasy at the probable consequences of the octennial act and hostile from at least 1780 onwards to the political aspect of the Volunteer movement. Because he was not politically minded himself, he seems to have been easily influenced by those who were, and to have kept his members for Strabane on a slacker rein than most borough patrons would have allowed. It is probable that in the 1768 parliament he was considerably influenced by his cousin, William Brownlow, the man who would have sat for Strabane had he not been elected for Co. Armagh; Abercorn would hardly have been prepared to return him for Strabane unless he was in sympathy with Brownlow's politics, since Brownlow was too distinguished and independent a member to trim his sails to any patron's wind.

Brownlow supported the government's contentious proposal for an augmentation of the army on the Irish establishment in November 1769, as did Hamilton of Dunamanagh (Claudius Hamilton's line is unknown). By the start of the 1771 session, however, Brownlow was in opposition, and was indeed the opposition candidate for the speakership; both Hamiltons were likewise in opposition, although it was noted by the Castle in 1772 that Hamilton of Dunamanagh had 'made many professions of support'. Castle lists later in this parliament raise the suspicion that Abercorn had become dissatisfied with the opposition politics of his members, a suspicion perhaps confirmed by his decision to discontinue Claudius Hamilton at the general election of 1776. At some stage – and the exact point in time is not clear – his instinctive conservatism proved too strong for the influence of Brownlow.

The role of Abercorn's members, Hamilton of Dunamanagh and Henry Pomeroy, in the first session of the parliament of 1776, is uncertain. During the free trade crisis of October–December 1779, at the start of the next session, they probably opposed the government, though whether this was consonant with Abercorn's wishes is also uncertain; Pomeroy, in particular, who had begun his parliamentary career with expressions of devotion to Abercorn's wishes, was at this time noted by the Castle as much under the influence of the Pomeroy family's principal patron, the duke of Leinster.

By February 1780, however, both Pomeroy and Hamilton were regarded by the Castle as supporters, at least on constitutional questions (so was Leinster at this particular period); and from then onwards the weight of the members for Strabane was always thrown into the government scale. Hamilton and Pomeroy opposed the Volunteer plan for parliamentary reform in December 1783 (in spite of the fact that it was seconded by

Brownlow) and supported the commercial propositions in August 1785 (in spite of the fact that they were opposed by both Brownlow and Leinster). By the time of Abercorn's death in 1789, the early opposition tradition of the members for Strabane, which had lasted at least until 1776 and probably until 1780, was long since forgotten, and a whiggish survey of the state of the parliamentary representation of Ireland in that year saw 'subserviency to court dictates' as the hallmark of the borough's members and its patron.

One unusual and complicating factor in the parliamentary conduct of the members for Strabane during the period 1764–89 was the relationship between Abercorn and Hamilton of Dunamanagh. This was not a normal patron–member relationship. Indeed, the Castle was often uncertain of the extent to which Hamilton's parliamentary conduct lay within Abercorn's control. The earliest castle list of the 1768 parliament states, correctly, that Hamilton had been returned by Abercorn and should 'be applied to through him'; and in October 1769 Abercorn was in fact applied to for Hamilton's vote on the augmentation, and by no less a personage than the British prime minister, the Duke of Grafton.

However, a Castle list of the period 1770–73 garbles this correct reading of the situation and comes to the conclusions, each of them wrong, that Hamilton, not Abercorn, controlled Strabane 'entirely'; that the other member, Claudius Hamilton, was Hamilton's brother; and that Claudius had been returned by 'his brother' and would vote as he directed. Such flagrant inaccuracy (which, incidentally, is a warning against relying on the evidence of Castle lists uncorroborated by information from other sources) would not have been possible if Abercorn had been asserting himself as Hamilton's patron. Subsequent lists of the 1768 parliament, relating to the period 1772–5, correct the inaccuracy and even claim that Abercorn was not going to return Hamilton again at the next general election. Abercorn, however, did return him again in 1776; and in the 1783 parliament, by which time Hamilton had been gratified with a baronetcy and the collectorship of Strabane, he was credited by the Castle with 'a seat for life' for the borough.

The cause of this uncertainty, which may have existed in the minds of Abercorn and Hamilton themselves as well as in the minds of Castle officials, was the agreement of 1764. At that time Abercorn had expressed the intention of always returning Hamilton, but had declined to commit his intention to paper, except in the most veiled terms, no doubt because he was afraid that the burgesses of Strabane might discover that their suffrages had been preempted. In the absence of a written agreement, there may have been a genuine doubt, particularly in Hamilton's mind, as to whether he sat for Strabane as a matter of favour or as a matter of right. After all, he was not an outsider, whose association with the borough derived from Abercorn; he was an erstwhile patron, who had transferred his interest in the borough to Abercorn for no greater consideration than a small, short-term loan.

In these circumstances, he was justified in regarding himself as being on a special footing with the new patron, although there can be no doubt that there was an element of deliberate misrepresentation in what he told the Castle. When Abercorn's back was turned he might claim to have 'a seat for life' which was not contingent on good behaviour; but in his correspondence with Abercorn there is no hint that he regarded himself as anything but Abercorn's nominee, bound to do Abercorn's bidding. Since he was on the spot, and Abercorn usually was not, he had considerable scope for such misrepresentation; and Abercorn for his part probably felt that a nominee so peculiarly placed as Hamilton was entitled to a greater degree of indulgence than that normally accorded by patrons to their members.

Abercorn's nephew and successor, the ninth earl and first marquess, was not similarly indulgent; in 1797 he dispelled the 'seat for life' myth by discontinuing Hamilton in the representation of Strabane. The special relationship which had existed between Hamilton and the Abercorn family up to the time of the eighth earl's death did not therefore long survive that event. It was a relationship which was peculiar to the eighth earl and was characteristic of the moderation and flexibility which he showed in other aspects of his handling of the borough of Strabane. In more general terms, it was a relationship which illustrates how complex the connection between patron and member could sometimes be.

The Marquess of Abercorn and Strabane 1789–1800

The advent of the ninth earl (in 1790 created first marquess) of Abercorn changed more than Hamilton's special status as MP for Strabane. Uncle and nephew were two men of very different stamp. It is not too much to say that, where the eighth earl was indifferent to politics, the first marquess was obsessed by them. The eighth earl, it is true, had laboured doggedly and patiently to recover political control of Strabane, but he had done so, not from political motives, but because he considered the reassertion of his control over Strabane corporation as a point of family honour, and because he found it difficult to administer his estate in and around Strabane with the corporation in hostile hands.

With the first marquess, on the other hand, political motives predominated. From the outset he declared that he 'meant to omit no honorable mode of increasing my parliamentary strength in the greatest possible degree'. The various 'honourable modes' included the outright purchase of any parliamentary boroughs which came on the market. In this period, demand for such assets greatly exceeded supply, and the first marquess succeeded only in purchasing Augher, Co. Tyrone, and failed in his negotiations over Philipstown (King's County), Donegal borough and, nearer at hand,

St Johnstown. This last borough closely resembled Strabane, in that it was on the Abercorn estate and had been alienated from the family by a coup de main on the part of local residents during the 1730s. The eighth earl had struggled to recapture it in vain, largely because the local man who eventually supplanted him as its patron, William Forward of Castle Forward, was sufficiently affluent to resist his counter-attack. St Johnstown, accordingly, passed with the rest of Forward's property into the possession of his daughter and heiress, who carried it by marriage into the Howard family and was mother of the second earl of Wicklow.

In 1790, the first marquess confided to Pomeroy: '[B]etween ourselves, I am trying to sound Lord Wicklow whether he will sell me St Johnstown. I cannot bear not to recover that family borough, if possible.' It did not prove possible. Their sense of dishonour at the loss of St Johnstown, and the high priority they accorded to its recovery, were among the few things the eighth earl and the first marquess had in common; their handling of Strabane borough illustrates well the difference between them.

Under the first marquess Strabane, instead of being the sole political concern of the Abercorn family, was converted into a mere province of a far flung political empire (although it must be admitted that the first marquess's empire was further flung in his own imagination than it was in reality); and the seats for Strabane, instead of being occupied concurrently by one member of the Abercorn family and one local man, in accordance with the tradition established in 1727, and broken only in 1761–8, were disposed of without regard to local sensitivities, in accordance with events which took place in other quarters of the Abercorn empire.

The change did not manifest itself at the general election of 1790. Abercorn seems to have felt himself free to discontinue either or both of the sitting members for Strabane, Hamilton and Pomeroy, but in fact he retained both, perhaps because the election took place too soon after his accession for his political schemes to have reached fruition. Hamilton thus survived to make a strong and not altogether unfavourable impression on a new member of the house of commons, Jonah Barrington, who recalled years later:

> Amongst those parliamentary gentlemen frequently to be found in the coffee-room of the House, were certain baronets of very singular character, who, until some division called them to vote, passed the intermediate time in high conviviality. Sir John Stuart [sic] Hamilton, a man of small fortune and large stature, possessing a most liberal appetite for both solids and fluids, much wit, more humour and indefatigable cheerfulness, might be regarded as their leader.

These qualities, unfortunately for Hamilton, were unlikely to endear him to the first marquess, who demanded more of his members than silent support at every ring of the division bell, and who was anxious to use his seats to attract into his political following men of eloquence and talent. In 1793 the Abercorn party proposed and supported full catholic emancipation (thus going far beyond the government measure of that year, which merely readmitted catholic voters to the parliamentary franchise). Hamilton seems to have followed the party line, but the report of Abercorn's political manager, the Hon. George Knox, nonetheless implied a criticism: '[I] find converts coming in very fast. Tom [Knox], John [Knox] and Pomeroy support it strongly in private. As to Sir J. Hamilton, I barely ever see him and never meet him in company.' (Clearly Knox was not one for 'high conviviality'.)

On another score, both members for Strabane contravened one cherished rule of the first marquess's political following, which was 'that the members of my particular boroughs should not hold places, [so] that there might be more room for the occasional gratification of such friends as voluntarily and irrevocably embarked with me'. In Pomeroy's case, Abercorn 'broke through my rule willingly . . . as he is the eldest son of a peer, with an income scarcely sufficient to exist upon'. No doubt he also broke through it willingly in Pomeroy's case because the Pomeroy family, through another kinsman, Lord Mornington, derived their political inspiration from Pitt. Abercorn himself had been a personal friend of Pitt since well before Pitt's rise to power, saw himself as his unofficial representative in Ireland (indeed, aspired to be the official one in Dublin Castle), and was building up his political connection specifically for the purpose of supporting Pitt's government – at a price.

On political grounds, therefore, Pomeroy was an appropriate MP for Strabane. He was not in fact re-elected in 1797, but this may only have been because his father, Lord Harberton, was in failing health and Pomeroy's tenure of a seat in the lower house unlikely to be of long duration. Sir John Hamilton was neither as appropriate nor as satisfactory a member as Pomeroy, and though he too lasted until 1797, in his case the wonder was rather that he had not been displaced in 1790 or called upon to resign his seat under the place act of 1793. Perhaps Abercorn, like his uncle before him, felt that the agreement of 1764 gave Hamilton some claim upon him, and only displaced him in 1797 because there were other candidates in the field whose claims were even stronger.

Abercorn's Nominations 1797–8

These claims derived from engagements entered into by Abercorn in the county politics of Tyrone and Donegal. Indeed, the people returned for Strabane in 1797–8 were both the victims of his miscalculations in these other quarters. The first of them, Nathaniel Montgomery Moore of Aughnacloy, Co. Tyrone, had been declared Abercorn's candidate for Co. Tyrone as early as May 1794. By May 1796 Abercorn had conceded that

Moore's candidature was hopeless. At that stage a compromise arrangement was made whereby Moore, to whom Abercorn had presumably pledged a seat, was to be returned for a borough controlled by a rival Co. Tyrone magnate, Lord Belmore. This arrangement must have fallen through; for when the general election took place in the summer of 1797, Moore was in fact returned by Abercorn for Strabane.

His partner in the representation of Strabane, Andrew Knox of Prehen, Co. Londonderry, was not returned for the borough until a bye-election in January 1798, having been unexpectedly defeated at the general election for Donegal, where he had stood as Abercorn's candidate. For him too the seat was a consolation prize and also probably the fulfilment of a pledge. The first marquess's disposal of the Strabane seats according to the fortunes of electioneering elsewhere was a striking departure from the custom of the eighth earl. The eighth earl had never set up a candidate for any other constituency, had not exploited the potential of his electoral influence in Tyrone and Donegal and had disposed of his votes there usually with a view to preventing a contest.

The man who was returned for Strabane along with Moore at the general election of 1797, and who subsequently made way for Knox early in the following year, was John Stewart of Athenree, Co. Tyrone, and his return and subsequent vacation of the seat were likewise dictated by events elsewhere. Although a fairly undistinguished lawyer, Stewart rose ultimately, but briefly, to be attorney-general as a result of the first marquess's influence and of the fact that most of the talent at the Irish bar was on the anti-government side during the union crisis. He had entered parliament as Abercorn's protege in 1794, and in 1797 was returned by Abercorn for six different borough constituencies, allegedly 'in order to give him consequence'. In the end, he chose to sit for Bangor, Co. Down, and vacated his seat for Strabane (and the other four constituencies as well), thus making room for Andrew Knox.

No doubt he was returned for Strabane only because Abercorn's intentions with regard to Knox were unknown at the time the Strabane return had to be made, and no doubt he was returned for the other constituencies as a seat-warmer also, and not for the purpose of giving him consequence. All the same, other instances of one individual warming so many seats at once are rare, if indeed they exist at all. The explanation probably lies in the peculiar circumstances of the 1797 general election, when money was tight and the traffic in seats sluggish. Presumably Stewart was used by the government as a means of holding open various returns for long enough to enable them to find government supporters who were prepared to pay the purchase price. Abercorn himself may well have been a case in point; probably he would not have purchased Stewart's return for Bangor if Stewart's seat for Strabane had not been needed for Knox. Strabane in 1797–8 is thus a good example of the tangled and misleading interrelationships which often subsisted among

8 The Growth and Development of Strabane 1800–1850

JOHN DOOHER

The events at the close of the eighteenth century had threatened community harmony in the Strabane area and divisions continued in the early decades of the nineteenth. The objectives and expectations from the United Irishmen movement and the fears engendered by it influenced attitudes and actions in the following years and created problems in the wider communities. The Union may have been seen by government as a part solution to Irish divisions but it was to prove incapable of reconciling divisions locally either in the short term or in a longer perspective.

Sectarian Conflicts

One of the expectations arising from the Act of Union had been Catholic Emancipation, the right of Catholics to become members of parliament and of local government. Such a proposal was totally rejected by the recently established Orange Order and sectarian conflict had become a major issue in many parts of Ulster in the later 1790s. The aggressiveness had initially been with the Orangemen in the immediate aftermath of the failed 1798 rising, and troops had been stationed in Strabane and Lifford to maintain the peace. By 1802 the conflict had re-emerged in the Strabane area, and Hamilton reported to Abercorn in April of the constant quarrels between Catholics and Orangemen. His letter suggested that many homes had been burned by the different factions and he warned Abercorn against too ready an acceptance of the petitions for help in rebuilding that would come flooding in, claiming that in his estimation most of those who had suffered were largely responsible by their own conduct for such revenge attacks. More worrying for Hamilton was the attitude of too many of the magistrates and most of the country gentlemen, who almost to a man 'show a disposition to support those who style themselves Orangemen'. A further letter in July emphasised a worsening of the conflict, made more difficult by the withdrawal of troops, and the agent reported that personal injuries were increasing at an alarming rate. In one incident it was said that a party of 200 men marched through a little town near Strabane on a fair day, with green branches in their hats, calling for Orangemen to fight and a minor riot ensued, with numerous serious injuries. Clearly the Catholic population had become much more assertive and Hamilton went on, in later correspondence, to blame the increased truculence of the Catholic population on the recent disbanding of soldiers, probably the militia. He had little doubt, however, that both groups were to be utterly condemned, especially by people of standing and property in the community:

> The Orangemen of this country are for the most part the most dissolute idle fellows, the very scum of the country and who in general were active United Irishmen. The other party are the most drunken and bigoted of the lowest class of Catholics. Their outrages have made the country fairs to be almost entirely deserted by women and by persons who were always in the habits of frequenting them.

As a magistrate Hamilton had to listen to complaints and demands for action from both sides and he clearly had little sympathy with either. Yet he was one of the few law enforcers that attempted to steer a middle road and the known partiality of many other magistrates could only exacerbate tensions and divisions.

There were frequent claims of Catholic plans for rebellion and Abercorn was likely to rely on a number of informants about possible danger points on the estates. Thus in 1803 Matthew Hood, manager of the Baronscourt estate, responded to a query by claiming that there was little to fear from a rebellion and that only the lowest dregs of the population were involved in any of the disturbances, with no real connection with politics. The re-establishment of a local yeomanry force that same year was partly to discipline the lawlessness of the local population and partly to provide a measure of reassurance against rebellion. No attempt seems to have been made to assess the possible repercussions on the local Catholic population and Hood rather glibly remarked later that year of the need to station the yeomanry in the Catholic district of Drumquin 'in case of disturbances'. Yet the widespread sectarian conflicts seem to have abated in the following years and it was not until 1806 that Hamilton again mentioned unrest, claiming that 'a strong disposition to riot has lately manifested itself among the Catholics around us'. He reported that a story had surfaced about a plot to rebel but this must have been little more than rumour since nothing more came of it. There did develop later in the year some opposition to tithes, with an attempt to levy them on potato crops, but this protest was not confined to any one section of the population and appears to have passed away fairly quickly. At the end of the year Hamilton was in a position to report that the country about Strabane remained undisturbed, no doubt in contrast to other parts where conflict was more open.

Yet nothing had been settled and events in 1808 demonstrated the growing sectarianism of community divisions, with the yeomanry playing a leading role. The origins of the dispute are again in shadow but it appears that an Orange parade through Strabane was prevented by the actions of a local group and that it was determined on a show of strength by the Orangemen on the 12 July. John J. Burgoyne, agent for Abercorn at this stage and soon to replace Hamilton as the person in charge at Strabane, reported that 'many riots have taken place between the Orange party and the country since, and many assaults committed' and attempts by government and magistrates to curtail marches had met with a very hostile response. A show of strength was arranged for Newtownstewart on 12 July, with the various yeomanry corps parading in support of the Orangemen. The leading county magistrate, Major Crawford, took command of the yeomanry and according to Hamilton's account, led the parade through Ardstraw and on to Strabane, where they paraded through all the streets before returning to Newtownstewart. It was further added that Crawford had been instructed by government the previous evening to take no part in the parade and to dissuade yeomanry corps from participating, but Burgoyne's report made some attempt at explanation by suggesting that Crawford's actions were 'in order I suppose to keep them within bounds'. It was little wonder that Catholics showed little faith in the yeomanry as an impartial defence force and the events were a demonstration to them of how much the ascendancy and magistracy was tied in with Orangeism. John Gamble, in his *Sketches of History, Politics, and Manners in Dublin and the North of Ireland*, in 1810, has provided an account of this same demonstration and highlights the eerie silence that greeted the invaders on their circuits of Strabane, while James Hamilton was so proud that his Strabane yeomanry corps had not taken part in the parade nor worn Orange lilies in their hats that he organised an impromptu celebration, consisting of fresh roasted salmon, which 'we washed down afterwards with a most amazing potation of whiskey punch, drinking every memorable and loyal toast that could be thought of'.

The story of political dissensions in Tyrone has yet to be fully researched and no doubt will show that Strabane had its stresses and divisions in the period. The Catholic Emancipation question was to play an important role until its resolution in 1829 and a report in the *Londonderry Journal* of April 1810 describes the divisions that the issue could engender at a public meeting called to discuss the matter in Omagh. Those who had summoned the meeting wished to pass a series of resolutions favouring a relaxation of penal laws against Catholics and one of the strongest advocates at the meeting was Major Crawford, the recent leader of the Orange yeomanry corps. Strong support for relaxation also came from James Sinclair of Hollyhill and the resolutions were passed with a substantial majority. Little came of this initiative, however, and a further public meeting at Omagh, this time of the freeholders of the county, came out against any immediate action on 'loose, unqualified, unconditional repeal of the remaining popery laws'. In later years similar resolutions were passed and in 1825 Sinclair found himself very much in the minority when he spoke in favour of emancipation at a public meeting of 'the nobility, gentry, clergy and freeholders of the county of Tyrone'.

Conflicts and Fair Day Riots

At local level sectarian conflict flared occasionally and by 1814 was intertwined with protest against tithes. Burgoyne reported on trouble in February and March, with 'the Urney mob' being blamed for the outbreaks. Military parties (yeomanry) were ordered to Magheracrigan, Derg Bridge, Killeter and Clady but this failed to halt the trouble, with the agent reporting to Abercorn in May of a riot at Magheracrigan fair. He believed that there was a concerted plan against the yeomanry and informed Abercorn that he had given them ammunition to protect themselves. Clearly the situation was tense, and in late August 1815 the Tyrone magistrates issued a strong proclamation against further violence at the local fairs. Their action was prompted by a riot at Dunnalong fair on 12 August and information of a planned showdown between the two factions at Dunamanagh fair on the 28 August. A force of military had been made available to help the magistrate uphold order and this had prevented the planned confrontation taking place. Yet it was only postponed and the following year a major fight took place, with one man killed and several badly wounded. Once again the magistrates of

Tyrone were called in to investigate and there were proposals made to take away the patent from Dunamanagh fair as a means of preventing future outrages. The difficulty was that the defeated party in one encounter would be marshalled for revenge at the next fair and it is clear that these had become battlegrounds in this period in many parts of Ulster.

The year 1822 seems to have been another very difficult period, with opposition to tithes an additional factor to the sectarian divisions. Rev. Hamilton of Donagheady was in frequent correspondence with government about the failures of local peace keeping and the level of intimidation to which he was being subjected. Local magistrate James Sinclair accepted that Hamilton was under threat but was not entirely sympathetic to his plight, believing that the searches of the excisemen for stills and the oath-bound natures of the Orange and Ribbonmen societies were contributory factors to the growth of unrest. These latter were apparently becoming more daring in their challenges to Orangemen and a report was sent of a group of Ribbonmen assembled near Plumbridge on 12 July 1822. A magistrate wrote to Dublin castle about a major Ribbonmen attack at Castlederg fair in November when Protestants were allegedly 'beat out of the fair', despite the intervention of troops. Two years later it was the magistrate that was being blamed for the unrest, with calls from the rector of Ardstraw and others for an investigation into the recent disturbances at Newtownstewart. It was claimed that Major James Crawford had not upheld the law impartially and that he had 'made himself obnoxious by his foolish interference'. Clearly there were many who still believed that different standards should be applied to lawbreakers from the different traditions and that Orangeism was not to be equated with Ribbonism when it came to law enforcement.

The passage of the Catholic Emancipation Act in 1829 did not please everyone and the *Strabane Morning Post* carried reports of meetings of Protestant protest groups in both Tyrone and Donegal. James Sinclair had been moved to insert an advertisement in the paper trying to dissuade the Protestant freeholders from being misled by the warnings and threats from many of their leaders but the resolutions had been passed by acclamation. Catholics had also had their demonstrations and resolutions in favour of emancipation, and sectarian divisions were likely to be widened as a result. The paper carried a report in July of an investigation into a minor riot in Strabane on 13 July when opposition had been mounted to an Orange procession through the town. It is possible, however, to read too much into these aberrations, and much has been made of the harmonious meeting of May 1830 when the local parish priest, Rev. Arthur McHugh, presided at a public dinner in thanksgiving for the support given by the Protestant traders and church leaders to the building of the Catholic chapel in Strabane. Much was made in the speeches of the liberal spirit and the harmonious relationships that existed in the town between the different religious groups and the high degree of co-operation that was evident in all spheres of local affairs. Even in the heyday of sectarian divisions there had appeared a greater degree of tolerance in Strabane than elsewhere in Tyrone. The inspector-general's reports for the county had suggested that party spirit prevailed widely but went on to report on an episode in June 1828 when a body of Freemasons marched into the town with weapons drawn and adorned with orange and blue scarves. On representations being made to their leaders, however, of the dangers of conflict, especially on a crowded market day, they dispersed quietly.

The success of emancipation, however, led to renewed attacks on tithes, and in 1832 there were concerted attempts to organise protests and refuse payments. The 'State of the Country' (National Archives, Dublin) papers are a collection of reports by the police and magistrates and Strabane is reported as strong in its opposition to tithes but also to county cess, imposed by the grand jury for roads, bridges and other communication requirements. In July the anti-tithe protest was considered especially strong and the slogan in many parts of the county was for 'half rent and no tithes'. Another focus for popular agitation in the period was against tolls, and an attempt to collect these on the road from Monaghan to Derry at Aughnacloy was strongly resisted. In the end the tithe issue was resolved by a commutation act, whereby they were no longer collected as a separate payment but merged in the rent. This, allied to a reduction in the sum required, effectively took the tithe question out of popular agitation and paved the way for its eventual abandonment in the disestablishment of the Church of Ireland in 1869. It also removed one of the main issues that Catholic and Dissenter had been united on in the previous decades.

Social Conditions – A 'Mini'-Famine in 1800

The years between 1800 and the Great Famine are often seen as the years when there was an inevitable approach to disaster, with steadily worsening conditions and growing poverty. Yet in many ways poverty was no worse nor more threatening than in the previous century, and the history of shortages and mini-famines in the eighteenth century bears out this picture. Strabane in 1798–9 was reportedly prospering and the linen market seemed set to keep expanding. Yet by September 1799 Hamilton was gloomily reporting on a 'most distressing season for farmers' and 'a sudden and unexpected fall in cloth and yarn' at the local market. Such a turnaround did not necessarily mean a famine, however, and it was not until the beginning of the new century, in February 1800, that Hamilton became really alarmist. The scarcity of provisions was forcing 'people of experience to dread everything short of a famine', while by May he was insistent that the poor were in desperation from the high prices and the lack of employment. Matthew Hood at Baronscourt made this same point forcefully to Abercorn:

> Provisions are now five times their usual price, but that is not the worst; there is no employment for the poor; every farmer etc is endeavouring to do his own business, as he considers the meat that a labourer consumes more valuable than his work.

What was even more worrying was the limited extent of the crop planted that year, with the fear that an abundant harvest could not end the cycle of shortage and high prices. Hamilton had once again called for a total ban on private distilling and a more rigid enforcement of the laws by the revenue officers and by March it was suggested that public opinion was forcing the poteen makers to cease their activities and conserve the food supplies. Hood claimed in May that the government action in stopping the malting of barley had prevented a famine but this was only a partial solution. A Strabane relief fund to purchase meal and sell it out at cost met with considerable approval, with over £800 subscribed in March 1800.

Acute poverty forced many families into begging in order to survive and for many this was a shameful necessity. *from* William Carleton's *Traits and Stories of the Irish Peasantry.*

The agents were equally concerned about the poor in the rural areas, especially in the approach to the summer months, when large-scale begging was widely practised in the countryside. The farmers had normally supported the cottiers through these hungry months of May to July but they were having difficulty meeting their own needs and the result was that many of the cottier families were starving, with Hamilton reporting that 'above two thirds of all the cottier houses in the country are deserted, and their families in crowds begging through the country'. Then there were those who were too proud to beg and Hood asked for support also for these starving householders. As in the town the main method was to buy meal and distribute it at cost to those who could buy and on loan to those who were destitute, and Hamilton congratulated himself on the success of his scheme, claiming by November 1800 that 'every shilling has been paid back'. Hood meanwhile had provided additional work on the estate, claiming in July 1800 that he was employing about 200 men and boys, most of whom could not have hoped to find work elsewhere.

There was a reluctance to believe that the scarcity would continue for a second year, and Hamilton was asserting as late as January 1801 that, while he did not believe there would be any real shortages, he felt nevertheless that the poor would probably suffer from high prices and that it 'may still be a little hard' for them. By March there was no longer room for doubt and Hood claimed that 'the poor are still in the most distressed state and the common beggars innumerable', while Hamilton had been forced to acknowledge that 'nothing can exceed the misery and wretchedness of the poor; there have been meetings in almost every parish in the neighbourhood and subscriptions organised for their relief: I do think some of the very poor will die of hunger'. James Sinclair attempted to enlist Abercorn's aid in helping the poor of Leckpatrick parish but James Hamilton cautioned against any acceptance of liability for that area, claiming that 'there are several poorer parishes on your lordship's estate'. A reported vestry meeting at Leckpatrick church in May 1801 to organise a relief collection for the parish saw Hamilton still against any direct assistance, with the poor there 'not as ill off as Ardstraw or Camus'. He claimed that the subscription to the soup kitchen in Strabane had proved a most beneficial measure and was concerned to minimise the extent of landlord contribution. A good harvest that year and an improvement in the linen trade effectively ended the distress and it was reported that beggars had become so selective by August that they would no longer accept potatoes as alms. This was both an inversion of the slogan about beggars not being choosers and a demonstration that actual starvation had been brought to an end. Rent arrears were now the growing concern of Hamilton and he asked for some leeway in allowing the poorer tenants clear their debts.

Food Scarcity in 1808

Another period of concern arose in 1808, when a bad harvest in 1807 and a very harsh winter created serious hardships, made worse by major flooding in late January. Food scarcity was only one part of the difficulty and Burgoyne reported on the acute shortage of fuel for heating during the inclement weather conditions, claiming that 'turf were actually sold for a halfpence each'. Once again there was a major crusade against the poteen makers, with steep fines being levied against those districts where stills were seized and it was remarked that the district of Glenmornan had recently been required to pay £200 for these offences. Relief measures were again set in train for the tenants on the estates, with Burgoyne seeking clarification on whether or not he should assist the cottiers as well as the tenants. The cottiers were generally sub-tenants of the farmers and it was not clear whether the landlord should extend his responsibilities by assisting them. Burgoyne felt that the cottiers were 'the most hurtful thing to an estate' but had also to accept that they were part of the prevailing economic system. Correspondence with Abercorn in the early summer months reported on the extent of food being made available and on the help being given to tenants to allow them to plant crops for that season and the assistance was sufficient to ensure that the crisis would not continue into a second year. The plentiful 1808 harvest was enough to bring prices down to the normal level and end the immediate crisis, though there must have been major concern in August when a major flood threatened the crops; according to reports the storm resulted in the destruction of eleven bridges in the Strabane neighbourhood, with only Newtownstewart and Strabane remaining intact. A helpful landlord and enterprising agent were clearly vital in controlling the periodic fluctuations in living conditions in the eighteenth and early nineteenth centuries and Strabane area was fortunate in the paternalistic help provided by the Abercorn family.

The Origins of Public Health –
A Fever Hospital Established

Poverty was endemic in pre-Famine society and the absence of state assistance placed a huge burden on the local communities. Public health was a source of much concern and many of the food shortages either caused or were the consequences of fever epidemics. In the eighteenth century county infirmaries had been erected to provide some degree of care for fever patients and others needing medical assistance, but the location at Omagh and the limited accommodation meant that the Tyrone hospital was of limited use to Strabane. Dispensaries or out patient treatment centres had also been established as a result of an act of parliament in 1805 but again considerable funding had to come from local resources. It was not until 1814 that a decision was made by the leading people of the town to build a fever or recovery hospital at Strabane and a fund-raising campaign was launched. A series of charity sermons was organised and reports in the *Strabane Morning Post* in 1815 provide details of the fund-raising efforts. Burgoyne in his reports to Abercorn gave the figures collected by each of the main religious denominations, with the Presbyterians raising £63, the Church of Ireland £60 and the Catholics collecting £51. Abercorn himself was expected to contribute and it was settled that the land for the new building should be provided 'on the Newtownstewart side of the town just on the rise of the hill at the pound'. The building erected continued to serve as a dispensary until the earlier part of the twentieth century and in the years after 1815 proved its value to the people of the town.

Famine and Fever 1816–18

A serious disease epidemic struck the area in late 1816 and throughout most of 1817 and many people died as a result. The origins were in another harvest failure in 1816 when exceptionally poor weather in the summer months destroyed a large portion of the crops and prevented the drying of turf necessary for heating and cooking. The consequent shortages were general throughout the whole country and the rise in food prices struck very forcibly against the poor. In March of 1817 Burgoyne was reporting to Abercorn 'that the distress of the poor is without precedent for they have neither food nor fuel', and by June he was pessimistic about the prospects for the coming winter: '[T]imes are not mending nor is there any prospect of it unless there is an abundant crop and even that will scarcely do it . . . the poor are absolutely starving.' One result of this was the vast increase in the number of starving beggars and the *Londonderry Journal* remarked in December 1817 on the 'extraordinary influx of beggars into the city at that early stage of the season'. Relief measures had been organised in the summer of 1817 and government had provided a grant to augment the money raised locally for relief. This was expended through local relief committees at parish level and was a combination of work and food at a reduced figure. Flax was given out to spinners to enable them to earn money and food at cost was provided to large numbers in the summer of 1817. It was not intended that relief alone should suffice to maintain the pre famine living standards but that it would be a supplement to prevent actual starvation, and many became increasingly emaciated during the hungry months of that summer.

By that stage, however, the dreaded fever had taken hold and Burgoyne reported in September 1817 that 'fever is still increasing very much over the face of the country and I would beg to suggest that your lordship subscribe towards those funds'. Reports from the newspapers at the time suggested that the problems of fever were being worsened by the beggars moving into the towns from rural areas and efforts were made to prevent the influx of these unfortunates into the towns. Fear was an important factor in the reaction of the urban leaders since the contagion of the fever threatened the well-off as well as the poor. The main Strabane dispensary doctor at the time, Dr Francis Rogan, has left a graphic account of the crisis in extracts from his recollections in 'An Essay on the State of Ulster in 1820' by Rev. John Graham, based closely on Rogan's published account. Rogan claimed that the establishment of a soup kitchen in the town in the spring of 1817 attracted many starving people from the country areas and that these beggars unwittingly brought the fever with them. Lodging houses at the upper part of the town had provided basic accommodation for a number of these beggars and the fever had taken hold in

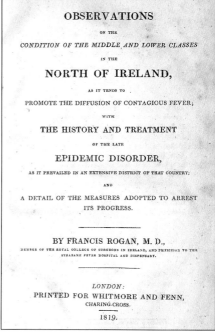

The title page from Dr Rogan's account of the famine and fever epidemic of 1816–1817 in Strabane and other areas in the North of Ireland. Dr Rogan worked in treating the fever in Strabane Fever Hospital in this period.

such premises. Even when public begging was prohibited and resident beggars badged in December 1817, as in the 1801 famine crisis, large numbers of non-resident poor stayed on in the lodging houses and sought relief by whatever means possible.

Rogan's account showed that the existing fever hospital was unable to cope with the numbers suffering in late July and early August, and a temporary hospital had to be fitted up in the courthouse. Money and nursing help were in very short supply and by September the lack of funds had become critical, with the *Strabane Morning Post* seeking support for a charity sermon by the Rev. John Graham in the parish church the following week. A sum of over £100 was raised through this appeal and the fever hospitals continued to deal with the starving population. It was clear that much work would yet be needed to eradicate the fever menace, and Burgoyne in November 1817 issued public notices that advice and medical assistance would be available in each of the manors of the Abercorn estate and provision made for a thorough cleansing of the houses in which fever had been reported. The people of Strabane also felt the need for further action and a public meeting was called at the Townhall for 18 December when proposals were to be put forward concerning regular contributions to a Poor Fund for the starving of the town. Clearly there were still considerable numbers suffering at this late stage and the dangers to the healthy inhabitants remained high:

> Those in private life are as equally subject to contagion as those whose doors are constantly open from their Trade; it is therefore proposed, that a Monthly Subscription should be entered into for the relief of the poor Inhabitants (the miserable situation of whom even at this moment is deplorable in the extreme), by which they should not be permitted to go through the streets for relief, but receive a monthly or weekly Distribution; and that all foreign Beggars should, if possible, be put out of town.

Early the following year normality returned and the numbers receiving treatment in the dispensary and fever hospital dropped to non critical levels. Relief remained, however, a constant drain and the annual reports from the fever hospital continued to urge the need for additional funding and wider and more regular contributions. The *Morning Post* of 11 February 1823 reported on one such general meeting of the governors of the Strabane dispensary and stated that 2,349 patients had been treated during the previous year, of whom 2,262 were cured. Fear was expressed that typhus fever seemed on the increase again and that constant vigilance was needed to ensure that it did not become an epidemic.

Further Famines and Fevers in the 1830s

The early 1830s did see a re-emergence of the famine/fever epidemics and the *Morning Post* provides some detail on the handling of the problems. The Penny Society had been set up following the 1817–18 epidemic to provide regular assistance to those in need and to prevent street begging becoming once again a part of everyday life. This charitable organisation was organised by ladies and provided food and clothing to the needy families of the town. Relief, however, was only provided after careful examination of the circumstances and the annual report in January 1830 made clear that every effort was made to assist the needy in self-help: flax was provided for spinning and housewives paid for the work done rather than provided with free food. Meal tickets and grocery tickets were provided to the old and the ill and householders encouraged to cleanse their homes and adopt more hygienic living conditions. Unemployment was stressed as the major problem besetting the poor and the report described graphically the unimaginable miserable hovels inhabited by the very poorest. The regular weekly collections for the Penny Fund had sufficed in good years, but the worsening economic situation in the late 1820s meant that in the crisis year of 1830 further collections were needed. There was a report of a charity sermon in July in aid of the relief funds and the report in January 1831 made clear that the year past had been one of 'awful and unprecedented pressure of the present distress'. The report went on to provide explanations for the almost total breakdown of the economy and painted a bleak picture of the situation. The 'complete breaking down of our linen manufacture' was augmented by the absence of male employment, the 'almost complete inoccupation of the females' and the very low wages on offer for any type of work.

The following year saw the town hit by a major flood and this again necessitated a relief programme. The *Morning Post* of 22 November 1831 described the flood as arising from a combination of melting snow and heavy rains and reported that Main Street, Castle Street, New Street and part of the Back Street had been flooded, as well as the Bridge End part of the town. A collection was taken up from the more prosperous inhabitants and a Mendicity Association organised for further fund raising by charity sermons in each of the main churches. A report stated that 'fuel and straw had been given out to more than 200 families whose houses had been inundated', as well as a distribution of food in the immediate aftermath of the flooding. The same report that gave notice of the church collections was unapologetic about the purpose of the funds and advocated liberal donations so as 'to prevent the much to be dreaded evil of street begging'. The total collection in the churches amounted to over £30 and this was to be used over the coming winter to relieve distress and help repair some of the flood damage of another severe season.

The Fever Hospital had been of immense benefit in the 1817 epidemic and was to be called upon in 1832 when the dreaded cholera reached Strabane. The hospital had depended on charitable donations and the Penny

Society had contributed to its upkeep through the years. An examination of the itemised accounts of the society shows that part of this funding was raised by fines imposed at the petty sessions for minor transgressions. Thus James Vance had to pay 10 shillings to the fever hospital when convicted of smashing a gate belonging to a Mr Hughes, while Margaret Toner, Owen McCullow, Hugh Mc Ginley and James Thompson were all convicted of assault, and fines ranging from 5 to 30 shillings were donated to the hospital. John James Burgoyne, Abercorn's agent, had donated fines levied on several people 'for cutting timber in Clougheen Wood and Strabane Glen' while linen merchant, Mr W. Gwynne, paid over a sum of 12 shillings which he had 'deducted from a weaver's wages for attempted embezzlement'. This must have been Strabane's nineteenth-century answer to community service and certainly few could question the worthiness of the recipient.

Cholera Epidemic 1832

In July 1832 the much-feared cholera had arrived in neighbouring counties and a Health Board was established to co-ordinate the preventative and relief efforts. An application was to be made to government for a £200 grant which would be necessary 'for the purpose of cleansing the houses, removing nuisances, preventing travelling beggars, providing fuel, straw, and nourishment for the poor of the District, and for the purchase of Blankets and Bedding for the Fever Hospital'. The town was divided into three districts, with an inspection group for each, and people suffering from fever were encouraged to seek help in the hospital. Clearly there was still a degree of resistance among the poor to admission to the hospital, and vigilance was necessary on the part of the inspection teams so that sufferers from the disease could be isolated. By October the *Morning Post* reported on the generous subscriptions to a relief fund for those families suffering from cholera and remarked that 'perhaps no town in Ireland has been more severely visited by Cholera than Strabane. In fact it has now the appearance of a deserted place', and the establishment of a soup kitchen to provide for over 800 persons on a daily basis was seen as essential in combating the crisis. October had seen the disease at its peak and by the end of the year the worst had passed. Details on the numbers of deaths are scanty but the figures from the Health Board for late September show up to seven per day dying from the disease. Even those figures are likely to be on the low side since they only account for deaths in the town area. It is unlikely that cholera made any distinction between urban and rural dwellers in its choice of victims. Contemporaries, however, were inclined to play down the impact of disasters and accept them as part of the natural order. Charity and relief measures were necessary to meet the crises but were brought to an end as quickly as possible.

Traveller Reports on Strabane in the
Early Nineteenth Century

Increasingly in the nineteenth century, travellers began to pay some attention to the living conditions of the working classes and John Gamble provided some detail about Strabane in his *Sketches of History, Politics, and
Manners in Dublin and the North of Ireland, in 1810*. He recorded that

> The houses of the respectable inhabitants are generally two stories, nor are
> any higher than three. Though many of the houses are old, they have a
> modern appearance; leaden windows have given place to sash ones and the
> projecting buttresses and old fashioned turrets have disappeared like the
> hands that reared them.

More descriptive was his account of the homes of the labouring classes,
which he found unable to praise:

> There is a species of squalid wretchedness, more akin to neglect than pover-
> ty – for in reality there was not poverty; they had the necessaries of life, and
> they who have the necessaries cannot be said to be poor. I have seen them
> at their meals, which are either of flesh meat or salt herrings, with potatoes
> and butter or milk . . . In their persons, however, they appear to be more
> cleanly; they shave tolerably regularly, and change their linen, perhaps,
> twice a week. The upper class of inhabitants are either merchants or shop-
> keepers; they carry on considerable business, and seem an industrious and
> respectable body of men.

These accounts were little more than fleeting impressions and Strabane was
of significance only because Gamble was a native of the town. His test of
poverty is of some interest and placed him firmly on the side of the well to
do. It appeared that the working class was not expected to rise above subsis-
tence levels and should be content with such a position.

Another traveller's report in 1833, that of A. Atkinson in *Ireland in the
Nineteenth Century*, gave considerably more scope to a description of the
town and its people, as a result of a visit made in 1830. He praised the growing prosperity of the town and attributed much of it to the canal and the
consequent improvement in communications with the wider world.
Mention was made of the weekly corn and linen markets, though it was stated that this latter had fallen much in recent years and the decline in this previous high earner had resulted in widespread poverty and spreading
mendacity. Atkinson went on to remark on the failure of the local magistrates to regulate the markets and establish proper and accessible locations
for the sale of goods. He was also highly critical of the operation of county
and local cess, with substantial variations in the sums demanded in neighbouring parishes and felt that the Rev. Hamilton of Strabane had some

explaining to do to justify the apparent inequalities. Atkinson's account then went on to look at what he headlined 'Charity and Sound Policy of Strabane' in the handling of food shortages in the summer of 1830. The scarcity of potatoes and oatmeal led to a rapid rise in prices and threatened serious shortages until the townspeople raised a collection and bought a large stock of oatmeal in Liverpool and Glasgow. This was then sold out at cost and prevented the anticipated rise in prices, as well as providing a supply of food for the most needy. What is most surprising in Atkinson's account was his claim that the merchants were the main instigators of the project, since it was this group who stood most to gain from scarcity and subsequent high prices. In this instance they were taking a highly principled and moral stance and must have felt under a degree of pressure to ignore the promptings of self-interest.

Linen Industry Collapse

What was also significant about the Atkinson account was the reported failure of the linen trade, the effects of which were felt in the whole of Ulster by the 1830s. Many families had depended greatly on the part-time earnings from both spinning and weaving, and the introduction of machine spinning had left the hand-loom weavers at the mercy of the factory owners. A major parliamentary inquiry in the late 1830s found clear evidence that the domestic basis of the linen industry had irretrievably collapsed, with major consequences for a large section of the rural population. At Dungannon the investigation found that 'the linen trade has greatly declined' and proceeded to Strabane, 'at one period the great yarn market of the counties Tyrone, Donegal, parts of Armagh, Derry and Down, and the point to which the yarn produced in Fermanagh, Cavan, Monaghan, Leitrim and even Sligo, was sent for sale. This trade is almost at an end, the introduction of mill-spun yarn having limited the market and the profits of hand-spun yarn.' A witness to the inquiry suggested that there was less than one tenth of the amount of webs offered for sale at the Strabane market compared to earlier years of the century and claimed that only those weavers working for a manufacturer could hope to survive in the existing climate. Gone were the days of the independent weaver and evidence to the inquiry added that the condition of weavers had deteriorated to the same level as that of the agricultural labourer. But it was the collapse of the earning potential of the cottage-based spinning that was to have most repercussions on the standard of living: the *Ordnance Survey Memoirs* for many of the Tyrone parishes in the mid 1830s stress the disastrous impact this had on the worsening poverty levels of many of the rural labouring families. A major investigation had been established in the early 1830s to assess the degree of Irish poverty, and the evidence of some of the leading people in the Strabane area left little room for doubt on either the extent of worsening poverty or the prime causes. Thus Rev. Arthur McHugh, parish priest of Camus and Clonleigh, reported that 'conditions had much deteriorated since 1815 due to the failure of the linen trade, high rents and low agricultural prices', while the Rev. F.L. Gore from Donagheady agreed that conditions had 'deteriorated in consequence of the decline in the linen trade and rent continuing nearly as high as before'. Rev. Gamble from Leckpatrick agreed that 'the condition (of the labourers) is much worse I should think'. Similar views came from Rev. Jones of Urney and from Rev. Hume of Leckpatrick and thus there was a general consensus that action was needed to remedy this worsening position.

Setting up the Workhouse

The problem arose over solutions, and the Irish Poor Inquiry reported in 1836 that the workhouse system, recently introduced in England, was unsuitable for Ireland, where the problem of regular and extensive poverty and semi-starvation was much more widespread. It came down finally to a question of cost: the British government was determined to impose the English system, whereby local property holders would be rated to pay for poor relief through a workhouse system. There was an outcry, mainly from large property owners, and the Tyrone Grand Jury passed a strong resolution against the introduction of this new Poor Law at their meeting in March 1838. According to the scheme, Strabane was to erect a workhouse and provide relief and a public meeting was convened in the town in November. At this meeting James Sinclair spoke strongly against the proposed measure and advocated instead a tax on absentee landlords who were doing nothing to help solve the ongoing problems of poverty and relief. Other strong condemnations of the proposed Poor Law and its effects on the local rates, as well as the burden it placed on hard-pressed property owners, were voiced by Rev. George Smithwick of Leckpatrick and by Major Humphreys, agent to the duke of Abercorn. Not everyone, however, was against the scheme and local lawyer Henry McCay made the point that the property owners were more concerned to save themselves money than to provide relief to the starving, and he advocated acceptance of the principle that the better-off should contribute towards the relief of the poor. The *Londonderry Journal* echoed McCay's arguments and asked for a fair trial for the new system, despite its rejection by property owners. In many ways, of course, the public meetings were little more than token protests, as the decision had already been taken: the Strabane Poor Law Union was set up in April 1838, and the building of the workhouse started in November of that year on land donated by Abercorn. Poor Law Guardians, drawn from property owners in the district, were to manage the workhouse and the Poor Law system. The Strabane building was completed by 1841, with the first admissions in November of that year. Only time would tell whether or not it would meet the needs of the poor in Strabane or whether it would collapse under the weight of destitution that a famine year would bring.

A Survey of Social Conditions 1844

This was a great period for governmental investigations and a further inquiry in 1844, the Devon Commission, travelled to different parts of the country taking evidence on the problems associated with land holding in Ireland. Strabane was one of the inquiry points and a number of local people were asked to provide evidence about the situation locally. James Sinclair was in no doubt that the lot of the labourers and cottier farmers was deteriorating in these years and was critical of the operation of the rating system under the Poor Law, claiming that the poorest divisions had to pay the highest rates while the better off districts that had not very many poor in their areas were levied at the lowest rates. He went on to observe that the workhouse at that stage, 18 April 1844, did not have many paupers and concluded that 'I do not think it will be ever half full'. Events in the following years would show how far off the mark his predictions were, but even then his conclusions were controverted by other witnesses. Robert McCrea of Grange had no doubt that labourers were 'as a whole in a very wretched state, whether as regards lodging, food or clothing' and was a strong advocate of a more supportive approach from the landlord class, especially in the making of improvements on the farms. Rev. William Browne, parish priest of Camus and Clonleigh, also provided evidence and was emphatic that the living standards of the smaller farmers and the labourers had declined and were still worsening. Work, he claimed, was in short supply, especially in agriculture, with poor prices forcing farmers to rely on their own labour rather than pay out wages. There had apparently been some little change in the linen trade and Rev. Browne suggested that 'this last winter we have had plenty of employment by the Belgians, who have introduced a new system of cleaning flax by hand labour, which has done more good than anything that has happened here for the last forty years'. It was his view of the Poor Law, however, that engaged most attention, when he declared that it had done more to injure the poor than anything else within his recollection. Rev. Browne's argument was that a number of landlords were anxious to get rid of the cottiers, in fear that they might become a burden on the rates, and this was leading to an increasing number of evictions. These evicted people then had to move into the towns, moving them away from potential work opportunities near the farmers.

Another witness at Strabane was Francis O'Neill, a linen bleacher at Burndennet, and he advocated government support for the reclamation of waste land as a means of stimulating employment and reducing destitution. His comments on the level of poverty locally were emphatic. It appeared that in 1843 a sum of £200 had been distributed to 500 poor families in the Leckpatrick parish from a fund under the direction of the clergy. They had called in the Poor Law Guardians and thus O'Neill's involvement and growing awareness of the extent of the problems of poverty:

> Until I went through that division I did not know that such destitution existed; for the parish is beyond the average, in point of comfort. There was a great want of regular and constant employment for able bodied men and women. Their houses in general are bad, and badly suited for health or comfort. I discovered cases where the family slept in the clothes they wore during the day, having no bed clothes. The cottiers in general are not well treated, nor are their wants and necessaries attended to as I think they should be.

Major Humphreys, Abercorn's agent, agreed in his evidence that the position of the cottiers was one of great difficulty but did not accept that the landlord or his agent had any influence over the situation nor did he accept the view of widespread poverty as painted by O'Neill and others. Mention was made of the recently established factory of Mulholland, Herdman and Co. and the 600 jobs that were being provided there, but Humphreys held out little hope of any action to improve the position of the cottiers and agricultural labourers. They and their families were to be the major sufferers in the famine that was to begin in the following year, and it is possible that the information collected by the Devon Commission, and its recommendations for extensive government intervention in extending cultivation in Ireland, might have done something to stave off the disaster of the Great Famine had there been enough time to implement the changes suggested.

The 1841 Census

The other main source of information on pre-Famine Strabane is the 1841 census and its portrayal of living conditions, as shown in the house classification. There were four house classes adopted for evaluating living conditions, with Class 1 being the best and Class 4 the worst. Class 4 houses were those with single rooms and generally a thatched roof, while Class 3 houses would have had two or three rooms and were single-storey. In the town area the population in 1841 was recorded as 4,704, with 628 of those described as visitors and 376 as servants. Omagh had an even higher number of visitors in a population of just under 3,000, so it is clear that large numbers not identified as being part of urban families were present at the census-taking. In the house descriptions, some questions can be asked.

The figures for house types were:

Class 1	68 (9 %)
Class 2	287 (37%)

Class 3	263 (34%)
Class 4	158 (20%)
Total occupied	776
Unoccupied	106

It is this last figure that is so puzzling. How do we explain the large number of unoccupied houses in an era when there was a rising or at least a stationary population? The less trustworthy 1831 census had given a population of 4,700 for Strabane, while an 1821 report had suggested 4,136. Where would the housing surplus have come from? Increasing poverty might certainly explain why so many families were prepared to accept a high level of overcrowding and the large number of visitors could be partly explained by lodgers, helping to offset the rent for the houses. The larger percentage of Class 2 houses would signify that there were many two-storey buildings and that slate was widely used in roofing in the towns. The Class 4 houses would normally have been found on the edges of the towns and these would have been the homes of labourers, many of whom might have worked seasonally at agricultural tasks in the nearby farming districts.

The census also provided detail on what occupation heads of families were involved in. Strabane's report showed that 126 were engaged in agriculture, 562 in manufacturing and trade and 184 in other non-specified lines of work. This latter category would have included professional people such as doctors, lawyers and schoolteachers, but overall the figures show the importance of trade and industry to the people of Strabane at that stage.

Literary standards were also assessed in this census and the figures showed that 40% of those aged five years and over could both read and write, with the figure for males in advance of that for females. Up to 26%, predominantly females, responded that they could read only, while 34% were recorded as being unable to either read or write. Female literacy was generally lower at this period, since women were not expected to engage to the same extent in trade or industry. In the whole Strabane barony, including the rural areas, the percentage figures for literacy were considerably lower, suggesting that the townspeople had an advantage in schooling opportunities or incentives. The barony figure for those able to read and write was 26%, while nearly 45% could do neither. The absence of schools and the constant struggle for survival would have reduced the relevance of education for many in the rural areas.

Housing also showed considerable differences between urban and rural areas. The table below shows both the whole barony, including Strabane town, as well as two rural parishes. (Note – The Strabane town section is removed from the Camus parish figures.)

HOUSING	STRABANE BARONY	CAMUS	LECKPATRICK
Class 1	120 (1%)	31 (1%)	5 (1%)
Class 2	2178 (17%)	88 (20%)	157 (18%)
Class 3	5514 (44%)	165 (38%)	377 (43%)
Class 4	4736 (38%)	174 (40%)	334 (38%)

It can be seen that while Class 2 houses predominated in the town, it was the Class 3 and Class 4 houses that were most usual in rural areas, and Camus was even worse off with regard to housing than Leckpatrick, having a greater percentage of the single-room cabins that denoted poverty and hardship. These Class 4 houses would generally have belonged to the labourers and cottiers; the farmers were often supposed to maintain these houses but rarely did so. It must also be remembered that while these figures appear rather shocking they paint a picture of relative prosperity for Strabane and Tyrone in general. Donegal and other counties on the western seaboard had a much higher percentage of Class 4 houses and were to suffer accordingly in the Great Famine.

It was clear then that Ireland was suffering economic stagnation in the mid nineteenth century and that poverty was widespread throughout society. Strabane had not grown in the previous decades even though the population of Ireland had risen sharply from 1800, clearly demonstrating that there were few opportunities for work in the town in the period. Manufacturing was on a small scale and the jobs in trade and marketing were limited. Sion Mills was only just emerging as a potential employment centre, and factory work would necessitate changes in outlook and social attitudes. Emigration must have been considerable, and the presence of emigration agents in the town of Strabane signifies that there were ample recruits in an impoverished population. Some progress had been made in public health and providing for the destitute, but there were many who saw little chance of escaping the poverty trap if they remained in Strabane.

The Great Famine in Strabane and District

The Great Famine began in 1845 but few at the time recognised the onset of a major catastrophe. In Tyrone the *Tyrone Constitution* reported in early September on the very promising crops, with the assertion that 'the crop of potatoes will be very abundant here'. Even as late as November the paper was still advising against any undue concern, and argued that the worst of the panic was on the decline, with every prospect of 'an abundance of potatoes both for use and for seed'. Not everyone felt so confident, however, and a Strabane public meeting was called in early December to assess the situation and plan for relief. It was estimated that the crops locally had suffered a loss of about one third and that every effort would be needed to prevent sharply escalating food prices the following spring and early summer. Present at the meeting were Lord Claud Hamilton MP, Major Humphreys, James Sinclair, Rev. James Smith, Rev. William Knox, Rev. Smithwick, Rev. Charles Douglas and Rev. Fr Conroy. Local guardians were requested to survey the crop losses. No action was decided on at this meeting and it was felt that the normal relief measures, augmented by the now functioning workhouse, should be sufficient to deal with the problems locally. There did not appear to be any rush yet to avail of the new Poor Law relief centre, and returns for January 1846 showed a figure of 251 inmates in the workhouse, an increase of only 22 on the previous year. By April of 1846 the figure for inmates was 250, the exact same as in the corresponding period the previous year.

One year's crop dislocation was not treated as unusual and a bumper crop in 1846 would have restored the balance. People watched the new potato crop anxiously, and in July 1846 the *Constitution* reported on the spread of the feared blight, with more alarming reports the following month: '[M]any fields are already quite destroyed and every morning affords additional evidence that the pestilence is rapidly extending its blighting influence; indeed the fear is becoming general that the whole crop will be totally lost.' By September the newspaper was appealing to all those with means to come forward and arrange a programme of help for a population staring into disaster. Sinclair summoned a distress meeting in Strabane and the attendance this time included Humphreys, Revs. Smithwick, Smith, Goudy, Atkinson, Conroy, William Browne, Porter and Chamber, with Dr Stewart, J.R. Auchinleck, James Cochrane and William Sigerson also part of the gathering. This was very much in the nature of a preliminary meeting to gauge the possible extent of distress and set in train relief measures. Major Humphreys spoke of the need for the wealthy to provide for the needy and issued a veiled warning that Abercorn would not provide carte blanche assistance but would be concerned primarily with his own tenants. Clearly, there were calls for an appeal to government for public works as a means of providing employment and purchasing capacity, but not everyone agreed with the direction of the meeting; a Mr Devlin claimed to be speaking for the working class and advised them to put no trust in landlords, who only wanted to improve their own lands. He proposed that the meeting should seek government help for the development of a ship canal to the Foyle and Derry and thus provide ample work for all in need of it. Rather than engage in divisive arguments, however, the meeting adjourned after having appointed a committee of clergy to assess the probable destitution during the following year.

This committee reported in early October, the main conclusion being that local relief could not possibly deal with the level of distress that would be met with and that an immediate application should be made for government relief funding. The figures given for the likely destitute in each parish were:

Estimated numbers of destitute 1846–1847

Camus	2047
Urney	1533
Leckpatrick	1134
Donagheady	2025

As a temporary measure, Fr Browne proposed the opening of a fund to buy provisions and selling out the food at cost to the families of those at present unemployed. Subscriptions would be collected by the clergy and leading men in both rural and urban areas and this measure would go some way to meeting the crisis in the short term. But this proposal met some opposition, with local barrister, John McCullagh, speaking against the proposal to establish a market for cheap food. This, he claimed, would be unfair to the farmers and merchants and would allow government to evade its responsibility to provide for the unemployed able-bodied labourer. People were being asked to tax themselves to support people who would be able to help themselves if sufficient work was made available. Clearly, this was a serious matter. The new poor law of 1838 had claimed to do away with the need for temporary relief measures by establishing a regular rate payment as part of support for the poor, and yet additional payments were being required at the first sign of crisis.

The town commissioners supported the idea of a ship canal and at a meeting on 9 October decided to lodge an application with parliament for special assistance on the project. It was argued that this would minimise the other public works necessary to deal with distress and reduce the potential rates burden, since otherwise public works would have to be paid for out of local taxation. There is no evidence that the proposal got the support of Abercorn, and it was soon made clear that parliament was not planning any large-scale exceptional expenditures to meet the Irish crisis. That relief would have to be paid for locally was the insistent message coming forward from parliament and thus the emphasis shifted to the local works programme to be approved by the magistrates. A report in the *Londonderry Standard* on 23 October 1846 provided details of the money voted for various schemes at the Strabane session: £30,000 was to be requested to help with the cost of the canal, on condition that there would be no burden on the local people. A similar proposal for £40,000 towards the construction of the railway through the district, to be redeemed later by the railway company, was also mooted but it was soon clear that government would have none of it. A further session the following week had to levy new rates on the various electoral districts and accept proposals for limited works on public roads and bridges. A sum was set aside for the building of a flood wall at Strabane while further measures proposed repairs to Ballcolman Lane and repairing footpaths and by-streets in the town. To administer these relief measures a relief committee appointed by government was required in each district, with the assistance and advice of the local board of guardians. The early appointments were:

Camus	Rev. James Smith; Mr Michael Ramsey
Urney	Rev. Robert Knox, JP
Leckpatrick	Rev. G . Smithwick; Rev. M. Chambers
Dunamanagh	Hon. Rev. Charles Douglas; Rev. John Monteith
Newtownstewart	John Rodgers, JP; J.G. Ramsey

These were the people who would assess the level of need of the various claimants and ensure that funding was properly directed. They would act in conjunction with the local poor law guardians and try to ensure that money went as far as possible and lasted as long as possible.

Growing Destitution 1847–8

The reports suggest that destitution soon made its appearance and by December 1846 Leckpatrick relief committee was expressing concern at the extent of the need in the area. A meeting called by the committee in early January of 1847 advocated the imposition of a further rate collection of one shilling in the pound on the inhabitants of the parish and thus signified that the situation was worsening. Strabane town had its own relief committee also in the period and there was a general acceptance that exceptional measures were needed in an exceptional situation. Abercorn was reportedly providing for the starving on the Baronscourt estate by the employment of up to 600 labourers and the provision of a soup kitchen, where 200 families were being supported four times weekly. In Urney parish the relief committee was working hard to overcome the destitution but the *Standard* reported in mid-March on the death by starvation of Patrick McDaid, an elderly man on the estate of 'an unsubscribing non-resident landlord'. The report added that he was receiving a weekly dole of 5 lb of meal, just like 200 other destitutes in the parish, and went on to allege that the recent dismissals of many workers from the Sion Mills had greatly augmented the problems of the parish and its relief committee. This latter claim was partly challenged in the following week, when a spokesperson for Herdmans claimed that the lay-offs were kept to a minimum but were necessitated by market conditions and would hopefully be only temporary. Such an explanation may have been justified by strict economics but was of little consolation to families deprived of income in the midst of a major crisis.

The worst period of crisis was in the winter and spring of 1847 and the term 'Black '47' was used to denote the suffering endured by the population at large. Strabane was probably more fortunate than many areas in having a concerned local leadership willing to take charge of relief measures and raise the necessary funding to carry them through. It was clear that from an early stage the local leadership had accepted that the existing Poor Law would be incapable of dealing with the immensity of the crisis and that outdoor relief in the traditional manner would be the most appropriate means of providing real help. The soup kitchens and the parish relief measures were important in keeping families together and preventing a rush on the workhouse, and government came to accept by the spring of that year that outdoor relief was necessary if the country was to get back to any semblance of normality. Strabane's leaders could take some consolation from the fact that they were prepared to look at famine relief practically, rather than being restrained by the theoretical concerns of an uncaring administration. Outdoor relief became the accepted method of dealing with the famine from the spring of 1847 and this continued until its sudden abandonment by government in July of 1848. Figures for Strabane poor law union in the early months of 1848 show just how critical it had become in the fight against starvation.

Average Weekly Outdoor Relief in Strabane Union 1848

MONTH	NO. OF FAMILIES
February	1129
March	1407
April	1582
May	1607
June	1301
July	1084

Government estimated that these figures represented only about 4% of the population in need of active assistance, but the figures are for heads of families only, and if we estimate that another four or five mouths might be depending on the soup or meal that was being made available, we get a truer picture of the destitution level. And if these families had been forced into the workhouse, the system would clearly have collapsed totally.

The Famine Workhouse

Strabane workhouse had come under severe pressure from the beginning of 1847 and was stretched to capacity for part of the year, despite the efforts of the relief committees outside. Only the most desperate sought the refuge of the workhouse, and there are numerous stories from the south and west of the country of whole families being denied admission because of overcrowding. Strabane did not have such problems, though there is one report of a family being refused help in December 1847 because they could not prove their entitlement to relief in Strabane union. The father and one of the children died, and the subsequent inquest made the master of the workhouse appear to have an uncaring attitude to those seeking support.

(See W.J. Carlin's account of this incident in Jack Johnston (ed.), *Workhouses of the North West*, WEA [1996].) In December of 1846 there was a noticeable increase in admissions, with 553 inmates, compared to a figure of 225 for the corresponding period in 1845. Thereafter there was a steady rise in admissions, and for the next three years the workhouse was often filled to its capacity of 800, and in fact had to increase the limit to 1,000 to help cater for the large numbers demanding help. The winter months were always the peak period, and the opening of a fever hospital in this period also helped reduce the pressure on the actual workhouse; previously, there had been no distinction between those in full health and those labouring under illness in the admissions, but the emergence of a virulent famine fever meant that separate provision had to be made for the very ill.

The high death rates in the workhouses in the winter of 1847 must have been a major deterrent to those needing relief, and Omagh had over one third of the workhouse inmates ill in the early part of that year, with more than 20 dying in one week. Strabane faced a similar problem by late March when 45 inmates had died during one week. This was sufficiently alarming to call for a special inquiry, and the guardians published their findings to allay the panic that had developed. It appeared from their report that of the 45 who had died, 32 were under ten years of age and 9 were over sixty years old. The main defence of the report was that 18 had died within ten days of admission to the workhouse, and that there was thus no fever epidemic in the hospital. It is certainly likely that families waited as long as possible before seeking admission to the fever hospital, and reports like the above would have made many delay still longer before entering what was increasingly like a death-trap.

The workhouse figures do not necessarily reflect the severity of the famine and the relative fall in residence figures after March 1847 was a reflection of the government's acceptance of the principle of outdoor relief. Some comparisons between the years 1846–8 are shown in the following figures for inmates in Strabane workhouse. These figures are monthly averages.

Workhouse Inmates

MONTH	1846	1847	1848
January	252	660	900
February	238	794	992
March	242	717	846
April	250	600	852

It is significant that the figures for 1848 are so much higher than for 1847, despite the fact that the potato harvest of the latter year had shown some improvement over the previous two years. Clearly the depth of famine had been such that it was going to take longer than one season to recover, especially since few people could afford to buy the seed necessary for planting the 1847 crop. And some parts of the country were even slower in recovering, with another harvest failure in 1848 delaying still further the longed for recovery. Despair must have been hard to avoid in these years and emigration seen as the only chance of longer-term survival, if the means could be found to move.

The Impact of the Famine on Strabane

So just how badly did Strabane suffer in these years? One guide is to compare the census returns of 1841 and 1851 in order to assess the major changes. The Strabane Poor Law Union in 1841 had a population of 36,251, and this would have risen by the onset of the famine to over 37,000. By 1851, however, the numbers had dropped to 30,367, a fall of over 16%. An even greater fall is seen in the number of occupied houses, with a decline from 6,399 to 5,157, or 19%. Clearly many families had to move from their homes in this famine period. The question is, What happened to them? Where did they go to? Clearly, migration is one answer, and that raises the question of where displaced persons would or indeed could have gone to for relief and safety. America, Britain or some of the urban centres in Ireland are the likely destinations of many of those who survived and moved.

Many towns saw a growth of population in these years, with labourers and dispossessed cottiers flocking for relief to the urban centres. In the Strabane case, however, this did not happen and the population of the town declined from 4,704 to 4,324 in the period, while other towns in Tyrone increased in size during the same years. Clearly there was little to attract the dispossessed from the rural areas into impoverished Strabane, and most moved further away when the decision to move had been made. It is likely too that part of the town's poor had been caught up in the famine and there would have been some population movement away from Strabane itself in the crisis years. We can see evidence of such movement if we examine an area on the outskirts of Strabane, for example the Townparks area in Leckpatrick parish. There the population had risen from 30 in 1841 to 261 in 1851, and the number of houses had risen from 3 to 42. A similar rise had occurred in the Townparks area of Camus parish. It seems likely that rough cabins were erected on the outskirts of the town and poor people had collected there, waiting for relief or preparatory to moving on. To compensate for this increase in the population on the outskirts of the town while showing a falling urban area population overall, according to the census figures, there must have been a considerable decline elsewhere in Strabane. The puzzling question is, Who did move? Was it the very poor or was it those above the poverty line escaping while they still could?

General statistics, even at parish or Poor Law Union level, can be misleading, as is again illustrated in the Strabane figures. It could be concluded that the population decline was somewhat under 20% and that the famine, therefore, had not very seriously impacted on the district. But an examination of townland changes can show a much deeper effect. In the portion of Ardstraw parish in the Strabane Poor Law Union, the total population decline was almost 25%, while the Baronscourt electoral division suffered a much higher fall of 44%. In Leckpatrick parish, townlands such as Backfence, Ballydonaghy or Ballyskeagh suffered losses of nearly 50% in population, with the population of Silverhill falling from 89 to 44 inhabitants. When we see that many of these areas suffered a corresponding fall in the number of inhabited houses, it is obvious that a large number of families were forced to move and seek new homes elsewhere. This was to have a lasting impact and for the following sixty years the population of most rural areas showed a steady fall and a continuous contraction in the number of occupied houses.

Strabane town fared little better and the figures for the rest of the nineteenth century saw a stagnation in population size. The figure for 1891 has to be treated with care, since the urban area was expanded from 253 acres to 1857 acres for this latter survey, and the increase in population was thus due to a larger statistical base.

Strabane Population Figures 1821–1926

YEAR	POPULATION
1821	4136
1831	4700
1841	4704
1851	4324
1861	4184
1871	4309
1881	4196
1891	5013
1901	5033
1911	5107
1926	5156

There was little evidence of an expanding town in the years after 1851, and any growth in one decade was likely to be short-lived. Continued emigration to the industrial centres of Britain and to the rapidly expanding United States ensured that the size and character of Strabane changed little in the second half of the nineteenth century, while its rural hinterland suffered a constant haemorrhaging of population and youthful initiative. The eighteenth-century promise was little more than a distant memory and comments such as that in the 1870 *Ulster Directory* that 'Strabane is a large and flourishing market town, the seat of important manufacturers' may have been pleasing to the inhabitants but far from an accurate portrayal of what was really happening.

9 Economic developments in Strabane 1800–1900

MICHAEL HARRON

Comprehensive data on the economy of Strabane and District in the nineteenth century are difficult to obtain. This leaves summaries which have appeared during the period in the form of directories. They are a valuable historical source and can provide a great deal of information on people and businesses, as well as descriptions of individual towns and villages. They also often give the names of local tradesmen, clergy and town officials. On the other hand they can contain errors, such as wrong locations of businesses, incorrect spelling of names, and may not be totally comprehensive in their coverage. Where dates are quoted, the information could be up to one year older than this, due to the time needed to compile, print and distribute the publication.

The first directory found to give details of Strabane appeared in 1820, and others followed at intervals until 1861, when the *Derry Almanac* started publication. This continued as a yearly volume up to the 1950s. Unfortunately, a complete series of this could not be located by the author and so no continuous record of the nineteenth century was available for this review.

The directory of 1820 states that Strabane was 101 miles north-west of Dublin, and this demonstrates the fact that the Irish unit of one mile was quite an amount longer than the Imperial measure, which is the standard at present. This usage continued throughout the century in the *Derry Almanac*, but Imperial measures were quoted in the *Belfast and Province of Ulster Directory* from 1854.

The chief feature of Strabane was that it had well-established and extensive markets. This was a summation of the economic nature of Strabane in that it was of a service type rather than an industrial base. The Industrial Revolution had begun in Great Britain during the 1700s and it spread to other parts of Europe and to North America in the early 1800s. As will be seen later, at the start of the century the only industry of note was that of linen manufacture. This, however, was probably of the 'cottage industry' arrangement. The introduction of the border with the Republic in the 1920s cut Strabane off from a major part of its overall marketing area and resulted in a rapid decline from which some commentators assert that it has never recovered.

The linen trade for cloth and yarn was of great importance, making Strabane in 1820 the third town in Ireland for the quality and quantity of that branch of manufacture. The provision trade (mutton, beef and pork) was also very extensive, the Strabane brands being highly esteemed both at home and abroad. The chief outlets were England and Scotland.

In 1856 Strabane ranked as the third in the county (though largest on the basis of population), and was progressing in size and commerce. By 1862 it was first and this continued up to at least 1878. The census of 1891 showed Strabane with a population of 5,013, whereas Omagh had 4,039, Cookstown 3,841 and Dungannon 3,812.

Infrastructure

In 1837 Lewis noted a number of improvements to the district in that new roads had been constructed to Derry, Newtownstewart and Castlefin, the bridge over the Mourne had been widened and that at Lifford extended. A title deed suggests that the Curley Hill road had also been upgraded around 1817, to make a new road to Dunamanagh.

In all publications the canal was identified as an important asset. By 1862 a Strabane Steamboat Company had been formed. This originated in the growing commerce of the town, and a wish to have a desirable transport for heavy goods between Derry and Strabane, by the canal and river. Before this, trade was carried on by lighters carrying about 20,000 tons annually between the two towns. The interest in these was bought up by the

ECONOMIC DEVELOPMENT 1800–1900   181

Company, and a steam dredge purchased to deepen the canal and river. A tug steamer was also purchased to carry on the traffic. The chairman was T.W.D. Humphreys, the secretary was James McFarlane, and the superintendent was Roderick Gormley. T.W.D. Humphreys resided at Milltown House and was a major landowner, as well as the estate manager for the Abercorn estate. James McFarlane lived at Melmount and was a smaller landowner. Roderick Gormley was an auctioneer, valuator and general commission agent at Patrick Street.

The railways also expanded throughout the century. In 1847 Strabane was linked to Derry and on to Belfast and Dublin by 1861. The Donegal railway, under various names, had expanded from Strabane to Stranorlar in 1863, Stranorlar to Donegal 1889, Donegal to Killybegs 1893, Stranorlar to Glenties 1894, with an additional line from Strabane to Derry (Donegal Railways) in 1900.

Communications

In 1824 the post office is recorded at Patrick Street but by 1839 was at New Street, where it remained until 1856. In 1839 at New Street, Andrew Jenkins, the postmaster, was noted as having a circulating library. In 1862 the post office address is stated as Abercorn Square, but this may have been a renaming of part of New Street. In 1881 it had relocated to Main Street and no address is reported after this. (An 1893 business was located in the 'old Post Office', Main Street.) Ireland's first telephone exchange was opened in Dublin in 1880, with five subscribers. In 1891 it was stated that telephonic communication had been established between Strabane and Derry and the first telephone numbers appeared in advertisements of 1893. These included S. Donnell & Co., wholesale and retail grocers and general merchants, with the telephone number 6A, William R. Orr, seed merchant and nurseryman, whose number was 12, and Robert Pollock, machine-made bread and biscuit manufacturer, whose number was 14A.

The first newspaper to be listed in the directories was the *Strabane Chronicle* in 1899, with Frank McMenamin as proprietor and editor. This publication started in 1896. Although it was not cited per se, the *Strabane Morning Post* was referred to in 1824 as being published by Carroll & Gray, Main Street.

Banking

In 1824 Strabane had a savings bank that was reported in 1846 as being in the Bowling Green. In 1854 it was in Cross House but by 1862 had moved to the Town Hall. In 1866 it appears to have changed to a loan fund, with an address in Main Street. It was still here in 1870. In this year the post

office had expanded its description to include savings bank. By 1839 branches of the Belfast and Provincial Banks had been established, both in Bowling Green Square. The latter remained here throughout the century. The Ulster Bank was in new premises that had just been completed in Abercorn Square in 1862. The comment was made that this circumstance was a pretty fair index of the material condition of the people. The Belfast Bank moved to new premises in Main Street in 1885. From 1874 there was

Strabane Town Hall as it looked in the later 19th century. This was originally erected in the mid-18th century as the market house in the days of the flourishing linen industry.
COOPER COLLECTION
PRONI, D.1422/5/10

a branch of the Northern Bank, open part-time in Main Street. A branch of the Hibernian Bank was reported from 1877.

Recreation and Culture

It was stated in 1839 that a public newsroom had opened in the Town Hall, and a circulating library at the post office. By 1862 a Christian association and newsroom had opened in Main Street. In 1870 this was followed by another in the Catholic Institute, Church Street. The latter may have been replaced in 1884 by the Strabane and Lifford library and newsroom.

A Literary and Debating Society existed in 1891 at Lifford Street (probably Lower Main Street and in the premises that had been used as the Christian Brothers' National School).

In 1887 the United Counties Club, with clubrooms at the Abercorn Arms Hotel, was recorded with the duke of Abercorn as president and the earl of Erne as vice-president.

The second half of the nineteenth century saw a great expansion in leisure facilities in Strabane. A cricket club existed in 1862, with the president being A.H. Campbell and the secretary J.J. Gray. Following the increasing national interest in cycling, 1891 saw a Cycling and Recreation Club appearing, with a clubroom at Irish Street. This was followed up in 1893 with new recreation grounds under the Strabane Recreation Park Company Ltd., with Chairman F.M. Steele and Secretary W.R. Orr.

In 1884 the Dog, Flower, and Poultry Show Association was formed, with the duke of Abercorn as president, and this started a comprehensive annual show.

The high status of Edward Gallagher, father of Andrew, is evident from the facts that in 1884 he was chairman of the Volunteer Fire Brigade, president of St Eugene's Catholic Temperance Society (see Social Matters), as well as a town commissioner (see Town Governance). By 1887 he was an assistant honorable secretary of the Dog, Flower, and Poultry Show Association.

Interest in music was evident from advertisements such as that in 1870 from P. McMahon, Castle Street, who advertised 'All kinds of Musical Instruments on hand'. In 1887 John Houston, Markethouse Street, cabinet and chair factory, advertised 'Harmoniums and Pianos always in stock', and in 1888 he added American organs. In 1900 James White, Main Street, advertised as an 'Importer of Musical Instruments', and George Reilly, Main Street, advertised a 'Musical Warehouse for all kinds of Musical Instruments.'

Social Affairs

A Total Abstinence and Benevolent Society was present in 1862 and was followed by a Temperance Association in the next year. The president of the former was T.N. Underwood, with W. McGuire as chairman, and N. Bradley as secretary. The treasurer of the latter was William Harpur and its secretary was Robert Smyth. The Total Abstinence and Benevolent Society appears to have been replaced by St Eugene's Catholic Temperance Society in 1884. The strength and growth of the temperance movement may also be partially a reason for the increase in temperance premises throughout the century (see Hotels and Inns).

Poverty was always present in Strabane and district, and action to alleviate this among Catholic children was extended in 1859, as reported elsewhere in this publication (see Strabane Convent). The Strabane chapter of the Society of Saint Vincent de Paul was established in 1862 and continues to the present day. The Strabane conference is called St Joseph's, and in 1865 there were only five conferences in the Derry diocese, two in Derry city, and one each in Omagh, Coleraine and Strabane.

The meeting place was in the choir of the church. The president in 1865 was Daniel O'Flaherty, Esq., MD, and he continued until 1873, when he was succeeded by William Devine. In 1873 Strabane had thirty-one active members and thirteen honorary members, with average attendance at meetings being eight. Its expenditure in the year 1872–3 was £16 19s 10d. Daniel O'Flaherty was a surgeon and apothecary in Main Street, while William Devine was a grocer and spirit dealer, as well as a publican and emigration agent, in Markethouse Street.

Services

Agents were representing four fire and life assurance companies in 1839, and this increased to six in 1856, twenty in 1881 and twenty-eight by 1900.

Strabane had a Volunteer Fire Brigade in 1884, with Edward Gallagher as its chairman.

Although the number of barbers fluctuated between one and five, the only one who was recorded over the long term was A. Quigley, Butcher Street, who appeared in 1874 and was still in business in 1900.

The number of undertakers varied from two in 1866 to five in 1900. In 1887 one of these was G.T. Laidlaw, Abercorn Square, who was also a cabinet maker, a furniture dealer, and a photographic artist. A G. Laidlaw was first recorded in 1870 solely as a photographic artist at Church Brae. By 1874 he had moved to Crossview House, Newtown, and in the same year he was musical conductor of the choir of the Good Templars' Lodge of the Primitive Wesleyan Methodist Chapel, Barrack Street. In 1881 he was classified as a photographer. The main thrust of his advertisement in 1887 was for picture framing. The author has seen photographs taken by this person but believes that there could have been a father and a son with the same first name, the latter signing himself as G.T. Laidlaw. He was last reported in 1891.

Laidlaw's advertisement also provided much detail concerning funerals. A cheap French-polished coffin cost £1. 10s for an adult size. Coffins could also be supplied in oak or lead, and hearses could be one- or two-horse. As a sign of increasing prosperity, Hood & Smyth, Commercial House, Newtownstewart, advertised in 1899 for four-horse hearses.

There were two or three printers throughout the century. In 1900 there were three, of which two were E.R. Gray & Sons and R.J. Blair, both of Main Street. Blair was first noted in 1884. Gray was first listed in 1824 as part of Carroll & Gray (and publisher of the *Strabane Morning Post*), Main Street, but in 1839 was listed as John Gray (an Australian agent), Main Street. In 1874 the proprietor was Miss Gray and she was noted up to 1885. The name became Gray & Co. in 1887. J.J. Gray died on 15 March 1888.

Hotels and Inns

The first hotel noted was that of Sarah Hamilton in 1824, with no address stated. In 1839 three were listed:

Simm's Hotel (Posting and Commercial), (Nicholas Simms), Castle Street
Wilson's Hotel (Abercorn Arms), Main Street
King's Arms Inn, Robert Irwin, Main Street

In 1846 Doherty's Hotel, operated by Neal Doherty in Bridge Street, and the Abercorn Arms in Main Street were described 'as well known establishments for comfort and respectability'. The latter was run by Robert Irwin.

By 1856 Neal Doherty appears to have been succeeded by Mrs Doherty, an Edward McKinney had 'The Grapes' in Castle Street, and Nicholas Simms had transferred the title of Abercorn Arms to his premises in Castle Street. James Henry Murphy, Main Street, had the Commercial Hotel. At Market Place, James Cullen was in 'The Stag', while Tom Watson had the 'Town Arms'. The 1858 directory noted a Thomas McSwegan, hotel-keeper, Abercorn Square.

In 1862 the directory showed five establishments:

Abercorn Arms, Castle Street: Nicholas Simms
Agricultural Hotel, Abercorn Square: Mrs Watson
Bowling Green Hotel: Mrs Kelly
Commercial Hotel: Alexander McClelland
Railway Hotel, Abercorn Square: J. Cullen

The 1870 survey had the same units with the addition of J.J. McElwaine's Farmers' Hotel, and James Gallagher's 'The Plough'. Mrs Kelly appears to have been succeeded by Miss Gregory. The latter hotel, however, is not cited from 1876 onwards.

The 1874 directory notes that the proprietor of the Abercorn Arms was now James Simms. In this year also was the first notification of Temperance premises. Some of these appear to have provided accommodation. The first two were :

Temperance Hotel (Ltd.), Main Street: Mrs Larmour
Temperance and Coffee Rooms, Abercorn Square: John Moody

Mrs Larmour was not listed in 1876 but Benjamin Purdon had the 'Temperance and Coffee Rooms' at Castle Street.

The number of this type had increased to five by 1889, all classified as temperance refreshment rooms:

Coyle David, Castle Street
Isaac Pollock, Abercorn Square
James Purdon, Castle Street
William Wray, Castle Street
John Kane, Castle Street

In 1900 there were two additional establishments of this nature:

Mrs Dowd, Ulster Cafe, Abercorn Square
James Ellis, Railway Road

In 1893 James Simms had expanded the title of his premises to Abercorn Arms and Country Club, indicating the presence of the United Counties Club, with the duke of Abercorn as president. This society was first mentioned in 1887.

Posting Establishments

This was another type of establishment that also provided accommodation, including stabling of horses. The hotels listed above, and many public houses, also had this facility, as indicated in advertisements of that time. In 1870 there were five:

Charles Gormley, Irish Street
James McCafferty, Main Street
John McCollum, Main Street
James McGee, Butcher Street
Francis McMenamin, Butcher Street

Expansion was continuous until 1900 when there were fourteen:

Edward Connolly, Main Street
Mrs J. Doherty, Main Street
Charles Doherty, Church Street
William Hackett, Lifford Street
John Kane, Castle Street
John McCollum, Main Street
Denis McDermott, Back Street
H. McDermott, Castle Street
Denis McElroy, Lifford Street (alias Lower Main Street)
James McGillion, Barrack Street
Patrick McIlroy, Bridge End
Mrs McMenamin, Castle Street
Thomas Quigley, Railway Road
Samuel Tease, Bridge End

Some of these also provided cars (probably jaunting) for hire.

Health

In 1820 Strabane had a dispensary and a fever hospital, built by subscription 1814–15, at Townsend Street. By 1900 the dispensary was listed in Newtown Road.

Health matters in the earlier part of the nineteenth century were complicated by the fact that physicians and surgeons were grouped together as a profession and very often they could also be classified as an apothecary (in modern times a dispensing chemist).

In 1820 there were four surgeons and one physician, namely Andrew Mease, New-town. Three of the surgeons were also apothecaries, as follows:

James Hunter, Markethouse Street (and apothecary)
William Leney, Main Street (and apothecary)
Bernard Rogan, Main Street (and apothecary)

By 1824 James Hunter and Bernard Rogan were not listed and James Swan, Main Street, had entered the list. Hugh G. Rogan was now surgeon to the dispensary. In 1839 the qualification MD had appeared, and by 1846 four of the six listed for Strabane had this entitlement.

In 1877, N. French, Main Street, was listed as an apothecary and surgeon. By 1881 H. French & Co., Main Street, was apothecary only, and in this year also Andrew McKinney (chemist) appeared. It may be of interest that an advertisement in the *Derry Almanac* of 1893 stated that French's had been established in 1770. This is an earlier date than that of 1797 stated in an advertisement for Gray, printer. (The date above the entrance door is 1797.)

The apothecary and druggist, J. Hill & Co., was established in 1884 in Castle Street, next door to the Abercorn Arms Hotel. During redevelopment of Castle Street, large parts of James Hill's premises and fittings were relocated to the Ulster American Folk Park, Omagh, and reconstructed there.

From 1887 to 1890 a dentist, J.J. Johnston, LDS, was attending at the Abercorn Arms Hotel every alternate Tuesday.

In 1899 P. Coyle, watchmaker, jeweller and goldsmith, Bridge Street, described himself as an optician. He also advertised himself as a naturalist, furrier and taxidermist.

Animal Health

The first veterinary surgeon was noted in 1881 as William Bryan, at Railway Road. Then, in 1890, G.B. McLay, MRCVS, Main Street, is recorded, and he was joined in 1893 by John L. Orr, MRCVS, at the Temperance Hotel, Abercorn Square. The latter had spent the previous three years in Kendal, England. These two continued up to 1900, John L. Orr having moved to Lifford Street.

Industry and Manufactories

In 1820 the linen trade was of great importance, and Strabane was considered to be the third most important centre in Ireland for the quality and quantity of that branch of manufacture.

In 1837 it was noted that cotton manufacture, corduroys and other fabrics, had ceased and the two bleach greens were not in use. A large ale and beer brewery was also recorded, presumably that of Smyth, Holmes & Smyth, Front Street, of 1820. By 1839 this establishment was referred to as Robert Holmes and the address changed to Meetinghouse Street. It produced ale and stout and most of its output was for local markets, with some being exported. This company continued into the twentieth century as Holmes & Co., Barrack Street. At one point, in 1874, it was known as Duncan & Dawson, Barrack Street.

In 1839 Mr David Smith, Main Street, was erecting a steam mill for meal and flour. The mill of Messrs Lyons & Co. for the manufacture of flax and cotton yarn was in operation (this may have been that at 'Seein', in which the Herdmans had invested in 1835). The bleachers were O'Bryen, Gwynn & Co., Main Street. There were two loom makers, indicating that some of the linen fabric may have been produced domestically.

By 1846 Gwynne and Co. were present as bleachers in Main Street, Mr F. O'Neill at Mountpleasant and Mr J. Scott at Spamount, as well as the flax and tow mills of Messrs Herdman and Co. at Sion Mills. Mr F. Rogan had a cotton works at Castlefinn. At Holyhill and Artigarvan, William Sigerson had a large manufactory for spades, shovels and other farming implements, and in the town, James Cooke & Co. was operating the Strabane Iron and

The Gallagher, Egan and Company textile factory continued in production until recent years when it finally shut down.
COOPER COLLECTION PRONI, D.1422/1/5

Brass Foundry. Mr John Patterson had oatmeal mills at Ballymagorry, and had been the first person to bring a vessel into the Strabane Canal direct from Scotland.

The Strabane foundry continued in operation into the twentieth century but experienced changes in ownership. In 1856 the foundry was operated by William Stevenson & Co., and this changed to James Stevenson in 1862. In 1891 J. Taylor had become the proprietor. It is highly probable that there was also a small foundry in Patrick Street, operated by Thomas Law, who described himself as a brassfounder. This report was made by one of his grandsons. At least one item made by him is in Canada.

Sigerson's spade factory may have had breaks in its operation. From 1856 until 1881 there is no mention of it. In the latter year the spade factory at Holyhill is noted as being operated by Andrew McGinnis. (He may have been a member of the family of Patrick McGinnis who was married to Jane Sigerson.) There is no further comment until 1887 onwards, when the name William Sigerson & Co., Holyhill, was used. (It has been reported that there is a spade on display in a museum in Anchorage, Alaska, United States, that bears the name McGinnis, but to date this has not been confirmed.)

In the latter half of the nineteenth century, the dominant manufacturing sector in Strabane became that of shirt manufacture. This was started by James Kennedy in 1848 and he remained in the business until 1888 when he sold his factory, in Barrack Street, to Stapley & Smith. At the outset, a training school was opened and in the space of four years the workers were capable of turning out 700 dozens of shirts per week, chiefly for the Scottish market. In 1888 the factory employed upwards of 1,000 hands, about 600 of whom resided in Co. Donegal, the remainder being resident in Co. Tyrone. The reports do not indicate that these employees were in-house. In fact, the size of the building, which still exists, could not have provided the space for such numbers. It is more likely that there was a small number in the unit and that the majority of the workers worked at home in the situation of a 'cottage industry'. Some indication of the scale of operations can be imagined from the fact that Kennedy stated, in an advertisement in 1870, that he had upwards of 80 machines in the factory and that operations there were supervised by him personally.

In 1862 there were five shirt agents, including James Kennedy, the number rising to six by 1870:

    John Arthur, Patrick Street (absent from 1889)
    T. Craig, Church Street (Miss Craig in 1888)
    James Duffy, Markethouse Street (absent from 1888)
    Gourlie & Sons, Derry Road (absent from 1877)
    James Kennedy, Barrack Street
    F. McCartney, Back Street (absent from 1874)

By 1889 the number was down to three:

    Miss Craig, Church Street,
    Stapley & Smith, Barrack Street
    Stewart & McDonald, Derry Road

This continued in 1900 when Miss Craig was not cited and Flannigan & Co., Main Street, made its entrance. This was the first mention of the company which was later to become famous in the twentieth century as Andy Gallagher's.

A town gas works had been constructed at Canal Basin by 1846 and the town now had gas lighting.

In 1862, McKinley & Son carried on extensive steam saw mills and chemical works at Canal Basin and continued until 1881, when they were succeeded by S.J. Moody & Co, who operated until 1887. The chemicals made or sold included pyroligneous acid, iron and red liquor, brown sugar of lead, sulphate of ammonia, wood naphtha, tar and charcoal. Some of these may have been sourced from the town gas works, which was adjacent to the premises. Pyroligneous acid, however, must have been made on site, since this product is derived from the distillation of wood. It consists of a mixture of methanol, acetone and acetic acid and was the starting material used in one of the earliest methods of obtaining acetic acid, more commonly known as vinegar. The 1885 Ordnance Survey map also shows two chemical works, one on each side of the canal. It has not been possible to identify any proprietor for the second one.

In 1887, Mr John Houston, Markethouse Street, had just completed a substantial cabinet warehouse that gave employment to a large number of hands, manufacturing a very wide range of furniture.

In 1870, P. Gillespie, Bridge End, was a rope and twine manufacturer. The classification in 1900 had changed to ropeworks, carried out by Charles Gillespie. The 1885 Ordnance Survey map shows a rope walk located at right angles to some buildings on the east side of the Broad Road (what is now called the Melmount Road) just past the present Melmount Villas.

In 1893, James McIvor & Co., Main Street, had started the manufacture of mineral water and this continued through to 1900.

Other smaller manufacturing businesses, such as coach-building and tanning, were in operation throughout the century. A few appeared briefly: for example Elizabeth King, Main Street, was a toy-maker in 1820.

There were six tobacco manufacturers in 1820 but only one in 1846, the last being Ephraim Campbell, Church Street.

There were two stay-makers in 1839, Jane Burrell, Castle Street, and Ann Dougherty, New Street.

Pat Holiday, Meetinghouse Street, was a reed-maker in 1820.

Walter Connison of Dunamanagh was a paper manufacturer in 1881.

Trade and Shops

The dominant business of Strabane, after the markets, was that of retailing and there were many different types of establishment. The largest sectors were the same as those in modern times, namely, the supply of food, clothing and alcoholic beverages.

One problem in analysing these is that many occurred in a number of different classifications and the mix could vary from year to year. When a new business started, it was quite usual for others to move into this, making assessments more difficult. A typical example is that there were three fruiterers in 1899 and eight the following year. A single year (1876) is examined later in detail.

The number of grocers increased from 25 in 1820 to a maximum of 59 in 1876. This then declined to 38 in 1900. Many were also confectioners, whose numbers steadily increased from 2 in 1820 to 7 in 1900.

There were 8 bakers in 1820 and their numbers grew to 15 by 1876. There was then a decline to 9 by 1900. This may have been associated with the development of bakery machinery, such as advertised by Pollock of Abercorn Square in 1893. It is of interest that those in 1900 included Doran's, Meetinghouse Street, McAnaw's, Market Place, and John W. Russell,

Church Street, who first appeared in 1899. These three survived well into the twentieth century. The progression of the first can be seen from the initial mention of James Doran, Lifford in 1839, to New Street in 1846. The next report is of Peter Doran, Meetinghouse Street, in 1870. He remained at this location through to 1900. Confirmation of the longevity of Doran's Bakery can be seen from the records of the business from 1837–73, held in the Public Records Office for Northern Ireland, Belfast. These documents include advertisements.

The number of drapers peaked in 1876 with 21 and then declined to 11 in 1900. A similar pattern is seen for clothes dealers, who numbered 4 in 1820, 12 in 1856 and 5 in 1900. The number of tailors rose from 7 in 1839 to 10 in 1884 and decreased to 5 in 1900. In 1862 James Kinch, Main Street, was so confident of his product that he advertised 'Fit or Forfeit.' On the other hand, the number of dressmakers rose from 12 in 1862 to 18 in 1876 and the same number at the end of the century. The advent of factory and machine-assisted production is suggested by M. Conroy, Main Street, advertising 'Ready-Made Clothing' from 1887, along with others in the years leading to the end of the century.

Boot and shoemakers numbered 9 in 1839, increased to 23 in 1870 and dropped to 12 in 1900. Again, this may have been the result of growth in machine-assisted manufacture. This is indicated by P. O'Brien, Main Street (mentioned elsewhere), advertising that he warranted genuine all articles stamped 'Irish Manufacture'. Linked to this trade may have been the appearance of 5 boot and shoeshops in 1870. This number increased to 12 in 1884 but declined to 9 in 1900. In 1876 it was noted that 4 of the boot- and shoemakers also operated boot and shoeshops. One of these, George Divin, Back Street, was also the only last-maker recorded. A possible member of his family was Miss Divin, a bonnet-maker.

There were 3 butchers in 1839, 13 by 1870, but only 7 by 1900. Three fish merchants appeared in 1890 and 4 in 1900.

In 1820 there were 27 publicans noted, the number increasing to 46 by 1876 but dropping to 43 in 1900.

An emigration agent is first noted in 1839, but there are citations in the *Londonderry Journal* of the 1770s. The number grew to six by 1884 and came down to four in 1900. A typical advertisement was that of 1877, in which R.T. Turbitt, Main Street, offered free and assisted passages to Canterbury, New Zealand, and Queensland, Australia.

A possible increase in legal business could have been the reason for the number of legal practitioners going from 5 attorneys in 1820 to 12 solicitors in 1899.

The application of science to agriculture could have led to the number of guano and seed merchants growing from 6 in 1866 to 17 in 1876 (12 in 1900).

Guano, however, had been available much earlier, since William Wright & Co., Main Street, advertised 'Genuine Peruvian Guano' in 1862, this being the type offered by all the dealers eventually. This company was also a grocer, druggist, coal merchant, timber and deal merchant, and an agent for the Life Association of Scotland Assurance Co.

The 1876 Directory

In order to review the multiple business activities in Strabane, the year 1876 was selected for evaluation since this year appears to have been the one when many business categories were at or around their peak in number. A leading businesswoman was Mrs Brown, Castle Street, who was a grocer, publican, baker, spirit dealer, guano and seed merchant, and emigration agent. Her wealth was such that, by 1890–95, she could far surpass other persons in her generosity towards the building and fitting out of the new Catholic Church of the Immaculate Conception. Filling most of the same business categories were Elliott & Crawford, Main Street, Daniel McAnaw, Market Place, and Samuel Gordon, Main Street. Elliott & Crawford was also a draper and haberdasher, a tailor, and operated a boot and shoeshop. Daniel McAnaw was additionally a confectioner and newsagent. William Wright & Co. has already been detailed earlier. Robert Smyth, Main Street, was a grocer and baker as well as a leather merchant.

Religion

The nineteenth century witnessed the replacement of many older buildings in the town. The Primitive Wesleyan Society opened a chapel in Barrack Street in 1830, and in 1814 a new, additional, Methodist chapel was built in Church Street, followed by St. John's Catholic Church, Townsend Street, in 1821. A second Catholic church was opened in 1846 at Melmount Road. (The 1835 Ordnance Survey map shows a Catholic chapel located at the lower end of Ballycolman Avenue. It has not been possible to find any reference to confirm this.) The First Presbyterian Church in Main Street was completed in 1871, and the new Christ Church, Bowling Green, in 1879. The sequence of churches was completed by the chapel at Strabane Convent of Mercy in 1881 and the Church of the Immaculate Conception in 1895.

The year 1868 saw the opening of the Convent of Mercy and its orphanage at Mount St Joseph, Barrack Street, followed by the first stage of St Catherine's Industrial School around 1871. In September 1897, five nuns from Strabane Convent of Mercy, and two girls from the convent boarding school, emigrated to South Africa and established a religious foundation in Mafeking in 1897.

In 1839 there was a Seceding meeting-house in Lower Main Street as a result of the 'Arian controversy'. This continued until 1858, when the premises were apparently purchased for the establishment of the Christian Brothers' National School.

Law and Order

Before 1814 Ireland had no 'police force' as such, although the parish vestries were empowered to hire a small number of constables. Public order was generally maintained by the army or by paramilitary forces such as the yeomanry. In 1814 Sir Robert Peel, then chief secretary for Ireland, introduced the Peace Preservation Force which was effectively the first nationwide Irish police service. The 1836 Constabulary (Ireland) Act replaced the Peace Preservation Force with the Irish Constabulary, which was later to become the Royal Irish Constabulary (RIC). In Strabane a constabulary station is first recorded for 1846 at New Street. By 1854 it appeared in Patrick Street and remained there until 1858. It 1862 it was located in Abercorn Square, where it remained until the end of the century.

The addresses also showed the interchangeability of the street names Patrick Street and Irish Street, a usage which has survived up to modern times. Although the 1835 Ordnance Survey map shows two distinct streets with these names, the author is confident that this was a mistake. The name Irish Street was then applied to what is now known as Castle Place.

Only one magistrate was noted for 1824, Edward Edie, Bridge End Street, and the number had increased to 9 in 1870 and 11 in 1884. By 1900 there were 19, but this may be a reflection of the apparent custom of appointing the chairman of the town commissioner as a justice of the peace, rather than any increase in levels of crime.

Schools

A list of national schools for Strabane and district was published in 1881 and reads as follows:

Artigarvan, Samuel McCleery, Master; Maggie Gut, Mistress
Bridge End, Patrick McGowan, Master; Susan McGowan, Mistress
Cloughcor, Michael McCullagh, Master; Cecilia Feely, Mistress
Convent of Mercy, Mount St Joseph, Mother Mary Atkinson, Superioress
Dunamanagh, James Rice, Master
Glenmornan, James Carton, Master
Killena, Dunamanagh, John O'Neill, Master
Meetinghouse Street, John Henderson, Master; Sarah Hannah, Mistress
Patrick Street, Robert S. Dunne, Master
Rabstown, Henry McDevitt, Master
Sion Mills, Thomas H. Thompson, Master; Eliza J. Creery, Mistress

Townsend Street, John McCaffry, Master
Tullywhisker, Charles Colhoun, Master
Urney, John Johnston, Master, Caroline Scott, Mistress

A Strabane school, possibly the early Technical College in the 1930s. Note the bench desks and the exposed inkwells.
COOPER COLLECTION, PRONI, D.1422/17/1

10 Mills and the rural economy

WILLIAM ROULSTON

On an island lacking any significant deposits of fossil fuels, in particular coal, the importance of water power in local industrial technology in Ireland cannot be overestimated. The aim of this chapter is to examine the different ways in which water power was harnessed in order to provide for local industries in north-west Tyrone. What is not provided here is a detailed examination of the technology used in these mills.

The remains of a paper mill near Ballymagorry

Corn Mills

Although there were undoubtedly corn mills in north-west Tyrone before 1600, we find the first documentary references to them in the plantation surveys of the early seventeenth century. By 1622 most of the manors in the Strabane area possessed their own mill. The Civil Survey of 1654–6 recorded nine corn mills in the barony of Strabane as well as two tuck mills. The Civil Survey also provides details on the value of these mills in 1640, just before the outbreak of the rebellion of 1641. The values ranged from only £5 for the mill in the manor of Derrywoon to £30 for the mill in the manor of Dunnalong. The mills in the manors of Strabane and Shean were jointly valued at £80. This would seem to indicate that the quantity of corn grown in the manor of Derrywoon was lower than in other parts of Strabane barony. More mills were built in the second half of the seventeenth century so that in the manor of Strabane alone the corn mills included Seein, Tullywhisker, Strabane and Douglas.

To each mill was attached a district known as the 'succan'. All tenants living within this district were bound by their leases to bring their corn to be ground at the appointed mill. They were also required to pay a proportion of their crop to the miller as 'mulcture'. A smaller proportion known as 'bannock' was paid to the under-miller. From 1747 we have a deed between John Pigott, tenant of the lands in the parish of Urney owned by the bishopric of Derry, and Adam Smyth, William Hunter and George Gwyn, by which Pigott leased to Smyth and the others the corn mill at Clady. The lessees were also permitted to collect the toll and 1/16 of all grain growing on the lands leased by Pigott. Here we see the miller's right to a proportion of the crop reinforced through a clause in his own deed.

It was important for the landlord that he retain ultimate control over his mills. In 1695 we have the then fifth earl of Abercorn granting to Thomas Maxwell of Strabane the townland of Knockroe, but reserving out of this the mill and one acre of ground with it. The construction of new mills was also regulated by the lord of the manor. In 1773 John Hood, the tenant of Douglas tuck mill, petitioned the eighth earl of Abercorn for permission to add a corn mill to his holding, claiming that he was being encouraged to do this by the farmers in the area. However, Abercorn responded to this request by insisting that Hood could not 'possibly be encouraged to build a corn mill during the present leases of Douglas and even Strabane mills'. He was obviously concerned that the erection of another mill in his manor of Strabane would be to the detriment of those already standing.

John McEvoy in his *Statistical Survey of the County of Tyrone*, published in 1802, noted 'no less than 124 mills in the county in 1800. Grist mills are the common names that mills go by, but this is understood only of such as prepare oatmeal and malt, and sometimes barley for bread, which was universally the case in 1800 and 1801.' However, McEvoy found it difficult to estimate just how many of these mills could be considered 'effective', as 'so many of them are perpetually out of order, some demolishing, others repairing, etc.' In fact it was McEvoy's opinion that 'about one hundred mills, kept fully employed, may be deemed sufficient for the county'.

The Freeholders and the Mills

One of the main issues concerning mills in the Abercorn estate in the middle of the eighteenth century was the question of whether the freeholders were obliged to grind their corn at the manor mills. By the late 1750s Abercorn had granted liberty to his ordinary tenants, i.e. those who held their farms by a twenty-one year lease, to go to any of the mills on the Abercorn estate. In fact, he seems to have gone even further than this, for in a letter to his agent, James Hamilton, dated 11 August 1758, he mentioned that he permitted his tenants to 'grind at any mill whatsoever, without regarding whose estate it was in'. However, because of a fear that some of the neighbouring landlords would take advantage of this by constructing additional mills on their own lands, Abercorn insisted that his tenants were only at liberty 'to go to any mill in their own manor, or to any mill in any other persons estate that was standing at the time they took their land'. Abercorn also pointed out to Hamilton that one of the reasons for 'exempting the tenants from service to mills was to put an end to their complaints against millers'.

However, it was a different story with the freeholders on the estate. Here we see Abercorn doing all in his power to ensure that the freeholders ground all their corn at his appointed mills. The freeholders held their lands by perpetual leases, usually dating from the early seventeenth century. These freeholds tended to be fairly extensive and could comprise several modern-day townlands. This meant that the freeholders themselves had large numbers of undertenants on their lands. Although the original freehold deeds contained a clause requiring the freeholder to grind all his corn at the appointed mill, by the middle of the eighteenth century it was becoming extremely difficult to enforce this rule. It also wasn't clear whether the freeholders' undertenants were also obliged to have their corn ground at a particular mill.

One of the mills on the Abercorn estate which particularly experienced this kind of difficulty was Burndennet, in the manor of Dunnalong. There were several freeholds in this manor, including Dullerton, the property of William Hamilton, MP for Strabane. In 1759, Abercorn gave instructions that the toll of Cloghogal and Dunnalong tenement was to belong to the corn mill in Magheramason, while the toll of the other freeholds was to belong to Bundennet mill. He was also insistent that the millers enter into a mutual agreement about the toll of the freeholds.

In the following year it was reported to Abercorn that, although the freehold of Dullerton was obliged to pay the 1/16 grain to the miller as 'mulcture' and the 1/64 grain to the under-miller as 'bannock', since 1744 the undertenants had refused to pay any more than the 1/21 grain. They also claimed that they were acting on the instructions of their landlord, William Hamilton. Before 1756 the mill had been rented by a tenant 'who, either out of friendship or for fear of the cost of the law, was content with what he got'. In 1770 James Hamilton reported to Abercorn that he had been told by two of the Dullerton undertenants that 'they never paid more than the twentieth grain, and if that was not taken they would go where they pleased for that they were not bound to any place by their leases; I do believe Mr Hamilton did neglect binding them'.

In February 1770 Abercorn explained his view of the situation to James Hamilton: 'The inconvenience complained of was that the freehold tenants, being bound to the mill or mills of the manor, went to which mill they pleased and the millers were induced to grind at an under value. To obviate this it was necessary to make the millers, in the same manor only, bind themselves to each other.' The solution seemed to be to make the freeholders support identified mills without increasing the burdens on the farmers. The following month Abercorn decided to set as the standard freehold toll the 1/20 grain. However, Abercorn's attempts to persuade the millers to reach agreements among themselves were met with stiff resistance, with the millers arguing that the freeholders and their under-tenants would simply take their grain elsewhere to be ground. It seems that the issue was never satisfactorily resolved, with regular correspondence on the issue of mills between Abercorn and his agent, James Hamilton, continuing into the 1780s. Even as late as 1783 we have Hamilton recommending that the 'grinding miller of any freehold that has not been appointed to him should return the whole toll to the [mill] farmer to whom it was appointed and receive for his trouble of grinding at the rate of 9d. a barrel which can be no inducement to him'.

Flax Mills

Almost as common as the corn mills, the flax mills, or scutch mills, of north-west Tyrone were an important part of the local economy, employing large numbers of workers and producing a commodity vital for the local linen industry. McCutcheon in his article on 'Water powered corn and flax scutching mills in Ulster' explains the purpose of the flax mill as follows: 'Flax is a bast fibre, from the stem of the flax plant, and has to be freed from the core by retting. When the retted flax is dried the stems can readily be broken and the unwanted *shows* beaten off by hand or by machinery in the process known as scutching.' The first water powered flax scutching mill was probably established near Belfast c. 1740. Within thirty years of this the first flax mills had been built in the Strabane district, at Shannony by James Kerr, and at Douglas by John Hood, the latter described as 'very good' by James Hamilton in 1773.

In 1802, McEvoy noted that the number of flax mills in Tyrone was 'not so numerous as the quantity of flax, raised in the county, seem to require'. Furthermore, McEvoy was of the opinion that, in general, they were not

Bleach Mills

The earliest reference to bleaching in the Strabane area comes in a deed of 1708 where John Henderson's 'blechery' in the Manor of Cloghogall (Leckpatrick parish) is mentioned. Nothing more is known about it. Another early attempt to establish a bleach works in the district was at Drumgauty, where in 1751 the tenant, James Hamilton, was in the process of building a bleach mill. This venture would appear to have been fairly short-lived. In 1779, Galbraith Hamilton of Ballyfatton wrote to the earl of Abercorn, pointing out that when he first became the tenant of Sion mill, nearly fifty years previously, it was with the intention of establishing a bleach green on the adjoining lands. This he had done at great expense to himself, but by 1779 it was becoming something of a burden to him. This bleach green seems to have been abandoned shortly afterwards, for in 1784 James Hamilton informed Abercorn that there were 'but two greens in this neighbourhood, Mr Edie's at Burndenet and a Mr Smyly's about two miles from this'. According to Hamilton the consequence of this was that '4/5 of our brown linen goes near 30 miles to be bleached'.

The bleach green at Burndennet had originally been established by John McCreery c. 1770. However, the expense of running this and the corn mill proved too much for him and he ran into serious debt. By the early 1780s the situation had become so serious that he was forced to sell his interest in the holding to Nathaniel Edie, a member of a well-established family from the Newtownstewart area. Edie laid out a great deal of money repairing the bleach mill, which had fallen into disrepair, and also rebuilding the corn mill on a more convenient site. He also repaid about £100 loaned to McCreery by Abercorn, and paid out at least as much in arrears. In 1787, he extended his holding by purchasing a farm of just under 24 acres from one of the neighbouring tenants. The enterprise became a thriving concern, and by 1791 it was reported that Edie was planning to expend £300 to £400 on a house at Burndennet and move to it as soon as possible. This he did, building Thornhill. (It was recently demolished.) Edie's efforts at Burndennet were recognised by Abercorn and he was rewarded with a three lives lease in 1791.

In 1802, McEvoy listed 27 bleach greens in Tyrone, 23 of which were in the barony of Dungannon. In the Strabane area he noted bleach greens operated by Smiley near Strabane, Quin at Douglas Bridge, and Sproule at Spamount. Strangely, he neglected to mention Edie's venture at Burndennet. Further bleach greens were established at Artigarvan, Fawney near

Dunamanagh, and Woodbrook, in Birnaghs townland near Newtownstewart. However, by the 1830s a number of these bleach greens had ceased to function. The *Ordnance Survey* memoir for the parish of Ardstraw, written in 1834, noted that the bleach green at Douglas Bridge was 'doing little except keeping the machinery in order', and there were only seven people employed at it. In 1835 the bleach mill at Woodbrook was converted to a flax mill. According to the First Valuation, compiled c. 1835, the bleaching concern at Artigarvan was in a state of 'dilapidation' and 'out of use', although only 14 years earlier it had been employing between 40 and 50 people.

Flour Mills

When John McEvoy was compiling his *Statistical Survey* in 1801–2, he was able to find only two flour mills in Tyrone, one near Dungannon, the other near Strabane. However, he found that 'the wheat manufactured in both is principally the produce of other parts, as at present very little of the grain is grown in the county.' In the late 1750s, when Seein corn mill in Liggartown was in need of rebuilding, Galbraith Hamilton was advised to add to it a wheat mill in the hope that it would encourage the cultivation of wheat in that area. Abercorn was in favour of the idea and loaned Hamilton £100. Hamilton also petitioned the Irish House of Commons in 1765 for financial assistance in building the mill. However, the venture did not prove successful and the only effect was to increase the expense for the mill farmer.

In the early 1780s Abercorn intervened personally and more than £1,000 was laid out on improving Seein mill. This included £39 for two French millstones and £36 for a stove for drying wheat. Abercorn even brought in Alexander Stewart to design and build it. Stewart was later to act as the clerk of works or resident architect during the building of Castle Coole, the residence of the earl of Belmore just outside Enniskillen. In 1828 this mill was rebuilt, but shortly afterwards became the site of the flax spinning mills owned by the Herdman family.

Other Mills: Spade, Paper and Tuck Mills

One of the responses to the increase in population and the resultant agricultural expansion of the pre-Famine period was the appearance in Ireland of the spade mill to cater for the rise in demand for hand tillage tools. McEvoy noted in 1802 that a spade mill was about to be built in Newtownstewart. By 1834 spade mills had been built in Hollyhill and Gorticrum Irish along the Glenmornan burn (and owned by the Sigerson family) while there was a spade foundry at Milltown, near Ardstraw.

In the early nineteenth century, a number of paper mills were established in the Strabane area. The earliest would appear to have been at

MacCrackens, near Ballymagorry, which is shown on the 1804 map of the Abercorn estate. Nearby, in Leckpatrick townland, another paper mill was built, while there were further paper mills at Tullyard and in Dunamanagh. The paper mill in Dunamanagh shared the same water-wheel as the flax mill in the townland. Paper mills used raw materials such as linen, straw wood or other fibrous material.

The Irish tuck mill corresponded closely to the fulling mill of Great Britain. 'Fulling', a term deriving from the use of fuller's earth, a natural detergent, was the name given to a process used to thicken cloth and give it a firm structure. Following this the cloth was then scoured or washed. Tuck mills served the local woollen industry, and when this declined in the aftermath of the rural depopulation caused by the Famine, most of the tuck mills fell into disuse. In the Strabane area tuck mills were very few and far between, the comment in the *Ordnance Survey* memoir for Ardstraw parish that 'sheep are scarce' probably going a long way to explain this.

The earliest mention of a tuck mill in the Strabane area comes in the 1622 plantation survey, where one is mentioned on Sir George Hamilton of Greenlaw's estate at Cloghogall (Leckpatrick parish). This mill is again mentioned in the Civil Survey of 1654–6, and it might possibly have been the tuck mill in Loughneas townland which continued in use until the middle of the nineteenth century. The Civil Survey also noted a tuck mill on the bishop's lands at Ardstraw. The only other tuck mills in the Strabane area that we know about were Douglas, tenanted in the 1770s by John Hood, and Birnaghs, built in 1808. McEvoy also drew attention to a manufactory in Strabane town owned by a Mr Ross which made 'corduroys, and other articles in the cotton way'.

Entrepeneurs and Milling in Strabane

McCutcheon, in his mammoth work, *The Industrial Archaeology of Northern Ireland*, described those involved in the bleaching industry as 'the first true capitalists in local industrial development' and that by the end of the eighteenth century many 'had become men of considerable wealth, with interests extending far beyond the linen trade'. McCutcheon obviously had in mind men such as Thomas Christy of Moyallan, Co. Down, who, by his will of 1780, bequeathed £2,000 to each of his grand-daughters, and to his two grandsons his 6000-acre estate in North Carolina.

The bleachers of north-west Tyrone were certainly not in Christy's category. Perhaps the most prominent bleacher in Strabane district was Nathaniel Edie, who played a significant role in the municipal government of the town of Strabane, and who seems to have been a fairly close ally of Abercorn. At the same time, Edie was already a man of some prominence in the district even before he took over the bleaching concern at Burndennet and whether it significantly increased his standing is not clear. Andrew Sproule was another prominent local industrialist. At Spamount, on the estate of Sir Edward Loftus, Sproule built two bleach mills and a corn mill in the early 1770s, laying out, it was believed, more than £2,000 on the venture.

The success of Edie's venture at Burndennet, in sharp contrast to McCreery's earlier failure, indicates the importance of strong capital backing when undertaking involvement in industries other than agriculture. Mills on their own were rarely, if ever, economically viable, and could usually only be maintained when run alongside a fairly substantial farm. The same was also true for orchards and fisheries. This was recognised by James Hamilton, who pointed out to Abercorn in 1781 that if 'orchards, mills and fisheries could be let in a lease with land, there would then be some security for payment'.

Hamilton wrote this at a time when mills, apart from bleach mills, were still generally seen as merely providing a service to the local community. However, by the end of the eighteenth century this perception was changing as commercial interests came increasingly to the fore. In the Strabane area this was evident at Seein where, as we have already seen, Abercorn laid out more than £1,000 on a flour mill in the early 1780s. However, because so little wheat was grown in the locality, and consequently it would take a long time for there to be any return on investment in the venture, James Hamilton was of the opinion that 'the man who would take these mills ought, I am told, to have £1,000 at least employed in that business'. Finding the right man was not an easy task, but eventually Abercorn told James Hamilton to let the mill to William Patterson, whom Hamilton had previously described as 'a cheerful honest man' who would 'make a faithful return of the produce of the mills'. Abercorn also instructed Hamilton to lend Patterson £300, interest free, provided that he paid off £100 of the principal each year on time.

The Abercorn letters contain frequent references to millers falling behind in rent payments. This could befall even the most reliable of millers. In 1781 James Hamilton informed Abercorn that 'Widow Lowther who holds Strabane mill used to pay her rent very punctually, but she now owes two years rent, £240'. Part of the reason for this was the fall in demand for malt which had previously 'brought her in a great deal, but the consumption of that here is very little, none but by beer'. The previous year Hamilton had pointed out to Abercorn that 'not near so much malt is distilled in this town [Strabane] as used to be, not the fifth part of it, owing to the strictness of the excise officers'.

Sion Mills

In 1836, Lieutenant I.I. Wilkinson, author of the *Ordnance Survey* memoir for the parish of Urney, noted: 'There is at this moment a most extensive flax

THE MILLS, SION MILLS, STRABANE.

Sion Mills in the 1930s

spinning mill being erected by a Belfast company, who have recently obtained by lease from Lord Abercorn the most advantageous site on the River Mourne.' The backers of the venture were the three Herdman brothers, James, John and George, and Andrew Mulholland. The site they were granted was that of the old Seein mill in Liggartown, where Abercorn had rebuilt the flour mill in 1828. Along with the mill site they were also granted one hundred acres of land at an annual rent of £200. The industrial complex that developed at Sion Mills was a considerable investment for the Herdmans and Mulholland, and within a few months £5,000 had been expended on the machinery alone.

When Mr and Mrs Samuel Hall visited Sion Mills in the early 1840s they were so impressed that they gave a detailed account of it in their book, *Tour in Ireland*. The following is an extract from it:

> In the county of Tyrone, and within a distance of little more than three miles from Strabane, is to be found one of the most interesting establishments it has ever been our good fortune to visit in any country . . . The mills are situated on the River Mourne which is one of the best water powers in Great Britain, the supply being not only large but constant. About eighty-horse power is now used to drive eight thousand spindles; yet but a small portion of the water is necessary for the purpose. Instead of the hot furnace, long chimneys, and dense smoke, rendering still more unhealthy the necessarily close atmosphere of manufactories devoted exclusively to the spinning of flax and tow into linen yarn, there is a clean, handsome, well-ventilated building, where nearly seven hundred of a peasantry, which,

before the establishment of this manufactory, were starving and idle are now constantly employed.

No doubt the Halls were allowing their own prejudices in favour of industrialisation to have free rein in this account, but early indications suggested that it was certainly an economic and social boon to the area. As the Herdmans continued to develop the mill complex so they developed the village of Sion Mills, building workers' cottages, churches, schools and other public buildings, and in the process created north-west Tyrone's very own New Lanark. The Herdmans themselves came to dominate the local scene and became heavily involved in liberal and later unionist politics in Tyrone. Herdmans Ltd remains a principal manufacturing business in this area, and as a major employer it plays a vital role in the local economy.

Conclusion: The Decline of Milling

The year 1834 did not mark the high point of milling in north-west Tyrone. The next few decades saw the construction of several more corn and flax mills. About 1850, David Smith built a flour mill at Artigarvan which the valuers described as 'furnished with elevators and with the requisites of a first class mill'. However, the latter part of the nineteenth century saw the beginning of the end. A number of mills marked on the first edition *Ordnance Survey* maps do not appear on the second edition of 1907. By the 1950s water-powered industry was all but finished in the district around Strabane. There were many reasons for this.

In the 1850s, when the Primary Valuation was being compiled, the valuer of Milltown corn mill, near Ballymagorry, described it in the following terms: 'I consider it a very bad take. I would put on [it] a higher value, but there are so many corn mills in this locality that they decrease the value of each other.' According to the same valuation, Tullyard flax mill, near Dunamanagh, had been 'worked very little for [the] last three years in consequence of the erection of other mills – worked not more than one month last year and employed only two scutching stocks'. Many mills catered for purely local needs: when this need ended the mill went with it. Developments in industrial technology left many mills behind; by the beginning of the twentieth century water was no longer the only means of generating power.

The countryside around Strabane still abounds with the remains of water-powered mills. They form an important part of our industrial heritage and as such should be preserved as reminders of a former age. In recent years a great deal of work has gone into restoring Silverbrook corn mill near Dunamanagh. It is hoped that this will allow visitors to gain an insight into the workings of a water-powered mill in the nineteenth century, as well as increasing their understanding of the life of the miller and his family.

Appendix

Water-powered mills marked on the first-edition *Ordnance Survey* maps (sheets 1–5, 6–10, 16 and 17) for north-west Tyrone, c. 1834:

CORN MILLS: Milltown (Donagheady), Tullyard (Donagheady), Leckpatrick (2), Knockanbrack, Milltown (Camus), Rousky (2), Liggartown, Clady, Donnygowen, Aghafad (Donagheady), Fyfin, Magheracreggan (2), Crew Upper, Ballyrenan, and Killymore. The first edition Ordnance Survey maps also mark a number of 'old' mills which, from other sources, would appear to have been corn mills. Old mills are shown in the following townlands: Magheramason, Binnelly, Coolermoney and Milltown (Leckpatrick).

FLAX MILLS: Drumgauty, Loughneas, Sandville, Altrest (2), Ballynabwee, Tullyard (Donagheady), Ballyheather, Artigarvan, Glentimon, Knockroe, Knockinallar (2), Killeen, Magheracreggan, Milltown (Ardstraw) and Ballyrenan.

TUCK OR CLOTH MILLS: Loughneas and Birnaghs

SPADE MILLS: Holly Hill, Gorticrum Irish and Milltown (Ardstraw)

PAPER MILLS: Leckpatrick and MacCrackens

BLEACH MILLS: Milltown (Donagheady) and Artigarvan (2)

RUINED MILLS: Camus (2) Carrigullin and Donnygowen

11 The Convent of Mercy and the Industrial School

MICHAEL HARRON

A postcard view of Strabane in the early twentieth century. Strabane Convent is in the background and the children helping with the harvest are possibly from the Industrial School attached to the Convent.

The Convent of Mercy has played a crucial role in the development of Strabane over more than a century and the work has encompassed a wide field. Apart from the major contribution made by the nuns to education in Strabane, not enough credit has been given for the charity and care they provided over more than eighty years to many unfortunate girls. It is hoped that this article will make the public more aware of this aspect of their work.

Introduction

The major problem in dealing with the history of Strabane Convent in general, and St Catherine's Industrial School in particular, is that very little exists in the form of documentation to assist a researcher.

By 1948 Sister Mary Magdalene Joyce had talked with all of the older nuns in the convent over a period up to that time and made a written record, which she continued editing until her death in 1985. Since that time the task has been undertaken by Sister Mary Ursula McHugh, who generously permitted the author access to her papers and the 'Annals of Strabane Convent'. These annals are mainly from memories and oral traditions and may not, therefore, be completely accurate.

In the case of St Catherine's Industrial School, the full admission records for every child who entered the school still exist and this article uses these, restrained only by the need for confidentiality and discretion. These records detail the condition of the children entering the school both in appearance and level of education. Most of them record the educational progression through the school and also what happened to girls for many years after they left.

Foundation

There is some evidence that three individual Catholic benefactors in Strabane had decided in 1859 (as reported in the *Tyrone Herald*, 19 June 1868) that an orphanage should be constructed for Catholic girls in Strabane, and they were the key persons in having the institution created. These were Mr James Kennedy, the shirt manufacturer, Mr Francis O'Neill, Mount Pleasant, a linen bleacher, and Mr John Carlin, a merchant, who had made his fortune in Canada some time previously.

In 1861 two deeds were executed which show that a building would be constructed as an orphanage, and the Sisters of Mercy would occupy it and care for and educate female Catholic orphans of Strabane. While this was the initial objective, provision was also made for the education of the more respectable (sic) Catholic females, from other places as well as Strabane.

Mr James Kennedy contributed 2 out of the 3 acres, 1 rood, and 6.5 perches of his own land, which he had purchased on 25 January 1857 from Charles James Brown (and others), a solicitor of New Inn, Middlesex, London. For this Mr Kennedy received the consideration of 10s, which in present-day coinage is 50p. The date on this deed is 9 July 1861. Mr Francis O'Neill contributed £500 sterling. Around the time of opening he also purchased 14 acres of adjacent land and donated this as a farm for the upkeep of the convent. Mr John Carlin assigned £50 per annum to be derived from his land, which he had purchased at Castletown, and also received a consideration of 10s. This land had been bought on 13 December 1857 from the Commissioners for the sale of Incumbered Estates in Ireland for £1,140 sterling and measured 32 acres and 1 rood. The deed in respect of this transaction was executed on 15 October 1861. On his death in 1883 this farm was inherited by the convent.

Although Very Rev. Dr Philip Devlin (1865–72) has been given credit for the approach to the Sisters of Mercy in Navan, Co. Meath, this is doubtful since the parish priest at the time of the execution of the deeds, which specified that the orphanage would be run by the Sisters of Mercy, was Very Rev. Fr William Browne (1840–64).

The foundation stone of the convent was laid and immediately the work of erection commenced, but after a few months operations ceased, principally through want of funds. For many years, no further steps were taken towards its completion. On his appointment to the parish, the Very Rev. Philip Devlin PP, VG, resumed the work and under his energetic direction construction progressed favourably. During this time numerous charity sermons were preached and bazaars organised to raise the additional funds needed for completion.

The convent was opened by Mother Catherine Atkinson (the mother superior of Navan) and along with Mother Xavier Brady, Sister Mary Evangelist Kearney, Sister Mary Columba Langan, and Sister Margaret White, a postulant, they arrived in Strabane for this purpose on 9 June 1868. Once the foundation was securely established, Mother Xavier Brady went back to Meath. Sister Margaret White's term of postulancy was completed and she was received into the novitiate 21 November 1869, taking the name of Sister Mary Joseph. She acted for many years as mistress of the national school.

The school for orphans was started up fairly quickly, since there is one recorded in the *Derry Almanac* of 1870 and the records of admissions to the industrial school for early 1870 note the admission of seven girls who had been at the Convent Female Orphanage School. In 1868 an act was passed setting up industrial schools for Ireland. According to the 'Annals', the statutory body responsible for the industrial schools approached the convent in Navan about setting one up. They could not assist and proposed that the Strabane community be approached instead. Mother Catherine Atkinson was quite enthusiastic and set about having premises specially designed and constructed for this purpose.

The 'Annals' state that Mother Atkinson needed £1,000 for the construction and that she approached Mr Francis O'Neill for assistance. He apparently was prepared to contribute £500 if she could raise an equal amount and it is claimed that this was successfully completed. However, the *Irish Builder* (1 November 1870) states that the estimated cost of construction would be not less than £1,800, which would be raised chiefly by donations from the charitable. Mother Atkinson is also described as being unremitting in her efforts to augment the resources of the institution. The planned increase in accommodation was to move from a provision for 40 to 150 children. This suggests that the original orphanage had a capacity for 40 orphans and that the planned industrial school would accommodate 150. This did not happen since the school was only licensed for 100.

The Industrial School was certified on 30 November 1869 for 100 girls but did not have its first admissions until January 1870, when it received 8, followed by a further 8 in February of the same year. At an early stage the nuns also initiated the education of other Catholic females within a boarding school. This is recorded as being in existence in 1881, at the dedication of the chapel.

In 1911 Rev. Mother Angela O'Neill opened a public steam laundry. Messrs Musgrave, Belfast, installed the machinery. Mother Magdalene, from the Mercy convent, Navan, came to give invaluable advice on the running of a public laundry. This laundry gave employment to women in the town. In 1928, owing to shortage of help, it ceased to be a public service but survived as the nuns' laundry until a few years ago.

Thus the nuns were carrying out a very complex operation at the convent. As well as the school for orphan girls, the industrial school and the girls' boarding school, they were running a separate orphanage and by 1883–5 they also had a school for boys. This may have been the start of the practice (continued into the second half of the twentieth century) where boys in Primary One and Two were taught at the convent before progressing to the boys' national school in Barrack Street.

The 1881 census showed 115 in the industrial school with 9 in the orphanage with a further 18 persons (records show 15 nuns). The report of the dedication of the chapel (*Derry Journal*, Monday 17 October 1881) in that same year claims that there were 300 girls in the industrial school and orphanage, but this appears unlikely. The same report refers to a boarding school, but the census data do not indicate the number of boarders. The 1891 census showed 118 in the industrial school, 30 boarders and a further 32 persons (convent records indicate 24 nuns). The 1901 census showed 90 in the industrial school and a further 31 persons (convent records show 27 nuns).

The Community of Sisters

The following table shows the development of the community of Sisters at Strabane Convent from its foundation throughout the nineteenth century:

YEARS	NO. OF ENTRANTS	TOTAL NO. IN COMMUNITY	REMARKS
1868		5	
1869	2	7	
1870–79	6	12	1 death 1876
1880–89	13	24	1 death 1882
1890–99	6	24	1 death; 5 to S. Africa, 1897
1900	1	25	

In 1897, five sisters and two girls from the boarding school travelled from Strabane to Mafeking, South Africa, to establish a foundation there. The pioneers of the missionary group who set out to establish the foundation at Mafeking were:

Mother Teresa Cowley from Dunshaughlin, Co. Meath
Mother Magdalene Dunne from Cashel, Co. Tipperary
Mother Stanislaus Gallagher from Omagh, Co. Tyrone
Sister Evangelist McGlynn from Stranorlar, Co. Donegal
Sister Gonzaga McDonagh, from Dublin

There were also three postulants in the group:

Margaret Coffey from Cashel, Co. Tipperary, who became Sister Joseph
Brigid McGlinchey from Glenfin, Co. Donegal, who became Sister Columba
Rose Helena Byrne from Lower Killeavy, who became Sister Patrick

All three of the reverend mothers had held offices of superior, assistant and novice mistress, respectively, in the convent at Strabane. Sister Gonzaga McDonagh died before they left Kimberley. Mother Teresa Cowley was elected superior of the new foundation.

On 1 July 1899 the school was opened at Mafeking with 50 day scholars and 5 boarders. In spite of the rumours of war, it made an excellent start but by October war was declared and those activities were suspended. The convent became a fort, and a bombproof shelter was dug near the hospital for the nuns, who now became nursing Sisters. For seven months of the siege, when not on duty at the hospital, the nuns lived in this dug-out. During their nursing service, Mother Mary Magdalene came across a soldier whom she had taught at the convent school, Strabane, when he was a schoolboy there. Johnny Hoynes recovered and on his return to Strabane was employed as a general worker at the convent for the rest of his life.

In more recent times Strabane answered another call to the African mission field. Towards the end of 1970, the Sisters of St Louis appealed to other congregations in Ireland for nuns to help them in their work in West Africa. They asked for nuns for a short period of about two years. Sister Dominic McDermott felt called to answer this appeal and having secured permission from her superior, Sister Mary Evangelist Farren, and Most Rev. Dr Farren, bishop of Derry, she set out for Nigeria on 6 November 1971. She was asked to go to Bida, Minna diocese, in what was then North-West State – now Nigeria State – to teach with two St Louis Sisters in a recently opened mission secondary school for girls.

In the years 1974–5 the Sisters of St Louis, due to lack of resources, were obliged to close one of the mission houses in the town of Minna, 100 miles from Bide. At their suggestion, Sister Dominic asked her community in

Strabane to consider sending nuns to Minna. The community agreed, and from those who agreed to work there, two Sisters, Vincent Lynch and Baptist Burke, were sent on the mission to Minna. They arrived in Nigeria on 15 March 1975, and together with Sister Dominic, became the little community of 'Gidan Rahama' (Mercy House) in Minna some days later. Sisters Vincent and Baptist (now known as Sister Susan and Sister Margaret) took up teaching in the local government secondary school and Sister Dominic (Shiela) in the teachers' college for women.

On 7 May 1922 after Exposition of the Blessed Sacrament in the convent chapel, Strabane, four Sisters left quietly for a new foundation in Buncrana, Co. Donegal. The nuns arrived in this little seaside resort without any fanfare of welcome and unobtrusively took possession of St Joseph's Convent of Mercy, as it is now called. It was a Sunday evening and the first guests to welcome them were Rev. Tom Agnew CC, and Rev. W. Elliott CC – both curates in Buncrana. The nuns in this new foundation were Mother de Pazzi Lynch, superior, Sister Josephine McLaughlin, principal of the national school, Sister Gertrude Normoyle, her assistant, and Sister Zita O'Duffy, to help with domestic duties. Buncrana, like Strabane, has flourished and triumphed down the years.

Mount St Joseph, Strabane, celebrated its centenary on 9 June 1968. Sisters from Mafeking, our African foundation, as well as nuns from Navan, Kells and Derry joined in the celebrations. The superior then was Sister Mary Evangelist Farren. From its humble beginning of five nuns, the Strabane community had grown to almost 'three score and twenty'. But unfortunately, with the decrease in religious vocations at the present time, numbers have declined. By 1998 a total of 167 women had entered the community at Strabane Convent, but 38 of these did not remain, most of them leaving before they had completed their novitiate. At the time of writing only 10 sisters remain in the new convent house, which opened in 1997. [The position has continued to change since the writing of this article. The convent building is now totally gone, with the likelihood that the site will be used in the coming years for housing. The remaining Mercy nuns have moved into a purpose-built house in the former convent grounds and the Order has ended its leadership of the education of girls in Strabane. ed.]

St Catherine's Industrial School

Industrial schools were established in response to concern about poverty in the first half of the nineteenth century, a concern which had led to the system of workhouses. Many people considered that the workhouses were unsuitable places for orphan children because they were forced to associate with criminals and developed similarly bad characters. In addition, various societies throughout Europe were establishing institutions which cared for poor children and also prepared them for the world of work. Legislation was passed for Scotland in 1854, and this was extended to England and Wales in 1866. The provision of industrial schools in Ireland was finally covered by the Act of 1868.

As already stated, St Catherine's Industrial School was certified on 30 November 1869, for 100 girls, but did not have its first admissions until January 1870, when it received 8, followed by a further 8 in February. The following table shows the growth of the school in its first decade. By the end of its second year the school had reached its registered capacity, but the records show that numbers could have easily exceeded this, since some girls did not leave at the end of their assigned time there but often stayed on. The reasons are not given but occasionally it is stated that they were employed in the laundry. This may have been a precursor to the commercial operation which the nuns started in the early 1900s.

YEAR	NO. OF ADMISSIONS	NO. OF DISCHARGES	TOTAL
1870	35	0	35
1871	7	1	41
1872	50	3	88
1873	22	4	106
1874	11	11	106
1875	8	13	101
1876	17	17	101
1877	23	15	109
1878	13	13	109
1879	15	16	108

The number of admissions per decade exceeded 100 from the start in 1871 up to the 1920s.

ADMISSIONS BY DECADE	
1870s	200
1880s	199
1890s	143
1900s	146
1910s	105
1920s	28
1930–46	13
TOTAL	834

The decline after 1920 may have been due to the partition of Ireland in 1921. From this point on the numbers entering the industrial school rapidly declined. But even though this was happening, there were still many poor children and orphans in the area and the nuns continued to accept these into their care and had 100 or more in the premises.

In 1876 an epidemic of fever broke out in the orphanage. Sister Mary Aloysius Joseph Higgins (Jane Higgins from Athboy, Co. Meath) nursed the fever-stricken children with the devoted care of a true Sister of Mercy but died on 9 October. It is not clear how long the fever had raged but a 10-year-old had died earlier on 10 May.

Where Did the Girls Come From?

Through the life of the school, girls were sent from a total of sixty four different towns and cities throughout Ireland. They were chiefly from Strabane and Derry city but ranged as far as Dublin.

The following table shows the principal places from which the girls were committed:

Place of commitment of girls (%) admitted to
St Catherine's Industrial School, Strabane

LOCATION	1870s	1880s	1890s	1900s	1910s	1920s	1930–46	TOTAL
STRABANE	22.5	10.6	31.5	24.0	29.5	53.6	30.8	23.5
DERRY	26.5	31.2	21.7	8.9	1.0		15.4	19.4
DUBLIN	4.0	2.0		5.5	36.2		7.0	
OMAGH	1.5	9.5	5.6	3.4	2.9	14.3	5.0	
BELFAST		1.0		24.7			4.6	
MOVILLE	9.5	6.5	2.1				4.2	
LIMAVADY	6.0	1.5	2.1				2.2	
LIFFORD			2.1	4.1	6.7	3.6	2.0	
DUNGIVEN		4.0	4.9	0.7			1.9	
DUNGLOE		1.0		6.8		10.7	1.8	
NEWTOWNSTEWART		2.0	5.6	0.7			1.6	
BUNCRANA	3.5	1.5	1.4				1.4	
CARNDONAGH	3.0	1.5		1.4			1.3	
OTHER PLACES	23.5	27.6	23.1	19.9	23.8	17.9	53.8	24.1

Where did the girls go to?

The records show that, in general, many of the girls were returned to their families, with a large number being licensed from around twelve years of age onwards. This was a procedure whereby a girl could be allocated to a suitable employer for work but remained under the supervision of the school until completion of the assigned term. In some cases the licence could be to the mother or another family member. Some are shown as going into employment at the end of their term in the school, usually as maids or servants.

Some highlights from the ninety-three girls who passed through the school (and were discharged) up to the end of 1879 were:

One became a monitor in the school but developed hip disease within four years and died two years later.
Another while in school was described as 'exemplary' and became a teacher in Liverpool.
One emigrated to California, another to New York and a further six to other parts of the United States of America.
One died in school at twelve years of age.
Two had to be transferred to a reformatory school: one within five days of committal; the other, described as 'most self-willed', after a year and six months.
Only one girl absconded from the school during these nine years.

Why Were the Girls Committed?

This table shows the grounds on which the girls were committed:

CAUSE	1870s	1880s	1890s	1900s	1910s	1920s	1930–46	TOTALS
ORPHAN	8.0	6.5		0.7	8.6			4.7
DESTITUTION	73.0	36.7	46.2	40.4	19.0	35.7		44.8
WANDERING	5.5	12.1	7.0	38.4	47.6	46.4	30.8	20.1
BEGGING	12.5	42.7	45.5	8.9	12.4		15.4	24.3
IN CRIMINAL COMPANY			0.7	8.9				1.7
ABSENT FROM SCHOOL							30.8	0.5
OTHER	1.0	2.0	0.7	2.7	12.4	17.9	23.1	3.8

Following the partition of Ireland, a decline in committals started, with just three admissions in 1946 for 'not attending school' and two in the same year for 'larceny'. The last two girls were discharged to their mothers in early 1949, thus ending the life of St Catherine's Industrial School. The associated orphanage also ceased within a further two years, and for some years the premises were adapted to provide accommodation for the boarding girls attending the convent grammar school.

Age distribution of girls (percentages) admitted to St Catherine's Industrial School, Strabane

AGE	1870s	1880s	1890s	1900s	1910s	1920s	1930–46	TOTALS
1					1.0			0.1
2					1.9	3.6		0.6
3					3.8	10.7		1.9
4					10.5	7.1		3.6
5	1.0	0.0	4.2	10.3	8.6	3.6	7.7	4.1
6	15.0	15.6	16.8	8.9	11.4	7.1		13.4
7	15.0	14.1	17.5	11.6	12.4			13.5
8	14.5	16.1	7.7	8.2	8.6	14.3	7.7	11.8
9	11.0	15.1	11.2	13.7	10.5	7.1		12.1
10	13.5	14.6	16.8	8.9	10.5	21.4	30.8	13.7
11	17.0	12.6	12.6	8.2	10.5	3.6	7.7	12.2
12	8.5	9.0	3.5	9.6	3.8	10.7		7.3
13	3.5	3.0	4.2	5.5	5.7	10.7	38.5	4.9
14	1.0	0.0	0.7	0.7	1.0		7.7	0.7

Some caution must be used in relying on this data since, for example, the child whose age is shown as one year and seven months is also shown as having a reading ability of first standard.

What Were the Family Sizes?

It is possible to analyse the relative sizes of the families from which the girls came. In many cases all of the girls in the family unit were committed and the following table shows an analysis of the family sizes:

Distribution of family sizes for girls (%) admitted to St Catherine's Industrial School, Strabane

FAMILY SIZE	1870s	1880s	1890s	1900s	1910s	1920s	1930–46	TOTALS
1	61.3	63.8	59.1	66.7	62.3	46.7	91.7	62.9
2	31.4	31.2	22.7	22.2	30.4	26.7	8.3	27.6
3	7.3	5.0	14.8	9.1	2.9	20.0		7.8
4			3.4	1.0	1.4	6.7		1.1
5				1.0	2.9			0.5

Finances

The raising of the capital costs has been mentioned earlier. Running costs were another matter. At the start of the programme of industrial schools, the Treasury paid 5s (25p in modern currency) for each child aged six years and over. This amount may have been increased in subsequent years. However, as can be seen from the relevant data above, St Catherine's had a significant number of girls under this age. As well as these, the orphanage was still in existence and had its complement of girls, and some of those discharged from the industrial school remained within the premises. Tradition suggests some charitable donations were received from benefactors but the nuns must have relied greatly on their own resources, which would have included the dowries with which each one entered the convent.

The nuns could not have managed all of the activities needed as well as attending to the requirements of their religious life without assistance. There are indications and there have been reports over the years that the older girls participated in many of the domestic duties of the institution.

Conclusion

The Sisters of Mercy, the convent of Mount St Joseph, St Catherine's Industrial School, the girls' orphanage, and the primary and post-primary schools established and operated by the Sisters of Mercy have demonstrated the great dedication and love given by them to the people of Strabane and district, and it is hoped that this brief article can pay some small tribute to this.

12 Parliamentary elections in North Tyrone 1885–1925

WILLIAM ROULSTON

In the preface to his book *The Soul of Ulster*, Lord Ernest Hamilton described North Tyrone as the scene of 'more closely contested elections than any other constituency in the kingdom'. Just glancing at the election results in North Tyrone between 1885 and 1911 bears out the truth in this assertion. Victories were rarely by more than one hundred votes, and in 1906 and 1907 the unionists lost, respectively, by nine and seven votes. The period 1885–1918 has been one of the most closely studied in Irish history. However, attention has rarely been focused on the events and activities in a particular constituency. This chapter seeks to rectify this by examining the

Lord Ernest Hamilton, MP for North Tyrone 1885–92

Background to the 1885 General Election

The 1868 general election was the last in Co. Tyrone in which the conservative landlord candidates were returned unopposed. At this time representative politics in Tyrone were controlled by the Abercorns and the Belmores, two aristocratic families with large estates in the county. The first challenge to their supremacy came in the by-election of 1873 when an independent conservative, J.W. Ellison Macartney, put himself forward as a candidate. Ellison Macartney had the backing of the Orange Order and campaigned on the issue of land reform. The landlords of Tyrone were extremely alarmed at Ellison Macartney's candidature and launched a particularly vociferous campaign against him. In the end, their candidate was returned by a majority of only thirty-six votes. However, in the general election of the following year Ellison Macartney was successfully returned as one of the two Tyrone MPs, the other being the conservative landlord candidate.

By the late 1870s the land question had come to dominate Irish politics, while the issue of Home Rule was also becoming increasingly important. Poor harvests and falling prices in 1878–9 only added to the situation. It was against this background that the 1880 general election campaign was fought. For the first time since the 1850s the Liberals decided to contest an election in Tyrone. Their candidate, E.C. Litton, made land reform the major issue in his campaign. The result of the election was victory for both Litton and Ellison Macartney, and meant that the landlord party, who had held both Tyrone seats just seven years earlier, no longer had a representative at Westminster. Litton's appointment as a land court commissioner necessitated a by-election in Tyrone the following year. However, this election again witnessed the defeat of the landlord candidate at the hands of a liberal one.

Parliamentary reform in the period 1883–5 transformed electoral politics in Ireland. As a result of the Franchise Act all adult male householders were given the vote. This dramatically increased the number of electors, giving many Catholics and labourers of all denominations the right to vote for the first time. The Redistribution of Seats Act saw the creation of four single-member constituencies in Tyrone – North, South, Mid and East. The effect of these legislative changes was to give the Home Rule movement a greatly enhanced chance of success in the forthcoming general election. The 1881 census had shown that in all the Tyrone divisions the number of Roman Catholics exceeded 50% of the total population. The total population of North Tyrone was 48,026, of which 25,623 were Roman Catholics. With regard to the Protestant population, Presbyterians outnumbered Anglicans by a ratio of roughly 3:2. It is worth emphasising this point as it was to have a crucial bearing on the election campaigns and results over the next three decades.

The General Elections of 1885 and 1886 in North Tyrone

By the beginning of 1885 there was a growing realisation within the anti-Home Rule camp that in order to counter the threat to the Union a united front was required which would cut across previous party affiliations. The leading liberal in North Tyrone was the industrialist, Emerson Tennant Herdman of Sion Mills, who in 1885 was the president of the Tyrone Liberal Association. He firmly believed that it was vital that Conservatives and Liberals should work together in order to defeat the nationalists.

The Conservatives of North Tyrone chose the marquis of Hamilton as their candidate for the December 1885 general election. The marquis was the eldest son of the duke of Abercorn, the largest landowner in Co. Tyrone and Ulster's leading grandee. The death of his father on 31 October 1885 saw the marquis elevated to the dukedom and his candidature was assumed by his younger brother, Lord Ernest Hamilton. The nationalists of North Tyrone chose as their candidate the prominent Home Ruler, John Dillon, but he was defeated by Hamilton with a fairly comfortable margin of 3,345 votes to 2,922. North Tyrone was the only constituency in the county to return a unionist, with nationalist victories in the other three. In the parliament of 1885 there were five Hamilton brothers. James, the eldest, sat in the House of Lords as duke of Abercorn, while his younger brothers Claud, George, Frederic and Ernest sat in the House of Commons. Lord Ernest was the only one to represent an Irish constituency.

Moves to unite the pro-Union forces in Ireland gathered pace in the aftermath of the 1885 election. In the election of that year, sixteen of the thirty-three seats in Ulster were won by conservatives, with the rest being taken by nationalists. None were won by liberals. The new duke of Abercorn played a leading part in drawing together the unionist groupings in northwest Ulster. On 9 January 1886 a meeting was held in Omagh under the chairmanship of Lord Abercorn which set up the Northwest Loyal Registration and Electoral Association (NLREA). Representatives from ten constituencies in the northwest, including the four Tyrone divisions, were invited to the meeting. Abercorn was elected president of the NLREA and it was decided that he would be advised by a directorate chosen annually from the constituencies through cooperation between Conservatives and Liberals.

E.T. Herdman was a strong supporter of the NLREA and a couple of weeks later, at the annual general meeting of the Tyrone Liberal Association, urged the Liberals to join with this new organisation in presenting a united pro-Union front. However, Herdman was strongly criticised for his conduct in the previous election campaign when he had supported Lord Ernest Hamilton and was accused of having acted without the sanction of the executive committee of the Tyrone Liberal Association. Herdman unashamedly defended his actions, but offered his resignation. One of the strongest opponents of a Conservative–Liberal alliance was T.A. Dickson who had been the Liberal MP for Tyrone between 1881 and 1885. Dickson believed that Conservative plans for a loyal union were 'a delusion and a snare to entrap and absorb the Liberal party'. After the meeting Herdman severed his links with the Tyrone Liberal Association. He became one of the principal figures in North Tyrone unionism over the next three decades. At the Ulster Convention of 1892 he described himself as 'the representative of a thriving, a happy and contented manufacturing community of nearly 2,000 engaged in the linen trade . . . on the fringe of dark Donegal'.

In the general election of July 1886 the NLREA promoted single pro-Union candidates in each of the Tyrone constituencies. Lord Ernest Hamilton again stood for the unionists in North Tyrone. On this occasion he was challenged by J.O. Wylie, a Presbyterian barrister. Wylie had nationalist backing while it was also hoped that he would win sufficient support from the Presbyterian tenant farmers to oust Hamilton. However, as Lord Ernest was later to reflect, this group disliked the idea of Home Rule even more than voting for a member of the landed aristocracy, and the duke's youngest brother was returned to parliament, though with a slightly reduced majority.

The Hamiltons and Electoral Politics in North Tyrone, 1886–92

Lord Ernest Hamilton was deeply disillusioned by parliamentary life. By his own admission he was an 'unwilling victim', only standing because his eldest brother, the original candidate, was forced to withdraw on the eve of the poll. Looking back at his parliamentary career forty years later, he lamented: 'The House of Commons, for the entry into which I had put myself to much inconvenience and a not inconsiderable expense, proved a disappointment to my expectations.' He made few contributions to parliamentary debate, though on one occasion joined with the Liberals in dismissing talk of civil war in Ireland as 'absurd and childish nonsense'. In order to relieve some of the boredom surrounding life at Westminster he would race with his brother on bicycles borrowed from dining room attendants. Not surprisingly, he retired from politics after one full parliamentary sitting, using the fact that he had married as his excuse.

At a time when the right to vote was limited by certain qualifications, one of the main activities for a constituency association, whether it be unionist or nationalist, was to ensure that every one of its supporters who was eligible to vote was actually on the electoral register. This was particularly important in a marginal constituency such as North Tyrone, and, consequently, success at the revision sessions, where difficult cases were decided before a court of law, was vital. Registration work was, however, a heavy financial burden for some local associations. The North Tyrone Unionist Association depended heavily on the duke of Abercorn for financial support. In 1890, of the total registration expenses of £750, the duke contributed £400. Even for a man of his means this was a considerable strain on resources. In March 1888 E.T. Herdman commented to Hugh de Fellenberg Montgomery that 'none of the Hamiltons wish to contest the seat as the duke thinks the amusement too costly'. Herdman was hoping to induce Montgomery, a leading unionist from Fivemiletown, to come forward as the unionist candidate for North Tyrone and had even approached the 'Belfast Party' for financial assistance to cover the costs of funding an election campaign and to pay some of the registration expenses.

As it turned out, however, the unionist successor to Lord Ernest Hamilton was actually his elder brother, Lord Frederic Spencer Hamilton, who had previously represented one of the Manchester divisions. While campaigning at Castlederg Lord Frederic made the rather surprising admission that he was a believer in the compulsory sale of estates as a means of resolving the land issue. Although brother to the largest landowner in Tyrone, Hamilton pointed out that he was not a landlord himself and so land reform would not affect him personally. Hamilton's advocacy of compulsory sale at this stage was remarkable given his class background and the fact that this issue was so controversial in a number of other constituencies, notably South Tyrone. In the heaviest poll yet in North Tyrone, Hamilton was elected ahead of the Presbyterian Liberal, the Rev. Professor James Brown Dougherty, though with a majority of only forty-nine.

In his autobiography, *Forty Years On*, Lord Ernest Hamilton related an interesting account of an event which supposedly took place after the result had been announced. He, his brother Frederic and a group of unionists were celebrating their victory in a hotel in Strabane when one of the leading nationalists in North Tyrone, Fr John McConnalogue, happened to pass by their door. In a fit of exuberance, Lord Frederic called out to the priest to join with them in their celebration. After a brief hesitation Father McConnalogue accepted the invitation and reputedly enjoyed an evening's conviviality with his political adversaries, with the suggestion by Lord Ernest that the cleric had enjoyed his fair share of Moët and Chandon. However, the story was entirely fictitious and when Lord Ernest brought out his book in 1925 Fr McConnalogue sued him for libel. The case was settled out of court, with Lord Ernest making a public apology and paying costs and damages to McConnalogue. Lord Frederic Hamilton retired from politics after just one parliament, and his failure to publish a farewell address provoked one correspondent to the *Tyrone Constitution* to accuse him of not having as much devotion to the constituency as other family members.

Charles Hemphill, Gladstonian Liberal, and the Elections of 1895 and 1900

In the lead up to the 1895 general election, it was anticipated that Dr Thompson of Omagh would be selected as the unionist candidate for North Tyrone. In 1892 he had unsuccessfully stood for the unionists in Mid Tyrone. However, his candidature in North Tyrone did not materialise, perhaps because Abercorn did not approve. Months later Abercorn was to write to the earl of Belmore concerning Thompson, stating that he was 'mad' about getting into parliament and 'very nearly played "hanky panky" in North Tyrone'. After 1895 Thompson's politics went through a radical transformation and in 1900 he stood as an independent nationalist in South Tyrone. He was unsuccessful on this occasion, but was eventually elected nationalist MP for North Monaghan.

The unionist candidate who was eventually selected to contest North Tyrone in 1895 was William Wilson, a local solicitor. In his election address Wilson pledged to support any measure which would secure the interests of the tenant farmer, but which would not damage those of the landlord. From the wording of Wilson's address it is clear that he was mindful of the patronage of the duke of Abercorn. His opponent was the Right Hon. Charles Hare Hemphill QC, who stood as a Gladstonian Liberal with nationalist backing. Hemphill was born in Cashel, Co. Tipperary, and married a granddaughter of the third earl of Harrington. Between 1892 and 1895 he was solicitor-general for Ireland. The result of the election was victory to Hemphill by 2,948 votes to 2,857. Soon after taking his seat at Westminster Hemphill was appointed to government office.

At the next general election, held in October 1900, Hemphill defended his seat against another member of the Wilson family – David J. Wilson. In his election address Hemphill described Wilson as a 'strong Tory, a Landlord's man and a determined opponent of Irish Nationality'. Wilson, for his part, made issue of the fact that Hemphill was a Tipperary man who had no real interest in the people of North Tyrone. At the same time, he went out of his way to insist that there was no personal animosity between the two candidates. The result of the election was another victory for Hemphill, though with a slightly reduced majority. According to the *Tyrone Constitution*, the result was a surprise to both sides as the unionists had had a majority on the register. The Liberal victory was, therefore, ascribed to unionist defections.

Catholic Unionist versus Presbyterian Liberal: the 1906 Election in North Tyrone

The general election of 1906 and the by-election of 1907 in North Tyrone produced two of the closest results ever seen in Ireland. The unionists of North Tyrone chose as their candidate Denis Stanislaus Henry KC. Born into a fairly well-to-do family from Draperstown and educated at public school in England and later at Queen's College, Belfast, Henry might appear to be a fairly typical unionist. However, in one important respect he differed from virtually all of his political allies – he was a Roman Catholic. He was no recent convert to unionism, however, and on at least one occasion during the 1895 election campaign in East Donegal, he shared the platform with the unionist candidate, E.T. Herdman.

In general, nationalist opinion of Henry was one of bewilderment, with the *Irish News* describing him as 'one of that weird class of creatures known as an Irish Catholic Unionist'. A correspondent to the *Derry Journal* addressed the following satirical verse to 'Brother Dinish':

> A Papist beating an Orange drum!
> Surely no slavery could be 'maner'?
> To what base uses you have come,
> In the hope of a North Tyrone Retainer!

It was also argued that Henry would receive no backing from the Orange Order in North Tyrone. This was proved entirely false by the subsequent declarations of support from the various lodges in the constituency. Indeed, only one, Newtownstewart, felt the need to draw attention to the fact that Henry was a Catholic.

Henry's opponent in the 1906 election in North Tyrone was William Heuston Dodd, a former secretary of the Ulster Reform Association, who stood as a Liberal with nationalist support. While Henry saw no difficulty with being both a Catholic and a unionist, Dodd made no secret of his Presbyterian background. In the hope of securing significant support from the Presbyterians of North Tyrone, Dodd was careful not to address the national question in explicit terms. In his election address he declared, 'I am in favour of a just measure of Self-Government for Ireland for the fullest extent consistent with the supremacy of Parliament and the integrity of the United Kingdom.'

One of the other important issues of the day was the question of whether there should be government-funded denominational universities in Ireland. Dodd couched his views on this in rather ambiguous terms, but Henry was in no doubt, declaring, 'I am not in favour of the establishment of a separate University for any one denomination, being convinced that it is essential to the future well being of this country that students of all religions should associate together during their university career.' Henry was also in favour of the introduction of legislation to increase the facilities given to occupying tenants for the purchase of their holdings by agreement.

Henry and Dodd knew each other from the Bar, and because of this the election campaign was remarkably free from ill-feeling on the part of the two candidates. There would also appear to have been few incidents between the two sets of supporters, though on one occasion an election meeting of Dodd's at Bready was disrupted by unionists. The fact that Dodd should have held an election meeting in Bready, a Protestant area, shows his determination to appeal across the religious divide. The result of the poll, held on 19 January 1906, was 2,966 votes for Dodd and 2,957 for Henry – a victory margin of only nine votes. Henry did not demand a recount and, although defeated, claimed a 'splendid moral victory'. The *Tyrone Constitution* noted that following the announcement of the election result Henry was 'not in the least cast down. Indeed he is in his customary radiant mood.' The newspaper did, however, demand an investigation into the methods used by the Catholic clergy in preventing people from voting for Henry. It also took some satisfaction from the fact that Dodd had not been able to capture the Presbyterian farmer vote.

North Tyrone's Closest Result: the 1907 by-election

Shortly afterwards Dodd was appointed a judge and this necessitated a by-election in North Tyrone which was to take place on 8 March 1907. By this time the Liberal government was well established and there was much speculation about proposals concerning Irish self-government. All sides – liberal, nationalist and unionist – saw the by-election in North Tyrone as a means of gauging opinion in Ireland on this subject, and it was to this background that the campaign was fought. The unionists lost no time in once again nominating Denis Henry as their candidate. His opponent was Redmond Barry KC, a native of Co. Cork and solicitor-general for Ireland since 1905.

Barry's candidature in North Tyrone was to the annoyance of certain sections of the nationalist population there, in particular the Ancient Order of Hibernians, who were disgruntled at the fact that they were continually having a Liberal candidate foisted on them as opposed to an out-and-out nationalist. The AOH was strong in North Tyrone, but they were given only cautious approval by the Catholic clergy and could not afford to antagonise them. The fact that Barry was himself a Catholic was enough to quell any dissension on this occasion. At the same time Barry was aware that championing the nationalist cause could cost him Presbyterian votes.

During the election campaign, nationalist criticism of Henry became increasingly scathing, and he was accused of seeking personal gain with Ireland's enemies. Henry, for his part, criticised the appointment of Dodd as a judge, claiming that his salary of £3,500 could have paid for 500 labourers' cottages. No effort was spared to try to bring as many supporters as possible to the polling booths. Almost all unionist outvoters came to vote, including a Mr W. Sinclair who travelled all the way from Buenos Aires in Argentina. Two nationalists died on their way to the poll. The result was even closer than the previous election, with Barry scraping home by a winning margin of just seven votes. Once again, Henry did not demand an election recount. After the election Henry addressed his supporters from the Abercorn Arms Hotel and declared, 'I was glad to come and fight your battle, and I have been manfully supported.'

For his efforts in North Tyrone Henry was presented with a silver tray inscribed with the following: 'This service of plate was presented to Denis S. Henry KC. by the Unionist women of North Tyrone in recognition of his two spirited contests in that constituency on behalf of the Union, 1906–1907.' In 1916 Henry was elected to Westminster as the unionist MP for the constituency of South Derry, and in 1921 he was appointed the first Lord Chief Justice of Northern Ireland. He died in 1925.

Financial Difficulties and the Two Elections of 1910

Thus by 1910 North Tyrone had become the most marginal division in Ireland; consequently success at the revisions was vital and the costs incurred huge. In order to clear off their debt, the North Tyrone Unionist Association sought help from the Ulster Unionist Council. In the discussions that followed it was decided that a united appeal to Conservative Central Office was appropriate. After much deliberation a plan was forwarded suggesting that if the duke of Abercorn subscribed £100 the Conservative Central Office ought then to contribute £200. Abercorn's intervention was decisive and eventually it was agreed that Central Office would send £200 if he and the local unionists raised £100 each.

The Ulster Unionist Council was keen that the North Tyrone Unionist Association contested the impending general election of January 1910. It had apparently been proposed that should the unionists of North Tyrone put up a candidate, Central Office would then contribute £600 to cover expenses. At this point Abercorn intervened, dismissing the proposed candidature of a local man, W.W. Barnhill, whom he believed was weak and unpopular, and arguing that E.C. Herdman, chairman of the North Tyrone Unionist Association, should stand instead. Abercorn was particularly incensed by the suggestion that, should his own son have been standing, he would have been expected to pay all the election expenses, which he was not in a position to do. Barnhill succumbed to the pressure and withdrew.

His replacement, E.C. Herdman, consented to stand for North Tyrone 'after much persuasion from friends'. He was the nephew of E.T. Herdman and was involved in the family business. At a meeting in Magheramason Herdman declared that he was 'neither an orator nor a politician, but he was a North Tyrone man and a businessman'. However, in the ensuing election Herdman was defeated by Barry by a margin of over 100 votes. Following the result, Herdman wrote, 'It is only right to say that I am very much disappointed that I obtained practically no support from the Nationalists, not even from those employed by my firm'.

Eleven months later another general election was called. At a large meeting of the North Tyrone Unionist Association in Strabane in late November, the candidature of Lord John Hamilton, fifth son of the duke of Abercorn and a captain in the Irish Guards, was announced and received with much enthusiasm. E.C. Herdman, addressing the meeting declared that he was glad the candidate was 'a member of a family which had always worked for the good, not only of North Tyrone, but the country generally'. However, not even the popularity of a son of the duke of Abercorn was enough to prevent another victory of the Liberal candidate, with Barry victorious by a majority of more than 130 votes.

After the election result was announced, Hamilton admitted that he was only a beginner in politics and was proud of his first efforts. In his letter thanking the unionists of North Tyrone for their support he wrote, 'The result of this election is a little disappointing, but the slight increase in the Nationalist majority is fully accounted for by so many of our Unionist voters being scattered all over the world and a large number of them found it quite impossible to get to North Tyrone in time to assist me.' The editorial in the *Tyrone Constitution* had already commented that 'having youth on his side, he will be a leader in the van of unionism in the days to come'. However, this was not to be, for on 6 November 1914 Lord John Hamilton was killed in action in France. Just to emphasise the North Tyrone Unionist Association's financial dependence on the duke of Abercorn, in January 1911 the duke sent a cheque for £652 to William Wilson, the unionist election agent, to cover the expenses of his son's election campaign. At the same time, the Duke did acknowledge Wilson's careful management of the election campaign and declared, 'I think the expenses are very moderate.'

The 1911 by-election and the Candidature of T.W. Russell

Barry was soon afterwards appointed Lord Chancellor, necessitating another by-election which took place in early October 1911. Thus North Tyrone experienced its third election in less than two years. Lord John Hamilton did not make himself available for this contest and the unionists of North Tyrone reverted to the tried and trusted E.C. Herdman. In the lead up to the election, the *Tyrone Constitution* drew attention to allegations made by

Sinn Féin, then a fringe nationalist grouping, that every Liberal or nationalist who had contested North Tyrone since 1886 had been rewarded with political or judicial office by the British government. According to Sinn Fein, North Tyrone was 'the one place in Ireland where 3,000 voters calling themselves Nationalists vote unanimously as the Castle directs them. It is not only the most degraded constituency in Ireland, but the most degraded constituency that Ireland has known in fifty years.' They were vehemently opposed to the selection of another 'placehunter' to represent the nationalist interest in North Tyrone.

The selection of T.W. Russell as a Liberal candidate was not without controversy. Russell was a Scot who came to Ulster to find employment, became involved in the temperance movement which drew him into politics, and in 1886 was elected unionist MP for South Tyrone. However, his advanced views on land reform drew him into conflict with the landlords of South Tyrone, so much so that following the 1900 general election he resigned from his local unionist party and founded the Ulster Farmers' and Labourers' Union and Compulsory Purchase Association. He fought the 1906 election with nationalist backing, which was enough to secure his return. However, in January 1910 he was defeated by the unionist, Andrew Horner KC. At the time Russell was the vice-president of the Department of Agriculture and Technical Instruction. Even after his election defeat he continued in his post and it was well known that the government was actively seeking to find him a new constituency.

The 1911 by-election campaign in North Tyrone took place when the political situation in Ireland, in general, was worsening as a result of the renewed discussions on Home Rule. The sense of impending crisis was reflected in Herdman's speech, following his selection, in which he declared that 'unionists must be prepared to take the field and fight as their forefathers had fought and if necessary die for their cause'. While campaigning in Magheramason, Herdman pointed out to his audience, 'You and I, gentlemen, have been represented for the last sixteen years by strangers of various political complexions whose chief merit is that we never see them again.'

The result of the election was a victory by Russell by 3,104 votes to 3,086. Because the nationalists had a majority of over 100 on the register, the result, though disappointing, was of some satisfaction to the unionists. Herdman was even to claim that the result was 'really a victory for the Union' and that several of the 'more sensible' nationalists had voted for him in preference to Russell. Looking at the response of the 210 unionist outvoters on the North Tyrone register, 134 of them managed to record their vote; 40 were abroad and couldn't make it; 9 gave acceptable excuses for their absence; the rest simply didn't bother. After the election the North Tyrone Unionist Association thanked the outvoters for their support, going so far as to attribute the 'great moral victory won by Mr Herdman to the splendid response

Appendix:

Election Results in North Tyrone, 1885–1911

YEAR	CANDIDATE	PARTY	RESULT
1885	Lord Ernest Hamilton	C	3345
	John Dillon	N	2922
1886	Lord Ernest Hamilton	U	3219
	James Owens Wylie	L	2867
1892	Lord Frederic Hamilton	U	3045
	Rev. Prof. James Dougherty	L	2996
1895	Charles Hemphill QC	L	2948
	William Wilson	U	2857
1900	Charles Hemphill QC	L	2869
	David J. Wilson	U	2814
1906	William H. Dodd KC	L	2966
	Denis S. Henry KC	U	2957
1907*	Redmond Barry KC	L	3013
	Denis S. Henry KC	U	3006
1910 (Jan)	Redmond Barry KC	L	3238
	Emerson C. Herdman	U	3136
1910 (Dec)	Redmond Barry KC	L	3170
	Lord John Hamilton	U	3038
1911*	Thomas W. Russell	L	3104
	Emerson C. Herdman	U	3086

Source: Walker, B.M., *Parliamentary Election Results in Ireland, 1801–1922*, Dublin (1978)
Key to parties: C, Conservative; L, Liberal; N, Nationalist; U, Unionist
* Indicates by-election

13 Local Government in Strabane 1800–1925

JOHN DOOHER

In early nineteenth-century Strabane there was little semblance of democracy, with the corporation firmly under Abercorn's control and the county administration under the grand jury system. Parish and manorial courts under the appointees of the landlord or the rector dealt with petty matters of law and order and obedience was expected from everyone in the lower orders. The Volunteer movement and the reformist demands of the United Irishmen had suggested that there might soon be greater participation in the decision making processes but the 1798 rebellion and the conservative reaction had ended the hopes of the reformers, for the time being at least. In the

Strabane Town Hall; the expenditure on the repairs for this renovation created much disquiet among a section of ratepayers in the years 1903–1904.
COOPER COLLECTION PRONI

early nineteenth century the Catholic question received most attention and it was not until its resolution in 1829 that attention swung back to other reform measures.

The Role of the Grand Jury

The grand jury was made up of the leading landowners in the county and dealt with roads, bridges and other aspects of communication, as well as raising money for a county hospital and gaol. Abercorn's agent was always part of the grand jury and was expected to protect the interests of the estate in the allocation of money or the imposition of county taxes or cess as it was then known. In 1807 James Hamilton informed Abercorn that he had applied for money for a new road through the estate and suggested that contact be made with neighbouring landlord, Lord Mountjoy, to strengthen the claim for the development. Burgoyne, Hamilton's successor as agent, was an active participant in Tyrone grand jury discussions and also participated in the Donegal presentments on behalf of Abercorn. In 1810 he complained bitterly about being left off the Donegal jury and insisted that his participation was a right because of Abercorn's landowning position in the county. In 1814 one independent juror had tried to question the allocation of money for the mail coach road from Omagh to Strabane but was told that this was a matter only for the landowners of the lands concerned, Abercorn and Mountjoy. Growing dissatisfaction with the grand jury system because of its undemocratic nature surfaced by the late 1820s, and government considered making changes in the composition of these important county bodies. It was proposed that a number of leading freeholders be included on the county juries in order to make them more representative but the leading property owners objected to any reduction in their control.

Strabane Protest Against County Cess

Increasingly, however, the county cess and its spending was being questioned, and a Strabane meeting in July 1832 came out against the level of the county tax and demanded that it be reduced. James Sinclair had chaired the meeting and it appeared that it had been summoned by the provost, Burgoyne, because of a protest poster at the recent market day encouraging the non payment of county cess. There were strong demands made that the legality of the latest increase in the rate of taxation be challenged in court and the meeting appointed a deputation to prepare a petition to the lord lieutenant for redress. The payment of a high taxation rate in addition to the tolls that all users of the roads were expected to pay made protest and opposition inevitable, and such signs of disapproval needed careful handling by those in authority. It is possible that Burgoyne did not attempt strongly enough to deflect this criticism of the grand jury because he soon lost his position as provost, being replaced in October of the same year by John Humphreys, recently appointed as agent to Abercorn. The landowners could not allow such public meetings to question the raising or allocation of money, and the preservation of the grand jury system was an important element in the anti-democratic crusade then gathering pace.

The Board of Guardians and the Poor Law

Other developments in central government administration gradually reduced the power of the grand jury system and the establishment of the Poor Law system in 1838 was to provide an alternative structure. The locally elected Boards of Guardians were given power over public health as well as the relief of poverty and this allowed public representatives some avenues for influencing developments. The guardians were themselves representative of the more prosperous sections of the farming community, with a fairly high property qualification for election, and with local magistrates automatically members of the board. By the 1890s the Boards of Guardians had responsibility for housing as well as public health and some of the landowners were increasingly worried about the potential high costs to local ratepayers, meaning themselves. Despite such reservations, however, the Boards of Guardians provided a degree of training in democratic control and paved the way for the more extensive democratic system introduced by the Local Government Act of 1898 which set up elected county councils and both urban and rural district councils. E.T. Herdman might complain in a letter to Lord Belmore in 1895 that too many Catholics were being appointed as magistrates, to the detriment of the administration of the law in the county and the downgrading of 'the superior type of Protestant magistrate', but he was powerless to arrest the march of time.

Strabane Town Commissioners

At local level the corporation had exercised control over the development of Strabane town but change was also happening there. The corporation had been controlled by the Abercorn interest for much of the latter part of the eighteenth century and remained in charge of the markets and trade in the early decades of the nineteenth century. The lack of economic advance in the period, however, led to calls for change, and the government in 1829 allowed for the appointment of town commissioners to provide for watching, lighting and cleansing of the streets. These commissioners were to be from the more prosperous ratepayers and were appointed for a term of three years. In the 1850s further power was delegated to the commissioners, with water supply and sewage disposal being part of their responsibilities, and by

Strabane Workhouse was managed by the Board of Guardians and later became the administrative centre for the Rural Council and after 1972 for the new District Council.

1874 further public health matters came under their control. In 1880 the property qualification for election as town commissioner was reduced to include all ratepayers, and the way was now opened for a more democratic system of authority. There were still areas of overlapping authority, however, with the commissioners, guardians or the grand jury responsible for aspects of public health and sanitary matters, and it became a question of each trying to avoid the responsibility and the cost. It took the Local Government Act of 1898 to sort out these areas of conflicting responsibilities.

In October 1829 a number of leading householders in Strabane petitioned the government for the establishment of commissioners in the town and Burgoyne, as chief magistrate and provost, was forced to call a meeting of the inhabitants to arrange for the election. There is no evidence that this action was opposed by the corporation but it is likely that it was seen by some of the former leaders as a dangerous move, even if the property qualification for election would ensure that only the wealthy were elected. The list of commissioners did not include any of the existing corporation members and appears to have been representative of the main commercial interests in the town. William Orr was elected chairman and Isaac Graham was appointed secretary to the commission, while other members included Samuel Morton, William Stevenson, David Smyth, Samuel Mathewson, Daniel Baird, James Adams, Hugh Hamilton, James Kerr, William Holmes, John Boyd, William Boyle, Joseph Henderson, Thomas Brown, Daniel Cook, Leslie Gault, Lighton Warnock, William Ramsay, William Doherty,

Charles Mc Cormick, and Nicholas Sims. The first duty was a valuation of the houses and this was completed by the end of the year, enabling the commissioners to levy a rate for improvements to be made. A priority seems to have been the piping of a new water supply and Orr publicly expressed his thanks to Burgoyne in July of 1831 for allowing the commissioners to use the water from his land. The potential of the commissioners to effect meaningful change was very limited, but it clearly demonstrated discontentment with the inaction of the previous administration in Strabane.

Agitation for Reform 1831

That discontent was taken a stage further in May 1831 when the issue of parliamentary reform was being actively discussed at parliamentary level and throughout the country. A group of Strabane's inhabitants had petitioned Burgoyne to call a public meeting to discuss the reform question but this had been refused and the town hall commandeered by the anti-reform group when the reformers had gone ahead and called their own meeting. Burgoyne had summoned a meeting on the anti-reform ticket and this included most of the clergy and a portion of the other leading citizens. It was claimed that reform would weaken the Union and endanger the position of the Protestant religion in Ireland, and it was argued that the people of Strabane should allow themselves to be guided by Abercorn and the elected representatives from Tyrone, both of whom were against reform. Letters to the *Morning Post* suggested that many of those favouring reform were former United Irishmen and therefore disloyal to the constitution, but a response letter accepted with pride the association with the Volunteers and the United Irishmen and claimed that many of Strabane's leading citizens had been caught up in the earlier reform movements. Most but not all of the town commissioners supported the reform party and a public statement issued by the pro-reform group denied the representative nature of the opposition – 'though there are among the requisitionists not less than ten clergymen of the established church, yet there are only eight inhabitants of Strabane', and one of these had earlier signed the reform petition. William Orr, chairman of the town commissioners, was main spokesman for the reformers and their petition in support was forwarded to Daniel O'Connell for transmission to parliament. The meeting also decided to support only a pro-reform candidate at the next election and rejected the slur that they were organising against Abercorn's interests. The inclusion of people like Patrick Boyle, Francis O'Brien and Francis O'Neill, and the involvement of leading citizens like Alexander Leney, MD, William Gwynn, Samuel Morton, Robert Porter and David Smyth demonstrated that the balance of power in Strabane had begun to shift and that the dominance of the former leadership was under serious threat. The abolition of the corporation just four years later emphasised just how much things were changing.

Investigating the Corporation 1833

Parliament had appointed commissioners in 1832 to investigate the existing role of corporations in Britain and Ireland and by October 1833 it was the turn of Strabane. Sir J.J. Burgoyne as provost was main witness and he outlined the position of the corporation and the main officers. The recorder, Mr Edward Edie, had charge of the books of the corporation and was paid £25 per year, while the provost had a salary of £70. The treasurer had £15 per year, while other salaried officers included a sergeant at mace, a constable, a beadle, an inspector of the corn market, a surveyor of the butter market, a crane master and a keeper of the town clock. The provost had previously held weekly courts but these had been discontinued and most matters were dealt with at the petty sessions. The existing corporation was named as: J.J. Burgoyne, James Hamilton, Rev. F. Brownlow, parish of Cumber, James Sinclair, Edward Edie, Alexander Auchinleck, General Sir John Hamilton, London, William Stevenson, Rev. Charles Douglas, rector of Donagheady and uncle of lord Abercorn, Rev. T. Burgoyne, curate at Donagheady and son of the provost, John Humphreys, Milltown, recently appointed as Abercorn's agent, Rev. Edward Bowen and John Fenton, Dublin.

It appeared from Burgoyne's evidence that the burgesses were elected by the other burgesses and that the freemen of the town had no input into the elective process. Abercorn decided on who should be provost and meetings were not called unless to appoint a new burgess or for the appointment of a new provost. A burgess was elected for life but could be removed by the other burgesses for ill conduct and the wishes of the freemen in common council could be ignored by the provost and his officials. Burgoyne's account suggested that the position of provost had been a matter of arrangement among Abercorn's agents, with himself succeeding James Hamilton who had succeeded Nathaniel Edie and with Rev. Stewart Hamilton, rector of Camus and brother of James Hamilton, also acting as provost for a period. William Stevenson, treasurer, outlined the main costs of the corporation in building the markets, in mending the sewers and improving the streets, in supporting public charities and in improving the town and showed a funding deficit of over £300, with salaries unpaid for the previous years. Much authority seemed to be held by the provost on what payments should be made and little attempt was made to seek the approval of the other corporation members.

Burgoyne was replaced as provost by John Humphreys, appointed agent for Abercorn the previous year just as the inquiry was getting under way and the new provost played little part in the examination. One issue did arise over funds earmarked for a school for the poor and apparently not used for that purpose by the clergymen of the established church, who had been given responsibility for its distribution. Humphreys claimed that he had spoken to the clergymen and pledged that the funds would henceforth be properly applied. The officers of the town commissioners and leading merchants and tradesmen were questioned about the administration of the town and their views on how it should be run and there was a degree of disparity about how burgesses should be elected, whether annually as for the provost or for life. There was little dispute, however, that a fairly high property qualification should be kept in place for the franchise but less unanimity about the level of wealth needed for election as a burgess. It was very clear that elections were seen as necessary and that the power of nomination had to be removed. Nowhere was it advocated that the corporation should be removed but there was broad acceptance that it should be more accountable to the townspeople and more concerned with the economic development of the area, rather than being a group of nominated people with little association with Strabane. Those who provided evidence to the inquiry included Burgoyne, Humphreys, Stevenson, James Sinclair, Isaac Graham, William Orr, Samuel Morton, Richard Gwynn, William Gwynn, James Cook, Samuel Colhoun, William Glasse, David Smyth, Andrew Jenkins, J. Mc Caffrey, James Graham, Charles Mc Cormick, Hugh Doherty, Patrick Boyle, Charles Conway, Hugh Hamilton and Francis O'Brien.

In 1835 the corporation was abolished and its powers transferred to the other local government agencies like the town commissioners and the grand jury, and soon to be supplemented by the Board of Guardians. As has been seen, the franchise for the commissioners and the guardians was deliberately limited and authority moved only to the middle classes. Responsibilities were also limited and ratepayers reluctant to sanction increased expenditure that they might have to pay for. One of the final acts of the corporation and the provost was to lower the charges on the canal barges, despite the opposition of the lightermen who partly owned the barges and depended on them for their livelihood. Humphreys, in his capacity as agent for Abercorn and provost of Strabane, threatened to purchase boats elsewhere and run these on the canal and it was agreed to reduce the charges as a means of stimulating trade and encouraging greater use of the waterway. An earlier meeting had called for support for the deepening of the canal and its extension further down the Foyle so that shipping could be brought directly to Strabane but this was to remain as an aspiration and the call was to be repeated in the early Famine period when public works were being announced. It was clear that trade was stagnating in the 1830s and that the canal had not lived up to expectations.

The Town Commissioners

The lists of town commissioners from the 1830s onwards show that the traders of the town were well represented and that the professional classes were prepared to become involved in managing local administration. In 1870 Oliver White was chairman of a 21-man committee, with Joseph Mc Kee as town clerk, while by 1875 the membership of the commissioners had been reduced to nine, with T.W.D. Humphreys as chairman and Edward Gallagher coming on as a new representative. The extension of the franchise in 1880 resulted in a changed council by 1882, when James Kennedy was chairman and Hugh Maguire town clerk. In 1890 Edward Gallagher was chairman and local solicitor, T.E. Nelson, was a newcomer to local government. He succeeded as chairman by 1897 and other additions later in the decade included John Devine, tea merchant, Charles Brown, publican, and P.J. O'Callaghan, butter merchant. One of the longest-serving members at that stage was Edward Duncan, while other relative newcomers included both John and Michael Mc Crossan. The Local Government Act of 1898 provided for a further review of the operation of how Strabane and area was to be administered and set up both an urban and a rural district council, with elections to the new bodies in 1899. That year also saw the first elections for a new county council to replace the old grand jury system that had survived from plantation times.

Setting Up the Urban Council 1899

The new urban council was due to be established during 1899 and the out-going town commissioners had expected to be re-nominated in the elections due in January of that year. A number of independents, however, threatened to destroy this arrangement and elections were forced, with the result that new members, John Mc Colgan, James Dunne, Peter Mc Kee, James White and Patrick Jordan joined existing members like T. E. Nelson, John Devine, John Elliott and Michael Mc Crossan. It appears that some at least of the new members were challenging for the leadership of the local nationalist community and a number of the independents were more radical in their views than the old guard had appeared to be. There was some dissatisfaction with the willingness to allow the unionist population a guaranteed share of the council seats. In the election for chairman, Mc Colgan was elected on the casting vote of Nelson against the nomination of Devine, who had been supported by Jordan, Mc Kee and Dunne. Following the election for the commissioners, a meeting in Strabane of the Peoples' Rights Association, under the chairmanship of local curate, Fr Mc Elhatton, was critical of the organisation of the nationalist movement locally, especially the arrangement with the Liberals over voter registration, and advocated a straight nationalist effort, free from any association with so-called moderate Protestants.

The new commissioners soon got their revenge when it transpired that the elected members had taken the wrong declaration and were asked by the local government board in Dublin to formally re-elect the chairman. Attendance at this meeting was small and Devine was appointed chairman without a contest. Mc Colgan's supporters probably remained away deliberately, knowing that they were bound to lose in the vote since White, who had missed the initial meeting, was known to support the Devine camp. He was elected vice-chairman, despite having declined the position when it had been offered under Mc Colgan's leadership, and for a period there were a number of verbal attacks and legal actions against former chairman, Edward Gallagher. The main running was made by Dunne, Mc Kee and Jordan, while the editor/owner of the *Strabane Chronicle*, Frank Mc Menamin, became increasingly satirical over the ongoing battle, with the result that he was finally barred from attending council meetings, when he supported a claim by John Elliott that the clerk, Hugh Maguire, had omitted a part of the minute of the previous meeting expressing confidence in a council employee who had been subject to attack by the new councillors. The new elections in January 1900 gave Mc Menamin the chance for revenge and his paper made no bones about who should be supported. Mc Crossan withdrew, while both Jordan and Mc Kee were faced by the old guard of Edward Gallagher, Charles Brown and Edward Duncan, and comprehensively defeated, according to the figures supplied by a gleeful Mc Menamin. These showed Gallagher 536, Brown 525 and Duncan 513, with Jordan on 276 and Mc Kee on 271. At the subsequent council meeting, Gallagher became chairman once again and the new urban council proceeded with a more noticeable degree of harmony for a period. Perhaps the *Chronicle* had less reason to highlight the areas of disharmony and only reported on the good news.

The new council had clearly decided to widen its areas of concern and a meeting of ratepayers was summoned in April 1900 to discuss improvements to the gasworks, sewerage system and the provision of housing. It was stressed by Gallagher that such improvements should not necessitate a major hike in rates but could be financed through loans and support from the local government board. Considerable discussion took place over whether the council should support a new gasworks or move towards electricity for lighting, and the suggestion of providing subsidised housing for the working classes was also mooted, with the problem of finding the necessary land for such development. The year 1900 also saw the retirement of Hugh Maguire, town clerk, and the appointment of a successor in T.B. Feely. This was done on the basis of open voting at council meeting, and Feely was only elected on the casting vote of the chairman after a three-way tie for the position, with Thomas Elliott and J.J. Mc Devitt being the other contenders. The use of the chairman's casting vote was referred to the local government board but they refused to intervene and the *Chronicle* described the public rejoicing at the confirmation of Feely's appointment, with a band parade and congratulatory public meeting. Having the right friends could be an important advantage in gaining public employment at the beginning of the twentieth century, and local government was to be plagued with allegations of malpractice from disappointed office seekers.

There had been general agreement that Strabane should be divided into four wards for election purposes and this was believed to provide for a degree of unionist representation. The scheme had not been approved, however, by the time the January 1901 elections came around and White, Colhoun and Nelson were due to seek re-election. The Catholic Association refused to accept that the unionists should be allowed a free run and nominated Thomas Mc Ivor and Michael Bannigan to contest the seats. This resulted in Strabane being without unionist representation during 1901 but the adoption of the ward scheme that year saw Thomas Elliott, W.C. Mc Devitte and James White being returned for the North Ward at the beginning of the following year. Further challenges did develop but these were mainly on social and economic issues, and in 1901 the establishment of a House League, to demand improved conditions for the housing of the poor, threatened the existing leadership. This was a short- lived movement that spread to other towns but the decision of many of the local councils to build houses for the working class helped to defuse their protest and they seem to have disappeared after 1906, when former secretary of the group, Eugene Conroy, was elected to the council. The urban council had decided as early as 1900 that the building of workingmen's houses was a priority and the local government board held a public inquiry in March of the following year. There was general agreement at this and the clergy of all denominations approved the proposed building programme. The House League contested the elections in the following years, when a section of the council retired by rotation, and had a number of successes in having their representatives elected.

The decision of the council to spend a large amount of money in the refurbishment of the town hall in the years 1903–4 drew considerable criticism and it became an issue at the 1905 elections. Following the elections, Gallagher was challenged as chairman by James Toner, solicitor, and only narrowly fought off the challenge to his position. The opposition claimed that the elections had shown the desire on the part of the townspeople for change and the anger at the disproportionate degree of expenditure on the town hall. At this remove it is difficult to be sure of the motives of people but the involvement of at least part of the anti-Gallagher group in the earlier Catholic Association might suggest that there was more than council expenditure engaging the attention of the opposition. In the event the opposition had their revenge when Gallagher declined to go forward for re-election the following year, and his position was filled by Eugene Conroy, formerly of the House League. The former chairman did not remain long outside, however, and returned to play an active role in urban affairs for a number of years. Conroy was elected as chairman in 1907 and remained a leading figure in the council and district for a considerable period. He was also a leading light in the AOH movement and had, therefore, considerable influence in the wider political field.

The Rural Council and Board of Guardians

The 1898 local government act had also set up rural district councils and the first meeting of the new Strabane Rural District Council took place in April 1899. This was made up of the members of the Board of Guardians elected under the poor law regulations and the initial meeting passed quietly, with Neil Bradley being elected chairman and Emerson T. Herdman as vice-chairman. In the election of the guardians the matter was somewhat complicated since part of east Donegal was included in the Strabane Poor Law Union and it became Strabane No. 2 Rural Council. Herdman was chairman of the guardians, with James Stewart as vice chairman and John O'Flaherty as deputy vice-chairman. Increasingly, however, local government bodies displayed a higher degree of nationalist-unionist rivalry and there were frequent conflicts over appointments of various officials. At the 1900 annual re-election of posts, the harmony of Strabane rural ended and strong political rivalry emerged. The establishment of Strabane Urban Council meant that the members from that area were no longer eligible to sit on the rural council and this was liable to effect the political balance. The nationalists decided to use their temporary majority to co-opt three members in place of the disqualified urban members and the unionist grouping protested strongly. The new chairman, Peter Clarke, refused to accept such protests and the changes were pushed through. At the subsequent meeting of the guardians, the co-option of the additional three nationalists was enough to sway the political balance, with the election of Daniel McCaffrey as chairman, again with strong unionist protests. Local government bodies were seen as having a degree of patronage over the various paid positions and this necessitated having control. There was the added bonus that the rural council chairman automatically became a member of the county council and this could change the political control there. It was little wonder then that unionists looked forward to the 1902 elections when the positions were reversed and unionism gained control, a position they were to retain until the local elections of 1920, when the proportional representation (PR) system was first used. Co-options were used by the majority party to strengthen its position and after each election up to three additional members were brought on to the council. These often included people such as E.T. Herdman, W.T. Miller and W.W. Barnhill; the latter was co-opted in 1908 and immediately afterwards elected as chairman of the rural council.

The county council was more remote in many ways and yet the reports of the meetings received extensive coverage in the local press. Rivalry between nationalism and unionism was intense at election times and the propaganda value of holding sway in Tyrone was seen as important in the wider political battles being fought out in the period. Unionism retained control in the period from 1899 to 1920, sometimes because they had the chairmanship of a majority of the rural councils, and nationalists were generally left demanding fair play in the allocation of posts and preferments. Patrick Mc Menamin was Strabane's elected representative on the county council but he came in for an increasing amount of criticism from the local press and from nationalist leaders for his independence in voting. In 1911 he was challenged for his position by Edward Gallagher and defeated. This was seen as a crucial period in the Home Rule struggle and it had been hoped that nationalism might gain control of the county council. There was deep disappointment when this did not happen and allegations made that in Omagh and other mid-Tyrone areas a section of the nationalist electorate refused to give their full support to the cause. Gallagher played a prominent part in challenging unionist domination and was no doubt considered a valuable party addition at that level. Success at county council level could provide a stepping stone for those with ambitions to serve the cause at parliamentary level.

Strabane Local Government and National Issues 1916–22

Local government had limited powers and responsibilities and generally functioned quite smoothly. It remained to a considerable extent the arena of the middle classes; and only at urban level did the working-class representatives have any prospect of election. Housing matters, street cleaning and sanitation remained the main issues, though national politics did sometimes intrude, especially in the period after 1912 when the Home Rule crisis was at its peak. Exclusion or partition appeared by 1914 as an emotive issue, while the outbreak of the First World War 1 was treated with broad agreement. The big change came from 1916 onwards, when the nationalist consensus on the best way forward began to dissipate and this was reflected at local level, with many more resolutions in favour or against the larger national issues. The 1916 Rising had few adherents in Strabane and the urban council passed a resolution in early May condemning the leadership of the rebellion and offering full support to John Redmond in his continued leadership of the nationalist cause. Shortly afterwards, however, the council passed a resolution demanding the release of all those detained in Strabane in connection with the Rising and paying particular attention to one detainee, Patrick Duncan, whose four brothers had fought in the British army, two of them being killed in action. In the following month attention switched to the partition question and Eugene Conroy, chairman, proposed that the council reject the Lloyd George scheme for six-county exclusion and demand that the council's delegates vote against the proposals at the nationalist conference at Belfast called to discuss the issue. Members at the council meeting on that occasion were Conroy, Michael Bradley, John Mc Dermott, Patrick Mc Collum, John Kelly, Thomas Knox Howie, Charles Brown, James White and John Perry, with James Mc Garrigle not present at that meeting. The unionist members proposed that no delegates be sent but Conroy refused to accept their amendment and the result was that Strabane's delegates were pledged to oppose the official nationalist line. Redmond had called for approval for the proposals and Joe Devlin had mobilised the AOH to support the official line. This must have posed difficulties for Conroy in his leading role with the Hibernians but others were caught in the same dilemma over an issue that was deeply felt in west Ulster. In the event the exclusion proposals were adopted at the Belfast meeting but later repudiated by Redmond when modified to placate Tory and southern unionist opposition. A series of nationalist protest meetings against Redmond and the proposals were organised throughout west Ulster and a short- lived Anti-Partition League was established, later to become the Irish Nation League. The Catholic clergy played a very active role in the protest movement and at the Strabane meeting in early July, both Conroy and Charles Brown spoke out against the partition scheme, while local parish priest, Monsignor John O'Doherty, claimed that 'there were some men from their own place who went to the conference (in Belfast) and voted for these proposals'. No doubt such people found it difficult in the following weeks, and the transfer of allegiance by the *Chronicle* to the more radical nationalism of the Nation League and then to Sinn Féin meant that thereafter little attention was given to those who continued to support the Home Rule cause locally.

It seems that the urban council was slower to adopt the new nationalism and in April 1917 the members decided to ignore an invitation to a conference in Dublin by newly elected Sinn Féin representative, Count Plunkett. At rural council level, unionist domination prevented any motions on the wider issues but by late 1916 there was some rancour over the appointment of a Presbyterian chaplain for the workhouse. It appeared that there was a degree of unionist opposition to the appointment of local minister, Rev. Clarke, and the urban council rowed in with a resolution in his favour. The matter was resolved at the following meeting and Rev. Clarke duly became the Presbyterian chaplain. There was some suggestion that the matter related to political disagreements six years previously and may have been in reference to the parliamentary election of 1911, when a Presbyterian, T.W. Russell, had been elected as liberal/nationalist MP for North Tyrone, or perhaps it was associated with disagreements over the 1912 Solemn League and Covenant. There must also have been some controversy in 1918 when the conscription crisis emerged in April and nationalists sought resolutions from all local bodies against the government scheme. A public protest in Strabane saw council chairman, Charles Brown, and former chairmen, Edward Gallagher and Eugene Conroy, make common cause with local Sinn Féin leaders in resolutions against the conscription scheme. Such former leaders, however, did not transfer to the new nationalist movement and their role in the forefront of local politics was seriously weakened through the growing radicalisation of the nationalist movement.

Local Government Changes, 1920

Local government held only limited attraction in the local press in the period 1919 to 1922, and attention was often concentrated on the events at national level. The urban council appears to have found it difficult to get away from the larger issues but faced some opposition in the early stages of 1919 from an organised labour movement. The establishment of a Strabane labour council in late 1918, with affiliations from a number of local unions, created another forum for political agitation, and by mid-1919 the labour council was demanding representation on the local council. There were a number of strikes by council employees and the chairman was forced to submit wage demands to arbitration in the early part of 1920. A town tenants defence league was established later that year to campaign for rent reductions and the new urban council had to face this increased militancy. Local government had been reorganised in 1919, and the first test was in the urban elections of January 1920. A combination of Sinn Féin and Labour saw a radical transformation in the membership of the urban council, with only the unionist members providing an element of continuity. New chairman was Sinn Féin activist, Mr S. Kennedy, and other party members included John Boyle, J. Mc Aleer and Edward O'Kane. Labour representatives included M. Furey, George Mc Dermott and Samuel Mc Guinness. Labels did not mean a lot, however, and Boyle was described as Sinn Féin/Labour when elected as chairman in January 1921. But what was without doubt was that the old guard had gone, for the moment at least, and a new generation had taken over at local level.

Change had also taken place at rural level and the May 1920 elections at rural and county council level were contested with intensity. Nationalists sought to prove that six-county partition was rejected by the majority in Tyrone, while unionists saw the county as pivotal to the success of a Northern Ireland state. The Sinn Féin organisation was fully mobilised in the elections and the Catholic clergy provided a high level of support in what was seen in many circles as an anti-partition crusade. The use of the PR election system was used for the first time and this proved decisive in key marginals. The outcome was victory for nationalists in both Strabane Rural District Council and Tyrone County Council and though there were legal challenges to some of the results the outcome remained unchanged. In Strabane Rural District Council, Charles Devlin became the new chairman with Daniel Mc Namee as vice-chairman, while the guardians saw the election of Edward Gallen and John Conway to the leading positions. The nationalist victory in the Strabane rural council was to prove decisive in the overall county situation, with the chairman providing the necessary majority at county council level. And equally significant was the fact that the elections at rural level had not seen the same degree of change of membership as at urban level. Some of the older members seemed content to accept the Sinn Féin label at election times but without showing any corresponding attachment to party policy.

Strabane Local Government and Partition

The independence of local councillors in Strabane was demonstrated most clearly in reactions to Dáil Éireann circulars in the latter part of 1920 and during 1921, when all local government bodies were required to declare their allegiance to the Dáil and break off relations with the local government board. Both Strabane rural and Strabane urban district councils continued to deal with the British local government board and finally, under pressure, submitted their accounts for audit. There was an acceptance of those aspects of Dáil policy that did not entail sanctions and financial penalties by the local government board, and thus both councils moved to support the Dáil boycott, announced in August 1920, against those Belfast firms that were allegedly supporting discrimination against Catholics. In one case, local traders, John Colhoun and Russell's Bakery, sought a meeting with the rural council and guardians over their tenders not being accepted. There were also resolutions passed against partition under the Government of Ireland Act, and in late 1921 both the rural council and the Board of Guardians declared allegiance to Dáil Éireann and rejected the authority of the Northern Ireland government. This move led to prompt action and both bodies were replaced by a commissioner at the beginning of 1922. The urban council, on the other hand, was more careful about the allegiance issue and avoided a clear declaration on the matter. They had attempted to serve two masters by sending copies of minutes of meetings to both the Dáil and to the Northern Ireland government and so managed to avoid dissolution. The decision of the ministry of home affairs in mid-1922 to end the PR electoral system made little difference to Strabane town and the urban council was quite willing to revert to the old four-ward system for the new council in 1923.

A general nationalist meeting in Strabane endorsed an agreed panel for the elections, with the result that there were no contests. The new council saw the reappearance of some of the older hands, with Charles Brown as chairman and both James Toorish and John Devine returning as councillors. John Boyle was now labelled as labour and other party followers were Robert Cunningham, Samuel Mc Guinness, Thomas Stewart, Michael Furey and John Kelly. John Perry, William Harpur and W.B. Smyth were returned as unionist representatives and one of the first actions of the new council was to protest against the recently introduced oath of allegiance for both councillors and council employees. In February another of the old-timers returned when Edward Gallagher was co-opted to replace Samuel Mc Guinness, who had died suddenly. Labour members protested against this co-option but were overruled and the 1923 council became increasingly like earlier models. The clerk was finally forced in March to end the practice of sending minutes of meetings to both the Dáil and the Northern Ireland government, and the resolution stated that henceforth they were to be sent only to Belfast.

The Boundary Commission and Strabane 1924–25

The decision of the northern government to end PR in local elections meant a redrawing of the boundaries and the rural and county elections were postponed until 1924. Nationalists protested strongly that the new electoral divisions were gerrymandered to suit unionism and refused to nominate candidates in the May elections. This did not prevent the councils operating and unionist members carried on without opposition. Strabane Rural District Council and Board of Guardians had been out of commission since early 1922 and they were now re-established, with little controversy to attract the attention of the newspapers. But political conflict had not ended and the imminent establishment of the Boundary Commission in the latter part of 1924 was sufficient to ensure continued disagreements. Control of local government was believed to be beneficial in helping to determine the award of the commission, and unionism appeared to be in the stronger position because of their control now over all of the rural councils and of the county council. At Strabane Rural District Council it had been at first intended to ignore the Commission and no written submission was made when requested at the end of 1924. There was a change of mind, however, by the spring of 1925 and the Strabane rural council appointed a deputation of W.T. Miller, Mr Rankin, Capt. Herdman and Robert Stevenson to attend the public sessions of the commission in Derry and work with Castlederg Rural District Council in opposing transfer of territory to the Irish Free State. This deputation, acting in conjunction with a North West Boundary

Defence Committee, went even further and claimed that a part of east Donegal should be brought into the area of Northern Ireland. The bottom line was that there should be no territorial transfer, but if the commission decided to move the border, then a part of east Donegal should be transferred to Northern Ireland.

For Strabane nationalists the commission also posed problems and the urban council was at first hesitant about how to approach it. In December 1924 the council decided to submit evidence and a joint deputation of John Devine, W.B. Smyth, Charles Brown and Thomas Stewart was appointed to draw up the submission. This highlighted the detrimental impact of the border on the town's economy and stressed the economic interdependence of Strabane and the Donegal hinterland. One problem for the Strabane nationalist leadership was the wider question of Tyrone and Derry and the demands for incorporation in the Free State. It would be relatively easy to make a case for the transfer of Strabane but that did not suit the wider nationalist interest, and the case had to be made for the whole county of Tyrone rather than for one part of it. The inclusion of W.B. Smyth, with his milling interests in Donegal as well as Tyrone, was seen as supporting the economic factors for changing the border, but it is noticeable that the unionist representative was not part of the deputation that made the case to the public sitting of the commission in June of 1925. Then the case for Strabane's economic dependence on Donegal was made by John Devine, Edward Gallagher and Mr O'Doherty, draper and outfitter. The wider case for Tyrone was left to the nationalist leadership of the county, based in Omagh and Cookstown. It is perhaps significant that there were more submissions from unionist viewpoints than from nationalists in the Strabane area, with the congregational committee of the Strabane Presbyterian Church, a Strabane Traders Association, and a group of unionist inhabitants of the parish of Urney all providing submissions in support of the inclusion of part of east Donegal in Northern Ireland and against the transfer of Strabane to the Irish Free State. In the event, the leak of the draft report of the Boundary Commission and its suppression at the request of the Irish government in December 1925, made the conflicting viewpoints of academic interest. The report, however, did recommend some transfer from east Donegal to Northern Ireland, with limited transfers in the other direction at Clady and Aghyaran.

So ended a tempestuous period for local government in Strabane and district which forced a reassessment of nationalist attitudes to the state of Northern Ireland. Much has been made of Strabane's losses resulting from the establishment of the border, but it has to be said that the economy of the area had been stagnating for a considerable period before then and the main losers in the post 1922 period were the traders who were deprived of a considerable part of their customer base. At local government level there was little that could be done and the general depressed state of the economy both North and South in the inter war years meant that Strabane, like many other towns throughout the country, made little progress and experienced considerable poverty. The workhouse remained, though with a much reduced role, and both urban and rural district councils continued to meet and disagree over appointments and the levels of rates needed to maintain a very skeletal public service. Political matters only occasionally intruded and councillors prided themselves on their general good sense and their service to the community. Few challenged for their posts and local democracy was rarely exercised when it became clear that existing councillors were hard to shift. The triennial elections came and went, with little disturbance to the status quo, and only the occasional bout of disharmony, when personality or political issues dictated an active stance.

A Fair Day scene in Strabane in the 1930s.
COOPER COLLECTION PRONI, D.1422/12/7

14 A Literary History of Strabane

JACK GAMBLE

The story of Strabane's literary history is one that reaches not only centuries back in time, but to far-off places. The earliest known writing in Strabane probably goes back to the fifteenth century, when the Franciscans founded a monastery in the town on a site which was later occupied by the old parish church in Patrick Street. Unfortunately, no examples of the calligraphic skill of the monks have survived.

Very little is known of this early period from a literary point of view, and in order to pick up the thread of Gaelic culture we have to turn to the great *Annals of the Four Masters* which records the building of O'Neill's castle in Strabane in 1575 and later the burning of O'Neill's town, Srath Bán, by Hugh O'Donnell in 1583.

However, by the year 1595 Turlough Luineach O'Neill was known to be a great patron and benefactor of rhymers, travelling poets and musicians.

Grays printing shop, one of the earliest printing concerns in Strabane but unlikely to have been in the ownership of the Gray family until the 1820s.

One of his bards, Ferdoragh MacAnamy, or MacConmidhe, is described in the Irish state papers as 'the richest rhymer in Ireland'. The family of MacAnamy (now McNamee) were hereditary poets of the O'Neills of Ulster.

The political history of Strabane gave the town a significance in the seventeenth century which is difficult to comprehend today, but this helps us understand the rise of an important printing and publishing industry there in the eighteenth and early nineteenth centuries in order to meet the requirements of political, social and educational progress. James I granted a royal charter to Strabane on 18 March 1613, establishing the town as a borough, with a provost and twelve free burgesses. On 8 August 1688 James II appointed a corporation in Strabane, though this was annulled by the Williamite succession and a new corporation appointed after the Treaty of Limerick.

The turbulent period in Ireland from the Flight of the Earls in 1607 through the plantation to the mid eighteenth century has left us with little knowledge of the literary history of the town. The rise of educational establishments in Strabane, the growth of the Volunteer movement and the need to spread political and religious information undoubtedly led to the development of the printing press locally.

By 1771 Strabane had become an important publishing centre. The *Strabane Journal*, or *General Advertiser*, was first issued in May of that year, a year before the *Londonderry Journal*, and appeared every Monday. John Alexander was the printer and possibly editor. He was succeeded in March 1801 by James Elliot. It is not known when the *Strabane Journal* terminated, but possibly shortly after 1801. Before the end of the eighteenth century Strabane was able to support two newspapers with a possible circulation of 400 copies per issue. The *Strabane Newsletter*, published by John Moore, Main Street, was probably in existence as early as 1788 but ceased publication about 1810. Mr A.A. Campbell records that around the year 1901 Mr Daniel McAnaw of Strabane, whose ancestors had printed and published many of the earliest newspapers, had in his possession copies of the earliest Strabane newspapers: however their present location, if they have survived, is unknown.

The *Strabane Morning Post* first appeared on 5 November 1811 (not March 1812, as stated in Campbell, *Literary History of Strabane*). It was published every Tuesday by Messrs Carroll and Foster (afterwards Carroll and Gray), priced at 5d. The proprietor was Daniel McAnaw and this paper may have survived until 1840. The motto of the paper was *Concordia Crescit*, the present motto of Strabane.

The Strabane Magazine, or *The New Magazine*, was a monthly journal of forty-eight pages and ran from January to December 1800. This journal contained accounts of the death of the Strabane historian Dr Crawford, of current literature and a lengthy account of the trials of Napper Tandy and the informer Jimmy O'Brien. The magazine was published and possibly edited by D. McAnaw. This journal like many others contained not only local but English and foreign news, and was complete with woodcut illustrations and advertising. Of special interest were the shipping notices for the port of Londonderry.

The Christian Enquirer, a weekly miscellany, was published and printed by Cowper Walker of Castle Street between Tuesday 8 May 1827 and Tuesday 29 April 1828. There were fifty-two issues, the content being largely polemical, including accounts of religious debates at Londonderry, the Arian controversy within the Presbyterian church, and a valuable 'Tour to Lough Derg' which appeared over a period of weeks.

It is interesting to note that the paper used to print these journals was possibly obtained from Ballyclare, Co. Antrim or Millfield, near Claudy, Co. Derry, and it is not very surprising that a small provincial town with a thriving newspaper industry should have produced the printer of the American Declaration of Independence in the person of John Dunlap.

Following the introduction of the printing press in Strabane in 1771 and the establishment of the newspaper industry, the first booklet appeared in 1779. It was *A Sermon Preached On Courage Or Moral Virtue*, and was delivered to the Strabane Rangers on 12 September 1779 by the Rev. William Crawford (minister in Strabane 1766–1800). The first four publications were addressed to members of the Co. Tyrone Volunteer movement in 1779 and 1780, particularly to the companies at Strabane, Finnwater, Urney, Omagh, Cappagh, and elsewhere, and from this we deduce that the printing presses at Strabane served a wide area from Derry to Omagh and Enniskillen, and via Lifford into Donegal. The stream of Volunteer sermons which followed, largely by Presbyterian ministers of Strabane and district, were of a strident nature, encouraging knowledge of the use of arms, questioning whether the magistrates were of divine appointment or not, and later turning to more serious theological matters.

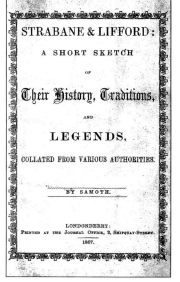

[O'Flanagan] *Strabane and Lifford*, 1867, only edition.

The year 1783 saw the publication of the most important book issued from the Strabane presses, namely *A History of Ireland From The Earliest Period*, addressed to William Hamilton Esq. by Rev. William Crawford, printed in Strabane by John Bellew. It was in two volumes containing over 768 pages, with a long list of approximately 1,380 subscribers, including at least three in America, accounting for around 1,500 copies. This gives some idea of the considerable ability of the printers to publish a work of this magnitude in the eighteenth century, though most of the titles published in Strabane had an average of only 100 subscribers.

Crawford's history was dedicated to Lord Charlemont, commanding officer of the First Tyrone Regiment of Volunteers, of which Rev. Crawford was chaplain. He wrote five books, three of which were published in Strabane. He came from a distinguished Presbyterian family, descended from Rev. Thomas Crawford, minister of Donegore (1655–70). He was ordained minister in Strabane on 6 February 1766 and his first published work was an antidote to Lord Chesterfield's *Letters To His Son*. It was published in London in 1776.

Crawford joined the Volunteer movement with patriotic zeal and visions of national independence, and his *History of Ireland* is valuable for the account he gives of the Volunteers and the secret societies of the Hearts of Oak and Hearts of Steel. Dr Crawford was instrumental in setting up the Strabane Academy in 1786. In October 1798 he resigned his charge of Strabane congregation and moved to Holywood, Co. Down. His contribution to the intellectual life of the town has been largely unrecognised.

Writing and printing in Strabane was not all serious politics and theology. Plays were published, among them *The Battle of Aughrim*, a tragedy in verse, printed by John Bellew in 1785. A comic opera by John O'Keefe entitled *Peeping Tom of Coventry* was also printed by John Bellew in 1786. By this time Bellew was so confident of his position as a premier printer and publisher that he called his establishment 'Shakespeare's Head'. It is not surprising that there was a demand for plays as well as sermons, as Miss Owenson (Lady Morgan), the famous actress and author of *The Wild Irish Girl* and other novels, resided in the town for three or four months in 1783, performing at the Little Theatre in Ball Court Lane, near Mr Smyth's steam mill. Her father was a friend of the Abercorn family and of Oliver Goldsmith, and was proprietor of the Old Crow Street theatre in Dublin.

The works which emanated from the printing presses of Strabane from 1779 until 1833 were numerous and varied, comprising history, politics, poetry, drama, literature, theology, songs and ballads. Plays, prose and polemic poured from the presses, printed by James Blyth (1779–80), James McCreery (1779), John Bellew (1783–9), John Alexander (1793), Andrew Gamble (*c.* 1795–1803) and several other lesser printers who printed commercial stationary and ephemera. The rarest work printed in eighteenth-century Strabane was a collection of sacred verse by the Most Rev. Dr Anthony Coyle, bishop of Raphoe, printed in 1788 by John Bellew, in two volumes. There are two known sets, one in the British Library and the other in the Shirley Library at Lough Fea, County Monaghan.

On the political side, it is believed that the United Irishmen in the 1790s planned to use the Strabane printers to publish revolutionary pamphlets before the 1798 rebellion. Though none were printed, two books of prophecies were printed in Strabane in 1795. Millennial in content, they promoted the ideals of a better life obtained by social and political change. In fact a millennial chapbook printed by Andrew Gamble at Strabane around 1795 entitled *Christ . . . Coming To Judgment* was confiscated and the chapman selling it at Gortin fair arrested, so great was the suspicion attached to any form of radical thought at that time.

A letter in the Abercorn papers helps us understand the political apprehension of the period. George Knox, writing from Strabane in 1793 to the duke of Abercorn regarding the United Irish paper, the *Northern Star*, stated that '[T]here are little clubs in almost every village in the north of Ireland who take the *Northern Star* . . . [T]hese clubs form Volunteer corps and distribute arms which are one day constitutional and another republican . . . [T]heir sentiments and principles are French.' (Abercorn papers, Knox to Abercorn, 16 March 1793).

The relaxation of the penal laws and the demand for Catholic Emancipation (obtained 1829) in the early nineteenth century saw a new readership emerge from the hedge and national school systems. New printers appeared like Carroll and Foster (later Carroll and Gray), Cowper Walker, James Canning, David Colhoun, Jenkins and others. The demand for cheap books was prodigious, and a new type of publication therefore began to emerge to entertain and educate the local readership.

Chapbooks or 'cheapbooks' were produced with entertaining titles such as *A Famous Song Called the Wedding of Ballyporeen* (1805), *The Sorrowful Lamentation of Jeremy O'Brien* (1806) and *The Farmer's Lament for the Downfalling Market* (1806) (nothing has changed!).

Political Songster, Strabane, 1816

The Orangemen and Freemasons also used the Strabane presses to produce their songs, and in 1812 a booklet printed by the Alexanders contained *A New Freemason's Song*, followed in 1815 and 1816 by *Patriotic Songster . . . of Loyal, Patriotic and Constitutional Songs*, edited by a Strabane man and printed by Joseph Alexander, containing 144 pages of Williamite and Orange songs and sold at the high price of 2s 1d for well-heeled buyers!

Most of the publications were issued uncut, sewn with thread and in plain wrappers. Broadsheets and ballad sheets were sold rolled, generally by hawkers or chapmen on the streets, and directly to the homes of the people. Often the chapmen would entertain the eager purchasers with a verse or two of the latest popular song composed by poets such as David Colhoun, otherwise known as *The Shepherd of Mary Gray* the name of a mountain near Newtownstewart. (David Colhoun, born Newtownstewart, 18 March 1747, claimed descent from Colhoun of Luss, Scotland. Well educated, he became a violin-maker and sheep farmer, and later overseer of the manor of Newtownstewart.)

From 1801 until 1853 the major output of the presses was once again

Presbyterian, with sermons by Revs. James and Samuel Gamble and Rev. William Dickey being the most popular in this period, approximately fifty publications being printed of various sizes. Undoubtedly one of the most interesting was a small Catholic booklet printed by Carroll and Foster in 1815, price 6d for forty-eight pages, entitled *The Devotions on the Stations of the Cross*, by Fr A. Parviliers SJ, translated from the French. The only known copy of this rare work was once shown to me by the late esteemed Mr Eddie McIntyre, former Donegal County librarian, who informed me that he thought this book had been used at a later date to perform the stations of the cross around the old Strabane workhouse.

The most important period for the printing of books and pamphlets in Strabane was 1799–1833. The considerable demand for printed works in the area in the late eighteenth century continued unabated, owing to the demand for books from circulating libraries such as that at Clady, as reported in the 1822 Sunday School Society for Ireland report.

From 1833 to 1892 only three small pamphlets were published, as well as the normal jobbing printing in the town. The arrival of the railway in 1847 caused a decline in the need for locally printed books, as readers could now obtain books more readily from further afield. However, local shops and printers continued to find a steady trade with the increase in the number of schools and circulating libraries and with the growth of commerce.

Strabane Booksellers and Printers

There is little information about the earliest booksellers in Strabane, though a Thomas Young and a John Dening, who was a merchant as well as a bookseller, were well established by 1750 and are known to have subscribed to some of the early Belfast printed books before publication, such as that of David Fordyce, *Dialogues Concerning Education*, printed in Belfast by H. & R. Joy in 1752 (both cited in J.R.R. Adams, *The Printed Word and the Common Man*, Belfast (1987), p. 26).

Andrew Gamble, merchant and bookseller, was a subscriber to a Newry printed book in 1775, though he would also have stocked Dublin, Belfast and other imprints for his local market (it is interesting to note that Andrew Gamble also sold porter at his bookshop in 1773 'on draught and bottled'!).

In 1787 there were at least three active booksellers in Strabane, namely John Alexander, John Bellew and James Anderson. John Bellew had opened a circulating library in Strabane in 1786, at a rate of 16s 3d per annum, but there was a special rate of 6s and a ha'penny per week which enabled a working man to obtain an occasional book. Alexander's bookshop and printing office in Strabane had their own engraved label in 1796, indicating a very successful and well-managed business.

In 1820 Mary Gamble was established as a bookseller and printer at Main

Street, Strabane. She may well have occupied the premises previously owned by Andrew Gamble and later owned by R.J. Blair. Her firm was listed in the *Commercial Directory of Ireland* for 1820, together with two other booksellers, namely Elizabeth Alexander at Market House Street and Carroll & Foster at Meetinghouse Street (est. 1812 – later Carroll and Gray, *c.* 1824). Mary Gamble issued her own bizarre book label of a classical semi-nude figure balanced on a wheel, *c.* 1840. None of these firms were listed in the *Pigot/Slater Directory* for Ireland in 1846, which listed the booksellers and printers in Strabane then as John Gray of Main Street, Andrew Jenkins of New Street and Cowper Walker of Main Street.

It is apparent that a great change had taken place by 1846–7. The old school of printers, publishers and booksellers had succumbed to the new industrial age, so that from this period the firms of Jenkins and Walker carried on the business of booksellers and stationers, with the printing shop of John Gray in Main Street now catering for the commercial printing needs of the town. (John Gray became the sole proprietor of the firm of Carroll and Gray, which had been established in 1824. Gray's printing shop, however, is probably the successor of one of the eighteenth-century printers, as there is a tradition which holds that the firm was founded in 1797.)

In twentieth-century Strabane the bookshops of Messrs Gray, Gormley and Blair served the town well in Main Street, with other shops in Market Street and Castle Street, and two newspapers still enjoy a wide circulation in the area, namely the *Strabane Chronicle* and the *Strabane Weekly News*.

We turn now to the lives and achievements of some Strabane printers and authors.

John Dunlap – Printer of the American Declaration of Independence 1776

John Dunlap is the name most widely connected with the history of printing in Strabane and a name widely known in the history of the struggle for American independence. He was born in Meetinghouse Street, Strabane, in 1747 and emigrated to Philadelphia when he was ten years of age. He lived in Philadelphia with his uncle, William Dunlap, who was one of the leading printers there at that time and who had just married a relation of the illustrious Benjamin Franklin. John later acquired his uncle William's printing house in 1768 after William became a minister. He was very ambitious, and in 1771 when he was twenty-four years old, he established the *Pennsylvania Packet* or *General Advertiser*. This paper became the first daily newspaper in the United States.

By 1774 Dunlap was a well-known and influential printer who had just been appointed printer to the Continental Congress. When the Congress, under the chairmanship of Charles Thomson from Maghera, drafted

A LITERARY HISTORY 257

Jefferson's manuscript of the Declaration of Independence, Thomson sent a copy in his own hand to Dunlap who printed it on 4 July 1776. How proud Dunlap must have been to see the names of some of his fellow countrymen – Charles Thomson from Maghera, John Hancock from Killyleagh, Charles Carroll of Carrollstown, Thomas Nelson and Thomas McKean, who were both natives of Strabane – on that great document which was to become a milestone in the history of the American people and nation.

John had to leave Philadelphia with many other revolutionaries on the occupation of the city in 1777. He joined a regiment of cavalry and became one of George Washington's bodyguards. After the war he acquired a large fortune and over 100,000 acres of land. He died on 27 November 1812 and was buried with full military honours. John Dunlap from Strabane, printer of the Declaration of Independence, was commemorated by a plaque at the site of his birth in Meetinghouse Street, erected in 1965 by Strabane Urban District Council.

William Starrat– Mathematical Genius

This remarkable scholar lived in Strabane in the early eighteenth century. William Starrat ran a private academy teaching arithmetic, algebra and geometry, with special reference to the application of mathematics to a career such as the army or surveying. He executed estate surveys and described himself as a 'philomath' – a student of mathematics and natural philosophy.(See chapter 5 for his role in estate mapping). Although his place of birth is not known, he apparently lived in Strabane for a considerable period: he is known to have carried out estate surveys in at least eight Irish counties from 1716, notably those in Fermanagh and Tyrone for the Brooke family and for the Creighton estate at Crom Castle, Fermanagh, and Lifford, Co. Donegal.

His major treatise undoubtedly influenced many young men to follow a military career. It was called *The Doctrine of Projectiles Demonstrated and Apply'd . . . in Practical Gunnery* and was first published by subscription and printed by S. Powell of Dublin in 1733 with folding plates; it was also print-ed by Philip Crampton, bookseller, of Dublin in 1746, also with plates and dedicated to the provost and fellows of Trinity College, Dublin. Among the list of subscribers' names are a number with Strabane associations, such as Mr Hugh Brown, Lt William Carleton, Andrew Crawford, William Calhoun, Guy Carleton, Mr William Delap, Hon. Capt. Gustavus Hamilton, William Hamilton of Dunamanagh, Mr Pat Hamilton of Strabane and others.

It is believed that William Starrat also wrote poetry and corresponded with William Ramsay (the 'Gentle Shepherd'), the famous Scottish poet, but substantive evidence of this is not presently available. His will was proven on

4 January 1769, so we can only assume that this influential scholar died shortly before this date.

Dr John Gamble – Surgeon and Author

The literary scene in early nineteenth-century Strabane was enlivened by the writings of Dr John Gamble, one of the foremost literary men of his day in Ireland. His books are now almost forgotten, apart from his accounts of his travels in Ireland (*c.* 1810–20).

He was born in Strabane around 1770 and was reared by his uncle, an apothecary, possibly in Main Street. He obtained a medical degree at Edinburgh, and a dissertation in the name of John Gamble on rheumatism – possibly his doctoral dissertation – was published there in 1793. He later served as a military surgeon in the Dutch campaign under Sir Ralph Abercrombie against the French in 1799. Considerably disillusioned by war, he lived in London for a time, returning to his native Strabane shortly before 1810.

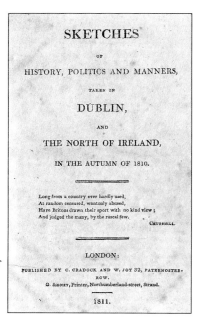

The first publication by Strabane born writer, John Gamble, and a moving commentary on social conditions in parts of Ulster in this period.

He took up writing and wrote three travel books about his journeys in Ireland, mainly in Ulster, and four works of fiction with an Ulster background. His journeys were lively, enthusiastic excursions on foot, horseback and by coach, chatting to all and sundry, gathering information, legends, humorous stories, and accounts of incidents and people. In his earliest book *Sketches of History, Politics and Manners Taken in Dublin in 1810*, published in 1811, we have a vivid description of Main Street, Strabane, and the 'lying clock of Strabane' which proclaimed the hour with 'more noise than veracity'. His sympathetic account of the trial of Robert Emmet so incensed the judge, the Right Hon. W.C. Plunket, that he took legal action against the Dublin distributors of the book, with the result that the book was suppressed. It was not until 1826 that a revised edition was published, with the offending paragraphs revised.

Dr Gamble had a deep sympathy and charitable regard for all his fellow countrymen. In his *Sketches* of 1810 he remonstrates that religious prejudice, which had for a while lain dormant in Ireland, is again unhappily 'revived'. Although a Presbyterian, he shows his appreciation of the beauty of Catholic music in his *View of Society and Manners in the North of Ireland* of 1812. In his revised *View* of 1818, addressing a peasant woman, he says: 'I am an Irishman, bred like yourselves on the potato ridge.' In contrast, we have an interesting account of his visit to Mavey Cann's parlour at Drumvallagh, and the meal of mutton, lamb and tongue, with candied gooseberries and rich pudding at a small farm near Clady, washed down with 'a tolerable port' and 'three immense jugs of whiskey punch'!

His love of Strabane is found at the beginning of each of his travel books where he begins by expressing his emotions on returning to the 'hills and dales of my youthful days'. His sense of place in writing is a positive theme taken up by his successors from William Carleton to Séamus Heaney.

Dr John Gamble's first novel, *Sarsfield, An Irish Tale*, was published in 1814. The hero is a young Irishman who, under the name of Glisson, is a French prisoner of war at Strabane. This was followed in 1815 by *Howard, A Novel*, in two volumes, which could be described as a 'rake's progress'. More interesting is his *Northern Irish Tales*, published in two volumes in 1818. This novel starts with the tale of Stanley, the son of a Derry alderman, and includes the famous story concerning Miss Knox of Prehen and her murder by Mr MacNaghten, together with a tale of the American War of Independence.

His final novel, *Charlton, or Scenes in the North of Ireland*, depicts with sympathy the views of the United Irishmen. The hero is a young surgeon who becomes a leader of the rebels at the battle of Ballynahinch. Cloaked under the name of Dimond is the Rev. James Porter of Ballindrait, who was hanged on 2 July 1798. Many quotations from Porter's famous satire, *Billy Bluff*, are included in this historical novel, and it was these lines from Charlton:

> Up the rocky mountain and down the rocky glen
> We'll keep them in agitation until the French come in

which are a possible source of inspiration for William Allingham, the Ballyshannon author's poem 'Up the Airy Mountain, Down the Rushy Glen'. Allingham was a clerk in the Provincial Bank in Strabane around 1841.

Dr John Gamble died in 1831 and is buried in the old burial ground at Leckpatrick. James Clarence Mangan, writing to Charles Gavan Duffy, said: 'Did you ever hear of Gamble, the author of *Northern Irish Tales*? He made a powerful impression on me . . . in my teens.' (Cited in O'Donoghue, *Life of JC Mangan* (1897), p. 145). It is tempting to suggest that our bachelor author may have lived beside Mary Gamble at 4 or 6 Main Street, where she carried on her bookselling business.

Cecil Frances Alexander – Hymn Writer

Although Cecil Frances Alexander, the world-famous hymn writer, was born in Dublin in 1818, she may be considered a Strabane lady. Her father, Major John Humphreys, was appointed land agent to the marquis of Abercorn so the family moved into Milltown House (Strabane Grammar School) in 1833. 'Fanny' became very involved in the life of the parish church (Camus-Juxta-Mourne) and, as her interest developed in philanthropic work amongst the poor and the children of the parish, so simultaneously her poetical genius began to blossom.

Three of her best-known hymns 'There Is a Green Valley Far Away', 'Once in Royal David's City' and 'All Things Bright and Beautiful' were written in Strabane prior to her marriage. In 1848 she published her *Hymns For Little Children.* The preface was written by John Keble and the proceeds went to support the newly opened school for deaf and dumb children in Strabane (1846).

Strabane printer's book label *c.*1796

Frances married the Rev. William Alexander DD in Strabane in 1850 and, following various appointments, her husband was appointed to the incumbency of Strabane parish church. A few years later William and Frances were devastated by the destruction by fire of the deaf and dumb school, with the loss of the lives of six children. They devoted the proceeds of their new volume of poems to the rebuilding of the school. This work was called *The Legend of the Golden Prayers,* and it contained the story of 'Stumpie's Brae', a well-known legend around Strabane at that time. It was about an old pedlar who sheltered for the night in a lonely cottage, and when he fell asleep the owner of the cottage and his wife determined to murder him in order to steal his purse and pack. They carried out the foul deed and then decided to carry him away in his pack. The poem tells the tale:

> The pack's owre short by twa gude span
> 'What'll I do?' quoth he –
> Oh, you're a doited, unthoughtful man
> We'll cut him off at the knee.

The guilty couple were haunted by Stumpie's ghost who followed them to America:

> In the woods of wild America
> Their weary feet they set;
> But Stumpie was there first, they say
> And he haunted them on to their dying day
> And he follows their children yet.

Mrs Alexander was greatly loved by people of all faiths. She died in Londonderry in 1895. Her husband, Bishop William Alexander (born Derry 1824), was a considerable author of theological books and shared with his wife a great love of poetry. A volume of their selected poems was edited by Dr A.P. Graves and published in Dublin around 1930. He published several volumes of poetry, including *St Augustine's Holiday* in 1886 and *The Finding of the Book* in 1900. William Alexander was ordained deacon in Derry in 1847 and it is not generally known that he nearly lost his life due to his labours among the poor in Derry during the Great Famine and fever epidemic which followed it. His colleague, Rev. R. Higginbotham, did in fact die from the effects of his exertions at that fearful time in Ireland. William Alexander was rector of Strabane from 1860 until 1867. He died in 1911.

Dr George Sigerson MD – A Literary Giant

Dr George Sigerson was born at Hollyhill, near Strabane, on 11 January 1836, the son of William Sigerson of Derry and his wife Nancy Neilson, a relative of the United Irishman, Samuel Neilson. His early education in classics was obtained privately from Rev. William Hegarty, later parish priest of Strabane. With this sound beginning he was sent to Letterkenny Academy and taught by Dr Crerard. He went on to St Joseph's College, Montrouge, France, and later studied medicine in Galway, Cork and Dublin, where he taught himself Irish.

He graduated in 1859 and was by this time enthusiastically involved in researching the old Irish sagas and legends. An assiduous researcher, his first book was a translation from the French into English of Charcot's *Treatise on the Disorders of the Nervous System*, published in 1857. This was followed by *The Poets and Poetry of Munster* (1860), a collection of Irish songs collected by John O'Daly and translated by 'Erionnach' (Dr Sigerson, using this pen name, was expressing his conviction that he was a fully accepted Irishman although of mixed Viking and Irish blood). His considerable interest in Irish politics, coupled with his literary skills, made him a force to be reckoned with in the columns of the *Freeman's Journal*, *The Irishman* and other influential nationalist journals. Perhaps George Sigerson's most influential work was his *History of the Land Tenures and Land Classes of Ireland*, published in 1871. This history and exposure of the anomalies which weighed against the peasant farmer had a profound effect on Gladstone's land reforming policies for Ireland.

George Sigerson's home at 3 Clare Street, Dublin, became a mecca for aspiring writers, poets and musicians; he was one of the founders of the Feis Ceoil and was president of the Irish Literary Society from 1893 until his death. His *Bards of the Gael and Gall* was first published in 1897 and is a tour de force, beginning with the Milesian invasion of Ireland. He produced an astonishing sequence of tales as he translated his way through the Cuchullain, Finn and Ossianic periods of Irish legendary history. He has been described as 'An Ulsterman of Viking race' and his *Modern Ireland*, published 1868, written under the pseudonym 'An Ulsterman', is still an extremely useful work of reference on a wide variety of Irish economic, social and national issues of the mid nineteenth century, as is his lesser known *Political Prisoners at Home and Abroad*, published 1890. He also wrote many articles under the pseudonym of Erionnach, as well as one under the name of Patrick Henry. His *Easter Song of Sedulius* was published in 1922.

An amusing fact about Dr Sigerson is that James Joyce was a student of his in the early 1900s, and Joyce, no doubt inspired by his impressive physical appearance, gave him a brief mention in both *Ulysses* and *Finnegans Wake* – immortal literary fame for this distinguished son of Strabane.

Dr Sigerson was one of the first senators of the Irish Free State and a fellow of the Royal University of Ireland. He was a friend of Isaac Butt MP from Ballybofey. His wife, Hester Varian, was also an author from a well-known Cork literary family, and his eldest daughter, Dora Sigerson (Shorter) was a considerable writer whose poem 'The Tricolour' was published in 1922.

Dr Sigerson died aged 89 on 17 February 1925, after a short illness. Here are some lines from his poem 'Far Away':

> Oh, fair the founts of Farranfore
> And bright is billowy Ballintrae,
> But sweet as honey, running o'er
> The golden shore of Far-away.

William Collins 1849–90 – Poet and Writer

William Collins was born in Strabane in 1840, the son of Thomas Collins who came to Strabane from the province of Munster. His father was an ardent nationalist and their home became a rendezvous for many noted northern nationalists of the time. William's love of poetry was awakened by a gift of a volume of Thomas Davis's poetry from a Castlefin pedlar. He ran away from home at the age of fifteen, taking an emigrant ship to Canada, where he settled in Bytown (now Ottawa), and was employed in farming and lumbering. He then began to write seriously and during the American civil war he moved to Cleveland, Ohio, where he fought for the federal army. In 1866 he took part in the Fenian raid on Canada, under General John O'Neill. His most famous poem from this period is entitled 'An Irish Rebel's Story', where we read:

> With one cheer for Mother Ireland
> On their serried ranks we pressed
> Sprang upon their massed battalions
> With our bayonets at their breasts.

Returning to Cleveland he wrote many articles and poems for the press, and his ability achieved widespread acclaim. In 1874 he went to New York to work on the editorial staff of the *Irish World*, and later he was connected with the *New York Tablet*. He wrote numerous poems, short stories and three novels, *Ballads, Songs and Poems*, New York (1876), *Dalaradia*, New York (1890), *Sybill, A Tale of the County Tyrone*, and *The Wild Geese*. All these are now very rare books, and we have been unable to locate copies of the last three titles.

One of the most nostalgic poems which Collins wrote is called 'A Sigh for Old Times'. The following are a few lines from the thirty-two known lines of this delightful poem:

> Oh God be with the good times when I was twenty one
> In Tyrone among the bushes where the Finn and Mourne run
> There's not a spot round old Strabane but memory treasures still
> From Milltown wide to Croghan's side but has my right good will
> The Curly Hill our playground was, our camp the Cottage Lea
> Within the glen where outlawed men in other days roamed free.

William Collins also wrote for the *Boston Globe* and the *New York Globe*. His *Summer In Ireland* was printed in *The Shamrock* on 8 September 1883. He died in Brooklyn, New York, on 4 February 1890. There is an interesting reference to him in the Strabane carnival booklet which was published in 1952.

Short Notes on Other Strabane Writers

Many and varied are the writers who have lived in Strabane over the years, including clerics, doctors, ordinary working men and women, and in recent years many young people writing poems for peace. Others are too numerous to mention, many of them anonymous writers who, without esteem or recognition, nonetheless kept their friends and fellow townspeople amazed and enthralled with their versatile verses.

In a more serious vein, at least two medical doctors who lived in Strabane gained considerable distinction through their writings.

Dr James Simms, 1741–1820, the son of a Co. Down Presbyterian minister, graduated at Leyden in 1764 and practised in Strabane from 1765 until 1772. His most famous work, *Observations on Epidemic Disorders and Fevers*, which was largely based on his medical observations in the Strabane area, was published in London in 1773, just after he had moved there. He wrote significant medical works, which were translated into French, German and Italian. In London he was held in high esteem and served for twenty-two years as president of the Medical Society. In 1802 he presented his valuable library to the society. He died in Bath in 1820.

Dr Francis Rogan, born in Strabane in 1787, was a notable successor to Dr James Simms in the medical annals of Strabane. He was an extremely careful statistician and epidemiologist and his carefully prepared reports on the health of the people, especially in the Abercorn estates and Strabane dispensary areas, became one of the keystones of the government medical reports. These reports concerned the contagious fever, smallpox and typhus epidemics between 1812 and 1819.

In 1819 Dr Rogan published his major work, *Observations on Contagious Fever*, which is based on his personal observations of the epidemic in the Strabane area. He died on 13 August 1854 and was buried in St Columb's Cathedral, Derry. There is a remarkable memorial to him just inside the porch of the cathedral.

Dr Thomas Carnwath, born in Strabane on 7 April 1878, is a lesser-known Strabane medical writer. He wrote many papers on public health, water supply and especially nutrition in the years before 1939. The Carnwath medal for social and preventive medicine has been awarded at Queen's University since 1956. Dr Carnwath died at Whitehead on 2 April 1954, and a paper by Dr J.H. Elwood about his life was published in the *Ulster Medical Journal* (Vol 51, No. 2, 1982).

Rev. James Porter, whose family had a long connection with Strabane, was born near Ballindrait, Co. Donegal, in 1753. He was ordained to the Presbyterian ministry at Greyabbey, County Down, in 1787. He became friendly with Samuel Neilson and other members of the Society of United Irishmen and his famous satirical letters in prose and verse on '*Billy Bluff and Squire Firebrand*', namely Lord Londonderry and other local squires in the Greyabbey area, were published in the soon-to-be-suppressed *Northern Star* United Irish newspaper. The offence to Lord Londonderry led to false charges being preferred against him of robbing a mail coach. He was tried by court martial and hanged in view of his residence and church on 2 July 1798. His sons rose to high positions in the United States judiciary.

A number of Strabane writers from the professional groups drifted into writing through their political involvement. One of these was Thomas Neilson Underwood, a native of Strabane, by profession a barrister. He played a prominent part in the Fenian movement in the 1860s. Together with Denis Holland he founded the Brotherhood of Saint Patrick and wrote prose and poetry for *The Irishman* and a play called *The Youthful Martyr*. He was a descendant of Samuel Neilson, the United Irishman and founder of the famous *Northern Star* newspaper. He died around 1876 and was buried at Glasnevin, Dublin.

Another Strabane man with journalistic ability was Bernard Quin (*c.* 1820–85), whose newspaper career began in Belfast on *The Vindicator*. The original editor of this paper was Charles Gavan Duffy. It represented

Catholic and Repeal opinion and ran from 1839 until 1848, when it was forced to close following a prosecution for libel. This remarkable northern paper emphatically pleaded for help during the Great Famine. An article dated 5 October 1846 states 'give us food or we perish, this is now the loudest cry in this unfortunate country'. Bernard Quin also worked for *The Mercury* and became editor of the Ennis-printed *Clare Journal*. He retired to Holywood, Co. Down, where he died on 17 August 1885.

A Presbyterian divine and author, the Rev. Dr William Fleming Stevenson, was born in Strabane on 20 September 1832, the son of a leading merchant in the town. He was educated privately in Strabane, and later at the Royal Academical Institution, Belfast, and at Glasgow university and Berlin and Heidleberg universities. He was licensed to preach by the Strabane presbytery in July 1855 and took up his first charge in Belfast. After the revival year of 1859 he proceeded to Rathgar, Dublin, and was married to a Miss Elizabeth M. Sinclair in 1865. He published *Praying and Working* in 1862, and a later edition of 1886 contains a useful biographical sketch. He also published a volume of hymns in 1873 and *The Dawn of Modern Mission* was published posthumously – a fitting tribute to a man who devoted his life to the promotion of foreign missions and who was instrumental in founding the Irish Zenana mission of the Irish Presbyterian Church in Gujarat, India. During his life Dr Stevenson formed a large library which was preserved in Assembly's College, Belfast, as the 'Stevenson Memorial Library'. He travelled very extensively and had many honours bestowed upon him, including an honorary doctorate, the moderatorship of the Irish Presbyterian Church, and the appointment as a senator of the Royal University of Ireland. After he died on 16 September 1886, it is recorded that 'an immense concourse of all creeds followed his remains to Mount Jerome cemetery in Dublin'. Dr Stevenson's *Life* was written by his wife and published in 1888 by Nelson's of London and Edinburgh.

As well as the named writers of a past age we cannot but mention those who wrote the stories and ballads which were sung, recited and remembered in Strabane by our forefathers, such as 'The Flower of Sweet Strabane', first published in a Derry newspaper by Dan McAnaw in 1909. This anonymous poem was published with an air in the *Northern Constitution* on 25 February 1928 by Sam Henry, the Coleraine folk tale collector:

> I've often been in Phoenix Park and in Killarney fair . . .
> But yet in all my travelling I never met that one
> That could compare with Martha, she's the Flower of Sweet Strabane.

The anonymous song 'Sunset on Croaghan' was collected and printed by Sam Henry at Coleraine in November 1935, while the splendid epic poem of unknown authorship entitled 'The Channel Fleet She Ploughs the Deep from Derry to Strabane' tells us about the Strabane canal in days gone by. These were the poems and writings of the ordinary people, using their free powers of self-expression without concern for the niceties of poetical structures, and how memorable they are.

From time to time an obscure name of an author or poet is suggested, but it hardly matters that we do not know the identity of the man called Devine from Strabane who penned the words:

> The first time I saw young Moorlough Mary
> Twas in the market of sweet Strabane.

More important is the fact that the songs and writings endure, though the authors are often forgotten. The story of the children of Strabane who wrote their poems for peace over the last thirty years is another part of the rich literary tradition of the 'fair town of the white plain'. 'Let Strabane flourish.'

15 Strabane in the Wider World
Famous People from the Area

JIM BRADLEY

Guy Carleton, 1724–1808

It is surely noteworthy that in the most important military engagement in the history of North America the opposing forces were under the respective commands of Strabane-born Carleton and Raphoe-born Montgomery. In this engagement Carleton's miniature army was initially forced to abandon Montreal. However, with a makeshift fighting force he defended the citadel of Quebec city and defeated its besiegers. Had he failed, Quebec would have become an American colony and Canada as we know it today would not exist.

Montgomery died leading his men in a final assault on the last days of the war. Thirteen years earlier at the siege of Havana he had been a captain in one English regiment, while Carleton was a colonel in another. Although they were both natives of this locality and had similar military backgrounds, it is not known if they ever met.

After Montgomery's funeral, Carleton sent on the dead soldier's watch and seal under a flag of truce to the American encampment for forwarding to Montgomery's widow. Carleton has been described as an enigma. Although trained to lead men in battle, he tried to avoid shooting American rebels whom he considered to be deluded Englishmen. To the consternation of the government he continually released prisoners of war. Some idea of Carleton's enlightened humanity can be gained from the following passage in a letter which he wrote on 10 August 1776:

> I have sent the rebel prisoners taken in this province (Quebec) to New York that they may from there return to their respective homes in the hope that the confinement they have undergone may have brought them to a sense of shame of their past crimes and proof given to the rebels still in arms that the way to mercy is not yet shut against them.

In 1778 Carleton resigned the Governorship of Quebec as a result of differences with Lord Germain, secretary of state for the colonies, but in 1782 he was brought out of retirement to act as commander-in-chief of the British forces in North America, in which capacity he was responsible in 1783 for the arrangements for the surrender of New York to George Washington and the evacuation of British troops from North America. (One of Washington's personal bodyguards during the three days of negotiations with Carleton was another Strabane man, Captain John Dunlap.)

Carleton was created Baron Dorchester in 1786 and appointed governor-in-chief of British North America. During his occupancy of this office, the Canadian Constitutional Act of 1791 was passed. Carleton's firm administration of the government at that time was responsible for the successful inauguration of the respective institutions established under the Act which are the foundations of modern Canada.

In 1773 Carleton had married Lady Maria Howard, third daughter of the earl of Effingham, who bore him nine sons and two daughters. He died suddenly on 10 November 1808 at Maidenhead. In his lifetime Carleton, otherwise Lord Dorchester, had brazenly defied the authority of his king and the English parliament, but at the time of his death he was recognised as one of the most decisive figures of the eighteenth century. He will be remembered as the soldier and statesman who more than any other person kept Quebec, and ultimately Canada, within the empire, not on Britain's terms but on those of the Quebecois – the people of Quebec.

General Richard Montgomery, 1737–75

Richard Montgomery was born in Raphoe on 2 December 1737. His father represented Lifford in the old Irish parliament in College Green and his brother afterwards sat for many years in that body as the MP for Donegal.

Montgomery entered the British army at the age of eighteen and served under General Wolfe at the taking of Quebec in 1759. He subsequently sold his commission in England (6 February 1772) and returned to Ireland before finally emigrating to America, settling at King's Bridge near Rhinebeck on the Hudson, where he purchased a 67-acre farm. In 1773 he married a Miss Livingstone, who was to survive him by fifty years.

When the American Revolution broke out, Montgomery, 'with the ardour of the people of his birthland' (*Field Book of the Revolution*), ranged himself on the side of the American rebels. In April 1775 he was selected as a delegate to the First Provincial Convention to New York and in the autumn of the same year he was appointed brigadier-general and ordered to join in the invasion of Canada.

As a result of the sudden illness of General Schuyler, the supreme command devolved onto Montgomery, who moved rapidly, forcing the army of General Guy Carleton to abandon Montreal on 12 November 1775. While leading his men in the final assault on Quebec, he and his principal aides were fatally wounded and their deaths so disheartened the rebels that they abandoned the expedition.

On the afternoon of 31 December 1775, the day of victory of the loyalist forces over the Americans, a hand was discovered sticking out of the snow-covered battlefield at Pres de Ville and the body, being extricated, was discovered to be that of Richard Montgomery.

In the Massachusetts Historical Collection, it was stated that at first Carleton refused to allow the remains of the first Irish general of the American forces the 'poor courtesy of a coffin', but the facts are that Carleton asked his chief of engineers, James Thompson, to have a 'genteel coffin prepared' and arranged for Montgomery's burial service at sundown on 4 January 1776, conducted by a military chaplain in the presence of Thompson and six other officers.

Montgomery's death was deeply felt in America and the Congress passed resolutions of sympathy to his family, expressive 'of its grateful remembrance, profound respect and high veneration'. It was also decided that a monument should be erected to his memory and this was placed in front of St Paul's Church, Broadway, NY, bearing the following inscription:

THIS
MONUMENT IS ERECTED BY ORDER OF CONGRESS
25TH OF JANUARY 1776
TO TRANSMIT TO POSTERITY A GRATEFUL REMEMBRANCE
OF THE PATRIOTIC CONDUCT, ENTERPRISE AND
PERSEVERANCE OF
MAJOR GENERAL RICHARD MONTGOMERY
WHO AFTER A SERIES OF SUCCESSES, AMID THE MOST
DISCOURAGING DIFFICULTIES, FELL IN THE ATTACK
ON QUEBEC, 31ST DECEMBER 1775
AGED 37 YEARS.

In 1818 Montgomery's remains were removed from their original resting place in Quebec and reinterred beneath the monument mentioned above.

James McCullagh 1809–47

James McCullagh, the eldest of fourteen children, was born in Landahussy, Plumbridge, the son of a farmer. At an early age the young McCullagh displayed extraordinary intellectual powers, and by the time he was seven years old he was able to solve difficult riddles and conundrums of every description.

Around 1818 the family moved to Strabane town, where James attended a school taught by Mr O'Brien, a talented mathematician and classical scholar, and where his genius soon displayed itself. It has been written that he devoted the time spent by other boys in play to the solving of mathematical problems, 'and that when Euclid was first placed in his hands he was not content merely committing the demonstrations to memory but also acquired a perfect understanding of the chain of reasoning in each proposition'.

When it was time to begin the study of classics McCullagh was sent to Rev. John Graham's classical school in Lifford and then to Rev. Rolleston's school in Strabane, where he was prepared for matriculation. At the age of fifteen he entered Trinity College as a pensioner, obtaining second place out of thirty candidates. At the examination in the same year for sizarship he was second out of ninety-five candidates.

In 1835 he was appointed professor of mathematics and in 1843 he was transferred to the chair of natural philosophy. The records of Trinity College state that the vast acquired treasures of his highly cultivated mind and his enthusiasm for his work attracted crowds of students to his lectures, and that an immense stimulus, which was felt in the University for many years afterwards, was given to the study of pure and applied mathematics.

McCullagh's chief claim to fame rests on the character of his geometrical work which was 'marked by an elegance, power and originality' which was to place him in the front ranks of the world's mathematicians. By 1838 he was a member of the Royal Irish Academy and in the same year he was awarded the Conyngham Gold Medal of the Academy for his paper 'The laws of crystalline reflection and refraction'. In making the presentation, Sir William Hamilton, the world-famous scientist, said: ' [W]hen your genius shall have filled a wider sphere of fame than that which it has yet come to occupy let this attest that minds were found which could appreciate and admire you early in your native country.'

Professor McCullagh acted as secretary of the Academy from 1842 to 1846 and contributed many of his learned papers to its proceedings. In many other ways his generosity and interest were of great service to the

Academy. In 1839 he presented the Cross of Cong and other archaeological treasures in his possession to its museum.

Sir William Hamilton's hopes for the wider sphere of fame for McCullagh were not to be fulfilled. In the general election of 1847, Professor McCullagh was a candidate for the representation of the University in parliament but was unsuccessful. The figures were:

G.A. Hamilton	728	Elected
F. Shaw	572	Elected
J. Napier	540	
J. McCullagh	373	

McCullagh's temperament was completely unsuited for the election contest. Worn out by overwork and no doubt feeling distressed at the undeserved rebuff at the polls, James McCullagh took his own life in his chambers in TCD on 24 October. His remains were interred quietly in his native parish of Badoney in keeping with his unassuming manner. His personal appearance is preserved in three pencil sketches by Sir F.W. Burton in the National Gallery, Dublin.

At the time of his death, his family was living at Curly Hill, Strabane, and remained there until his sister Isabella, the sole survivor, returned to the old home in Landahussy, where she died on 31 December 1894. In response to her wishes, the family vault at Badoney was sealed after her interment, and a marble slab was erected bearing the names of the family members interred therein.

In accordance with her further wishes a brass tablet was placed inside the parish church inscribed:

THIS TABLET IS ERECTED BY

ISABELLA McCULLAGH

IN LOVING MEMORY OF HER DEAR BROTHER

JAMES McCULLAGH

FELLOW OF TRINITY COLLEGE DUBLIN, WHO AFTER A SHORT

AND BRILLIANT CAREER AT THE IRISH

UNIVERSITY, WHERE HE CARRIED OFF THE HIGHEST HONOURS,

DIED IN DUBLIN

A.D. 1847

AT THE EARLY AGE OF 36.

HIS WORKS ARE HIS MONUMENT,

THEY SHALL ENDURE.

1894

One of McCullagh's brothers, Andrew, emigrated to the United States and was a member of Congress for Wisconsin for some years before his death in 1882.

James Wilson, 1787–1850

James Wilson, grandfather of President Woodrow Wilson, was born on 20 February 1787 at Dergalt, Strabane, and emigrated to America in 1807. On the voyage out he met a young girl from Sion Mills named Annie Adams and they were married in the Fourth Presbyterian Church in Philadelphia on 1 November 1808.

Wilson had served his time as a printer in Strabane, and in Philadelphia he soon found work on the staff of a leading Democratic newspaper, *The Aurora*, to whose editorship he succeeded after five years.

In 1815 he moved to Ohio where, although not a lawyer, he became a judge of the Court of Common Pleas, as a result of which he was known in later life as Judge Wilson. He was elected to the Ohio State legislature and later became a member of the US Senate.

In 1832 he founded the *Pennsylvania Advocate* in Pittsburgh, in which paper he campaigned unceasingly for the abolition of slavery and announced that he would not accept advertisements asking for information as to the whereabouts of runaway slaves.

At the time of his death on 23 October 1850, in his sixty-fourth year, after an attack of 'Asiatic cholera', he was publicly described as 'one of the most distinguished men of his community'.

James Wilson was the father of ten children, the youngest of which, Joseph Ruggles, born 1822, became a distinguished Presbyterian minister. Joseph Ruggles Wilson married Jessie Woodrow from Carlisle, and their third child, Woodrow, born in 1856, became president of the United States from 1912 to 1921. (President Wilson died in Washington on 3 February 1924.)

The Wilson ancestral home at Dergalt was acquired by the National Trust and is now under the care of the Ulster American Folk Park and Strabane District Council.

Matthew Mease, 1729–87

Matthew Mease was born in Strabane in 1729 and reared by his uncle Matthew in Gortinmore, Ballindrait, Lifford. Matthew Mease Sr made a will in 1746 whereby, after making several pecuniary bequests, part of his property was devised to his nephew and namesake. Long before the testator's death, however, the young Matthew emigrated to Philadelphia, to be joined later by his brothers James and John.

Unlike his brothers, who were early members of the First City Troop of Cavalry in Philadelphia, Matthew entered the fledgling American navy and served under the famed Paul Jones. In a fierce naval encounter in 1779 between Jones's vessel and the *Seraphis* from Flanborough Head, Matthew, who was his ship's purser, wanted to be more than an idle spectator. He requested from Jones, and received, the command of the quarterdeck guns, which duty he faithfully discharged until carried below after being dangerously wounded in the head by a flying splinter.

Matthew Mease died in Philadelphia in 1787. His name is on the list of original members of the Friendly Sons of Saint Patrick.

John Mease, 1740–1826

John Mease was born in Strabane in 1740 and emigrated to America in 1754, where he became one of the most important shipping merchants in Philadelphia. He was an early and ardent friend to the cause of American independence and one of the original members of the First City Troop of Cavalry. On a memorable night in American history, 25 December 1776, he was one of twenty-four of that corps who crossed the Delaware with the troops under General George Washington.

John Mease was one of five men detailed to the service of keeping alive the fires along the line of the American encampment at Trenton to deceive the enemy while the Americans marched by a private route to attack its rearguard. He served with the troop until the end of the war and suffered great loss of property in his warehouses and dwelling. For the last thirty years of his life he was one of the admiralty surveyors of the port of Philadelphia and died in 1826 at the advanced age of eighty-six years.

John Mease was the only man who continued into the nineteenth century to wear the old three-cornered hat of the Revolution and was familiarly called 'the last of the cocked hats'.

He was survived by his wife Esther and son James Jr, born 11 August 1771, who became a renowned American physician, scientist and author. In August 1790, while still a student, James Mease published the first of a series of learned articles on hydrophobia. During his lifetime he wrote, edited and compiled numerous medical works, but he was principally remembered in the US for his contributions to literature unconnected with his profession.

James Mease Jr died in Philadelphia on 14 May 1846 and was buried in the grounds of the Third Presbyterian Church in that city.

James Mease, 1732–85

James Mease was born in Strabane in 1732 and emigrated to America around 1750. With his brothers John and Matthew he soon became an activist in the struggle for American independence. He was a founder member of the First City Troop of Philadelphia and became a member of the powerful Committee of Correspondence on 18 June 1774. He was also a member of a secret revolutionary committee known as the Committee of Safety (a nomenclatural forerunner of the notorious Committee of Public

Safety that would later spread terror in the French Revolution).

In November 1775 James Mease was made paymaster and treasurer of the Continental army. In 1776 following the evacuation of New York by the British the American Congress made a number of changes in its appointments, one of which was that a separate department should be established to supply clothing to the army. The department was to be headed by a clothier-general and the initial appointment went to James Mease. His performance in that office may be estimated by the phrase coined by the American soldiers to describe the sickness associated with inadequate clothing – they were, they grimly joked, dying of the Meases.

Mease, who in civilian life was a prominent Philadelphia merchant, had canvassed Washington personally for the appointment with the sycophantic wish that 'God grant that your future success may in all things be equal to your merits'. Some months later Mease was explaining to a very disgruntled Washington how it happened that one of his regiments had been outfitted in red uniforms (the same colour as their British opponents). On a previous occasion he had been called before Washington to explain the absence of uniforms of any colour.

Although James Mease was not entirely to blame for the shortages (supply wagons were being constantly intercepted and their contents irregularly appropriated), the low level of competence in his administration obliged Washington, under severe pressure from his senior officers, to request Congress in August 1778 to replace Mease. Due no doubt to the esteem in which the Mease brothers were held by the members of Congress, action on Washington's request was delayed until July of the following year.

There was no long-standing estrangement between Washington and James Mease, for in 1780 the latter was subscribing £5,000 in gold coins to provide clothes for the army, and he was one of the select few who dined with Washington in Evan's Tavern, Philadelphia, on the evening of 1 January 1782.

James Mease died in Philadelphia in 1785 and was survived in the city by his brothers John and Matthew. A further brother, Robert, remained in Strabane, where his son, Andrew, and grandsons Andrew Jr, William and James were educated (by Rev. Burgoyne in Lifford and Rev. Rollestone in Strabane) before graduating in TCD.

The names of Robert and Andrew Mease are mentioned in the list of Protestant Dissenters in Strabane in 1775. Although the Meases had distinct Presbyterian leanings (a Matthew Sr had bequeathed £3 in his will in 1746 towards the building of a meetinghouse in Ballindrait) they continued to remain in the Church of Ireland, as otherwise their descendants could not attend any university in Ireland in the eighteenth century. The Meases who emigrated to America became openly Presbyterian while those who remained in Ulster were only 'occasional Dissenters'.

On 1 January 1782, the Friendly Sons of Saint Patrick held a dinner in Evan's Tavern in Philadelphia to mark the presentation of a gold medal, the insignia of the Society, to George Washington, the president of the state and Congress. Accompanying the president were the minister of finance, the Chief Justice, the speaker of the House of Assembly and leading American generals then in Philadelphia. In addition to the distinguished guests there were present thirty-five members of the Society. It is surely noteworthy that these included four Strabane-born emigrants – John Dunlap and the three Mease brothers.

All four had taken an active part in the American Revolution as soldiers, and, on one single occasion on 17 June 1780, they subscribed £13,000 in gold and silver to the Bank of Pennsylvania for the supply of provisions to the American army. This was a very substantial amount – equivalent to several millions of pounds in today's money. (The individual subscriptions were James Mease £5,000, John Mease £4,000 and John Dunlap £4,000.)

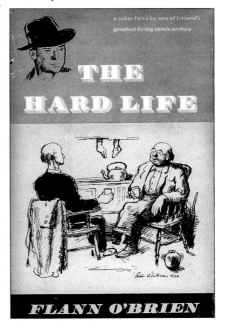

Brian O'Nolan (Flann O'Brien/Myles na Gopaleen), 1911–66

The Hard Life, dust jacket designed by Séan Ó Sullivan RHA

Prior to 1986 the name and fame of Brian O'Nolan was little known in the Strabane district. In the early 1980s the responsible authorities were deliberating on suitable names for the various streets and cul-de-sacs of a new housing estate at Melmount, and when the name O'Nolan was put forward it was quickly passed over – a further instance of 'the prophet not being honoured in his own country' – and at a time when the reputation of Brian O'Nolan, the leading satirical writer in this century in English and Irish, was posthumously gaining international acclaim.

It was fitting therefore that the local Arts Advisory Committee should decide on a modest attempt to gain belated recognition of O'Nolan's genius in the town of his birth. To this end it decided in 1986 to adopt, as the central theme of its annual arts festival, a programme of events relating to the life and times of Brian O'Nolan, and with the support of the District Council a symposium was held in October of that year which was attended by the surviving members of O'Nolan's family and some of his distinguished literary contemporaries. As part of the itinerary a commemorative plaque was unveiled at his birthplace at 15 Bowling Green, and a new housing estate at Magirr was formally designated O'Nolan Park. [It appears from the research of Jack Gamble that the O'Nolan family also lived for a period at Tulach na Gréine, Derry Road (ed.).] Appropriately, in the year in which the first international literary workshop on the writings of Brian O'Nolan was being held in Dublin, public tribute was paid to his memory in the town for which, uncharacteristically, he had an abiding affection.

Brian O'Nolan, who has been described as 'one of the funniest writers to use the English language in this century', was born on 5 October 1911, the third of a family of twelve born to Michael Victor O'Nolan of Omagh and Agnes Gormley, of the well known Gormley family of Strabane which, until recent times, carried on a newsagency and stationary business at Main Street and Market Street. The full roll call of the O'Nolan family was Gearóid, Ciarán, Brian, Róisín, Fergus, Kevin, Maeve, Nessa, Nuala, Shiela, Michael and Niall. The children's Christian names are evidence of the fact that, although a customs surveyor by profession, the father was an Irish language enthusiast by inclination. (Michael O'Nolan was also elected the first chairman of the Tyrone County Board of the GAA in 1904, an office he held until 1908, and was chairman of the Ulster Council of the GAA from 1904 to 1907.) Michael's brothers, who included a professor of Irish at Maynooth and a Carmelite priest, were all versed in Latin and Greek and were well-known writers in Irish.

On the mother's side the Gormley brothers were also talented, George and Eugene as writers, and Tom and Joe as musicians and composers. Tom became a professional violinist and was part of the folklore of Strabane in his later days as an alcoholic musical genius before dying almost forgotten in a local psychiatric clinic. Joe will be remembered by the older generation as the conductor of the town choral group 'The Good Companions' and the producer and conductor for many years of the former St Pat's Operatic Society.

If antecedents count for anything, it was obvious that the O'Nolan children would benefit from the learned, literary and musical backgrounds on both sides of their family. After a much-sheltered childhood at Bowling Green and later at Ballycolman Avenue, where they were privately tutored, the three eldest brothers, Ciarán, Gearóid and Brian entered Blackrock College at the same time and won many class prizes, earning for themselves studious reputations in an institution renowned for its distinguished alumni.

After graduating with a BA Honours degree (in English, German and Irish) and an MA in Celtic studies from UCD (where he had become the foremost contributor to the college magazine *Cothron na Féinne*, Brian entered the Irish Civil Service, where he ultimately became private secretary to three successive government ministers and in which he was to remain until his dismissal in 1954. On the sudden death of his father in 1937, he became the principal support of his younger brothers and sisters. The necessity of holding down a full-time responsible position prevented O'Nolan from taking up writing as a full-time occupation and made his prolific literary output all the more remarkable.

Brian wrote his first novel, *At Swim-Two-Birds*, in 1938 under the pseudonym 'Flann O'Brien'. The work, which was published in 1939, was admired and acclaimed by James Joyce, Graham Greene, Samuel Beckett and Dylan Thomas. Despite this high level of literary appreciation the book on its first publication was not a financial success, principally due to the outbreak of the Second World War and the subsequent destruction of the publisher's stocks when their premises in London were destroyed by German incendiary bombs in August 1940.

Brian O'Nolan made his earliest recorded appearance in the columns of the *Irish Times* in 1938, but his first contribution under the pen-name 'Myles na Gopaleen' did not appear until 1940. For almost a quarter of a century his column 'Cruiskeen Lawn' appeared regularly in English and Irish. Satirical and controversial, it was accused of 'poking fun at the national tongue', but the reaction from its readers was not always unfavourable. The most significant comment came from P. Ó hAodha, who wrote:

> I have been reading the Irish that is printed in our newspapers for many years and I do not remember ever having seen an article which called forth a single comment, be it praise or blame, from the readers. That should be a sufficient defence for your contributor – if indeed he needs any.

To set language enthusiasts at each other's throats, and in impeccable Irish, was the type of dubious success that was to attach to all his works during his lifetime. Brian's relationship with the *Irish Times* was not always happy. It was a standing editorial order that the 'Myles copy' was to be closely scrutinised for libel, scurrility and double meanings. The alteration and rejection of offending columns, and the corresponding reduction in the paltry remuneration paid to the author, infuriated Myles, who would never admit that he had libelled anyone.

The only occasion of libel recorded against the column followed an attack by Myles against the Dublin Institute of Advanced Studies, founded by Eamon de Valéra. The head of the Institute was Professor Edwin Schroedinger, a world-famous mathematician, who gave an address to the Institute on 'Science and Humanism', which Myles understood to be a proposition that there was no logical basis for belief in a Divine Being.

At the same time another luminary of the Institute, Professor T.F. O'Rahilly was advancing the hypothesis that there were two different Christian missionaries to Ireland who had been confused historically as one figure – Saint Patrick. In a scathing witticism much enjoyed in Dublin,

Myles wrote that the Institute 'was seeking to prove that there were two Saint Patricks and no God'. When the director of the Institute sued the paper, the matter was settled out of court on payment of £100.

O'Nolan's second novel, *The Third Policeman*, written in 1940, was not published until after his death, when it was immediately hailed as a masterpiece of comic invention. *The Hard Life* (described as 'an exegesis in squalor'), written in 1941 and dedicated to Graham Greene, was not published until 1961. *An Béal Bocht*, written in 1941, his only lengthy work in Irish, was translated into English in 1973 as *The Poor Mouth. The Dalkey Archive*, published in 1964, was dramatised by Hugh Leonard under the title *When the Saints Go Cycling In* and was presented at the Dublin Theatre Festival in 1965. In 1943 two other works, *Faustus Kelly* and *Thirst*, were produced at the Abbey Theatre where his uncle, Fergus O'Nolan, had been a producer twenty years earlier.

A difficult and morose man and a long-time habitual drinker, Brian O'Nolan saw his vocation in life as 'the chastisement of the folly and the hypocrisy of modern day Ireland'. In his later years he scoffed at the Americans, scholars and thesis writers, beating a pathway to Dublin in search of James Joyce. Twenty-five years on, a new generation of students of English literature are coming to Ireland to research the works of Flann O'Brien and Myles na Gopaleen.

It was a fitting irony that the author of so much outrageous fantasy should die on All Fool's Day, 1966. Plagued for much of his life by sickness, alcoholism and a perennial shortage of cash, he was to write in the days before his death from cancer in a Dublin hospital:

> . . . that anyone who has the courage to raise his eyes and look sanely at the awful human condition must realise finally that a tiny period of temporary release from intolerable suffering is the most that any individual has the right to expect.

He was survived by his wife Evelyn (née McDonnell), a Civil Service colleague whom he married on 2 December 1948. During his lifetime, in which he suffered frequent literary rejection, and since his death, countless articles and many books have been published on the life and times of Brian O'Nolan.

The list of authors and contributors reads like a literary Who's Who and includes the names of Dylan Thomas, Anthony Burgess, Brendan Behan, Seán O'Faoláin and Benedict Kiely. When J.B. Morton, 'Beachcomber' of the *Daily Express*, died some years ago, Bernard Levin, the famous literary critic and TV personality, referred to him as 'a brilliant satirical writer, second only to Myles na Gopaleen'.

Despite his irascibility Brian always remained loyal to his family and close friends and cherished memories of his childhood and subsequent holidays in

Strabane, which he once described as 'the happy-go-lucky town at the confluence of two tumbling rivers'. His brother Ciarán was to write later that the days that he and Brian and Gearóid spent by the Mourne were the happiest of their lives, 'particularly the hours spent in the long grass of the river bank while the sun seemed to stand still in the cloudless summer sky and they could hear the distant clank of mowing machines and the faint hum of the turbines in the linen mill . . .'

Brian O'Nolan was buried following Requiem Mass on 4 April 1966, in Kilmacud parish church. At the graveside the rosary was recited in Irish but there was no oration.

At the time of writing all of the Flann O'Brien novels and plays are in print, as are *The Poor Mouth* and three collections of the *Cruiskeen Lawn* columns by Myles na Gopaleen. The latest of the many books about him are *Flann O'Brien: An Illustrated Biography* by Peter Costello and Peter van de Kamp, published in 1987, and the first full-length biography, *No Laughing Matter: The Life and Times of Flann O'Brien,* by his personal friend Anthony Cronin, author, poet and critic, published by Grafton Books, 1989.

Alexander Ector Orr, 1831–1914

Alexander E. Orr (the son of William Orr and Mary Moore) was born in Strabane on 2 March 1831.

At the age of nineteen he emigrated to the US and by 1861 he was deeply involved in the commercial life of New York City. In 1889 he was elected president of the New York Chamber of Commerce, an office he was to hold for the next five years. In 1894 he was appointed a member of the Rapid Transport Commission created by the state legislature to draw up plans for a comprehensive transport system for New York City. At the first meeting of the Commission he was elected president, and, after four years of intensive work under his direction, plans were completed for a subway system, construction of which was commenced in 1900.

In 1904 the first trains began to run on the New York subway and at the official opening of the system in that year the principal address was given by Alex Orr. Referring to the event, an editorial in *World Work* commented: '[I]t's a cheerful fact that the costliest municipal undertaking ever constructed in the world has been free from corruption and free from political management – in New York too without scandal – and much of the credit for this historic achievement belongs to Alexander E. Orr.'

Orr was for many years president of the New York Assurance Company and held many important positions in the commercial life of the city. For fifty years he acted as treasurer to the Long Island diocese of the Protestant Episcopal Church, prudently managing its many complicated financial affairs, and was its most generous benefactor. He died on 3 June 1914.

Eddie McIntyre, 1918–83

Eddie McIntyre, who provided much of the inspiration for this book, was born in Co. Donegal in 1918, the eldest son of Andrew McIntyre, the first Donegal county librarian. Eddie became assistant to his father in 1936 and his belated appointment as county librarian in 1968 was welcomed by a multitude of well wishers in the north-west.

While McIntyre Sr was responsible for the fine collection of rare books, particularly Irish historical works, in the possession of the Donegal library and which he purchased over the years on a shoestring budget, his son became an authority on the whole collection and unstintedly put the benefit of his knowledge at the service of history students and casual readers.

Eddie wrote many articles on local history for various magazines and periodicals and for many years contributed a perceptive weekly column to a local newspaper.

A founder member and past president of the Donegal Historical Society, he successfully undertook the mammoth task of comprehensively indexing the complete set of Donegal Historical Annuals from their inception to the date of his retirement – a work that has been of immense benefit to those interested in research in the wide range of learned articles contained in these annuals.

His untimely death in the year after his retirement in 1982 was an event of special sorrow not only in Strabane, the town in which he had made his home, but throughout the north-west and especially Lifford, in which he was reared and which he knew so intimately.

The following is part of the concluding paragraph of an article by Right Rev. George Otto Simms, former archbishop of Armagh and primate of Ireland, entitled 'Growing up in Donegal' (*Irish Life,* published by O'Brien Press, Dublin, 1979):

> Lifford's Carnegie Library in the old courthouse served the county. Here the biographies, history and literature were on the open shelves for browsing. The story of the county and of Ireland was not confined to books, for the friendship of Andrew McIntyre helped me to appreciate the culture and traditions he so clearly loved.

There was magnetism in his storytelling. The soft voice from the north of the county spoke of books and writers with an intimacy and affection that held the listener fascinated and admiring. I often thought of the manner in which he related all that the county had produced in song and saga and had given to the world of literature.

His critical appreciation, lively with humour, sparkled as he showed me the range of his studies. With but little persuasion I might have become a librarian.

George Otto Simms, 1910–92

The former archbishop of Armagh and primate of Ireland was born in 1910 into a family which came from England in the early seventeenth century as part of the Ulster plantation and whose descendants are still to be found resident in the substantial Georgian house known as 'Combermore' on its commanding site overlooking the Foyle.

James Sime and John Sime his son are mentioned in the Church of Ireland census of 1659 as living near Castlefin. Early in the last century the family transferred to Strabane where they became proprietors of the town's principal hotel. George Otto was the third son of John F.A. Simms, who was the originator of a legal dynasty that still flourishes in the Strabane area, and whose father-in-law was German-born Otto Stange, from whom the future archbishop derived his middle name.

At the age of five George Otto entered the Prior School in Lifford and four years later he enrolled at a preparatory school in Surrey where his uncle was a vicar. In 1935 he graduated from Trinity College, and, following his ordination in 1936 as a Church of Ireland minister, was appointed a curate in Saint Bartholomew's parish, Dublin. In 1938 he was persuaded to take up the appointment of chaplain to Lincoln Theological College and two years later was appointed dean of residence in TCD, which office he combined with lecturing in classics, running the Church of Ireland training college and numerous other activities.

In 1962 he was appointed bishop of Cork, Cloyne and Ross and four years later was elevated to Dublin. Finally in 1969, and somewhat reluctantly, he accepted the office of archbishop of Armagh and primate of Ireland, at a time when the northern troubles were just beginning. The political trauma in which he was then unwillingly involved imposed an ever-increasing strain on a man whose natural instincts were always inclined towards matters of a spiritual and scholarly content.

Happily married to Mercy Felicia Glynn for many years, Dr Simms has long been recognised as one of the most distinguished figures in the Church of Ireland. Although not renowned as a historian, as was his late brother, Professor James Gerald, the former archbishop has won special distinction as the leading authority on the Book of Kells, and his mellifluous tones were often heard on television and radio and in lecture halls throughout the country, as he held audiences enthralled with his brilliant, and occasionally humorous, word picture of our most famous manuscript.

In an absorbing and nostalgic article in *Irish Life* (O'Brien Press, Dublin), Dr Simms wove a multi-coloured tapestry of 'growing up' in Lifford and Strabane in the early 1920s and his feeling for his native place can be gauged from the following extracts:

> . . . growing up in the valley with the hills in front of us and behind us,

was a gentle, quiet process . . . we ranged freely enough in what were country surroundings with the town life of Strabane but a mile away in the bordering county of Tyrone . . . the rivers that glinted in the sunlight on a wintry morning, seen from our windows, through the bare branches of the trees, lent distinction to the Lifford/Strabane neighbourhood. The stately flowing waters shaped the valley.

The Mourne and the Finn met before our eyes and formed the broader Foyle, sending it on its way to Derry and the lough beyond, a stretch of some fifteen miles. Often in flood, rich in fish, majestic in their onward flow, we found these waterways as they dominated the landscape, friendly and companionable. Not with the eye of the tourist or of the visiting stranger but with familiarity and affection we named and claimed as part of our life these rivers and their tributaries, the heather hills and each peak of their ranges. Purple headed Knockavoe and the sprawling contours of green topped Croghan were special and constant companions.

As Others Saw Us –
Descriptions and Views on Strabane

Ireland From The Air, Benedict Kiely, London (1985)

Where the Finn river, coming from the long and lovely Lough Finn in the heart of the Donegal highlands, meets the Mourne water from Co. Tyrone to form the Foyle are the towns of Lifford and Strabane. The big bridge that joins them is one of the chief gateways to the wonders of Donegal. This unfortunate border that separates them has meant that Strabane has been exposed to more than its share of the irrationalities of our time, even to an attempt at aerial bombardment. Perhaps the towns are best known through a lovely song:

> But farewell till bonny Lifford where the sweet Mourne waters flow
> And likewise to my brown haired girl since I from her must go
> As down Lough Foyle the waters boil and my ship stands out from the land
> I'll say farewell and God bless you, my Flower of Sweet Strabane.

There is also the song about Moorlough Mary whose lover first glimpsed her at the market of sweet Strabane, where 'the hearts of all the men she did trepann . . .'

Northern Ireland – Soldiers Talking, Max Arthur, London (1987)

Strabane is really the pits of the world. It's the most bombed area of Northern Ireland – it really is. It's the worst place you've ever seen in your life. The people are so hostile there. I went there one day after someone had left a suspicious bag which the police thought had a device in it. As I was walking there was a bunch of bloody yobboes behind me and because there wasn't enough police on patrol they started prodding me. I ran – I couldn't do anything else. I went back later to the device and as I was walking down I could hear these jeers 'Die you bastard' and 'I hope you get fucking blown up'. Very sociable people.

Ireland in 1834, Henry D. Inglis, London (1835)

Strabane I found a remarkably neat and pretty looking town with several streets, which contained excellent houses and capital shops. In spite of the obstacle offered to improvement by the refusal of the Marquis of Abercorn to grant good leases, the town advances nevertheless. There is an excellent retail trade, and an improving linen trade which averages a sale of about 500 pieces weekly. I saw little or nothing of rags in Strabane; there was a respectable look about the people and everything else. The poverty-stricken appearance of Irish towns was fast disappearing. I perceived that I was verging towards the north, and getting among a different race of men. I heard few complaints of want of employment, and ten pence is the usual rate of wages.

Post Chaise Companion (1830s)

Strabane is a large populous and tolerably well built town on the river Mourne half a mile from its confluence with the River Finn and the same from Lifford which is in view and renders this situation one of the most beautiful spots in Ireland. It contains many gentlemen's houses and gives the title of Viscount to a branch of the noble family of Hamilton as Lifford does to that of Hewitt.

Lifford has a barrack for a troop of horses.

Irish Sketch Book, W.M. Thackeray (1843)

Through a coach window starred with mud and ice, while horses were changed, we saw a dirty town called Strabane.

The Tyrone, Fermanagh and Donegal Directory 1913, Omagh (1913)

Strabane, beautifully situated on the River Mourne about twelve miles from the city of Londonderry, is an important town in the county of Tyrone with a population of over 5000. It is one of the best market towns in the North West of Ireland for flax, pork, butter and grain. The market days are Tuesday and Wednesday (flax), Tuesday being the principal. The most important fairs are held on the 1st of February, 12th and 13th of May, 1st August and 12th and 13th November. A monthly fair is held on the first Thursday of every other month.

Strabane has direct railway communication with Dublin, Belfast and Londonderry and is a junction of the Donegal Railways, which is a narrow gauge railway running through the picturesque gap of Barnesmor to Donegal, and the favourite watering resort of Killybegs. There is also a branch line from Stranorlar to Glenties. One of the latest improvements is a railway line to Londonderry via Dunamanagh striking out at Waterside and a new railway line has been running across the Foyle at Lifford since January, 1900, calling at Raphoe and Convoy and coming to its destination at Letterkenny. Strabane means to rival Portadown in the matter of railway connection. There is also communication with Londonderry for goods by means of a canal which joins the river Foyle at a point about four miles from the town. The existence of the Canal is obviously of considerable advantage to Strabane, keeping low the freight on goods.

The principal public buildings are the Parish Church, the First Presbyterian Church, the Convent of Mercy, the Union Workhouse, the Ulster, Belfast, Hibernian and Provincial banks, the Masonic Hall, the Academy, the Roman Catholic Church, and a new town hall has been completed which presents a commanding appearance facing Main Street. There is a clock which lights up at night.

A new Technical School has been built over the entrance to the flax market and has been opened by T.W. Russell, MP, for winter classes.

A View of Society and Manners in the North of Ireland, 1812,
Dr J. Gamble, London (1813)

It was evening; the setting sun shed his rays on the hill which was opposite to me and threw a ray of glory on the distant mountains. The lower part of the town surrounded by water, appeared like a city in a lake or like a Venice in miniature. The neat little cottages of the upper part, as I caught a partial view of them through the trees, realised the visions of the poet and transported me, as it were to Arcadia. I do not say that Strabane will appear so to everybody; short sighted persons have a kind of second sight; they do not see what others see, but to make amends, often see what others do not. Much of this magic colouring, however, dissolves on entering the town. What was beautiful in perspective loses its charms contemplated at hand. Strabane, like most pictures, many men and some women, appears to most advantage at a distance.

Extract from the minutes of Strabane Board of Guardians, 1850s:
A. Leney, surgeon

Mr Wallace and I have examined the Main Street of the town of Strabane and find it generally speaking in a filthy state and most injurious to the health of the inhabitants and likely to produce epidemic disease and we are ready to carry out any instructions we may receive from the Board of Guardians for the removal of these nuisances. We propose making examination of the entire town as we are satisfied that, bad as the part alluded to is, there are other places even still worse.

The National Commercial Directory of Ireland, Slater & Co. (1846)

The environs of Strabane are replete with interest and beauty; the hills and the mountains, the valleys and the streams, contending for the palm of the picturesque. The Mourne river that leaves the town, and, with the Finn, forms at Lifford the Foyle, is one of the most beautiful rivers in Ireland; and the valleys of these rivers vie with one and another in luxuriance and loveliness. The town consists of ten principal and several smaller streets; the houses are generally well built, and many of them are spacious and handsome, especially in such of the streets as are of most recent formation.

Since 1831 great improvements have been made; the town has been gas lighted, new roads to Londonderry, Newtownstewart and Castlefin have been constructed; the bridge over the Mourne has been widened and three arches added to that which bestrides the Foyle. The appearance of the town altogether is strikingly pre-possessive, and its aspect rendered additionally pleasing by the thriving orchards and gardens attached to the houses skirting the town, producing apples, pears and cherries in abundance.

16 A History of the Church of Ireland and of Methodism in Strabane

CANON FREDERICK FAWCETT

Before we consider this aspect of life in our fair town (Strabane – 'the fair plain'), a few introductory words on the origin of Protestantism. The word Protestant comes from two Latin words, *pro*, before, and *testare*, to testify.

The early church taught the apostolic faith as found in the Bible. Unfortunately however, during the course of centuries, especially in the Middle Ages, new doctrines and practices began to appear. As a result a great protest movement grew within the church in various places throughout Europe. Men such as Martin Luther (Germany), Calvin (Switzerland), Hus (Bohemia) and Cranmer (England) became leaders of the movement which gave birth to most of the Protestant churches and sects. It was not for the purpose of destroying the Church of the time, rather its aim was positive – to purge the church, to declare, to testify before the people the teaching and the doctrine of the primitive church. Unfortunately the church fragmented,

Church of Ireland. An early twentieth century postcard view.

caused by disagreement over the nature of that teaching and its government.

Hence the unhappy divisions of today. The earnest prayer of Christians in all sections of the church is that of Jesus himself – that all may (once again) be one in hope and doctrine, one in charity.

With this background let us now consider first the Church of Ireland in Strabane. Again we must look briefly at the title; the name points to our lovely island land, to the ancient Celtic church founded by St. Patrick, AD 432–461, a church both Catholic and Apostolic, giving those qualities of today's church and as a result of the Reformation it is now, in addition, Protestant and Reformed.

The first church in the Strabane area was possibly that at Camus, the 'curved townland', on the river Mourne. It dates back to St Colgan, a pupil of the great St Columba, to the year AD 585 and a ruin now marks the spot. We read that it was old and ruinated in 1622; indeed from AD 585 to 1622 the history of the parish – Camus-Juxta-Mourne – is hidden from view, but we can be sure that during all those years children were baptised, marriages celebrated and burial services recited for the living in the presence of the silent dead.

In 1642, just after the start of the great rebellion, the old church at Camus was in hopeless ruin, but a 'fayre Church' was being built in Strabane, started sometime before 1619 by James, earl of Abercorn, for this parish and possibly also for Leckpatrick. It stood in the old churchyard, now bounded by Patrick Street and Church Street, perhaps on the site of a short-stay Franciscan Monastery allegedly founded in the fourteenth century.

At this point it behoves us to refer to a dramatic far-reaching event that happened in our country following the rebellion and the defeat of the O'Neills and the O'Donnells and their leaving the realm of Ireland – the Flight of the Earls. By doing so they were held to have forfeited their feudal right to their lands. Plans were laid to plant six of Ulster's nine counties with settlers from Britain, so came the Hamilton family with their seat at Baronscourt and their fortifying and developing of the town of Strabane. The native people for the most part did not attend the Church of Ireland but remained loyal to the Roman Catholic Church for several reasons, one of great importance being that the Bible and the Book of Common Prayer were not translated into Irish, the language of the people, and another that the Reformation movement originated in England. Many clergymen were uneducated and, due to the shortage of clergy, held several parishes. The new settlers were for the most part Calvinists or Presbyterians who at the beginning strengthened the Church of Ireland in Ulster and, we may be sure, that part of it in Strabane. They later had to withdraw that support, for they had little love for bishops or Prayer Book worship, but we must move on in time. We should also note the claim by Bishop Downham in 1630 that Strabane was a refuge for Scottish Catholics.

Following the surrender of the town to James II in 1688, the church was made a hospital by King James' army, and much defaced, but was well repaired (1693). The utensils for the communion were saved. Lewis records in his *Topographical Survey* of 1837 that the church had been enlarged from time to time and 'is now a handsome cruciform structure in the Grecian style, with a cupola (dome), and the arms of the founder were over the principal entrance'. There is a photograph of it in the vestry room of the present parish church. Eleanor Alexander, however, describes it as an ugly old parish church – with square high pews, a three decker (pulpit) and a desolate chancel. The parish had been united with Leckpatrick in the period 1666–1702 when John Sinclair was rector.

The Building of Christ Church, Strabane

In 1849, near the end of the Great Famine, which, it appears, did not have the same severity in Camus parish as elsewhere in Ireland, it was stated in a memorial to the ecclesiastical commissioners that visitors declared it to be the dirtiest church they had ever been in. It was also in a state of disrepair, although the Church of Ireland population was about 1,200 in the 1860s. It was time, therefore, to replace the 260-year-old church with a new building. The then rector, William Alexander, purchased a site in the Bowling Green – it is said that it was the location of one of the three castles round which Strabane developed. It was not until 1879, after five years of building, that the church, costing £6,503 3s 1d, was ready for consecration. The architect was Mr John Kennedy MRIAI and the style was early English Gothic, the stonework being limestone. It was a memorial church built in memory of the Rev. James Smith, a much-loved and esteemed rector of the parish, 1835–1860. It was consecrated by another former rector, the then bishop of Derry, William Alexander, a scholar of note, a poet of no mean order, a preacher of great power, loved and esteemed by clergy and laity, a great churchman and later a great archbishop of Armagh and primate of all Ireland, in a Church that had just been disestablished in 1869, when

Christ Church

the union of Irish and English churches, formed in 1801, was dissolved and the former deprived of land income and property. At that time the Church of Ireland commanded the loyalty of little more than one eighth of the population of Ireland . The laity, through small in number, rallied to their church and in Camus-Juxta-Mourne the rectory at Camus and some of the land was bought back: later another rectory was purchased in Strabane, to be succeeded in 1961 by the present one in Newton Street. Bishop Alexander's wife was formerly Cecil Frances Humphreys, whose father, Major Humphreys, was land steward to the duke of Abercorn and lived at Milltown House, now Strabane Grammar School. Three of her most famous hymns were written in Strabane prior to her marriage:

> 'There Is a Green Hill Far Away'
> 'Once in Royal David's City'
> 'All Things Bright and Beautiful'

Her poem 'The Burial of Moses' is one of the finest poems in the English language. Her practical sympathy and self-denying help enriched the lives of all around her, especially the poor, the oppressed, the homeless, and the deaf and dumb children, whose school on the Derry Road was destroyed by fire with the consequent loss of so many little lives, causing her great sorrow. Strabane is justly proud to be associated with such a famous husband and wife.

In the 1870s the sexton was John Alexander and in 1900 a son, Lyons, was appointed to the position and held it until 1957 – a long and faithful service. He was very skilled at playing hymn tunes on the memorial chime of bells, he could play the organ and also sang alto or tenor in the choir. In 1885 Mr David Hamilton was appointed secretary to the select vestry, serving for sixty years – perhaps a record in the Church of Ireland. Another longserving parishioner was Capt. J.C. Herdman who was hon. treasurer of the parish for fifty years, 1907–1957. Yet another was Mr Charles Campbell who served on the vestry for fifty years and died in 1878. In 1894 the church population was stated to be 804, in 199 families. In 1914 at the outbreak of the First World War, numbers had fallen to 761. The annual report of 1916 states that fifty men from the parish were serving in HM forces, while by the following year sixty are recorded, with four deaths from warfare. The church population at the time of partition, which did not alter the boundaries of our parish, was approximately 750, with attendances of 162 at the morning service and 174 at the evening.

A Church of Ireland school was built in 1714 beside the old church in Patrick Street, now the Craig Memorial Hall, founded by the earl of Abercorn. In 1895, with the aid of the duke of Abercorn, a new school was built in the Bowling Green beside the church – the Abercorn Memorial – a tribute to the generosity of the duke: later the school received a generous legacy from Mr John Perry and was renamed the John Perry Memorial. In 1964 it was replaced by a new parish hall, retaining his name.

On Tuesday 30 October 1979, the centenary service of the church was held, when the preacher was the Most Rev. G.O. Simms PhD, DD, archbishop of Armagh and primate of All Ireland. He had close family ties with Strabane, and the bishop of the diocese, who succeeded Dr Simms in the primatial city, the Rt. Rev. R.H.A. Eames LLB, PhD, now Lord Eames, dedicated many valuable memorial gifts, including beautiful stained glass memorial windows, to complete the others, also of great beauty; they were given by Miss Martha Harpur in memory of her parents and by Mr Thomas McNeill in memory of his wife Kathleen. To these were added in 1995 two more, with scenes from Mrs Alexander's hymns (centenary of her death), given once again by the generosity of Miss Harpur in memory of her sister Kathleen and Mr Thomas McNeill, her brother in law.

Civil disturbances – the Troubles – broke out in 1969, lasting up to the present. The church and hall suffered damage and some of our parishioners lost their lives and limbs. A considerable number moved away from the parish, resulting in a 55% decrease in numbers. At present there is a uneasy peace and we pray with the members of the other churches in Strabane that these terrible days and happenings may come to an end and Christ the King of Peace may reign as he leads us all into the twenty-first century.

Rectors of Camus-Juxta-Mourne

1535	Odo MacBard	1765	George McGhee
1620	Alexander Spicer	1769	Adam Harvey
1622	Henry Noble	1793	Robert Graham
1636	William Kingsmill	1800	Theophilus Brocas
1638	Robert Semple	1804	Stewart Hamilton
1656	Robert Brown	1833	George Smithwick
1659	William Keynes	1835	James Smith (Canon)
1661	John Whitworth	1860	William Alexander (Archbishop)
1662	Philip Johnson	1867	Mervyn Wilson
1663	James Harwood	1894	Alexander Henry Delap (Canon)
1668	John Sinclair	1918	Thomas Baird (Archdeacon)
1703	David Jenkins	1956	Ernest William Lovell (Canon)
1729	Robert Downes (Bishop)	1987	Frederick William Fawcett (Canon)
1734	William Hamilton		

Other Parishes and Churches in the Strabane District

Donagheady

Dunamanagh Church in the parish of Donagheady is dedicated to St James. The parish can claim considerable antiquity, with the name derived from

CHURCH OF IRELAND AND METHODISM   291

Domhnach Caoide, the church of St Caidinus, one of the companions of Columbanus. The church figures in Archbishop Colton's visitation report of the fourteenth century, and the present church was built in 1879 to replace an earlier building erected in 1788. The parish was in the patronage of the earl of Abercorn and a list of rectors from the time of the plantation is as follows:

1622	Robert Sempill	1860	George John Thomas
1635	Robert Stanhope	1871	Frederick James Clark
1656	Robert Semple	1897	James Henry Gatchell
1658	John Hamilton	1924	Thomas Kelly
1661	William Crofts	1931	John Ernest Doyle
1665	James Hamilton	1937	Robert Henry Egar
1689	Andrew Hamilton	1943	Samuel Chadwick
1753	(Hon.) George Hamilton	1960	Robert John Stanley
1753	George Bracegirdle	1963	William Doherty
1768	James Hamilton	1971	John Bavaria Boden
1781	Andrew Thomas Hamilton	1978	Edward Thomas Dundas
1825	(Hon.) Charles Douglas	1984	William Creighton McNee
1857	(Hon.) Douglas Hamilton Gordon	1991	Frederick Lawrence Graham

Leckpatrick and Dunnalong

The name of the parish Leckpatrick, the 'stone of Patrick', is said to have come from an ancient rocking stone near the former rectory. The present church, dedicated to St Patrick, was built in 1815 and enlarged nineteen years later – which may account for its unusual shape and orientation. Unusual too is its imitation plantation style and its box pews. The church built in 1815 replaced a much smaller building dating back to plantation times and it was reported to have been burned by King James' retreating army in 1689 but rebuilt by 1693.

Dunnalong Church, dedicated to St John, was built and consecrated in 1866 just before disestablishment. It was originally carved out of Donagheady parish and was joined with Leckpatrick in 1921. The name Dunnalong, meaning 'fort of the ships', suggests a place of some importance in earlier times.

1622	Henry Noble	1788	Jocelyn Ingram
1625	Alexander Spicer	1793	Alexander Clotworthy Downing
1636	Henry Kingsmill	1812	Francis Brownlow
1638	Richard Wakefield	1830	Samuel Law Montgomery
1657	John Adamson	1832	Robert Hume
1661	John Whitworth	1835	George Smithwick

1662/3	James Harwood		1853	Charlton Maxwell
1665	John Sinclair		1872	William Macklin Edwards
1703	James Goodlat		1883	Alexander George Stuart
1727	Robert Jenkins		1886	Robert Burroughs
1730	Philip Downes		1897	William George Rennison
1730/1	Paul Read		1926	Thomas Alexander Hickson Moriarty
1742/3	James Clewlow		1944	Ernest Harley Hadden
1751	James Ingram		1979	Alan Ernest Tilson
1765	Richard Leslie		1990	Henry David Ferry

Urney and Sion Mills

The name Urney denotes an oratory or prayer house and appears in Colton's visitation records as Furney. The church was reported in ruins in 1622 but was apparently rebuilt, being destroyed in 1689 by King James' army but soon after restored. A new church was built in 1734 and repaired and restored in 1809, with the present church being erected in 1865.

The Church of the Good Shepherd at Sion Mills was erected in 1909 and succeeded an earlier church dedicated to St Saviour that had been built in 1889 and is still in use as a parish hall. The rectors from the plantation period onwards were:

Canon Fawcett, rector of Camus Juxta Mourne, 1987–1999

1617	Isaac Wood		1814	James Jones
1637–8	William Kingsmill		1835	Robert Hume
1657	James Wallace		1849	Benjamin Bloomfield Gough
1661–2	Thomas Buttolph		1862	Charles Seymour
1671–2	John Leslie		1872	William Olphert
1700–01	David Jenkins		1899	John Olphert
1729	Robert Downes		1921	Richard Scandrett
1740	William Henry		1953	William Edwin Davey
1768	William Beresford		1968	Gerard James Alexander Carson
1780	William Foster		1986	Raymond Craigmile Thompson
1789	John Pomeroy		1992	John Raymond Stafford
1794	Robert Fowler		1999	David Skuce
1813	Charles Knox			

(Further details on the curates of these parishes and other details of their history are included in the recently updated book, *The Clergy of Derry and Raphoe*, originally published as *Derry Clergy and Parishes* in 1937 by Canon Leslie and brought up to the present by Canon Fawcett and Rev. Crooks. This valuable publication also contains comprehensive details about the other parishes and churches in the Strabane area, while further information is included in Canon Gebbie's work *Historical Survey of a Parish: Ardstraw 1600–1900.*)

The Methodist Church in Strabane

The eighteenth century is often called a time of deadness in the Church of England. It was the beginning of the Industrial Revolution, the population grew rapidly and there was need for new methods of evangelism because the existing parochial system could not cope. It was this problem that John Wesley, son of a Church of England Rector and a priest of that Church, set himself to meet. He was influenced by the Moravians with John Hus, the reformer, as their mentor, and by another reformer of the Church, the learned Dutch theologian Arminius, with his teaching on the free will of man in contrast to Calvinism. Wesley's doctrines were substantially those of the Church of England. The name 'Methodists' was given to a small group of students at Oxford University, including John Wesley, because of the exact regularity of their lives, led according to the Book of Common Prayer, as well as their studies. Although Wesley ordained preachers and sanctioned bishops he died as a Church of England clergyman – they, however, could not minister in that Church as they were not episcopally ordained. This led to a separate church, which in its early years broke up into various bodies. There are more than 12 million Methodists in the world today. The church is governed by a Conference with a president, and with subordinate district synods. The local clergy belong to circuits and are moved every few years to new charges.

John Wesley came by sailing ship to Dublin every second summer when he would tour Ireland for four months. He travelled on horseback, riding sometimes 200 miles in the day. He would preach anywhere, courthouse, schoolhouse, church or in the open under a tree. He usually spent a week in Londonderry on his Irish tours. He passed through Strabane a number of times, the first perhaps in 1785, when he remarked that 'if Strabane receives the gospel nothing is too hard for God!' He stopped here on at least three other occasions and in 1787, when it appears he was well received, he preached to a congregation in the Town Hall. George Brown of Creevy is the first local Methodist known to have preached in the Strabane area. In 1774 he preached by moonlight to a great congregation near Strabane, then part of an enormous Londonderry circuit. The Methodist preachers from time to time met with opposition from the local Church of Ireland clergy.

Many people we are told 'turned to God from idols to serve the living and true God'. In 1813 Strabane became a separate circuit which had 640 members and in the next year, 1814, a preaching house and manse were built beside the graveyard of the parish church in Patrick Street, a most unpopular site with ministers. Controversy arose in the wider Methodist movement – as far as John Wesley was concerned, the Methodists were a group within the Church of Ireland and were almost under contract to attend their parish churches on two Sundays in the month and to receive the Holy Communion there. As the years passed they wanted it in their own services, so Conference in 1816 gave leave to eight circuits, one in Strabane, to administer within such the Holy Communion. The Rev. Adam Averell held out for 'simple original Methodism' inside the Church of Ireland. This gave way to the meeting of the Primitive (original) Wesleyan Conference in 1818 and a Primitive Wesleyan Chapel was opened in Strabane in 1830 – about where the present health centre is in Barrack Street. The split continued until 1878 and there was a Primitive Wesleyan Society in the town throughout those years.

The *Parliamentary Gazeteer* for 1837 gives the following figures for Sunday services:

MORNING AND EVENING ATTENDANCE

Primitive Methodists	60/70 – at both
Wesleyan Methodists	40/50: 150/200
Presbyterians	400 – at both
Church of Ireland	600/700 at both
Roman Catholics	1200/1300 at both

(1830 – town population 4,700)

The year 1834 is reported to have been a good one in both Methodist societies in Strabane, with a revival blessing circuit.

The 1798 rebellion disturbed Methodist work as it did every other aspect of society. Roman Catholic Emancipation came in 1829 and the first Roman Catholic church was built in Strabane – St John's – in 1819 with all local clergy attending the opening ceremony and drinking the loyal toast to the king. The Methodists did not take part in political agitation. John Wesley had made it clear that good Christians are good citizens. He urged people to keep the law and obey them that have rule over them, and keep the peace – as do Methodists to this very day.

Bad harvests and poor trade led up to the years of the 'Great Hunger' and famine throughout Ireland in 1845–9, when the potato crops failed. Strabane did not suffer initially, this being a reasonably prosperous area. The recently opened workhouse, built to accommodate 800, had to cater for 1200 at the height of the famine. Membership of the Wesleyan Society fell by more than 25% during the famine years, leaving just 485 members. The Rev. H.J.F. Ranson, writing in 1911, suggested that hundreds carried the good seed with them, enriching Methodism in other parts of the world.

Building the Methodist Church, 1900

The Methodist church at Railway Road, Strabane, opened in 1900 to replace the earlier building at Church Street

In 1878 the Primitive and Wesleyan connection was re-established. Many Primitive circuits had Church of Ireland and Presbyterian members and feared to lose them if Methodists became a separate 'Church'.

With Gladstone as British prime minister, the Church of Ireland was disestablished in 1869. After that it was no longer patriotic to keep the link with the Church of Ireland. Primitive Methodists might as well have the sacraments from their own preachers. The Primitive Chapel in Strabane was sold and was demolished only in recent years. Repairs were made to the Wesleyan Church in 1882, with the Church of Ireland select vestry and Presbyterian businesses now having an input. The manse and chapel were eventually sold, the manse to be used as a dwelling house and the chapel as a forge. Both properties, situated just off Church Street, are still in use. The present manse was built in the Derry Road between 1887 and 1890 during the ministry of Rev. Thomas Rutherford. Despite the renovations of 1882, a new church building was required. Rev. Hugh McGahie saw it built at a cost of £1,200. It was opened on Friday 7 December 1900, on a site on the Railway Road rented from the duke of Abercorn. Buttresses were added in 1920. The Church halls were built in 1932 at a cost of £420, Rev. H.J.F. Ranson being then the minister. Throughout the years there have been strong links with Stranorlar, Newtonstewart and Castlederg, with the sharing of ministers. Strabane became in 1975 part of the Londonderry mission circuit and various recommendations were made, including the sale of Strabane Manse. This has not yet happened. In 1982 the ground rents from the Abercorn estate for both church and manse were bought by the Strabane society for £100 each, Mr Alex C. Smith playing a key role in the purchase.

A significant feature of early Methodism was the 'cottage meeting'. They became annual events when neighbours gathered in a house for a meeting presided over by a Leader or a preacher. A substantial meal usually followed.

Minister followed minister down the years. The highest official honour ever done to a minister serving in the Strabane circuit came in 1953 when the Rev. R.L.M. Waugh was elected president of the Methodist Church in Ireland. Manse families continued to contribute to Church life after they moved away from Strabane. Four sons of the manse were all ordained in the Church of Ireland – Robert Collier, Earnest Clayton, and brothers George and John Knowles. The former became archdeacon of Derry. Another manse son, Charles Ranson, became a distinguished theologian in the United States and later served as a president of the Methodist Church in Ireland.

Lay leaders play an important part in Methodism – Smiths, Sweeneys and Russells amongst others including Mr Percy Colhoun, a leader for many years who also played the organ unpaid for at least thirty years and in 1965 installed a bigger organ.

Others served as both society and circuit stewards, among them Mr Cecil Russell, first chairman of the reconstructed district council, who prepared the communion elements for a life-time.

Strabane Methodism claims to be the first church in the town to have a Sunday school – and to have supported temperance work. For many years, watch night services, ushering in the New Year with prayer, have been a feature.

Strabane town centre was flooded on the night of 21 October 1987. The Methodist Church was flooded to a depth of over 6 feet (nearly 3m). In restoration some changes and improvements were made. The major decision was to put a screen at the back of the church to give a larger reception area. The church was reopened by the president of the Methodist Church, Rev. Stanley Whittington, on 24 September 1988. It is also a vote of confidence for the future. In recent years, with the Troubles and unemployment in the area, Methodist numbers, in common with the Protestant churches in general, have gone down. Strabane Methodist church is now linked with the new Methodist Church at Magheramason.

The Methodists have given much to the Universal Church of Christ with their care for the poor and outcasts; also the great hymns of John and Charles Wesley, his brother, which are sung and loved by all Christian people. Unity with their mother Church of England is now much nearer and we pray for it and for the unity of all Christian people in Strabane and throughout the world, for so our master Jesus Christ prayed – that they all may be one – with their own identities, we may be so bold to add.

Ministers who have served in the Railway Road church

1889	Rev. Hugh McGahie	1947	Rev. Robert A. Knowles
1901	Rev. Thomas Knox	1952	Rev. R.M.L. Waugh (President)
1904	Rev. John G. Whittaker	1957	Rev. Walter Hill
1907	Rev. Henry J.F. Ranson (President)	1961	Rev. W. Moore Lispett
1910	Rev. Richard Green	1969	Rev. H.N. Medd
1913	Rev. Henry Frackleton	1969	Rev. Fred Twinem
1921	Rev. Horatio C. Collier	1975	Rev. R. Mervyn McClean
1923	Rev. C.H. McCartney Clayton	1975	Rev. Thomas A. Johnston
1926	Rev. Joseph D. Ritchie	1976	Rev. David Mullan
1929	Rev. William T. Dennison	1981	Rev. Kenneth J. Robinson
1933	Rev. Irvine Kirkpatrick	1986	Rev. S. Wesley Blair
1938	Rev. John Bertenshaw	1994	Rev. McAllister
1942	Rev. Robert Ferguson	1998	Rev. Daphne Twinem

Presbyterian Church & River Mourne, Strabane.

17 Strabane Presbyterianism

WILLIAM ROULSTON

The early seventeenth-century plantation of Ulster firmly established a strong and vibrant colony of Scots in Strabane barony. However, it was not until the latter part of the century that organised Presbyterianism developed in the area. Although there was a significant Catholic element among the early Scottish tenantry, encouraged by a number of the leading landlords, particularly Sir George Hamilton of Greenlaw, it is probably true to say that most of the planters in the Strabane area were Protestant. At least one of the earliest Protestant clergymen in the barony was a Scot – Robert Semple, who ministered at Donagheady and later in Camus parish. Precisely where he stood theologically is not clear though Bishop Downham of Derry had no doubts, describing Semple as an 'honest man and a preacher'. We catch only fleeting glimpses of non-conformity in Strabane in the period before 1641. On one occasion William Kennah of Strabane was fined £5 for providing lodgings for John McClelland who had been excommunicated by the

Presbyterian church in Meetinghouse Street. This church was accidentally destroyed by fire on Christmas Day 1938 and the congregation moved for service to the Second Presbyterian Church at Leepers Brae.

Established Church in County Down. Around the same time Bishop Bramhall of Derry was in conversation with the provost of Strabane and inquired after a certain non-conformist. On being told that he was a young merchant of the town the bishop indignantly replied, 'A young man! He is a young devil.'

In 1641, rebellion broke out in Ireland, and the following year an army of Scots under General Robert Munro landed at Carrickfergus and established the first Irish presbytery there. In 1644, John Adamson, who was probably the son of Principal John Adamson of Edinburgh University, was sent by the General Assembly of the Presbyterian Church of Scotland to north-west Ulster. He subsequently became minister of Leckpatrick and was the first clergyman based in this area who is known to have held Presbyterian beliefs. During the Commonwealth, when Cromwell ruled as Lord Protector, a number of non-conformist clergymen served parishes in the Strabane area and received their income either from the tithes of the parish or from a state salary. In the town of Strabane Robert Brown ministered on an income of £40 per annum, later increased to £60. His successor, William Keyes, previously minister of Raswell, Cheshire, received the far greater income of £140. Other non-conformist clergymen in the Strabane area included John Hamilton at Donagheady, James Wallace at Urney and William Moorecroft at Ardstraw and Badoney. However, in 1660, with the restoration of the monarchy and the established church these men were all forced to leave their churches, having refused to conform to the episcopal form of church government.

The Emergence of Organised Presbyterianism in the Strabane Area

The 1660s witnessed a period of great persecution of Presbyterians at the hands of the Established Church, and in 1667 a large number of Presbyterians from the Strabane area were excommunicated by the bishop of Derry. According to the order for their expulsion, non-conformity was defined as 'not only absence from church, but baptising by unlicensed ministers'. Another excommunicant, John Boyd of Ardstraw, was further charged with ploughing on Christmas Day and condemning the ecclesiastical government. For a time Presbyterians were forced to meet for worship in secluded, out-of-the-way places, while their ministers lived as virtual outlaws.

By the 1670s restrictions were more relaxed and Presbyterians were able to meet openly and even construct their own meeting-houses. Our main source of information on the Presbyterian Church in Strabane and district at this time comes from the minute-book of the Laggan presbytery which covers the period 1672–1700. All the congregations in the Strabane area were under the care of this presbytery, which had been constituted as far back as 1654. The first mention that we have of the construction of a Presbyterian place of worship in this area comes in August 1672 when Robert Cowan of Donagheady reported to presbytery that their meeting-house had been completed. It was situated in the townland of Altrest.

The main difficulty for the congregation at Urney as far as constructing their own church building was concerned was agreeing among themselves where it should be built. Attempts at resolving the differences by presbytery proved unsuccessful, for although it had been agreed in 1676 that 'the meeting-place be removed a little further upwards to the quarter land of Urney, and built in Spring next', three years later the matter was again brought to the attention of presbytery. On this occasion, while the congregation could agree on where to build their meeting-house, they ran into another difficulty. The site that they had chosen was located on land owned by the bishop of Derry, and while he granted them permission to build a church on his land – surely a sign of the more liberal times they were living in – his tenant, Mathew Babington, refused to allow them to do so.

The debate continued and in October 1679 a meeting of presbytery was held in Urney at which it was decided that it was 'not meet to remove the meeting-house out of the townland where it now is; & yet they find it meet to remove it out of the place where it now stands'. The following September it was reported to presbytery that a new meeting-house had been built at Tullymoan, presumably in the townland where the previous church had stood. The people from the upper end of the parish, however, remained discontented. The Presbyterians of Ardstraw, on the other hand, seem to have avoided the disputes that so afflicted the Urney congregation; the only reference to their meeting-house in this period comes in 1695 when it was reported to presbytery that it had been rebuilt on the site that the previous building had stood on.

Financial Problems with the Congregation at Strabane

The main problem facing the Strabane congregation in this period was their apparent inability to provide sufficient financial support to their minister, the Rev. Robert Wilson. In 1675 Wilson appeared before presbytery and asked them to 'declare him transportable' because of his difficulties at Strabane. His congregation stated that they could pay him no more than £25 per year, and that was only because ten men paid most of it. In order to try to remedy the situation they suggested that 'half the parish of Leck[patrick], and that part of the parish of Ardstra which lies contiguous to them upon the east side of the river Morn may be stirred up to joyn with them.' By July 1676 Wilson's position at Strabane had still not improved and so the presbytery judged 'him not necessarily obliged to stay there'.

However, his congregation were keen to retain his services and even promised to build him a meeting-house. In October of that year Wilson agreed to stay on until at least the following May and it was reported to presbytery that he would 'stretch himself as far as he can to gratify them in their desire'. Wilson was in fact to remain at Strabane for a further thirteen years. The apparent poverty of the Strabane congregation is surprising given that most of the leading merchants of the town in the second half of the seventeenth century were Presbyterian. The situation at Strabane was by no means unique, however, with all the congregations in the area finding it difficult to give their ministers sufficient financial support. In 1674, the Donagheady congregation promised to provide for their minister a house and garden free of rent, and in addition 'an acre of medow & two acres of corn & grass for a horse & two or three cows free & as much more of the land for payment for his use as he pleases'.

The troubles of 1689–91 weighed heavily on the pastorate of the Presbyterian church in the Strabane area with three of its ministers dying in Derry during the siege – Robert Wilson of Strabane, John Hamilton of Donagheady, and David Brown of Urney. The meeting-house in Strabane would also appear to have been destroyed, for in September 1693 it was reported to presbytery that a new church building would be finished within the next two weeks. This church was located in what became Orchard Street, and continued in use until 1871 when a new church was built; the building was subsequently used as a school. The original Presbyterian meeting-house in Strabane had been built on the west side of the Bowling Green.

Strabane Presbytery in the Eighteenth Century

In June 1717 at a meeting of the General Synod of Ulster a decision was made to reorganise the Presbyterian Church in north-west Ulster, and thereby bring into existence the Presbytery of Strabane. The congregations included in this Presbytery were Strabane, Ardstraw, Urney, Donagheady, Ballindrait, Derg, Omagh, Badoney and Pettigo. The first meeting of this newly constituted Presbytery was held in Strabane on 17 August 1717 when Rev. Samuel Halliday was chosen as moderator. The minutes of Strabane Presbytery have survived for the period 1717–40 and provide a fascinating insight into the workings of the Presbyterian Church in rural Ulster in the first half of the eighteenth century.

Much of the business of Presbytery was taken up with disciplining its members and there are numerous references to individuals being reprimanded for adultery, non-attendance at church, slander, etc. Strange though it may seem today a great deal of presbytery's time was given over to settling disputes regarding the seating arrangements within its churches. Virtually all of the congregations experienced these unseemly squabbles and presbytery was continually trying to resolve the difficulties presented by these disputes. In April 1718 presbytery even brought in a local landlord, William Hamilton of Dunamanagh, to assist in regulating the seating arrangements in Donagheady meeting-house.

The Presbyterian Church and Emigration

Large numbers of Presbyterians left Ulster in the eighteenth century for North America, and the district around Strabane was no exception to this. Shortly before the presbytery of Strabane had come into being the minister of the Strabane congregation, the Rev. William Holmes, had left for America. He had in fact been in America before, and it was shortly after returning from this first trip abroad that he was ordained minister of Strabane in December 1692. His son married a sister of the American statesman and scientist, Benjamin Franklin.

The pages of the minute book of Strabane Presbytery are littered with passing references to emigration and its implications for the congregations within its bounds. Those planning to emigrate would often petition presbytery for a certificate testifying to their credentials as good Presbyterians. This would enable them to join a Presbyterian congregation in America without having to undergo a rigorous examination of their character and religious beliefs. In December 1718 John Alison came before presbytery desiring such a testimonial as he was preparing to emigrate. Presbytery decided not to issue him with one until just before he was ready to leave and then only conditional on his continued good behaviour.

In July 1720 Isaac Taylor, who two years previously had been ordained minister in Ardstraw as a 'colleague' to Mr Halliday, announced his desire to go to America, citing financial hardship as the principal reason for his wanting to do so. The Presbyterians of Ardstraw were at first adamant that he should stay, though in the end they reluctantly granted him permission to go there temporarily. He stayed two years and in his absence 'scandalous reports' were spread about his behaviour in America. However, on his return to Ardstraw he was able to produce certificates from the church in America, and so was able to convince the presbytery that the allegations made against him were 'groundless and false'. Seven years later Taylor shocked presbytery by abandoning his flock in Ardstraw and joining the Established Church. He later became a Church of Ireland curate in the parish of Ardstraw.

According to the minutes of the presbytery, emigration from the Castlederg area was so heavy that it was placing the financial position of the congregation there under severe strain. Emigration also had implications in other, more unusual, ways. In 1730, presbytery rebuked John Patterson and Mary Atchison for marrying without making sure that Atchison's former husband, who had emigrated to America, was definitely dead.

Boundary Disputes Between Congregations

It would appear that in its early days the Presbyterian Church in the north-west tried to make each congregation fall within the bounds of a single parish. However, this did not always turn out to be the case. For example, the parish of Leckpatrick did not have its own Presbyterian church until 1836. The result was a number of boundary disputes between congregations in Strabane Presbytery. A seemingly long running dispute between the congregations of Urney and Strabane was brought to a head in August 1722 when commissioners from Strabane renewed their request that those Presbyterians living within a quarter of a mile of the bridge over the Mourne on the Urney side of the river be joined to their congregation. They were, however, unsuccessful in their bid. Undeterred, they continued to make representations to presbytery on this matter, and in 1724 Mr Wilson of Strabane reported that those Presbyterians from Urney who had been disjoined from the Strabane congregation continued to attend the meeting-house in the town even though they had been offered money for their seats. In 1726, the session of Strabane was instructed by presbytery not to collect stipend from any families living in the parish of Urney, 'otherwise they will be held disorderly'.

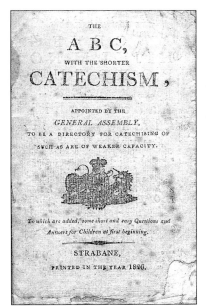

Presbyterian Catechism

A further boundary dispute involved the congregations of Strabane and Donagheady. In May 1729 a deputation from Donagheady came before the sub-synod of Londonderry and complained that several members of their congregation were attending worship in Strabane. The boundary between the congregations was defined as being the burn, now known as the Glenmornan River, which begins in Moorlough and crosses the road at Ballymagorry. With this definition the dispute seems to have been resolved.

Disputes Within the Urney Congregation

A previous section dealt with a dispute within the Urney congregation in the late 1670s over the siting of their meeting-house. In the 1720s history repeated itself as the same issue engulfed the congregation and threatened to tear it apart. In late summer 1724 the Presbyterians of Urney voted to move their meeting-house from Tullymoan to a new site, those principally in favour of this coming from the lower end of the parish. However, following a challenge to the result of the ballot, they decided to ignore the original result and refer the matter to the presbytery. The original decision of the people of Urney to take some sort of affirmative action may have been prompted by the rather damning report presented to presbytery in August of that year which described how the congregation were 'sinking in their ability' and looked 'upon themselves as entirely incapable to support a Gospel ministry among them'. Presbytery resolved that 'the melancholy condition of the congregation is to be taken into consideration'.

The matter concerning the proposed relocation of the meeting-house in Urney came before presbytery in November 1724. Following an intensive debate it was decided that the new meeting-house was to be built at Peacockbank, and that for the time being the minister was to preach once a month in the upper end of the parish. It was also resolved that the people from the lower end of the parish should provide all the stone needed to construct the new church, but that the people from the upper end should play their full part in the building work. The following February a deputation from the upper end of the parish appeared before presbytery and requested that the proposed move should not take place. Presbytery decided to defer any decision on the matter until a later stage, but suggested that in the meantime all quarrying and drawing of stone and timber should cease; whether the people from the lower end heeded presbytery's suggestion is not clear.

In May 1725 the dispute was brought before the sub-synod of Londonderry who upheld the wishes of the people of the lower end of the parish to have the site of the meeting-house moved to Peacockbank. Strabane Presbytery passed a similar resolution in August 1725 and instructed William Holmes, the minister of Urney, to begin preaching at Peacockbank. The people from the upper end of Urney remained defiant with many refusing to attend worship at Peacockbank and others deserting to the neighbouring congregation of Donoughmore, Co. Donegal. In May 1728 we find the matter again before the sub-synod of Londonderry who again recommended that all of the Urney congregation should attend the meeting-house in Peacockbank.

How much damage had been done to the congregation is not clear, but they had at least avoided the open split that a number of other congregations in the Strabane area were to experience in the ensuing decades of the eighteenth century. The church at Peacockbank had, in fact, a very short history, for in October 1740 we find John Pigott of Dublin, the then owner of the quarterland of Urney, demising to the Rev. Victor Ferguson, minister of Strabane, an acre of land known as the 'three-angled or three-cornered field . . . to erect and build a meeting house thereon'. Ferguson was acting on behalf of the Presbyterians of Urney and had agreed with Pigott a nominal rent on the property of 6s per annum. Because the minutes of presbytery end just a short time before this, we have simply no idea why the people of Urney should have decided to build a new place of worship less than twenty years after the construction of the previous one.

Divisions Within the Congregations of Ardstraw and Donagheady

Schism, as A.T.Q. Stewart has pointed out in his book *The Narrow Ground*, is 'the inevitable consequence of attaching so much importance to the right of individual conscience', and the church in Strabane and district has certainly not been free from this phenomenon which has afflicted Presbyterianism from its very inception. In the course of the eighteenth century, several Presbyterian congregations in this area experienced disputes which culminated in splits and the creation of breakaway churches. In August 1733 Andrew Welsh was ordained minister of Ardstraw. This was to the dissatisfaction of a large section of the congregation who the following year came before the General Synod and requested that they be erected into a separate congregation, claiming to have over 200 families on their side. Their petition was rejected by the synod. The dispute was brought to the attention of the synod for a second time in 1735 and again the following year, but in 1737 it was reported that the malcontents in Ardstraw had submitted to Welsh's teaching.

This harmony did not last long and in November 1739 it was reported to the Strabane Presbytery that a number of families had withdrawn from Ardstraw and were holding their own meetings, with ministers supplied by the presbytery of Letterkenny. The dispute was debated at the General Synod of 1740, though without resolution, and eventually with no common ground between the two sides it was decided to establish a second congregation in the parish of Ardstraw. This congregation, known as Clady or Alte-Clady, was placed under the care of the Letterkenny Presbytery, and in 1746 Alexander Miller was ordained as its first minister. In 1749, he was deposed 'for a pretended clandestine marriage and other abnormalities'. After carrying on illegally for some time, he emigrated to America in 1751 where he continued to get into trouble.

The congregation of Donagheady also experienced a serious rupture in 1736–41, which culminated in the congregation splitting into two separate divisions. In 1736 the Rev. Thomas Winsley, minister of Donagheady Presbyterian Church for the previous thirty-seven years, died. The basis of the ensuing dispute was the inability of the congregation to come to any agreement over the choice of their next minister. However, underlying this was the rivalry that existed between the earl of Abercorn and his distant relative, William Hamilton of Dunamanagh. Between them they owned nearly all of the parish of Donagheady, and with the congregation more or less divided along geographical lines it is difficult to imagine that the enmity between these two men did not have an indirect bearing on the dispute.

The situation gradually deteriorated, reaching its lowest point in a riot in the church during a Sunday service. Fortunately, William Hamilton of

Dunamanagh, a member of the Donagheady congregation, used his influence to good effect by ensuring that this event was not investigated by the civil courts. By 1741, with still no resolution in sight, the Synod of Ulster sanctioned the separation of the congregation into two different parts. The congregation which continued to meet in the old church became known as First Donagheady, and in July 1741 the Rev William Armstrong was ordained minister. The new congregation was called Second Donagheady, and in August 1741 their first minister, the Rev. Robert Wirling, was installed. The ridiculousness of the situation was compounded by the construction of the Second Donagheady meeting-house barely 200 yards from the old church.

The Volunteers, United Irishmen and the Presbyterian Church in Strabane and District

The Presbyterian church in Strabane and district came through the tumultous 1790s virtually unscathed. A number of ministers had been involved in the Volunteer movement, including the Rev. William Crawford of Strabane, whose *History of Ireland*, published in 1783, gives a valuable insight into the various political movements of the time. He was present at the Volunteer convention in Dungannon in February 1782 which called for legislative independence for Ireland, and the following year was involved in the movement for parliamentary reform. Crawford was also responsible for establishing an academy at Strabane in 1785 to provide a sound education for those students preparing for the Presbyterian ministry.

We know of only one minister in the Strabane area who was involved in the United Irish movement – the Rev. William Dunlop of Badoney and later of Strabane. His political sympathies almost cost him his life, for on one occasion, while acting as a courier for the United Irishmen, he ran into a company of militia. Adopting an air of officialdom he managed to bluff his way through and escape. He wrote several patriotic songs and was described by the Rev. E.E.K. McClelland in his book, *Friendly Strabane*, as 'a warm-hearted swashbuckler'.

The Secession Church of Strabane and District

Up until the middle of the eighteenth century, all Presbyterian congregations in Strabane and district were connected with the Synod of Ulster. However, by the latter part of that century the Secession Church had gained a footing in the area. The origins of this denomination go back to a split in the Established Church of Scotland in 1712 over the issue of official patronage. The arrival of the Seceders in Ulster came at a time when many Presbyterians were becoming increasingly concerned with the doctrines espoused by a number of their clergy and had turned to Scotland for spiritual guidance.

Little is known of the early history of the Secession Church in this district, but some time before 1781 moves were made to establish a congregation at Ardstraw. The first Secession minister was the Rev. Thomas Dickson of Aughentaine. To begin with Dickson also ministered at Sixmilecross, but by 1784 his time was solely taken up by Ardstraw. Around 1791 the Seceders of Ardstraw established an outstation at Castlederg. In 1833, Dergbridge, as it was then known, was erected into a separate congregation and is now called Second Castlederg.

In 1798 the Presbyterian church at Badoney was vacant and the subsequent election of the Rev. Charles Hemphill resulted in a serious split in the congregation. Those who disapproved of Hemphill withdrew from Badoney, forming themselves into a separate congregation and building a meeting-house at Corrick. At about the same time a Seceder society was formed in Donemana (Dunamanagh) and the two groups put out a joint call to the Rev. Robert Reid. In 1800 he was ordained Secession minister of the congregations of Donemana and Corrick. While the Corrick section prospered, the Donemana side declined, so much that in 1836 the church building was described as 'ruinous' and what was left of the congregation worshipped in a local public house. We have no further mention of this congregation and presumably it was allowed to lapse.

In September 1816 the Rev. James Gamble was ordained minister of a Secession church in Strabane. The origin of this congregation, which worshipped in a meeting-house on the Derry Road next to the courthouse, is not known. Gamble continued to minister at Strabane until 1836 when he was suspended for reasons unknown. He left Strabane and later turned up as minister at Cloughey, Co. Down. In 1826 the Secession church began a mission in Newtownstewart and a congregation was soon established. The following year a meeting-house was built on a site granted free by the earl of Blessington and the Rev. John Martin of Markethill was ordained its first minister. In 1840, the Seceders and the Synod of Ulster congregations, with a very small number of exceptions, united. Since then the governing body has been known as the General Assembly of the Presbyterian Church in Ireland. However, there continued to be two separate Presbyterian congregations in Strabane town for another seventy years.

The Covenanting Congregation at Bready

The Covenanter or Reformed Presbyterian Church established itself in the area immediately north of Strabane in the middle of the eighteenth century. As with the Secession Church, it originated in Scotland and gradually spread to the north of Ireland. Before it was organised on a more formal basis its adherents met in small societies scattered across the countryside. There were a number of societies in the Bready area as well as a group in Strabane, and to begin with the Scottish Reformed presbytery, formed in 1743, supplied them with travelling ministers. Twenty years later the Irish Reformed presbytery was established and in May 1765, at an open air service near Mountcastle, William James of Faughanvale was ordained minister of a Covenanter congregation which covered a large area of the Foyle Valley, and which at that stage did not have its own church building.

The following year a meeting-house was built at Bready on a site granted free of rent forever by the earl of Abercorn. During a Sabbath service in 1786 this building collapsed, fortunately without anyone being injured. A new church was quickly erected in its stead. The outreach work of Bready Reformed Presbyterian Church included a mission station at Mulvin near Victoria Bridge. In 1844 Mulvin became a Covenanter congregation in its own right, although it was not until 1872 that it was granted independent status by the Western presbytery.

In 1840 a split occurred in the Reformed Presbyterian Church when a section of its membership claimed the right to vote in parliamentary elections. The Covenanters had traditionally avoided involvement in all forms of civil government and this included non-participation in elections. Those who wished to vote withdrew from the main body of the church and formed the Eastern Reformed Presbyterian Church, consisting of nine congregations, one of which was at Waterside, Londonderry. A number of Covenanters from Bready joined this church, but finding the journey to Derry inconvenient, resolved to build their own meeting-house at Cullion. Although their numbers were small, the church they built was capable of seating 300 and became known as 'Gormley's folly' after William Gormley, one of the most enthusiastic members of the congregation. In 1860, differences arose between the congregation and their minister, the Rev. Samuel Patton, which were serious enough for Patton to refuse to conduct services at Cullion, confining himself to the Waterside church. Soon afterwards the congregation at Cullion ceased to exist and most of its members returned to Bready. The church building was demolished a few years ago.

Unitarianism in Strabane

The Arian controversy, which raged within Presbyterianism in the 1820s and early 1830s, was not without its consequences in Strabane. The debate centred on the doctrine of the Trinity. Those who rejected the belief that there are three persons in the Godhead were known as the Unitarians, and in 1830 they withdrew from the Synod of Ulster. The presbytery of Strabane took up an uncompromising stance on the issue, and declared in 1834 that: 'It is wholly inconsistent with the character of an Elder of our Church in any way to encourage the Unitarian doctrine.' The clerk of session of the Strabane congregation was forced to resign his position for publicly espousing Unitarianism. A number of Presbyterians in Strabane actually seceded and formed their own congregation which had its meeting-house in Lower Main Street. However, the history of Unitarianism in the town was short, and we have very little information on this congregation.

Nineteenth-century Church Expansion in Strabane and District

The nineteenth century was an era of expansion for the Presbyterian Church in the Strabane area with the establishment of a number of new congregations. In 1802, Presbyterians living in the vicinity of Newtownstewart petitioned the Synod of Ulster to be erected into a separate congregation. This request was granted, and in 1804 John McFarland was ordained minister there. In 1824, he was suspended by presbytery for the irregular celebration of marriage and resigned his charge two years later. Ironically his successor, the Rev. Charles Adams, was suspended for similar misconduct in 1842. In 1831, a congregation was formed at Douglas when the Presbyterians living in that area separated from Clady. About 1830 the Synod of Ulster established a mission station at Donemana. The outreach work prospered at the expense of the aforementioned Secession congregation, and in 1833 Donemana was erected into a separate charge. In 1876 a new church was built on the site of the former Secession meeting-house.

Although small in number the Presbyterians of the Glenelly Valley had their own distinct identity, and this was recognised in 1835 by the Synod of Ulster when they were erected into a congregation in their own right. The following year the Rev. John Moore was ordained minister there. He was a strong supporter of the Orange Order, and on one occasion after a particularly Orange sermon, was viciously attacked on his way home from church and left for dead. He never fully recovered from this assault, but was able to continue ministering at Glenelly until 1869.

At the General Synod of Ulster of 1836 it was reported by the presbytery of Glendermott that a number of families in the parish of Leckpatrick had requested that they be created a separate congregation. The request was granted and a church building was completed by the end of the year. Prior to this the Presbyterians of Leckpatrick had been divided between Strabane and Donagheady. In 1842, the presbytery of Omagh established a congregation at Gortin, and Matthew Logan, who had been working in the district for some time, was ordained minister. In response to the rapid growth of Sion Mills in the middle of the nineteenth century a Presbyterian congregation was established here in 1866.

The Establishment of a Congregation at Magheramason

In June 1875 a deputation appeared before the Glendermott Presbytery and requested that a new congregation be established at Magheramason. The petitioners argued that no Presbyterian church existed within four miles of Magheramason, and this after all was in an area almost exclusively Presbyterian. The enthusiasm of the people of this district to have their own Presbyterian church can be gauged by the fact that nearly £900 had already been subscribed for building purposes. Their request was turned down by presbytery who instead recommended that a preaching station be established at Magheramason. Undeterred the deputation decided to appeal the decision of presbytery and presented their case to the General Assembly a few weeks later. However, the appeal was rejected and the ruling by presbytery upheld.

The affair dragged on, and in August 1877 the petitioners went ahead and commenced building a church at Magheramason on a site granted by the duke of Abercorn. The following February the Presbyterians at Maghermason sent a memorial to the Glendermott Presbytery asking for ministers to preach to them. The Committee of Inquiry set up to look into this request found that many of the signatories to the memorial were not actually Presbyterians and did not intend attending church in Magheramason. The request was consequently turned down.

The case again came before the General Assembly in June 1878 with Victor Love of Foyleside representing the people of Magheramason. The ensuing debate was lively with Love arguing the necessity of having a Presbyterian congregation in that district, and his opponents rejecting the idea. One of the strongest detractors of the proposal was the Rev. George Magill of Second Donagheady who believed that the people of that area simply could not afford their own minister. However, in the end the General Assembly agreed to the establishment of a congregation there. The opening service in the new church, the construction of which was almost entirely due to the efforts of the people of that area, took place on 17 November 1878, and the following year the Rev. Thomas Boyd was ordained its first minister.

A Presbyterian Champion

On 20 March 1833, the Rev. Alexander Porter Goudy was installed as minister of the Presbyterian Church in Strabane. Although a native of the Ards peninsula, he was a grandson of the Rev. James Porter who was from Ballindrait, and who had been executed in 1798 for supposed involvement in United Irishmen activities. Before moving to Strabane, Goudy had previously ministered for a short time at Glastry, Co. Down. By the time of his death twenty-five years later he had become possibly the best-known Presbyterian minister of his age. Although Goudy had already come to notice as one of the authors of *A Plea to Presbytery*, a defence of the Presbyterian form of church government, it was his involvement in the Presbyterian marriages controversy of 1844 which made him a household name all over Ulster. His strenuous defence of Presbyterian rights helped to overturn a law which declared invalid marriages between members of the Church of Ireland and Presbyterians when the ceremony was performed by a minister of the latter denomination. A noted orator and political satirist, Goudy was also involved in the campaign for tenant rights. However, in December 1858, aged only 49, his life was cut short.

The 1859 Revival in Strabane and District

Some mention needs to be made here of one of the most significant events in the history of the Presbyterian Church in the nineteenth century – the 1859 Revival. Its impact on congregations in the Strabane area was significant, with happenings reported on a weekly basis in the *Tyrone Constitution* throughout the summer of that year. At Badoney events associated with the Revival appear to have been particularly intense: at one prayer meeting in July there were nearly thirty conversions; the following Sunday the attendance was so large – reputedly more than 1,200 individuals – that the meeting had to be held in a neighbouring garden. At a subsequent meeting there were nearly thirty cases of physical prostration; this feature was also noted at services in Donagheady. The impact of the 1859 Revival was also felt in more subtle ways. In 1861 the session of Leckpatrick Presbyterian Church decided to hold communion services quarterly instead of half yearly because of the dramatic increase in numbers since 1859; the previous year there had been 190 people at communion, the highest attendance then experienced.

Twentieth-century Developments in the Presbyterian Church in Strabane and District

The twentieth century has seen a number of significant developments in the history of the Presbyterian church in Strabane and district. Of great importance was the union of the two Presbyterian congregations in the town of Strabane in 1911. The question of unity had originally arisen nearly forty years previously at a time when First Strabane was vacant. In May 1873 the minister of Second Strabane, W.A. Russell, wrote a letter to the session of First Strabane suggesting amalgamation. Nothing was forthcoming from this request; indeed, it was unanimously rejected. Interestingly, when union did eventually take place the only serious objections came from members of Second Strabane. However, the actual process of uniting the two congregations ran with a remarkable smoothness, helped by the good relationship between the Rev. Edward Clarke and the Rev. C.K. Toland, ministers of, respectively, First and Second Strabane. Both men served as ministers in the combined charge until the death of Mr Toland in 1916. The respect with which this man was held in the local community was exemplified by the fact that men of every class and creed were in attendance at his funeral.

As a result of a disastrous fire on Christmas Day 1938 Strabane Presbyterian Church was burnt to the ground. Nine months later the Second World War began and plans to rebuild the church were put on hold. During this time the congregation used the former Second Presbyterian Church building as their place of worship. Rather than rebuild the church on its former site, the majority of the congregation voted in 1945 to move to a fresh site on the Derry Road. However, it was to be a further twelve years before the new church was finished. It was designed by Thomas Houston, and has been described by the architectural historian, Alistair Rowan, as 'a large pink brick hall, nicely handled, in a modern Scandinavian idiom'. As a reminder of the past the bell from the old church was placed in the tower of the new building.

The Presbyterian Meetinghouse, Leepers Brae: formerly Strabane Second Presbyterian Church

Several years before the union of the congregations in Strabane, the Presbyterians in Newtownstewart had joined forces, building a new church in 1909–10 on the site of the original meeting-house of 1804. Two previous attempts at uniting the two congregations, the first in 1877 and a second in 1900, had been unsuccessful. Changed economic circumstances and a significantly reduced membership forced the two Donagheady congregations to give serious consideration to union in the early 1930s. Despite some opposition union was effected on 1 January 1933, with the united congregation using the Second Donagheady church building as their place of worship. The twentieth century has also seen several congregations becoming united charges, i.e. sharing the same minister with one or more churches, but retaining their own separate identity. Examples of this include Ardstraw and Douglas, united in 1946, and Newtownstewart and Gortin, united in 1970. Also in 1970 the three congregations of Badoney, Corrick and Glenelly were grouped together under the ministry of the Rev. Robert Watts.

The latter part of the twentieth century has also witnessed the appearance of a further brand of Presbyterianism in this area with the establishment of a Free Presbyterian congregation at Castlederg. In 1976, Castlederg Free Presbyterian Church bought the church building at Mulvin from the Reformed Presbyterian Church and established a further congregation there. The size of the congregation of Bready Reformed Presbyterian Church was substantially increased in 1990 following the closure of the church in Clarendon Street, Londonderry, and the removal of its members to Bready.

Although the twentieth century has been very much a period of consolidation for the Presbyterian Church in Strabane and district, contrasting with nineteenth century, which, as we have seen, was an era of expansion, the Presbyterian ethos in the area remains strong. From unpromising beginnings nearly 350 years ago, the Presbyterian church established itself by the latter part of the nineteenth century as the dominant Protestant denomination in this part of north Tyrone, a position it continues to hold to the present day.

18 The Catholic Church in Strabane since *c.* 1600

JOHN DOOHER

The Pre-Plantation Church

The position of the Catholic Church in the Strabane area in the reformation and pre-plantation period is very much hidden from view and only glimpses are available through folk memory and pieces of information recorded at the very end of the age in question. The very foundation of Strabane through the establishment of a Franciscan monastery in the town has been called into question, with Fr Ciaran Devlin asserting that the Third Order only came to the town in the latter half of the seventeenth century, though previously having monasteries at Corrick, Pubble and Scarvagherin.

Opening of the Grotto, 1950. This was the site of the earlier Church of St John, opened in 1821.

(Henry H. Jefferies and Ciaran Devlin (eds.), *History of the Diocese of Derry from Earliest Times*, Dublin [2000]). There were certainly earlier monastic sites in the district and many of the present day parishes probably owe their boundaries to a medieval monastery. The evolution of the diocesan and parish structures that became familiar in the post reformation era probably dates only from the twelfth century and it was in 1254 that Derry became the centre rather than Maghera or Ardstraw from where the bishops had previously exercised authority. The move had much to do with the changing power of the Gaelic chieftains and the growing supremacy of the O'Neill clan in central Ulster in the later middle ages. Parishes also evolved from the control exercised by sub clans over territory and the ergenachs, the tenants of church lands and the leading clerical families in the district, were an important group in the pre plantation church. The ergenachs were generally appointed from within a distinct family group and exercised authority on behalf of the bishop in that district. It is difficult to determine whether these ergenachs had any religious training but they appear to have been regarded as the clergy of the pre reformation church. In *the Survey of the Clergy of Derry and Raphoe* by Canon Leslie lists are provided of rectors, vicars and ergenachs for the various parishes. Thus Urney parish had names like John O'Casey, Donal Mac Ward, Donal O'Brien, Odo O'Carolan, Donal O Kelly and Magnus O'Gormley as clerical leaders in the fifteenth and sixteenth centuries. Ardstraw parish was served by clerical families such as McColgan, O'Carolan, O'Boyle and O'Farran while the only decipherable name mentioned for Camus was Odo Mac Ward: it was stressed, however, that the clerical leaders for Urney also covered Camus for most of the period. In Leckpatrick parish names like John McCallion, Patrick O'Duffy, Patrick O'Brien and Phelim O'Carolan appear while Donagheady was served by clerics such as Patrick McColgan, Donal O'Carolan, William O'Hegarty and Bernard O'Divin. The survival of many of these names to the present day suggests that the clergy were drawn from the local families and it is known that many regarded the positions as belonging to the family group, with a strong degree of succession from father to son or uncle to nephew. These were the people responsible for the provision of what church services were available in those unsettled times and church buildings were rudimentary in most cases. The remains of earlier monastic sites generally sufficed as centres for formal religious practice and for the burial of the dead though it is very likely that holy wells and other pre-Christian sites may have also provided centres for popular religious ceremonies.

The Reformation Brought to Ireland

The introduction of the reformation to Ireland and the spread of English control in the sixteenth century was to bring major changes to religious practices, with monasteries and clergy in the religious orders feeling the earliest effects. Until 1600 west Ulster had been sheltered from the growing Anglicisation of the country but the weakening power of the O'Neill–O'Donnell alliance made change inevitable. In 1601 one of the earliest casualties of the growing English power was the killing of Bishop Redmond Gallagher at Cumber in attempting to escape from the invading English forces and the beginning of the plantation programme a few years later was to greatly increase the rate of change. Bishop Montgomery had been appointed to introduce the ideas of the reformation to north-west Ulster and his survey of the Derry diocese in 1607 provides historians with considerable information on the state of religion in Strabane area at that time. It is clear that he wished to know the full value of his new diocese and was very concerned at ensuring that the traditional church lands in the various parishes was reserved for the new church leadership and not dissipated in plantation grants. Less attention was paid in the survey to the state of the churches and it is likely that most were in ruins at the end of a period of major upheaval and warfare. Yet what Montgomery's survey shows is that nearly every parish had an officiating priest and these were to provide a problem for Montgomery and his successors. Attempts were made in the early stages to persuade them to function as clergy for the new religious administration and firm action taken against the monks and friars of the religious orders. Thus in Derry a number of Dominicans were executed or imprisoned for refusal to adopt the new religious practices while others were driven to seek refuge in more rural and isolated areas (Jefferies and Devlin, *History of the Diocese of Derry*). The parochial clergy were to be the next to suffer in the land confiscations and transfers of the plantation period.

The 1607 Survey of Clergy

The Montgomery survey shows that most of the parishes in the Strabane area had their quota of priests in 1607. In Donagheady the incumbent was Terence O'Devenny (more likely Devine) while Denis O'Farren was also in position. In neighbouring Leckpatrick the two officiating clergymen were Cormac O'Cleary and Eneas Mac Eneaney. A similar name was found in Camus, with Muiris MacEneaney being in charge, while Urney was under the authority of Finian Mac Ward and Terence O'Farren named for Ardstraw. One difficulty is that the names were recorded from the Irish and present-day scholars are at the mercy of the translation and spelling of Bishop Montgomery and his scribes. Yet it is clear that at the beginning of the plantation period most parishes had priests in position and Montgomery's first task was to interview these and seek their support in the introduction of the new religious practices. It seems clear that very few accepted his offer of continued employment, since the early plantation

THE CATHOLIC CHURCH SINCE *C.* 1600   317

records show a major change in names of officiating clergymen. A survey by Bishop Downham in 1622 provides detailed information on the fledgling Church of Ireland in the Strabane district and we learn that the church at Donaghkiddy (Donagheady) had 'sufficient walls but remains uncovered'. The clergyman was Robert Sempill and some progress had been made in improving attendances at services. At the same date Henry Noble was rector in Leckpatrick and he appears to have later transferred to Camus in place of Alexander Spicer who had gone the other way. Ardstraw parish had John Richardson as rector while Isaac Wood was in charge in Urney. Clearly a new generation of clergy was established in power in the parishes of the Strabane barony and the traditional church families were deprived of power and position in the post plantation scheme of things.

Catholics in Strabane 1628

Bishop Downham became increasingly perturbed at the failure to remove Catholicism from the district in these plantation years and reported in 1622 that 'priests were placed in every parish to celebrate the Mass and other priestly functions and who, though they be rude, ignorant and vicious fellows, yet carry the natives after them generally'. No doubt the opportunities for religious training for Catholic priests were limited but Downham felt that the laws were too weak and the military leaders insufficiently committed to adequately ensure the removal of the Catholic religion. A few years later, in 1628, he returned to the same theme, with the claim that Owen MacSweeney and his successor, Terence O'Kelly, were 'doing much harm in the town of Strabane'. He went on to allege that Strabane businessmen like James Farrell, 'the chief harbourer of priests and Jesuits', Andrew Hadaway – 'an apostate, a malicious papist', James Crawford, agent to the countess of Abercorn and Robert Algeo, agent to Sir George Hamilton, were the main leaders in the Catholic revival, allowing their houses to be used for Sunday masses, with numerous Irish and about forty Scottish attending regularly. Frequently Mass was celebrated at the house of Sir George Hamilton himself and these Scottish papists were largely to blame for the failure of the reformation in the Strabane district (see R.J. Hunter (ed.), *The Plantation of Ulster in the Strabane Barony*, Derry [1982]). It is doubtful, however, whether things were as clear-cut or as favourable to Catholics as Downham alleged and other evidence suggests that Catholicism in the Derry diocese suffered severely in the seventeenth century. There was no bishop resident in the diocese from 1601, on the death of Redmond Gallagher, until the late eighteenth century, and authority was exercised by vicar apostolics. One such was Terence O'Kelly who remained in control of the Derry diocese from 1629 until 1670, when he was removed by Archbishop Oliver Plunkett. O'Kelly became infamous for his priestly immorality but the fact that he remained in power so long illustrates the probable lack of alternatives. He was protected for much of the period by the Catholic Hamilton family and appears to have lived mostly in the parish of Urney, a traditional power base for the O'Kelly family in the pre plantation period. Strabane was somewhat distinctive in this period in having a Catholic-friendly landlord group in power but toleration was best maintained by adopting a low profile and keeping out of the limelight. The Cromwellian settlement, however, following the decade of rebellion from 1641, was to bring about major changes and a further deterioration in the position of the Catholic Church in the district.

The Outlawed Church: 1650s–1670s

The success of the Cromwellian campaign by 1651 ensured that a new plantation and further land confiscation would take place and the Civil Survey, carried out in the following years to determine the existing ownership of land, showed that the former Catholic Hamiltons were in danger of losing much of their influence and land in the Strabane area. Little toleration would be extended in the new regime and this period from 1651 until the 1670s saw renewed persecution and a religion driven underground in many areas. This is probably the beginning of the era of the mass rocks and the absence of clergy made life difficult. Mass was said at irregular intervals by travelling clergy, generally from some of the religious orders, and there was a high price on their heads. Folklore suggests that a number of priests suffered the death penalty while celebrating mass, with a Fr Nugent in Leckpatrick being allegedly shot at the altar. Legend also tells of a Catholic college established by the Hamiltons near Artigarvan being sacked and destroyed and the inmates put to death, with the Malison Bridge (the cursed bridge) allegedly named after this deed (Walter Hegarty, *Leckpatrick Parish and its History*). Another priestly fatality is said to have occurred at Calhame, near Donneyloop in the Urney parish, when a Fr Ward died from injuries received while trying to escape the attentions of priest-hunters and it is likely that these events could be placed in the years after 1650. Mass was being celebrated in clandestine fashion in woods and glens while existing church and monastic sites, almost always in ruins through the ravages or time or the depredations of war, remained in demand as burial sites for the local population.

Further Persecution, 1681

In the year 1681 renewed efforts were made to round up Catholic clergy and a report of that time records the names of a number of priests wanted for treason and implicated in the alleged plotting of Oliver Plunkett. We learn that James Devine of Donagheady, James O'Kelly of Ardstraw and James McConnolly of Badoney were among a group of Derry diocese clergy wanted by the authorities. Catholics were blamed for the unsettled state of the country and the activities of outlaw Tories in places like Tyrone and Armagh persuaded many in officialdom that the role of the Catholic Church in fermenting unrest necessitated punitive action against the leadership. Franciscan and Dominican clergy were particularly susceptible to government actions and it is likely that the attempts to re-establish congregations at places like Strabane and Derry drew a swift response from government (see Oliver Rafferty, *Catholicism in Ulster, 1603–1983*, Dublin [1984]). Dean Brian McGuirk, vicar apostolic, was one of those arrested in Derry and suffered a period of imprisonment during which the government attempted unsuccessfully on three occasions to have him convicted of exercising papal authority and plotting treason. Clearly there were many among the protestant population who were unwilling to accept the official line on the treasonable activities of the Catholic leadership.

Short-term Toleration 1685–91

There was a short-lived period of toleration from 1685, when James II became king in England, and a rudimentary structure of clerical involvement in the various parishes may have been restored. The defeat of the Jacobite cause in the Williamite wars, however, ensured that toleration of Catholicism would be short-lived and in 1696 we have evidence that a number of Catholic clergy were imprisoned in Strabane gaol. A letter was sent from the prisoners to the Protestant bishop of Derry, William King, seeking his intervention to secure their release. They complained that no charge had been made against them and they sought relief from the financial burdens of imprisonment, some of them 'being mendicants and thereby unable to defray our charges'. The letter was signed by John McNally, Badoney, James O'Hegarty, Fahan, Tagh O'Luinsechan, Leckpatrick and James Mc Connolly, Badoney. It seems likely that they were released at this stage but the passage of a new series of penal laws in the following years was to seriously weaken once again the security and prospects of the Catholic clergy in Ireland in general and also in Strabane. The 'strolling' or 'mendicant' clergy, the name given to those in the orders like the Franciscans and Dominicans, were first to feel the effects of the new laws and were banished from the country on pain of death. In the early stages the parish clergy were accorded a measure of toleration, on condition that they registered with the government and pledged loyalty to the new regime. In 1704 the first of the registrations took place and this has provided historians with some evidence of just who was ministering to the people in these years.

Registration of Clergy 1704

The 1704 list demonstrates a degree of continuity from earlier records. Tagh O'Luinsechan was priest in Leckpatrick, as he had been in 1696 while a prisoner in Strabane, and he was registered as living at Fyfin in Glenmornan and aged fifty-five years. Local legend talks of an altar/mass rock at Fyfin and it appears that this priest remained as pastor of the parish for a considerable period. James O'Devin was registered for the parish of Camus and aged forty-eight. This is possibly the same James Devine who was being sought by government in 1681 while ministering in Donagheady, though the age given in 1704 would suggest a very young priest in the earlier episode. Fr Devine was registered as living at Bernagh (Bearney) and folklore talks of an altar for saying mass being in that area during the eighteenth century. It is likely that use was also made of the nearby Camus church ruins and grave-yard for religious services and especially burials during this period of penal law deprivation. James O' Kelly, aged sixty-four, was registered for Ardstraw, just as he had been in 1681, and a John McConnolly, aged seventy, was reported ministering at Badoney. This is likely the James McConnolly of 1681 and it is clear that a considerable number of priests retained their parochial cares in the period . New figures appearing in government records were Bryan O'Hegarty, aged forty-eight, and ministering at Donagheady, with a residence at Aughafad, while Cornelius O'Mongan was registered for Urney and Termonamongan and aged fifty-four years. It is very likely that Fr Mongan, clearly a descendant of the traditional church family in the Aghyaran/Killeter district, was not a recent addition but had evaded the attentions of government in the earlier years and was now testing the new law on registration (Diarmaid O'Doibhlin, 'Penal Days', in Jefferies and Devlin, *Diocese of Derry*).

The Penal Laws in the Eighteenth Century

Such toleration as suggested in the 1704 registration act did not survive long, however, and the next fifty years were to see a continuation of govern-ment action and punitive sanctions. Information is limited to scattered ref-erences and more attention needs to be given to oral tradition in the various districts. Diarmaid Doibhlin has examined Gaelic poetry from the period and feels that folk memory is a key element in reconstructing the past. The issue of whether the penal laws were seriously enforced in the period is addressed by Oliver Rafferty who has no doubt that Ulster Catholics were distinctly more disadvantaged than their fellow Catholics in the rest of the country, both in material and cultural terms. In 1714 there was an attempt-ed round up of priests in the Derry and Raphoe dioceses and a survey by the Protestant bishop of Derry in 1731 painted a bleak picture of

THE CATHOLIC CHURCH SINCE *c*. 1600   321

Catholicism in the area in that year. There were only nine identified mass houses in the diocese, with mass being said mostly in the open or in some sort of shed. The report went on to deal with the state of the clergy and the uncomfortable situation of both them and the ordinary laity.

> There is not ordinarily above one priest that officiates in any of the mass houses. And there are in the whole diocese about twenty-six or twenty-seven priests who are commonly resident, some of which have two or three parishes under their care . . . We are frequently infested with strolling Friars and Regulars, who say mass from parish to parish as they pass, in the open fields or in the mountains, and gather great numbers of people about them . . . mass is sometimes performed in the neighbouring cabins when the weather is extremely bad . . . There are not any Popish schools; sometimes a straggling schoolmaster sets up in some mountainous parts of some parishes, but upon being threatened, as they constantly are, with a warrant, they generally think proper to withdraw. [O'Doibhlin, 'Penal Days', in Jefferies and Devlin, *Diocese of Derry*]

It is unlikely that those mass houses that did exist were anything more than modified sheds but the picture of open air worship is fairly clear. And it is equally evident that the contribution of the friars and monks to the religious observances of the ordinary people was important. These would have been the preaching clergy and we should see here the genesis of the parish missions that were to be such a feature of life in the nineteenth and twentieth centuries. Again the absence of churches was partly overcome by the celebrating of mass in the peasant cottages and the tradition of the 'Stations' survives in many of the rural parishes to the present day. In an era when priests were not always available and travel was difficult, the station mass was a crucial feature in Catholic religious observances. In 1744 there was a general order closing mass houses in Ulster but this was a short-term panic measure occasioned by the Jacobite threat from Bonny Prince Charlie in Scotland, and from its defeat in 1746 a greater spirit of official toleration was evident. Yet it was toleration not a right and both clergy and laity had to pursue a cautious line for a considerable period yet.

The Religious Census of 1766

A further survey in 1766 demonstrated a Catholic church weak and impoverished and yet surviving through the bad times. This religious census was carried out by the Church of Ireland and details provided of the numbers of families in each of the main religious groups in the various parishes. In Leckpatrick there were said to be 287 'papist' families with one priest in residence, though too old to minister to the people. That task was undertaken by another non-resident priest. The old priest has been identified as a

Fr Hegarty, possibly a nephew of the Fr Brian Hegarty who had been registered in 1704 for Donagheady, since both parishes were united at this stage for administration purposes. The same report for Donagheady recorded that there were 353 Catholic families, with one priest and no friar. It is likely that this was the curate for the combined parishes and the same person who was the non-resident priest officiating for Leckpatrick. In the account for Camus there were said to be 210 papist families, with Robert McCawell (Campbell?) as the parish priest. He did not reside in the parish but was said to have a large chapel there. It is likely that this Fr McCawell also served as priest for Urney parish and he may have lived in that area. But the suggestion that there was a large chapel in the Camus parish raises problems over its location and seems contrary to the tradition that Catholic worship was held in a barn before the establishment of the church in Meetinghouse Street in the early nineteenth century. What happened to this large church between 1766 and the end of the century? (PRONI, *1766 Religious Census*). The figures would also suggest that Strabane town did not have a sizeable Catholic population at that time and that the growth in that denomination mainly occurred in the following century.

The Ending of Persecution

By the 1770s the penal laws were greatly relaxed and a number removed in the early 1780s. This provided the opportunity for church reorganisation and also church building, and the final years of the eighteenth century saw much progress. One of the major figures in this period of growth has to be Dr Philip McDevitt, appointed bishop of the Derry diocese in 1766 and successor to John McColgan. McDevitt was the first bishop since the plantation period able to live openly in his diocese and he lived most of his life in Urney, where he established a seminary for the training of students for the priesthood. This was a demonstration of just how far the penal laws had fallen into disuse since the establishment of schools had earlier been seen as one of the areas most frowned upon by the authorities. This seminary was the equivalent of the secondary schools and would have been the next stage from the hedge schools that had continued to exist despite efforts to disrupt them. Students for the priesthood would have got a good grounding in Latin and possibly theology at the seminary and would have gone from there to complete their training at one of the European colleges. Clearly there was a considerable financial commitment in training for the priesthood and clergy would have been drawn from the better off farming class or from business families. Tyrone novelist William Carleton wrote of a person leaving his area to go to Maynooth to study for the priesthood in his famous *Traits and Stories of the Irish Peasantry* and how the whole community contributed to the cost of the student's education. Another of his tales, *The Poor Scholar*, told of how boys intending to join the priesthood had to go to the hedge schools of Munster to finish their schooling before going off to Europe to complete their education. It seems likely that the Urney seminary provided for such a schooling in the north-west, and reports suggested that intending clergy from Raphoe and Derry dioceses made use of the facilities on offer. It is also likely that some students were ordained directly from the seminary and some went from there to further study in the Irish college in Rome. One such recorded case was of Charles O'Donnell, nephew of Bishop McDevitt and his successor as bishop of Derry, who left Urney in 1777 on his way to Rome to complete his clerical education. His diary account provides details of the journey and the stops made at friendly houses en route, as well as listing the contents of his saddle bags: these included '9 shirts of fine linen, 6 ditto of coarse kind, 8 socks, 9 pairs of stockings, 2 pair of breeches, 2 flannel waistcoats, 1 French grammar, 2 Irish hymn books, 2 pocket handkerchiefs, 6 pairs of ruffled sleeves' (O'Doibhlin, *Diocese of Derry*). The cost of equipping a student for study abroad would have proved too much for most Irish families in the period and it is clear that the clergy were largely drawn largely from the better-off sections of the Catholic population, with nephews and cousins succeeding almost as a matter of family inheritance like the erenagh system in pre-plantation times.

Expressions of Loyalty 1798

The seminary at Urney must have been a major boon for the whole diocese and helped Bishop McDevitt greatly in his reorganisation of the church structure following the penal period. It is clear that McDevitt felt that they must show loyalty to the state authorities and participate where allowed in the political affairs of the nation. Thus in 1780 McDevitt and thirteen priests presented the Volunteer corps at Strabane with a sum in excess of £39 as a demonstration of Catholic support for the movement even though Catholics were not permitted to join the Volunteers or carry arms. In 1793 McDevitt and the clergy of the Derry diocese warned their flocks of the dangers of revolutionary organisations and the misleading messages of paid agitators (Rafferty, *Catholicism in Ulster*). The letters from Strabane agent, James Hamilton, to Abercorn in the 1790s stressed the peaceful demeanour and loyalty of the Catholic population in contrast to what he termed the disloyalty of the Presbyterians, though the mask slipped somewhat in the weeks immediately preceding the 1798 rebellion, when Hamilton reported that 'the priests, at least all I know, have been particular in giving the most loyal advice to their flocks that could be wished, *in public*, but it would be a very easy matter if they were inclined to give them a contrary admonition, *in private . . . .*' Clearly the spirit of the penal code still lingered in the minds of some even if the worst of the restrictions had been removed and it was difficult for the Catholic clergy to be more forthright in supporting the government. In the immediate aftermath of the 1798 rebellion it was reported that Dr McHugh, parish priest of Urney, had forwarded to Hamilton a loyalty petition signed by his parishioners for transmission to Abercorn, and a week later Fr McBride, parish priest of Ardstraw, had also sent in a petition stressing loyalty to government and this one had 1,400 signatures of loyalty. Hamilton advised that Abercorn should acknowledge the petitions and build on these demonstrations of loyalty and support. It is clear then that the Catholic church leadership in the Strabane area wished to retain the goodwill of the Protestant administration and that involvement in radical politics was condemned. That policy was continued by Charles O'Donnell when he became bishop of the diocese in 1799, so much so that he earned the nickname 'Orange Charlie' for his continued association with the Protestant leadership in Derry in the early years of the nineteenth century.

The Era of Church Building from the 1790s

The removal of the penal laws led to a more open church and this became epitomised by the period of church building in the late eighteenth and early nineteenth centuries. Such a programme must have meant major sacrifices by the Catholic population but would have been recognised as a major advance on the mass rocks and open air altars of the penal period. Active local leadership was a necessary requisite for church building and we can assume that those parishes where it occurred must have been in a strong position. Two of the earliest in the Strabane area seem to have been Ardstraw and Leckpatrick. The church at Glenock, near Newtownstewart, was built in the 1780s, with Fr McBride as pastor there. One difficulty for church building was finding the land, and this necessitated a willingness on the part of the landlord to allow the erection of a Catholic chapel. Friendly relationships with the leading members of the established church would have proved useful and thus the desire of Fr McBride in 1798 to show that Catholics could be trusted. In the bicentennial publication, *The Parish of Ardstraw East, 1785–1985*, it was suggested that the building of St Eugene's church at Glenock in 1785 was supported by the whole community and that protestant farmers helped transport the materials for the building. This would have been a replacement for the mass house or 'scalan', said to have been in use in Gallon in the eighteenth century, and the name was for long preserved in the local name, the 'Mass House Hill'. The original church at Glenock was apparently a very basic structure, a rectangular building with a thatched roof, and it had to be modified and enlarged as early as 1823.

The Church of the Apple Tree

The first church in Leckpatrick parish was erected in the early 1790s, probably 1793, at Glenmornan, with the land being made available by Abercorn. This chapel appears to have been erected near the site of an open air mass centre in the area and Dr George Sigerson wrote in the later nineteenth century of the folk tradition of mass celebrated at the 'Church of the Apple Tree'. This has been identified as being in close proximity to the chapel site, seen on the 1830s Ordnance Survey map as being partly on the site of the present chapel. It is likely that the first church was largely a wooden structure and was probably built by the voluntary labour of the local population – that is, the people of the two parishes of Leckpatrick and Donagheady. The choice of Glenmornan as the chapel site probably owed much to its location, in a strongly Catholic area and unlikely to cause offence to nearby Protestant families. It was part of a large area stretching through Altishane to Belix and Doorat that was out of the limelight and seen as inaccessible to outsiders. Thus it would have been a place of refuge in penal times and could now build on that tradition in the new era of openness. The priest responsible for this building was probably a Fr Rogan, about whom little is known, with popular tradition saying that he died in 1804 while on a sick call at Gorticrum. The original church was replaced in 1879 by a stone building which remains to the present as the chapel for the area. Folk tradition suggests that it served as a burial ground for the surrounding parishes for a considerable period in the nineteenth century and this serves to highlight its importance as one of the earliest post-penal establishments.

Church Building in Leckpatrick/Donagheady

A number of mass rocks/altars have been identified by Fr Hegarty as centres of religious practices in the Leckpatrick parish in the penal era and these included Hollyhill, Fyfin and Clochcor. A church was erected there in 1823 on land provided by the Abercorn family and said to be adjacent to the open air site, the 'altar green', where mass had traditionally been celebrated. References were made in the Abercorn letters to a mass house at Clochcor and it is likely that the church in 1823 replaced this building rather than bringing the congregation in from the open air. This Clochcor church would have served both the northern parts of Leckpatrick parish and also the more northerly parts of Donagheady; parish priest at the time was Fr William O'Kane and he also had charge of the Donagheady parish. Evidence suggests that the early chapel building was basic and that the altar area and porch had to be added to or repaired as early as the 1840s. The church itself had to be substantially renovated in 1895 when Fr Sam Connolly appealed for urgent support to prevent the roof collapsing. No doubt this was part of the fund

STRABANE THROUGH THE AGES

raising drive, the need to present the building in a dangerous condition, but the fact that Fr Connolly felt it necessary to make major repairs just months after his appointment signifies that the condition must have been quite serious. There is less information about the Donagheady building programme, but the chapel at Killenagh was erected in the early years of the nineteenth century while a church at Aughabrack must have been erected somewhere in the 1830s. This was very much a wooden structure and it was totally replaced in 1899 by the present church building, just after Fr McGlinchey had become parish priest and Donagheady and Leckpatrick had been made separate parishes again from 1891. There are again traditions of mass rocks having been used in the parish from penal times and the one at Ballykeery is said to have been used frequently, possibly by the travelling priests.

Developments in Urney and Mourne

In the parish of Urney open air mass had been celebrated at Scelpy near the site of the present Donneyloop chapel and there are suggestions that the townland of Inchiney also provided a refuge for religious practice during the penal times. The site of the death of Fr Ward at Calhame may also have been used for celebrating mass and it is claimed that the first church building was erected by a Fr Nugent as early as 1733. This is unlikely to have been anything like a modern church and may have been some sort of sheltered accommodation in a secluded part of the parish. Burials had continued at the original church site at Urney, this being a common experience right up to the nineteenth century with Catholic and Protestant sharing the same graveyard, albeit different parts of it. The establishment of the seminary at Clady by Bishop McDevitt in the latter part of the eighteenth century suggests that a high degree of toleration existed in that area and it seems likely that the parish would have had a chapel within its bounds. Fr Hegarty, in his account of Urney parish in 1933, suggests that the chapel at Donneyloop was rebuilt in 1824 when Fr Neal J. O'Donnell was the priest in charge. Clearly this would suggest that there had been a chapel at the Donneyloop site for a considerable period prior to that and that it may have been one of the earliest buildings in the diocese. The Ordnance Survey maps of the 1830s also show another church in the parish, at Ballycolman lane in Strabane. The Melmount area was part of the Urney parish until 1938 when it was created as the parish of Mourne. There is surprisingly little information about this early Ballycolman church and it is possible that it may have been what had been called in penal times a mass house, to avoid undue attention and ensure that there was no problem over the lease. The site of this early church was near what is now Landsdowne Park and it was replaced in 1846 by the old Melmount church, located at the upper end of the present graveyard. The priest associated with this Famine period chapel was

Fr Paul Bradley, previously parish priest in Plumbridge and succeeding Fr Denis McDevitt as pastor in Urney in 1844. He did not remain long in his new charge and transferred to Gortin in 1847. This Famine period chapel appears to have been very incomplete, however, and tradition tells of additional work being done in the late 1860s and early 1870s by parish administrator Fr James Connolly, later to succeed as parish priest in 1877 when the previous incumbent, Fr Edward McBride, died. Urney remained the centre for the parish until 1906, when Fr John McElhatton purchased a parochial house at Melmount and this became the focus for the new parish of Mourne when it was created in 1938 (see Edward Daly and Kierán Devlin, *The Clergy of the Diocese of Derry: An Index*; Eddie McIntyre, Strabane Carnival magazine; and John McCrory, *Melmount 85*, souvenir publication).

The First Strabane Chapel at Meetinghouse Street

That Strabane parish was the last to erect a church in this post penal period must mean that the priests and congregation were satisfied with the arrangements in place at the end of the eighteenth century. It seems that the priest in charge of Camus and Clonleigh in 1800 was a Fr Mongan and little else is known of him except his death in 1808. He is said to have lived in Lifford and it was under his guidance that the chapel at Murlog was built about 1791. On the Strabane side it is claimed that at the turn of the century mass was celebrated at a Protestant-owned barn at Liskey Road and that this had been offered as an alternative to the open air mass that had been the practice prior to this (see Michael Harron, 'Christianity and Catholicism in Strabane before 1895', in *The Church of the Immaculate Conception Strabane, 1895-1995*). Mass rocks at Curly Hill and earlier at Cavanalee and Bearney had been used during the penal era, and clearly the old church site at Camus had continued to be used for burial right up to the late nineteenth century. Another mass rock is reported from Roundhill and Fr Hegarty, in his account for Leckpatrick, describes the location under a giant oak tree with the 'mass hollow' providing the space for the congregation. The location of the mass house or chapel recorded in the parish in 1766 is unknown but we must assume that it existed since it is recorded in what was a fairly detailed survey. If folk tradition is correct it must have been short lived as a chapel and the people of Strabane were clearly in need of a building by the early years of the nineteenth century. Fr Arthur McHugh was transferred to the parish in 1808 from Urney, and it was under his guidance that the land for a chapel was acquired at Townsend Street from Mrs Bannigan, a tenant of Lady Tottenham whose approval had to be sought for the erection of the church. The church was opened in 1821 and reports from contemporary accounts suggest that Mr John Carroll, senior partner in Carroll and Gray, printers and publishers of the *Strabane Morning Post,* contributed substantially to the building costs. In 1830 a charity sermon was held in the chapel to help clear the debt of the original building and the erection of an altar in 1828 and once again John Carroll was recorded as the main funder. This seems to have been the solemn dedication of the church to St John since the newspaper report suggested that four bishops were present for the ceremonies – Dr McLaughlin, Derry, Dr Kelly, Armagh, Dr Crolly, Down and Connor, and Dr McGettigan, Raphoe – and donations were acknowledged from a number of Protestant businessmen in the town and district. Further work was done in 1837 with the building of a tower, and another charity sermon by the 'celebrated Tom Maguire' was organised to clear the debt. Clearly, many in Strabane's Catholic population in the early years of the nineteenth century were in no position to contribute towards the building of a chapel and this may account for the piecemeal building programme and the need for outside stimulants to encourage the liquidation of debt incurred (see John Dooher, 'Building the Church of St John in Strabane', in *The Church of the Immaculate Conception, Strabane*, 1995).

Emancipation Completed

Thus by the 1830s the Catholic population was well on the way to equality and the building of churches was part of this striving for equal rights. The other main area was education and the establishment of the Urney seminary in the late eighteenth century was one demonstration of the necessity for proper training for the clergy. It was also a move on from the hedge school educational system that had been the main option for the Catholic population for so long. An educational survey in 1825 revealed that there were still many schools carried on in poor cabins and often conducted by untrained and untried teachers. Some schools were supported by Protestant missionary groups or by organisations like the Kildare Place Society and the London Hibernian Society that were very much concerned to promote religious education through the Bible. The establishment of the National Schools system in 1833 owed much to the pressure from the Catholic hierarchy and the Catholic leadership, determined after a period of uncertainty to use the new system to help in the drive for equality. Funds were sought from the National Board to pay for the establishment of schools in many of the parishes and it is from the 1840s that the development of primary education on a widespread basis can be dated. There was a growing readiness to challenge the monopoly of the Established Church and this challenge was openly voiced, in particular at a famous public challenge in Derry courthouse in 1828, when a number of Catholic theologians took on their Protestant counterparts in debate. The 1820s was an era of Protestant revivalism and also the age of O'Connell, when Catholic Emancipation was demanded and reluctantly granted in 1829 despite much opposition in both Ireland and

Britain. Good relations may have been apparent at local level but there were also many areas of dispute and controversy.

Active Clerical Participation

The changed role of the Catholic clergy at local level can be seen in their involvement as equals in the social and economic issues of the 1830s and 1840s. Dr McHugh had contributed to the Poor Inquiry into social conditions in the 1830s, while Fr William Browne, parish priest of Camus since 1843 and previously curate in Urney, provided information to the Devon Commission in 1844 when it was examining living conditions among the farming population. He was critical of the landholding families and their abuse of power in evicting Catholic tenants from farms in order to make way for Protestant tenants. In the Famine period he played a leading role in the local relief programme and worked alongside the other clergymen and local leaders in attempting to distribute supplies to the neediest. Fr McLaughlin, parish priest in Leckpatrick/Donagheady, had played an important role as chaplain in the Strabane workhouse when it opened in 1841, and his successor, Fr Bernard McKenna, was to continue to play a role there in providing for the pastoral and educational requirements of the Catholic inmates. At the wider level the role of the Catholic laity was also changing, and while John Carroll may have been influential in the 1820s, he was joined by others from the 1830s onwards. William Sigerson was seen by 1850 as an important local manufacturer while linen bleacher Francis O'Neill had also provided evidence to the Devon Commission and was clearly an influential figure in Strabane by the following decade. It was not long before they were to become town commissioners in the administration of Strabane, but restrictive property qualifications meant that it was not until the 1870s that Catholic representatives were elected in proportional terms. The big change came in 1899 when the first urban council was established and this was under nationalist/catholic control throughout its existence. The 1911 census figures gave a Catholic population in Strabane urban area of 3,750, or 73% of the total.

Building the Town Chapel 1895

The 1890s had seen evidence of this improved position for Catholics with the building of the impressive new church for the town, dedicated in 1895 as the Church of the Immaculate Conception. It was designed to rival, if not surpass, the new Christ Church building by the Church of Ireland and to move away from the poverty image of the earlier chapel of St John, which had collapsed by this stage. Luckily the chapel in the Convent of Mercy was available for a period for the Catholic parishioners of Strabane. The new

Strabane's Catholic Church, opened in 1895, was a testimony to the growing wealth of the Catholic middle class in the later 19th century.

building was cathedral-like in appearance and one of the proud boasts of Fr O'Hagan was that all the money had been raised for the new church and the parish and community was without debt, despite the massive expenditure. Gratitude was expressed at the opening to local business leaders and others in the Catholic community for their generous donations, but it was also stressed that Fr John Mc Elhatton, the curate, had contributed substantially by going on a fund raising mission to the United States, where he had earlier spent a number of years ministering. The 1895 dedication was a far cry from the piecemeal stages in the completion of the Church of St John and a demonstration of the progress made during the nineteenth century by the Catholic population (Michael Kennedy, 'The building and opening of the Church 1890–95', in *Church of the Immaculate Conception*, 1995).

Local Leaders of Stature

One of the key factors in the improved position for the Catholic community was the long service of many of the parish priests. In Leckpatrick/Donagheady parishes, Fr Bernard Mc Kenna was in charge from 1847 until his death in 1891, while Fr James Connolly was pastor of Urney from 1868 until his death in 1904. Camus had more frequent changes, with William Browne lasting from 1843 until 1864, followed by Philip Devlin and William Hegarty until 1884, when Hugh O'Hagan became parish priest and he was in charge until 1906 when Charles McHugh was appointed and served for only two years before being appointed bishop. He was succeeded by Fr John O'Doherty, later to be Monsignor, and he remained in charge until 1934. Another leading figure in the area was Fr John McConalogue, parish priest in Ardstraw West from 1892 until 1898 when he moved to Termonamongan, where he remained as pastor until his death in 1933. Leckpatrick parish had also a long-serving parish priest when it and Donagheady were divided in 1891. In 1893 Fr Sam Connolly became parish priest and he remained in charge until his death in 1931, while in Donagheady Fr John McGlinchey remained in charge from 1895 until 1928. In Ardstraw parish Rev. John Keys O'Doherty, one of the earliest historians of the diocese, had served as both curate and parish priest from 1870 until 1890 when he became bishop of Derry. Each of these leaders were strong personalities and remain very much alive in popular tradition in the various parishes.

Community Leadership

A number of the clergy became partially involved in the political life of the area in the late nineteenth and early twentieth centuries and often played crucial roles at election times. Parliamentary elections in North Tyrone were very closely contested in the period and clergy from all sides of the religious divide became involved in supporting their respective sides. One of the least controversial area should have been in voter registration and Fr John McConalogue played a key role in the Catholic Registration Committee, whose job was to ensure that all potential voters were registered. It is said that Fr McConalogue had a close friendship with Michael Davitt, founder of the Land League, and this led him into supporting the Home Rule movement. The Registration Committee, however, were not welcomed by everyone and Strabane curate and later parish priest in Urney, Fr John McElhatton, was critical of the readiness of the moderates to make common cause with Liberals against unionism. These divisions surfaced at times in Strabane urban council but were stilled somewhat when Dr McHugh became bishop in 1908. He was unequivocal in his support for the Home Rule movement up until 1916 and publicly backed Redmond in 1914 over the Irish Volunteer movement. Thereafter he moved closer to the emerging Sinn Fein position but intervened less directly in political matters. Mc Hugh in late 1921 supported acceptance of the Treaty but did not publicly seek its endorsement.

Emphasis on Religious and Moral issues

Other clergy in North Tyrone were equally involved in the political issues of the day. Fr Connolly participated actively in the North Tyrone elections of 1906 and 1907, while Fr John O'Doherty was a strong advocate for the Liberal candidate, T.W. Russell, in the 1911 by-election. It is said that Fr McGlinchey was active in support of the rights of the AOH to have a demonstration in Dunamanagh in 1909, and both himself and Fr Connolly are reputed to have encouraged support for Sinn Féin candidates in the 1920 local government elections. Fr O'Doherty was active in support of the Gaelic League in Strabane in the early decades of the century and a number of the curates were also involved in the cultural revival. The opposition used these examples of clerical involvement to attack the nationalist movement and its overly Catholic leanings, but the involvement of many of the Protestant and Presbyterian clergy in the unionist movement was an effective counter-argument. Politics, religion and social progress were seen by many as being intertwined and local religious leaders were expected to be in the forefront. The division of nationalism after 1916, with the emergence of Sinn Fein and republicanism to challenge the constitutional nationalism of the old Home Rule movement, forced the withdrawal of the clergy from active participation in political matters except when there was consensus among the various nationalist strands. Thus in the protests against the gerrymandering schemes of the unionist government or at the failure of the Boundary Commission to take Tyrone out of the state of Northern Ireland, the Catholic clergy were able to provide a degree of leadership and support to the wider nationalist cause. The Treaty and partition had, however, effectively ended the years of open clerical participation in political matters and saw a withdrawal to areas of moral and spiritual concern.

Thus the circle had almost turned fully in the years between 1600 and 1922, from a period when the Catholic church and its leaders had been banished from the country and from any role in the decision-making process through to the confident years of the later nineteenth century when the Church had been closely involved in the everyday life of the community and then on to the post-partition period when voluntary exclusion from the political nation had become the order of the day. But the Church had moved from being peripheral to centre stage and equality was no longer a pious hope but an insistent reality.

19 River, Road and Rail
Communications and Transport

MICHAEL KENNEDY

Thou hast set them their bounds
which they shall not pass,
nor turn again to cover the earth
He sendeth the springs into the rivers
which run among the hills

Psalm 104 v. 9

River

Although it is nowhere documented the oldest way through Strabane is the water way – the River Mourne.

The map of probable routes of the first explorers and settlers in Northern Ireland indicated the routes along the Lagan, Bann, Strangford, Carlingford and the Foyle rivers. From the Foyle the penetration inland continued by boat along the Mourne, Finn and Strule waterways, and the river basins southwards as far as Lough Erne. By the evidence of worked flint, the valley of the Foyle had early settlers. Island McHugh near Baronscourt, one of the oldest island dwellings found, provides evidence not only of the presence of early man but also of how he was learning to adapt himself to difficult surroundings. Military historian Richard Doherty points out that the Danes used the river as far as Dunnalong from whence they made forays inland and up river to explore the territory. Evidence exists to show that the river was used up the Finn as far as Castlefinn and 'barks' were carrying heavy loads up the Foyle as far as Lifford. However, the river was tidal as far as Lifford bridge, and for several months in a dry summer it was unnavigable. It was not a reliable or dependable option for transport.

Canoes Found

The finding of the dugout canoes thrown up by the flood waters on the point of the Finn in 1991 provided evidence of the importance of the river crossing from early times. The misshapen logboat was dated around mid-to-late fifth century according to experts counting the tree-rings in the remaining timbers. The finds were fairly short, lightweight 'coite' (meaning a cot) logboats with delicate and ornate rowlocks. The oldest such logboat ever found was in the river Quoile near Downpatrick; it was 4,500 years old. Evidence would point to their popular use between the years 2000 BC and AD 1300. By the eighteenth century they had all but disappeared due to the dearth of suitable oak trees, which had been felled during the sixteenth and seventeenth centuries for the manufacturing of barrel staves or provision of charcoal for ironmasters' furnaces.

The crest of Strabane shows a boatman (in a boat not dissimilar to the dugout canoes) and symbolises the river, the ferry and the fishing rights of the Marquis. An early source states 'there was a boat for men and horses at Strabane on the river Mourne for the passage . . . upon any inundation or swelling of the river.' In 1614–15 the Lindsay brothers skippered a ship called *The Gift of God* belonging to the marquis of Abercorn between Derry and Lifford.

Roads and Settlements

Many centuries ago, the terrain of Ireland was a wild and hostile stretch of land. The north-west was especially so as it was sparsely populated; a mere 500,000 people were estimated to live in Ireland in the twelfth century. There were no towns and few settlements. Those settlements which did exist were mostly religious foundations, such as monasteries or friaries, around which a cluster of dwellings arose. From the Bronze Age there were circular lake dwellings known as crannogs, built on rows of piles in the lake bed and covered with layers of brushwood and stones (the nearest known crannog to Strabane was found at Baronscourt). Access to these was initially by dugouts and later by boats.

Around Strabane there was the settlement at Camus on the banks of the Mourne. Others were situated at Ardstraw and at Urney. It is claimed that a friary existed at Strabane from early in the fourteenth century. These settlements were within walking distance and could be accessed by following the rivers. There is evidence of this from Curtis in *A History of Medieval Ireland from 1086 to 1513* in which he describes a journey in 1397 from Armagh to Derry by Archbishop Coulton of Armagh. Arriving from Cappagh at Ardstraw, the vicar and erenaghs had to provide for his men and horses. The following day he set off for Urney where similar provision had to be made for his retinue.

Few people had reason to travel outside their immediate district. According to St Patrick travel was hazardous because of wild men, wild beasts, outlaws and robbers. Bogs and woodlands had to be avoided; travellers sought out gravel ridges and high places to point the way, and moved along river basins. Since there were few bridges, there were favoured crossings or fords which were shallow in summer, but often inaccessible in winter. There are two examples of these fording places, one across the Mourne below the bridge, another across the river to Lifford. Sea routes and main rivers were used where possible. There was a recognised network of river and mountain crossing routes across west Ulster, but the road and track conditions were primitive. The land was divided into separate, autonomous units known as tuaths, each headed by a rí or king. Travelling through these tuaths without protection was ill-advised. Examples of these are well illustrated by Red Hugh O'Donnell's journey north from Dublin after escaping from prison, and then the retreat of the two Hughs from Kinsale across the full length of Ireland. On both occasions they suffered great hardship at the hands of some warlike clansmen on their route north.

Most movement around the country was on foot along simple trails. On occasion, horses were used to carry heavier gear. Wheeled vehicles were used from *c.* 2000 BC in Northern Europe. Clergy, monks, small traders and prospectors used two- and four-wheeled carts, with solid disk wheels. Important, well-to-do people travelled on horse-drawn wheeled vehicles. One group in the social system, known as the Aos Dána, which included those skilled in poetry, learning and crafts, travelled freely because they were protected by local rulers. In Celtic times a 'carbat', a word derived from the Latin 'currus' meaning chariot was used as a means of transport during peaceful times. It was the more common use of these that demanded the development of the rough damp tracks into better roads. The early road system had different types of roads such as a 'slige', which was a main road used by wheeled vehicles, a 'ramut', which was traditionally an avenue to a fort, a 'set', a 'rot' and a 'bóthar', which was a cattleway. The people of the tuath were legally obliged to maintain the 'slige' road and 'ramut' free of brushwood and water weed. This tradition prevailed into the 1760s when the Dublin government introduced a system of taxation to provide for new roads.

As the population increased, and the number of settlements spread across the countryside, a network of villages and monastic settlements, and later shelters, grew up that provided hospitality for travellers. Irish society developed into a pastoral economy that became parochial and self-sufficient. The cow provided most of the clothing, food and drink. Crops were planted to supplement the main diet of dairy produce. Bread, porridge and beer were in common use. Most villages in the plantation period had their own breweries. Iron was taken from the bog ores and pins; iron knives and other implements were manufactured locally. As the pastoral economy developed, markets called 'aonachs' were held periodically to market livestock, food and produce.

Exceptions to this local independence were travelling smithies, stonemasons and carvers, who visited the country to sell their skills. Salt was distributed around the country and stone had to be transported some distances. Where possible, heavy materials such as stone were transferred by water, as these were slow, inconvenient and expensive to move.

Military Influence

By the 1600s and due to the Nine Years War, the movement of large armies of men made better roads more essential. Well-beaten tracks were reported by the lord deputy and his army, as trains of bullocks and horsetracks of merchandise and victuals were driven into the deeper countryside. Beyond the roads there were 'sill' bogs, thickets, forests, rough and treacherous overgrown ground. The Docwra military map of 1600 shows part of the Strabane barony between Strabane and the port of Derry. The map shows clearly the fortified towns of Lifford, Dunnalong and Derry. Strabane is shown as in 'ruynes'. Lines of communications were obviously maintained along the Foyle and Mourne rivers. It is interesting to note that to this day the two main routes from Derry to Strabane still straddle the river on both sides.

The Plantation

In 1608 Sir Josias Bodley was asked to prepare a report on the garrisons and forts in which troops could be garrisoned in order to protect the plantation settlements against the Irish. During the next two years, 'Inquisitions' or inquiries were held by government officials to provide information on the ownership of land, and this survey and those that followed by Carew and Pynnar led to maps and charts being drawn of each area, estate and county. Every 'ballybo', 'tate' and 'poll', as well as all castles, forts, rivers, lakes, woods, bogs, roads and landmarks were now recorded for the first time. The survey of Tyrone 1622, for example, indicates that there was a bridge over the 'water wch runneth by the said mill at the charges of the late Earle of Abercorne. A sufficient boate [exists] for men & horses at Strabane upon the river of Morne for passage upon any inundacon or swelling of that river', showing that the ford was the usual crossing method.

On 18 April 1688 King James II arrived in person in Strabane and passed on to the fort at Lifford. He continued on his route to Derry and returned to Strabane on 20 April. Indications are that James made this journey on horse with his army on foot.

The planters began to clear this land to bring it under cultivation. By the eighteenth century, when a period of peace prevailed, trade expanded uninterrupted and so there was a need to improve access for communications and goods. This led to an increase in the use of horses, horse-drawn carriages and eventually stagecoaches. There was an increase in the movement of people around the country. For example the judiciary had to come from Derry by coach with an armed guard to Lifford, the military travelled the country to preserve peace and order, and many linen merchants visited all areas where the flax trade was carried on.

Transportation

Transport throughout Tyrone in the 1700s was by means of a 'wheel-barrow', a vehicle used for the carriage of produce and the import of 'goods'. The 'wheel-barrow' was a small wooden cart or car drawn by a 'mountainy horse', a native breed of small horse. This cart was a crude vehicle which was extremely robust and particularly suited to carrying goods cheaply over the rough terrain around Strabane. The cost of carrying goods between Strabane and Dublin was 6s per hundredweight (cwt.) in winter and 5s per cwt. in summer. The firmer ground in better weather was obviously less time-consuming and less onerous for the driver and horse.

As indicated earlier, roads at that time were not the responsibility of local authorities but were the duty of each householder of towns and villages. In the countryside farmers were also expected to maintain the road surface. This policy was implemented by requiring each person to be available for 6 days per annum for work. If a citizen owned a horse then the horse had to be made available also. By the 1760s this compulsory labour was replaced by a tax levied on all citizens for road-building and maintenance of surfaces. There is evidence to show that the main road through Strabane from Derry to Omagh was in very poor condition at that time. However, the introduction of the mail coaches led to the necessary improvements. These coaches had glass windows and lined interiors and travelled at a speed of 5 miles per hour.

In 1761 an infamous event occurred near Strabane which highlighted the story and the dangers of travel. A coach belonging to a Mr Knox, travelling from Prehen to Rathmullan, stopped at the inn at Cloughcor to change horses and allow refreshments for the weary travellers. Having set off again, the coach travelled approximately 100 yards up the road towards Strabane when a band of men ambushed the travellers. The leader of the highwaymen was John MacNaghten, who was seeking to abduct Ms Mary Ann Knox, daughter of the coach owner, who was travelling with her father. In the course of the ambush Mr Knox and Mary Anne were shot. MacNaghten, who was wounded in the skirmish, fled but was subsequently captured, taken to Lifford Gaol and eventually hanged on the 'great road' between Strabane and Lifford.

Evidence from Trade Directories

Samuel Lewis's *Topographical Dictionary of Ireland*, published in 1837, noted that Strabane was 12 miles south-south-west (SSW) from Derry, 14 miles north-west (NW) from Omagh, 107 miles north-north-west (NNW) from Dublin on the mail coach road, and 'at its junction with that from Sligo to Londonderry'. (It is interesting to note these distances in comparison to present-day milage.) This directory notes that great improvements had been made to the roads to Derry, Newtownstewart and Castlefinn. The old stone bridge between Strabane and Lifford was built in 1730. In 1788 a bridge was built over the Mourne and in 1823 this was widened. Another three arches were added to Lifford bridge. These points would indicate an increase in the volume of traffic. Chief imports listed were lumber, iron, staves, groceries and general merchandise. Exports included wheat, oats, barley, flax, pork, beef, eggs, groceries and general merchandise. More than 1,000 tonnes of beef and 2,000 barrels of cured pork were prepared for the English markets. Considerable quantities of ale and beef were sent to Derry, Donegal and Coleraine. These imports and exports would indicate that Strabane and district was a prospering community and would explain why there was such a need for improved road and river communications.

Mail Coaches

In 1798 the Rev. James Porter, a native of Ballindrait, and a supporter of the rising was hanged for treason on a trumped-up charge of robbing the Royal Mail coach. It is worth noting that by 1808 coaches had copper-lined bodies for bullet-proofing. Mail coaches had two armed guards to prevent highway robbery, which had become prevalent. The guards were armed with polished brass blunderbusses and loaded pistols. Sometimes up to six armed dragoons rode with the coach. By 1810–20 highway robbery had been virtually stamped out.

From 1805 the mail coach travelled twice per week from Dublin to Derry, stopping at Strabane. John Gamble, a well-known writer from Strabane, tells of his experience in 1810 when the wheel slipped into the ditch. In 1834 there were two coaches and two caravans daily through the town. By this time road conditions had improved so dramatically that they were superior to those in England. An indication of the volume of passenger travel is given by the statistic that 3,000 travelled from Dublin to Derry by mail coach in that year. Others travelled by stagecoach and public car. John O'Donovan, in his investigations for the *Ordnance Survey* memoirs, relates that at Strabane he got down off the coach to look for a glass of whisky, as he was soaked through. Noting the demand for the vacated seat, he promptly returned to his seat. From 1847 there was a significant change in that much mail was carried by the train service through Strabane. The development of railways therefore damaged the trade of coaches, which became less popular for carrying freight and passengers and very slowly began to disappear.

Road and Transport Improvements

By the 1830s road transport had increased significantly, and a corresponding improvement in road conditions due to the Board of Works. The new Lifford road was built between 1827 and 1828. According to Pigot's *City of Dublin and Hibernian Provincial Directory* in 1824, £20,000 was granted for minor repairs to roads and bridges in the Strabane district. In the years 1833–6, there were nine services out of Derry alone. By 1850s the Bians (Bianconi Cars) were running to Letterkenny. The yellow and crimson livery, with the names of the towns served printed in gold on a red background, became a prominent feature of transport calling at Strabane. A noteworthy feature of the service was the fine, strong, well-bred horses used. The Halls (authors of *Ireland: its Scenery and Character*), who called at Sion Mills on their way around Ireland, praised the quality of service provided by Bianconi. The tariff was one penny farthing per mile, and as the general labourer received between 6d and 8d the rate was still beyond most. Bianconi's cars eventually became feeders to the railways and then carried Royal Mail. The Bians were eventually replaced by 'omnibuses'.

An advertisement on 10 December 1824 announced the opening of a new hotel at Bridge Street by Mr William Boyle: ' . . . hopes for strict attention to business, with moderate charges, that Gentlemen travelling will find it in their interest to give it a trial. N.B. steady post horses, comfortable chaises and jaunting cars, with careful drivers, on the shortest notice.' An advertisement which appeared in the *Strabane Morning Post* on 21 December 1824 read: 'To be sold, a handsome inside Jaunting Car, nearly new, with good cushions and harness. Apply to Mr. Daniel Cook or Mr. Francis Larmour.'

Along with the latter, Francis Larmour, a coach-builder of Main Street, were other names and trades associated with travel and transport at that time such as J. Sunderland, a coach-maker of Main Street, John Moody, a saddler and harness-maker, and Alexander Scarff, wheelwright and cart-maker.

In 1870 the trade directory indicates that there were ten principal streets or roads in the 'flourishing town of Strabane'. Goods were conveyed by canal to Derry by the Strabane Steamboat Co. Ltd., three or four times per week. The superintendent was Roderick Gormley, who had his office at the Canal Basin. By 1894 the superintendent was James Richie (*Royal Commercial Directory of Ireland*, Slater & Co., 1894). Slater describes Strabane as a large flourishing town on the mail road from Derry to Dublin with an important station on the Great Northern railway line and a junction with the Finn Valley railway.

The *Belfast Directory* of 1901 related that 'the Steamboat Co. do a very large and profitable business under the able management of Mr. James McFarlane M.P.' James Simms at that time owned the Abercorn Arms, 'the only first class hotel in Strabane' and ran a posting establishment with 'post horses with careful drivers'. He also advertised 'a magnificent new hearse (two or four horses) with glass panels open or closed'.

In the *Omagh Almanac & Co. Tyrone Directory* of 1895, the directory for Strabane listed E. Connor of Bridge Street and S. Wade & Son, Main Street, as coach builders. Wade & Sons advertised a coach building firm offering 'a good selection of new and second hand vehicles "always in stock" and carriages in all the newest design built to order. Repairs neatly, promptly and cheaply executed.' A new entry appearing in the directory – that of emigration agents – listed three agents, Andrew Hamilton of Main Street, William Mitchell of Main Street and Alexander Moore of Railway Road. There were also five horseshoers and blacksmiths, five saddle and harness-makers and twelve posting establishments.

The 1895 directory also indicated that Strabane had direct railway communications with Dublin, Belfast and Londonderry, and was a terminus for the Finn Valley railway, which ran from Strabane to Stranorlar, 'from whence there is a narrow gauge railway running through the picturesque gap of Barnesmore to Donegal. There is also communication with Londonderry for goods by means of the canal which joins the river Foyle at the point about 4 miles from the town. The existence of the canal is obviously of considerable advantage to Strabane, keeping low the freight on goods.'

The Canal

The canal basin as it appeared in the 1930s. By that stage the canal was already facing closure as an uneconomic method of transportation

The advent of waterways known as canals as a concept dated from the 1730s; Newry was built in 1742, followed by an upsurge in canal-building which saw the opening of the Tyrone and Lagan, the Grand, the Shannon Navigation, the Barrow and Boyne. Unlike the natural waterway of the Foyle, Finn and Mourne, a man-made structure from the Foyle to the centre of Strabane was to play a significant part in the early development of the town. The ninth earl (first marquis) of Abercorn in the early 1790s had an idea of linking his landed estate around Strabane to the outside world of England, Europe and the colonies. His vision led to the building of the canal off the Foyle into the heart of Strabane. This concept made an impact on the commerce of the town and changed the appearance and street pattern of Strabane, leading to the development of land to the north of Church Street and Castle Lane. Abercorn Square was designed in the early 1800s and warehouses started to appear around the Canal Basin. Derry Road, Leepers Brae, Patrick Street and the 'Slip' started to take shape as commercial prosperity was realised.

The building of the Strabane Canal began on 1 March 1792. The marquis employed Mr John Whally of Coleraine to oversee the work. Richard Owen was employed to provide engineering expertise and a crew of 70 men worked on the project. The canal was dug along a straight track from Dysert on the east bank of the River Foyle 8 miles south of the port of Derry. The canal was 4 miles 6 chains long (approximately 4.25 miles) and was brought into the north end of Strabane through the townlands of Ballydonaghy, Greenlaw and Dysert. The canal was completed in 1796 to great rejoicing among the townfolk, who greeted it with great optimism for the commercial future. The canal, which cost £11,318 to build, included two sets of lock gates. These were in the lower reaches of the canal: the one close to the Foyle measured 117 feet long, 24 feet wide and 6.5 feet deep; the upper lock was shorter, measuring 108 feet long, 24 feet wide and 7 feet deep.

The first traffic sailed into the canal on 21 March 1796. The *Captain Quigley*, owned by a Mr Fleming, was the first boat to arrive at the quay in the centre of the town and was greeted by a most enthusiastic crowd, who anticipated that the opening of the canal would herald a great future for the commercial business of Strabane.

A levy of 2s per ton carried was imposed on all merchandise transported on the canal. Business men considered this tariff too high and thus began a history of difficult trading for the various companies who managed the waterway. The enterprise seldom realised a worthwhile profit, raising between £2,000 and £3,000 per annum but repaying loans and rentals of £400 to £500. Barges and lighters (manned by two men) were used to ferry coal, steel, iron and timber from the port of Derry into Strabane; agricultural produce, wheat, oats, beef, butter, eggs and barley were exported out of Strabane. In the vicinity of the canal there grew up various working plants including a brewery, a chemical works, a flour mill and a saw mill. Initially, the gas works was established at the head of the canal (Weir's yard), latterly 400 yards approximately down the canal adjacent to Bog Road. The gas works had a private berth to allow for the unloading of coal used in the preparation of gas and coke. Labourers who worked on the canal earned approximately 6s per week.

The Canal Company traded for 40 years from 1820 to 1860. The Strabane Steamboat Navigation Co. took out a new lease for 30 years and in 1890 new owners called the Strabane Steamboat Co. assumed responsibility. Due to poor turnover in profit margins, little was invested in the upkeep of the canal and it fell into disrepair. A Board of Trade inquiry in 1898 imposed a much-reduced levy of 6d per ton on all tonnage; by this time the channel was very shallow and the locks were in poor condition and seeping water. By 1910 there was less than 2 feet of water in parts. The canal was thus described as unnavigable and peak tonnage by now was less than 20,000 per annum. In 1912 the duke of Abercorn sold out his share in the canal and brought to an end the long association of his family with the Strabane Canal. In 1921 the canal was taken over again by a new company known as the Strabane & Foyle Navigation Co. The steam tug known as the *Shamrock* was used to tow lighters up to the canal, where horses on a path took over to tow the barges into the town. By 1920 the diesel and petrol engines had taken over to propel the barges along the canal.

The 1930s and 1940s saw the total neglect of the canal, and as the water dried up several barges were left in the dry dock or moored on shallow water at the head of the canal close to Smyth's Mill. The canal was officially closed in 1962, although the upper end had already been filled in with hard core and rubble by that stage. Today little but stories and reminiscences remain of a venture that never really took off.

A Story of My Grandfather, by Daniel Crampsie

It is of an old captain who had nearly gone blind
he sailed from Londonderry to sweet Castlefinn
he had an old boat and he sailed her so fast
you would have thought the old devil was nailed to the mast.
He passed a steamboat the race he did run
and with 50 horse power he sailed into the Finn.
Now this old boat is well loaded with sugar and tea
and the best of French flour as I heard them say.
Its up through Clady she cuts a fine show
and into the Finn with her brandy and rum
and over Marachaghan and now it is so near day
and the Castlefinn ladies is wanting their tea.
The next day the quay porters' shout here old Crampsie's back
he had scarcely time to be up at the wreck.
Now you could search Londonderry and likely Strabane
and among all these old lightermen to pick such a man-
the bet I would make with the crown of the Queen
that such an old lighterman never was seen.
Now that he is gone and his old bones rotten
his memory in Derry will never be forgotten.

The Railways

One crucial reason why the Strabane Canal never reached full potential as a commercial venture was that within 50 years of the opening a new railway system was built to network the north-west and provide cheaper, faster, more reliable and economic means of transportation. The first work out of Derry was surveyed in 1837, reaching Strabane in 1847 and Omagh in 1852. In the area corresponding approximately to the large roundabout on the Strabane bypass, the old Strabane railway station stood. In 1847 Robert Stephenson, son of the famous inventor, George Stephenson, was employed to survey the land south of Strabane. Already the Londonderry and Enniskillen railway track, authorised by parliament in 1845, joined Strabane to Derry and now building had begun to reach Sion Mills, Newtownstewart and eventually Omagh in 1852. A railway bridge had to be built over the Mourne where Branch Road meets Lower Main Street (then known as Lifford Street), and rail crossing gates were located across the main road from Strabane to Lifford. By 1854 it was possible to travel from Derry to Enniskillen by train. Within five years the rail link had been made with Belfast and Dundalk. In 1865 the Great Northern Railway Co. took over management of the rail network from Derry to Belfast.

Development of the Donegal System

Further developments were also taking place to the west of Strabane. Between 1861 and 1906 eleven acts and orders of parliament were passed to authorise the building of railways in south and west Donegal. Broad gauge tracks (measuring 5 feet 3 inches) were laid from the town to Stranorlar in 1863 by the Finn Valley Railway Co. The railway bridge built over the Mourne in 1846 carried both rail companies and branched off beyond the railway crossing at Urney Road. The line from Stranorlar to Lough Eske (Druminin) was built by the West Donegal Railway Co. Both the Finn Valley and the West Donegal were owned mainly by local wealthy merchants.

It is interesting to note that in 1861 the method of transporting the rails to the Finn valley was by river. Six small craft were chartered to carry 1,085 tons of rails as far as Castlefinn. The *Joseph*, *Kate*, *Samuel Roper*, *Countess of Morley*, *Furness Buss* and *The Hope* must have been a fine sight sailing up the Foyle and into the Finn laden down with the rails that would eventually put these boats out of business. The first sod was turned on 9 September 1861 at Castletown outside Strabane by Lord Abercorn. Although the track was expected to be completed in nine months there were many holdups. Approximately 600–650 men were employed in the building, which eventually cost £70,000 or £5,300 per mile. Within the first sixteen weeks of opening in 1863 there was a disappointing return, with the company recording 14,904 passengers carried. In 1864, the first full year of trading, the Company grossed £3,441.

An 1892 act of parliament led to the amalgamation of the Finn Valley with the West Donegal Railway Co. There followed a rapid expansion which eventually linked Strabane to Killybegs in 1893 and Glenties in 1894. The Midlands Railways helped finance the Derry line into the Waterside in 1900 via Ballymagorry, Dunamanagh, and New Buildings in an effort to compete with the GNR line to Derry. The line out of Strabane station was laid north between the Foyle and the GNR tracks. After a half mile it curved east up an embankment, over the GNR track, bridged the Bog Road and then the Strabane Canal. It then turned north again to run parallel with the Derry Road. It crossed a bridge 400 yards south of Ballymagorry before running into the village station at Station Road. Approximately 400 men were employed on the building of this line which cost £13,000. By December 1899, seventeen bridges had been completed out of a total of twenty-four.

The long embankment across the valley north of the town caused a few engineering problems due to the soft damp nature of the subsoil. The line was a single track except for a passing loop at the intermediate station at Dunamanagh.

The idea of linking Strabane to Letterkenny had been promoted for about forty years by local business interests such as Herdmans but had been vehemently opposed by the Londonderry & Swilly Railway Co. which ran a line from Derry via Letterkenny to Burtonport. Eventually in 1904 Strabane was linked by rail with Letterkenny and a stretch of over 125 miles of track linked Strabane to most parts of Donegal. Another bridge had to be erected over the Foyle at the north end of Lifford. This was an impressive red metal structure. By now Strabane was one of the most important rail centres in the north of Ireland, as it brought together several companies and two different gauges. So busy was the station that a fifth platform had to be built to cater for the increasing traffic.

In 1870 a scheme was proposed to build an independent line into a station at Railway Road (adjacent to the Canal). An English consultant was hired to survey the plans. He suggested that the line should diverge 1 furlong (220 yards) from the existing junction, run parallel to the Irish North Western Railways (INWR) line, crossing the Mourne by a new bridge. The line would then bypass Strabane station on the west side and proceed north of the station to curve back towards the town centre to the terminus at the top of the canal. The proposal failed in the Commons in 1871 due to the opposition from the INWR. The earl of Erne, a major shareholder in the INWR, was blamed for the fall of the order.

In 1893 some of the proposals were granted. Previously the track to Stranorlar had been the broad 5 foot 3 inches gauge (to save on the expense of building another bridge out of Strabane station), where it joined the narrow 3 foot line. Eventually the full Co. Donegal railway was regauged to run on the narrow track and another bridge was built over the Mourne 50 yards down river and west of the broad gauge bridge. To avoid further payment of rent for the use of the station to the GNR they decided to build their own, but to build it adjacent to the main station to facilitate interchange of traffic. Instead of using a mixed gauge track over the existing bridge, Donegal Railways decided on complete independence by building another bridge west of the existing one. The contract for the new bridge was awarded in October 1893 to Edward Manistry of Dundalk at a cost of £2,450. The station house building went to Campbell & Son, Belfast to be completed by late 1894. Six furlongs (3/4 mile) of new rail track was laid out of the station. On the weekend of 13–15 July construction gangs toiled to successfully regauge the line to Stranorlar. On Monday 16 July Finn Valley reopened as a narrow gauge line.

An act of parliament in 1906 allowed the GNR & Midlands railways to acquire the Donegal Railways Co. A joint committee of three members from each was set up to run the company. It was this committee under B.L. Curran, who had been manager since 1943 (Henry Forbes had managed from the inception until 1943), which was ordered to close down the surviving lines in 1959 after a public inquiry. By this time the Glenties run had already converted to a road/bus service. The lines were lifted in 1960 and the last to go was the one which had opened first – the line between Strabane and Stranorlar.

It is interesting to note that in order to involve the local population and to test interest in the railway system the grand jury (the precursor of the county council) was given power to guarantee the interest payable on railway shares. If the railway company lost money or was unable to afford the payment of interest on the shares the grand jury would levy people in areas served by the railway and this levy was paid to the shareholders.

The early influence of rail may have affected a young Strabane man called Alexander Ector Orr who emigrated to America in 1850 at the age of 19. In New York plans were drawn up for fast commuter transport for the busy growing city. Orr was elected president of the Rapid Transit Commission and personally supervised the building of the first subway in 1904, at which the Strabane man made the keynote address.

The Castlederg and Victoria Bridge Tramway

On 9 May 1852 rail services were available through Victoria Bridge on the Derry to Enniskillen railway. In 1860 Sir Robert Ferguson, then MP for Derry city, sponsored a bill in parliament which led to the Tramway Act. Sadly he died shortly after that on 13 March 1860. He was instrumental in securing the act which led to the building of the Castlederg & Victoria

No 4 Hudswell Clarke 2-6-0 (1904)

Bridge tramway (CVBT) which was opened in 1884 by the marquis of Abercorn after four years of construction by Dixon of Belfast. Ferguson had the line already surveyed at his own expense. The first engineer appointed was J.G. Barton. The tramway measured 7 miles and 5 chains, was a single narrow-gauge line and only worked one engine in steam on most occasions. On special occasions two trains were run and crossed at either of the two loops at Spamount or Crew. Since only one engine was in steam, no signalling system was necessary. The journey took 30–35 minutes. The station and goods depot in Castlederg was at William Street to the north of the town. At Victoria Bridge the CVBT shared the yard, cattle pens and water tank with the GNR. The company continued to trade but struggled to make ends meet. There were few commuters and little industry. An examination of statistics shows that the tramway made little impact on the growth of Castlederg. During the 1914–18 war the tramway benefited when potatoes from the Castlederg area were in great demand and were conveyed to the main line by tramway.

The rolling stock included engine No. 1, called *Mourne*, which was in service until 1904; the No. 2 engine, *Derg*, was scrapped in 1912 and the *Kitson*, No. 3, was built in 1891 and used until 1928. Engines 1–3 had a black livery. Engine No. 4 was a 2–6–0 from Hudswell Clarke, built in 1904 at a cost of £1,600 and had a temporary name plate with *Victoria* on it. This engine and a number of wagons were bought by the Clogher Valley Railway Co. Engine No. 5, called *Castlederg*, was used as the lifting train in 1934. It had been purchased in 1912 to replace the *Kitson*, No. 2. Engines 4 and 5 had a brick red livery, with a quarter inch vermilion yellow trim. A *Beyer Peacock 2–4–0T* was bought in 1928 to replace No. 3, *Hunslet*, and gave five years good service after modification and a derailment. It retained the Northern Counties Company (NCC) crimson lake colour.

In 1924 a new paraffin-driven railcar was built by local men Pollard, Doherty and Graham in the Castlederg workshop. It seated twenty passengers and had standing room for eight. On Christmas Day 1927 the CVBT made history by putting into service the first ever diesel traction engine to be run in Ireland. It was taken on loan from the Stoke firm Kerr, Stuart & Co. at a sale price quote of £1,350. It was retained until May 1930 but out of 137 days it was operational on 70 only. The diesel experiment was not successful on the CVBT.

The 1920s and early 1930s saw greater competition from local road haulage services such as Roberts, Donaghey, Simpson and Charlton. The establishment of the border in 1921, the outbreak of 'foot and mouth' which prevented cattle being moved, the British coal strike of 1926 and the depreciating stock all added to the difficult existence of the Tramway. After a strike from 31 January to 8 April 1933 which affected the GNR and the CVBT, the future looked poor. A meeting of the directors was held on

The End of the Railways

Just as the age of water had given way to the advent of steam and rail, so again did technology interfere with a thriving industry. Railways were slowly eroded as road conditions were improved and from 1935 the Northern Ireland Road Transport Board introduced larger lorries and buses to replace the rail cars. Government policy played a hand in the fate of the railways as investment was directed first at road development and secondly road transport fleets to be known as Ulster Transport, at the expense of railways. In 1955 the first signs of a run down showed when the narrow gauge between Derry and Strabane closed down. By 1959 all the Donegal Railway Company lines had closed. By 14 February 1965 the last broad gauge train pulled out of Strabane station despite a rearguard action by towns and communities west of the Bann. The Derry line was closed and the track lifting trucks moved in to remove the last remnants of a much-cherished mode of transport.

Bus Service

Motor vehicles arrived in Ulster in the late 1890s. In 1903 Lord Leitrim operated a road bus service from Rosapenna to Strabane, known as the Lord Leitrim Co. The service only survived for a short period but the date of closure is unrecorded.

From 1924 motor buses and charabancs began to appear, maintaining a maximum speed of a mere 12 m.p.h. Mr H. Brook & Co. (Ireland) Ltd. set up his company in 1924 and in 1926 it was renamed the Six Counties Motor Co. Ltd. On the appointment of N.W. Brodie as local manager a fleet of two AECs and two Berliets operated on a service between Derry, Strabane and Sion Mills. On 1 October 1926 the Roberts Brothers had a service between Strabane, Sion Mills, Victoria Bridge and Castlederg. The service provided three double workings per day, two of which extended to Killeter. The GNR ran a twenty-seater Dennis G. built in 1929, registration number UI2194, also on the route. Another service operated between 1927 and 1930 by Mr W.F. Hill and Miss Marlowe of Omagh ran a twenty-seater Reo between Omagh, Baronscourt and Strabane. C.H. Donaghey from Omagh set up a bus service in November 1929 to run from Omagh to Derry through Strabane. He had four double workings daily and also had four shorter runs from Derry to Strabane. Eventually Brook withdrew from the run and Donaghey held a monopoly on this trade route. On 5 May 1927

H.M.S. Catherwood, one of the biggest operators in Northern Ireland, inaugurated a twice daily service from Belfast to Derry via Armagh and Omagh. The 110 miles took 5 hours 35 minutes. In the following year, due to the lack of custom, the run went only as far as Omagh and passengers transferred onto Donaghey's Dreadnought bus service. Between 1927 and 1935 many small companies sold out to larger ones. Recommendations made by Felix Pole's *Transport Conditions in Northern Ireland*, Belfast (1934) led to public road service transport for passenger and freight being set up under one owner. In August 1930 GNR acquired the six buses used by the Roberts brothers, three Chevrolets, two Dennis and one Gilford. On 20 June 1931 GNR took over Donaghey's business of two Commers and four Gilfords. And in 1934 the map of NCC railway and bus routes linked Strabane with Derry and Dunamanagh and Newbuildings. On 16 July 1935 the Northern Ireland Transport Board was set up and the Board took over sixty different bus operators. Eventually all services to Derry, Omagh and other destinations were taken over by the NITB.

Road Improvements

With the closure of the railways in 1959 and 1965 the government had promised a significant financial investment in transport facilities to and from the north-west. There had been a growing dependency on road transport as freight and passengers were ferried by Ulster Transport and private hauliers. The number of individual car owners had shown significant increases following a trend which has continued into the 1990s. The main roads between Derry through Strabane to Omagh were upgraded. The much-promised motorway network got as far as Dungannon on the M1 and to Randalstown with the M2. A new road was constructed between Strabane and Ballymagorry with an overhead bridge between the old Derry Road and Barnhill Road. With the dismantling of the old railway 'Tin' bridge on the Melmount Road between Strabane and Sion Mills, the road was straightened and made safer at that point.

Traditionally the main route through the centre of Strabane was two-way around the Bridgend Corner along Main Street, Castle Street and Abercorn Square around the old Pagoda. In 1968 the Pagoda was removed as it was a regular target for vandals. Traffic movement through the narrow Market Street/Townhall areas and around the Town Hall was always a difficult manoeuvre. The destruction of the Town Hall in 1972 was a great loss to the history and architectural heritage of the town but it did open up the rather narrow streets. The first one-way plan came into effect in the 1970s to cope with the larger containers snarling up these narrow streets. Abercorn Square, Castle Street and Castle Place, Lower Main Street, Eden Terrace, Market Street and Townhall Street all became one-way. In 1985 the Butcher Street,

Market Street and Townhall Street area of the town was completely demolished under a £500,000 town centre improvement scheme carried out by local contractor, Mr. Billy Doherty. A total of 117 houses were removed and a new shopping centre, public amenities and car parking built. With the removal of the east side of Market Street, through traffic was now redirected two-ways around Shiels' Corner, along Market Street through Abercorn Square. Castle Street, Castle Place and Main Street became one-way in the opposite south direction as was lower Church Street. In 1991 under further town centre improvements, Castle Street became a pedestrian precinct. In 1996 the Bowling Green area was given a face lift and also saw the erection of marble plaques in recognition of famous Strabane people. Railings enclosed an attractive car parking area for several dozen vehicles. In 1997 the old cattle market was converted temporarily into a large car park, to add to the parking facilities at Canal, Railway Road, Upper and Lower Main Street and Butcher Street.

Strabane Bypass

The Strabane bypass which was to be built after 1965 was not opened until 1992. The two-year project saw the building of a 2.3km stretch of road which bypassed the town of Strabane to the west from the northern point at Derry Road to the bottom of Melmount Road and Urney Road. The project cost in excess of £2 million and was partly financed by the European Regional Fund. It crosses the townland of Maagirr, the River Mourne by means of a new 150-foot bridge, the Lifford Road at the Camel's Hump, the old Bog Road and the previous Strabane Canal. Work was completed by Milligan Brothers, Edenderry, P. Bradley Ltd., Derry, and Woodvale Construction, Omagh. The new road was officially opened by Northern Ireland Minister Mr Richard Needham. Although serving to alleviate the traffic congestion through the town, especially at rush hours and holidays, it is already inadequate for the increased volume of through traffic. Public funding is unlikely to be found for the extension of this scheme in the near future.

Flood Defence

In the early hours of Thursday 22 October 1987, after thirty-six hours of continuous rain the water wall at Lower Main Street gave way to a devastating flood which covered the whole inner town area, Waterside and outlying areas of Bog Road and Derry Road. This area had a history of flooding from as far back as 1682, again in 1816 and in this century in 1909, 1929, and 1948. The water wall built some eighty years earlier proved incapable of withholding the force of water and despite the provision of 3,000 sandbags

The changing face of the Strabane Derry Road – as it was in c. 1910 through the village of Ballymagorry
COOPER COLLECTION
PRONI, D.1422/5/8

by morning many of the domestic and commercial properties in the town were under water. Properties in Main Street, Castle Street and Castle Place, Abercorn Square and Railway Road, Eden Terrace and Lower Main Street all experienced flood damage. As a result of much protest, followed by negotiating between the local Council, Department of the Environment and the European Economic Council a sum of £7 million was agreed for the erection of a new flood wall defence. Work was started in 1989 at the upper reaches of the town adjacent to the golf course at the Holmes and by 1991 the project was completed as far as the Lifford Road. Although the large concrete fortification is not an environmentally friendly sight, it is hoped that this flood wall will protect the property and the people of Strabane for many years to come, bearing in mind the words of Psalm 104.

20 Education in Strabane

MICHAEL KENNEDY

Developments in Education

The Earl of Abercorne holdeth a thousand acres, called Strabane. Upon this there is built a very strong and fair castle but no bawne, and a school-house of lyme and stone. There is also a church in building, the walls whereof are about five feet high, but hath been at a stay ever since the late Earl dyed. There is also about this castle a town built consisting of eighty houses, whereof a great many of them are of lyme and stone very well and strongly built; there are many other good timber houses; in these houses there are a hundred and twenty families which are able to make two hundred men, every one having arms for his defence; also there are three water mills for corn on this proportion.

The North-west Agricultural College situated off Orchard Road near where the Fir Trees Hotel now stands.

This information was supplied by the 1619 Pynnar Report which was carried out to determine the progress made in the precinct of Strabane, which had been allocated to Scottish 'undertakers', in the years after the plantation of Ulster. The undertakers were given the responsibility for ensuring that their tenants had built houses and amenities in their newly established towns and villages, in accordance with their settlement agreements. The school in question was most likely a single storey thatched, large rectangular cottage, built of lime and stone. No further information is provided.

An early reference to the appointment of a teacher, showing the involvement of the burgesses, is taken from the minute book of Lifford Corporation 1744. There is a record of a Thomas Bargoine being appointed on 10 October as teacher in the school in Lifford.

> We the warden and free burgesses have met in order to choose a schoolmaster for the said borough in the room of Mr John Cowen deceased and accordingly have made choice of the Reverend Thomas Bargoine as a fit person to be schoolmaster of the said school of Lifford.

An extract from the *Londonderry Journal* on 11 July 1772 advertised that

> William Drysdale, formerly usher for many years in one of the most reputable academies in London, has opened a school near the Market House, Strabane, where he teaches writing in all the hands viz. German text, secretary, old English, Italian and Roman wherein good judges have allowed him to excel; is master of accounts and book-keeping; teaches English only gramatically. His terms are very reasonable.

Mr Drysdale's wife was also available to teach several branches of needlework. A footnote was added as follows: 'The morals of the pupils will be strictly superintended.'

Within six months Mr James Jordan established another educational institution for young men in the town. His advert also appeared in the *Londonderry Journal*, on 1 January 1773. He offered instruction for young gentlemen to read English after the most approved method, and writing in all the hands at 7s 6d by the quarter, entrance 2s 8d. He also taught 'arithmetic, merchant accounts and the most branches of the mathematics at 11s 4d by the quarter, entrance 5s 5d.'

His footnote is worthy of mention as he claimed to have real practice of book-keeping in an 'eminent' house in Dublin, which rendered his abilities in teaching this subject 'superior to those [of teachers] who were only acquainted with the theory.'

These two cases indicate that private education was attracting teachers who had experience in London and Dublin, to set up practice in places like Strabane. Their rates were expensive, and only basics were being taught.

STRABANE THROUGH THE AGES

Furthermore, maths teaching was considered to be more expensive than English.

The cost of tuition is important to note in the light of the following comments from the Survey Memoirs for the North-West of Ireland Agricultural Society. George D. Mansfield surveyed the parish of Leckpatrick in 1821 and on 8 October wrote :

> A very general wish for education does prevail . . . poverty appears the only barrier . . . a spirit of enquiry is abroad. The Scriptures are in the hands of most people. Their very pursuits render a certain degree of education necessary; buying and selling cloth yarn constantly, a knowledge of arithmetic is required and a weaver can calculate his 7d 3 farthings or his 15d 3 farthings a day for his 52 or his 102 yards as accurately as the merchant who purchases it.

Mansfield indicated that there were about seven schools operating in the area in 1821. The London Hibernian Society had established a school on the estate of Mr Sinclair. The Rev. Brownlow provided the salary for the schoolmaster in another. The other schools were financed by the subscriptions of the pupils, a practice described as 'very precarious'. The schools were teaching English, writing and arithmetic and the cost ranged from 7s to 2s per quarter according to the progress of the pupils and the qualifications of the teachers:

> Habits of decency and order are observable amongst the children of the poor who are educated, foreign from those who are uneducated. The one is the rational accountable being, the other the idle mischievous and inconsiderate creature who, from want of proper employment, is constantly engaged in either what is useless or wicked.

Mr Mansfield would certainly not be noted for his caring and sympathetic attitude towards the less fortunate members of this community, but significantly sees education as the great influence in changing 'creatures' into 'decent children'.

The *Pigot Directory* of 1824 reported the existence of three academies in Strabane. Mr Francis O'Brien ran the Mercantile and Mathematical School at Bowling Green, Mr Robert Creighton had established an 'English' school in New Street and a 'Day School for Ladies' had been set up in Patrick Street by the Misses Lees. There also existed a 'Female Charity School' under the patronage of Mrs S. Hamilton, which 'gratuitously educates 70 children. Another free school educates and clothes 12 poor boys and the same number of girls. This is supported by a donation of £32 per annum and by public contributions.'

The development of Abercorn Square had been a direct result of the opening of the canal in 1796 and Creighton's 'English' school had been opened on New Street, which was the street leading from the Square to the older part of the town at Castle Place. A further significance of the canal was the introduction of navigation onto the curriculum of Mr Greer's school on Main Street. This 'English, Mathematical and Mercantile School', advertised in the *Strabane Morning Post* on Tuesday, 17 July 1827, was opened for business that month. Mr Greer taught reading, writing, English grammar and history (ancient and modern), geography, arithmetic and book-keeping, Euclid's elements, trigonometry, algebra as well as navigation.

It is interesting to note that Mr Greer describes his method of instruction as peculiar since he combines 'gentleness and long experience with the most persevering attention to the improvement of those who may be committed to his care, [which] will, it is presumed, ensure a certain and satisfactory progress.' In the light of the present changes in educational accountability, which are aimed at involving parents to a much greater extent, it is interesting to read that Mr Greer addresses himself particularly to parents and guardians of children, 'that they will find it in their interest to unite with him and he pledges himself to show even in the tenderest age of youth, an improvement hitherto unknown here'. Of further interest is the first ever reference in Strabane education to 'night classes', a tradition which has continued in the technical schools to this day. 'An evening class will be formed for young Ladies in Writing, Accounts, English, Grammar and Mental Arithmetic.'

The records in J.B. Leslie's work, *Derry Clergy and Parishes*, Enniskillen (1937), indicate that a Bluecoat School existed in the town in 1829. Eight years later there was a total of thirteen boys attending; the school had an income of £30 per annum. Such schools existed in England and Ireland, and were so called because of the distinct uniform worn by the pupils.

An earlier academy school had been established in Strabane in 1785 by local Presbyterian minister, Rev. William Crawford, a noted scholar and writer whose two-volume *History of Ireland* was published at Strabane in 1783. This new school appears to have been a scientifically and practically orientated establishment and cost a considerable amount to set up. Crawford had appealed to James Hamilton in October 1786 to help in defraying the costs and Hamilton's letter to Abercorn provides details on the school and its progress. According to this report it had been going from the previous November and about sixteen young men attended, 'chiefly from the country about, some from some distance'. There had been public examinations of the pupils in February and late April, with 'languages, mathematics and philosophy' being subject to testing. Hamilton reported that the pupils had acquitted themselves well and stated that he relied for his information on Mr Burgoyne, himself the teacher in the local Church of Ireland school. The main reason for the new appeal was for equipment to help develop the practical subject areas and Hamilton was in no doubt that it was a worthy cause. Rev. Crawford had earlier sought and got the support of the leading local people in his project and had contributed substantially from his own meagre resources but much new equipment such as air pumps, microscopes, and telescopes were required if the school was to progress. It is likely that Abercorn did contribute towards the new Academy and it was for a few years recognised by the Synod of Ulster as a training school for potential Presbyterian ministers. It did not long survive, however, and A.A. Campbell in his *Literary History of Strabane* suggested that the school ended around 1791, possibly due, he claims, to Rev. Crawford's withdrawal from active participation in radical politics. Strabane writer John Gamble paid tribute to the work of Rev. Crawford in his *Sketches of the North of Ireland 1810* and claimed that poverty finally drove him to accept a call to minister in Holywood, Co. Down, in 1798, where he died in 1801. It is possible that the minute book of the Strabane Presbyterian congregation may contain further information on this early Academy and its demise and help clarify this promising educational experiment of the late eighteenth century.

In 1831 Lord Edward Stanley, the Irish chief secretary, introduced proposals for a new national system of elementary education for Ireland. The non-sectarian part of the proposals was rather ambitious and from the beginning, had little chance of succeeding. He proposed a united system of education in which children of all denominations would be educated together – Church of Ireland, Presbyterian and Catholic. One hundred and sixty years on, the government has relaunched Stanley's plan in the form of integrated schools. Stanley's plan resulted in several schools being set up in the Strabane area in the following years.

Statistics from the 1841 census indicated the level of literacy in the town of Strabane. There were 770 males and 580 females at or above 5 years who could read and write; 304 males and 531 females at or above 5 years could read but not write; 389 males and 651 females at or above 5 years were found unable to read or write. These statistics do not indicate the extent of ability in the core skills.

A few year later, in 1845, a school for the education of the deaf and dumb was established by the Derry and Raphoe Diocesan Institution. At first it was housed in rented accommodation, but after 6 years, in 1851, a permanent school was built on the Derry Road at a cost of £600 and the matron of the school was Ms Susan Boyd. In 1848 a slim volume of hymns was published by a young Strabane lady called Fanny Humphreys, who lived at Milltown House. The Hymn Book was called *Hymns for Little Children* and contained three hymns which were to become famous throughout the world. They were 'All Things Bright and Beautiful', 'Once in Royal David's City', and 'There is a Green Hill Far Away'. The preface of the book was written by John Keble who noted that part of the proceeds from the book were to go towards the building programme of the new school for the deaf

EDUCATION 357

and dumb. Fanny Humphreys, better known as Cecil Frances Alexander, and her sister had taken an active part in the education of these less fortunate children and, through their work, the school eventually catered for twenty children, some of whom came from further afield than Strabane, to board in the school. In 1856 the *Slater Directory* indicated that Mr George Dowling was headmaster. Support for this educational establishment was by voluntary contribution.

In addition to the national schools listed, the *Slater Directory* of 1856 refers to several other institutions. An infant school had been opened at Derry Road, under Mistress Charlotte Woods. Martha Brown ran an academy on Market Street, Rev. Charles Allen's school was listed as Irish Street and Rebecca Anderson had a school on Main Street. Interestingly, Ms Anderson is also included as schoolmistress at the Poor Law Union Workhouse on Derry Road.

Miss Brown, previously of Market Street, had moved to Abercorn Square to establish a Young Ladies D & B (Day and Boarding) School. This school, later run by Miss Worthing, offered a curriculum of English, French, mathematics, music and art. Rev. T. Patterson was the principal of a Classic and Commercial School at Irish Street. Miss White continued with her infant school at Derry Road for several years before it became known as Mrs Baxter's, in 1872. Misses Dillon and Glasse took ladies' music classes. The name of Dillon continued to be associated with music tuition at the family home at Upper Church Street until the late 1950s. Meanwhile Master Charles Matthews was principal of the Church of Ireland Parochial School at Patrick Street.

In 1893 a small private school, catering for up to thirty pupils, was opened by a Mr Bamford BA on the Derry Road. He taught English, French, mathematics and classics and prepared his pupils for public examination. His reputation for academic excellence was known far and wide and many professional men received their early schooling in Mr Bamford's establishment.

In 1916 Mr Bamford, who had continued his education establishment at Derry Road (at the bottom of McDermott's Lane), purchased premises at Main Street, Lifford, and transferred his school there. This school remained open until 1925. His daughter, Mrs Frankie Dunne, continued to live there until the 1960s.

Although the next reference is by way of an aside, and has a national context rather than a local one, a reference to the curriculum of 1894, as laid out in the *Handbook of School Management*, makes interesting reading. In the present climate of central administration and statutory prescribed curriculum, entry no. 452 in this handbook, referring to the teaching of geography, is worthy of note:

The teacher may make these lessons attractive and even amusing to the children, by introducing a few interesting particulars regarding some of the countries or their productions. Lapland – dreadfully cold country – little men and women – night two or three months long – five or six families live together in one warm snug house all the time, and never stir out – day three months long – little people in sledges (explain) – reindeer-plenty of snow and ice. China – great numbers of people (Chinese) – very clever at many kinds of handicraft – tea (describe tea plant and show how tea is got). United States – many people in Ireland have friends there . . . Nigeria – hot weather – swamps – great long grass – large trees – people black as ink, thick lips, wooly hair, very small flat noses, some are cannibals (explain).

In section 454 an interesting parallel to present day programmes of study is included: 'The outlines and leading features of the map of the world which the programme requires the third class children to know, may be said to consist of the following.' There followed a list of items which had to be taught by the teacher and learned by the pupils.

The 1895 *Strabane Directory* listed the academies and schools of Strabane. The Academy at Derry Road was listed, with Mr Kerr as headmaster, F.M Steele Jr and Miss Moody as assistants. Bamford's was included; the convent under 'Mrs' Atkinson, superioress, appeared in the directory; and two ladies' Boarding and Day Schools, one under Miss Worthington at Abercorn Square, the other Miss Kearney's at Canal Basin. Music teachers were listed as Miss McKee, Miss Kearney, Miss Moody, Mrs A. Boyle, Miss Worthington, Miss Gordon of Stragullen, Mr M. Hamill and Miss Connolly. Some of the music teachers were also teaching in other schools. Mr W. McKew was the master of the Bowling Green Parochial School, Barrack Street was under Mr F. Durnien, Mr William Edgar was in charge of First Presbyterian, which was described as 'just completed and looking magnificent'. Later, Miss Young was mistress in this school which became synonymous with her name.

The town Educational Board was included in this directory and included the chairman, Right Rev. H. O'Hagan, the vice-chairman, Rev. E. Clarke, and Rev. A.H. Delap, T.E. Nelson LLD, John McCrossan TC, Charles Brown, TC, E. Duncan, and Rev. Father McLaughlin PP. It is worth noting that the churches of the town were well represented on this public body.

National Elementary and Primary Education

Three national schools and one parochial school had been established during the 1850s. Mr W.A. McGonagle was the headteacher of the Church of Ireland Parochial School at Patrick Street, adjacent to the plot on which now stands the Church of Ireland. There were two national schools for Catholics in the town, one for boys and girls at Townsend Street under Mr John

McCaffry and the other at Bridge End under Mr P. McGowan. The school at Townsend, known as Strabane No. 1, had been established in 1855 and had 110 pupils on the rolls: 61 males and 49 females. Mr McCaffry was paid a princely sum of £20 per annum and his wife Anne received £8 for her teaching commitment. A national school had been established at Orchard Street under the direction of Mr J. Henderson and catered for boys and girls, mainly from the Presbyterian denomination. In February 1854 it was noted that a new teacher, Margaret Ann Queate, was appointed to this school, referred to as Strabane No. 2, joining Mr Henderson and his brother. A supply of books was donated to support the curriculum.

In 1858 the Irish Christian Brothers were invited to set up a school in the town. The Most Rev. Dr Kelly, bishop of the Derry Diocese, made an application on behalf of Rev. William Brown, parish priest of Camus-Juxta-Mourne. Rev. Brown had bought a Dissenting meeting-house at Lower Main Street and three Brothers arrived in Strabane in July to open their school. The first director of the school was Brother Thomas Neaton. An adjoining residence was rented for seven years, at a cost of £15 per annum, for the Brothers. They served the people of the town for a mere 21 years, leaving in 1879. There is a lack of detail about their contribution to education in Strabane, which was not in keeping with the work of this Order in other towns. No reason has been advanced for their departure. We do know, however, that Brother Thomas was still in post as superior in 1865 and reference is made to Rev. William Hegarty, parish priest of Strabane 1872–83 (presumably after their departure), making payment of 9 shillings premium on fire policy 416385, to insure for £500 'on a building brick or stone built and slated known as the Christian Brothers School and situate Main Street, Strabane' and for £100 'on desks, seats, globes, books, maps and fixtures therein'. The school, in more recent times, belonged to Mr James Magee and was well known as the 'Lower Rooms', used as a billiards and snooker hall.

In 1867 Dr Devlin, parish priest of Camus and Clonleigh, was concerned about the lack of educational opportunity for the poor of his parish. He appealed for assistance to the mother superior of the Sisters of Mercy in Navan, Co. Meath, and made the journey to Navan to escort the Sisters to Strabane. Mr Francis O'Neill, Mount Pleasant, Burndennett, offered Dr Devlin the beautiful site for the convent. On 9 June 1868 five Sisters of Mercy, under the direction of Mother Mary Atkinson, arrived from Navan and took up residence in the new convent buildings which the townspeople had prepared for them. An elementary school, known as Mount St Joseph Convent, had been built by James Kennedy, Mount Kennedy, within the convent complex, to accommodate 100 pupils. The first mistress was Rev. Mother Joseph White, from Co. Meath; she was followed by Sister Ligouri O'Grady, from Stratford, London. By 1895 this school was totally inadequate and a new building, to house 500 children, was designed and built by

Mr Paul Kane of Bridge End. Other principals to serve in the convent elementary school were Sister Gertrude Normoyle from Rathkeale, Co. Limerick, Sister Gerard McDaid from Derry, Sister Magdalene Joyce from Ballyhaunis, Co. Mayo, Sister Teresa Faller, who was German by birth, and Sister Ignatius Murray from Newry.

In 1990 St Anne's Primary School finally replaced the convent primary school, which had operated in the convent grounds for 130 years. Sister Carmel Fanning, principal of the old school, continued as principal of the new, modern and most attractive school at Newtownkennedy Street. In 1997, on the retirement of Sister Carmel, Mrs Maura Shannon succeeded her and became the first lay principal of the 'convent' primary school. Now in 1999 the school caters for 285 girls.

In 1907 Fr McElhatton, parish priest of Melmount, set up an elementary school on the site of the present St Mary's Hall, in Bridge Street. The school was placed under the protection of St John the Evangelist and the Sisters of Mercy, under Sister Mary Morrissy, were invited to staff it. She was followed in 1930 by Sister Mary Mannion, who was recalled from Buncrana, to take up the post. In 1932 Rev. William Devine set about finding a site to build much needed larger school premises, and in 1935 Most Rev. Dr Bernard O'Kane, bishop of Derry, opened a new St John Bosco's Junior School, at the bottom of Ballycolman Lane (on the present site of the health centre), to replace the old St John's.

In 1878 the numbers on the rolls at Strabane national schools were 398. Approximately 155 of these attended the Townsend Street School, under Mr John McCafferty. In that year it was noted that the manager, Rev. William Hegarty, granted a salary application of £25 to assistant teacher, Anne Quinn.

The *Omagh Almanac & Co. Tyrone Directory* of 1885 lists the academy, Mount St Joseph, Mrs Baxter's Infant School, Miss Brown's Day and Boarding School, Miss Risk's Ladies' School of Derry Road and ladies' music classes. The parochial school at Patrick Street was now under Mr Dunne while the master and mistress of the 1st Presbyterian were Mr McClements and Miss Hannah. In 1887 the *Derry Almanac* listed a new national school at Barrack Street, Strabane, which replaced the one at Townsend Street.

This school, consisting of three classrooms and built at a cost of £845, opened its doors on 3 May 1886, and originally admitted 99 boys. By the end of the first year the numbers had increased to 156. The first headmaster of the school was a Mr Felix Durnien who trained as a teacher in St Patrick's, Drumcondra.

The first 10 boys out of 99 names to appear on the Barrack Street roll on 3 May 1886 were as follows:

Charles Kelly   Chapel Street

William McGonigle	Broad Lane
Joseph McGonigle	Broad Lane
John Mahon	Barrack Street
Patrick Grahames	Chapel Street
Thomas McHugh	Main Street
John McGranaghan	Railway Road
Hugh Henderson	Chapel Street
Thomas Gallagher	Spring Hill
Hugh Duncan	Barrack Street

Felix Durnien retired in August 1912 from Barrack Street and was replaced, on 1 October of that year, by local man, Mr Andy Doherty. Master Doherty had been a pupil and monitor at Barrack Street, before going to train as a teacher at Drumcondra. He joined the staff of the school in 1895. There were 150 boys on the rolls in that year when he took over. During these years, and long after his death, on 30 March 1941, at the age of 59, the school was known as 'Doherty's School'.

Mr Andy Doherty was succeeded by Mr Paddy Deehan, a Derry man, who had been appointed to the school on 13 December 1926. When he became principal, there were 4 teachers and 236 boys attending the school, a ratio of 1 teacher to every 59 boys! He was much respected in the area for his teaching ability and was held in high esteem by his pupils. The numbers at Barrack Street Boys School had outgrown the small building, which had originally been designed for three classes. It was not unusual for an Inspector to find over 50 pupils in a class. A new building programme was begun by the Right Rev. Mon. Agnew PP. Sadly, Paddy Deehan did not survive long enough to see the new extension. He died in 1956. He was succeeded, as principal, by another Derry man, Mr James S. Kelly. On 25 September 1956 the enlarged school, costing £30,000, was opened and dedicated by the bishop of Derry, Most Rev. Dr Farren. The new school had 6 classrooms, 6 teachers and was to cater 'comfortably' for 350 pupils!

In 1981 James S. Kelly retired. He had supervised the first extension of Barrack Street School and saw the student body expand to a roll of 300. He was succeeded by local man, Mr P.J. Hassan, a former pupil of the school. Mr Hassan, also chairman of Strabane Urban Council for a period, had spent three years abroad lecturing in mathematics in the Seychelles Training College in the Indian Ocean. As principal he promoted many educational innovations and encouraged the use of the new computer technology in classrooms. During his time as principal the school also ventured abroad on previously unheard of educational trips to Paris and London. Sadly Mr Hassan's time as principal was restricted to a mere three years and he died suddenly in December 1984. It was left to the newly appointed principal, Mr John Doherty, to lead the celebrations which heralded the 100th birthday of Barrack Street. And a fine celebration it was. Past pupils rallied in Strabane from all parts of the world. Those who could not be present attended in spirit and participated in the 'Where are they now?' project, which clearly indicated that a small school like Barrack Street had influences in every corner of the globe. Once again sadness was felt on 5 December 1986 when Mr Doherty passed away at a young age. Mr Dominic McDermott was appointed principal in 1987 and presently holds the post. The school has 247 boys on the rolls and has 12 teachers.

In 1882 the duke of Abercorn sold a site on the Derry Road to a number of prominent Strabane men who built the non-denominational Academy School. It was opened in 1884 and, under the 1885 Educational Endowments Act, the scheme to endow the Strabane Academy was drawn up and approved. Mr Aeneas Kerr MA, formerly of Queen's University, was appointed as headmaster and his assistant was Mr David Morton. Others to join this school staff in later years were Mr England, Mr Philander Baines, Mr Alexander Baines and Mr John Humphries. The curriculum had a classical dimension and included Greek, Latin, and French as well as English and mathematics. Many prominent scholars owed their good start in life to the education at the Strabane Academy. Noteworthy amongst these were Professor John Maguire who taught Mr Eamon de Valéra at Blackrock College, Dublin, Rev. Nicholas Simms, Church of Ireland, and Sir William Taylor, eminent Dublin surgeon of his day.

In 1964 an expansion in school places was required for the population on the north side of the town and district. The new controlled primary school, built by the Western Education and Library Board, below the Strabane Hospital, on the Derry Road, saw the final demise of the Academy, which had served the community so well for eighty years. Mr Sam Stirling, the last principal of the Academy, was appointed as principal of the new primary school. Mr Tom Bratton transferred from Ardstraw Primary School to take over on the retirement of Mr Stirling and was principal of the school until his appointment to the DENI Inspectorate in 1991. Mr David Canning, previously principal at Bready Primary School, was appointed as head teacher. There are 205 pupils at present on the rolls of the school. The old Academy building continues to function as an educational institution, offering pre-apprenticeship training as part of the North West Institute of Further and Higher Education.

The growth of the town on the south side of the River Mourne determined the need for an increase in the number of school places. The Bridge End primary school had been run by the Sisters of Mercy from 1907 as the old St John's National School, on the site of the present St Mary's Hall. In 1935 it was replaced by the Bridge End Convent School, dedicated to St John Bosco by Most Rev. Dr O'Kane. It catered for girls and boys up to first standard (primary 3). The boys then transferred to Barrack Street Boys and the girls to the convent primary. In 1969 the nuns, who had served the parish so well, finally severed links with education in that part of the town. In 1960 St Mary's Primary was opened at Melmount for the boys of the parish of Mourne. The first principal was Mr Michael Cassidy, who retired in 1983 and was succeeded by Mr Patrick Quinn, and then by the present headmaster, Mr John McGinley. On 2 September 1972 St Mary's Girls Primary School was opened to cater for the girls of the Melmount area. The school opened under the principalship of Ms Eleanor Devine with an enrolment of 450 girls and a staff of 15 teachers. The current headmistress is Ms Dympna McNamee. There are presently 597 boys and 612 girls attending the two St Mary's Primary Schools.

Vocational Education

From the early 1920s technical education had been available at the technical school at Upper Main Street (on the site possibly of the first castle, later to become Gallagher's shirt factory, at the end of Brigade Terrace) for some years under Miss Galvan, the principal. In 1927 Mr T.J. O' Carroll succeeded her as principal. He is well remembered as a great teacher and strict disciplinarian who used the phrase, 'D'ye see? D'ye follow?' Under his dynamic and inspired leadership the enrolment of the school increased and soon it became necessary to find and develop another site. In 1937 the new technical school was opened on spacious grounds at Derry Road. This school offered basic technical subjects, woodwork, engineering, commerce, and domestic science at both day and night classes. A modern gymnasium, the first in Strabane, was erected at the rear of the building, adjacent to the new playing fields. In 1942 Mr T.J. Carroll was dismissed by the Strabane and Castlederg Regional Educational Committee, after attempting to set up a Gaelic language class in the school. He was succeeded as principal by Mr Sam Rainey. In 1973 the technical school came under the management of the Western Education and Library Board and Mr Sean Diamond was appointed principal. Courses continue on this campus, although, in 1988, it was incorporated into the North West Institute of Further and Higher Education.

For years Strabane had a proud tradition of providing vocational education for those who wished to pursue a career in agriculture. The North West Agricultural School was situated on the outskirts of the town, on the Melmount Road. It provided residential courses for females in domestic science, cookery, dairying and poultry. From the 1911–12 records of the Department of Agriculture and Technical Instruction of Ireland, an agricultural institute for north-west Ulster was to be set up, as a result of a meeting in Derry on 22 August 1911. Representatives from County Commissions of Donegal, Derry, and Tyrone, and the vice-president and officers from the department, agreed to the provision of an Institute to run Courses of instruction in agriculture for young men, and in domestic economy, butter-making and poultry-keeping for young women. The department was to meet the cost of all buildings, equipment and furniture, the appointment and payment of staff, and the general management of the institute. The school opened in 1914 with places for twenty-four students.

Firstly, under Miss Martin, who retired in 1958, then under Mr Moreland Ingram (1958–66), the school offered three or four courses per year, lasting thirteen weeks at a time. In the late 1950s the school was renamed the Strabane Agricultural College. Mr Ingram distinguished himself further at this time by being appointed area (All-Ireland) chairman of the Round Table. Mr Tom Gibson took over the principalship in 1966 and, as courses for females became less viable, he once again opened up the college to males, who followed courses in livestock, crop development and husbandry. On the adoption, by the Ministry of Agriculture, of the policy of one agricultural college per county, it was decided to close the Strabane campus in 1971, with preference given to Loughry College, Cookstown. In 1972 the property had become a target for vandals and the house was destroyed by a terrorist bomb. The Fir Trees Hotel now dominates the grounds on which stood the school.

Grammar Education

In 1928 the Sisters of Mercy obtained permission from the bishop of Derry to open a school at Mount St Joseph for secondary education. Under the patronage of Our Lady of Mount Carmel, a grammar school for girls, dedicated to St Anne, was established in a building purchased from the Kennedy estate in 1924. In the first year there were 4 staff and 80 girls. Mother Augustine Comber was the first principal, from 1928 to 1934. The building was fitted with a new science laboratory and facilities for domestic science. As a result of the partition arrangements and the border which was established through the Strabane hinterland, pupils at the new grammar school studied either of two syllabi, depending on which examination they intended to sit. By 1940 there were 126 pupils on the rolls; by 1948 this number had increased dramatically to 192. It is interesting to note that in 1956–7 the numbers were reduced to 151, due to the opening of the new Milltown Grammar School.

As the number of pupils reached the 200 mark, 210 in 1965, there was an obvious need for a new school, which was agreed by the Board of Governors on 6 May 1965. In 1968 the school moved to new premises, costing £191,278, under the leadership of Sister Cecilia Morrissy, from Kilrush, Co. Clare, who had been principal since 1934, and the school continued to expand with numbers currently in excess of 400. Sister Angela Kelly was appointed principal in 1970 until 1972, when Sister Evangelist Farren, from Buncrana, took over. The school broke with the tradition of appointing from within the Order when the present principal, Mr Vincent Power, took over from Sister Margaret McConalogue in 1989.

In 1956 a non-denominational grammar school for boys and girls was opened at Milltown House, previously the home of the earl of Abercorn's land agent. Frances Humphreys, better known as Cecil Frances Alexander, had lived there with her father, Major Humphreys, in the 1840s. Previously the boys and girls had obtained second-level education in Omagh, Derry and at the convent grammar school in Strabane. The school was designed originally to cater for 89 pupils. The first headmaster was Mr James Wilson. By 1959, after extensions had been added to the house, it had increased to 225 pupils. Mr Wilson retired in 1976 and was succeeded by Mr David Todd. He was appointed at a time when the school had 252 pupils. There are currently 21 teaching staff, 2 part time staff and there are now 350 pupils. Mr Todd retired in 1996. He was succeeded by Mr Lewis Lacey who had been vice-principal in Foyle and Londonderry. Pupils are drawn from the town, from Omagh, Castlederg, Derry and East Donegal.

Secondary Intermediate Education

In 1958 St Colman's Secondary Intermediate for boys was opened at Melmount at a cost of £150,000. It was the first of its kind in Co. Tyrone. The school was built to cater for pupils within a 10-mile catchment area, embracing Castlederg, Newtownstewart, Donemana, Sion Mills and Tyrone areas in the direction of Derry. The first principal was Mr John Maultsaid, formerly of St Columb's College, Derry. There was a staff of 16 teachers and in the first year there was an enrolment of 480 boys. Mr Jack Gallagher, also of St Columb's College, took over in 1963 when Mr Maultsaid transferred to the newly built St Joseph's School in Derry. In 1978 Mr Patrick J. Grimley, one of the original members of staff, assumed the role of headmaster. Among the original staff was a young John Hume who was subsequently to play a leading role in the political scene in Northern Ireland as MP and MEP for Foyle. The school numbers increased rapidly and at one stage there were almost 1000 pupils and 59 staff. Mr P.J. Grimley retired in 1994 and was succeeded by Mr Michael G. Kennedy. There are currently 921 pupils on the rolls and 58 staff.

In the following year, 1959, a similar school for girls, Our Lady of Mercy Girls Voluntary Intermediate, was built by the Mercy Nuns on the Springhill side of town, at a cost of £145,000. The school was built to cater for 600 girls and was opened by Bishop Farren on 6 February 1960. Sister Evangelist of the Mercy Order was the first principal and held the post for fourteen years. In 1973 Sister Evangelist retired and another nun of the Order, Sister

Monica, was appointed. After eleven years as principal, during which time the school numbers increased and an extensive building programme was undertaken, Sister Monica retired. Sister Marie took over in 1984 and continued as headteacher for five years. The next principal, Miss Mary Ward, had spent several years teaching first in Our Lady of Mercy, and then in St Colman's High School; she returned to take over from Sister Marie in 1989. There are currently 32 teachers on the staff and 434 pupils. In 1999 Ms Mary Ward retired and was succeeded by Mrs Anne McGarvey from Omagh who had previously served as vice-principal in St Brigid's High School in Omagh and St Ciaran's, Ballygawley.

In September 1964 the new Controlled Secondary Modern School was opened on a site along the Derry Road and Mr Ernie Cave was appointed as headmaster. Mr James Thompson from Ballymoney took over from Mr Cave, who transferred to Lisnasharragh in Belfast. In 1990 Mr Alan Brown succeeded on the retirement of Mr Thompson when there were 450 pupils attending this school. It occupies a 13-acre site and includes attractive playing fields, a heated indoor swimming pool and a large youth wing. The original 14 staff has now been increased to 29, with a student population of 359, in 1996.

Special, Nursery and Other Educational Establishments

In June 1868 a Catholic orphanage was opened at the Convent of Mercy. It had originated in 1859 through the inspiration of three prominent businessmen, Francis O'Neill, James Kennedy and John Carlin. James Kennedy made the land available and the others contributed substantial financial grants towards the building and upkeep of the institution. In 1869 the convent also received a government grant for the setting up of St Catherine's Industrial School, which opened on 30 November 1869. This was not an orphanage, but a facility for unfortunate and destitute girls who needed help, care and attention. They were to be trained in housecraft, home management, economy, knitting, crochet and embroidery. Initially there were 36 children registered from Strabane and district. By 1903 the numbers had grown substantially and a new wing was built. A further extension was needed by 1907. The 'Grey Building', made up of workrooms and dormitories, children's kitchen and scullery was built, using the bricks from the recently demolished Lifford jail, to cater for 130 girls.

In 1911 Rev. Mother Angela set up a public laundry, which provided much-needed employment for the older girls of the school and many women from the town community.

In 1928 a fee-paying preparatory school for junior pupils was opened, in conjunction with the recently established grammar school. Pupils followed a curriculum similar to that of the elementary schools, but were offered specialist tuition in music, art, physical education and French. The school became unviable, due to falling numbers, and closed in 1957.

Special education had been offered for children with severe physical and mental problems. The first unit had been set up in 1962 in upstairs accommodation at Abercorn Square, and consisted of two classrooms and three staff. Twenty pupils were catered for. Mr Brendan Keogh was appointed principal. In 1972 Roundhill House, set in its own grounds, formerly belonging to the Lawson family, was converted into a special unit and provided adequate accommodation for forty pupils. In 1989 a custom built school and adult centre was opened in the grounds of Strabane Hospital. On the retirement of Mr Keogh, Mrs Kincaid was appointed principal. The school now caters for thirty-five children.

Nursery or pre-school education was provided for children in the Railway Road in temporary accommodation from 1948 until 1953. In 1978 the new Ballycolman Nursery School was built by the Western Education and Library Board and opened in September 1979. Mrs Deirdre McLaughlin was appointed principal of the school which caters for seventy-five pupils, aged three and four, who attend on a full-time or part-time basis.

In 1973 the Western Education and Library Board opened the first teachers' centre on the grounds of the technical college at Derry Road. This was to be a base for in-service training and a resource centre for teachers to prepare materials. In 1982 new premises were secured at Khiva House (former home of Sam Rule, a well-known seed merchant of the town), Urney Road, where it continues to provide a service for local teachers.

The Area Development Plan, which was drawn up to prepare Strabane for the twenty-first century, identified education as a vital section of the report. Further projected population increases and housing development in the southern sector (towards Sion Mills) of the town will create demands for additional primary school facilities in this area over the period of the Development Plan. In order to facilitate this need a school site has consequently been zoned, adjacent to the proposed bypass, and access to it should be provided from the Melmount Road. This site, between Lisnafin and Melmount Gardens, has also been identified for the provision of a special school and nursery unit. A further nursery unit has also been proposed for the Derry Road. These proposals are subject to funding from the Department of Education.

Extensions at St Colman's High School and Strabane Convent Grammar have been proposed for the period of the plan but recent proposals by the Catholic Council for Maintained Schools (CCMS) to rationalise post primary education provision in the maintained sector in the Strabane area have caused the indefinite postponement of such expansions.

An enterprising venture in pre-World War II Strabane

21 The Arts in Strabane

MICHAEL KENNEDY

Introduction

Written events from the *Annals of the Four Masters* tell us of the important social events in the home of The O'Neill at Strabane Castle. Bardic festivals were of great prestige value to the clans, and a lavish festival and the hospitality offered to the travelling bards always rewarded by poems in praise of the generous chieftain. The O'Neills held their bardic festivals annually and they welcomed guests from all over Ireland. Traditionally they held this event at the period of the Nativity celebrations. Much praise was showered on successive members of this family; great was their reputation for hospitality throughout the country. Music, poetry and storytelling were provided

THE ARTS 369

for entertainment and sumptuous food was laid on.

The only other early allusion to musical tones was in reference to the church bells calling the faithful to prayer at Urney or Ardstraw.

Such an early account, whether factual or fictitious, could as easily describe the inhabitants of the town of Strabane throughout the last century and beyond. Strabane is well known for its entertainment; one has only to mention the names of Cecil Frances Alexander, Paul Brady, Hugo Duncan, the Clipper Carlton, Strabane Concert Brass or the Lifford Players and immediately people appreciate the enjoyment these people provided.

In a survey of this type it is possible only to touch on the outstanding moments of entertainment and theatre over the years. In the future more comprehensive surveys may be made of the great moments of sport and entertainment of our town. Here are some of the important events, personalities and venues.

Ball Court Alley Theatre

From the eighteenth century the town had grown apace and the corporation, wishing to house themselves in an edifice in keeping with their importance, erected in 1752 a Town Hall, then known as the Market House. The Town Hall referred to later was greatly altered and improved and stood on the same site at the top of Main Street and Market Street. About the same time a theatre existed at Ball Court Alley, later Mill Lane, which was a narrow laneway connecting Barrack Street and Meetinghouse Street. The building was not impressive and was described as 'indifferent, the decoration being more ingeniously conceived than happily executed'. The theatre was regularly hired out, sometimes for a season, by travelling actors. One Robert Owenson, a friend of Oliver Goldsmith and known to David Garrick, is said to have taken the Ball Court Alley Theatre for several seasons before moving on to own the Crow Street Theatre in Dublin. He later enjoyed a successful dramatic career in London. The theatre fell into disrepair in the 1800s. A factory and terraced houses for the factory workers were built on the site, between Kennedy Street and Mill Street.

Cecil Frances Alexander

Throughout the English speaking world and even beyond the hymns of Cecil Frances Alexander are known and loved. It is not so well known that three of her best known hymns were written in Strabane, when she lived at Milltown House. The hymns were 'Once in Royal David's City', 'There is a Green Hill Far Away', and 'All Things Bright and Beautiful'. They were printed in a collection published in 1848 entitled *Hymns for Little Children*. She was born Cecil Frances Humphreys in Dublin in 1818. In 1832 her father secured the position of land agent for the Marquis of Abercorn. It was the inclusion of her hymns in Sir Henry Baker's *Hymns, Ancient and Modern* that brought her worldwide recognition. She married Rev. William Alexander in 1850 in Christ Church, Bowling Green, and then went to live in the parish of Termonamongan, outside Castlederg. Rev. Alexander was later transferred to Fahan, then Strabane in 1860. Frances Alexander died at the bishop's palace in Derry in 1895, months before her husband was elevated to the position of primate of All Ireland.

St Patrick's Hall

In 1939 the premises previously occupied by the English shirt company of Stapley and Smith, and more recently owned by local brothers John and Patrick McGinley, was converted to a place of entertainment and parish hall and renamed St Patrick's Parochial Hall. It became a popular centre for dancing and ceili, panto, opera, drama, guest teas, Silver Circle Draws, table-tennis, card playing, bowls, bingo, snooker, billiards and draughts and has been commonly known as St Pat's hall. The Billiards Club staged exhibitions featuring celebrities such as world champion Joe Davis. Early celebrities such as Victor Sylvester and Michael O'Duffy were brought to Strabane. Well known artists such as the Wolfe Tones, Dana, The Clipper Carlton Showband, the Melody Aces, Johnny Quigley and Johnny Flynn later appeared on stage.

In 1949 St Patrick's Operatic Society was formed and managed to produce a show each year such as *Les Cloches de Corneville* and *The Gondoliers*. *The Gondoliers* featured Fidelma Doherty, Dessie Devlin, Magdalene Forbes and Eddie Devlin. In 1952 the Society produced *The Mikado* with Patsy Gallagher playing Nanki Poo and Fidelma Doherty as Yum-Yum. The conductor was Joe Gormley.

The year 1959 opened with *Babes in the Woods* in St Patrick's Hall, starring Tommy Burns, Jim Tinney as the Dame, Patsy Gallagher and P.J. Hassan. The cast included Pauline Norry, Celine McElroy, Maura Houston, Fay Pooley, Liz Doherty, Shiela McNamee, Bridie Duncan, Ann Duncan, Rosaleen Quinn and Lorna Doherty. Musical direction was by Sister Ursula and Mary Harley.

Joe Gormley features throughout as a musician, conductor and composer. In 1960 he composed 'My Own, My Ireland' for the tenor Patrick O'Hagan, who had been doing a season at the Theatre Royal in Dublin. Earlier Michael O'Duffy used another of Joe Gormley's scores to record 'Wee Hughie'. Joe was remembered for his long, knee-length black coat and wide-brimmed hat.

In 1961 *Aladdin* was produced by Joe Gormley. This was Joe's first attempt at panto and sadly it was his last ever production. It featured an excellent

Frances Quigley, later to win gold medals at the All-Ireland drama festivals with the Lifford Players, as the principal boy.

The 1969 Panto *Mother Goose* is seen as a watershed in the tradition of entertainment in St Patrick's. The producer was Jim Foley, then principal of Scraghy Primary School. His musical director was local teacher John Doherty. *Mother Goose* had an array of talent in a large cast – Jimmy Tinney played Mother Goose, Geraldine Corry played Jenny, Frankie McGonagle played Sir Hugh Neek, while Columba Caulfield, Vera McGillion, Eamon Quigley, Mickey Wilson, Michael Kennedy, Helen Cunningham and Martin Burns were listed in a show which played to packed houses throughout the week. The show was so successful that it was performed in Castlederg and Killygordan and was also staged in St Columb's Hall, Derry, where it received a rapturous welcome in the *home* of panto!

In 1983 Fr Andy McCloskey met the Hall committee to convey a message from the then PP, Rev. Fr John Farren, that the time was right to begin an overhaul of the old St Pat's. Four years and £300,000 later the new St Pat's Hall opened its doors to the public.

In 1987 St Pat's presented *Hickory Dickory Dock*, produced by Aodh McCay and with musical direction by Mary Harley in the surroundings of the recently refurbished St Pat's Hall. The cast included Tommy Burns as the Wizard, Eamon McAteer, Bill Kennedy, Marian Devine, Columba Caulfield, Leo McBride, Phelim O'Hagan, Briege Bradley, Vera McGillion, Ann Bradley, Paddy Curran, Fr Andy McCloskey as Dame Foxtrot, Kevin Doherty and Aussie Bryson as Snowdrift.

Strabane Carnivals

In close association with St Patrick's Hall of the 1950s were the legendary fund-raising carnivals which were first organised from 1952 by Rev. Fr Michael McHugh and his committees. Lasting one week at first the programme started with a band parade around the streets, children in fancy dress, dances of the nations, and games and sports. The guest of honour on Sunday 20 July 1952 was Pa McCooey of BBC radio and Group Theatre fame. On Monday there was a wrestling exhibition and dog show. Ireland's leading tenor Dermuid Troy featured in concert; Wednesday was Ladies Day with mannequin parades, fashion contest, handicraft and baking competitions. Thursday night featured the carnival masked ball with Hugh Toorish and J. McCafferty. Former World Flyweight Champion Rinty Monaghan was the special guest at the grand boxing tournament, with J. O'Connor, national champion, and Maxie McCullough, Golden Gloves champion, among the stars in the ring. After a 'Grand Sale of Work' on Saturday the carnival closed on Sunday 27 July with the 'Grand Irish Finale', with dancing, singing, music and recitation.

The 1953 carnival opened with guest of honour Major-General H. MacNeill, organiser of *An Tostal*, followed by a 'Grand Concert' featuring Liam O'Connor and the great Sean McGuire. A garden party for the ladies was a favourite event with style on display worthy of an Oscars evening in Hollywood. Another new feature was the gymkhana for horse lovers. The boxing tournament featured the Irish Army team taking on all comers, including international Terry Milligan and John McNally. The masked ball was repeated with a barbecue supper at midnight.

The 1954 carnival lasted for two weeks and followed similar programmes to the previous years. A 'Car Treasure Hunt' was an innovation, the gymkhana was a major event, a special golf competition was held on the new course at Ballycolman, an open air Whist Drive was organised, and there was nightly dancing in the new 2,500-feet maple floor marquee. The garden party was held in the convent grounds and a special Aerideacht Mór was held on closing day.

The final carnival was held from 10 to 24 July 1960. The activities were similar to previous years with sporting competitions, whist drives, an Irish day to finish and talent competitions. Music again was provided by bands such as the local Topliners, Charles Kelly, Jimmy Sturrock, the Comets, Richard Fitzgerald's Céilí Band, Maurice Lynch, Tommy Mac, Eber Clarke, the Platters Showband and the Merry Macs.

The carnival days were days of great community spirit throughout the town and district, and brought people from far and near to enjoy the events and the fun of the fairground when it was a true novelty.

Opera

The first light opera production, *The Mikado*, was produced in 1911. Mr Cathal O'Byrne was brought from Belfast to play Nanki Poo; all other principals were played by local talent. A Derry newspaper report of Strabane's opera said:

> When it was announced that a company of Strabane Amateurs intended producing the *Mikado* in Derry, there were a few superior people who argued that the thing could not be done. If Derry, they said, could not venture on anything half so difficult as Gilbert & Sullivan's racy Japanese Opera, Strabane dare not do so. Strabane, however, did so, and those of the superior people who attended the performance in St Columb's Hall must have confessed rather shamefacedly that Derry could not have done anything like so well. In fact so admirably put on was the opera that the performance would have reflected credit on Belfast, Dublin or any large centre in the country, with an extensive area from which to draw talent.

The founder of the first Operatic Society was Mr E. Stevenson who was appointed as conductor of the orchestra. With the financial and moral support of others high standards of productions were maintained. Costumes were supplied by Messrs Simpson, Covent Garden, London, and from 1923 Mr H. Minshull of the Queen's Island Operatic Society was hired to produce the operas. The orchestra was very lavish, consisting of over twenty instrumentalists from the Derry-based British Army Regimental Band. Among the regiments were the Royal Scots Fusiliers, the Cheshire Regiment and the Rifle Brigade.

The early Operatic Society lapsed only to be resurrected in 1936 under the conductorship of Mr M. H. Franklin, BMus, with a splendid production of the comic opera *Les Cloches de Corneville*. On Franklin's appointment as organist at Limerick Cathedral, the Society again ceased to exist.

On Friday 21 and Sunday 23 April 1939, a concert consisting of five numbers from *The Mikado*, followed by a vocal and instrumental entertainment, was held in St Patrick's Hall. The proceeds were in aid of parochial funds. The accompanist on these nights was Mr Andy Doherty, the dance music was provided by Mr Bernard Connolly and the choir conductor was Mr Andy Doherty. *The Mikado* numbers were provided by Barrack Street School choir with Pat McColgan, Charlie McGowan, Art O'Hagan and Declan Doherty singing solos from *The Mikado*, Sadie Vaughan danced a jig and step dance, Deirdre Doherty sang 'Bless This House', and Pat Cannon sang 'The Garden Where the Praties Grow'.

The Town Hall

On Saturday 4 March 1972 Barney McCool, in his lament of the passing of the Town Hall, recorded the following in the *Strabane Weekly News*:

> On its stage appeared many travelling companies of actors and artistes from all parts of Great Britain and Ireland, and even further, playing everything from Shakespeare to *Conn the Shaughran* or *The Pope in Killybuck*. Many who have since become literally world-famous received their 'baptism of fire' on the stage of the Town Hall, for it was often said: If you could please Strabane you could please anywhere. Among those of recent years have been Stephen Boyd, the film star, J.G. Devlin, and the redoubtable James Young, to name but a few.

Not all were 'foreigners', however; there was always a great spate of talent in Strabane, both musical and dramatic. As some local poet once said:

> The town is full of actors, and the folk are music mad,
> they run an opera once a year, and a panto called 'Sinbad',
> there's a Repertory Company who put on a play for fun,
> they possess some brilliant talent, just look at 'Feeley' Quinn.

True enough the town was full of actors – and actresses – then and the pantomimes were great crack. The well-known 'Feeley' was ever a tower of strength, not forgetting Scobie McCosker and Paddy McNamee and the much-lamented Charlie Feeley, and who could ever forget those beautiful and talented Scott sisters?

There was a grand orchestra too, with New Zealander 'Sammy' Stevenson and Miss Annie Keatley among the violinists, and of course Daisy McAnaw on the piano, who, if she were not accompanying a pantomime, was equally at home doing the same for an operetta like *Iolanthe* or *The Gondoliers*. Yes indeed, the musical talent was widespread, and provided you turned up on the stage during the week, nobody bothered where you went on a Sunday. No mention of the musical talent that the Town Hall housed in its time would be complete without the aptly named Good Companions male choir, formed by the late Joe Gormley, which spanned not only religious divides, but embraced a wide variety of occupations. Among its ranks were a chemist, a grocer, an egg merchant, a house-painter, a farmer, banker – even a Customs man from Lifford – and, all unknowingly, a future BBC executive in the person of the late Reggie George. As far as I can remember, they actually broadcast from the stage of the Town Hall and I heard them myself many miles away.

In the mid 1950s Frank Nugent, a thespian of some talent, arrived and proceeded to produce a series of high-quality plays, including *Mungo's Mansion* and *Quinn's Secret*. *Autumn Fire* was the first production by Frank Nugent. The actors included the producer himself, Frances McNerney, a teacher in Barrack Street Boys, A. McGill, Marie Vaughan of Butcher Street, Sean and Molly Brady, both teachers, John McColgan, Afric Doherty of the Bowling Green and Alfie Gallagher. Another group called the Milltown Players at that time produced *The White-headed Boy* in the Town Hall in February 1953, featuring Elizabeth Canavan, Jack Duffy, Mary Muhan, Willie Elliott, Kitty Kearney, Michael Gallagher, Bridget Harron, Patsy McGuire, Eileen Canavan, Patsy McGarrigle, Eugene Doherty, Joe Doherty, Edward McCallion and Willie Harron.

The Pallidrome

The Pallidrome was built by the Cooper family in 1910–11 at Railway Road. Originally it was a cinema and later turned into a dance hall and a place of entertainment. As a dance hall it featured top dance bands and show bands from all over Ireland. Local groups such as the Clipper Carlton spent their formative years on stage here and other regulars such as the Royal, Capitol, Cadets, Joe Dolan and Dickie Rock drew capacity crowds to the Railway Road. For years the annual highlight was the Hunt Ball when local dignitaries dressed in their finest gathered to celebrate.

In 1933 the Cooper family acquired the site of Barry's Hotel in Main Street and built the Commodore Cinema which was in use until the early 1970s.

Bridgend Hall

The Bridgend Hall was previously used as a school and was converted in 1956 for use as a local parish venue. It was used for activities such as bingo, concerts, Sunday night dances and meeting place for scouts, briginis (Brídíní) and local bands.

A notable series of entertainment revues took place held during the 1950s. The last of the 'Revues', organised and directed by Dr Sullivan, was held at Bridgend in 1959. This featured among others local talent such as Anita McGarrigle, Marie McColgan, Kathleen Logue and her sister Lily, Pauline Norry and her sister Anita, both of whom achieved national recognition on TV and radio.

In January 1964 *The Good Old Days*, modelled on the then successful TV programme from the Leeds Musical Hall, was held by Fr John Convery in St Mary's Hall. Among those dressed up for the occasion were Mrs Cissie Donaghey, Mrs Dooher, Mrs Mary McGillion, Miss Mary Meehan, Miss Kathleen Kearney and Miss Marie Mullen.

The Melmount Centre

Built in 1985 the Melmount Centre is a formidable building, provided to serve the local community. There is seating capacity for approximately 550 people, and it boasts meeting rooms, a lecture room seating 250, snooker and all-purpose rooms, as well as offices, a kitchen and a bar area. Early entertainment on the agenda included the Clipper Carlton, Roly Daniels, Rock Stewart, Memories, Dicky Rock, *Aladdin* by the Glebe Primary School, *Oliver* by St Mary's Boys, the Lifford Players and the Puddle Alley Players. Quiz nights, bowls, talent competitions and back-to-back are all popular with the public.

In 1987 panto time came to Melmount with the performance of *Dick Whittington and His Cat*. In the very successful and enjoyable show, John McGinley played the part of King Rat, Fidelma Hassan the Fairy Godmother, Oliver Rouse as Idle Jack, Brigette Conroy as Joy, Clare Rafferty as Dick and Anthony Callaghan as Cat. Arthur McGarrigle played a very convincing Rosey O'Grady, James McGurk was Lord Mayor, Stephen Doherty was Mate, Brian McGrath played Captain, and Cahir Doherty was Alderman Fitzwarren.

Panto time returned to the Melmount Centre in February 1988 with the production of *Cinderella*.

Clipper Carlton, widely hailed as the first of the showbands of the 1950s and 1960s era.

Showbands

On Wednesday night 22 May 1985, music enthusiasts of Strabane had the opportunity to take a trip down memory lane when they were treated to a musical extravaganza in the Fir Trees Hotel. The occasion was to welcome back the Clipper Carlton showband. They proved to their home fans (often the most critical) that they had lost none of their old flair for entertaining.

Hugh Toorish, a pianist, was the leader of the Carlton Dance Orchestra in the 1940s. Then a small group with Packie McDevitt, Peter Dunleavy, Fido Molloy and Hugh Toorish, they were well known in the area for quality music. Hugh had for forty years played the organ in St Mary's Church, Melmount. He had been a member of the local Operatic Society, he played tenor roles in Gilbert & Sullivan under the late Sammy Stevenson (his favourite singer was Count John McCormack). He played with the Connolly Orchestra before breaking away to form his own group in which he was resident organist.

THE ARTS   377

The band was formed in December 1949 by 'Big' Hugh, with Hugh Quinn on cornet, Michael O'Hanlon on drums (he received a call from Hugo Quinn from Sion who asked, 'Is that you, Mickey? You're in boy! You play tomorrow night.'), Art O'Hagan, and Terry Logue on tenor sax, later to become manager of the well-known Victors showband. They were paid 75 s for their first night. Victor Fleming from Letterkenny joined the band to play trombone and piano and was responsible for musical direction. They became known nationally as the band that put 'show' into 'showband'. 'They simply didn't sit on chairs, sullen and snug, playing music, while couples danced. They jumped and laughed, sang and talked their way to stardom and money', as a local reporter once described them.

Later in 1953 they were joined by locals, Fergie O'Hagan, a 'large, jovial man with a butch haircut and a resonant voice like a bee around a honey pot' and Dominic Sheerer. Dom had met Vic Fleming when the Clippers were playing at the Galtymore Hall in Cricklewood, London, and told him he was a singer and played the guitar. Later, in Strabane, while Art was sick, Dom, who was home on holidays, joined temporarily and stayed.

It is claimed that the name Clipper was thought up by an inebriated barman in Fintona and no one quite remembers why. I prefer to believe the name came from the Clippertone cornet which Hugo Quinn played. But in July 1954 the Clipper Carlton was described by a leading Dublin reporter as 'six young Strabane men who provided a feast of unorthodox music' at the Crystal Ballroom, Dublin. Their programme included 'Down by the River Side', 'The Place Where I Worship', and Mickey O'Hanlon doing 'Blueberry Hill' and the 'Jolson Story'.

In 1958 they were invited for the first time to play in the United States. Michael O'Hanlon, who refused to travel by air, set sail for New York three weeks early from Cobh in Cork. The group arrived in Idlewild Airport, New York, in October, and commenced their first coast-to-coast tour of the USA. The group consisted of Hugo Quinn, Dom Sheerer, Terry Logue, Mike O'Hanlon, Art O'Hagan, Victor Fleming, Hugh Toorish, Fergie O'Hagan, and Vic Craig as manager. The highlight of the tour was at the St Nicholas Arena in New York, in which they played before an audience of 6,000 people. For the boys from Strabane this must have been a daunting ordeal but a great tribute to their ability.

Other highlights included playing at the opening of Harry McGuirk's Shamrock Ballroom in New York in 1959. During their US tour in March of that year, Steve Schickel of the Chicago Tribune wrote that the Clippers 'were about the best showband your reporter has ever heard in his more than 10 years of covering amusement events'. A fine compliment indeed! And on Scottish Cup Final night in Glasgow, so great was the interest that the traffic in Sauchiehall Street was stopped because the crowd was so big. An estimated 2,000 people were unable to get into the dance. To prevent an incident, the band rigged up amplification and presented their 'Juke Box Saturday Night' routine from the open balcony. In 1960 they again played Boston, Toronto and London. One of their greatest moments however was at the Ulster Hall in Belfast in April 1962 when they played with the great Louis Armstrong. By 1963 the Clippers were drawing average crowds of 6,000 per week, at 6 s per head. In September 1963 they had a five-week tour of the US, including New York, Chicago, Boston, Philadelphia, San Francisco and Hollywood. One outstanding feature of that tour was the Lonnie Donegan skiffle 'Rock Island Line', with Fleming on piano, Logue on drums, Sheerer on guitar, Art O'Hagan on bass and Mickey O'Hanlon on washboard.

By 1966 the band was re-formed after a three-year gap. A special custom-built bus was commissioned and a new managerial team of Vic Craig and Maurice Cassidy undertook the arrangements. The new line-up had Fleming, Quinn, Logue, O'Hanlon, Art O'Hagan and Dom Sheerer on stage and after weeks of non-stop 12-hours-a-day practice, on 3 June they played at the Floral Hall, Belfast. Due to the seamen's strike their new suits, ordered from Leeds, arrived just before they went on stage. By 30 September they were again voted into the ratings in the top five bands and described as 'still the best entertaining unit in the country' by the *Donegal People's Press*. In October they appeared on a 45-minute RTE spot and proceeded on tours of Chicago and Las Vagas in the States, and Hammersmith, Harringay and Holloway in London. Disappointingly, their 1967 promised recording session never took place.

In all they toured the US on six occasions and played in Ohio, Hollywood, Missouri, Las Vagas, Dubois, Wyoming, Laramie, Nebraska, Texas, California, New York, Boston and Philadelphia. In Canada they appeared in Toronto, in Germany in Frankfurt, and in France they played in Paris and Cherbourg.

Along with the Clippers, other local bands at that time included the Jimmy Sturrock Band, well known in the 1960s with Hughie Blee, Jimmy Sturrock, Willie Maguire, Reba Callaghan, Eddie Milligan, Tommy McGarrigle, Tommy McColgan, Jimmy Sturrock (Junior), Tony Gallagher and Jim Pearson. The Bill Quinn Trio in the 1960s featured Tony Gallagher, John Wilson, Bill Quinn. The Molloy All-Stars Dance Band included Willie Patsy and Danny Molloy, Mickey Christy, L. McGlinchey, B. Barr and P. McCauley. By 1962 the personnel had changed somewhat and the line-up read as follows: Willie Molloy, John Wilson, Charlie Friel, Bill Quinn, Harry Vance, George McKane, David Laird and Eddie Milligan.

The Columba Gallagher Showband in the 1950s and 1960s included Columba Gallagher, Charlie McCauley and Fergie O'Hagan, who found fame and fortune with the Clippers, Cecil McBride, Jackie Wolfe, Michael Gallagher, Billy McAnaw and Johnny Campsie. The group later added

Hughie Blee, Tommy McColgan, Adran McDevitt, Tony Gallagher, Michael McDaid, Sean McDevitt. The Topliners in the 1950s consisted of Sean Porter, Pat Morris, Len Gray, John Gallagher, Vincie Bonner, Willie Christy, Mickey Christy. The Stumpers Group in the 1960s were led by Paddy McGarrigle. And who could forget the Rockville Stompers of the 1970s who provided some fun, music and interest in the drab dark depressing streets of Strabane. The Playboys showband has been in business since the 1960s, when Charlie Friel played with musicians such as Noel Guthrie, who found fame with the Wolfe Tones, Kieran McDonnell, later ordained as Father Kieran, James Doherty, Terri Murphy, Pat Morris and Brian McGee from Derry. In 1989, when they released their single 'We can make it', the line-up included Charlie with Billy D'Alton, Joey Messanger and Brogan McGinty.

In 1950 John Devine, a mechanic from Newtownstewart, joined up with the McNamee brothers, Eugene and Eddie, and Gene Turbett from Omagh to form the Mourne Dance Band. The band of four played at local 'hops' and on Saturdays brought in two others to play the Star Ballroom in Omagh. David Coyle joined as resident vocalist and the band renamed themselves the Melody Aces and became well known all over Ireland, toured the UK and made US trips in 1959, 1961 and 1963 which included visits to Boston, New York, Philadelphia, Chicago, as well as Toronto. John played keyboard, Eddie the clarinet, Jim the saxophone, and Gene the trumpet, with Eugene on drums. Their first Dublin booking was at Rolestown Hall in Swords. This was followed with bookings in the Olympic, Crystal and Ballerina. Gradually the band was increased to eight musicians, with Patsy McGonigle joining on trombone and then Shay Hutchinson on guitar.

The Lifford Players

In 1952 Rev. Fr Augustine Gillespie, a curate in the parish of Camus and Clonleigh, brought together the founding members of the Lifford Players, who were officials of Donegal County Council and Lifford Post Office, and he became the first chairman. Terry O'Doherty was a founder member and is still active on the boards as actor and producer. The Players took part in their first festival in 1956 with *Thy Dear Father*, having presented George Shiel's *The Fort Field* in 1952, O'Casey's *Shadow of a Gunman* in 1953, *Lock of the General's Hair* the following year and, in 1955, *Is the Priest at Home*, a show which they repeated in 1959. The Lifford Players also presented *Glenkeeran* in the Town Hall in that year. Among their later shows were George Shiel's *Macook's Corner* in 1969, which won the Ulster Festival at the Opera House in Belfast, ironically after coming runner-up in Ballymoney in the Shiels section, which featured only two plays in this confined section!

The Lifford Players in *Macooks Corner* in 1969.

In 1982–3 Lifford won the Premier Award at the Opera House and Moneyglass Drama Festival, and followed this with a first-ever win at Athlone in the All-Ireland Esso Trophy with their re-run of the popular *McCook's Corner*. This was followed-up by an invitation to perform six nights at the Peacock Theatre in Dublin.

Lifford chose *Wood of the Whispering* as their festival play in 1985, a three-act play by M.J. Molloy, depicting the depopulation of rural Ireland, set against the background of emigration. Sanbatch Daly was played by Aussie Bryson, Con Kinsella was played by Frank McGillion, Ann Shiels played Sadie Tubridy and Jim Bradley played Stephen Lanigan. This performance won at Moneyglass, Carrickmore, Athlone and then at the International Festival at Dundalk. As a result of this success, Lifford performed their festival winning show at the Abbey for six nights.

In total, Lifford players have won three All-Ireland titles, two Ulster titles and the prestigious Carroll's International Drama Award.

Strabane Drama Festival

April 1987 witnessed the opening of the first ever Drama Festival in Strabane, held in St Patrick's Hall, Barrack Street. The Festival Director, Aodh McCay, saw months of planning come together with the launch of the seven-day festival. Among the plays presented during that first week were Joseph Tumelty's *All Soul's Night*, *Lovers* and *Translations* by Brian Friel, while the Butt Players presented *Sive* and the second Keane play, *Chastitute*, was performed by the Mercury Players, Dublin. The Lifford Players emerged overall winners, collecting no less than six awards out of ten.

After ten successful years, in 1997 Strabane welcomed adjudicator Tom Doherty from Derry to assess the line-up of plays, which included *Run for your Wife* by Puddle Alley, *Summer* by Theatre 3, *Blue Remembered Hills* by Castleblaney, *The Enemy Within* by The Lifford Players, *Les Liaisons Dangereuses* by Blackwater Theatre Co., *No Comet Seen* by Silver Apple Drama, *Of Mice and Men* by Slemish, *Lovers Meeting* by Coolera and *Canaries* by Olivian Players of Dublin.

The 1999 festival was opened by the Creggan Players who took on the Shiel play *The Rugged Path*. Puddle Alley performed *Stella by Starlight*, a Bernard Farrell play presented outside Dublin for the first time. Other productions on stage in 1999 included *The Last Yankee* by Arthur Miller, presented by Theatre 3, Newtownabbey, while CB Players from Belfast presented *Extremities*, Newtownstewart Backburners presented the popular Tomelty's *All Soul's Night*, and *Wedding Fever* was brought by the Letterkenny Players. Theatre 3 won the Blue Riband with *Last Yankee*.

Puddle Alley Theatre Group

This group was set up in 1991 to appear in the one-act drama circuit. The first production was Hugh Leonard's *Last of the Mohicans*. Encouraged by this, the group ventured into the full-length productions and presented *I Do Not Like Thee, Dr. Fell* and *Canaries*. This further encouraged Puddle Alley to join the festival circuit, which they did, successfully, with *The Last Apache Reunion*. The group won four festivals, including the prestigious City of Derry Overall trophy. This led to an invitation to compete in the All-Ireland Finals in Tralee. In 1997 *Run for Your Wife* won the confined sections in all five drama festivals in which Puddle Alley took part – Strabane, Derry, Ballyshannon, Ballinamore, Cavan – and also the Blue Riband at Ballyshannon. The cast included Maria Doherty as Mary Smith, Eugene McMenamin as Detective Porterhouse, Bill Kennedy as Stanley Gardner, Aodh McCay was John Smith and Fr Paul Porter as Detective Troughton.

The play *Why Not Stay for Breakfast*, by Gene Stone and Ray Cooney, finished in second place in the 1998 All-Ireland confined finals.

STRABANE THROUGH THE AGES

The year 1999 saw Puddle Alley perform *Stella by Starlight*. The Group took the Confined section at the local Strabane Drama festival, with Aodh McCay winning the Best Actor category. They went on to win the confined sections in Castleblaney, Ballyshannon, Cavan and Dublin and collected a range of awards for acting and stage management.

St Eugene's Brass Band

In the early years of the present century the foremost musical family in the north-west was undoubtedly the Connolly family of Strabane. Teachers by day, they formed the Connolly's Dance Band by night and were much in demand across the country, playing regularly in palatial homes such as Baronscourt and Manorvaughan. Dan Connolly was the oldest and he was a zealot for brass band music. It was he who formed and tutored the first brass and reed group, which was only equipped with a poor collection of second-hand instruments. In 1928 St Eugene's Band was formed in the Backroom in Barrack Street, and for forty years this remained the home of the band. The second-hand instruments gave way to splendid new silver-plated instruments. The first conductor was Charlie Boyle and original members included George and Pat Madden, Paddy Mullen, James and Tommy McGarrigle, Barney Mulhern, Hugh Doran, Patsy McColgan, Jimmy Sturrock. Typical music on the band's agenda was Gilbert & Sullivan melodies, light opera, and Irish and American selections.

In 1948 Charlie Boyle left the band after a rift, which led to a number of other regulars leaving. Mickey Boyle took over the baton. Recognised throughout Ireland as one of the country's foremost musical combinations, St Eugene's was in constant demand to lead parades, processions and play at functions. The band won many trophies at Feiseanna for a wide-ranging repertoire.

St Eugene's Brass Band appeared in concert in 1985 to produce the 'Big Band Sound'. Appearing in the Fir Trees Festival Concert were M. Boyle, B. Forbes, G. Gallagher, P. McLaughlin, C. McGarrigle, J. Boyle, J. Blee, J. O'Kane, M. Canavan, J. McGarrigle, R. Doherty, A. O'Neill, P. McGlinchey, A. McGarrigle, M. Boyle (conductor), L. McCosker, B. McDevitt and M. Reynolds.

St Joseph's Brass Band

On 29 November 1997 St Joseph's celebrated its Golden Jubilee birthday in the Everglades in Derry. Formed in 1948 after a split in the ranks of St Eugene's, St Joseph's has advanced to become one of the foremost brass and reed outfits in the North West. The early tradition was built up by Charlie Boyle, Mickey Boyle, Willie Maguire, George Early, Patsy Early and Tommy

Barr. It is interesting to note that Patsy McColgan was a founder member of St Eugene's in 1928 and St Joseph's in 1948. Hugo Quinn who distinguished himself with the Clippers served his apprenticeship with the 'Joes'. Charlie was appointed as 'conductor' in the early days and the band practiced twice per week. He was conductor in the 1950s and the 1960s. Jim Quinn followed Charlie as musical director and in 1959 George Early took over. Other directors included Pat Boyle, Willie Maguire, Michael Doherty, Michael Early and Noel Barr. Much fund-raising – including the Pallidrome dance on Christmas Night and Midsummer's dance – was necessary to equip the band with new instruments. The idea of uniforms was discussed many times but was resisted for many years until 1965.

The first band room was an old loft at the canal. It was so cold that members sat around and practised in their overcoats and scarves. The Forresters Hall beside Packie McDevitt's shop in Townhall Street was most fondly associated with the band. The band has played around Ireland and is fondly remembered in Sligo, Donegal, Waterford and Dundalk. Many of the players have graduated to play in operas, pantos and musicals.

As a major highlight of the fiftieth anniversary, St Joseph's played host to the world-famous Black Dyke Brass Band in concert in St Patrick's Hall on 14 June 1997. Under the baton of James Watson, the band featured Robert Childs on euphonium and Matthew Baker on cornet in a programme which thrilled a capacity crowd at the Barrack Street venue. The 'Broadway Brass' was an impressive second half medley, 'Fantas' by Hummel was performed by Childs, and the 'Via Appia' from the *Pines of Rome* was a brilliant finale to one of the great nights in St Pat's.

Strabane Concert Brass

Strabane Concert Brass was formed in 1979 as an extension of the very successful Tyrone Youth Band. In 1981 they achieved their first success when they won the Brass Band League Senior Championship and the Northern Ireland Bands Association contest. The reward for this success was an invitation to appear in the European Championship at the renowned Albert Hall in London and at Darlington in the Brass in Concert Championship. The band continued this success throughout the 1980s by winning the League Championship on several occasions, and 1986 in Glengormley they beat the favourites Templemore by one point to take the title. The 1986 group included for the first time Nuala Crilly, the first female to take her place in the band. The band guested on high-profile TV programmes such as Harry Secombe's *Highway* and *Songs of Praise*. The 1990s have been particularly successful. In 1990 the band again represented Ireland at the European Championships at Falkirk in Scotland. The Brass Band League was secured again in 1992, and in April 1993 Strabane won again in Belfast,

384 STRABANE THROUGH THE AGES

a victory which led to the European Championships in Switzerland. In 1993 the Band won the NIBA for the first time since their historic win of 1981. In May 1994 the band represented Ireland in the European Championships at Montreux in Switzerland. The band again qualified for the European Championships in the spring of 1997.

Some of the band's most successful musicians have moved on to greater things. Damien Harron has played with Grimethorpe in the National Championships, and with the famous Black Dyke and Faireys bands, British and National Champions. Barry Callaghan joined Carlton Main Frickley, Francis Magee played with CWS in Scotland, and Derek McGillion, now back with the band, had a spell with the William Davis Band. Dominic Winters and Stevie McGowan made history by attending the Brass Band course in Salford College, the first from Northern Ireland to be accorded the honour. An interesting statistic to note is that in 1994 all but 4 members of the band were pupils or ex-pupils of St Colman's High School; there were 3 civil servants in the band, 2 joiners, a painter, a manager in a supermarket, a lab assistant, a factory worker and 8 teachers; 6 members were in further education and a further 6 were still at school.

In March 1999 the band again broke new ground when they performed at the prestigious 'Peace and Reconciliation Service' in Liverpool Metropolitan Cathedral and later at a Peace Concert in the Parr Hall in Warrington in front of an audience of 2000. Stephen McGowan, who plays cornet with the band, was appointed to the world-famous Black Dyke Mills Band in March 1999.

Harry Gault, music tutor with the Western Education and Library Board, has been credited with the tuition work done with many youths in this area, and his work in St Colman's High School is well documented. His untimely death in 1996 was a great loss to the youth and music lovers of this area in which he had worked so successfully for twenty-five years. The driving force behind the success of Strabane Concert Brass has undoubtedly been Mr Terry Doherty, head of music in St Colman's High School.

Strabane Arts Festivals

The Strabane festival of 1975 was opened by the then Chairman of Council, Mr John McKelvey. He introduced a week of culture in which Strabane people were treated to many outstanding events, such as the Bart Players performing *A Breath of Spring* in St Colman's High School, 'Grand Irish American Dance' in the festival marquee, and music by Sharon and the Entertainers. Queen's University Belfast Fringe Theatre presented a puppet show, there was a concert for senior citizens at the Presbyterian hall at Derry Road, and the Western Counties Youth Brass played at Melvin.

Strabane Festival 1983 featured a line-up including Strabane Concert

Brass, Londonderry Amateur Operatic Society, Pat Deery and Johnny Mitchell (Country & Western), Artie McGlynn and Nollaig.

The Arts Festival of 1984 consisted of Flann O'Brian's *Yer Man and the Brother* by Tom McCabe, Quarterdeck, Isosceles, the traditional group Curlew, a Country & Western night with Hugo Duncan, Brian Coll, Pat Deery and Eileen King, *Lay up Your Ends* by Charabanc Theatre Company, and a final night with Strabane Concert Brass, the McCafferty Singers and Caviar. The opening parade had support from St Joseph's, St Patrick's Murlog and Oliver Plunkett Accordion Band.

In 1985 the arts festival was held from 9 to 23 October. Again the line-up included a variety of entertainment with Eamon Morrissey doing Flann O'Brian, Francis Canning on piano, Philip Jones (Brass), Cran traditional group, Chris Ward in cabaret, *Now You're Talking* by Charabanc, Ann and Francie Brolly in folk at St Colman's, Apex Jazz in the golf club, and 'Make Mine Country' with Brian Coll, Eileen King and Hugo Duncan.

The music festival at Melvin Park in 1985 attracted Hard Contact, featuring Mickey Campbell, Freddie Semple, Pipe McGlinchey, Dougie McGonagle, and Charlie McCosker on drums; Steel Claw, with Benny Hunter, Gerard Walsh, Speedy Rouse and Joe Hudson took part in the festival and then went into studio with Pete O'Hanlon to produce a tape. Star Brass and Cunla featured, the Wild Geese dropped in by parachute and Aidan 'Cookie' Dunne and Danny Rouse shaved off their beards for charity. Quarterdeck, featuring Strabane man Sean McCarron on saxophone, had a very successful tour of Europe.

In 1986 Council Chairman James O'Kane opened the fourth arts festival, organised by Festival Director Raymond Kirk and Arts Chairman Declan Doherty. The programme included Freddie White, Matt Molloy, Artie McGlynn, Monty Sunshine, Black Mountain Blue Grass, Apex Jazz, Rascals, Strabane Concert Brass, Jazz Gazette, Brian Coll, Eileen King, Brendan Quinn, Hugo Duncan and St Eugene's Silver Band.

Jazz has never been a popular form of music in Strabane. The group Jazz Gazette first played in the Fir Trees in 1985 and were pleasantly surprised by the warm reception they received. They featured Van Morrison's 'Moon Dance', 'Sweet Georgia Brown', and 'New York, New York', with Tommy McColgan on vocals. They also featured in the Melvin festival, in Sligo, Derry, Belfast, and at many bookings in Donegal. The group included Ian McGowan on guitar, Mark Bradley on trumpet, Peter Doherty on trombone, bass and vocals, and Joe Gillespie on drums. Additions to the group were Gerard Bradley on piano, Michael Canavan on sax and clarinet, and Ronan Doherty on trombone.

In 1987 Strabane paid a tribute to three ambassadors who had distinguished themselves in their respective fields; Paul Brady, Hugo Duncan for music and Felim Egan for art. This was part of the 1987 arts festival which also featured Barnbrack, Francis Canning, Jazz Gazette, Eamon Morrissey, Noel McBride and *Somewhere Over the Balcony* by Charabanc and *The Tail of the White Giant* by Northern Black Light Theatre Puppet Show.

Paul Brady

Strabane-born Paul Brady, who has been described as a highly influential figure in rock music, is a multi-talented artiste with over thirty years of experience in the music profession. In 1986 he was voted 'best vocalist' and 'best songwriter'. Paul's breakthrough was with the folk group The Johnstons, who had a series of records and TV appearances. Paul moved on to join the very popular Planxty, before crossing over from folk music and launching a solo career as a music writer and performer in rock music. Among his early album releases were *Back to the Centre* and *Hard Station*. His major successes as a song writer have been 'Steel Claw' and 'Paradise is Here', which were recorded by Tina Turner. His later release of *Primitive Dance* has also been a tremendous success.

Hugo Duncan

Hugo started singing at Barrack Street School and then at St Colman's and also in the church choir: he sang in concerts and talent competitions, and joined the Dermot Dunne Céilí Band, later moving onto the Aranville, Comets, and the Melody Aces. At the age of nineteen he joined Frankie McBride and the Polka Dots, later called the Tallmen. Hugo featured on *Reach for the Stars* on RTE and finished runner-up to the late Fran O'Toole.

In 1971 he recorded 'Dear God' which reached No. 1 in the Irish charts on Homespun records. He later recorded 'Brady from Strabane' about a man who was hired out at the hiring fair at Strabane by the farmer named Brady.

Another major success was his solo recording of the 'Wedding Song', which also reached No. 1. At present he is a popular presenter for Radio Foyle, Radio Ulster and Ulster Television, while still continuing his good work for local and national charities.

Phelim Egan

Phelim Egan from Strabane has been described as 'one of Ireland's leading contemporary painters' and 'the current great white hope of Irish painting'. Phelim first discovered art at Barrack Street Primary School, polished it up at St Colman's, and perfected it at Belfast, Portsmouth, at the Slade School for Fine Art in London and finally Rome. In 1981 Phelim was commissioned by Strabane Arts Advisory Committee to produce a painting and his work is exhibited in the waiting room of the health centre at Upper Main

Street. He has been in receipt of the Patrons Award in 1979, the Guinness Peat Aviation Award for Emerging Artists, Premier Award 1981–3. In 1984 he was commissioned, with composer Roger Doyle, to produce a collaborative work to celebrate the European Music Year by the Douglas Hyde Gallery.

From the evidence presented in this chapter, the people of Strabane throughout the ages have been privileged to have enjoyed entertainment of the highest quality by people so talented that they could hold their own with the best. From Hugo Duncan's No. 1 hits to internationally renowned singers such as Tina Turner singing Paul Brady's material, Lifford Players winning All-Ireland titles and the Clipper Carlton leading the field in showband music, Strabane can rightly claim a place among the entertainment elites of Ireland.

22 Strabane in the Twentieth Century 1900–1950

BRIAN CARLIN

Expansion or Stagnation?

Throughout the twentieth century the fortunes of Strabane and its people have been both many and varied. Life for many has changed dramatically since the 1900s. The centre of the town itself has seen many changes, planned and unplanned. Many businesses have come and gone. The population of the town has risen steadily, and subsequently, the need for both public and private housing has increased. Strabane has reached many milestones and often with great sadness. The demise of the railways is arguably the most notable. When one looks back to a bygone era it is often with a great fondness for a time long since gone. According to the *Belfast & Ulster Directory* of 1899 Strabane is described as 'a market town in Co. Tyrone . . .

Strabane in the era of World War II when most of the Ballycolman/ Melmount area was still green fields.

one of the largest and most populous towns in the county and its environs are replete with interest and beauty.'

Few would argue with this description yet perhaps more interestingly the *Directory* continues with a list of the businesses and trades to be found in Strabane – most of which are alive now only in fading memories. The *Directory* states that 'The Belfast Banking Company Ltd., the Provincial Bank of Ireland, the Ulster Bank and the Hibernian Bank all have branches here and there is a Savings Bank. The Northern Bank branch opens on Tuesdays and Wednesdays only.'

On reading further, we find that

> The Steamboat Co. do a very large and profitable business under the able management of Mr. J. McFarlane. The Town Hall is too small. The shirt trade is extensively carried on. Messrs. Stapley and Smith have erected a very large factory in Barrack Street and Messrs. Stewart McDonald & Co. of Glasgow have a very large factory on the Derry road. Mr. R. Pollock operates a steam bakery in Abercorn Square. The Flax markets which are held on Wednesday are the largest in the district and are attended by buyers from every part of the province. Being the centre of a rich agricultural county, the grain market on Tuesday is very large and important.

When one reads the listed businesses/trades one can see that Strabane was indeed thriving and it is a great sadness that a lot of these have long since

STRABANE THROUGH THE AGES

gone. Some of the most notable and interesting are as follows:

The Post Office was listed at Main Street with Mr J.J. Pakenham as postmaster. The RIC were in Abercorn Square with Robert Dunlop (DI) and Mr Sheridan as head constable. The Poor Law inspector was M. Hicks and the Excise Office was to be found on Abercorn Road.

Solicitors listed included some familiar names. They range from James A.F. Simms, J. Colhoun, John Elliott, Thomas Elliott, P. Gallagher, R. Burke, W. P. Moody, John McCay, T.E. Nelson, P.H. O'Brien, Thomas H. Risk (an unfortunate name for a solicitor!) to W. Wilson.

The listed businesses/trades are also interesting, both for unusual occupations and the location of the premises. Main Street must have been an exceptional street with varied trades being carried on. Some examples are as follows.

Andrew Aiken	Saddler	Main Street
John Anderson	Merchant	Main Street
Patrick Bannigan	Nurseryman	Chapel Street
R.J. Blair	Printer, Newsagent, Stationer, Bookseller	Main Street
L. Bradley	Grocer, Baker	Back Street
Clarke & Co.	Wholesale Wine & Spirit	Back Street
John Colhoun	Grocer	Main Street
J. Connolly	Spirit Dealer	Abercorn Square
Mrs Connor	Milliner	
Mrs Crawford	Draper	
Thomas Dillon	Butcher	Back Street
Divine & Co.	Tea Merchant	Main Street
J. Donnell	Coal & Timber Merchants	
J. Donnelly	Butcher	Markethouse Street
Ellen Dowd	Ulster Hotel	
Elliott & Sons	The Castle	
W. Finlay	Watchmaker	Castle Street
Dr French	Apothecary	Main Street
John Gillespie	Bookseller	Main Street

Of the 49 persons listed, almost half (19) are located on the Main Street. One may notice familiar family businesses and peculiar spelling, e.g. Divine (tea merchants). Undoubtedly the town at that time was thriving as a commercial centre.

As Strabane continued to grow and prosper changes to the everyday lives of the people became more evident. In 1902 gas supplies first became available after the building of the gasworks. Three years later, in 1905, the water wall was built from the Bridge to Lower Main Street. Quite obviously this was to offer some protection from the recurring floods which had previously affected Strabane. However serious flooding still occurred in 1906, 1909, 1929, 1948 and more recently 1987. It wasn't until this most recent disaster that a proper flood defence was built and a new reinforced wall was completed.

In 1908 the National Telephone Company laid the first telephone cables and so Strabane gained a much speedier access to the outside world. However it was not until 1936 that electricity was supplied to the town. Five years earlier pedestrians and vehicle owners of any description must surely have noticed when, on 17 August 1931, Abercorn Square was resurfaced with concrete. A year later the Pagoda, so loved by many, replaced the old memorial to the marquis of Abercorn and the Coffee Stand.

The War Years brought to Strabane and surrounding districts a tightening of belts and shortages. The post-war world saw the advent of the welfare state and Strabane benefited accordingly.

Since the start of the twentieth century Strabane's population has shown a rise, especially in the years since 1926, and with accelerated growth from the 1950s onwards. The post-war years witnessed a rapid development in house building, particularly from the 1950s onwards, and Appendix 1 shows the development of public authority housing in the second half of the twentieth century. This has been accompanied by an equally rapid expansion of private housing since the 1960s and such developments help to explain the near doubling of the town's population over a 40-year period, with the 1990s showing a total near 12,000. Census figures for the years up to 1991 are given in the following table and it is estimated that the figure in the year 2000 is in excess of 13,000.

1911	5107
1926	5156
1937	5600
1951	6619
1961	7783
1966	8812
1971	9413
1981	10340
1991	11670

(Note: the figures for 1971 and more especially for 1981 are suspect since there was a degree of organised boycott of the census enumeration in these years due to political agitation.)

As time marched on, however, Strabane failed to keep pace and in the 1950s the slow and lingering decline of the railways became more evident. The rise and fall of the railways has been very much documented but in the

1950s it was realised that from assuming a position of great importance Strabane found itself in the programme of closure. By 31 December 1959 all the narrow-gauge Co. Donegal railways had been closed down. Many factors were to blame, including depression in trade, changing modes of transport, the border and the Ulster Transport Authority. Ultimately it all ended on 14 February 1965 when the last train pulled out of Strabane station.

The Northern Ireland Fire Authority was formed in 1950. In 1951 the new authority decided that the premises in the old flax mill in Barrack Street were unsatisfactory and a proposed move to Branch Road was scheduled. In 1957 the new fire station was built, and in 1991 it was upgraded. On yet another sad note for those of us who cherish the past, the old fire siren sounded for the last time in 1996 when it changed to a new high-tech pager/bleeper system.

The arrival of Adria Ltd, a hosiery factory, in Strabane in 1961 promised a brighter future and there was considerable development in the later 1960s. The onset of the Troubles, however, meant that the progress was not sustained and Strabane suffered accordingly. The physical destruction of much of the town and the failure of local leadership to provide economic guidance left Strabane as the employment black spot of Western Europe.

Yet life was not all bad and some of the older citizens look back at their youthful days in the 1930s with a fair degree of nostalgic affection. It is the custom now to record memories from earlier days and many tall tales have emerged into print. The following accounts of life in the 1930s comes from interaction among a group of pensioners at the luncheon club organised by

The Customs Post on the Strabane Lifford border, an ever present reminder of the impact of partition

Melmount Community Care, and attempts to incorporate a number of different and sometimes conflicting accounts.

Boys and girls left school at the age of fourteen and generally went straight into work. Working in a shop was well thought of but wages were relatively low, with 10 shillings weekly being considered generous for the apprentice. On the other hand piece work in the factory at Sion Mills seemed much better by comparison, with girls earning from 15 to 25 shillings per week. Those on set wages in the factory, however, started at only half that figure, though they could expect to move upwards as they gained experience. Domestic service was still a major source of employment for many girls but wages were low, with £1 a month along with board being considered the average.

Those boys not able to find work in the shops and service sector often had to look for seasonal work with the local farmers and again wages were low. For a young boy just leaving school the norm was 5 shillings per week along with meals, though there was often an increase at the busier seasons like spring and harvesting when workers were in bigger demand.

Apprenticeships to the various crafts were much-prized positions but often these were closed shops, and only relatives of the existing craftsmen were taken on for a five-year apprenticeship programme. Wages were very low for much of this period and it was only when the workers were 'out of their time' that they could hope to earn a living wage. One example was of a cobbler who started off as an apprentice at 2s 6d per week and this had only risen to 5 shillings after three years. In the building trade it was a little better, with the apprentice starting off at 4d per hour, giving a total of 16s 8d for a 48-hour week. After five years he had progressed as a qualified tradesman to 1s 8d per hour, with a weekly packet of £3 15s 9d.

It is clear that house buying would have been out of the question for most young married couples and the sharing of the parental home was a customary start to married life. One correspondent claimed that there was little severe poverty and that all who wanted work could get it, but it has to be said that the rewards were slight and often uncertain. Work on the land was notoriously seasonal and even the factories had their periods of short time. The construction industry had not yet taken off and the system of apprenticeship meant that admission was strictly limited. The railways and the canal were sources of work for some but once again jobs tended to run in families and the gradual run down of these ensured that opportunities were limited and work often uncertain, especially in the canal.

Some non-natives came to Strabane to find work, and the railways were one of the employment areas where outsiders might be found. One former white-collar employee described his early experiences in 1940 when his wages were £1 10s 10d per week. Lodgings, however, cost £1 5s per week, while the train fare home to Belfast at the weekend was a further 5s 10d.

This meant that his mother had to subsidise him with about 5s per week, with the result that movement to find work would have been beyond the reach of many. It was little wonder that the boat to Scotland or England appeared attractive to many of the younger generation and that the early years were spent getting enough money to make the move.

The outbreak of the Second World War in 1939, however, caused a hiccup in the emigration race and some of the older generation speak disparagingly of the returning emigrants rushing to avoid the introduction of conscription in Britain. Yet the number of those returning must have been quite small, since they would have known that there were few prospects for employment at home and even less across the border, where the war years saw major shortages despite the neutrality of the Free State. Conscription was not extended to Northern Ireland either and enlistment in the armed forces continued on a voluntary basis. The textile industry was given a boost by war needs and the opening of a munitions factory at Sion Mills helped provide some additional work. Farmers also benefited with the increased tillage crop quotas and this in turn increased the demand for agricultural labourers. Rationing did much to control prices and shortages were supplemented by a thriving cross-border smuggling trade in the Strabane district. The whole topic of the impact of the Second World War on the local economy, and the supplementary issue of the impact of the customs border on cross-border trade and the local efforts made to bypass the official structures, needs much fuller investigation and treatment; it is hoped that this will be researched and documented by some enterprising local historian in the near future.

PEACHES
(SLICED)
IN LIGHT SYRUP

NET WEIGHT 6 LBS.

PACKED BY
NORTH WEST CANNERS LTD.
STRABANE, CO. TYRONE, ULSTER

An advertisement from the Strabane Cannery which closed down after the fire in the 1950s.

This sparse treatment of a major subject area has meant perforce that it is little more than a glimpse into aspects of the life and times of the community about two generations ago. Stagnation was the keyword as far as Strabane in the twentieth century is concerned, and though there was a brief flurry in the 1950s and 1960s with the introduction of Adria and an extensive programme of house building, the basic infrastructure of the town's economy remained underdeveloped. Emigration continued at a high level in the 1950s and 1960s and the growth in the later decades was led more by rural depopulation than by a vibrant urban scene. Local government could do little to ameliorate the situation and the onset of the Troubles from 1969 saw the destruction of much of the traditional fabric of the town. Later historians will have to judge whether the town at the end of the twentieth century is on the threshold of greater things or in a continued stage of relative stagnation.

Appendix

The following is a list of streets/estates with their year of construction. Where a street/estate is listed twice, it is assumed that further developments took place after the initial construction.

1934	Townsend Street
1936	Bridge Street, Barrack Street (1953, 1978–81), Melmount Villas, Council Terrace, Brigade Terrace, Church View
1950	Owenreagh Drive, Owenreagh Pass, Urney Road, St Mary's Drive, St Mary's Place, Melmount Villas, Knockavoe Crescent, Koram Square, Drumman Court, Meenashesk Place, Melmount Road, Croaghan View, Mourne Avenue, Mourne Place, Dublin Road
1953	Fountain Park, Newtownkennedy Street, Fountain Street
1954	Marian Park, Townsend Street
1955	Finn View
1956	Mount Carmel View, Pearse Gardens, Sigerson Place, St Colman's Drive
1957	Delaney Crescent, Olympic Drive, Beechmount Avenue
1958	Fountain Park
1960	Fountain Terrace
1961	Patrician Villas
1963	Columban Terrace, Gartan Avenue, Iona Villas, Mount Sion
1964	Newtown Place, Newtown Street
1965	Inisfree Gardens
1966	Casement Place
1968	Alexander Place, Brigade Terrace Flats, Castlemurray, Riverside Terrace, St John's Place
1969	Fountain Street
1970	Drumrallagh
1971	New Ballycolman Estate, Lisnafin
1973	Chestnut Park
1976	Kennedy Street, Meetinghouse Street (1976–9), Mill Street
1977	Bridge Street (1977–80), Magirr Park, Springhill Park (1977–1980), Waterside Street (1977–87)
1979	Newtownkennedy Street, Townsend Street (1979–83)
1980	Townsend Terrace (1980–83)
1981	Orchard Street (1981–2)
1982	O'Kane Terrace, Collins Walk, Gallany Court (1982–4), Gormley Crescent, Carlton Drive (1982–8), Fleming Way
1984	Patterson Park
1985	Carlton Crescent
1986	O'Nolan Park (1986–7)
1989	Ard-na-lee Park (1989–92)
1995	Oakland Park

23 Corridors of Memories
Personal Recollections

JIM BRADLEY — 1985

Looking back down the long avenue of the years, my mind's eye can recall a scene on an autumn day in 1926 – my earliest memory. The occasion was the funeral of Fr James O'Kane, parish priest of Urney for sixteen years. The obsequies were taking place at Melmount, in the presence of a concourse of mourners drawn from the extensive parish of Urney, as it then was, embracing Castlederg, Doneyloop and Sion Mills, as well as the area forming the present parish of Mourne.

Jim Bradley pictured with Fr. Anthony Mulvey, family friend and parish priest in Melmount during the 1980s.

I remember being taken as a four-year-old to stand outside the old St Mary's in the midst of an overflow congregation. The solemnity of the occasion impressed itself on the memory of all who were there, and lest they should forget some time later, many homes in the parish, including our own, began to display gilt-framed photographs of the late parish priest. The cameo centrepiece was surrounded by a lengthy poem of doubtful merit, the opening lines of which I can still recall:

> No tongue or pen can ever tell the sorrow, grief and pain,
> caused by the death of our good priest, Reverend James O'Kane.

My next recollection of life in the parish was equally memorable – the great flood of 1929 when the Mourne breached the transverse rampart (since heightened and strengthened at Melvin Park) and a solid wall of water swept across the meadows to inundate the low lying houses in the Bridge End to near ceiling height, imprisoning entire families in the upstairs of their dwellings for three full days. Although the flood happened suddenly, at noon, on an October Sunday, it was not unexpected. All through the previous night there was uproar, with the squealing of pigs being hurriedly evacuated from the many back-yard piggeries at Bridge Street and Urney Road, to Elliotts' farmyard at Myrtle Hall. Nobody slept. Many times during the night and the next morning, anxious voices were heard inquiring 'Is the bankin' all right?', until around noon we heard the dramatic alarm 'The bankin's burst' – a phrase that was to be repeated in the same street in 1948. In those hard times before the introduction of social security benefits, the Bridge End parishioners spent a real 'winter of discontent' drying out their homes, aided only by the limited resources of the St Vincent de Paul Society and a relief fund totalling £50.

As a result of the flood the Bridge Street convent school (on the site of the present St Mary's Hall) was unfit for some months and the only accommodation available was in a disused factory in the neighbouring parish (now St Patrick's Hall). The Bridge End school, with four classrooms, never fully recovered from the flood, and in 1934 Dr O'Kane, the bishop of Derry,

Bridge Street flooded in 1929

blessed and opened its replacement, a new school built on undeveloped parochial lands known as the 'Mullen' field.

Two memories of that opening day remain, which may be worth telling. It was arranged that the children should remain seated in their classrooms until the bishop, priests and nuns should enter, to be greeted by the infants of each classroom with a specially composed salutation. I was the sole acolyte on the day and after carrying the holy water container for the bishop at the outdoor ceremonies, I was deputed by the late Fr Willie Devine to stand in the hallway and stop the public coming into the school until after the ceremonies. However, there were two entrance doors and I could only guard one. Too late, I spotted an irrepressible parishioner, long since deceased, slipping into the school through the other door and proceeding directly into the nearest classroom.

The moment she opened the door, thirty young voices burst out singing their joyous welcome and were well into the first verse before they could be silenced by their panic-stricken teacher. The commotion caused Fr Devine to make a hurried departure from the VIP tea party in the nuns' room to politely evict the offending parishioner and, not so politely, to admonish me for my failure to 'hold the fort'.

The second memory of the day was overhearing the bishop's misgivings on the non-traditional construction of the school. He was a better theologian than a building technician, for, over fifty years later, the same building is in excellent condition. In fact it was only abandoned as a school because of the accommodation problems created by the post-war expansion of the parish. That school became O'Neill's Octopus Sportswear factory. (It is still in use as part of the Mourne Health Centre [ed.].)

Fr Devine, often referred to as 'The Major', was, despite his occasional lapse into mild eccentricity, an indefatigable worker. An ex-Army chaplain, with several distinctions for bravery in the 1914–18 War, he had ministered in the Far East, and was author of several distinguished works, including a history of the Catholic Church in China, entitled *The Four Churches of Peking*. In the hard days that marked the mid 1930s, he spearheaded the erection of the new school, the graveyard extension and the renovation of the old St Mary's. He was later responsible for the erection of the first Catholic Church in Sion Mills, the parochial house there, and the adjoining church hall.

Before he took up residence in Sion Mills, he lived in 'The Barn' at Ballycolman (the present home of Danny Shiels). He was not happy with the practice of some of the parishioners attending the late Mass in the town church instead of the earlier Mass in Melmount, and although he could not very well denounce the practice, he effectively discontinued it by a simple stratagem. At 11.00 a.m. on occasional summer Sundays, he strode down from the 'The Barn' through 'The Laurels', to Strabane Bridge, where, dressed in ankle-length cassock and continental cape, he read his daily Office while pacing backwards and forwards on the upstream footpath of the bridge.

Although the good priest never lifted his eyes from the breviary, many a self-conscious townward bound Mass-goer felt it necessary to slip furtively across on the other footpath, while at the same time developing a sudden interest in the down-river vista. Needless to say, the attendance at our parish Mass had well improved by the end of that particular summer.

Another memory from 1934 is of serving at the first Mass on the new marble altar which replaced the old wooden one, in St Mary's Church. It was on a summer Saturday, the day before the new altar was to come into use with full ceremonial. The occasion was the Requiem Mass for the aged and last member of the oldest family in the parish – a Miss Bradden from Flushtown, who had died in hospital. The beautiful mosiac around the new altar was laid in two stages, and, during the work on the sanctuary, the old altar had been taken out of use in the body of the church. But on this Saturday it had been removed and Fr Ryan had to use the new altar. The new marble steps were very slippery and the rather short-sighted curate had some difficulty because he was used to the old altar steps, which were completely carpeted. Later that morning he was to officiate at Miss Bradden's burial in the old Abbey Churchyard at Urney – the last Catholic interment there.

Until the coming of electricity to the town in 1936, only a few houses possessed 'wireless sets' around which we clustered to hear boxing and other broadcasts. One willing host, who readily allowed his kitchen to be swamped by the men and boys of the parish for these broadcasts, was universally and paradoxically nicknamed 'The Unknown', and the pre-broadcast 'conversazione' in his home was invariably more interesting than the actual broadcast. One evening the man of the house, whose hospitality was equalled only by his gullibility, agreed to and implemented the daft suggestion of a local wiseacre that the inside of the wireless set should be disinfected to guard against malaria and other tropical diseases that 'could be caused by germs coming in from foreign radio stations'.

For many years the Melmount congregation was principally drawn from Bridge Street, Urney Road and lower Ballycolman. We were collectively referred to by the rest of the townspeople , sometimes derisively, as 'Bridge End people' or 'the wans from over the Bridge'. We certainly had a close-knit community up to the post-war years when there were still green fields from 'the corner' to Melmount, along both the Melmount and Ballycolman roads. It was open country, too, out from the small terrace houses on Urney Road.

In the mid 1930s the parish had a very talented football team rejoicing in the unlikely name of 'Linfield', which was vehemently opposed by all 'the town' teams and their supporters from the 'Fut o' the town' to the 'Head o' the town'. So intense was the rivalry surrounding a local Cup Final that

This church of St Mary at Melmount Church was built in the 1840s and replaced in 1970 by the present St Mary's, Melmount.

'Linfield's' opponents refused to play 'over the bridge', in Mourne Park, and succeeded in their demand that the venue should be the Brandywell grounds of Derry City Football Club.

It was a measure of the local community spirit that three buses and Mickey (Senior) McShane's car were required to take the Bridge End supporters to the Brandywell – almost half of the able-bodied men and youths of the parish. The other half stayed behind to prepare the bonfires and other 'welcome home' festivities for the once again victorious Bridge End team. The same street corner that would in more recent years be the location of more significant conflagrations involving buses, bread vans and other vehicles, was the scene that night of the greatest rejoicing of our early years.

Members of the team, all from the parish, were Willie Falconer, Mickey McConnell, Tony Gallagher (deceased), Mickey Bradley, Ted Begley (deceased), Paddy White (deceased), Frankie Donaghy (deceased), and John Flood. The hero of the night was the gentle and handsome six footer, Ted Begley, soon to die slowly and painfully as a consequence of a later football injury. The unheeding 'heart-throb' of all the girls around, Ted was an inveterate card player who carried his pack of cards everywhere, except when unfailingly going to Mass or evening devotions. Many a time he put the playing cards in the saddlebags of our bikes or into a recess in the graveyard wall, before going into the Church.

After a football accident, his leg was put in plaster for six weeks or so, and when this was removed, a fatal infection was discovered. Those of us who knew him can recall how he chatted about football and more serious topics nightly, while calmly awaiting death, and we truly believe that if there are saints' graves in Melmount, one of them is surely the unmarked plot that holds his earthly remains.

In our small community, the death of any parishioner was an important event and not always a mournful one. Following a long-established custom, one of the shutters on Louis Kane's pub would not be taken down during the three days of mourning. According to the age of the deceased and circumstances of the death, there would be at least two well-attended 'wake nights' with a plentiful supply of snuff, clay pipes, tobacco and cigarettes laid on for the callers to the house. Wakes sometimes involved an incongruous mixture of piety and the none-too-edifying wakehouse games such as 'My Man Jack', now happily consigned to the limbo of forgotten customs.

In 1938 the parish of Urney was redefined. Castlederg and Doneyloop were separated from Sion Mills and Melmount, which were then formed into the new parish of Mourne. Around the same time Fr George Faulkner came to Melmount as parish priest to serve as pastor until his retirement twenty-eight years later. It was during his pastorate that great physical changes took place in the new parish. Up to the mid 1930s, there were only six houses from Melmount Villas to the church on the east side of the Melmount Road. These comprised three picturesque thatched cottages, Greenfield House (which was the wartime location of Londonderry Girls' High School), the Forbes' Cottage and Beechmount House.

On the west side of the road there were no houses from 'Prospect' (then owned by the late John Reilly, always the most generous benefactor of the parish) to the old parochial house. The upper Ballycolman Lane, as it was then called, really was a lane with only a few cottages and two larger houses, one of which would later become Strabane Golf Club. To our minds the most notable landmark on the Lane was the 'Ivy Pillar' – the legendary remains of an abbey said to have been founded by an obscure St Colman some 800 years before the establishment of the town.

All the land on both sides of the upper Melmount Road was parochial land and was part of a former demesne which had in the last century been extensively planted with a splendid collection of native trees which in summertime formed an enclosed leafy avenue along the main road to the church. In those tranquil years many teenagers attended evening devotions almost as regularly as Sunday Mass. There were few distractions in those days, and anyway we could not afford them.

In the course of the monthly holy hour, Fr Faulkner was certain to recite the Irish *Te Deum*. In our seats away up in the gallery of the church, we never failed to have a wry chuckle when the good priest intoned the final line of the following stanza:

Thanks be to God for the rain and the sunshine

> Thanks be to God for the hail and the snow
> Thanks be to God when our pockets are empty
> Thanks be to God when agin they o'erflow.

An overflowing pocket was a condition we had never experienced!

In pre-war days, the Melmount curates lived in the 'priest's house', two doors from the present Labour Exchange, on the Urney Road. Many people still remember Frs Ryan, Chapman and Sheerin living there, in succession, in the 1930s. On the creation of the new parish, no curate was allotted for the Melmount end of the parish.

During the Second World War, building restrictions were imposed which lasted right through the 1940s and there was no housing development, either in the public or private sector, and consequently no growth in the parish population. So, at the close of the war and for some years after, the Bridge End part of the parish remained substantially the same in size and population as it was in the early 1930s.

As elsewhere in Ireland, the outbreak of the war accelerated the flow of emigration from the parish and many of the friends of our youth were attracted by the employment in England. A few were destined never to return and became the forgotten casualties of war, on land and sea and from German air raids on their adopted cross-channel cities. Otherwise parish life went on as usual despite rationing and the 'black-out', and the occasional excitement, generated by the US military police post located for the duration of the war in the large, unoccupied houses at the corner, now owned by the King sisters.

During the 'black-out' the only light permitted in the old church after dusk was from a partially lit candelabra. One memory prompted by the recollection of those nights in the dimly lighted church is of a variety show touring the north-west which had run into financial trouble. The manager of the show had appealed to Fr Faulkner for the use of the old schoolhouse, by then known as St Mary's Hall, as an inexpensive venue for a week or two to 'keep the show on the road'. On compassionate grounds the hall was let free of charge to the penniless but talented group of professionals which included Kay Maloney, later to have her own RTE show. Among the galaxy of stars temporarily stranded in the Bridge End was a young tenor named James McKenna, who was then being daily tutored in the hall by Vittorio Forte, a brilliant hard-working, Belfast-Italian pianist. Our own keyboard artist, Hugh Toorish (for many years parish organist, and the founder of the *Clipper Carlton* showband) always supplied his piano on loan to the hall for all musical occasions, and his inevitable friendship with the 'professionals' led to the young tenor agreeing to sing at evening devotions in Melmount.

On the night, the darkened interior of the church enhanced the dramatic effect of the singer's magnificent rendering of Gounod's 'Ave Maria' before the Rosary, and his singing of the hymns during and after benediction. Not all the members of the small congregation on that winter's night were suitably impressed – one irascible parishioner, long since gone aloft, assailed the organist and soloist at the foot of the gallery steps with the indignant query, 'What was all that gouldrin and shoutin' about?' Despite this more than critical assessment of his talent, the same young man was shortly afterwards touring internationally as the leading tenor of the Carl Rosa Opera Company.

In 1948 disaster struck again with a repeat performance of the 1929 flood and once again Hugh Toorish's piano had to be hoisted by John O'Kane Sr and his strong sons to the safety of the sturdy parlour table in Hugh's Bridge Street home, the traditional priority in pre-flood preparations. Appeals to the Stormont government for assistance for the twice-stricken Bridge End families were unsuccessful and again they had to bear the burden of drying out their homes and belongings out of their own meagre resources. As in 1929, not one single family moved residence as a result of the flooding, either through loyalty to the street and the parish, or because there was no alternative accommodation available.

Other memories of the 1940s are of superb entertainment by artists from the north-west and local artists in St Mary's Hall, with the help of the late David Coyle and others now gone to their eternal reward, and of the annual parochial sports, featuring nationally acclaimed athletes such as Mickey Doherty of St Colman's Drive, then an All-Ireland sprint champion. I also recall open air concerts and ceilidheanna on the lawn of the old parochial house – with double summer time it was then clear daylight to midnight. Do I dream or were the summers of long ago as glorious as I like to remember them?

In the immediate post-war years, expansion of the parish began with the construction of Knockavoe Crescent, followed by the Riversdale (Trust) Estate, the Aluminium Bungalows and Croaghan View/Mourne Avenue.

Fr Michael Conway was appointed Fr Faulkner's first curate and he was followed by Frs John McCullagh and Michael Flanagan, and subsequently by the distinguished theologian and author, the Rev. Sean O'Doherty, DD, PhD, whose sudden death in the parish in 1954 brought the most distinguished gathering of clerics in the history of the parish to the old St Mary's. The beautiful sanctuary in the old church was the setting for a solemn Requiem Mass presided over by the primate of All Ireland, Cardinal D'Alton, in the presence of prelates, monsignori and clergy from many parts of Ireland.

The building boom in the parish was at its height when Fr J.F. Convery arrived in 1954, to begin a twenty-year stint of totally dedicated priestly and fund-raising activities made necessary by the construction of St Colman's Secondary School and the two new primary schools, the reconstruction of

St Mary's Hall, and finally the replacement of the old St Mary's Church and parochial house by the fine modern church and priests' residences.

On Fr Faulkner's retirement in 1966, Fr Patrick Dillon became parish priest and he was to spend eleven eventful years as pastor of one of the fastest-growing parishes in the diocese of Derry. In 1974 Fr Convery moved to Strathfoyle as parish priest, to start afresh on the task of building up a structure of that completely new parish. Fr Convery was followed as curate by Fr Joe O'Connor, and then Fr John Doherty, whose eventual departure was a great loss to the musical life of the parish, as he inspired the Ventures II choir which made a successful recording. Other popular and hard-working curates of recent memory were Frs Peter McLaughlin, John Farrell and Charlie Logue.

The most recent reshaping of the parish was in 1974 when the newly appointed bishop, Most Rev. Dr Edward Daly, established Sion Mills as a separate parish. The challenge of meeting the spiritual and temporal needs of Melmount parish was passed on to a Fr Anthony Mulvey, who became parish priest in June 1978. It is not appropriate in this journey into the past to dwell upon his service to the parish and the district from the moment of his arrival. His considerable achievements, with the assistance of his present curates, Frs O'Kane and McGuinness, and the consequent vitality of this young and ever-growing parish, will surely figure largely in the reminiscences of some of our youthful parishioners when it is their turn to look down the corridor of memories.

(This article was published in *Melmount '85*, at the opening of the new parish-built Melmount Centre.)

Acknowledgements, Notes and Sources

CHAPTER 1

Colm Tóibín, *Walking Along the Border*, 2nd edn., London (1988)
John Toland, *A Critical History of the Celtic Religion and Learning, Containing an Account of the Druids*, London (1740; new edn. 1814)
R.R. Madden, *The Shrines and Sepulchres of the Old and New World*, London (1851)
Lebor Gabála Éireann: The Book of the Taking of Ireland, ed. and trans. R.A.S. Macalister, Dublin (1939–56), 5 vols.
Annála Ríoghachta Éireann: Annals of the Kingdom of Ireland, by the Four Masters, from the Earliest Period to the Year 1616, ed. John O'Donovan, Dublin (1851), 5 vols.
Whitley Stokes, *The Tripartite Life of St Patrick*, London (1887), 5 vols.
Samuel Lewis, *A Topographical Dictionary of Ireland*, London (1837), 2 vols. and atlas
Séamus MacManus, *The Story of the Irish Race*, Old Greenwich (1921)

CHAPTER 2

Annála Ríoghachta Éireann: Annals of the Kingdom of Ireland, by the Four Masters, from the Earliest Period to the Year 1616, ed. John O'Donovan, Dublin (1851), 7 vols.
Manus O'Donnell, *Beatha Choluim Cille*, trans. A. O'Kelleher and G. Schoepperle, Urbana, IL (1918)
Lord Ernest Hamilton, *Elizabethan Ulster*, London (1919)
'Book of Howth', in *Calendar of the Carew Manuscripts, Preserved in the Archiepiscopal Library at Lambeth, 1515–1624*, ed. J.S. Brewer and W. Bullen, London (1871) 6 vols.
'Lord Deputy Chichester: notes of remembrances', in *Calendar of the State Papers Relating to Ireland*, London (1860–1912), 13 vols.

CHAPTER 3

Primary sources

Acts of the Privy Council of England, London (1890–1907)
Annála Ríoghachta Éireann: Annals of the Kingdom of Ireland, by the Four Masters, from the Earliest Period to the Year 1616, ed. John O'Donovan, Dublin (1851), 7 vols.
Calendar of the Carew Manuscripts, Preserved in the Archiepiscopal Library at Lambeth, 1515–1624, ed. J.S. Brewer and W. Bullen, London (1867–73), 6 vols.
Calendar of the State Papers Relating to Ireland, 1509–1603, London (1860–1912), 13 vols.
Sir Henry Docwra, 'A narration of the services done by the army deployed to Lough Foyle, etc.', ed. John O'Donovan, *Miscellany of the Celtic Society*, Dublin (1849)

Secondary sources

S.G. Ellis, *Tudor Ireland: Crown, Community and the Conflict of Cultures, 1470–1603*, London (1985)
Cyril Falls, *Elizabeth's Irish Wars*, London (1950)

406   STRABANE THROUGH THE AGES

——, *Mountjoy, Elizabethan General*, London (1955)
Lord Ernest Hamilton, *Elizabethan Ulster*, London (1919)
G.A. Hayes-McCoy, *Irish Battles*, Belfast (1990)
——, *Ulster and Other Irish Maps c. 1600*, Dublin (1964)
Hiram Morgan, *Tyrone's Rebellion*, Dublin (1993)
John O'Doherty (Rev.), *Derriana*, Dublin (1902)

CHAPTER 4

Acknowledgements

The author wishes to thank, somewhat belatedly, Bob Hunter, then of Magee University College (University of Ulster), and Bill Crawford, then of the Public Record Office of Northern Ireland, who in the late 1960s introduced him and others to the delights of researching the history of the Strabane area. Special thanks are extended to Bob Hunter who, during the past years, has added to the author's knowledge of the Plantation period, as well as guiding him to sources post 1641, and to Hamilton Thompson for providing information on the Sinclairs of Hollyhill.

Sir William Petty, *The Political Anatomy of Ireland* [1691], IUP reprint, Shannon (1970)
T.W. Moody, F.X. Martin and F.J. Byrne (eds.), *A New History of Ireland,* iii: *Early Modern Ireland, 1534–1691*, Oxford (1976)
Thomas Bartlett and Keith Jeffrey (eds.), *A Military History of Ireland*, Cambridge, (1996)
Jonathan Bardon, *A History of Ulster*, Belfast (1992)
William Nolan, Liam Ronayne and Mairéad Dunlevy (eds.), *Donegal: History and Society*, Dublin (1995)
G.A. Hayes-McCoy, *Scots Mercenary Forces in Ireland, 1565–1603*, Dublin/London (1937)
O.P. Rafferty, *Catholicism in Ulster, 1603–1983*, London (1994)
Edward Daly and Kieran Devlin, *Diocese of Derry, An Index*, Dublin (1997)
T.W. Moody and J.G. Simms (eds.), *The Bishopric of Derry and the Irish Society of London, 1602–1705*, Dublin (1968), 2 vols.
J.S. Reid, *History of the Presbyterian Church in Ireland*, 2nd edn., Belfast (1853)
James McConnell and S.G. McConnell, *Fasti of the Irish Presbyterian Church, 1613–1840*, Belfast (1951)
George Hill (Rev.), *The Plantation in Ulster 1608–1620*, Belfast (1877)
J.T. Gilbert (ed.), *A Contemporary History of Affairs in Ireland from 1641 to 1652*, Dublin (1879–80), 6 vols.
Michael Perceval-Maxwell, *The Scottish Migration to Ulster in the Reign of James I*, London (1973)
P.S. Robinson, *The Plantation of Ulster: British Settlement in an Irish Landscape, 1600–1670*, Dublin (1984)
R.J. Hunter (ed.), *The Strabane Barony During the Ulster Plantation, 1600–1641*, Derry (1982)
R.C. Simington, *The Civil Survey,* AD *1654–1656,* iii: *Counties of Londonderry, Donegal and Tyrone*, Dublin (1937)
J.H. Gebbie, *Ardstraw (Newtownstewart): Historical Survey of a Parish, 1600–1900*, Omagh (1968)
John Anderson, *Memoirs of the House of Hamilton*, Edinburgh (1875)
George Hamilton*, A History of the House of Hamilton*, Edinburgh (1933)
Earl of Belmore (Somerset Richard Lowry Corry), *Parliamentary Memoirs of Fermanagh and Tyrone, 1613–1885*, Dublin (1887)
A.A. Campbell, *Notes on the Literary History of Strabane*, Omagh (1902)
E.E.K. McClelland (Rev.), *Friendly Strabane*, Strabane (1959)
F.W. Fawcett (Rev.), *Christ Church, Strabane: Centenary*, Strabane (1979)

ACKNOWLEDGEMENTS, NOTES AND SOURCES   407

David Killen, *Through All the Days: A Presbyterian Heritage, Strabane, 1659–1994*, Strabane (1994)

M.G. Kennedy, *By the Banks of the Mourne: A History of Strabane*, Strabane (1996)

CHAPTER 5

J.L. McCracken, 'The social structure and social life, 1714–60', in T.W. Moody and W.E. Vaughan (eds.), *A New History of Ireland,* iv: *Eighteenth-century Ireland, 1691–1800*, Oxford (1986)

David Dickson, *Artic Ireland: The Extraordinary Story of the Great Frost and Forgotten Famine of 1740–41*, Belfast (1997)

John Dooher, 'A Strabane famine in the 1740s', in *Concordia*, iv (1997)

Corporation Records from the 18th Century, PRONI typescript, Belfast (1971)

Abercorn correspondence, PRONI [MSS]

CHAPTER 6

[A more detailed account of the events of the 1790s and the impact of the 1798 rebellion can be found in John Dooher, 'Strabane and the north west in the decade of rebellion', in *Ulster Local Studies*, xix, no. 1 (1997) while the failure of rebellion is dealt with by Brendan Mac Suibhne in an article – 'Up not out: why did north west Ulster not rise in 1798' – in Cathal Poirteir (ed.) *The Great Rebellion of 1798*, Cork (1998)]

A.A. Campbell, *A Literary History of Strabane*, Omagh (1902)

W.H. Crawford, *Domestic Industry in Ireland*, Dublin (1972)

John Dooher, 'Strabane and West Ulster in the Decade of Rebellion', in *Ulster Local Studies*, xix, no. 1 (1997)

Abercorn correspondence, PRONI [MSS]

Rebellion Papers, National Archives, Dublin [MSS]

J.H. Gebbie, *Introduction to the Abercorn Letters*, Omagh (1972)

Brendan Mac Suibhne, 'Up not out: why did north west Ulster not rise in 1798?', in Cathal Póirtéir (ed.), *The Great Rebellion of 1798*, Cork (1998)

Londonderry Journal (from 1772)

CHAPTER 7

The principal source is the Abercorn papers, PRONI D/623 and T/2541. For detailed footnote references, see Malcomson, 'The Politics of "Natural Right": the Abercorn Family and Strabane Borough, 1692–1800', in *Historical Studies*, X (Galway, 1976).

CHAPTER 8

John Gamble, *Sketches of History, Politics, and Manners in Dublin and the North of Ireland, in 1810*, London (1811; new edn. 1826)

A. Atkinson, *Ireland in the Nineteenth Century*, London (1833)

John Graham, 'An essay on the state of Ulster in 1820', *Strabane Morning Post*, Strabane (1820–21)

Francis Rogan, *Observations on the Conditions of the Middle and Lower Classes in Ireland, with the History and Treatment of the Late Epidemic Disorder*, London (1819)

Report of the Inquiry into Handloom Weavers, Parliamentary papers, London (1839)

Report of the Commissioners for Enquiring into the Condition of the Poorer Classes in Ireland: Appendix, Dublin (1836)

Devon Commission Reports on the Occupation of Land in Ireland, Dublin (1845), 4 vols.

State of the Country Papers, National Archives [MSS]

W.J. Carlin, 'Strabane workhouse', in Jack Johnston (ed.), *Workhouses of the North West*, WEA (1996)

Census of Ireland 1841 & 1851, Parliamentary papers, London (1842, 1852)

W.E. Vaughan and A.J. Fitzpatrick (eds.), *Irish Historical Statistics, Population 1821–1971*, Dublin (1978)

Newspapers

Tyrone Constitution, 1845–
Strabane Morning Post
Londonderry Journal, 1772–
Londonderry Standard

CHAPTER 9

Many persons and organisations assisted with providing facts and publications for this evaluation, and thanks are due to them. In particular I would like to express my gratitude to: Mrs. Attracta Harron, Librarian, Strabane Branch Library; The Librarian, University of Ulster, Magee College, Derry; Local History Section, Library Headquarters, WELB, Omagh; Local History Section, Central Library, Derry; Central Library, Belfast; Public Records Office for Northern Ireland, Belfast; Rev. J. Clerkin, formerly P.P., Church of the Immaculate Conception, Strabane; Mr. David Killen, *Strabane Weekly News*, Omagh, Co. Tyrone.

Most of the information contained in this review was abstracted from the *North West Advertiser* (commonly known as the *Derry Almanac*), published in Derry, for the following years:

1862, 1863, 1870, 1874, 1876–8, 1884, 1885, 1887–9, 1890, 1891, 1893–7, 1899 and 1900.

Commercial Directory of Scotland, Ireland, and the Four Most Northern Counties of England for 1820–21 & 22, J. Pigot & Co., Manchester (1820)
City of Dublin and Hibernian Provincial Directory, J. Pigot & Co., Manchester (1824)
S. Lewis, *A Topographical Dictionary of Ireland*, London (1837), 2 vols. and atlas
New Directory of the City of Londonderry, Derry (1839)
Belfast and Province of Ulster Directory, Belfast (1854, 1856, 1858, 1866)
National Commercial Directory of Ireland, Slater & Co., Manchester (1846)
The Royal Commercial Directory of Ireland, Slater & Co., Birmingham (1856, 1870, 1881)
Guide to County Sources, PRONI, Belfast, (1997), 2 vols.
Strabane Carnival Programme (1952)
Archives of the Church of the Immaculate Conception, Strabane
David Killen, *Through All the Days: A Presbyterian Heritage, Strabane, 1654–1994*, Strabane (1994)
M.G. Kennedy, *By the Banks of the Mourne: A History of Strabane*, Strabane (1996)
Strabane WEA Reminiscence Group, *Railway Days in Strabane* (1992)

CHAPTER 10

Unpublished sources

PRONI, D/623 and T/2541, Abercorn estate papers; VAL/1B, Townland valuation books, 1830s; VAL/2B, Primary valuation books, 1850s
Registry of Deeds, Dublin (1956–84) 3 vols.

Published sources

Angélique Day and Patrick McWilliams (eds.), *Ordnance Survey Memoirs of Ireland,* v: *Parishes of Co. Tyrone* I, 1821, 1823, 1831–6, Belfast (1990)
Angélique Day and Patrick McWilliams, *Ordnance Survey Memoirs of Ireland*, xxxix: *Parishes of Co. Donegal* II, 1835–6, Belfast (1997)
Marian Gunning, 'The development of Sion Mills', in *Concordia*, iv (1997)
S. Lewis, *A Topographical Dictionary of Ireland*, London (1837), 2 vols. and atlas
John McEvoy, *Statistical Survey of the County of Tyrone*, Dublin (1802)
R.C. Simington (ed.), *The Civil Survey, AD 1654–1656,* iii: *Counties of Londonderry, Donegal and Tyrone*, Dublin (1937)

W.A. McCutcheon, *The Industrial Archaeology of Northern Ireland*, Belfast (1980)
Mr and Mrs Hall, *Ireland: its Scenery and Character*, London (1841–3), 3 vols.

CHAPTER 11

[It would not have been possible to carry out this review without the generous assistance and time given by Sister Mary Ursula McHugh of Strabane Convent of Mercy.]
'Annals of Strabane Convent', 1868–1989
Admissions Registers of St Catherine's Industrial School, 1870–1949, 3 vols.
Joseph Robins, *The Lost Children: A Study of Charity Children in Ireland, 1700–1900*, Dublin (1980)
Jane Barnes, *Irish Industrial Schools, 1868–1908: Origins and Development*, Blackrock (1989)

CHAPTER 12

Unpublished sources

PRONI, D/623, Abercorn papers; D/3007, Belmore papers; D/627, Montgomery papers

Newspapers

Tyrone Constitution

Published sources

Lord Ernest Hamilton, *The Soul of Ulster*, London (1917)
——, *Forty Years On*, London (1925)
Alvin Jackson, *The Ulster Party: Irish Unionists in the House of Commons, 1884–1911*, Oxford (1989)
W.J. Roulston, 'Landlordism and unionism in Tyrone, 1868–1910', in H. Jefferies and C. Dillon (eds.), *Tyrone: History and Society* (2000)
D.C. Savage, 'The origins of the Ulster Unionist Party, 1885–6', in *Irish Historical Studies*, xii, no. 47 (1961)
B.M. Walker, *Parliamentary Election Results in Ireland, 1801–1922*, Dublin (1978)
B.M. Walker, *Ulster Politics: The Formative Years, 1868–86*, Belfast (1989)

Theses

D. Burnett, 'Unionism and the new century', PhD thesis, Queen's University, Belfast (1995)
John Dooher, 'Tyrone nationalism and the question of partition, 1910–25', MPhil thesis, University of Ulster, Coleraine (1986)
A.D. McDonnell, 'The 1918 general election in Ulster, and the biography of a candidate, Denis Henry', PhD thesis, Queen's University, Belfast (1983)
A.D. McDonnell, *The Life of Sir Denis Henry: Catholic Unionist*, Belfast (2000)

CHAPTER 13

Strabane Morning Post, Strabane (from 1811 to 1840)
The Ulster Directory, Belfast (various years from 1850 to 1900)
The Strabane Chronicle, Strabane
The Strabane Chronicle and *Ulster Herald* (Omagh)
The Tyrone Constitution and *Strabane Weekly News*, (Omagh)
Geoffrey Hand (ed.), *The Report of the Irish Boundary Commission*, Shannon (1969)
Virginia Crossman, *Local Government in Nineteenth Century Ireland*, Belfast (1994)
John Dooher, 'Tyrone nationalism and the question of partition, 1910–25', MPhil thesis, University of Ulster, Coleraine (1986)

CHAPTER 16

George M.C. Ruddock, *History of Strabane Methodist Church*, Strabane (1988)

410 STRABANE THROUGH THE AGES

J.B. Leslie (Rev.), *Derry Clergy and Parishes*, Enniskillen (1937) [Revised edn. (including Raphoe), Belfast (1999)]

F.W. Fawcett (Rev.), *Christ Church, Strabane: Centenary*, Strabane (1979)

Kenneth Milne, *The Church of Ireland: A History*, Dublin (1966)

CHAPTER 17

Primary Sources:

PRONI, MIC/637/6, Minutes of the Laggan Presbytery, 1672–1700

PRONI, CR/3/26, Minutes of the Strabane Presbytery, 1717–40

PRONI, CR/3/46/2, Minutes of the Sub Synod of Londonderry, 1706–36

Records of the General Synod of Ulster, 1691–1820, Belfast (1890), 3 vols.

Registry of Deeds, Dublin (1956–84) 3 vols.

Secondary sources:

Badoney Presbyterian Church, 1844–1994 (1994)

Thomas Croskery and Thomas Witherow, *Life of the Rev. A.P. Goudy, D.D., 1809–58*, Dublin (1887)

S. Ferguson (Rev.), *Brief Biographical Sketches of Some Irish Covenanting Ministers*, Londonderry (1897)

J.H. Gebbie (Rev.), *Ardstraw (Newtownstewart): Historical Survey of the Parish, 1600–1900*, Omagh (1968)

[F. Hay (Rev.)], *Leckpatrick Presbyterian Church, 1836–1974* (1974)

A History of the Congregations in the Presbyterian Church in Ireland, Belfast (1982) [supplement and index, 1996]

David Killen, *Through All the Days: A Presbyterian Heritage, Strabane, 1659–1994*, Strabane (1994)

A. Lecky (Rev.), *Roots of Presbyterianism in Donegal* [repr. Omagh, 1978]

J.B. Leslie (Rev.), *Derry Clergy and Parishes*, Enniskillen (1937) [Revised edn. (including Raphoe), Belfast (1999)]

A. Loughridge (Rev.), *The Covenanters in Ireland*, Belfast (1987)

E.E.K. McClelland (Rev.), *Friendly Strabane*, Strabane (1959)

R.S.K. Neill, *A Short History of First Castlederg Presbyterian Church*, Omagh (1993)

Alistair Rowan, *North West Ulster: The Counties of Londonderry, Donegal, Fermanagh, and Tyrone*, Harmondsworth (1979)

J. Rutherford (Rev.), *Donagheady Presbyterian Churches and Parish*, Belfast (1953)

A.T.Q. Stewart, *The Narrow Ground*, Belfast (1997)

D. Stewart (Rev.), *The Seceders in Ireland*, Belfast (1950)

[John Turner], *Magheramason Presbyterian Church, 1878–1978*, Omagh (1978)

CHAPTER 18

Edward Daly and Ciaran Devlin (eds.), *The Clergy of the Diocese of Derry: An Index*, Dublin (1997)

Henry Jefferies and Ciarán Devlin (eds.), *History of the Diocese of Derry from Earliest Times*, Dublin (2000)

O.P. Rafferty, *Catholicism in Ulster, 1603–1983*, Dublin (1994)

J.B. Leslie (Rev.), *Derry Clergy and Parishes*, Enniskillen (1937) [Revised edn. (including Raphoe), Belfast (1999)]

Walter Hegarty, *Brief History of Leckpatrick* (1935)

Walter Hegarty, *Rambles in Urney* (1933)

Michael Kennedy (ed.), *Centenary Booklet of the Church of the Immaculate Conception*, Strabane (1995)

R.J. Hunter (ed.), *The Plantation of Ulster in the Strabane Barony*, Derry (1982)

ACKNOWLEDGEMENTS, NOTES AND SOURCES   411

Evidence given to the Devon Commission: *Devon Commission Reports on the Occupation of Land in Ireland*, Dublin (1844)
Report of the Commissioners for Enquiring into the Condition of the Poorer Classes in Ireland: Appendix, Dublin (1836)
Strabane Carnival Magazines (1958–60)
Melmount '85, souvenir publication
The Parish of Ardstraw East 1785–1985, bicentennial publication

CHAPTER 19
G.A. Hayes-McCoy (ed.), *Ulster and Other Irish Maps c.1600*, Dublin (1964)
Strabane Lifford Notes (1970s and 1980s)
County cameo by Oscar, *Strabane Chronicle* (9 February 1974)
Samuel Lewis, *A Topographical Dictionary of Ireland* (1837), 2 vols. and atlas
City of Dublin and Hibernian Provincial Directory, J. Pigot & Co., Manchester (1824)
Belfast Street Directory, Belfast (1901)
Omagh Almanac (1886, 1895)
Thom's Almanac, Dublin (1845)
Strabane WEA Reminiscence Group, *Railways Days in Strabane* (1992)
Kevin B. Nowlan, *Travel & Transport in Ireland*, Dublin (1993)
The Royal Commercial Directory of Ireland, Slater & Co., Birmingham (1856, 1894)
E.M. Patterson, *The Co. Donegal Railways*, 2nd edn., Newton Abbot (1969)
E. Curtis, *A History of Medieval Ireland from 1086 to 1513*, London (1923)
M.G. Kennedy, *By the Banks of the Mourne: A History of Strabane*, Strabane (1996)
E. Haslett, *A Social History of Northern Ireland*, Belfast (1960–)
E.M. Patterson, *The Castlederg & Victoria Bridge Tramway*, Newtownards, Co. Down (1998)
Steve Flanders, *The Co. Donegal Railway*, Leicester (1996)

CHAPTER 20
'Pynnar Survey (1619)', ed. Walter Harris, *Hibernica: or, Some Ancient Pieces Relating to Ireland, etc.*, Dublin (1747–50), 2 Parts
H. Hackett, '100 years in education in Strabane', Strabane Carnival Programme (1952)
M. Kennedy, *A History of Strabane* (1965)
C. Montague, *A History of Barrack St. School* (1984)
P.W. Joyce, *A Handbook of School Management*, Dublin (1894)
'Mansfield Survey (1821)', in Angélique Day and Patrick McWilliams (eds.), *Ordnance Survey Memoirs of Ireland, North West Tyrone*, v: *Parishes of Co. Tyrone* I, 1821, 1823, 1831–6, Belfast (1990)
Minute Book, Lifford Corporation (1744)
City of Dublin and Hibernian Provincial Directory, J. Pigot & Co., Manchester (1824)
Strabane Lifford Notes (March 1984)
Strabane Morning Post (July 1827)
Londonderry Journal (11 July 1772)
The Royal Commercial Directory of Ireland, Slater & Co., Birmingham (1856)
Angélique Day and Patrick McWilliams (eds.), *Ordnance Survey Memoirs of Ireland*, v: *Parishes of Co. Tyrone* I, 1821, 1823, 1831–36, Belfast (1990)
Area Development Plan, 1986–2001

CHAPTER 21
Strabane Carnival Programmes (1951–60)
Strabane Lifford Notes, nos. 1–239 (1982–6)
Strabane Chronicle
Strabane Weekly News
The Herald (cross-border community newspaper)

412 STRABANE THROUGH THE AGES

J. Bradley, 'Random recollection', in *St. Patrick's Hall, A Tradition Renewed* (1987)
J. Bradley, 'Corridors of memoirs', in *Melmount '85*

SELECT BIBLIOGRAPHY – JACK GAMBLE

Adams, J.R.R. *The Printed Word and the Common Man*. Belfast (1987)
Alexander, Mrs Cecilia Frances. *Hymns for Little Children*. London (1862)
——, *Poems by C.F. Alexander*, ed. with preface by William Alexander DD. London (1896)
Alexander, E. *Primate Alexander*. London (1913)
Annála Ríoghachta Éireann: Annals of the Kingdom of Ireland, by the Four Masters, from the Earliest Period to the Year 1616, ed. John O'Donovan. Dublin (1851), 5 vols.
Bradley, Jim. 'Myles naGopaleen', in *Concordia* (1993), pp. 60–62
Breslin, H. 'Ballads and jobbing printers', in *Mourne Review* [Strabane], i (1992)
Brown, S.J. *Ireland in Fiction*. Dublin (1919)
Campbell, A.A. *Notes on the Literary History of Strabane*. Omagh (1902)
Campbell, A.A. 'Bibliography of Dr John Gamble', in *Irish Book Lover*, i, no. 2 (1910), pp. 20–21.
Clissman, A. *Flann O'Brien*. Dublin (1975)
Collins, William. *Ballads, Songs and Poems*. New York (1876)
—— *Dalaradia*. New York (1890)
Costello, Peter and Peter Van de Kamp. *Flann O'Brien: An Illustrated Biography*. London (1987–9)
Crane, R.S. and F.B. Kaye. *A Census of British Newspapers and Periodicals, 1620–1800*, London (1927; reprinted 1966)
Crone, John S. (ed.) Article in *Irish Book Lover*, vii (1916), pp. 131 ff.
Crone, J.S. *A Concise Dictionary of Irish Biography*. Dublin (1937)
[Darwin, Kenneth]. *Gray's Printing Press, Strabane*. National Trust, Belfast (1967) [Article on John Dunlap]
Dix, E.R. McC. *List of Books & Pamphlets Printed in Strabane in the Eighteenth Century*. Dublin (1901)
—— *The Irish Book Lover*, iv (1913) pp. 48, 114–16, 134–5; vii (1916) pp. 68–9, 91 [articles on printing in Strabane in the nineteenth century]
Gamble, John. *Disputatio Medica . . . De Rheumatismo*. Edinburgh (1793)
—— *Sketches of History, Politics, and Manners in Dublin and the North of Ireland, in 1810*. London (1811; new edn. 1826)
—— *A View of Society and Manners in the North of Ireland, 1812*. London (1813)
—— *Sarsfield, An Irish Tale*. London (1814) 3 vols.
—— *Howard, A Novel*. London (1815), 2 vols.
—— *Northern Irish Tales*. London (1818), 2 vols.
—— *Views of Society and Manners in the North of Ireland, 1818*. London (1819)
—— *Charlton, or Scenes in the North of Ireland*. London (1823), 3 vols.
Hayes, Richard (ed.) *Manuscript Sources for the History of Irish Civilization*. Boston (1965), 11 vols.; Supplement (1979), 3 vols.
—— *Sources for the History of Irish Civilization. Articles in Irish Periodicals*. Boston (1970), 9 vols.
Hogan, R. (ed.) *Macmillan Dictionary of Irish Literature*. London (1979)
Hopper, K. *Flann O'Brien*. Cork (1995)
[Hutchison, W.R.], *Strabane Rural District Council, Official Guide*. Belfast (1969)

ACKNOWLEDGEMENTS, NOTES AND SOURCES 413

Lovell, E.W. *A Green Hill Far Away: A Life of Mrs Alexander*. Dublin (1970)

Fawcett, F.W. *Christ Church, Strabane, Centenary*. Strabane (1979)

Madden, R.R. *History of Irish Periodical Literature*. London (1867), 2 vols.

McGilloway, Ken. 'George Sigerson M.D.', in *Mourne Review* [Strabane], i (1992), pp. 73 ff.

Munter, R.L. *The History of the Irish Newspaper, 1685–1760*. London (1967)

McClelland, E.E.K. (Rev.) *Friendly Strabane*. Strabane (1959)

O'Brien, G. 'The first Ulster author: John Gamble, 1770–1831', in *Éire Ireland, A Journal of Irish Studies*, xxi, no. 3 (1986) pp. 131–41

O'Casaide, Séamus. *A Typographical Gazetteer of Ireland*. Dublin (1923)

O'Donoghue, D.J. *The Poets of Ireland*. Dublin (1912)

O'Leary, John. *Recollections of Fenians and Fenianism*. London (1896), 2 vols.

O'Nolan, Brian. *At Swim-Two-Birds*. London (1939 and 1980)

—— *An Beal Bocht*. Dublin (1941)

—— *The Hard Life*. London (1961, 1966 and 1986)

—— *The Dalkey Archive*. London (1964 and 1976)

—— *The Third Policeman*. London (1967 and 1986)

—— *The Poor Mouth*. London (1973 and 1986)

—— *Stories and Plays*, ed. C. Cockburn. London (1973 and 1986)

O'Nolan, K. *The Best of Myles*. London (1968 and 1989)

O'Nualláin, Ciarán. *Óige an Dearthar*. Dublin (1973)

Sigerson, George. *The Poets and Poetry of Munster*. Dublin (1860)

—— *Modern Ireland*. London (1869)

—— *Political Prisoners*. London (1890)

—— *Bards of the Gael and Gall*. London (1907)

—— *The Last Independent Parliament of Ireland*. Dublin (1919)

—— *The Easter Song of Sedulius*. Dublin (1922)

—— *Songs and Poems*, intr. by Padraic Colum. Dublin (1927)

Strabane Carnival Programme (1952)

Strabane, Co. Tyrone: The Official Guide. Burrow & Co. Ltd., Cheltenham (*c.* 1930)

Wallace, Valerie. *Mrs Alexander: A Life*. Dublin (1995)

Waterloo Directory of Irish Newspapers and Periodicals, 1800–1900. Waterloo, Canada (1986)

Whelan, Kevin. Article on Strabane imprint, in G. Long (ed.), *Books Beyond the Pale*. Dublin (1996), p. 118

Witherow, Thomas. *Historical and Literary Memorials of Presbyterianism in Ireland*. Belfast (1879–80), 2 vols.

Select Bibliography

Index of Articles 1991–1997

MOURNE REVIEW (1991)

Michael G. Kennedy	Strabane through the lens
David Cannin	Half hanged MacNaghten
John Dooher	Coffins for the poor
Jimmy Quigley	Youthful days – lasting memories
Hugh Breslin	Ballads & jobbing printers
E. Lovell	Cecil Frances Alexander
Kate McAllister	Strabane Library – A visit to the local collection
W.J. Carlin	Disaster of the Strabane narrow gauge
John Mills	Turlough Luineach O'Neill
Ken McGilloway	George Sigerson M.D.

CONCORDIA (2ND SOCIETY JOURNAL 1993)

John Dooher	Reformers, religion & realism
Patsy McCormack	Memories of a 'Glen' navvy
Hugh Breslin	The Hamiltons of Ballyfatton
Eddie MacIntyre	Rev. James Porter – A hero of '98
Jimmy Quigley	The hiring fair
Ciara Canning	The hiring fair
Michael G. Kennedy	A history of education in Strabane
Declan Doherty	The late Jim Bradley – A tribute
Jim Bradley	Myles Na Gopaleen
John Dooher	Life & work in Donagheady in the 1820s
W.J. Carlin and John Dooher	Crossing the Mourne in ancient times
Terry McBride	Ardstraw poet of long ago

THE CHURCH OF THE IMMACULATE CONCEPTION (1995)
(CENTENARY BOOKLET)

Michael Harron	Christianity & Catholicism in Strabane before 1895
John Dooher	Building the Church of St. John in Strabane
Michael G. Kennedy	The building & opening of the Church 1890–1895
Michael G. Kennedy	1895 was a very good year

Michael Harron	The parish records & town surveys 1895
Compiled	The Omagh Almanac 1895
John Dooher	Local leaders in Strabane in the 1890s
Rev. James Clerkin	Parish priests & curates of the Immaculate Conception
Rev. Oliver Crilly	Memories
John Dooher, Michael G. Kennedy] Joint	Revs. O'Hagan, McElhatton, McHugh, O'Doherty
Rev. James Clerkin	] authors McGettigan, Agnew, McCauley, Farren, Clerkin
Michael G. Kennedy	The Consecration of the Immaculate Conception
Michael G. Kennedy	Well, I didn't know that

CONCORDIA (1995)

Rev. Canon W. Fawcett	A history of the diocese of Derry
John McGinley	The races at Carricklee
Hugh Breslin	Half-timers
John Mills	Canada's cotton king – a Strabane emigrant prospers
John Dooher	Commit thy work to God – Sinclairs of Holyhill
Charles Montague	Courtrai Park
John Mills	Guy Carleton – soldier & statesman
Malachy McGarrigle	Buildings of Strabane past & present
John Dooher	A tribute to a seanchaí
Michael G. Kennedy	The Strabane Canal
John Dooher	Dunamanagh – The disputed origins
Séamus Ua Domhnaill	The Court is in session

STRABANE HIRING FAIRS – MEMOIRS, VIEWS, ATTITUDES (1996)

W.H. Crawford	Strabane Corporation: fairs & market rights
W.H. Crawford	Fairs & markets in Ulster: the origins
Ann O'Dowd	Market for youth – the hiring fair
Jonathan Bell	Farm servants in Ulster
Roy Hamilton	Memories of Strabane hiring fairs in the 1920s
Lochlinn McGlynn	Market for youth
Jimmy Quigley	The hiring fair
Patrick Gallagher	Paddy 'the Cope' Gallagher remembers
Patrick McGill	The calvary of North Tyrone
Claire Cunningham	Experiences of the hiring
Patrick McGill	Memories of the hiring – A bad master
Paul Kerr	A change of heart
Sinead Cassidy	Hired – An imaginary experience
Sinead Ayres	Government & the hiring fairs
Anonymous	The Rocks of Bawn
John Dooher	The Strabane hiring fair: A critical review

CONCORDIA (1997)

Michael Cox	Education in Strabane 100 years ago
William Roulston	The archaeological fabric of an Ulster barony
Anne Marie Neeson	The Poor Law in practice
Rebecca (McDaid) Longhorn	John McCrossan, the Evish bard
John Dooher	A Strabane famine in the 1740s
Roise Mairead Rua Coll	The hiring fair in Strabane
Alice Milligan	The hiring fair in Strabane
Marian Gunning	The development of Sion Mills
W.J. Carlin	Death on the line
Thomas Patton	Carthorse to champion
The National Trust	End of an era at Gray's

OTHER LOCAL AND RELATED PUBLICATIONS

Michael G. Kennedy	*By the Banks of the Mourne: a History of Strabane* (1996)
W.J. Carlin et al.	*Railway Days in Strabane*, WEA People's History (1992)
W.J. Carlin et al.	'The Strabane workhouse', in Jack Johnston (ed.), *Workhouses of the North West*, WEA People's History (1996)
John Dooher	Strabane and the north west in the decade of rebellion', in *Ulster Local Studies*, xix, no. 1 (1997)
John Dooher	'Famine and fever in north-west Ulster 1817–18', in *Due North*, i, no. 1 (1999)
John Dooher	'Holyhill', in W.H. Crawford and R.H. Foy (eds.), *Townlands in Ulster* (1998)
David Killen	*Through All the Days: a Presbyterian Heritage* (1994)
William J. Roulston	'Landlordism and unionism in Tyrone, 1868–1910', in H. Jefferies and C. Dillon (eds.), *Tyrone: History and Society* (2000)

Index

Abercorn, countess of (17th c.), 317
Abercorn, Duke of (James Hamilton), 183, 220, 222, 223, 226, 230, 342, 362
Abercorn, Hamilton, marquis of (1884), 346
Abercorn, Lady (1751), 85
Abercorn, Lord (1861), 344
Abercorn, 1st Earl of (James Hamilton), 9, 59–60, 61, 63, 64, 130, 352–353
    enlarged holdings, 65
    estate of, 61–62
Abercorn, 2nd Earl of, 1st Lord Strabane (James Hamilton), 65
Abercorn, 3rd Earl of, George Hamilton, 70, 72
Abercorn, 4th Earl of, 5th Lord Strabane (Claud Hamilton), 72, 75, 76–77, 78, 131
Abercorn, 5th Earl of (Charles Hamilton), 78, 131, 197
Abercorn, 6th Earl of (James Hamilton), 77, 134, 136
Abercorn, 7th Earl of (James Hamilton), 305–306
Abercorn, 8th Earl of (James Hamilton), 134, 149
    change of politics, 131–133
    estate management, 82–96
    influence in Strabane, 97–129
    mills, 198–199, 203
    political crisis, 1732, 133–135
    political influence, 143–145
    schools, 355–356
    struggle with Corporation, 135–140
    and Volunteers, 141–142
Abercorn, 9th Earl of, 1st Marquis (John James Hamilton), 145–150, 323, 341
    sectarian conflict, 152
Abercorn estates, 79, 82, 83, 84, 91–92
    bog utilisation, 90–91
    duty work, 89–90
    estate management, 87–88
    ground rents, 296
    natural resources, 88–89
    and Strabane Corporation, 85–87
    tithes, 93–96
Abercorn Memorial school, 289–290
Act of Union, 129, 149, 151–152
Adamnain, St, 12
Adams, Annie, 272
Adams, Rev. Charles, 309
Adams, James, 235
Adamson, John, 71, 299
Adria Ltd, 392, 394
Aedh Finnliath, High King, 13–14
Aghyaran, Co. Tyrone, 248, 320
Agnew, Monsignor, 361
agriculture, 78, 102–103
Alexander, Rev. Andrew, 114
Alexander, Cecil Frances, 259–261, 289, 356–357, 365, 69–370
Alexander, Eleanor, 288
Alexander, Elizabeth, 256
Alexander, John, 115, 251, 253, 255, 289

Alexander, Joseph, 254
Alexander, Lyons, 289
Alexander, William, Bishop of Derry, 260–261, 288, 370
Algeo, Robert, 66, 70, 317
Alison, John, 302
Allen, Rev. Charles, 357
Allingham, William, 259
Altishane, Co. Tyrone, 325
American War of Independence, 112, 268, 269, 273
Ancient Order of Hibernians, 225, 229, 242, 244, 332
Anderson, James, 255
Anderson, Rebecca, 357
Angela, Rev. Mother, 366
Annals of the Four Masters, 5, 20, 22, 32, 41, 48, 55, 250, 368
Anne, Queen, 132
Anti-Partition League, 244
Antrim, County, 128
apprenticeships, 393
Ardstraw, Co. Tyrone, 14, 15, 29, 32, 58, 70, 75, 153, 155, 158, 317, 335, 369
    bleach green, 201
    Catholic clergy, 315, 316, 319, 320, 324, 331
    emigration, 111–112
    Great Famine, 177
    monastery, 11
    plantation, 62
    Presbyterians, 299, 300, 301, 302, 305, 312
    road, 89–90
    school, 362
    Secession Church, 307
    tithes, 93, 94
    tuck mill, 202
Area Development Plan, 367
Armagh, County, 60, 108, 141, 143, 165
Armstrong, Rev. William, 306
Arthur, Max, 282–283
Artigarvan, Co. Tyrone, 9, 188, 200, 201, 318
    mill, 205
    'rocking stone,' 4
arts, 368–387
Arts Advisory Committee, 275
arts festivals, 384–386
assurance companies, 184
Atchison, Mary, 302
Athenree, Co. Tyrone, 148
Atkinson, A., 164
Atkinson, Captain, 52
Atkinson, Mother Catherine, 209, 358
Atkinson, Mother Mary, 359
Atkinson, Rev., 171
Auchinleck, Alexander, 237
Auchinleck, J.R., 171
Auchinleck, William, 96
Aughabrack, Co. Tyrone, 326
Aughafad, Co. Tyrone, 320

Aughentaine, Co. Tyrone, 307
Augher, Co. Tyrone, 54, 145
Aughnacloy, Co. Tyrone, 147–148
Aughrim, Battle of, 77
Averell, Rev. Adam, 294

Babington, Mathew, 300
Backfence townland, Co. Tyrone, 177
Badby, Captain, 52
Badoney, Co. Tyrone, 10, 35, 271
   Catholic clergy, 319, 320
   Presbyterians, 299, 301, 306, 311, 312
   Secession Church, 307
Bagenal, Marshall, 29
Bagenal, Sir Nicholas, 24
Baines, Alexander, 362
Baines, Philander, 362
Baird, Daniel, 235
Ball Court Alley Theatre, 369
Ballindrait, Co. Donegal, 301, 310, 338
Ballyclare, Co. Antrim, 252
Ballycolman, Co. Tyrone, 10, 367, 398
   Bellicolman, 90
Ballydonaghy townland, Co. Tyrone, 89, 177, 341
Ballyfatton, Co. Tyrone, 69, 70, 73, 75, 90, 200
Ballykeery, Co. Tyrone, 326
Ballymagorry, Co. Tyrone, 93, 100, 120, 202, 303
   mills, 189, 205
   railway, 344
   road, 349
Ballyshannon, Co. Donegal, 52, 53
Ballyskeagh townland, Co. Tyrone, 177
Bamford, Mr, 357, 358
Bangor, Co. Down, 148
banking, 181–183, 389
Bannigan, Michael, 241
Bannigan, Mrs, 327
barbers, 184
Barclay, Mr, 125
Barclay, provost, 138
Barcley, Robert, 96
Bargoine, Thomas, 353
Barnesmore, Co. Donegal, 6
Barnhill, W.W., 226, 243
Baronscourt, Co. Tyrone, 25, 69, 70, 89, 90, 92, 152, 157, 287, 334
   buses, 348
   crannog, 335
   Great Famine, 173, 177
Barrack Street School, 360–362, 373
Barrington, Jonah, 146
Barry, Redmond, 225–226
Barton, J.G., 347
Bassett, Captain, 52
Baxter, Mrs, 357, 360
Beard, Andrew, 73
beggars, 104–105, 119, 157, 160–161
Begley, Ted, 400–401
Belfast and Province of Ulster Directory, 180
Belix, Co. Tyrone, 325
Bellew, John, 252, 253, 255

Belmore, Earl of, 148, 201, 223, 234
Beltany stone circle, 2–3
Beltrim, Co. Tyrone, 141
Benburb castle, 36
Bernagh (Bearney), Co. Tyrone, 320, 327
Bianconi cars, 339
Bill Quinn Trio, 378
billeting, 129
Bingley, Captain Ralph, 49
Birnaghs townland, Co. Tyrone, 200–201, 202
Birsbean, John, 64
Birsbean, William, 70
Blair, R.J., 185, 256
bleach mills, 200–201
Blessington, earl of, 110, 307
Blewart, George, 75
Bloomfield, gardener, 92–93
Bluecoat School, 355
Blyth, James, 253
Board of Guardians, 234, 238, 242–243, 246, 247, 284–285
Board of Works, 339
Bodley, Sir Josias, 336
Bodley survey, 59
Bolles, Sir John, 41, 42, 43, 46–47, 48, 50–51, 52
   letters of, 49–50
Book of Invasions, 54
booksellers, 255–256
Boundary Commission, 247–249, 332
Bowen, Rev. Edward, 237
Bowling Green Parochial School, 358
Boyd, John, 78, 235, 299
Boyd, Marion, 60
Boyd, Susan, 356
Boyd, Rev. Thomas, 310
Boyd, Sir Thomas, 59–60, 65
Boyle, Mrs A., 358
Boyle, Charlie, 382
Boyle, John, 245, 247
Boyle, Patrick, 236, 238
Boyle, William, 235, 339
Boyne, Battle of the, 77
Bracegirdle, Rev., 95
Bradden, Miss, 399
Bradley, Fr Paul, 327
Bradley, Jim, 380
   recollections, 396–404
Bradley, Michael, 244, 400
Bradley, Neil, 184, 242
Bradley, P., Ltd, 350
Brady, Paul, 369, 386
Brady, Mother Xavier, 209
Bramhall, Dr John, Bishop of Derry, 62, 66, 299
Bratton, Tom, 362
Bready, Co. Tyrone, 225, 307–308, 313, 362
brewery, 43–44, 188
Bridge End school, 397–398
Bridgend Hall, 375
Bridges, Sir Matthew, 131
Brodie, N.W., 348

INDEX   419

Brook, H., 348
Brooke family, 257
Brotherhood of St Patrick, 264
Brown, Alan, 366
Brown, Charles, 239, 240, 244, 245, 247, 248, 358
Brown, Charles James, 208
Brown, Rev. David, 301
Brown, George, 293
Brown, Hugh, 257
Brown, Martha, 357
Brown, Miss, 360
Brown, Mrs, 193
Brown, Robert, 299
Brown, Thomas, 235
Brown, Rev. William, 359
Browne, Fr William, 167, 171, 172, 209, 329, 331
Browne, Hugh, 85–86
Browne, John, 64, 66
Browne, Robert, 71
Brownlow, Rev. F., 237, 354
Brownlow, William, 101–102, 107, 141, 143–144
Bryson, Aussie, 380
Buncrana, Co. Donegal, 212, 360
Burgoyne, John James, 153, 158
    Corporation inquiry, 237–238
    county cess, 233–234
    fines, 163
    poor relief, 159, 160, 161
    reform movement, 236
    town commissioners, 235
Burgoyne, Mr, 355
Burgoyne, Rev. T., 237
Burke, Sr Mary Baptist, 212
Burndennet, Co. Tyrone, 167, 359
    bleach green, 200, 202–203
    mill, 198
Burns, Tommy, 370, 371
Burrell, Jane, 191
Burton, Sir F.W., 271
bus service, 348–349
Butler, Mary, 68
Butt, Isaac, 262

Caidinus (Caoide), St, 9–10, 291
Calhame, Co. Tyrone, 318, 326
Calhoun, William, 257
Campbell, A.A., 356
Campbell, A.H., 183
Campbell, Ephraim, 191
Campbell & Son, Belfast, 345
Campbell, Charles, 289
Camus, Co. Tyrone, 10, 66, 72, 158, 166, 167, 237, 317, 335, 359
    Camus-Juxta-Mourne parish, 58, 73, 260, 289, 290, 359
    Catholic clergy, 315, 316, 320, 322, 327, 329, 331
    churches, 287, 288
    Great Famine, 173, 176
    housing, 170
    monastery, 8
    Presbyterians, 298

tithes, 96
Canada, 267–268, 269
canal. see Strabane Canal
Cann, Mavey, 258
Canning, David, 362
Canning, James, 254
Cannon, Pat, 373
canoes, 334
Cappagh Volunteers, 252
Carey, Mr, 95
Carleton, Guy, 257, 267–268, 269
Carleton, Lt William, 257
Carleton, William, 322–323
Carlin, John, 208, 366
Carlton Dance Orchestra, 376
carnivals, 371–372
Carnwath, Dr Thomas, 264
Carrickfergus, Co. Antrim, 54, 59, 68, 299
Carricklee, Co. Tyrone, 29
Carroll, Charles, 257
Carroll, John, 327–328, 329
Carroll and Foster, Messrs, 251, 254, 255, 256
Carroll and Gray, Messrs, 327
Cary, Tristram, 107–108
Cassidy, Maurice, 378
Cassidy, Michael, 363
Castle Coole, Co. Fermanagh, 201
Castle Gore, Co. Tyrone, 134
Castlederg, Co. Tyrone, 50, 53, 155, 348, 365, 370, 371, 396
    Free Presbyterians, 313
    Methodism, 296
    Presbyterians, 302
    RDC, 248
    Secession Church, 307
Castlederg and Victoria Bridge tramway, 346–348
Castlefin, Co. Donegal, 19, 28, 188, 281, 334, 344
    road, 180, 338
castles, 16
Castletown East, Co. Tyrone, 29, 208
Catherwood, H.M.S., 348–349
Catholic Association, 241
Catholic Confederacy, 68
Catholic Council for Maintained Schools, 367
Catholic Emancipation, 117, 147, 151–152, 154, 254, 328–329
    Act, 1829, 155–156
Catholic Registration Committee, 331
Catholics, 77–78, 121, 127, 159, 287, 319. see also education; tithes
    church building, 324–329
    as electors, 219, 229
    first church, 294
    Hamilton family, 61, 66, 70
    as magistrates, 234
    and militia, 110
    and partition, 244, 246
    and politics, 331
    priests exiled, 71
    publications, 255
    registration of clergy, 1704, 320

420 STRABANE THROUGH THE AGES

religious census, 1766, 321–322
in Strabane, 66, 314–332
pre-Plantation, 314–316
tenants, 100
United Irishmen, 128
Cavan, County, 139
Cavanalee, Co. Tyrone, 79, 327
Cave, Ernie, 366
Cecil, William, 42, 48, 49–50
Celts, 6–7
Census, 1841, 168–170
Census, 1891, 180
Chamber, 171
Chamberlain, Sir John, 41
Chambers, Rev. M., 173
chapbooks, 253, 254
Chapman, Fr, 402
Charlemont, earl of, 117, 188, 252–253
Charles I, King, 66, 67, 69
Charles II, King, 68, 69, 70, 71–72, 75
Charleton, Colonel, 117, 118
Charleton, Richard, 142
chemical works, 190–191
Chichester, Lord Deputy, 35, 36
Chichester, Sir Arthur, 54
Christ Church, Bowling Green, 193, 288–290, 329
Christian Brothers, 194, 359
Christian Enquirer, 252
Christianity, 7–13
Christy, Thomas, 202
Church of Ireland, 71, 72, 92, 114, 156, 159, 230, 294, 295, 317, 328
history in Strabane, 286–293
and Presbyterians, 298–299, 302, 311
tithes, 93–96
Church of Ireland Parochial School, 357, 358
Church of the Immaculate Conception, 193, 329–330
Cinel Connail, 6, 11
Cinel Owen, 6–7, 11
Civil Surveys, 17th c., 61, 69–70, 75, 196–197, 202, 318
Clady, Co. Tyrone, 70, 76, 79, 248, 255, 259, 305, 326
mill, 197
Presbyterians, 309
clans, 6–7
Clarke, Peter, 242
Clarke, Rev. Edward, 244–245, 312, 358
Clayton, Earnest, 296
Clipper Carlton, 369, 374, 375, 376–378
Clochcor, see also Cloughcor, Co. Tyrone, 325
Clogher, Co. Tyrone, 61
Cloghogall (Cloughogle), Co. Tyrone, 62, 113, 137, 198, 200
tuck mill, 202
Clonleigh, Co. Tyrone, 8, 14, 15, 71, 166
Cloughcor, Co. Tyrone, 88, 338
Clougheen Wood, 163
Cloughey, Co. Down, 307
Cochrane, James, 171
Colepepper, Elizabeth, 73
Coleraine, Co. Derry, 65, 184, 338

Colgan, St, 8, 287
Colhoun, 241, 246
Colhoun, David, 254
Colhoun, John, 84, 88–89, 91–92, 92, 102, 106
Colhoun, Percy, 296
Colhoun, Samuel, 238
Colhoun, William, 96
Colley, Henry, 133
Collier, Robert, 296
Collins, William, 262–263
Colman, St, 10, 401
Colmcille, St, 8, 21
Colton, Primate, 11
Columba, St, 287
Columba Gallagher Showband, 378–379
Comber, Mother Augustine, 364
Commodore Cinema, 375
Commonwealth, 69–71
Conkill townland, Co. Tyrone, 70
Connison, Walter, 191
Connolly, Bernard, 373
Connolly, Dan, 382
Connolly, James, 331
Connolly, Fr James, 327
Connolly, Miss, 358
Connolly, Fr Sam, 325–326, 331, 332
Connolly family, 382
Connor, E., 340
Conroy, Eugene, 241, 242, 244, 245
Conroy, M., 192
Conroy, Rev. Fr, 171
Controlled Secondary Modern School, 366
Convent of Mercy, 193, 207–217, 329, 358–360, 362–365
orphanage, 366
Convery, Fr John, 375, 403, 404
Conway, Charles, 238
Conway, John, 246
Conway, Fr Michael, 403
Cook, Daniel, 235, 340
Cook, James, 238
Cooke, James, & Co., 188–189
Cookstown, Co. Tyrone, 180, 248
Cooper family, 374, 375
Coote, Sir William, 69
Colton, Archbishop, 291
Corickmore, Co. Tyrone, 10
Corrick, Co. Tyrone, 307, 312, 314
Corry, Geraldine, 371
Coulton, Dr, Archbishop of Armagh, 335
county cess, 156, 233–234
courts, 107–108, 126, 127, 232
Covenanting Congregation, 307–308
Covert, Captain Humphrey, 44
Cowan, Robert, 300
Cowley, Mother Teresa, 211
Coyle, Dr Anthony, bishop of Raphoe, 253
Coyle, David, 403
Craig, Vic, 377, 378
Craig Memorial Hall, 289
Crampsie, Daniel, 343

INDEX 421

Crampton, Philip, 257
crannogs, 334–336
Crawford, Andrew, 257
Crawford, C., 125
Crawford, James, 66, 317
Crawford, Major James, 153, 154, 155
Crawford, Patrick, 64
Crawford, Captain Patrick, 59
Crawford, Rev. Thomas, 253
Crawford, Rev. William, 114, 117, 252–253, 306
    school, 355–356
Creevy, Co. Tyrone, 293
Creighton, Mr, 106
Creighton, Robert, 354–355
Creighton estate, 88, 133, 257
Crerard, Dr, 261
Crewe (Crowe), Co. Tyrone, 75, 347
Crolly, Dr, Bishop of Down and Connor, 328
Cromwell, Oliver, 69, 71, 299, 318
Cromwell, Richard, 71
Crowe (Crewe), Co. Tyrone, 75, 347
Cullen, James, 185
Cullion, Co. Tyrone, 93, 308
Culmore, Co. Derry, 33, 40, 41, 47
Cumber, Co. Derry, 48, 237, 316
Cunningham, Robert, 247
Curly Hill, 180, 327
Curran, B.L., 346
Cuthbert, Alan, 73

Dail Eireann, 246, 247
Daly, Dr Edward, Bishop of Derry, 404
Davis, John, 136
Davis, Thomas, 262
Davitt, Michael, 331
de Burgh, Sir John, 15–16
De Courcy, John, 11
De Danann, 5
de Valera, Eamon, 277, 362
deaf and dumb school, 260, 289, 356–357
Declaration of Independence, 252, 256–257
Deehan, Paddy, 361
Defenders, 126
Delap, Rev. A.H., 358
Delap, William, 257
Delap family, 73
Dening, John, 255
dental care, 188
Derg, Co. Tyrone, 127, 301
Dergalt, Strabane, 272
Derry, 33, 47, 54, 55, 61, 68, 69, 89, 105, 107, 108,
    112, 184, 248, 293, 304, 337, 340, 371
    buses, 348
    canal, 171
    Catholic clergy, 319, 320, 323
    diocese, 11, 71, 316–317
    education, 365
    emigration, 122
    fortified, 41, 44, 336
    illegal distilling, 121
    plantation town, 63

railway, 343, 344, 348
Reformed Presbyterians, 308
Rising, 1641, 67
roads, 180, 338
siege of, 76–77, 301
size of, 65
Derry (Londonderry), County, 165
Derry Almanac, 179–180, 187, 209, 360
Derry and Raphoe Diocesan Institution, 356–357
Derry Journal, 210, 224, 251
Derrywoon (Dirrywoon), Co. Tyrone, 62, 69, 70, 84,
    110, 197
Desert (Dysert), Co. Tyrone, 107, 341
Desmond, earl of, 27, 29
Devine, Eleanor, 363
Devine, James, 319
Devine, John, 239, 240, 247, 248
Devine, Mr, 266
Devine, William, 184
Devine, Fr William, 360, 398–399
Devlin, Charles, 246
Devlin, Fr Ciaran, 314
Devlin, Dessie, 370
Devlin, Eddie, 370
Devlin, Mr, 171
Devlin, Rev. Dr Philip, 208–209, 331, 359
Devon Commission, 167–168, 329
Diamond, Sean, 363
Dickey, Rev. William, 255
Dickson, Rev. Thomas, 307
Dickson, T.A., 221
Dillon, Fr Patrick, 404
Dillon, John, 220
Dillon, Miss, 357
disease, 79–80, 104, 159–161
    cholera, 162–163
dispensary, 187
Divin, George, 192
Docwra, Sir Henry, 33–34, 40–44, 47, 49, 50, 51, 58
    assessment, 55
    final stages of war, 53–55
    in Tyrone, 52–53
Dodd, William Heuston, 224–225
Dog, Flower, and Poultry Show Association, 183
Doherty, Andy, 361, 373
Doherty, Billy, 350
Doherty, Declan, 373, 385
Doherty, Deirdre, 373
Doherty, Fidelma, 370
Doherty, Hugh, 238
Doherty, John, 361–362, 371
Doherty, Fr John, 404
Doherty, Maria, 381
Doherty, Mickey, 2, 403
Doherty, Neal, 185
Doherty, Terry, 384
Doherty, Tom, 381
Doherty, William, 235
Doibhlin, Diarmaid, 320
Dominican order, 316, 319
Donagheady, Co. Tyrone, 9–10, 58, 62, 67, 72, 89,

166, 237
Catholic clergy, 315, 316, 319, 320, 322, 325–326, 329, 330–331
churches, 290–291, 325–326
Hamilton rector, 125–126
Irish population, 78
Presbyterians, 298, 299, 300–303, 309–312
divisions, 305–306
sectarianism, 155
tithes, 93, 94–95, 96
United Irishmen, 127
Donaghey, C.H., 348, 349
Donaghmore, Co. Tyrone, 15, 76
Donaghy, Frankie, 400
Donegal, County, 105, 110, 132, 139, 155, 165, 170, 190, 338, 365
Abercorn in politics, 147–148
Boundary Commission, 248
grand jury, 233
militia, 91
railway, 340, 344–345
United Irishmen, 126, 128
Donegal Historical Society, 280
Donegal Railways Company, 345–346, 348
Donegal town, 13, 28, 69, 280
borough, 145
siege, 52–53
Donegore, Co. Tyrone, 253
Donemana. see Dunamanagh
Donnell, S., & Co., 181
Donnelly, Terence, Dean of Armagh, 24
Donnyloop, Co. Donegal, 318, 326, 396, 401
Donoughmore, Co. Donegal, 304
Doorat, Co. Tyrone, 325
Doran's Bakery, 191–192
Dougherty, Ann, 191
Dougherty, Rev. Professor James Brown, 222
Douglas, Co. Tyrone, 127
bleach green, 200, 201
mills, 197, 199, 202
Presbyterians, 309, 312
Douglas, Hon. Rev. Charles, 171, 173, 237
Douglas Burn, 79
Dowling, George, 357
Down, County, 128, 165
Downham, Dr, Bishop of Derry, 287, 298, 317
Drumgauty, Co. Tyrone, 200
Drumleen, Co. Tyrone, 19
Drumquin, Co. Tyrone, 153
Drumvallagh, Co. Tyrone, 258
Drysdale, William, 353
Dublin Institute of Advanced Studies, 277–278
Ducart, Mr, 107
Dullerton freehold, 198–199
Dunamanagh (Donemana), Co. Tyrone, 62, 78, 92, 127, 134, 138, 191, 200, 257, 332, 365
fair, 108, 154–155
Great Famine, 173
mills, 202, 205–206
MP, 141
Presbyterians, 309

railway, 344–345
road, 180
Secession Church, 307
Duncan, Edward, 239, 240, 358
Duncan, Hugo, 369, 386
Duncan, Patrick, 244
Dungannon, Baron of, 29
Dungannon, Co. Tyrone, 15, 59, 60, 63, 105, 165, 180, 200, 201, 349
Barony, 36, 56
Convention, 114, 117
Dungiven, Co. Derry, 31, 53
Dunlap, Captain John, 73, 122, 252, 256–257, 268, 275
Dunlap, William, 256
Dunleavy, Peter, 376
Dunlop, DI Robert, 390
Dunlop, Rev. William, 306
Dunn, James and Robert, 93
Dunnalong Castle, 29, 33, 34, 35, 41
Dunnalong (Donelong), Co. Tyrone, 13, 16, 24, 28, 69, 72, 76, 88, 91, 93, 108, 334
1640 survey, 70
abandoned, 56
Battle of, 50–52
bog, 90
church, 291–292
development, 43–44, 61–62
fair, 154
fort layout, 44–47
fortified, 336
garrison size, 52
mill, 197, 198
O'Gallagher killing, 48–49
poor relief, 113
trade, 79
Dunne, James, 239, 240
Dunne, Mr, 360
Dunne, Mrs Frankie, 357
Durnien, Felix, 358, 360, 361
Dutton, Captain, 50, 53
Dysert (Desert), Co. Tyrone, 107, 341

Eames, Lord, 290
Edgar, William, 358
Edie, Edward, 194, 237
Edie, Nathaniel, 118, 123, 124, 125, 129, 200, 202–203
Edie, William, 89, 90
education, 71–72, 352–367, 403–404
grammar, 364–365
primary, 358–363
secondary intermediate, 365–366
vocational, 363–364
Educational Board, 358
Educational Endowments Act, 1885, 362
Edwards, Hugh, 134
Edwards, Rev. Mr, 125
Edymore, Co. Tyrone, 79, 88
Egan, Phelim, 386–387
Elagh castle, Co. Doneagal, 40

INDEX   423

elections, 131–150
 1768, 110
 1885, 219–221
 1885-1925, 218–230
 1886, 220–221
 1906, 224–225
 1907, 225–226
 1910, 226–227
 1911, 227–229
 1918, 229–230
 1920, 245–246
 1924, 247
 Catholic participation, 332
 reform movement, 236–237
 registration of electors, 221–222
electricity, 391
Elizabeth I, Queen, 22, 26, 32, 35, 42, 53, 54–55
Elliot, James, 251
Elliott, John, 240
Elliott, Thomas, 241
Elliott & Crawford, 193
emigration, 170, 176, 177, 394, 402
 agents, 192
 Presbyterians, 302, 305
 18th c., 110–112, 121–123
Emmet, Robert, 258
Enagh castle, Co. Derry, 52, 54
England, Mr, 362
Enniskillen, Co. Fermanagh, 69, 201, 343, 344
Environment, Department of the, 351
Erne, Earl of (1871), 345
Erne, Earl of (1887), 183
Erne, Earl of (18th c.), 107
Essex, earl of, 26–27
Eugene, St, 10–11
Eunan, St, 12
European Regional Fund, 350
evictions, 118–119, 167
Ewarts, William, 73

Fahan, Co. Donegal, 319
fairs, 108, 127, 152
 riots, 154–156
Falconer, Willie, 400
Faller, Sr Teresa, 360
famines, 80, 82–84, 103–104, 112–113, 119, 156–159, 160, 162. see also Great Famine
Fanning, Sr Carmel, 360
Farrell, James, 66, 317
Farrell, Fr John, 404
Farren, Dr, Bishop of Derry, 211, 361, 365
Farren, Fr John, 371
Farren, Sr Mary Evangelist, 211, 212, 364–365
Faughanvale, Co. Derry, 308
Faulkner, Fr George, 401–402, 403, 404
Fawney, Co. Tyrone, 200
Feeley, Charlie, 374
Feely, T.B., 240–241
Fenians, 262, 264
Fenton, Dr, 125
Fenton, John, 237

Ferguson, Sir Robert, 346–347
Ferguson, Rev. Victor, 304
Fergyshill, John, 75
ferries, 79, 88–89, 334
Finlay family, 79
Finn river, 79, 334, 341, 344
Finn Valley Railway Co., 340, 344
Finnwater Volunteers, 252
Fire Brigade, 184, 392
First Presbyterian Church, 193
First Presbyterian school, 359, 360
First Valuation, 1835, 201
First World War, 227, 229, 243–244, 245, 289
Fitzwilliam, Viceroy, 25–26, 30, 31–32, 33
Fivemiletown, Co. Tyrone, 222
Flanagan, Fr Michael, 403
flax mills, 199–200
Fleming, James, 102
Fleming, Mr, 342
Fleming, Victor, 377, 378
Flight of the Earls, 36, 55, 58, 251, 287
Flood, John, 400
flooding, 105–106, 119, 159, 162, 296, 397–398, 403
 defences, 172, 350–351, 390–391
flour mills, 201
Floyd, Captain, 52
Foley, Jim, 371
football, 399–400
Forbes, Henry, 346
Forbes, Magdalene, 370
Fordyce, David, 255
Forward, William, 146
Fowler, Rev., 126–127, 128
Foyle river, 5, 79, 238, 333–334, 336, 341
 bridge, 106–107
 ferries, 88–89
 fishing, 88
France, 112, 122
franchise, 110, 229, 238, 331
Franchise Act, 1883, 219
Franciscan order, 10, 314, 319
 Strabane, 17–18, 20
Franklin, M.H., 373
Free Presbyterian Church, 313
free trade, 114–117
Freeman's Journal, 261
Freemasons, 156, 254
friaries, 17–18, 335
Friendly Sons of St Patrick, 273, 275
Furey, Michael, 245, 247
furniture manufacture, 191
Fyfin, Co. Tyrone, 320, 325

Gaelic Athletic Association (GAA), 276
Gallagher, Andy, 190
Gallagher, Edward, 183, 184, 239, 240, 241–242, 243, 245, 247, 248
Gallagher, Hugh, 29, 30
Gallagher, Jack, 365
Gallagher, James, 185
Gallagher, Patsy, 370

424   STRABANE THROUGH THE AGES

Gallagher, Bishop Redmond, 47–49, 316, 317
Gallagher, Tony, 400
Gallen, Edward, 246
Galvan, Miss, 363
Gamble, Andrew, 111, 253–254, 255, 256
Gamble, Jack, 276
Gamble, Rev. James, 255, 307
Gamble, John, 78
Gamble, Dr John, 164, 258–259, 284, 339, 356
Gamble, Mary, 255–256, 259
Gamble, Rev., 166
Gamble, Rev. Samuel, 255
gas lighting, 190
Gault, Harry, 384
Gault, Leslie, 235
Gavan Duffy, Charles, 259
George, Reggie, 374
Gibson, Tom, 364
Gillespie, Fr Augustine, 379
Gillespie, P., 191
Glasse, Miss, 357
Glasse, William, 238
Glebe Primary School, 375
Glendermott, Co. Derry, 309, 310
Glenelly Valley, 309, 312
Glenmornan, Co. Tyrone, 158, 201, 320, 325
Glenmornan river, 303
Glenock, Co. Tyrone, 324
Glynn, Mercy Felicia, 281
Goodler, John, 70
Gordon, Jean, 65
Gordon, Miss, 358
Gordon, Samuel, 193
Gore, Rev. F.L., 166
Gormley, Joe, 370–371
Gormley, Roderick, 181, 340
Gormley, William, 308
Gormley family, 256, 276
Gorticrum, Co. Tyrone, 201, 325
Gortin, Co. Tyrone, 62, 254, 309, 312, 327
Gortinmore, Ballindrait, Co. Donegal, 272
Goudy, Rev. Alexander Porter, 171, 310–311
Government of Ireland Act, 246
Grafton, Duke of, 144
Graham, Isaac, 235, 238
Graham, James, 238
Graham, Rev. John, 270
Graham, Rev., 126–127
grand jury, 105, 233, 238, 239, 346
Grange, Co. Tyrone, 10, 167
Graves, Dr A.P., 261
Gray, E.R., & Sons, 185
Gray, J.J., 183
Gray, John, 256
Great Famine, 168, 170–177, 261, 265, 288, 294, 329
    impact on Strabane, 176–178
Great Northern Railway Co., 344, 345
Greenbrae fishing, 88
Greene, Graham, 277, 278
Greenlaw, Co. Tyrone, 298, 341
Greer, Mr, 355

Gregory, Miss, 186
Grianan Aileach, 14
Griffith, Arthur, 229–230
Grimley, Patrick J., 365
Gwyn, George, 197
Gwynn, Richard, 238
Gwynn, William, 236, 238
Gwynne, W., 163

Hadaway, Andrew, 317
Hall, Mr and Mrs S.C., 204–205, 339
Halliday, Mr, 302
Hamell, John and Christian, 73
Hamill, M., 358
Hamiltons, *see also* Abercorn
Hamilton, Rev. Andrew, 125–126
Hamilton, Andrew (1630), 67
Hamilton, Andrew (1895), 340
Hamilton, Anthony, 75
Hamilton, Archdeacon, 102
Hamilton, Cecilia, 72
Hamilton, Hon. Charles, MP, 134, 136, 150
Hamilton, Claud, 110
Hamilton, Claud, Lord Strabane, 65
Hamilton, Lord Claud, MP (1845), 171
Hamilton, Lord Claud, MP (1885), 220
Hamilton, Sir Claud, 59–60, 60–61, 70
    estate of, 62
Hamilton, Claudius, MP, 141, 143, 144
Hamilton, David, 289
Hamilton, Dr, 94
Hamilton, Elizabeth, 75
Hamilton, Lord Ernest, MP, 27, 28, 31, 218, 220,
    221–223
Hamilton, Lord Frederic Spencer, MP, 220, 222–223
Hamilton, Rev. Frederick, 95
Hamilton, Galbraith, 200, 201
Hamilton, George, 127
Hamilton, George, 4th Lord Strabane, 69, 70, 72, 73
Hamilton, Hon. George, MP, 136, 150
Hamilton, Lord George, MP, 220
Hamilton, Sir George, of Dunnalong, 69, 70, 73, 76
Hamilton, Sir George of Greenlaw, 59–66, 202, 297,
    317
Hamilton, Hon. Gustavus, 131, 132, 133
Hamilton, Hon. Capt. Gustavus, 257
Hamilton, Hugh, 61, 235, 238
Hamilton, James, agent, 61, 78, 96, 139, 140–141, 237
    Act of Union, 129
    brother stands for election, 110
    and burgesses, 124
    on Catholic loyalty, 323–324
    Crawford's school, 355–356
    on emigration, 111–112
    and grand jury, 233
    hospital, 105
    mills, 198, 200, 203
    poor relief, 156–158
    poteen, 120–121
    provost, 125
    rent arrears, 118–120

on sectarian conflict, 152, 153, 154
on United Irishmen, 126–127
and Volunteers, 113–118, 142
Hamilton, James, 3rd Lord Strabane, 65, 69, 70
Hamilton, Colonel James, MP, 73, 75, 77
Hamilton, Rev. James, 95
Hamilton, James Jr, 125, 126
Hamilton, Janet, 60–61
Hamilton, John, agent, 100
  hospital, 105
  navigation, 107
  poverty relief, 103–104
  protests, 109
  seneschals, 107–108
Hamilton, John, MP, of Dunamanagh, 125, 138–140,
    141, 143–144, 146–147
  and Abercorn, 144–145
  petition, 149
Hamilton, General Sir John, 237
Hamilton, Lord John, 227
Hamilton, John (1618), 61, 63–64
Hamilton, John (1666), 73, 77
Hamilton, John (1762), 93
Hamilton, Katherine, 73
Hamilton, Marion, 67
Hamilton, Pat, 257
Hamilton, Patrick, 73, 78
Hamilton, Rev. John, 72, 299, 301
Hamilton, Rev., 155
Hamilton, General Richard, 76, 77
Hamilton, Mrs S., 354
Hamilton, Sarah, 185
Hamilton, Rev. Stewart, 126, 237
Hamilton, William, 61, 62, 63–64, 64–65, 69
Hamilton, William, MP, of Dunamanagh, 92, 96,
    134–135, 135–137, 150, 198–199, 257, 305–306
Hamilton, William, of Ballyfatton, 75
Hamilton, William, of Dunamanagh, 302
Hamilton, William, provost, 85
Hamilton, Rev. William, 96
Hamilton, Sir William, 62–63, 68, 70, 270
Hamilton family, 71, 80, 287, 308, 310, 325. see also
Abercorn estates
  1640 survey, 70
  control, 1770-1800, 96–129
  electoral influence, 230
  electoral influence, 1886-92, 221–223
  family tree, 74
  political control, 1770-1800, 130–150
  political crisis, 1732, 133–140
  poor relief, 158–159
  protection of Catholics, 318
Hancock, John, 257
Hannah, Miss, 360
Hansard, Sir Richard, 8, 55
Harberton, Lord, 117, 147
Harley, Mary, 370, 371
Harpur, Martha, 290
Harpur, William, 184, 247
Harry Avery's castle, 16
Hassan, P.J., 361, 370

Hatch, Henry, 102
Health Board, 163
health care, 159–161, 162–163, 187
hearth tax returns, 1666, 72–73, 78–79
Hearts of Oak (Oakboys), 108–109, 253
Hearts of Steel (Steelboys), 109, 253
Hedge Masons, 126
Hegarty, Fr Brian, 322
Hegarty, Fr William, 261, 322, 325, 327, 331, 359, 360
Hemphill, Charles, 223, 230
Hemphill, Rev. Charles, 307
Henderson, J., 359
Henderson, John, 200
Henderson, Joseph, 235
Henry, Denis S., 224–226, 230
Henry, Sam, 265
Henry VIII, King, 21
Herdman, E.C., 226–227, 227–229
Herdman, Emerson T., 220–221, 222, 224, 226–227,
    234, 242, 243
Herdman, Captain J.C., 247–248, 289
Herdman & Co., Messrs, 188, 204–205, 345
Herdman family, 173, 201
Herkes, Alex and Thomas, 78
Hervey, Dr, Bishop of Derry, Earl of Bristol, 106, 117
Hicks, M., 390
Higginbotham, Rev. R., 261
Higgins, Sr Mary Aloysius Joseph, 214
highway robbery, 338–339
Hill, W.F., 348
Holiday, Pat, 191
Holland, Denis, 264
Hollyhill (Holyhill), Co. Tyrone, 70, 75, 87, 154, 188,
    189, 201, 325
Holywood, Co. Down, 253, 265
Holmes, John, 73
Holmes, Rev. William, 77, 302, 304
Holmes, William, 235
Holmes & Co., 188
Home Rule, 219, 220–221, 224–225, 243, 331, 332
Hood, John, 197, 199, 202
Hood, Matthew, 152–153, 156–158
Hood & Smyth, 185
Hopkins, Dr Ezekiel, Bishop of Derry, 75
Horne, Robert, 96
Horner, Andrew, 228
hospitals, 105, 159–161, 162–163, 187
hotels, 185–186, 339–340
House League, 241, 242
housing, 125, 164, 168–170, 241, 391, 394, 403
  development, 99–100
Houston, John, 183, 191
Houston, Thomas, 312
Hovenden, Henry, 54
Howie, Thomas Knox, 244
Hoynes, Johnny, 211
Hudson, Dr, 94
Hume, John, 365
Hume, Rev., 166
Humphreys, Major John, agent, 166, 168, 171, 234,
    237–238, 259–260, 289, 365

426 STRABANE THROUGH THE AGES

Humphreys, T.W.D., 181, 239
Humphries, John, 362
Hunter, William, 197

illegal distilling, 103, 120–121
Inchany (Inchiney), Co. Tyrone, 14, 326
industrial schools, 212–213
industry, 188–191
infirmaries, 104–105
Inglis, Henry D., 283
Ingram, Moreland, 364
Irish Builder, 209
Irish language, 363
Irish Literary Society, 261
Irish Nation League, 244
Irish News, 224
Irish North Western Railways, 345
Irish Parliamentary Party, 229–230
Irish Reformed presbytery, 308
Irish Times, 277
Irishman, The, 261
Irwin, Robert, 185
Island McHugh, 16, 54, 334

Jacobite war, 91–92
James, Rev. William, 308
James I, King, 34, 57, 59, 61, 65, 251
James II, King, 75–77, 131, 251, 288, 291, 292, 319, 337
Jefferson, Thomas, 256–257
Jenkins, Andrew, 181, 238, 254, 256
Jimmy Sturrock Band, 378
Jones, Rev., 166
Jordan, James, 353
Jordan, Patrick, 239, 240
Joyce, James, 262, 277, 278
Joyce, Sr Mary Magdalene, 207–208, 360
Kane, Louis, 401
Kane, Paul, 359
Kearney, Miss, 358
Kearney, Sr Mary Evangelist, 209
Keatley, Annie, 374
Keble, John, 260, 356
Kelly, Dr, Archbishop of Armagh, 328
Kelly, Dr, Bishop of Derry, 359
Kelly, James S., 361
Kelly, John, 244, 247
Kelly, Mrs, 185–186
Kelly, Sr Angela, 364
Kenaghan townland, Co. Tyrone, 75, 87
Kennah, William, 298–299
Kennedy, Bill, 381
Kennedy, James, 189–190, 208, 239, 359, 366
Kennedy, John, 288
Kennedy, Michael G., 365
Kennedy, S., 245
Keogh, Brendan, 367
Kerr, Aeneas, 362
Kerr, James, 199, 235
Kerr, Mr, 120–121, 358
Keyes, William, 71, 299

Kildare Place Society, 328
Kilkenny Confederacy, 68
Killen, Robert, 102
Killenagh, Co. Tyrone, 326
Killeny and Eden estate, 62–63, 70
Killeter, Co. Tyrone, 320, 348
Killydonnell, Co. Tyrone, 22
Killygordan, Co. Donegal, 371
Killymoon, County Tyrone, 142
Kilmacrenan, Co. Donegal, 59, 61
Kincaid, Mrs, 367
Kinch, James, 192
King, Dr William, Bishop of Derry, 78, 319
King, Elizabeth, 191
Kinsale, Battle of, 34, 53
Kirk, Raymond, 385
Knockavoe, Battle of, 19–20, 22
Knockincligh castle, 36
Knockroe townland, Co. Tyrone, 197
Knowles, George and John, 296
Knox, Andrew, 148
Knox, George, 254
Knox, Hon. George, 147
Knox, John, 147
Knox, Mary Ann, 108, 338
Knox, Mr, 125, 338
Knox, Rev. Robert, 173
Knox, Tom, 147
Knox, Rev. William, 171

labour council, 245
Labour Party, 245, 247
Lacey, Lewis, 365
Laggan Force, 67–68, 69
Laggan presbytery, 299–300
Laidlaw, A.G., 184–185
Laidlaw, G.T., 184
Land League, 331
land reform, 219, 228
Landahussy, Plumbridge, Co. Tyrone, 270
Langan, Sr Mary Columba, 209
Largie, Co. Tyrone, 70
Larmour, Francis, 340
Larmour, Mrs, 186
Law, Thomas, 189
law and order, 107–108, 194
Leckpatrick, Co. Tyrone, 8, 10, 58, 65, 66, 73, 75, 78, 200, 287, 317
 Catholic clergy, 315, 316, 318, 320, 321–322, 324–326, 329, 330–331
 churches, 77, 291, 324–326
 congregation, 71, 72
 Great Famine, 173, 176
 mearing dispute, 87
 paper mill, 202
 parish, 288
 poverty, 158, 166, 168
 Presbyterians, 299, 300, 303, 309, 311
 schools, 354
Lees, the Misses, 354
Leicester, Robert, 20

INDEX 427

Leinster, Duke of, 143, 144
Leitrim, Lord, 348
Leney, Alexander, 236, 284–285
Leslie, Dr, bishop of Raphoe, 71
Leslie, J.B., 355
Leslie, John, 70
Letterkenny, Co. Donegal, 64, 105, 305, 345
library, 183
Lifford, Co. Donegal, 8, 13, 29, 30, 33, 47, 60, 64,
71–72, 88, 152, 268, 272, 327, 334
bridge, 106, 180, 338
captured, 43
castle, 20–22, 26–27, 28, 34
Common Council, 99
defences, 44, 55, 59, 91, 336
development, 106, 107
Dispensary, 104
education, 270, 357
jail, 108, 338, 366
library, 280
parliamentary representation, 133
railway, 344
road, 339
United Irishmen, 128
Williamite wars, 76
Lifford Corporation, 353
Lifford Players, 369, 371, 375, 379–380, 381
Liggartown, Co. Tyrone, 201, 204
Limerick, Treaty of, 77, 251
Lindsay brothers, 334
Lindsiee, Robert, 63
Linen Board, 101
linen industry, 79, 83, 84–85, 87, 91, 102–103, 121,
158, 180
collapse of, 165–166
crisis, 101–102
sales figures, 123–124
19th c., 188
and US war, 113
Lisdivin, Co. Tyrone, 61, 70
Lislap, Co. Tyrone, 61
literacy, 169, 356
Literary and Debating Society, 183
literary history, 250–266
Little Theatre, 253
Litton, E.C., 219
Lloyd George, David, 244
local government
1800-1925, 232–249
changes, 1920, 245–246
and national issues, 243–245
and partition, 246–247
Local Government Act, 1898, 235, 239
Loch Finne, 5
Loftus, Sir Edward, 203
Logan, Rev. Matthew, 309
Logue, Cardinal, 229
Logue, Fr Charlie, 404
Logue, Terry, 377, 378
London Hibernian Society, 328, 354
Londonderry *see* Derry

Londonderry, Lord, 264
Londonderry & Swilly Railway Co., 345
Londonderry Journal, 111, 112, 121, 154, 160, 166,
192, 353
Londonderry Standard, 172
Lough Foyle, 13–14, 39–40, 106
Loughneas, Co. Tyrone, 61
Love, John, 78
Love, Victor, 310
Lowry, Andrew, 2
Lowry, Robert, 138, 139
Lowther, Widow, 203
Lurgan, Co. Armagh, 101–102, 107, 141
Lynch, Mother de Pazzi, 212
Lynch, Sr Mary Vincent, 212
Lynne, William, 61–62, 70
Lyons, Messrs, & Co., 188

McAleer, J., 245
MacAnamy, Ferdoragh (MacConmidhe), 251
McAnaw, Daisy, 374
McAnaw, Daniel, 193, 251, 252, 265
McAnaw's, 191–192
Macartney, J.W. Ellison, 219
McBride, Fr Edward, 128, 324, 327
McCafferty, John, 360
McCaffrey, Daniel, 242
McCaffrey, J., 238
McCaffry, Anne, 359
McCaffry, John, 358
McCausland, John, 133, 134
McCausland, John Jnr, 137–140
McCausland, Mark, 136
McCausland, Mr, 85, 125
McCausland, Oliver, 135–137, 137
McCausland, Captain Oliver, 131, 132, 133
McCausland family, 149
McCawell, Robert, 322
McCay, Aodh, 371, 381, 382
McCay, Henry, 166
McClelland, Alexander, 185
McClelland, John, 298–299
McClements, Mr, 360
McClintock, John, 87–88, 88–89, 90, 92
McCloskey, Fr Andy, 371
McColgan, John, 239, 240
McColgan, John, Bishop of Derry, 322
McColgan, Pat, 373
MacColla, Alasdair and Ranald, 68
McCollum, Patrick, 244
McConalogue, Fr John, 222, 331
McConalogue, Sr Margaret, 365
McConnell, Mickey, 400
McConnolly, James, 319, 320
McCool, Barney, 373
McCormick, Charles, 236, 238
McCosker, Scobie, 374
McCrackens, Ballymagorry, 202
McCrea, Robert, 167
McCreery, James, 253
McCreery, John, 200, 203

McCrossan, John, 239, 358
McCrossan, Michael, 239, 240
McCullagh, Andrew, 271
McCullagh, Isabella, 271
McCullagh, James, 270–271
McCullagh, John, 172
McCullagh, Fr John, 403
McCullow, Owen, 163
McDaid, Patrick, 173
McDaid, Sr Gerard, 360
McDermott, Dominic, 362
McDermott, Sr Dominic, 211–212
McDermott, George, 245
McDermott, John, 244
McDevitt, Fr Denis, 327
McDevitt, J.J., 241
McDevitt, Packie, 376, 383
McDevitt, Dr Philip, Bishop of Derry, 322, 323, 326
McDevitte, W.C., 241
McDonald, Stewart, & Co., 389
McDonnell, Evelyn, 278
McDonnell, Lady Agnes, 24–25, 26, 27–28, 32
MacDonnells, 23
McElhatton, Fr John, 239–240, 327, 330, 331, 360
McElwaine, J.J., 185
McFarland, Rev. John, 309
McFarlane, James, 181
McFarlane, James, MP, 340, 389
McGahie, Rev. Hugh, 295–296
McGarrigle, James, 244
McGarvey, Anne, 366
McGettigan, Dr, Bishop of Raphoe, 328
McGhee, George, 134, 135, 137, 138
McGillion, Frank, 380
McGinley, Hugh, 163
McGinley, John, 363, 370
McGinley, Patrick, 370
McGinnis, Andrew, 189
McGlinchey, Fr John, 326, 331, 332
McGonagle, Frankie, 371
McGonagle, W.A., 358
McGowan, Charlie, 373
McGowan, P., 358
McGuinness, Fr, 404
McGuinness, Samuel, 245, 247
McGuire, W., 184
McGuirk, Dean Brian, 319
McHugh, Fr Arthur, 128, 155, 166, 327
McHugh, Fr Charles, 331
McHugh, Dr, Bishop of Derry, 324, 329, 331
McHugh, Sr Mary Ursula, 208
McHugh, Fr Michael, 371
McIntyre, Andrew, 280
McIntyre, Eddie, 255, 280
McIvor, James, & Co., 191
McIvor, Thomas, 241
McKean, Thomas, 257
McKee, Hugh and Daniel, 70
McKee, Joseph, 239
McKee, Miss, 358
McKee, Peter, 239, 240

McKelvey, John, 384
McKenna, Fr Bernard, 329, 330–331
McKenna, James, 402–403
McKernan, 107–108
McKew, W., 358
McKinley & Son, 190
McKinney, Edward, 185
McLaughlin, Deirdre, 367
McLaughlin, Dr, Bishop of Derry, 328
McLaughlin, Fr, 358
McLaughlin, Fr (1895), 329
McLaughlin, Sr Josephine, 212
McLaughlin, Fr Peter, 404
MacLochlainn, Donnail, 14–15
MacLochlainns, 11, 14
McMahon, P., 183
McMahons, 24
McMenamin, Eugene, 381
McMenamin, Frank, 181, 240
McMenamin, Patrick, 243
MacNaghten (McNaughten), John, 338
McNally, John, 319
McNamee, Daniel, 246
McNamee, Dympna, 363
MacNamee, Ferdoragh, 24–25
McNamee, Paddy, 374
McNamees, 251
McNaughten trial, 108
McNeill, Thomas, 290
MacRickard, Cane Ballogh, 53
McShane, Mickey, 400
MacSweeney, Owen, 317
MacSweeny Fanad, 49, 50
McSwegan, Thomas, 185
Mafeking, South Africa, 211
Magee, Daniel, 75
Magee, David, 70, 72, 75
Magee, George, 75
Magee, James, 359
Maghera, Co. Derry, 315
Magheracrigan, Co. Tyrone, 84
Magheramason, Co. Tyrone, 198, 227, 228, 296, 310
Magill, Rev. George, 310
Magirr townland, 350
Maguire, Hugh, 239, 240
Maguire, Professor John, 362
Maguire, Tom, 328
mail coaches, 338–339
Malison Bridge, Co. Tyrone, 318
Maloney, Kay, 402
Mangan, James Clarence, 259
Manistry, Edward, 345
Mannion, Sr Mary, 360
Mansfield, George D., 354
Marie, Sister, 366
Markethill, Co. Armagh, 307
markets, 84–85, 87, 97, 99
Marlowe, Miss, 348
martial law, 127
Martin, Miss, 364
Martin, Rev. John, 307

INDEX 429

mass houses, 321
Mathewson, Samuel, 235
Matthews, Charles, 357
Maultsaid, John, 365
Maxwell, James, 68
Maxwell, Mr, 117
Maxwell, Thomas, 197
Maxwell, William, 140–141
Mease, James, 273–275, 275
Mease, James Jr, 273
Mease, John, 273, 275
Mease, Matthew, 272–273
Mease, Robert, 274
Meenashesk mountan, Co. Tyrone, 128
megalithic tombs, 3, 4
Mellifont, Treaty of, 54
Melmount, 326, 327, 360, 363, 396
    Mourne parish, 401–404
    school, 365
Melmount Centre, 375
Melmount Community Care, 393
Melody Aces, 379
Mendicity Association, 162
Mercantile and Mathematical School, 354
Mergoh, Art, 53
Merriman, Captain, 32
Mervyn, Audley, 131
mesolithic period, 2
Methodists, 127, 193
    list of ministers, 297
    in Strabane, 293–297
middle ages, 13–16
Midlands Railways, 344, 345
Milesians, 5, 6
militia, 91, 92, 110, 152
Millberry, Co. Tyrone, 138
Miller, Rev. Alexander, 305
Miller, W.T., 229–230, 243, 247–248
Millfield, Co. Derry, 252
Milligan Brothers, 350
mills, 196–206
    corn mills, 196–197
    decline of, 205–206
    entrepreneurs, 202–203
    and freeholders, 198–199
Milltown, Ardstraw, Co. Tyrone, 201, 205, 237
Milltown Grammar School, 364, 365
Milltown Players, 374
Minshull, H., 373
Mitchell, William, 340
Moderall, John, 73
Moderwell, Andrew and Robert, 73
Molloy, Fido, 376
Molloy All-Stars Dance Band, 378
monasteries, 8–10, 14, 15, 314, 315, 336
Mongan, Fr, 327
Mongevlin Castle, Co. Donegal, 28, 76
Monica, Sister, 365–366
Monro, General, 68
Monteith, Rev. John, 173
Montgomery, George, 139, 141

Montgomery, George, Bishop of Derry, Raphoe and
    Clogher, 48, 58, 316
Montgomery, Hugh de Fellenberg, 222
Montgomery, General Richard, 267, 268–270
Montgomery family, 133
monuments, 2–5
Moody, John, 186, 340
Moody, Miss, 358
Moody, S.J., & Co., 190–191
Moorcroft, William, 70–71
Moore, Alexander, 340
Moore, John, 251
Moore, Rev. John, 309
Moore, Nathaniel Montgomery, 147–148
Moorecroft, William, 299
Moorlough, Co. Tyrone, 88, 303
Morgan, Lady, 253
Morning Post, 236
Mornington, Lord, 147
Morrissy, Sr Cecilia, 364
Morrissy, Sr Mary, 360
Mortimer, Edmund, 19
Morton, David, 362
Morton, Samuel, 235, 236, 238
Mossom, Robert, Bishop of Derry, 72, 73
Mount St Joseph Convent, 193, 207–212, 359–360,
    364–365
Mountcastle, Co. Tyrone, 308
Mountjoy, Lord (1715), 133
Mountjoy, Lord (1807), 233
Mountjoy, Lord (16th c.), 39
Mountjoy, Omagh, Co. Tyrone, 29, 42, 52, 53, 54
Mourne, Co. Tyrone, 79, 107
    bridge, 180
    parish, 326–327, 401–404
Mourne Dance Band, 379
Mourne Health Centre, 398
Mourne river, 5, 333–334, 336, 341
    bridge, 338
    bridges, 350
    floods, 397
    ford, 337
    railway bridge, 343, 345
Muldoon, John, 229
Mulholland, Andrew, 204
Mulholland, Herdman and Co., 168
Mulvey, Fr Anthony, 396, 404
Mulvin, Co. Tyrone, 308, 313
Murlog, Co. Donegal, 327
Murphy, James Henry, 185
Murray, Sr Ignatius, 360
music, 183, 357, 358
    bands, 382–384
Mussey, Hugh, 53

national schools, 194–195, 328, 356, 358–363
natural resources, 88–89
Neaton, Brother Thomas, 359
Needham, Richard, 350
Neilson, Nancy, 261
Neilson, Samuel, 264

430 STRABANE THROUGH THE AGES

Nelson, T.E., 239, 241, 358
Nelson, Thomas, 257
neolithic period, 2
Newcome, Mr, 46
Newry canal, 107
Newton O'Donnell castle, 19
Newtown, Co. Tyrone, 61, 89
  castle, 35, 55, 56
  development, 100, 125
Newtownstewart, Co. Tyrone, 15, 16, 19, 23, 53–54,
    60, 76, 79, 110, 133, 159, 224, 229, 254, 365
  bleach greens, 200, 201
  Catholic church, 324
  Great Famine, 173
  linen market, 124
  Methodists, 296
  Oakboys battle, 108
  plantation, 61, 62
  poor relief, 102, 113
  Presbyterians, 70–71, 309, 312
  railway, 343
  Rising, 1641, 67
  road, 89, 180, 338
  sectarianism, 155
  surrender, 1601, 52
  United Irishmen, 127, 128
  Williamite wars, 77
  yeomanry demonstration, 153–154
Newtownstewart Backburners, 381
Nicholson, Dr, bishop of Derry, 82
Nigeria, 211–212
Nine Years War, 32, 33–34, 39–56, 58, 336
  Battle of Dunnalong, 50–52
  Bishop Gallagher killed, 47–49
  Dunnalong fort, 44–47
  final stages, 53–55
  O'Doherty submission, 47
  O'Donnell submission, 42–44
  in West Tyrone, 52–53
Nisbitt, Nathaniel, 85–86, 88–91, 100, 101, 110, 136
  on poverty, 102
  on tithes, 93–94
Nobel, Henry, 66
Normans, 15
Normoyle, Sr Gertrude, 212, 360
Norry, Pauline, 370
North Tyrone Unionist Association, 222, 226, 227,
    228–229
North West Agricultural School, 363–364
North West Boundary Defence Committee, 248
North West Institute of Further and Higher Education,
    362, 363
Northern Constitution, 265
Northern Ireland Fire Authority, 392
Northern Ireland Road Transport Board, 348
Northern Ireland Transport Board, 349
Northern Star, 254, 264
Northland, Lord, 105
Northwest Loyal Registration and Electoral Association
    (NLREA), 220–221
North-West of Ireland Agricultural Society, 354

Nugent, Christopher, 75
Nugent, Fr, 318, 326
Nugent, Frank, 374

O hAodha, P., 277
O'Brien, Francis, 236, 238, 354
O'Brien, Gwynn & Co., 188
O'Brien, Muireartach, High King, 11
O'Brien, P., 192
O'Byrne, Cathal, 372
O'Cahan, 44, 49, 52, 53–54
O'Cahan, Donal, 34
O'Cahan, Rory, 31
O'Cahans, 41, 58
O'Callaghan, P.J., 239
O'Carroll, T.J., 363
O'Cleirigh, Micheal, 31
O'Connell, Daniel, 236, 328
O'Connor, Fr Joe, 404
octennial act, 109, 143, 149
O'Daly, John, 261
O'Devin, James, 320
O'Divine, Captain Murragh, 67
O'Doherty, Monsignor John, 331, 332
O'Doherty, Cahir, 34, 47, 50, 54, 64
O'Doherty, Sir Cahir, 55, 58–59, 60
O'Doherty, Hugh Boy MacDavitt, 47, 49, 50
O'Doherty, Fr John Keys, 331
O'Doherty, Monsignor John, 244
O'Doherty, Mr, 248
O'Doherty, Phelim Oge, 47
O'Doherty, Rev. Sean, 403
O'Doherty, Sir John, 40, 47
O'Doherty, Terry, 379
O'Dohertys, 14
O'Donnell, Art, 33–34
O'Donnell, Calvagh, 21, 22–23, 30
O'Donnell, Charles, Bishop of Derry, 323, 324
O'Donnell, Conn McCalvagh, 25, 26–27, 27, 28, 33
O'Donnell, Hugh, 22, 25, 26, 27, 28–29, 29–30, 33
O'Donnell, Hugh Dubh, 23
O'Donnell, Inion Dubh, 25, 27–28, 33
O'Donnell, Joan, 27, 29
O'Donnell, Manus, 20–21, 27
O'Donnell, Fr Neal J., 326
O'Donnell, Niall Garbh, 34, 40, 47, 51, 55–56
  submission of, 42–44
O'Donnell, Niall Mac Conn, 30
O'Donnell, Red Hugh, 28, 33–34, 40, 54, 58, 335
  Donegal siege, 52–53
  and Turlough Luineach, 30–31, 32
O'Donnell, Rory, earl of Tyrconnell, 21, 34, 54, 55
O'Donnells, 14, 30, 316
  internal divisions, 33
  O'Neill rivalry, 15–16
  14th-15th c., 19–20
O'Donnelly, Daniel, 75
O'Donovan, John, 339
O'Duffeme, Brian Groome, 62
O'Duffemes (Devines), 78
O'Duffy, Michael, 370

INDEX 431

O'Duffy, Sr Zita, 212
O'Flaherty, Daniel, 184
O'Flaherty, John, 242
O'Gormleys, 7
O'Grady, Sr Ligouri, 359
O'Hagan, Art, 373, 377, 378
O'Hagan, Fergie, 377
O'Hagan, Fr Hugh, 330, 331, 358
O'Hagan, Patrick, 370
O'Hammill, Patrick, 68
O'Hanlon, Michael, 377, 378
O'Hanlons, 58
O'Hegarty, Bryan, 320
O'Hegarty, James, 319
O'Kane, Dr Bernard, Bishop of Derry, 360, 362,
    397–398
O'Kane, Edward, 245
O'Kane, Fr, 404
O'Kane, James, 385
O'Kane, Fr James, 396
O'Kane, John, 9, 403
O'Kane, Fr William, 325
O'Keefe, John, 253
O'Kelly, James, 319, 320
O'Kelly, Terence, 71, 317–318
O'Kelly family, 318
O'Luinsechan, Fr Teig/Tagh, 78, 319, 320
Omagh, Co. Tyrone, 15, 53, 54, 76, 109, 184, 220,
    223, 229, 243, 248, 365
    burnt, 1741, 83
    buses, 348, 349
    education, 365
    Great Famine, 175
    hospital, 105, 159
    linen market, 124
    meeting on penal laws, 154
    population, 180
    Presbyterians, 301
    railway, 343
    road, 89
Omagh Volunteers, 252
O'Mellan, Friar, 67–68
O'Mongan, Cornelius, 320
O'Neill, Rev. Mother Angela, 210
O'Neill, Sir Art, 32, 36, 40–42, 44
O'Neill, Catherine, 25
O'Neill, Con Bacach, 19–20, 22
O'Neill, Cormac, 32, 44
O'Neill, Sir Cormac, 52
O'Neill, Cormac McArt, 34–35
O'Neill, E., 188
O'Neill, Francis, 167–168, 208, 209, 236, 329, 359,
    366
O'Neill, Gordon, 68, 75
O'Neill, Colonel Gordon, 75, 76, 77
O'Neill, Sir Henry Oge, 59
O'Neill, Hugh, 35
O'Neill, Hugh, Earl of Tyrone, 21, 29–30, 58. see also
Nine Years War
    agreement with Turlough Luineach, 37–38
    battle of Dunnalong, 50–51

surrender, 53, 54–55
O'Neill, Hugh Boy, 54
O'Neill, John (Shane Mac Con Bacagh), 76
O'Neill, Niall Connolly, 19, 23
O'Neill, Owen Roe, 68
O'Neill, Sir Phelim, 60, 66–67, 67–68, 75
O'Neill, Shane, 22–23, 24, 25, 29
O'Neill, Turlough, 44, 53, 55, 56, 59, 60, 63
O'Neill, Turlough Luineach, 23–32, 29–30, 34, 40, 41,
    46, 51, 58, 59, 250–251
    agreement with earl of Tyrone, 37–38
    and English administration, 26–28
    as middleman, 30–32
    Strabane burnt, 28
O'Neill, Turlough Magnylson, 52, 53
O'Neill, Turlough McArt, 35–36
O'Neill, Turlough Oge, 59, 60
O'Neills, 7, 11, 14, 315, 316, 368–369
    dispossessed, 35–36
    internal divisions, 33–34
    O'Donnell rivalry, 15–16
    14th-15th c, 19–20
O'Nolan, Brian, 275–279
O'Nolan, Ciaran, 278–279
O'Nolan, Michael Victor, 276
opera, 372–373
optician, 188
O'Rahilly, Professor T.E., 277–278
Orange Order, 127, 128, 152, 155, 219, 224, 254, 309
Ordnance Survey map, 1885, 191
Ordnance Survey Memoirs, 165, 203–204, 339
Orighealla, 7
Ormond, Duke of, 73
orphanage, 366
Orr, Alexander Ector, 279, 346
Orr, James, 118
Orr, William (1753), 96
Orr, William (1829), 235, 236, 238
Orr, William R., 181, 183
Our Lady of Mercy Girls Voluntary Intermediate,
    365–366
Owen, Richard, 341
Owenson, Miss, 253
Owenson, Robert, 369

Pagoda, Strabane, 349, 391
Paisley, Lord, 134, 135
Pakenham, J.J., 390
Pallidrome, 374–375
paper mills, 201–202
parliament. see elections
partition, 180, 243–244, 332
    effects of, 246–247, 248–249
Parviliers, Fr A., 255
Paton, Mr, 71
Patrick, St, 7–8, 10, 277–278, 335
Patterson, John, 189, 302
Patterson, Robert, 135
Patterson, Rev. T., 357
Patterson, William, 203
Patton, Rev. Samuel, 308

432　STRABANE THROUGH THE AGES

Paulett, Sir George, 55, 58
Peacockbank, 304
Peel, Sir Robert, 194
Pellissier, Rev., 102
Pemberton, T., 125
penal laws, 82, 92–93, 110, 154, 254, 319, 320–321
  end of, 322–323, 324
Penny Society, 162–163
People's Rights Association, 239–240
Perkins, Major Richard, 72
Perrott, Sir John, 28–29
Perry, John, 244, 247, 290
Pettigo, Co. Donegal, 301
pharmacies, 187
Philipstown, King's County, 145
photography, 184
Pigot Directory, 354
Pigott, John, 197, 304
Pitt, William, 147
Playboys showband, 379
Plumbridge, Co. Tyrone, 62, 155, 270, 327
Plunket, Right Hon. W.C., 258
Plunkett, Archbishop Oliver, 71, 317, 318
Plunkett, Count, 244
Poak, Frederick, 89
Pole, Felix, 349
policing, 194
Poll Money Ordinance, 73
poll tax, 1660, 78
Pollock, Robert, 181, 191, 389
Pomeroy, Henry, 125, 141, 143–144, 146, 147
Poor Inquiry, 329
poor relief, 102–105, 113, 118–120, 156–157,
  167–168, 234
population size, 169, 176–178, 180, 391
Porter, Rev. James (1798), 259, 264, 310, 338
Porter, Fr Paul, 381
Porter, Rev. (1846), 171
Porter, Robert, 236
post office, 181, 183, 390
posting establishments, 186–187
poteen, 120–121, 157, 158
Powell, S., 257
Power, Vincent, 365
Prehen, Co. Derry, 148, 338
prehistory, 1–5, 334
Presbyterians, 66, 68–69, 77, 159, 230, 248, 287
  1859 revival, 311
  boundary disputes, 303
  congregations, 70–71, 72
  education, 356, 359
  as electors, 219–220
  emigration, 302
  merchant class, 109
  penal laws, 78, 92–93, 110–111
  publications, 255
  Secession Church, 306–307
  in Strabane, 298–313
  tithes, 94
  United Irishmen, 127–128
  and Volunteers, 114, 116

Priestly, Michael, 90, 99–100, 106
Primary Valuation, 205
Primitive Wesleyan Society, 193, 294, 295
printers, 185, 255–256
proportional representation, 242, 246, 247
protest movements, 108–109
Pubble, Co. Tyrone, 10, 314
Puddle Alley Theatre Group, 375, 381–382
Purdon, Benjamin, 186
Pynnar Report, 352–353

Queate, Margaret Ann, 359
Quigley, A., 184
Quigley, Frances, 371
Quin, Bernard, 264–265
Quinn, Anne, 360
Quinn, 'Feeley,' 374
Quinn, Hugh, 377
Quinn, Hugo, 377, 378
Quinn, Mr, 200
Quinn, Patrick, 363
Quoile, river, Co. Down, 334

Rabb family, 79
Rafferty, Oliver, 320
railways, 172, 181, 339, 340, 343–346, 391–392
  end of, 348
Rainey, Sam, 363
Ramelton, Co. Donegal, 67
Ramsay, William, 235, 257
Ramsey, J.G., 173
Ramsey, Michael, 173
Randalstown, 349
Rankin, Mr, 247–248
Ranson, Charles, 296
Ranson, Rev. H.J.F., 294, 295
Raphoe diocese, 11, 12, 69, 112, 132, 320, 323
Rash, Co. Tyrone, 76
Rathmullan, Co. Donegal, 49, 338
Redistribution of Seats Act, 219
Redmond, John, 243, 244, 331
reform movement, 236–237
Reformation, 315–316
Reformed Presbyterian Church, 307–308
Reid, Rev. Robert, 307
Reilly, George, 183
Reilly, John, 401
relief works, 171, 172–173
Restoration, 71–72
Ribbonmen, 155
Richie, James, 340
Rising, 1641, 67, 128
Rising, 1916, 243–244
Risk, Miss, 360
river transport, 106–107
roads, 89–90, 334–336, 339
  bypass, 350
  improvements, 349–350
  maintenance, 337–338
Roberts, Edward, 70
Roberts Brothers, 348, 349

Rocking Stone, 4
Rockville Stompers, 379
Rodgers, John, 173
Rogan, Dr Francis, 160–161, 264
Rogan, F., 188
Rogan, Fr, 325
Rolleston, Rev., 270
rope manufacture, 191
Ross, Mr, 202
Roundhill, Co. Tyrone, 327, 367
Rowan, Alistair, 312
Royal Irish Academy, 270–271
Royal Irish Constabulary (RIC), 194, 390
Rule, Sam, 367
Russell, Cecil, 296
Russell, John W., 191–192
Russell, T.W., 228–229, 245, 332
Russell, Rev. W.A., 311
Russell's Bakery, 246
Rutherford, Robert, 122
Rutherford, Rev. Thomas, 295
Ryan, Fr, 402

St Anne's Primary School, 360
St Catherine's Industrial School, 193, 207, 212–217,
    366
St Colman's Secondary School, 365, 366, 367, 384, 403
St Eugene's Brass Band, 382
St Eugene's Catholic Temperance Society, 183, 184
St John Bosco Primary School, 360, 362–363
St John's Catholic Church, 193, 329, 330
St Johnstown (St Johnston), Co. Donegal, 76, 127, 136,
    150
    borough, 131, 132, 146
St Joseph's Brass Band, 382–383
St Mary's Primary Schools, 363, 375
St Patrick's Hall, 370–371
St Patrick's Operatic Society, 370
St Vincent de Paul Society, 184, 397
Samthainn, St, 9
Scarff, Alexander, 340
Scarvagherin, Co. Tyrone, 10, 12, 18, 314
Scelpy, Co. Donegal, 326
Schroedinger, Professor Erwin, 277
Scotland, 78, 111
    Catholics from, 287, 317
    Jacobite rebellion, 91–92
    planters from, 59–61
    pre-plantation settlers, 55, 59
    refugees to, 67
    Secession Church, 306–307
    trade with, 63–64, 79, 80, 189
Scott, J., 188
Scott sisters, 374
Scottish Reformed presbytery, 308
Scraghy, Co. Tyrone, 371
Secession Church, 193–194, 306–307, 309
Second World War, 277, 312, 391, 394, 402
sectarian conflict, 108–109, 127, 151–156
Seein. see Sion Mills
Semple, Robert, 298

Seven Years War, 110
Shannon, Maura, 360
Shannony, Co. Tyrone, 199
Shean. see Sion Mills
Sheerer, Dominic, 377, 378
Sheerin, Fr, 402
Sheridan, Mr, 390
Shiels, Ann, 380
Shiels, Danny, 398
ship canal, 171, 172
shirt manufacture, 189–190
shops, 191–193
Shorter, Dora Sigerson, 262
showbands, 376–379
Sian. see Sion Mills
Sidley, Captain, 52
Sigerson, Dr George, 261–262, 325
Sigerson, William, 171, 188, 189, 329
Sigerson family, 201
Silverhill townland, Co. Tyrone, 177
Sime, James and John, 281
Simms, Dr James, 263–264
Simms, Most Rev. Dr G.O., 280, 281–282, 290
Simms, James, 186, 340
Simms, Professor J.G., 281
Simms, John F.A., 281
Simms, Nicholas, 185
Simms, Rev. Nicholas, 362
Sims, Nicholas, 236
Sinclair, Elizabeth, 265
Sinclair, James, 154, 155, 158, 166, 233, 237, 238
    Great Famine, 171
    social conditions, 167
Sinclair, John, 88, 90, 95, 108, 288
Sinclair, Rev. John, 72, 75, 76, 77
Sinn Fein, 228, 229–230, 244, 245–246, 331, 332
Sion Mills, Co. Tyrone, 70, 90, 115, 123, 170, 173,
    188, 201, 203, 220, 272, 339, 365, 367, 396
    buses, 348
    Catholic church, 398
    church, 292
    development of, 203–205
    employment, 393
    mills, 197, 200, 204
    munitions factory, 394
    parish, 401, 404
    Presbyterians, 309
    railway, 343
    road, 349
Sisters of St Louis, 211
Six Counties Motor Co. Ltd, 348
Sixmilecross, Co. Tyrone, 307
Slater Directory, 357
Smiley, Mr, 200
Smith, Alex C., 296
Smith, David, 188, 205
Smith, Rev. James, 171, 173, 288
Smithwick, Rev. George, 166, 171, 173
Smyth, Adam, 197
Smyth, David, 235, 236, 238
Smyth, Holmes & Smyth, 188

434 STRABANE THROUGH THE AGES

Smyth, Robert, 184, 193
Smyth, W.B., 247, 248
social activities, 183–184
Solemn League and Covenant, 68–69, 245
solicitors, 390
songs, 265–266
Southwell, Edward, 132–133
spade mills, 201
Spain, 51, 53, 55, 58, 68
Spamount, Co. Tyrone, 188, 200, 203, 347
Spicer, Alexander, 66
sports facilities, 183
Sproule, Andrew, 200, 203
standing stones, 3, 5, 17
Stanhope, Rev. Edward, 67
Stanley, Lord Edward, 356
Stapley and Smith, Messrs, 190, 370, 389
Starrat, William, 87, 257–258
Steele, F.M., 183, 358
Stephenson, Robert, 343
Stevenson, E., 372–373
Stevenson, James, 97, 189
Stevenson, Robert, 247–248
Stevenson, Sammy, 374, 376
Stevenson, William, 235, 237, 238
Stevenson, Rev. Dr William Fleming, 265
Stewart, Alexander, 201
Stewart, Dr, 171
Stewart, James, 142, 242
Stewart, John, 148
Stewart, Hon. Richard, 133
Stewart, Sir Robert, 67, 68, 69
Stewart, Thomas, 247, 248
Stewart, William, 64
Stewart, Captain William, 59, 61
Stewart, Sir William, 67, 68
Stirling, Sam, 362
stone circle, 2–3
Strabane, Co. Tyrone, 152, 197
   arts and entertainment, 368–387
   burnt, 28, 59
   Catholics in
      church building, 327–330
   charter, 131, 251
   Corporation of, 64–68
   descriptions of, 282–285
   foundation of, 17–37
   hospital, 162–163
   list of streets, 395
   plantation town, 63–64
   poor fund, 119–120, 161
   roads, 350
   in ruins, 34
   under 1st marquess, 146–150
   17th c., 72–75, 77–78
   18th c.
      development, 81–96
      leadership, 96–129
      MPs, 143–145
   19th c.
      development, 151–177, 179–195

   political control, 130–150
   20th century, 388–394
   town improvement scheme, 349–350
   traffic, 349–350
   undertakers, 60–61
Strabane, Lady, 67–68, 69
Strabane & Foyle Navigation Co., 342
Strabane Academy, 362
Strabane Agricultural College, 364
Strabane and Castlederg Regional Educational
Committee, 363
Strabane Arts Advisory Committee, 386
Strabane Canal, 79, 99, 104, 106, 107, 124, 125,
      180–181, 189, 342, 350
   Abercorn Square, 354–355
   barge charges, 238
   construction, 341–343
   transport, 340
Strabane Castle, 16, 23, 29, 30, 31, 32, 102
   partial demolition, 33
Strabane Chronicle, 181, 240, 241, 244, 256
Strabane Concert Brass, 369, 383–384
Strabane Convent Grammar, 367
Strabane Corporation, 82, 99, 234, 251
   Abercorn struggle with, 133–140
   abolition, 236–238
   financial dependence on Abercorn, 131
   political influence of Abercorn, 132–133
   reconstructed, 76
   records of, 150
   river transport, 106–107
   18th c., 85–87
   tithes, 96
   town growth, 124–126
Strabane Drama Festival, 381
Strabane Glen, 163
Strabane Hospital, 367
Strabane Iron and Brass Foundry, 188–189
Strabane Journal, 115, 118, 251
Strabane Magazine, 251–252
Strabane Morning Post, 155, 159, 161–163, 181, 185,
      251, 327, 340
Strabane Newsletter, 251
Strabane Poor Law Union, 166–167, 176–177
Strabane Presbytery, 300–302
   expansion, 309–310
   20th c., 311–313
Strabane Rangers, 114, 252
Strabane Rural District Council, 242–243, 246
   Boundary Commission, 247–248
   and partition, 246–247
Strabane Steamboat Co. Ltd, 180–181, 340, 342, 389
Strabane Steamboat Navigation Co., 342
Strabane Traders Association, 248
Strabane Urban District Council, 239–242, 329
   Boundary Commission, 248
   and national issues, 243–245
   and partition, 246–247
Strabane Volunteers, 114, 115–118, 142, 252
Strabane Weekly News, 256, 373
Stranorlar, Co. Donegal, 296

INDEX 435

Strule, river, 334
Stumpers Group, The, 379
Sullivan, Dr, 375
Sunderland, J., 340
Sydney, Lord Deputy, 25, 26
Synod of Ulster, 306

Talbot, Richard, earl of Tyrconnell, 75
Taughboyne, Co. Donegal, 70, 95, 102
Taylor, Isaac, 302
Taylor, J., 189
Taylor, Sir William, 362
telephones, 181, 391
Temperance Association, 184
Termonamongan, Co. Tyrone, 320, 331, 370
Thackeray, W.M., 283
Thompson, Dr, 223
Thompson, James, 163, 366
Thomson, Charles, 256–257
Tighernach, 10–11
timber, 79, 88, 163
Tinney, Jim, 370, 371
Tirenemuriertagh, Co. Tyrone, 61
tithes, 93–96, 109, 155, 156
tobacco manufacture, 191
Todd, David, 365
Toland, Rev. C.K., 312
Toner, James, 241
Toner, Margaret, 163
Toorish, Hugh, 376–377, 402, 403
Toorish, James, 247
Topham, James, 131, 132
Topliners, The, 379
Total Abstinence and Benevolent Society, 183–184
Tottenham, Lady, 327
town commissioners, 234–236, 238, 239
Town Hall, 97, 349, 369
    refurbishment, 241–242
    stage productions, 373–374
town tenants defence league, 245
Townparks, 87
trade, 191–193, 338, 340, 390
tramways, 346–348
transport, 336, 337–338
travellers' descriptions, 164–165, 282–285
Trinity College Dublin (TCD), 94, 270, 271, 281
tuck mills, 202
Tullyard, Co. Tyrone, 70, 202, 205
Tullymoan, Co. Tyrone, 300, 303
Tullywhisker mill, Co. Tyrone, 197
Turbitt, R.T., 192
Tyrconnell, 22
Tyrone, County, 63, 108, 132, 139, 155, 165, 170
    Abercorn in politics, 147–148
    Great Famine, 176
    special jury, 137
    survey, 1622, 337
    United Irishmen, 128
Tyrone, Lord, 136
Tyrone Constitution, 222–223, 225, 311
    elections, 227–228, 229

Great Famine, 170, 171
Tyrone County Council, 239, 246
Tyrone Herald, 208
Tyrone Liberal Association, 220–221
Tyrone Youth Band, 383

Ui Fiachrach, 7, 11
Ui Meic Cairthinn, 7
Ulster American Folk Park, 188, 272
Ulster Convention, 1892, 221
Ulster Custom, 119
Ulster Farmers' and Labourers' Union, 228
Ulster Plantation, 34, 35–36, 56, 57–64, 336–337
    categories of grantees, 59
    crises of 1640s, 66–69
    Strabane district, 60–61
Ulster Reform Association, 224
Ulster Transport, 348, 349, 392
Ulster Unionist Council, 226
undertakers, 184–195
Underwood, Thomas Neilson, 184, 264
Unitarianism, 308–309
United Counties Club, 183
United Irishmen, 109, 126–129, 152, 232, 236,
253–254, 261, 264, 306, 310, 324
United States of America (USA), 330
    emigration to, 110–112, 121–123, 177, 302, 305,
        346
university question, 224–225
Urney, Co. Tyrone, 15, 71, 90, 126, 197, 317, 369
    agriculture, 78
    bridge arrests, 86
    Catholic clergy, 315, 316, 318, 320, 322, 324,
        326–327, 329, 331
    Catholic seminary, 322–323, 326
    churches, 326-327, 329, 292
    graveyard, 399
    Great Famine, 173
    nunnery, 9
    O'Kane funeral, 396–397
    parish, 400
    poverty, 166
    Presbyterians, 299, 300, 301, 303–304
    Strabane jurisdiction, 137
    United Irishmen, 128
Urney Foresters, 114
Urney Fort, 14
Urney Volunteers, 252
Ursula, Sr, 370

Vance, James, 163
Varian, Hester, 262
Vaughan, Sadie, 373
Venables, Colonel, 69
veterinary care, 188
Victoria Bridge, 308, 348
Vikings, 13–14, 334
Vindicator, The, 264–265
Volunteer movement, 109, 112–118, 143–144, 232,
236, 252–253, 306
    and Abercorn, 141–142

436 STRABANE THROUGH THE AGES

Catholic support, 323

Wade, S., & Son, 340
wakes, 401
Walker, Cowper, 252, 254, 256
Walker, Rev. George, 76
Wallace, James, 71, 299
Ward, Fr, 318, 326
Ward, Mary, 366
Warnock, Lighton, 235
Washington, George, 268, 273, 274, 275
Watson, Tom, 185
Watts, Rev. Robert, 312
Waugh, Rev. R.L.M., 296
Welsh, Rev. Andrew, 305
Wensley, Thomas, 89
Wentworth, Thomas, 66, 67
Wesley, Charles, 297
Wesley, John, 293, 294, 297
West Donegal Railway Co., 344
Western Education and Library Board, 362, 363, 367, 384
Whally, John, 341
White, James, 183, 239, 240, 241, 244
White, Rev. Mother Joseph, 209, 359
White, Miss, 357
White, Oliver, 239
White, Paddy, 400
Whittington, Rev. Stanley, 296
Wickow, Earl of, 146
Wilde, George, bishop of Derry, 71
Wilkinson, Lt I.I., 203–204
Willes, Chief Baron, 82

William of Orange, 75–77
Williamite war, 75–77, 81, 131, 251, 319
Willis, Captain Humphrey, 30, 31, 43, 44, 50
Wilson, David J., 223
Wilson, James, 122–123, 272, 365
Wilson, Joseph Ruggles, 272
Wilson, Mr, 303
Wilson, Rev. Robert, 71, 72, 76, 77, 300–301
Wilson, William, 223, 227
Wilson, Woodrow, 122–123, 272
Windsor, Captain, 51
Winsley, Rev. Thomas, 305
Wirling, Rev. Robert, 306
Wisher, Captain, 68
Wood, Andrew, 94
Woodend, Co. Tyrone, 70, 90, 100
Woodgate, Mr, 125
Woods, Charlotte, 357
Woodvale Construction, 350
workhouses, 166–167
    Great Famine, 171, 174–176
    Presbyterian chaplain, 244–245
    school, 357
Worthing, Miss, 357
Worthington, Miss, 358
Wright, William, & Co., 193
Wylie, J.O., 221

Yellow Ford, Battle of the, 39
yeomanry, 126, 153–154, 194
Young, Miss, 358
Young, Thomas, 255

Strabane History Society wishes to acknowledge the donation from each of the following towards the costs of the publication of this history

Michael Bradley (publican)
Felix O'Neill (publican)
Crawford, Scally and Co. (solicitors)
Wilson and Simms (solicitors)
John Fahy and Co. (solicitors)
Mc Canny and Keohane (solicitors)
Colm McLaughlin (menswear and outfitters)
Jim McFadden (newsagent)
First Trust Bank
Bank of Ireland
Hugo Duncan (broadcaster and entertainer)
Pat McColgan (McColgan's Foods Ltd.)
Mark Patton (Patton's paints)
Michael Quigley (Funeral Director)
Sean McGoldrick (publican)
Michael McAteer (pharmacist)
McElholm and Co. (accountants)
Philip Brown (jeweller)
Shiels Brothers (furniture suppliers)
Adria Ltd.